Kaplan Publishing are consta[n]...
ways to make a difference to y[our]...
exciting online resources real[ly]...
different to students looking f[or]...

G000122955

This book comes with free EN-gage online resources so that you can study anytime, anywhere.

Having purchased this book, you have access to the following online study materials:

CONTENT	ACCA (including FFA,FAB,FMA)		AAT		FIA (excluding FFA,FAB,FMA)	
	Text	Kit	Text	Kit	Text	Kit
iPaper version of the book	✓	✓	✓	✓	✓	✓
Interactive electronic version of the book	✓					
Fixed tests / progress tests with instant answers	✓		✓			
Mock assessments online			✓	✓		
Material updates	✓	✓	✓	✓	✓	✓
Latest official ACCA exam questions		✓				
Extra question assistance using the signpost icon*		✓				
Timed questions with an online tutor debrief using the clock icon*		✓				
Interim assessment including questions and answers		✓			✓	
Technical articles	✓	✓			✓	✓

* Excludes F1, F2, F3, FFA, FAB, FMA

How to access your online resources

Kaplan Financial students will already have a Kaplan EN-gage account and these extra resources will be available to you online. You do not need to register again, as this process was completed when you enrolled. If you are having problems accessing online materials, please ask your course administrator.

If you are already a registered Kaplan EN-gage user go to www.EN-gage.co.uk and log in. Select the 'add a book' feature and enter the ISBN number of this book and the unique pass key at the bottom of this card. Then click 'finished' or 'add another book'. You may add as many books as you have purchased from this screen.

If you purchased through Kaplan Flexible Learning or via the Kaplan Publishing website you will automatically receive an e-mail invitation to Kaplan EN·gage online. Please register your details using this email to gain access to your content. If you do not receive the e-mail or book content, please contact Kaplan Flexible Learning.

If you are a new Kaplan EN-gage user register at www.EN-gage.co.uk and click on the link contained in the email we sent you to activate your account. Then select the 'add a book' feature, enter the ISBN number of this book and the unique pass key at the bottom of this card. Then click 'finished' or 'add another book'.

Your Code and Information

This code can only be used once for the registration of one book online. This registration and your online content will expire when the final sittings for the examinations covered by this book have taken place. Please allow one hour from the time you submit your book details for us to process your request.

Please scratch the film to access your EN-gage code.

Please be aware that this code is case-sensitive and you will need to include the
[d]ashes within the passcode, but not when entering the ISBN. For further technical
[s]upport, please visit www.EN-gage.co.uk

Paper P6

Advanced Taxation
(Finance Act 2012)

EXAM KIT

KAPLAN
PUBLISHING

British Library Cataloguing-in-Publication Data

A catalogue record for this book is available from the British Library.

Published by:

Kaplan Publishing UK

Unit 2 The Business Centre

Molly Millar's Lane

Wokingham

Berkshire

RG41 2QZ

ISBN: 978 0 85732 689 8

© Kaplan Financial Limited, 2012.

Printed and bound in Great Britain.

Acknowledgements

The past ACCA examination questions are the copyright of the Association of Chartered Certified Accountants. The original answers to the questions from June 1994 onwards were produced by the examiners themselves and have been adapted by Kaplan Publishing.

We are grateful to the Chartered Institute of Management Accountants and the Institute of Chartered Accountants in England and Wales for permission to reproduce past examination questions. The answers have been prepared by Kaplan Publishing.

CONTENTS

Key features in this edition

In addition to providing a wide ranging bank of real past exam questions, we have also included in this edition:

- An analysis of all of the recent examination papers.

- Paper specific information and advice on exam technique.

- Our recommended approach to make your revision for this particular subject as effective as possible.

  This includes step by step guidance on how best to use our Kaplan material (Complete text, pocket notes and exam kit) at this stage in your studies.

- An increased number of enhanced tutorial answers packed with specific key answer tips, technical tutorial notes and exam technique tips from our experienced tutors.

- Complementary online resources including full tutor debriefs and question assistance to point you in the right direction when you get stuck.

June and December 2011 and June and December 2012 – Real examination questions with enhanced tutorial answers

The real June 2011, December 2011, June 2012 and December 2012 exam questions with enhanced "walk through answers" and full "tutor debriefs", updated in line with legislation relevant to your exam sitting, are available on Kaplan EN-gage at:

www.EN-gage.co.uk

You will find a wealth of other resources to help you with your studies on the following sites:

www.EN-gage.co.uk

www.**acca**global.com/students/

INDEX TO QUESTIONS AND ANSWERS

INTRODUCTION

The style of current Paper P6 exam questions has changed recently and significant changes have had to be made to questions in light of the legislative changes in recent Finance Acts.

Accordingly, many of the old ACCA questions within this kit have been adapted to reflect the new style of paper and the new rules. If changed in any way from the original version, this is indicated in the end column of the index below with the mark *(A)*.

Note that the majority of the questions within the kit are past ACCA exam questions, the more recent questions (from 2005) are labelled as such in the index.

The pilot paper is included at the end of the kit.

KEY TO THE INDEX

PAPER ENHANCEMENTS

We have added the following enhancements to the answers in this exam kit:

Key answer tips

All answers include key answer tips to help your understanding of each question.

Tutorial note

All answers include more tutorial notes to explain some of the technical points in more detail.

Top tutor tips

For selected questions, we "walk through the answer" giving guidance on how to approach the questions with helpful 'tips from a top tutor', together with technical tutor notes.

These answers are indicated with the "footsteps" icon in the index.

ONLINE ENHANCEMENTS

 Timed question with Online tutor debrief

For selected questions, we recommend that they are to be completed in full exam conditions (i.e. properly timed in a closed book environment).

In addition to the examiner's technical answer, enhanced with key answer tips and tutorial notes in this exam kit, online you can find an answer debrief by a top tutor that:

- works through the question in full

- points out how to approach the question

- how to ensure that the easy marks are obtained as quickly as possible, and

- emphasises how to tackle exam questions and exam technique.

These questions are indicated with the "clock" icon in the index.

 Online question assistance

Have you ever looked at a question and not known where to start, or got stuck part way through?

For selected questions, we have produced "Online question assistance" offering different levels of guidance, such as:

- ensuring that you understand the question requirements fully, highlighting key terms and the meaning of the verbs used

- how to read the question proactively, with knowledge of the requirements, to identify the topic areas covered

- assessing the detail content of the question body, pointing out key information and explaining why it is important

- help in devising a plan of attack

With this assistance, you should then be able to attempt your answer confident that you know what is expected of you.

These questions are indicated with the "signpost" icon in the index.

Online question enhancements and answer debriefs will be available from Spring 2012 on Kaplan EN-gage at:

www.EN-gage.co.uk

TAXATION OF INDIVIDUALS

TAXATION OF CORPORATE BUSINESSES

ANALYSIS OF PAST PAPERS

The table below summarises the key topics that have been tested in the new syllabus examinations to date.

Note that the references are to the number of the question in this edition of the exam kit.

In addition, the Pilot Paper is produced in its original form at the end of the kit.

	Jun 08	Dec 08	Jun 09	Dec 09	Jun 10	Dec 10
IHT						
Lifetime gifts	Q20	Q21	Q22, Q31	Q23, Q32	Q3, Q33	Q24, Q34
Death estate			Q31		Q33	
Diminution in value			Q22			Q24
Business property relief/ agricultural property relief	Q20	Q21	Q22	Q23		
Gift with reservation						
Consequences of lifetime giving		Q21	Q22	Q23	Q3, Q33	Q24, Q34
Overseas aspects		Q29	Q31		Q33	Q34
Trusts						
Description					Q33	
Tax treatment		Q29			Q33	
CGT						
Basic computations	Q45	Q21	Q11, Q22	Q23, Q32		Q24, Q48
Shares		Q21			Q13	
Reorganisations						
Liquidations						
Capital gains tax reliefs:						
Incorporation relief					Q13	
Entrepreneurs' relief			Q11		Q13	Q48
Gift relief			Q22	Q23		Q24
PPR relief				Q32		
Overseas aspects of CGT	Q20	Q30		Q32		
Income Tax						
Personal tax computations	Q45	Q29, Q30, Q46	Q6, Q31	Q7, Q32, Q47	Q3, Q33	
Redundancy payments		Q46				
Share options and share incentives		Q46			Q3	
Calculation/discussion of benefits	Q20	Q29		Q47	Q13, Q33	Q48
Employed v self employed		Q46				Q49
Property business profits			Q31		Q33	
Overseas aspects of income		Q30	Q31			Q34

	Jun 08	Dec 08	Jun 09	Dec 09	Jun 10	Dec 10
Self Employed Income						
– Opening year rules				Q7	Q12	
– Closing year rules						
– Capital allowances			Q6	Q7	Q13	
– Trading losses			Q6		Q12	
– Partnerships			Q6			
Badges of trade				Q32		
Self assessment				Q23		Q24
Sole trader versus Company					Q12	
Corporation Tax						
Anti-avoidance – trading loss relief	Q55					Q60
Loan relationships			Q57		Q59	
Close Companies				Q47		Q48
Purchase of own shares	Q45					Q48
Personal service company		Q46				Q49
Groups	Q55	Q56		Q58	Q59	Q60
Consortium Relief	Q55					
Capital gains implications inc. rollover	Q55	Q56		Q47, Q58	Q59	Q60
Pre entry cap loss						Q60
Overseas Aspects	Q55		Q57		Q59	
Extraction of profits from company (salary vs. dividend)						
Reorganisations						
Transfer pricing		Q56	Q11			
Sale of shares vs. assets		Q56				
Administration		Q56	Q11			
Financial Planning						
Investments			Q31			
Pensions			Q31		Q3	
EIS/VCT	Q40		Q31			
Stamp Duty/SDLT	Q55	Q29	Q11	Q32		Q60
VAT						
Registration/deregistration			Q6		Q12	
Schemes				Q7		
Partial exemption	Q40	Q29			Q59	Q49
Groups		Q56	Q11			
Overseas aspects		Q56	Q11			Q60
Land and buildings	Q40, Q55			Q58	Q59	
Ethical issues	Q55	Q29	Q31		Q33	Q60

KAPLAN PUBLISHING

ANALYSIS OF MOST RECENT EXAMS

The table below summarises the key topics that have been tested in the most recent exams.

Note that the references are to the number of the question in the original exam. These exams can be found, with enhanced "walk through answers", updated in line with legislation relevant to your exam sitting, on Kaplan EN-gage at:

www.EN-gage.co.uk

	Jun 11	Dec 11	Jun 12
IHT			
Lifetime gifts	Q4	Q2, Q4	Q1
Death estate	Q1	Q4	Q1
Diminution in value		Q4	
Business property relief/ agricultural property relief	Q1		Q1
Gift with reservation		Q2	
Consequences of lifetime giving	Q4		Q1
Overseas aspects	Q1		Q1
Trusts			
Description			
Tax treatment	Q4	Q4	
CGT			
Basic computations	Q1, Q4	Q2, Q3	Q1
Shares	Q1, Q4		
Reorganisations	Q4		
Liquidations			
Capital gains tax reliefs:			
Incorporation relief			
Entrepreneurs' relief	Q1	Q2, Q3	
Gift relief	Q1, Q4	Q4	
PPR relief		Q2	
Overseas aspects of CGT		Q2	
Income Tax			
Personal tax computations	Q1, Q3	Q2	Q3, Q4
Redundancy payments			Q4
Share options and share incentives		Q3	
Calculation/discussion of benefits		Q1, Q3	Q3
Employed v self employed			
Property business profits	Q1		
Overseas aspects of income		Q2	Q1, Q3

	Jun 11	Dec 11	Jun 12
Self Employed Income			
– Opening year rules	Q3		Q4
– Closing year rules		Q2	
– Capital allowances			
– Trading losses	Q3	Q2	
– Partnerships	Q3		Q4
Badges of trade			
Self assessment			Q1
Sole trader versus Company			
National Insurance Contributions			Q4
Corporation Tax			
Anti-avoidance – trading loss relief			
Loan relationships		Q5	
Research and development			Q5
Intangible assets			Q2
Close Companies		Q1	
Purchase of own shares			
Personal service company			
Groups	Q2, Q5	Q1, Q5	Q2, Q5
Consortium Relief			Q2
Capital gains implications inc. rollover	Q2	Q1, Q5	Q2
Pre entry cap loss			
Overseas Aspects	Q5		
Extraction of profits from company (salary vs. dividend)			
Reorganisations			
Transfer pricing	Q5		
Sale of shares vs. assets			
Administration	Q2	Q1, Q5	Q2, Q5
Financial Planning			
Investments			
Pensions			Q4
EIS/VCT	Q4		Q4
Stamp Duty/SDLT	Q1		Q1
VAT			
Registration/deregistration		Q2, Q5	Q3
Schemes		Q1	
Partial exemption	Q2	Q5	Q2
Groups		Q5	
Overseas aspects			Q2
Land and buildings			Q2, Q3
Ethical issues	Q2	Q1	Q1

EXAM TECHNIQUE

- Use the allocated **15 minutes reading and planning time** at the beginning of the exam:
  - read the questions and examination requirements carefully, and
  - begin planning your answers.

  See the Paper Specific Information for advice on how to use this time for this paper.

- **Divide the time** you spend on questions in proportion to the marks on offer:
  - there are 1.8 minutes available per mark in the examination
  - within that, try to allow time at the end of each question to review your answer and address any obvious issues

  Whatever happens, always keep your eye on the clock and **do not over run on any part of any question!**

- Spend the last **five minutes** of the examination:
  - reading through your answers, and
  - **making any additions or corrections**.

- If you **get completely stuck** with a question:
  - leave space in your answer book, and
  - **return to it later.**

- Stick to the question and **tailor your answer** to what you are asked.
  - pay particular attention to the verbs in the question.

- If you do not understand what a question is asking, **state your assumptions**.

  Even if you do not answer in precisely the way the examiner hoped, you should be given some credit, if your assumptions are reasonable.

- You should do everything you can to make things easy for the marker.

  The marker will find it easier to identify the points you have made if your **answers are legible**.

- **Written questions**:

  Your answer should have:
  - a clear structure
  - a brief introduction, a main section and a conclusion.

  Be concise.

  It is better to write a little about a lot of different points than a great deal about one or two points.

- **Computations**:

  It is essential to include all your workings in your answers.

  Many computational questions require the use of a standard format:

  e.g. income tax computations, corporation tax computations and capital gains.

  Be sure you know these formats thoroughly before the exam and use the layouts that you see in the answers given in this book and in model answers.

- **Reports, memos and other documents**:

  Some questions ask you to present your answer in the form of a report, a memo, a letter or other document.

  Make sure that you use the correct format – there could be easy marks to gain here.

PAPER SPECIFIC INFORMATION

THE EXAM

FORMAT OF THE EXAM

Number of marks

Section A: 2 compulsory scenario-based questions:

Question 1	35
Question 2	25
Section B: 3 20 mark questions, 2 only to be answered	40 marks in total
	————
	100
	————

Total time allowed: 3 hours plus 15 minutes reading and planning time.

Note that:

- There will be four marks for professional skills in question one.

- Every Paper P6 (UK) exam will include an ethical component for approximately five marks. The examiner has stated that questions on ethics will be confined to the following areas:

  - prospective clients

  - conflicts of interest

  - disclosure of information to HM Revenue & Customs

  - money laundering

  - tax irregularities

  - tax avoidance

  - tax evasion.

  The ethical component of the exam will appear in Section A.

- Apart from the above, any subject may be tested anywhere in the exam for any number of marks.

- The exam will not just test P6 knowledge: F6 knowledge is still highly examinable, but will be tested in a more advanced way.

- The requirements of a Section A question may be presented in one of two different ways:

  - given in full at the end of the question, or

  - a brief overview can be provided at the end of the question with a reference to the detailed requirements in the body of the question.

PASS MARK

The pass mark for all ACCA Qualification examination papers is 50%.

READING AND PLANNING TIME

Remember that all three hour paper based examinations have an additional 15 minutes reading and planning time.

ACCA GUIDANCE

ACCA guidance on the use of this time is as follows:

This additional time is allowed at the beginning of the examination to allow candidates to read the questions and to begin planning their answers before they start to write in their answer books.

This time should be used to ensure that all the information and, in particular, the exam requirements are properly read and understood.

During this time, candidates may only annotate their question paper. They may not write anything in their answer booklets until told to do so by the invigilator.

KAPLAN GUIDANCE

As there is some choice in Section B, there is a decision regarding which one of the optional questions to drop, together with the decision of which order you should attempt the questions.

Therefore, in relation to P6, we recommend that you take the following approach with your reading and planning time:

- **Skim through the whole paper**, assessing the level of difficulty of each question.

- **Write down** on the question paper next to the mark allocation **the amount of time you should spend on each part.** Do this for each part of every question.

- **Decide which optional question to drop and the order** in which you think you will attempt each question:

  This is a personal choice and you have time on the revision phase to try out different approaches, for example, if you sit mock exams.

  A common approach is to tackle the question you think is the easiest and you are most comfortable with first.

  Others may prefer to tackle the longest questions first, or conversely leave them to the last.

  Psychologists believe that you usually perform at your best on the second and third question you attempt, once you have settled into the exam, so not tackling the bigger Section A questions first may be advisable.

  It is usual however that student tackle their least favourite topic and/or the most difficult question in their opinion last.

  Whatever your approach, you must make sure that you leave enough time to attempt all questions fully and be very strict with yourself in timing each question.

- **For each question** in turn, read the requirements and then the detail of the question carefully.

  Always read the requirement first as this enables you to **focus on the detail of the question with the specific task in mind.**

  For computational questions:

  Highlight key numbers/information and key words in the question, scribble notes to yourself on the question paper to remember key points in your answer.

  Jot down proformas required if applicable.

  For written questions:

  Take notice of the format required (e.g. letter, memo, notes) and identify the recipient of the answer. You need to do this to judge the level of sophistication required in your answer and whether the use of a formal reply or informal bullet points would be satisfactory.

  Plan your beginning, middle and end and the key areas to be addressed and your use of titles and sub-titles to enhance your answer.

  For all questions:

  Spot the easy marks to be gained in a question and parts which can be performed independently of the rest of the question. For example, tax payment dates, ethical issues, laying out the answer in the correct format etc.

  Make sure that you do these parts first when you tackle the question.

  Don't go overboard in terms of planning time on any one question – you need a good measure of the whole paper and a plan for all of the questions at the end of the 15 minutes.

  By covering all questions you can often help yourself as you may find that facts in one question may remind you of things you should put into your answer relating to a different question.

- With your plan of attack in mind, **start answering your chosen question** with your plan to hand, as soon as you are allowed to start.

 Always keep your eye on the clock and do not over run on any part of any question!

DETAILED SYLLABUS

The detailed syllabus and study guide written by the ACCA can be found at:

www.**acca**global.com/students/

KAPLAN'S RECOMMENDED REVISION APPROACH

QUESTION PRACTICE IS THE KEY TO SUCCESS

Success in professional examinations relies upon you acquiring a firm grasp of the required knowledge at the tuition phase. In order to be able to do the questions, knowledge is essential.

However, the difference between success and failure often hinges on your exam technique on the day and making the most of the revision phase of your studies.

The **Kaplan complete text** is the starting point, designed to provide the underpinning knowledge to tackle all questions. However, in the revision phase, pouring over text books is not the answer.

Kaplan Online fixed tests help you consolidate your knowledge and understanding and are a useful tool to check whether you can remember key topic areas.

Kaplan pocket notes are designed to help you quickly revise a topic area, however you then need to practice questions. There is a need to progress to full exam standard questions as soon as possible, and to tie your exam technique and technical knowledge together.

The importance of question practice cannot be over-emphasised.

The recommended approach below is designed by expert tutors in the field, in conjunction with their knowledge of the examiner and their recent real exams.

The approach taken for the fundamental papers is to revise by topic area. However, with the professional stage papers, a multi topic approach is required to answer the scenario based questions.

You need to practise as many questions as possible in the time you have left.

OUR AIM

Our aim is to get you to the stage where you can attempt exam standard questions confidently, to time, in a closed book environment, with no supplementary help (i.e. to simulate the real examination experience).

Practising your exam technique on real past examination questions, in timed conditions, is also vitally important for you to assess your progress and identify areas of weakness that may need more attention in the final run up to the examination.

In order to achieve this we recognise that initially you may feel the need to practise some questions with open book help and exceed the required time.

The approach below shows you which questions you should use to build up to coping with exam standard question practice, and references to the sources of information available should you need to revisit a topic area in more detail.

Remember that in the real examination, all you have to do is:

- attempt all questions required by the exam

- only spend the allotted time on each question, and

- get them at least 50% right!

Try and practise this approach on every question you attempt from now to the real exam.

EXAMINER COMMENTS

We have included the examiners comments to the specific new syllabus examination questions in this kit for you to see the main pitfalls that students fall into with regard to technical content.

However, too many times in the general section of the report, the examiner comments that students had failed due to:

- "misallocation of time"

- "running out of time" and

- showing signs of "spending too much time on an earlier questions and clearly rushing the answer to a subsequent question".

Good exam technique is vital.

THE KAPLAN PAPER P6 REVISION PLAN

Stage 1: Assess areas of strengths and weaknesses

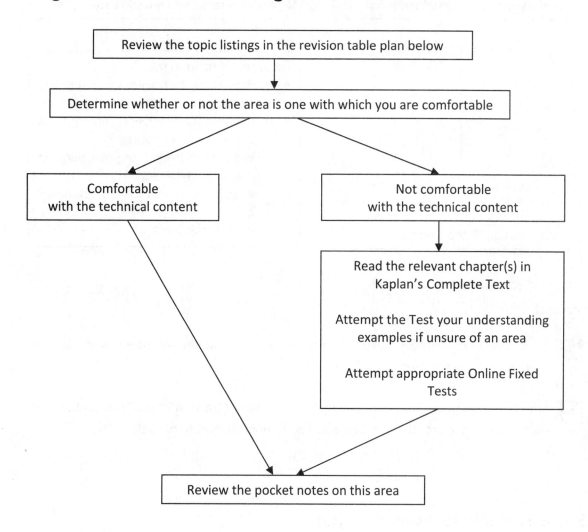

Stage 2: Practice questions

Follow the order of revision of topics as recommended in the revision table plan below and attempt the questions in the order suggested.

Try to avoid referring to text books and notes and the model answer until you have completed your attempt.

Try to answer the question in the allotted time.

Review your attempt with the model answer and assess how much of the answer you achieved in the allocated exam time.

Fill in the self-assessment box below and decide on your best course of action.

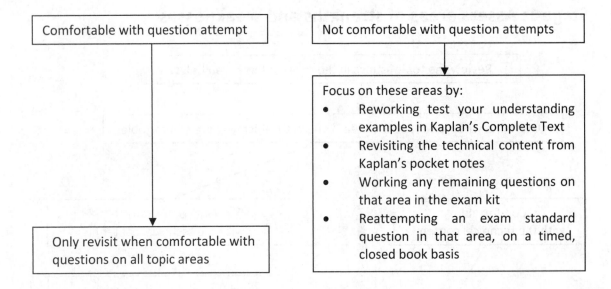

Note that :

 The "footsteps questions" give guidance on exam techniques and how you should have approached the question.

 The "clock questions" have an online debrief where a tutor talks you through the exam technique and approach to that question and works the question in full.

Stage 3: Final pre-exam revision

We recommend that you **attempt at least one three hour mock examination** containing a set of previously unseen exam standard questions.

It is important that you get a feel for the breadth of coverage of a real exam without advanced knowledge of the topic areas covered – just as you will expect to see on the real exam day.

Ideally this mock should be sat in timed, closed book, real exam conditions and could be:

- a mock examination offered by your tuition provider, and/or

- the pilot paper in the back of this exam kit, and/or

- the last real examination paper (available shortly afterwards on Kaplan EN-gage with "enhanced walk through answers" and a full "tutor debrief").

THE DETAILED REVISION PLAN

Very few of the recent P6 exam questions focus on just one area of tax.

This is especially true of the big, compulsory scenario questions, which often test several different areas.

This revision plan aims to lead you through a selection of the best questions, broadly grouped by the areas covered, and will ensure that you revise all of the key topics.

It is especially important that you practise the more recent questions, as the current examiner has his own particular style.

Familiarisation with his style of questions will help to make sure that you are as well-prepared as possible for the real exam.

Topic	Complete Text Chapter	Pocket note Chapter	Questions to attempt	Tutor guidance	Date attempted	Self assessment
Corporation tax				Corporation tax is often an area that students struggle with, but in recent exams has regularly formed the basis of one of the compulsory scenario questions. For this reason, it would be a good idea to start by revising corporation tax to ensure that you have enough time to cover it thoroughly.		
Basics	22-24	15	Q50 Juglans Ltd and Larix Ltd (a)	Q50 part (a) is useful as a warm-up and covers the basic computation with capital allowances, with the twist that the company could either prepare accounts for a short period then a 12 month period, or for a long period.		
Losses, anti-avoidance re trading losses c/f; Losses groups; Consortia; Rollover relief; VAT: land and buildings and overseas aspects; Ethics	24 27, 29 27 9 20 16	15 16 27 8 14 11	Q50 Juglans Ltd and Larix Ltd (b), Q55 Saturn Ltd, Q60 Daube Group	The corporation tax scenario questions will often involve a group of companies; VAT is a regular feature too. Use your Kaplan pocket notes to make sure that you are happy with all the different group definitions and implications before attempting these questions. You must also learn the reliefs available for the various types of losses, as it is easy to get these confused. Rollover relief is the only capital gains relief available to companies, making it a highly examinable area.		

Topic	Complete Text Chapter	Pocket note Chapter	Questions to attempt	Tutor guidance	Date attempted	Self assessment
				VAT on land and buildings is a favourite area, and regularly features in questions. Q50(b) is a gentle warm-up before attempting Q55 and Q60; full-blown scenario questions from recent exams. Don't worry if you find these hard – these questions will get easier with practice. There are walkthrough answers to help you if you get stuck. Note that stamp duty and ethics often represent easy marks in this type of question.		
Gains groups; Sale of shares versus sale of assets; Admin; VAT: groups and overseas	27, 29 27 22 21, 27	16 15 16, 17	Q56 Particle Ltd Group	Another big scenario question covering disposal of a subsidiary through sale of its shares or assets. Look at the mark allocations here to gauge how much you need to write. The corporation tax admin is pure F6 knowledge, highlighting how important it is that you retain this knowledge. This question covers some other popular areas of VAT: groups and overseas aspects. Use your Kaplan pocket notes to refresh your memory.		
Gains groups, Degrouping charges; Rollover relief; VAT: land and buildings	27 27 9 20	16 16 8 14	Q58 Automatic Ltd	This question covers some quite specific areas. There is a good written section on degrouping charges here.		

Topic	Complete Text Chapter	Pocket note Chapter	Questions to attempt	Tutor guidance	Date attempted	Self assessment
The Capital taxes	The key capital taxes are capital gains tax and inheritance tax. Inheritance tax often features as part of both a compulsory question and an optional question, often linked with capital gains tax.					
Inheritance tax basics; Income tax basics; Trusts	11-13 1 14	8 1 10	Q16 Alex	Q16 is a good question to start with, covering the basic calculations and includes a straightforward income tax computation in part (a), and a written section on trusts. Trusts often feature as a small written section.		
Inheritance tax: further computations; Business property relief (BPR); Admin	11-12 12 13	8 8 8	Q20 Kepler	This question includes popular complications: the diminution in value principle and BPR. BPR features in nearly every exam, so you must learn the conditions in detail. Also use your Kaplan pocket notes to make sure that you learn the payment dates for inheritance tax, particularly payment by instalment.		
Inheritance tax versus capital gains tax; Agricultural property relief; BPR; Gift relief; Principal private residence relief; Planning	13 12 12 9 9 13	8 8 8 6 6 12	Q14 Joan Ark, Q22 Fitzgerald and Morrison Q21 Ernest and Georgina Q3 Dokham (b)	One of the examiner's favourite tricks is to test both the inheritance tax and capital gains tax implications of lifetime gifts, and there are many questions on this area. Q14 is not in current exam style, but is a great question as it covers most of the calculations and reliefs available for both IHT and CGT. Before attempting this question, make sure that you revise the CGT reliefs thoroughly, and try not to get IHT and CGT confused!		

Topic	Complete Text Chapter	Pocket note Chapter	Questions to attempt	Tutor guidance	Date attempted	Self assessment
				Note that part (ii) of this question, on the advantages of lifetime gifts, is very general. You will probably have to apply this knowledge in an exam question, and just pick out the points which are relevant. Have a go at Q22, a real past exam question from the optional section of the exam. This question covers gift relief for CGT in detail. Then try Q21 – but think carefully before you answer! The individuals are not married. Q3(b) also covers lifetime gifts, but with a slightly less obvious requirement.		
Test question			Q19 Crusoe	Try answering this one under exam conditions.		
Income tax				Income tax is not likely to be tested on its own at P6, but will often feature as part of a bigger question. For many of the questions set at this level, the examiner will not require you to do a whole income tax computation, but rather to start part way through. For example, you may have to calculate just the tax on some extra income, working in the margin. Be prepared to write about employment benefits as well as doing calculations.		
Property income; Employment benefits: share options, loans, use of assets; CGT: PPR relief; Ethics	3 2 9 16	1 2 6 11	Q2 Clifford and Amanda	A two part question, with part (a) on CGT and PPR relief, part (b) on income tax. Lease premiums are a tricky area, so you may want to revisit the test your understandings in the complete text before attempting this question.		

Topic	Complete Text Chapter	Pocket note Chapter	Questions to attempt	Tutor guidance	Date attempted	Self assessment
				The examiner will often ask for explanations of how benefits are taxed. Think about how you would calculate the benefit, then write the process down in words, make sure your advice is clear and concise. Note the easy marks for ethics again.		
Termination payments; Share incentive plan;	2 2	2 2	Pilot Q5 Vikram Bridge	Parts (a) and (b) of this question cover CGT and IHT. Redundancy payments often feature as part of a bigger question. Share schemes are frequently tested, as they are not examined at F6.		
Marginal tax computations; CGT vs. IHT; Gift with reservation	13 12	8 8		The last part of the question involves calculating extra tax on a dividend –by working in the margin		
Personal financial planning				You may be asked to advise on suitable investment products in the exam, particularly tax efficient forms of investment. Again, this is not likely to form the basis of a whole question, but will generally be combined with other areas.		
Enterprise investment scheme (EIS);	3, 9, 15	6, 12	Q40 Gagarin	This is really two completely separate questions: one on EIS and the other on VAT.		
VAT on land and buildings, capital goods scheme	20	14		Use your Kaplan pocket notes to revise the conditions for EIS before attempting this question – you need a detailed knowledge of the rules to pass.		
Venture capital trusts (VCTs); Pensions;	3, 15 4	12 3	Q31 Charleston Dance, Q28 Coral (a)	The rules for VCTs are very similar to the EIS rules, but you need to learn a few subtle differences.		
Furnished holiday lettings (FHL);	3	1		Pensions and FHL were covered at F6, but still appear in questions at P6.		
IHT overseas aspects; Investment through a company;	13	8		Try Q31 to exam time; you need to be very focused to complete it in the time available.		
Ethics	16	11		If you don't finish, don't panic – remember that you only need to get half of it right to pass. It is worth attempting it fully though, as it is a good question.		

Topic	Complete Text Chapter	Pocket note Chapter	Questions to attempt	Tutor guidance	Date attempted	Self assessment
				Again, note the easy marks for ethical issues at the end of this question. Q28(a) is a higher-skills question on pensions, requiring you to apply the rules to a scenario.		
Test question			Q33 Poblano	Try attempting this question to exam time.		
Overseas aspects of personal tax	Overseas aspects for individuals are very popular in the exam, often appearing in optional questions but also sometimes in the compulsory scenario questions. Before attempting these questions, use your Kaplan pocket notes to revise the definitions of residence, ordinary residence and domicile, and make sure that you can explain how a person's status affects the way they are taxed.					
Income tax	10	9	Q28 Coral (b)	Q28 is a good test of your knowledge of the income tax rules for non UK domiciled individuals. Make sure you apply the rules to the scenario.		
Income tax and capital gains tax	10	9	Q30 Boson	This is a great question to use to revise the temporary absence rules for CGT, with some income tax aspects too. It contains a mixture of words and numbers and, as usual, you must apply the rules to the scenario to score well. Don't worry about (b)(iii) regarding the rate of return - this was only worth 3 marks and is not something which is tested regularly.		
Inheritance tax; Income tax	11 10	9	Q25 Ming Wong	A comprehensive test of your knowledge of the rules regarding domicile, deemed domicile and the implications for inheritance tax and income tax. This question is more computational in nature than those seen in recent exams.		

Topic	Complete Text Chapter	Pocket note Chapter	Questions to attempt	Tutor guidance	Date attempted	Self assessment
Business scenarios	There are lots of business scenarios for the examiner to test, and because of the many aspects of tax that apply, these often feature as big, compulsory questions. Much of the knowledge required is basic F6 knowledge, but you must make sure you keep this knowledge up to date.					
Commencement of trade with basic income tax; NICs;	17	13	Q39 Adam Snook	This is a scenario involving an individual selling some assets to raise the money to start a business as a sole trader.		
CGT: takeovers;	8	5		There are many easy marks available for basic knowledge – the hard part is finding the relevant information and structuring your answer.		
VAT: land and buildings;	20	14		There is a walkthrough answer for this question to give you further guidance, if needed.		
IHT re lifetime gift	11	8				
Cessation of trade;	18	13	Q10 The Stiletto Partnership	Although this question actually deals with the incorporation of a partnership, it only covers the income tax and NIC implications – so is really just a question about cessation of trade with two alternative cessation dates.		
Partnerships;	19	13				
NICs;	18	13		There are some tricky points regarding the personal age allowance, but don't get too bogged down with these aspects of the question.		
Corporation tax residence;	22	17		Make sure you are happy with the basics regarding the split of partnership profits, closing year assessments, and the NICs payable by self-employed individuals.		
VAT overseas aspects;	21	17		Part (b) is a good written question on various overseas aspects of tax.		
Income tax residence	10	9				

Topic	Complete Text Chapter	Pocket note Chapter	Questions to attempt	Tutor guidance	Date attempted	Self assessment
Incorporation; CGT:	18	18	Q13 Vine (a) and (b);	Incorporation is a popular scenario as there are many different tax implications.		
Incorporation relief, Entrepreneurs' relief	9 9	6 6	Pilot Q3 Stanley Beech (a)	The previous question covered the income tax aspects of incorporation – these cover some of the other areas, particularly the CGT aspects with some planning points.		
Employed versus self employed;	2	12	Pilot Q2	Before attempting this question you may want to revisit the test your understandings covering VAT for a partially exempt business.		
Lease versus buy;	25	18	Pilar Mareno	Follow the examiner's instructions – he guides you through the calculations in the correct order. An excellent question.		
VAT: partial exemption	20	14				
Test question			Q29 Nucleus Resources	Try attempting this question to exam time.		
Family companies and planning scenarios				The following are also common scenarios that you need to be familiar with, although areas such as IR35, purchase of own shares and liquidations tend to only come up every few sittings in the exam.		
Business structure: unincorporated versus company; Loss reliefs;	26 24, 27	18 13, 15	Q12 Desiree	Before attempting these questions, you may want to use your Kaplan pocket notes to revise loss reliefs and the opening year assessment rules for individuals.		
VAT registration	20	14	Q44	Try not to confuse unincorporated businesses (individuals) and companies; the computations for individuals are all based around the tax year, whereas companies are taxed based on their chargeable accounting period.		
Close companies; Ethics	26 16	18 11	Banda Ross	Q12 is very straightforward, so have a go at that first.		

Topic	Complete Text Chapter	Pocket note Chapter	Questions to attempt	Tutor guidance	Date attempted	Self assessment
				Before attempting Q44 make sure you learn the rules for close companies: most small family companies are close. Again – note the easy marks for ethics!		
Business structure: Unincorporated versus company; Losses; Husband and wife tax planning: VCT; IHT for lifetime gift; Self assessment	26 17, 24 5 15 11 16	18 13, 15 12 11 8 11	Q27 Arthur and Cindy Wakefield	This question covers a number of areas. Business structure for a loss-making business is tested here again, but this time without calculations; You can save time in the husband and wife income tax planning section by performing your calculations in the margin. The IHT part of this question covers the pre-owned assets anti-avoidance legislation, which is not often tested. The self assessment rules are pure F6 knowledge, but still important.		
Extraction of funds from a company	26	18	Pilot Q3 Stanley Beech (b)	Extraction of funds from a company is an area you should be familiar with, but this question illustrates how the examiner likes to test common topics in a less obvious way.		
IR35	26	18	Q46 James (b)	You may want to revisit the test your understandings covering the calculation of deemed salary under IR35 before attempting this question.		

Topic	Complete Text Chapter	Pocket note Chapter	Questions to attempt	Tutor guidance	Date attempted	Self assessment
Purchase of own shares	26	18	Q45 Spica (a)	Make sure you learn the conditions for purchase of own shares before you do this question.		
Liquidations	8, 26	5, 18	Q43 Carver Ltd (b)	Although this question covers liquidations, it is mainly about the difference in tax treatment between dividends and capital gains.		

Note that not all of the questions are referred to in the programme above.

We have recommended an approach to build up from the basic to exam standard questions.

The remaining questions are available in the kit for extra practice for those who require more questions on some areas.

TAX RATES AND ALLOWANCES

SUPPLEMENTARY INSTRUCTIONS

1. You should assume that the tax rates and allowances for the tax year 2012/13 and for the Financial year to 31 March 2013 will continue to apply for the foreseeable future unless you are instructed otherwise.

2. Calculations and workings need only to be made to the nearest £.

3. All apportionments should be made to the nearest month.

4. All workings should be shown.

INCOME TAX

		Normal rates %	Dividend rates %
Basic rate	£1 – £34,370	20	10
Higher rate	£34,371 – £150,000	40	32.5
Additional rate	£150,001 and above	50	42.5

A starting rate of 10% applies to savings income where it falls within the first £2,710 of taxable income.

Personal allowances

		£
Personal allowance	Standard	8,105
Personal allowance	65–74	10,500
Personal allowance	75 and over	10,660
Income limit for age related allowances		25,400
Income limit for standard personal allowance		100,000

Car benefit percentage

The relevant base level of CO_2 emissions is 100 grams per kilometre.
The percentage rates applying to petrol cars with CO_2 emissions up to this level are:

75 grams per kilometre or less	5%
76 grams to 99 grams per kilometre	10%
100 grams per kilometre	11%

Car fuel benefit

The base figure for calculating the car fuel benefit is £20,200.

Individual Savings Accounts (ISAs)

The overall investment limit is £11,280, of which £5,640 can be invested in a cash ISA.

Pension scheme limits

Annual allowance	£50,000
Lifetime allowance	£1,500,000

The maximum contribution that can qualify for tax relief without evidence of earnings is £3,600.

Authorised mileage allowances: cars

Up to 10,000 miles	45p
Over 10,000 miles	25p

Capital allowances: rates of allowance

Plant and machinery (WDA)	%
Main pool	18
Special rate pool	8

Motor cars	
New cars with CO_2 emissions up to 110 grams per kilometre (low)	100 FYA
CO_2 emissions between 111 and 160 grams per kilometre (medium)	18
CO_2 emissions above 160 grams per kilometre (High)	8

Annual investment allowance (AIA)	
First £25,000 of expenditure No AIA on cars	100

CORPORATION TAX

Financial year	2010	2011	2012
Small profits rate	21%	20%	20%
Main rate	28%	26%	24%
Lower limit	£300,000	£300,000	£300,000
Upper limit	£1,500,000	£1,500,000	£1,500,000
Standard fraction	7/400	3/200	1/100

Marginal relief

Standard fraction $\times$ (U – A) $\times$ N/A

VALUE ADDED TAX

Standard rate of VAT	20%
Registration limit	£77,000
Deregistration limit	£75,000

INHERITANCE TAX

Tax rates

£1 – £325,000		Nil
Excess	– Death rate	40%
	– Lifetime rate	20%

Taper relief

Years before death	Percentage reduction %
Over 3 but less than 4 years	20
Over 4 but less than 5 years	40
Over 5 but less than 6 years	60
Over 6 but less than 7 years	80

Nil rate bands

	£		£
6 April 2009 to 5 April 2013	325,000	6 April 2002 to 5 April 2003	250,000
6 April 2008 to 5 April 2009	312,000	6 April 2001 to 5 April 2002	242,000
6 April 2007 to 5 April 2008	300,000	6 April 2000 to 5 April 2001	234,000
6 April 2006 to 5 April 2007	285,000	6 April 1999 to 5 April 2000	231,000
6 April 2005 to 5 April 2006	275,000	6 April 1998 to 5 April 1999	223,000
6 April 2004 to 5 April 2005	263,000	6 April 1997 to 5 April 1998	215,000
6 April 2003 to 5 April 2004	255,000		

CAPITAL GAINS TAX

Rates of tax	– Lower rate	18%
	– Higher rate	28%
Annual exempt amount		£10,600
Entrepreneurs' relief	– Lifetime limit	£10,000,000
	– Rate of tax	10%

RATES OF INTEREST

Official rate of interest:	4.0%
Rate of interest on underpaid tax:	3.0%
Rate of interest on overpaid tax:	0.5%

NATIONAL INSURANCE CONTRIBUTIONS
(not contracted out rates)

			%
Class 1	Employee	£1 – £7,605 per year	Nil
		£7,606 – £42,475 per year	12.0
		£42,476 and above per year	2.0
Class 1	Employer	£1 – £7,488 per year	Nil
		£7,489 and above per year	13.8
Class 1A			13.8
Class 2		£2.65 per week	
		Small earnings exception limit £5,595	
Class 4		£1 – £7,605 per year	Nil
		£7,606 – £42,475 per year	9.0
		£42,476 and above per year	2.0

STAMP DUTY LAND TAX

£150,000 or less	0%
£150,001 – £250,000	1%
£250,001 – £500,000	3%
£500,001 or more (2)	4%

(1)   For residential property, the nil rate is restricted to £125,000.

(2)   For residential property, where consideration exceeds £1 million the rate is 5% and where it exceeds £2 million the rate is 7%.

STAMP DUTY

Shares	0.5%

TIME LIMITS AND ELECTION DATES

Income tax

Election / claim	Time limit	For 2012/13
Agree the amount of trading losses to carry forward	4 years from the end of the tax year in which the loss arose	5 April 2017
Current and prior year set-off of trading losses against total income (and chargeable gains)	12 months from 31 January following the end of the tax year in which the loss arose	31 January 2015
Three year carry back of trading losses in the opening years	12 months from 31 January following the end of the tax year in which the loss arose	31 January 2015
Three year carry back of terminal trading losses in the closing years	4 years from the end of the last tax year of trading	5 April 2017
Set-off of loss on the disposal of unquoted trading company shares against income	12 months from 31 January following the end of the tax year in which the loss arose	31 January 2015
Transfer of assets eligible for capital allowances between connected parties at TWDV	2 years from the date of sale	

National Insurance Contributions

Election / claim	Time limit	For 2012/13
Class 1 primary and secondary – pay days	14 days after the end of each tax month under PAYE system	19th of each month
Class 1 A NIC – pay day	19 July following end of tax year	19 July 2013
Class 2 NICs – pay days	50% on 31 January and 50% on 31 July or Monthly by direct debit	
Class 4 NICs – pay days	Paid under self assessment with income tax	

Capital gains tax

Election / claim	Time limit	For 2012/13
Replacement of business asset relief for individuals (Rollover relief)	4 years from the end of the later of: – the tax year in which the disposal occurred – the tax year in which the acquisition of the replacement occurred	5 April 2017
Holdover relief of gain on the gift of a business asset (Gift relief)	4 years from the end of the tax year in which the disposal occurred	5 April 2017
Disapplication of incorporation relief	2 years from the 31 January following the end of the tax year in which the business is transferred If sell all shares by 5 April following tax year of incorporation: Time limit 12 months earlier than normal claim date	31 January 2016 31 January 2015
EIS Reinvestment relief	5 years from 31 January following the end of the tax year in which the disposal occurred	31 January 2019
Entrepreneurs' relief	12 months from 31 January following the end of the tax year in which the disposal occurred	31 January 2015
Determination of principal private residence	2 years from the acquisition of the second property	

Self assessment – individuals

Election / claim	Time limit	For 2012/13
Pay days for income tax and Class 4 NIC	1st instalment: 31 January in the tax year 2nd instalment: 31 July following the end of tax year Balancing payment: 31 January following the end of tax year	31 January 2013 31 July 2013 31 January 2014
Pay day for CGT	31 January following the end of tax year	31 January 2014
Filing dates Paper return Electronic return	Later of 31 October following the end of the tax year or 3 months after the issue of the return Later of 31 January following the end of the tax year or 3 months after the issue of the return	31 October 2013 31 January 2014
Retention of records Business records Personal records	5 years from 31 January following end of the tax year 12 months from 31 January following end of the tax year	31 January 2019 31 January 2015
HMRC right of repair	9 months from date the return was filed	
Taxpayers right to amend a return	12 months from 31 January following end of the tax year	31 January 2015
Error or mistake claim	4 years from the end of the tax year	5 April 2017
HMRC can open an enquiry	12 months from submission of the return	
HMRC can raise a discovery assessment – No careless or deliberate behaviour – Tax lost due to careless behaviour – Tax lost due to deliberate behaviour	 4 years from the end of the tax year 6 years from the end of the tax year 20 years from the end of the tax year	 5 April 2017 5 April 2019 5 April 2033
Taxpayers right of appeal against an assessment	30 days from the assessment – appeal in writing	

Inheritance tax

Election / claim	Time limit	For 2012/13
Lifetime IHT on CLTs – pay day	Gift before 1 October in tax year: Following 30 April Gift on/after 1 October in tax year: 6 months after the end of the month of the gift	30 April 2013
Death IHT : on lifetime gifts within seven years of death (CLTs and PETs) and on the estate value	6 months after the end of the month of death	
Deed of variation	2 years from the date of death – in writing	
Transfer of unused Nil rate band to spouse or civil partner	2 years from the date of the second death	

Corporation tax

Election / claim	Time limit
Replacement of business asset relief for companies (Rollover relief)	4 years from the end of the later of: – the accounting period in which the disposal occurred – the accounting period in which the acquisition of the replacement occurred
Agree the amount of trading losses to carry forward	4 years from the end of the chargeable accounting period in which the loss arose
Current year set-off of trading losses against total profits (income and gains), and 12 month carry back of trading losses against total profits (income and gains)	2 years from the end of the chargeable accounting period in which the loss arose
Surrender of current period trading losses to other group companies (Group relief)	2 years after the claimant company's chargeable accounting period
Election for transfer of capital gain or loss to another company within the gains group	2 years from the end of the chargeable accounting period in which the disposal occurred by the company actually making the disposal

Self assessment – companies

Election / claim	Time limit
Pay day for small and medium companies	9 months and one day after the end of the chargeable accounting period
Pay day for large companies	Instalments due on 14th day of: – Seventh, Tenth, Thirteenth, and Sixteenth month **after the start** of the chargeable accounting period
Filing dates	Later of: – 12 months from the end of the chargeable accounting period – 3 months form the issue of a notice to deliver a corporation tax return
Companies error or mistake claim	4 years from the end of the chargeable accounting period
HMRC can open an enquiry	12 months from the actual submission of the return
Retention of records	6 years from the end of the chargeable accounting period

Value added tax

Election / claim	Time limit
Compulsory registration Historic test: – Notify HMRC	30 days from end of the month in which the threshold was exceeded
– Charge VAT	Beginning of the month, one month after the month in which the threshold was exceeded
Future test: – Notify HMRC	30 days from the date it is anticipated that the threshold will be exceeded
– Charge VAT	the date it is anticipated that the threshold will be exceeded (i.e. the beginning of the 30 day period)
Compulsory deregistration	30 days from cessation
Filing of VAT return and payment of VAT	End of month following the return period

Section 1

PRACTICE QUESTIONS

TAXATION OF INDIVIDUALS

EMPLOYMENT

1   BENNY KORERE

Assume today's date is 1 December 2013.

Benny Korere has been employed as the sales director of Golden Tan plc since 1999. He earns an annual salary of £32,000 and is provided with a petrol-driven company car which has a CO_2 emission rate of 167g/km and had a list price when new of £22,360. In August 2010, when he was first provided with the car, Benny paid the company £6,100 towards the capital cost of the car. Golden Tan plc does not pay for any of Benny's private petrol and he is also required to pay his employer £18 per month as a condition of being able to use the car for private purposes.

On 1 December 2013 Golden Tan plc notified Benny that he would be made redundant on 28 February 2014. On that day the company will pay him his final month's salary together with a payment of £8,000 in lieu of the three remaining months of his six-month notice period in accordance with his employment contract. In addition the company will pay him £17,500 in return for agreeing not to work for any of its competitors for the six-month period ending 31 August 2014.

On receiving notification of his redundancy, Benny immediately contacted Joe Egmont, the managing director of Summer Glow plc, who offered him a senior management position leading the company's expansion into Eastern Europe. Summer Glow plc is one of Golden Tan plc's competitors and one of the most innovative companies in the industry, although not all of its strategies have been successful.

Benny has agreed to join Summer Glow plc on 1 September 2014 for an annual salary of £39,000. On the day he joins the company, Summer Glow plc will grant him an option to purchase 10,000 ordinary shares in the company for £2·20 per share under an unapproved share option scheme. Benny can exercise the option once he has been employed for six months but must hold the shares for at least a year before he sells them.

The new job will require Benny to spend a considerable amount of time in London. Summer Glow plc has offered Benny the exclusive use of a flat that the company purchased on 1 June 2010 for £165,000; the flat is currently rented out. The flat will be made available from 1 September 2014. The company will pay all of the utility bills relating to the flat as well as furnishing and maintaining it. Summer Glow plc has also suggested that if Benny would rather live in a more central part of the city, the company could sell the existing flat and buy a more centrally located one, of the same value, with the proceeds.

On 15 March 2014 Benny intends to sell 5,800 shares in Mahana plc, a quoted company, for £24,608. His transactions in the company's shares have been as follows:

		£
June 2003	Purchased 8,400 shares	10,240
February 2006	Sale of rights nil paid	610
January 2011	Purchased 1,300 shares	2,281

The sale of rights, nil paid, was not treated as a part disposal of Benny's holding in Mahana plc.

Benny's shareholding in Mahana plc represents less than 1% of the company's issued ordinary share capital. He will not make any other capital disposals in 2013/14.

In addition to his employment income, Benny receives rental income of £4,000 (net of deductible expenses) each year. He normally submits his tax return in August but he has not yet prepared his return for 2012/13. He expects to be very busy in the later part of 2013 and is planning to prepare his tax return in late February 2014. He does not intend to file electronically.

Required:

(a) Calculate Benny's employment income for 2013/14. (4 marks)

(b) (i) Advise Benny of the income tax implications of the grant and exercise of the share options in Summer Glow plc on the assumption that the share price on 1 September 2014 and on the day he exercises the options is £3.35 per share.

Explain why the share option scheme is not free from risk by reference to the rules of the scheme and the circumstances surrounding the company. (4 marks)

(ii) List the additional information required in order to calculate the employment income benefit in respect of the provision of the furnished flat for 2014/15.

Advise Benny of the potential income tax implications of requesting a more centrally located flat in accordance with the company's offer. (4 marks)

(c) Calculate Benny's capital gains tax liability for 2013/14. (3 marks)

(d) State the implications of Benny missing the 31 October filing deadline for his 2012/13 paper tax return and identify the penalties and interest that may arise if he submits the tax return in accordance with his plans. (4 marks)

You should assume that the rates and allowances for the tax year 2012/13 apply throughout this question. (Total: 19 marks)

2 CLIFFORD AND AMANDA (ADAPTED)

You have received the following email from your manager, John Jones.

From	John Jones
Date	13 July 2013
To	Tax senior
Subject	Clifford and Amanda Johnson

I have just had a call from a prospective new client, Clifford Johnson. He and his wife are thinking of using us as tax advisers and during the course of the conversation I have made some notes which are attached to this e-mail.

Clifford is looking for some capital gains tax advice with regard to the disposal of a house. He has given me all of the relevant details we require at this stage.

Clifford has also informed me that his wife, Amanda, would like some income tax advice as her remuneration package is due to change. On her behalf he has supplied me with all the relevant details.

I have requested that I meet with both Clifford and Amanda next week to discuss their issues and I will be confirming the meeting with them by e-mail tomorrow.

Please can you review the attachment and prepare some notes for me to take to the meeting.

In your notes can you make sure you include the following:

(i)   A calculation of Clifford's capital gains tax liability for 2013/14 on the assumption that the Oxford house, together with its entire garden, is sold on 31 July 2013.

Please make some reference to the relevance of the size of the garden in your calculations.

(ii)   Some brief notes on the capital gains tax implications of the alternative of selling the Oxford house and garden by means of two separate disposals as proposed.

Do not bother to do any calculations on this option at this stage though.

(iii)   A calculation of Amanda's income tax payable for the tax year 2012/13.

(iv)   Some brief notes explaining the income tax implications for Amanda for the tax year 2013/14 of the additional benefits offered by her employer, Shearer plc.

Please can you also draft me a paragraph suitable for me to copy and paste into in my e-mail to Clifford tomorrow explaining our firm's policy when acting on behalf of both husband and wife.

We should also express any reservations we have in accepting and acting upon information supplied by Clifford in relation to Amanda's affairs.

Thanks

John Jones

The notes taken by your manager and attached to the e-mail are set out below:

To	The files
From	Tax manager
Date	13 July 2013
Subject	Clifford and Amanda Johnson – prospective new clients

Proposed meeting	w/c 15 July 2013
Clifford	Aged 54
Amanda	Aged 45
Date of marriage	1 February 2003

Oxford house

- Clifford moved into Amanda's house in London on the day they were married.

- Clifford's own house in Oxford, where he had lived since acquiring it for £129,400 on 1 August 2001, has been empty since the date of marriage, although he and Amanda have used it when visiting friends.

- Clifford has been offered £284,950 for the Oxford house and has decided that it is time to sell it.

- The house has a large garden such that Clifford is also considering an offer for the house and a part only of the garden.

- He would then sell the remainder of the garden at a later date as a building plot. His total sales proceeds will be higher if he sells the property in this way.

- Clifford is a higher rate taxpayer who has realised taxable capital gains in 2013/14 in excess of his capital gains tax annual exempt amount

Action required

Clifford would like to know:

- What his capital gains tax liability would be if he sold the house and its entire garden on 31 July 2013 for the offered price of £284,950, and

- The implications of his proposed two-part sale.

Amanda's current employment package

- Amanda began working for Shearer plc, a quoted company, on 1 June 2012 having had a two year break from her career.

- She earns an annual salary of £136,600 and was paid a bonus of £15,750 in August 2012 for agreeing to come and work for the company.

- As Amanda has made no pension provision to date Shearer plc agreed as part of her remuneration package to contribute £60,000 to a registered pension scheme on her behalf. This contribution was made on 1 September 2012.

- On 1 August 2012 Amanda was provided with a fully expensed company car, including the provision of private petrol, which had a list price when new of £23,400 and CO_2 emissions rate of 169 grams per kilometre.

- Amanda is required to pay Shearer plc £22 per month in respect of the private use of the car.

- In June and July 2012 Amanda used her own car whilst on company business. She drove 720 business miles during this two month period and was paid 34 p per mile.

- Amanda had PAYE of £47,785 deducted from her gross salary in the tax year 2012/13.

Amanda's increased employment package

- After working for Shearer plc for a full year, Amanda becomes entitled to the following additional benefits:

  - The opportunity to purchase a large number of shares in Shearer plc on 1 July 2013 for £3.30 per share. It is anticipated that the share price on that day will be at least £7.50 per share. The company will make an interest-free loan to Amanda equal to the cost of the shares to be repaid in two years.

> – Exclusive free use of the company sailing boat for one week in August 2013. The sailing boat was purchased by Shearer plc in January 2011 for use by senior employees and costs the company £1,400 a week in respect of its crew and other running expenses.
>
> **Amanda's other income**
>
> – Amanda received the following income from quoted investments in 2012/13:
>
> | | £ |
> |---|---:|
> | – Dividends in respect of quoted trading company shares | 1,395 |
> | – Dividends paid by a Real Estate Investment Trust (out of tax exempt property income) | 485 |
>
> – On 1 May 2012, Amanda was granted a 22 year lease of a commercial investment property.
>
> – She paid the landlord a premium of £6,900 and also pays rent of £2,100 per month.
>
> – On 1 June 2012 Amanda granted a nine year sub-lease of the property.
>
> – She received a premium of £14,700 and receives rent of £2,100 per month.
>
> **Action required**
>
> According to Clifford, Amanda would like to know:
>
> – Her income tax liability for 2012/13, and
>
> – The income tax implications of additional employment benefits she will receive in 2013/14.

Required:

(a) **Prepare the notes requested by your manager.**

The notes should address all the issues and include the calculations you think are required.

The following marks are available for the four parts to be addressed:

    (i) **Clifford's capital gains tax liability if he accepts the offer price.** **(5 marks)**

    (ii) **An explanation of the capital gains tax implications of two separate disposals.** **(3 marks)**

    (iii) **Amanda's income tax payable for the tax year 2012/13.** **(11 marks)**

    (iv) **Explanation of the income tax implications of the additional employment benefits.** **(6 marks)**

Additional marks will be awarded for the presentation of the notes and the effectiveness with which the information is communicated. **(2 marks)**

You should assume that the rates and allowances for the tax year 2012/13 apply throughout this question.

(b) **Draft the paragraph to insert in your manager's e-mail concerning the ethical issues of acting on behalf of both a husband and his wife.** **(4 marks)**

                                             (Total: 31 marks)

3   DOKHAM (ADAPTED) *Walk in the footsteps of a top tutor*

 Timed question with Online tutor debrief

Dokham requires advice on his pension position at retirement, the rules relating to enterprise management incentive (EMI) schemes and the tax implications of his mother helping to pay his children's school fees.

The following information has been obtained from a telephone conversation with Dokham.

Dokham:

–   Is 39 years old and married with two children.

–   Is domiciled, resident and ordinarily resident in the UK.

–   Has been offered a job by Criollo plc.

–   His mother, Virginia, has offered to contribute towards Dokham's children's school fees.

The job offer from Criollo plc:

–   Dokham's salary will be £70,000 per year.

–   Criollo plc will make annual contributions of £8,000 into Dokham's personal pension scheme.

–   Criollo plc will invite Dokham to join the company's EMI scheme.

Dokham's pension arrangements:

–   Dokham has not made any pension contributions to date.

–   Dokham intends to make gross annual contributions of £11,000 into a registered personal pension scheme.

The EMI scheme:

–   The scheme will have five members including Dokham.

–   Criollo plc will grant Dokham an option to purchase 26,200 shares at a price of £9·00 per share. This will represent a holding of less than 1% of the company.

–   The option can be exercised at any time until 31 December 2018.

–   Criollo plc's current share price is £9·53.

Dokham has requested explanations of the following in respect of the job offer from Criollo plc:

–   What would be the difference for me, from a tax point of view, if Criollo plc increased my salary by £8,000 instead of contributing into my personal pension scheme and I made additional gross annual pension contributions of £8,000?

–   What benefits will I receive from the pension scheme, how will they be taxed and when can I receive them?

–   Why might Criollo plc have told me that it is 'not possible' to increase the number of shares I can purchase within the EMI scheme?

- What are the tax implications for me when I exercise my EMI share option and when I sell the shares?

Virginia:

- Is 68 years old.

- Is domiciled, resident and ordinarily resident in the UK.

- Has taxable income of more than £120,000 per year.

- Owns a portfolio of quoted shares that is worth more than £500,000.

- Uses her capital gains tax and inheritance tax annual exemptions every year.

- Is considering three alternative ways of contributing towards Dokham's children's school fees.

The three alternative ways of contributing towards the children's school fees:

- Make a one-off gift to Dokham of £54,000 in cash.

- Make a one-off gift to Dokham of 9,800 shares (a holding of less than 1%) in Panatella plc, a quoted company, worth £54,000.

- Make a gift to Dokham of £8,000 in cash every year for the next seven years.

Required:

(a) **Provide the information requested by Dokham in respect of the job offer from Criollo plc as set out above.** **(9 marks)**

(b) **Explain in detail the possible tax liabilities that could result from the three alternative ways proposed by Virginia to contribute towards the children's school fees.** **(11 marks)**

(Total: 20 marks)

 Calculate your allowed time, allocate the time to the separate parts...................

UNINCORPORATED BUSINESSES

4   BOB

Assume today's date is 15 May 2013.

In March 2007, Bob was made redundant from his job as a furniture salesman. He decided to travel round the world, and did so, returning to the UK in May 2009. Bob then decided to set up his own business selling furniture. He started trading on 1 October 2009. After some initial success, the business made losses as Bob tried to win more customers. However, he was eventually successful, and the business subsequently made profits.

The results for Bob's business were as follows:

Period	Tax Trading Profits/(losses) £
1 October 2009 – 30 April 2010	3,500
1 May 2010 – 30 April 2011	(18,000)
1 May 2011 – 30 April 2012	41,040

In 2012/13, Bob required additional funds for his business, so he raised money in three ways:

(1) Bob is a classic car enthusiast and he has collected a number of cars over the last 20 years as well as having acquired a number by inheritance. To raise money he sold a number of pieces from this collection. Each one raised between £4,000 and £6,000. He obtained the sales by creating a website and advertising the cars.

Bob has not declared these transactions as income, as he believes that the proceeds from selling the cars are non-taxable.

(2) He disposed of two paintings and an antique silver coffee set at auction, realising chargeable gains totalling £24,120.

(3) Bob took a part time job in a furniture store on 1 January 2011. His annual salary has remained at £12,790 per year since he started this employment.

Bob has 5,000 shares in Willis Ltd, an unquoted trading company based in the UK. He subscribed for these shares in August 2008, paying £3 per share. On 1 December 2012, Bob received a letter informing him that the company had gone into receivership. As a result, his shares were almost worthless. The receivers dealing with the company estimated that on the liquidation of the company, he would receive no more than 10p per share for his shareholding. He has not yet received any money.

Required:

(a) Write a letter to Bob advising him on whether or not he is correct in believing that his car sales are non-taxable.

Your advice should include reference to the badges of trade and their application to this case. **(9 marks)**

(b) Assuming that the income from the sale of the cars is not treated as trading income, calculate Bob's taxable income and gains for all relevant tax years, using any loss reliefs in the most tax-efficient manner, and quantify the tax saved.

Your answer should include an explanation of the loss reliefs available and your reasons for using (or not using) them. **(12 marks)**

Assume that the rates and allowances for 2012/13 apply throughout this part of the question.

(c) State any reliefs Bob could claim regarding the fall in value of his shares in Willis Ltd, and describe how the operation of any such reliefs could reduce Bob's taxable income. **(4 marks)**

(Total: 25 marks)

5 GLORIA SEAFORD (ADAPTED)

Gloria Seaford is UK resident and ordinarily resident but is not domiciled in the UK. She has owned and run a shop in the UK selling books, cards and small gifts as a sole trader since June 1999.

Gloria will be 66 on 4 January 2014 and, with this in mind, on 1 November 2013 she started looking for a buyer for the business so that she could retire. She has received an offer of £335,000 for the shop premises from Ned Skillet who intends to convert the building into a restaurant.

The following information has been extracted from her client files and from a recent meeting with Gloria.

Gloria's business

– purchased current premises, which were built in 1993, in July 2012 for £267,000

– registered for value added tax

– plans to sell the shop premises to Ned on 28 February 2014 and cease to trade on that day

– estimates that on 28 February 2014 she will be able to sell the shelving and other shop fittings to local businesses for £1,400 (no item will be sold for more than cost)

– has agreed to sell all inventory on hand on 28 February 2014 to a competitor at cost plus 5%. This is expected to result in sales revenue of £8,300

– only other business asset is a van that is currently used 85% for business purposes. The van is expected to be worth £4,700 on 28 February 2014 and Gloria will keep it for her private use

– tax adjusted trading profit for the year ended 31 October 2013 was £39,245

– forecast tax adjusted trading profit for the period ending 28 February 2014, before taking account of the final sale of the business assets on that date and before deduction of capital allowances, is £11,500

– Gloria has overlap profits brought forward of £15,720.

Capital allowances

– the tax written down value on the capital allowance general pool at 31 October 2013 was £4,050

– purchased equipment for £820 in November 2013

– the tax written down value of the van at 31 October 2013 was £4,130.

Other income in 2013/14

– taxable retirement pension of £5,312 received

– bank interest of £13,500 was credited to her bank account.

Capital assets and capital disposals

– on 1 November 2011 Gloria inherited the following assets from her aunt.

	Probate value £
Painting	15,200
17,500 shares in All Over plc	11,400

- sold the painting in May 2013 and realised a gain of £7,100

- at the end of April 2012 Gloria received notification that All Over plc, a quoted trading company, was in receivership and that there would be a maximum payment of 3 pence per share

- unused capital losses as at 6 April 2013 of £31,400.

Investment opportunities

- Eric Sloane, a business associate of Gloria, has provided her with the details of a number of investment opportunities including Bubble Inc, an investment company incorporated in the country of Oceania where its share register is maintained

- Gloria plans to buy a 2% share in Bubble Inc in May 2014, and expects to receive dividends of £12,000 per annum from 2014/15, which she will leave in an overseas bank account

- There is no foreign tax withheld on these dividends

- Gloria paid Eric £300 for his advice.

Required:

(a)   State the value added tax implications of the sale by Gloria of her business assets and cessation of trade.

Calculations are not required for this part of the question.   (3 marks)

(b)   Compute Gloria's total income tax and national insurance liability for 2013/14.

(7 marks)

(c)   (i)   Compute Gloria's capital gains tax liability for 2013/14 ignoring any claims or elections available to reduce the liability.   (4 marks)

(ii)   Explain, with reasons, the relief available in respect of the fall in value of the shares in All Over plc, identify the years in which it can be claimed and state the time limit for submitting the claim.   (3 marks)

(d)   (i)   Explain the options available to Gloria in respect of the UK tax on the dividends paid by Bubble Inc.

You should calculate the tax payable under each alternative for 2014/15, assuming that Gloria's other income remains the same as in 2013/14, and advise which basis should be chosen.   (8 marks)

(ii)   Explain the capital gains tax and inheritance tax implications of a future disposal of the shares.

Clearly state, giving reasons, whether or not the payment made to Eric is allowable for capital gains tax purposes.   (4 marks)

You should assume that the rates and allowances for the tax year 2012/13 apply throughout this question.

(Total: 29 marks)

 Online question assistance

6 SIMONE (ADAPTED) *Walk in the footsteps of a top tutor*

Simone is a partner in the firm Ellington and Co. She is seeking advice on the tax efficient use of her share of the partnership's loss for the year ended 5 April 2013. Simone intends to establish a new business and is considering the need to register for the purposes of value added tax (VAT).

The following information has been obtained from a meeting with Simone.

Simone's income and capital gains:

–   Dividends received of £12,600 in the tax year 2011/12, £10,800 in the tax year 2012/13 and £nil in subsequent years.

–   Share of profits from Ellington and Co for the year ended 5 April 2012 of £48,200.

–   Capital gains of £94,000 on the sale of a portfolio of quoted shares on 1 February 2013.

Ellington and Co:

–   Has been trading for many years.

–   Has two partners; Ellington and Simone. A third partner, Basie, retired on 28 February 2013.

–   Made a loss in the year ended 5 April 2013.

–   Is budgeted to make tax adjusted trading profits of no more than £25,000 per year for the next few years.

–   Is registered for the purposes of VAT.

Ellington and Co – results for the year ended 5 April 2013:

–   The firm made a tax adjusted trading loss, before deduction of capital allowances, of £90,000.

–   The firm purchased office equipment on 1 December 2012 for £21,200.

–   The balance on the capital allowances main pool as at 5 April 2012 was £700.

Ellington and Co – profit sharing arrangements:

–   From 6 April 2012 until 28 February 2013

	Ellington		Simone		Basie
Annual salaries	£15,000		£11,500		£13,000
Profit sharing ratio	3	:	2	:	2

–   From 1 March 2013

	Ellington		Simone
Annual salaries	£14,000		£14,000
Profit sharing ratio	1	:	1

Simone's new business:

–   Simone intends to start trading on 1 September 2013.

–   Taxable trading profit is budgeted to be approximately £1,500 per month.

–   Taxable supplies are expected to be between £75,000 and £95,000 in the first year.

– Simone does not wish to register voluntarily for VAT.

Required:

(a) (i) Calculate Simone's share of the tax adjusted trading loss for the year ended 5 April 2013; **(5 marks)**

(ii) State the alternative strategies available to Simone in respect of her share of the taxable trading loss for the year ended 5 April 2013. **(3 marks)**

(iii) Explain, using supporting calculations where necessary, which of the strategies will save the most tax and calculate the total tax saved via the operation of this strategy.

Your calculations should be based on the assumption that the tax rates and allowances for the year 2012/13 apply to all relevant years. **(8 marks)**

(b) Explain when Simone would be required to register and to start charging her customers VAT and, in relation to this, comment on the relevance of Ellington and Co being VAT registered.

You are not required to prepare calculations for part (b) of this question.

(4 marks)
(Total: 20 marks)

---

7 **ELLROY (ADAPTED)** *Walk in the footsteps of a top tutor*

Ellroy started an unincorporated business on 1 October 2013. He requires advice on his choice of accounting date, a possible change of accounting date and the use of the flat rate scheme for the purposes of VAT (value added tax).

The following information has been obtained from telephone conversations with Ellroy.

Ellroy:

– Is 47 years old.

– Is considering either a 31 March or a 30 September year end in 2014 and future years for his new business.

– Receives a share of profits from a partnership of more than £165,000 per year.

The budgeted trading profits of the business:

– It should be assumed that the profits set out below will accrue evenly in each trading period.

– The profits before deduction of capital allowances but after all other tax adjustments have been made are:

	£
Six months ending 31 March 2014	13,100
Year ending 31 March 2015	87,200
Year ending 31 March 2016	74,400

– Ellroy's only capital expenditure will be the purchase of two vans at a total cost of £22,000 in June 2014.

The VAT position of the business:

–   The budgeted annual turnover and expenses of the fully established business are:

		£
Turnover (all standard rated)		100,000
Expenses:	standard rated	21,000
	zero rated	3,000
	outside the scope of VAT	5,000

–   All the figures exclude VAT.

Required:

(a)   (i)   Calculate the difference in the total income tax and national insurance that will be payable by Ellroy for the first three tax years of the business depending on whether he adopts a 31 March or 30 September year end;

(8 marks)

(ii)   Explain the tax implications, including the effect on Ellroy's taxable profits for 2016/17 if, having initially adopted a 31 March year end, he were to change his accounting date and prepare accounts for the six months ending 30 September 2016.

You should consider the possibility of both rising and falling levels of profitability.   **(7 marks)**

(b)   Explain, by reference to the budgeted annual turnover and expenses of the fully established business and with the aid of supporting calculations, the maximum flat rate percentage that can apply to Ellroy's business such that it would be financially beneficial for him to join the flat rate scheme.   **(5 marks)**

You should ignore the 1% discount for the first 12 months of registration.

(Total: 20 marks)

CHANGING BUSINESS SCENARIOS

8   DELIA JONES

Delia Jones, aged 42, has been running a successful restaurant business as a sole trader since 1 September 2002. She has recently accepted an offer from Fastfood Ltd, an unconnected company quoted on the Alternative Investment Market, to purchase her business.

Fastfood Ltd would like to complete the purchase on 31 March 2013, but are prepared to delay until 30 April 2013 should this be beneficial for Delia. The purchase consideration will consist of either cash or ordinary shares in Fastfood Ltd.

The following information is available:

(1)   Delia's tax adjusted trading profits are as follows:

	£
Year ended 31 August 2011	65,400
Year ended 31 August 2012	77,200
Period ended 31 March 2013 (forecast)	58,500
April 2013 (forecast)	9,000

The figures for the years ended 31 August 2011 and 2012 are adjusted for capital allowances, whilst those for the period ended 31 March 2013 and for April 2013 are before taking account of capital allowances.

Delia has overlap profits brought forward of £24,200.

(2)   The forecast market values of Delia's business assets at both 31 March 2013 and 30 April 2013 are as follows:

	£
Goodwill	125,000
Freehold property (A)	462,000
Freehold property (B)	118,000
Fixtures and fittings	240,000
Net current liabilities	(95,000)
	850,000

Freehold property (A) cost £230,000 in 2002. Freehold property (B) was purchased during June 2010 for £94,000. The goodwill has a nil cost.

(3)   The tax written down value of the fixtures and fittings at 31 August 2012 was £114,000. Fixtures and fittings costing £31,000 were purchased on 15 December 2012. All of Delia's fixtures and fittings qualify as plant and machinery for capital allowances purposes, and are being sold for less than original cost.

(4)   Delia has unused capital losses of £12,400 brought forward from 2011/12.

(5)   Delia currently has no other income or outgoings. Her investment income will be £45,000 p.a. for 2013/14 onwards, regardless of whether the consideration is taken as cash or shares.

(6)   Delia will not become an employee or director of Fastfood Ltd. If the consideration is in the form of shares in Fastfood Ltd, then Delia's holding will represent 7.5% of the company's share capital. Delia will sell the shares at regular intervals over the next ten years.

(7)   Both Delia and Fastfood Ltd are registered for VAT.

Required:

(a)   **Assuming that the business is sold on 31 March 2013 with the consideration being wholly in the form of cash:**

   (i)   **Calculate Delia's trading income assessment for 2012/13.** **(5 marks)**

   (ii)   **Calculate Delia's CGT liability for 2012/13.** **(6 marks)**

   (iii)   **Advise Delia of the VAT implications arising from the sale.** **(2 marks)**

(b)   **Advise Delia as to the income tax, CGT and NIC implications of:**

   (i)   **Delaying the sale of the business until 30 April 2013.** **(7 marks)**

   (ii)   **Taking the consideration wholly in the form of ordinary shares in Fastfood Ltd, rather than as cash.** **(7 marks)**

You should assume that the tax rates and allowances for 2012/13 apply throughout.

(Total: 27 marks)

9 DAVID AND PATRICIA

(a) Assume that today's date is 1 December 2012.

David is 35 years old and married to Patricia who is 32 years old. The couple have one child who is six years old.

David has been employed since 2002 earning £3,750 per month (monthly PAYE deducted £670). He will have no other income in the tax year 2012/13. From 6 April 2013 he will have a source of property business income of £45,000 per year.

David intends to cease his current employment on 31 December 2012, and start trading as a self-employed businessman on 1 January 2013 preparing accounts to 31 March each year. His business plan shows profits in the region of £60,600 per year, before any payment to his wife, Patricia.

Patricia has been employed as a bookkeeper since 2004, earning £1,100 per month (monthly PAYE deducted £95). She will also cease her current employment on 31 December 2012 and will keep the books and prepare the accounts for David's business from 1 January 2013. She will continue to work the same number of hours per week as she does in her current employment.

David would like some advice on the taxation implications of involving his wife, Patricia, in his business either as an employee, or, alternatively, by taking her into partnership.

David has never previously had dealings with HMRC, so would also like details as to when he should notify HMRC about his new business for income tax purposes; when his 2012/13 self assessment income tax return is due; and how he should pay the income tax due on the profits made by the business in both the first and subsequent years.

Required:

(i) **Evaluate the taxation implications for David of:**

(1) David employing his wife Patricia, and

(2) taking her into partnership.

Support your answer with calculations of the income tax (IT) and National Insurance Contributions (NIC) payable, based on the expected trading results for a full year of operation and the tax rates and allowances for 2012/13.

(11 marks)

(ii) **State the information David requires concerning tax administration.**

(4 marks)

(b) Assume that today's date is 1 May 2013.

David decided to form a partnership with his wife, Patricia, sharing profits and losses equally, and to adopt a 31 March year end for accounting purposes.

The business in fact showed a loss of £40,000 in the three month period to 31 March 2013, but profits of £60,600 per annum are still anticipated for future years.

Required:

Identify the loss reliefs available to David and explain which of the available reliefs would be most beneficial for him to claim.

Support your answer with calculations of the income tax (IT) saving achieved in each case. **(10 marks)**

Assume that the tax rates and allowances for 2012/13 apply throughout this question.

(Total: 25 marks)

10 THE STILETTO PARTNERSHIP (ADAPTED)

Assume today's date is 6 June 2013.

Clint, Ben and Amy are three partners in The Stiletto Partnership, who shared the profits of the business equally.

On 28 February 2013 the partners sold the business to Razor Ltd, in exchange for shares in Razor Ltd, with each former partner owning one third of the new company.

The following information has been extracted from client files and various telephone conversations with the partners.

The Stiletto Partnership

– Recent tax adjusted trading profits are as follows:

	£
Year ended 30 June 2012	107,124
1 July 2012 to 28 February 2013	96,795

– Estimated partnership's tax adjusted trading profits for the period from 1 March 2013 to 30 April 2013 would have been £20,760.

Clint Toon

– Aged 65 on 5 October 2012.

– Retired when the business was sold to Razor Ltd.

– Concerned that if the sale of the partnership, and his retirement, had been delayed until 30 April 2013, his total tax liability would have been reduced.

– His only other income is gross pension income of £8,100 per year, which he began receiving in the tax year 2011/12.

– Does not work for Razor Ltd and has not received any salary or dividends from the company.

– Overlap profits were £14,250 from when the partnership began trading.

Razor Ltd

– UK resident company that manufactures industrial cutting tools.

– On 1 July 2013, Razor Ltd will subscribe for the whole of the ordinary share capital of Cutlass Inc, a company newly incorporated in the country of Sharpenia.

– It is intended that Cutlass Inc will purchase partly finished tools from Razor Ltd and customise them in Sharpenia.

– It is anticipated that Cutlass Inc's annual taxable total profits will be approximately £120,000.

– Ben and Amy will be the directors of Cutlass Inc, although Ben will not be involved in the company's business on a day-to-day basis.

Amy Peters

– Currently resident, ordinarily resident and domiciled in the UK.

– Intends to spend one or two weeks each month in the country of Sharpenia looking after the company's affairs.

– The remainder of her time will be spent in the UK.

– She has employment contracts with both Razor Ltd and Cutlass Inc and her duties for Cutlass Inc will be carried out wholly in Sharpenia.

– Cutlass Inc will pay for Amy's flights to and from Sharpenia and for her husband and baby to visit her there twice a year.

The tax system in the country of Sharpenia

– The system of income tax and corporation tax in the country of Sharpenia is broadly similar to that in the UK although the rate of corporation tax is 38% regardless of the level of profits

– There is a double tax treaty between the UK and Sharpenia based on the OECD model treaty

– The clause in the treaty dealing with company residency states that a company resident in both countries under domestic law will be regarded under the treaty as being resident only in the country where it is effectively managed and controlled

– Sharpenia is not a member of the European Union.

Required:

(a) (i) Calculate Clint's taxable trading profits for the tax years 2012/13 and 2013/14 for both of the alternative retirement dates (28 February 2013 and 30 April 2013). **(3 marks)**

(ii) Analyse the effect of delaying the sale of the business of the Stiletto Partnership to Razor Ltd until 30 April 2013 on Clint's income tax and national insurance position.

You are not required to prepare detailed calculations of his income tax or national insurance liabilities. **(4 marks)**

(b) Draft a report as at today's date advising Cutlass Inc on its proposed activities.

The report should cover the following issues:

(i) The rate at which the profits of Cutlass Inc will be taxed.

This section of the report should explain:

– the company's residency position and what Ben and Amy would have to do in order for the company to be regarded as resident in the UK under the double tax treaty

– the meaning of the term 'permanent establishment' and the implications of Cutlass Inc having a permanent establishment in Sharpenia

- the rate at which the profits of Cutlass Inc will be taxed on the assumption that it is resident in the UK under the double tax treaty and either does or does not have a permanent establishment in Sharpenia. **(9 marks)**

(ii) The UK value added tax (VAT) implications for Razor Ltd of selling tools to and purchasing tools from Cutlass Inc. **(2 marks)**

(iii) The extent to which Amy will be subject to income tax in the UK on her earnings in respect of duties performed for Cutlass Inc and the travel costs paid for by that company. **(5 marks)**

Appropriateness of format and presentation of the report and the effectiveness with which its advice is communicated. **(2 marks)**

You should assume that the income tax rates and allowances for the tax year 2012/13 and the corporation tax rates and allowances for the Financial year 2012 apply throughout this question.

(Total: 25 marks)

11 FRANK COLTRANE (ADAPTED) *Walk in the footsteps of a top tutor*

An extract from an e-mail from your manager is set out below.

I attach a letter from Frank Coltrane who is about to sell the unincorporated business (known as 'Alto') that he has owned and operated since 2006.

I would like you to prepare notes on the tax issues raised by Frank for me to use at a meeting we are going to have later this week. I set out below some thoughts I have had which you should refer to when preparing your notes.

(i) Capital gains tax

I have calculated that Frank's capital gains on the sale of the unincorporated business will be £420,000 and I'd like you to assume that the Tenor plc shares will be sold for £1,400,000 on 31 July 2016. Because the sale of Alto will be Frank's only chance to get Entrepreneurs' relief we have agreed that he will disclaim incorporation relief so please prepare your calculations on this basis. By the way, Frank has capital losses brought forward as at 6 April 2013 of £155,000.

Frank may be willing to gift some shares in Tenor plc to his wife prior to both of them selling their shares on 31 July 2016. Please include a summary of all of the tax implications of such a gift and the maximum potential tax saving. Both Frank and his wife are resident, ordinarily resident and domiciled in the UK.

(ii) Corporation tax

Keep your comments brief and specific to Soprano Ltd. Soprano Ltd has trading losses brought forward as at 1 August 2012 of £65,000. I have reviewed the consolidated financial statements of Tenor plc and can confirm that the group is large for all aspects of corporation tax.

(iii)   Value added tax (VAT)

      Don't forget that the supply of baby clothes is zero rated.

Please keep your notes brief and clear so that I can find my way around them during the meeting.

Alice

The letter from Frank Coltrane is set out below.

---

                                             1 Garden Walk
                                               Manchester

Ms A Peters
F & G Co
Manchester

                                              28 May 2013

Dear Alice

You'll be pleased to know that I've finally agreed a deal with the management of Tenor plc and that the company is going to buy my 'Alto' business on 31 July 2013 for £1,350,000 despite my recent poor results.

I'm delighted with the price even though they will only pay me £200,000 in cash with the balance in shares in Tenor plc. My shareholding in Tenor plc will be less than 1% and we have agreed that I will not sell the shares until I leave the company's employment (although I am allowed to give shares to my wife if I wish).

As you know, Tenor plc is a very large quoted company (it has 34 wholly owned UK resident trading subsidiaries). I'm going to be put in charge of Soprano Ltd, one of the smallest subsidiaries, that makes and sells baby clothes.

Soprano Ltd is expected to have taxable trading profits (it has no other income or capital gains) of at least £80,000 and possibly as much as £110,000 on turnover of £500,000 for the year ending 31 July 2013.

We have agreed a fixed term employment contract from 1 August 2013 until 31 July 2016 with an annual salary of £135,000.

Now that the deal is done I need the following from you.

(i)   A calculation of the amount of capital gains tax I will have to pay in respect of both the sale of my Alto business and the shares in Tenor plc and when the tax will be payable in each case.

(ii)   I have no experience of corporation tax. Please let me have a brief explanation of the taxable periods of Soprano Ltd, its tax rates and the dates on which the tax will be payable.

       Soprano Ltd buys services from two other subsidiaries of Tenor plc. There has been a proposal that the prices charged to Soprano Ltd in the future should be increased in order to reduce its effective rate of corporation tax. Is this a sensible suggestion?

(iii)   Please let me have your interpretation of the value added tax (VAT) position of Soprano Ltd as I keep getting confused in my discussions with the management of Tenor plc. As you know, I pay VAT annually on the cash basis in respect of my Alto business.

       Why does Soprano Ltd prepare its VAT returns monthly on the accruals basis?

> Also, why do the other Tenor plc companies charge VAT on the services supplied to Soprano Ltd when all the companies are wholly owned by Tenor plc?
>
> Finally, what is the VAT position when Soprano Ltd purchases raw materials from countries in South America?
>
> Thanks in advance for your help.
>
> Frank

Required:

Prepare the meeting notes requested in the e-mail from your manager. The following marks are available.

(i)	Aspects of capital gains tax together with all of the tax implications of the potential gift to Frank's wife;	**(8 marks)**
(ii)	Aspects of corporation tax;	**(11 marks)**
(iii)	Aspects of value added tax.	**(6 marks)**

(Total: 25 marks)

12   DESIREE (ADAPTED) *Walk in the footsteps of a top tutor*

 Timed question with Online tutor debrief

Desiree requires advice on whether she should run her new business as an unincorporated sole trader or via a company together with the financial implications of registering voluntarily for value added tax (VAT).

The following information has been obtained from a meeting with Desiree.

Desiree:

–   Resigned from her job with Chip plc on 31 May 2013.

–   Had been employed by Chip plc on an annual salary of £60,000 since January 2010.

–   Has no other income apart from bank interest received of less than £1,000 per year.

–   Intends to start a new business, to be called Duchess, on 1 September 2013.

The Duchess business:

–   The business will sell kitchen equipment and utensils.

–   Market research consultants have estimated that 80% of its sales will be to commercial customers.

–   The consultants were paid fees in November 2012 and March 2013.

Budgeted results of the Duchess business:

–   The budgeted tax-adjusted trading profit/(loss) for the first three trading periods are:

	£
Ten months ending 30 June 2014	(46,000)
Year ending 30 June 2015	22,000
Year ending 30 June 2016	64,000

– The fees paid to the market research consultants have been deducted in arriving at the loss of the first period

Desiree's financial position:

– Desiree has not yet decided whether to run the business as an unincorporated sole trader or via a company.

– Her primary objective when deciding whether or not to operate the business via a company is the most beneficial use of the loss.

Registration for VAT:

– The turnover of the business is expected to exceed the VAT registration limit in January 2014.

– Desiree would consider registering for VAT earlier if it were financially advantageous to do so.

– Desiree will import some of her products from outside the EU, but is unsure of the VAT treatment.

Required:

(a) (i) Calculate the taxable trading profit or allowable trading loss of the business for each of the first three taxable periods for the following alternative structures:

  • the business is unincorporated;
  • the business is operated via a company. **(4 marks)**

 (ii) Provide Desiree with a thorough and detailed explanation of the manner in which the budgeted trading loss could be used depending on whether she runs the business as an unincorporated sole trader or via a company and state which business structure would best satisfy her primary objective.

  You are not required to prepare detailed calculations for part (ii) of this part of this question or to consider non-taxation issues. **(9 marks)**

(b) Explain in detail the financial advantages and disadvantages of Desiree registering voluntarily for VAT on 1 September 2013 and the VAT consequences of the imports from outside the EU, assuming she is VAT registered. **(7 marks)**

(Total: 20 marks)

 Calculate your allowed time, allocate the time to the separate parts....................

---

13   VINE (ADAPTED) *Walk in the footsteps of a top tutor*

 Timed question with Online tutor debrief

Vine requires advice on capital allowances, the incorporation of his business together with a subsequent sale of some of his shares, and the tax implications of measures intended to encourage his employees to become involved in a marketing strategy.

The following information has been obtained from a meeting with Vine.

Vine:

– Is 38 years old.

– Purchased a supermarket and began trading on 1 January 2013.

– Will make no capital disposals other than those referred to below.

– Has capital losses brought forward at 6 April 2013 of £6,900.

Vine's plans:

– Vine intends to incorporate the supermarket business, as detailed below, for commercial reasons.

– In June or July 2014 Vine intends to sell 20% of the new company to his store manager for £64,000.

– Vine is developing a marketing strategy called 'the active supermarket'.

– In October 2013 a false ceiling will be installed in the supermarket premises in order to conceal electrical wiring and water pipes.

The incorporation of Vine's business:

– All of the assets and liabilities of the business will be transferred to a new company, Passata Ltd, on 31 July 2013.

– Passata Ltd will be wholly owned by Vine.

– The consideration paid by Passata Ltd will be:

– the maximum amount of cash that can be paid without giving rise to a capital gains tax liability; and

– the issue of 1,200 £1 ordinary shares to Vine in respect of the remainder of the value of the business.

– The cash will be left on a loan account payable to Vine.

The assets and liabilities to be transferred to Passata Ltd:

	Cost	Value	Tax written down value on 31 July 2013
	£	£	£
Premises	205,000	260,000	–
Equipment	55,000	35,000	22,000
Trading inventory		11,000	–
Liabilities		(10,000)	–
Goodwill	Nil	24,000	–
		320,000	

– All of the equipment qualifies for capital allowances and no item is valued at more than cost.

The active supermarket:

– Passata Ltd will purchase six bicycles for a total of £2,400.

– The bicycles will be made available on loan to all employees for travelling to and from work and for making deliveries to customers.

– Employees will be paid 15 pence per mile if they use their own bicycles to make deliveries to customers.

– To help to enable those employees with children to start work earlier, Passata Ltd will provide childcare vouchers of £40 per week.

– On the first Monday of each month employees who cycle to work will receive a free breakfast.

– Each breakfast will cost Passata Ltd £8.

Required:

(a) Explain:

   (i) the capital allowances implications for Vine of the transfer of the equipment to Passata Ltd; and

   (ii) whether or not the false ceiling to be installed in the supermarket premises will qualify as plant and machinery for the purposes of capital allowances.

   (4 marks)

(b) Calculate the chargeable gain arising on the proposed sale of the shares to the store manager and suggest a minor change in relation to the sale that would reduce the capital gains tax due. **(9 marks)**

(c) Outline the tax implications for Passata Ltd and its employees of the active supermarket marketing strategy. **(7 marks)**

You should ignore value added tax (VAT) when answering this question.

(Total: 20 marks)

 Calculate your allowed time, allocate the time to the separate parts...................

CAPITAL TAXES

14 JOAN ARK

Joan Ark, aged 76, has asked for your advice regarding the following gifts that she has made during 2012/13.

(a) On 30 July 2012 Joan made a gift of 250,000 ordinary shares in Orleans plc, a quoted company into a discretionary trust for the benefit of her granddaughters.

On that day the shares were quoted at 146p – 150p, with recorded bargains of 140p, 144p, 149p and 155p.

Joan originally purchased 200,000 shares in Orleans plc during 1997 at a cost of £149,000. Joan also bought 75,000 shares on 15 August 2010 for £69,375 and has subsequently bought 10,000 shares on 21 July 2011 for £14,800.

Orleans plc has an issued share capital of 10 million ordinary shares and Joan has never been a director or employee of the company.

(b) On 15 July 2012 Joan gave 20,000 of her 40,000 ordinary shares in Rouen Ltd, an unquoted trading company, to her son Michael. Rouen Ltd has an issued share capital of 100,000 ordinary shares. Joan's husband also owns 40,000 ordinary shares in the company.

On 15 July 2012 the relevant values of Rouen Ltd's shares were as follows:

Shareholding	Value per share
	£
100%	22.30
80%	17.10
60%	14.50
40%	9.20
20%	7.90

Joan purchased her 40,000 shares in Rouen Ltd during 1999 for £96,400. Her husband works for the company but Joan does not.

(c) On 4 November 2012 Joan gave her grandson an antique vase worth £18,500 as a wedding present. Joan purchased the vase during 1997 for £14,150.

(d) On 15 January 2013 Joan gave agricultural land with an agricultural value of £175,000 to her son Charles. Joan had purchased the land during 2001 for £92,000, and it has always been let out to tenant farmers.

The most recent tenancy agreement which started in June 2003 will soon come to an end, and Joan has obtained planning permission to build residential accommodation on the land. The value of the land with planning permission is £300,000.

Charles owns adjoining agricultural land, and the value of this land will increase from £210,000 to £250,000 as a result of the gift.

(e) On 31 March 2013 Joan made a gift of her main residence valued at £265,000 to her daughter Catherine. However, as a condition of the gift, Joan has continued to live in the house rent free.

The house was purchased on 1 July 1991 for £67,000, and Joan occupied it as her main residence until 31 December 1995. The house was unoccupied between 1 January 1996 and 31 December 1999, and it was rented out as furnished accommodation between 1 January 2000 and 31 December 2010.

Since 1 January 2011 Joan has again occupied the house as her main residence.

Joan has not previously made any lifetime transfers of assets. She is to pay any IHT and CGT liabilities arising from the above gifts.

Required:

(i) **Advise Joan of the IHT and CGT implications arising from the gifts made during 2012/13.**

Your answer should be supported by appropriate calculations, and should include an explanation of any reliefs that are available.

You should ignore the instalment option and the effect of the annual exemption for IHT purposes and the annual exempt amount for CGT purposes.

Marks for this part of the question will be allocated on the basis of: 5 marks to (a), 5 marks to (b), 3 marks to (c), 5 marks to (d), 7 marks to (e)

(ii) **Explain the main advantages of an individual making lifetime gifts for IHT purposes and the main factors to be considered in choosing which assets to gift.** **(6 marks)**

Joan is a higher rate taxpayer for income tax purposes.

(Total: 31 marks)

15   DEE LIMITED (ADAPTED)

You have received the following memorandum from your manager, Lucy Sawry.

To	Tax senior
From	Lucy Sawry
Date	8 June 2013
Subject	David and Debbie Dee

As you know, David Dee, a longstanding client of ours, died last month. His wife, Debbie, is very concerned about her own mortality and has rung me to talk about inheritance tax planning.

I have had a long conversation with her and she is coming in to see me tomorrow to discuss her affairs further.

In preparation for this meeting please can you read the notes I have left on your desk this morning and prepare some notes for the meeting to include the following:

(a) Explain the IHT implications and calculate the IHT that will be payable as a result of David's death.

✳ Don't forget to include calculations of any tax arising on any lifetime transfers he made and consider whether you think any reliefs will be available.

(b) Explain the IHT implications and calculate the IHT that would be payable if Debbie were to die today (i.e. 8 June 2013).

At this stage we will have to assume that no tax planning measures have been taken and that there has been no change in the value of any of the assets since David's death.

Also include the due dates of when the IHT would be payable and by whom.

wife

(c)   Assuming that Debbie will survive until July 2017, list the key lifetime IHT planning measures that we could recommend to Debbie and quantify the likely tax savings that can be made as a result.

As we don't have a crystal ball, for simplicity, you can assume that the rates and allowances for 2012/13 continue to apply for the foreseeable future.

Please make sure that your notes are brief and clear to follow and leave them on my desk as I will be rushing back in at 6pm to pick them up to read tonight in advance of the meeting.

Many thanks

Lucy Sawry

The schedule left on your desk and referred to in the e-mail summarises the family's history and financial affairs as follows:

The Dee family

David	Aged 72	Died May 2013
Debbie	Aged 66	In good health
Andrew	Aged 37	Son of David and Debbie
		Engaged to be married to Julia
		Shareholder and Managing Director of Dee Ltd
Allison	Aged 32	Daughter of David and Debbie
		Married to Maurice
		Two children aged 2 and 4
		Lives in Spain in a villa gifted to her by Debbie in June 2011
		Shareholder of Dee Ltd
		Does not work for the company

Lifetime gifts by David

February 2006	Holiday cottage in the UK worth £70,000 to Andrew
	– The gift was on the condition that David was allowed to occupy the cottage for two months per year, which he did up to the date of his death.
	– The value of the cottage is now £150,000.
June 2007	£333,000 into a discretionary trust
	– David paid the IHT due.
February 2008	Shares in Dee Ltd to his children
	– 20% interest to Andrew
	– 10% interest to Allison

Lifetime gifts by Debbie

June 2011	Villa in France worth £205,000
	– Current value has fallen to £113,000 as a result of exchange rate movements.

Dee Limited

- Family trading company
- Set up by David and Debbie in 1982
- Very successful business
- Currently worth £1,260,000 (unlikely to change in value in the foreseeable future)
- Shareholdings in May 2013:

	Shares	%
David	3,000	60
Debbie	500	10
Andrew	1,000	20
Allison	500	10

- The value of shareholdings in Dee Limited on the relevant dates were as follows:

	On gift (Feb 2008) £	At death (May 2013) £
100% holding	900,000	1,260,000
90% holding	730,000	1,022,000
70% holding	475,000	665,000
60% holding	405,000	567,000
30% holding	175,000	245,000
20% holding	110,000	154,000
10% holding	50,000	70,000

The assets owned by David and Debbie

- In addition to shares in Dee Ltd, the couple owned the following assets in May 2013 (i.e. at the date of David's death):

	David £	Debbie £
Family home (jointly owned)	275,000	275,000
Cash deposits	60,000	40,000
Paintings	12,000	6,300
Death in Service policy	200,000	–
Quoted shares in Don plc	125,000	25,000
(a 6% holding for David and 1% for Debbie)		

- The wills of David and Debbie currently leave all assets to the surviving spouse.
- On the death of the second spouse, all assets are to pass to the children in equal proportions.

Required:

Prepare the notes requested by your manager.

Marks are available for the components of the Notes for the Meeting as follows:

(a) **Explanation of the IHT implications and calculation of the IHT that will be payable as a result of David's death.** **(12 marks)**

(b) Explanation of the IHT implications, calculation of the IHT that would be payable if Debbie were to die on 8 June 2013 and statement of the due dates for payment and who is to pay the tax. **(6 marks)**

(c) List of lifetime inheritance tax (IHT) planning measures that could be recommended to Debbie with quantification of the tax savings that can be made. **(7 marks)**

Additional marks will be awarded for the clarity with which the information is presented and explained. **(2 marks)**

(Total: 27 marks)

16 ALEX (ADAPTED)

Assume today's date is 20 February 2013.

Alex, a widower, died on 5 February 2013, aged 85 years. His will leaves £150,000 to charity and the remainder of his assets split in equal shares to his son, Brian and his daughter, Beatrice, who support his decision to benefit charitable causes.

The assets comprised in Alex's estate were as follows:

	Market Value 5 February 2013 £
Residence	475,000
Building society account	15,000
NS & I EASA account	55,000
NS & I savings certificates	180,000
Various chattels	40,000
Shares in Touriga Ltd	Note 1
Shares in Nacional plc	Note 2
Other quoted investments	115,000

Notes

(1) Touriga Ltd is an unquoted trading company. Alex bought his 2,450 ordinary shares (representing 35% of the issued shares) in September 2010 for £8.50 per share. The shares were worth £11.00 per share at the time of his death.

(2) Nacional plc is a quoted company in which Alex held 20,000 shares (representing less than 1% of the issued shares) at the time of his death. On 5 February 2013, the shares were listed ex div at 624p – 632p with marked bargains at 625p, 629p and 630p. A dividend of 18 pence per share was declared on 5 December 2012, and was received on 11 February 2013 by the executors.

Alex had made two lifetime gifts. The first was a villa in Spain. This was given to Brian in July 2007. The value at that time was £338,000. In addition, Alex settled an equal amount on a relevant property trust in March 2008. Alex agreed to pay any tax due on the gifts.

Prior to his death, Alex had the following income in 2012/13:

	£
Pension (gross – PAYE deducted at source £1,184)	11,740
Building society interest received	1,280
NS & I EASA interest received	370
Dividends received (other than from Nacional plc (Note 2 above))	8,100

Brian, Alex's son, is aged 58, is in poor health, and is not expected to live more than a few years. His wife died ten years ago, since when he has lived alone. He owns a house, currently worth £400,000 with an £80,000 mortgage outstanding and has other assets in the form of cash investments worth £80,000, and personal belongings worth £50,000.

Consequently, Brian has no need of his inheritance from Alex and so intends to gift his share of his father's estate to his two children, Colin and Charlotte, in equal shares.

Colin, who is 20, is in his second year at university, but Brian is worried that his son will spend all of the money at once. Charlotte, who is 17, is still at school but is likely to go to university in the near future.

Again, Brian worries about the money being spent unwisely, and therefore wishes to use some form of trust to control the capital sums gifted to both his children. Brian has made no lifetime gifts to date.

Required:

(a) Calculate the income tax (IT) payable/repayable for Alex for the income tax year 2012/13. **(5 marks)**

(b) Calculate the inheritance tax (IHT) liabilities (including any additional tax due on his lifetime gifts) arising on the death of Alex, and quantify the inheritance (after tax) due to Brian and Beatrice.

Assume that Alex's wife utilised all of her nil rate band when she died. **(10 marks)**

(c) (i) Explain how Brian could use a trust to maintain control of the capital he intends to gift to Colin and Charlotte following Alex's death and the inheritance tax (IHT) treatment of the trust. **(4 marks)**

(ii) State, giving reasons, what other inheritance tax (IHT) planning advice you would offer Brian with regard to setting up a trust for Colin and Charlotte with the assets he has inherited. **(3 marks)**

(Total: 22 marks)

17   MABEL PORTER

Mabel Porter is 76 years old and in poor health. Her husband, Luke, died on 1 June 2013 and she has no children.

Luke fully utilised his nil rate band for inheritance tax purposes during his lifetime.

In her will, Mabel has left the whole of her estate to Bruce and Padma, her brother's children. Bruce and Padma have always visited Mabel regularly although, since emigrating to South Africa in January 2010, Bruce now keeps in touch by telephone.

Mabel owns the following assets:

	Probate value 1 June 2013	Market value Today	Estimated at 30 June 2018
	£	£	£
House and furniture		325,000	450,000
Rolls Royce motor car		71,000	55,000
Diamond necklace		70,000	84,000
Cash and investments in quoted shares		120,000	150,000
Assets inherited from her husband, Luke:			
40,000 ordinary shares in BOZ plc	44,500	77,000	95,000
Land in the country of Utopia	99,000	75,000	75,000

Mabel has decided to give a substantial present to both Bruce and Padma on each of their birthdays on 1 February 2014 and 5 March 2014 respectively. She does not want to gift any asset that will give rise to a tax liability prior to her death and hopes that the gifts will reduce her eventual inheritance tax liability.

Bruce and Padma have agreed to sign any elections necessary to avoid tax arising on the gifts. It can be assumed that the market values of the assets will not change between now and when these gifts are made.

Mabel will give Bruce either the shares in BOZ plc or the land in the country of Utopia.

Luke purchased the shares in BOZ plc on 1 March 2010. BOZ plc is a quoted manufacturing company with an issued share capital of 75,000 ordinary shares. It owns investment properties that represent 8% of the value of its total assets. The land in Utopia consists of a small farm that has always been rented out to tenant farmers. It was purchased by Luke on 1 May 2009 and has an agricultural value at today's date of £58,000.

Mabel will give Padma either the Rolls Royce or the necklace.

Mabel purchased the Rolls Royce, new, in June 2008, for £197,000. She inherited the necklace from her grandmother in April 1988; its probate value at that time was £21,500.

Mabel's only lifetime gift was a gift of £210,000 to a discretionary trust on 1 May 2007 and she does not intend to make any further substantial gifts between now and her death. Mabel has capital losses of £15,100 as at 5 April 2013.

Required:

(a) **Explain the immediate capital gains tax and inheritance tax implications of each of the four possible gifts.**

Quantify the capital gain or loss and the potentially exempt transfer in each case and comment on the availability or otherwise of any reliefs. **(12 marks)**

(b) **Mabel has two objectives when making the gifts to Bruce and Padma:**

1 **To pay no tax on any gift in her lifetime; and**

2 **To reduce the eventual liability to inheritance tax on her death.**

Advise Mabel which item to gift to Bruce and to Padma in order to satisfy her objectives. Give reasons for your advice.

Your advice should include a computation of the inheritance tax saved as a result of the two gifts, on the assumption that Mabel dies on 30 June 2018. **(10 marks)**

(c)   Without changing the advice you have given in (b), or varying the terms of Luke's will, explain how Mabel could further reduce her eventual inheritance tax liability and quantify the tax saving that could be made.   **(3 marks)**

You should assume that the rates and allowances for the tax year 2012/13 will continue to apply for the foreseeable future.

(Total: 25 marks)

   Online question assistance

---

18   ALVARO PELORUS (ADAPTED)   *Walk in the footsteps of a top tutor*

Two years ago Alvaro Pelorus moved to the UK with his family to look after his father, Ray, who has recently died.

Alvaro requires some help in sorting out his father's tax affairs and is also concerned about his own liability to UK capital taxes. Alvaro and his family expect to return to their home in the country of Koruba in October 2013 once Ray's affairs have been settled.

The following information has been extracted from client files and from telephone conversations with Alvaro.

Alvaro Pelorus

–   Aged 47 years old, married to Maria.

–   The couple have two children, Vito and Sophie, aged 22 and 19 years respectively.

–   Alvaro and Maria have lived in the country of Koruba since 1986 and are both domiciled in the country of Koruba.

–   On 1 July 2011 the family moved to the UK to be near Alvaro's father, Ray, who was very ill.

–   Alvaro and Maria are UK resident, but not ordinarily resident in the UK in the tax years 2011/12 and 2012/13.

–   There is no double taxation agreement between the UK and Koruba.

Ray Pelorus

–   Has been seriously ill and has not worked for the last three years.

–   Died on 1 February 2013.

–   UK domiciled, lived in the UK for the whole of his life.

Lifetime gifts by Ray

–   1 May 2009 gave Alvaro 95 acres of farm land situated in the UK

  –   market value of the land was £273,000, although its agricultural value was only £120,000

  –   Ray had acquired the land on 1 January 2001 and granted an agricultural tenancy on that date

  –   Alvaro continues to own the land as at today's date and it is still subject to the agricultural tenancy.

- 1 August 2012 gave Alvaro 6,000 shares in Pinger Ltd

- shares were valued at £195,000

- Pinger Ltd is a UK resident trading company

- gift relief was claimed in respect of this gift

- Ray had acquired 14,000 shares in Pinger Ltd on 1 April 2001 for £54,600, which represents a 4% interest in the company.

Assets owned by Ray on 1 February 2013

- UK assets, valued at £870,000 after deduction of all available reliefs.

- A house in the country of Pacifica valued at £94,000.

- The executors of Ray's estate have paid Pacifican inheritance tax of £1,800 and legal fees of £7,700 in respect of the sale of the Pacifican house.

- Ray left the whole of his estate to Alvaro.

Alvaro's capital assets and capital disposals

- Owns the family house in the UK, shares in UK and Koruban companies, and commercial rental property in the country of Koruba.

- In 2012/13 he made the following disposals of assets:

1 September 2012	sold the 6,000 shares in Pinger Ltd for £228,000
1 October 2012	sold 2,350 shares in Lapis Inc, a company resident in Koruba, for £8,270
	purchased 5,500 shares in the company on 1 September 2007 for £25,950
1 December 2012	transferred shares with a market value of £74,000 in Quad plc, a UK quoted company, to a UK resident discretionary trust for the benefit of Vito and Sophie
	had purchased the shares on 1 January 2012 for £59,500.

- Has not made any other transfers of value for the purposes of UK inheritance tax.

Maria's capital assets and capital disposals

- Only significant asset owned is the family home in the country of Koruba.

- Has not made any transfers of value for the purposes of UK inheritance tax.

Required:

(a) Calculate the inheritance tax (IHT) payable as a result of the death of Ray Pelorus.

Explain the availability or otherwise of agricultural property relief and business property relief on the two lifetime gifts made by Ray. **(8 marks)**

(b) (i) Explain how Alvaro may be assessed for capital gains tax purposes in 2012/13. **(7 marks)**

(ii) Calculate Alvaro Pelorus's capital gains tax liability for the tax year 2012/13 on the assumption that all available reliefs are claimed. You should assume that all of Alvaro's overseas income is remitted to the UK. **(8 marks)**

(c)   (i)   Explain the inheritance tax (IHT) implications and benefits of Alvaro Pelorus varying the terms of his father's will such that part of Ray Pelorus's estate is left to Vito and Sophie.

State the date by which a deed of variation would need to be made in order for it to be valid.   (3 marks)

(ii)   Identify any further planning opportunities available to Alvaro Pelorus in order to minimise the UK inheritance tax (IHT) due when he dies.

He does not wish to make any lifetime gifts other than to his wife, Maria.

(6 marks)

You should assume that the rates and allowances for the tax year 2012/13 continue to apply for the foreseeable future. Alvaro is a higher rate taxpayer for income tax purposes.

(Total: 32 marks)

19   CRUSOE (ADAPTED)

Crusoe has contacted you following the death of his father, Noland. Crusoe has inherited the whole of his father's estate and is seeking advice on his father's capital gains tax position and the payment of inheritance tax following his death.

The following information has been extracted from client files and from telephone conversations with Crusoe.

Noland – personal information:

–   Divorcee whose only other relatives are his sister, Avril, and two grandchildren.

–   Died suddenly on 1 October 2013 without having made a will.

–   Under the laws of intestacy, the whole of his estate passes to Crusoe.

Noland – income tax and capital gains tax:

–   Has had taxable income of £20,000 per year since the tax year 2006/07.

–   Sales of quoted shares resulted in:

–   Chargeable gains of £7,100 and allowable losses of £17,800 in the tax year 2013/14.

–   Chargeable gains of approximately £14,500 each tax year from 2006/07 to 2012/13.

Noland – gifts made during lifetime:

–   On 1 December 2005 Noland gave his house to Crusoe.

–   Crusoe has allowed Noland to continue living in the house and has charged him rent of £120 per month since 1 December 2005. The market rent for the house would be £740 per month.

–   The house was worth £240,000 at the time of the gift and £310,000 on 1 October 2013.

–   On 1 November 2010 Noland transferred quoted shares worth £260,000 to a discretionary trust for the benefit of his grandchildren.

Noland:

-   Probate values of assets held at death:

	£
Portfolio of quoted shares	370,000
Shares in Kurb Ltd	38,400
Chattels and cash	22,300
Domestic liabilities including income tax payable	(1,900)

-   It should be assumed that these values will not change for the foreseeable future.

Kurb Ltd:

-   Unquoted trading company

-   Noland purchased the shares on 1 December 2011.

Crusoe:

-   Long-standing personal tax client of your firm.

-   Married with two young children.

-   Successful investment banker with very high net worth.

-   Intends to gift the portfolio of quoted shares inherited from Noland to his aunt, Avril, who has very little personal wealth.

Required:

(a)   Prepare explanatory notes together with relevant supporting calculations in order to quantify the tax relief potentially available in respect of Noland's capital losses realised in 2013/14.   **(4 marks)**

(b)   State the immediate tax implications of the proposed gift of the share portfolio to Avril and identify an alternative strategy that would achieve Crusoe's objectives whilst avoiding a possible tax liability in the future.

State any deadline(s) in connection with your proposed strategy.   **(6 marks)**

(c)   On the assumption that the administrators of Noland's estate will sell quoted shares in order to fund the inheritance tax due as a result of his death, calculate the value of the quoted shares that will be available to transfer to Avril.

You should include brief notes of your treatment of the house and the shares in Kurb Ltd.   **(10 marks)**

You should assume that the tax rates and allowances for the tax year 2012/13 apply throughout this question.

(Total: 20 marks)

20   KEPLER (ADAPTED)   *PET*

Kepler gave his nephew, Galileo, 600 shares (a 30% holding) in Messier Ltd on 1 June 2009. On 1 May 2013, Kepler died and left the remaining 1,400 shares in Messier Ltd to Galileo. Galileo intends to move to the UK from the country of Astronomeria to participate in the management of Messier Ltd.

The following information has been obtained from client files and meetings with the parties involved.

Kepler:

-   Died on 1 May 2013.

wiy
- Was UK resident, ordinarily resident and domiciled.

- Has two nephews; Galileo and Herschel.

- In his will he left 1,400 shares in Messier Ltd valued at £546,000 to Galileo and the residue of his estate valued at £480,000 to Herschel.

Kepler – Lifetime gifts:

- 1 February 2008   Gave a house to Herschel valued at £311,000.

- 1 July 2008   Gave a watch costing £900 to each of his two nephews.   PET

- 1 June 2009   Gave 600 shares in Messier Ltd to Galileo. PET

Messier Ltd:

- Unquoted company that transports building materials.

- Incorporated in the UK on 1 February 2000 when Kepler subscribed for 2,000 shares, the whole of its share capital.

Messier Ltd – Value of an ordinary share:

	1 June 2009	1 May 2013
– As at	£	£
As part of a 100% holding	485	570
As part of a 70% holding	310	390
As part of a 30% holding	230	260

Messier Ltd – Asset values:

	£
– As at 1 June 2009	
Premises	900,000
Surplus land rented to third party	480,000
Vehicles	100,000
Current assets	50,000

Galileo:

- Resident, ordinarily resident and domiciled in the country of Astronomeria where he has lived since birth.

- Lives in rented accommodation in Astronomeria.

- Intends to sell two paintings in order to provide funds to go towards the cost of relocating to the UK and purchasing a house here.

- Has a full time employment contract with Messier Ltd commencing on 1 September 2013.

- Intends to stay in the UK for at least five years.

The two paintings:

- Are situated in Astronomeria and are worth approximately £20,000 each.

- Have been owned by Galileo since 1 May 1998; their cost is negligible and can be ignored.

Employment contract with Messier Ltd:

- Galileo will be paid an annual salary of £52,000.   Higher Tax payer.

- Messier Ltd will assist Galileo with the cost of relocating to the UK.

Required:

(a) (i) Calculate the inheritance tax payable (if any) by Galileo in respect of:

(1) the gift of shares in June 2009, and

(2) the inheritance of shares in May 2013; **(8 marks)**

(ii) Explain why Galileo is able to pay the inheritance tax due in instalments, state when the instalments are due and identify any further issues relevant to Galileo relating to the payments. **(4 marks)**

(b) Prepare a reasoned explanation of how any capital gains tax arising in the UK on the sale of the paintings can be minimised. **(2 marks)**

(c) (i) Explain how Messier Ltd can assist Galileo with the cost of relocating to the UK and/or provide him with interest-free loan finance for this purpose without increasing his UK income tax liability; **(3 marks)**

(ii) State, with reasons, whether Messier Ltd can provide Galileo with accommodation in the UK without giving rise to a UK income tax liability. **(3 marks)**

(Total: 20 marks)

21 ERNEST AND GEORGINA (ADAPTED) *Walk in the footsteps of a top tutor*

Ernest intends to sell a capital asset on 1 February 2014 and wishes to maximise his after tax sales proceeds. He is also seeking advice on his inheritance tax position and on his will.

The following information has been obtained from a telephone conversation with Ernest and from client files.

Ernest:

– Is 54 years old and unmarried.

– Lives with Georgina, who is 48 years old, and her adult daughter, Eileen.

– Earns a salary of £130,000 per year.

– Has as yet made no disposals of capital assets in the tax year 2013/14.

– Intends to sell either an oil painting or 7,700 shares in Neutron Ltd on 1 February 2014.

Oil painting:

– Ernest inherited the painting on the death of his uncle on 1 May 2009 when it was worth £23,800.

– Ernest's uncle purchased the painting on 1 July 1995 for £19,500.

– The painting is expected to be worth £47,000 on 1 February 2014.

Shares in Neutron Ltd:

– Qualified for income tax relief under the enterprise investment scheme (EIS) although Ernest did not claim any relief.

– 1 April 2006 Ernest subscribed for 18,600 shares at £8·90 per share.

– 1 March 2008 Ernest received a 1 for 4 bonus issue.

-      1 July 2011   Ernest purchased his full entitlement under a 1 for 10 rights issue at £4.20 per share.

-      The shares are expected to be worth £5 each on 1 February 2014.

Neutron Ltd:

-      Has an issued share capital of two million £1 ordinary shares.

-      Is not quoted on any stock exchange.

-      Manufactures and distributes radiation measuring equipment.

Inheritance tax planning and wills:

-      Neither Ernest nor Georgina have made any lifetime gifts.

-      In his will, Ernest has left the whole of his estate to Georgina.

-      In her will, Georgina has left the whole of her estate to Eileen.

-      Ernest and Georgina wish to minimise their total inheritance tax liability.

-      They are willing to make lifetime gifts to each other but not to Eileen or any other person or organisation.

Current market values of assets owned:

	Ernest £	Georgina £
Family home	620,000	–
Antiques and works of art	400,000	60,000
Investment property	380,000	–
Shares in Neutron Ltd	127,875	–

Required:

(a)   **Prepare calculations of the after tax sales proceeds that would be realised on the proposed sale of the painting and on the proposed sale of the shares on 1 February 2014.**

     You should assume that Ernest will make any necessary beneficial claims or elections.   **(7 marks)**

(b)   **Prepare brief notes explaining the inheritance tax liabilities that will arise on the deaths of Ernest and Georgina if no action is taken to reduce such liabilities; identify any actions that could be taken in order to reduce these liabilities and explain the inheritance tax and capital gains tax implications of these actions.**

     You are not required to prepare detailed calculations for part (b) of this question.

               (13 marks)

You should assume that today's date is 1 December 2013 and that the rates and allowances for the tax year 2012/13 apply throughout the question.

               (Total: 20 marks)

22 FITZGERALD AND MORRISON (ADAPTED) *Walk in the footsteps of a top tutor*

Fitzgerald and Morrison, two clients of your firm, require advice on the capital gains tax and inheritance tax implications of gifts they propose to make in the next few months. They are both higher rate taxpayers.

Fitzgerald

Gift of shares in Jay Ltd on 1 October 2013:

- To be made to Fitzgerald's nephew, Pat.

- Comprises the whole of Fitzgerald's 9% shareholding.

- Fitzgerald inherited the shares from his mother on 1 February 2013 when their market value was £32,000.

- The shares are expected to be worth £127,500 on 1 October 2013.

Jay Ltd

- An unquoted manufacturing company.

- Values of the company's assets as at 1 October 2013

	£
Premises	740,000
Plant and machinery (each item is worth more than £6,000)	160,000
Quoted company shares	250,000
Motor cars	30,000
Net current assets	80,000

Pat's plans:

- Pat is an employee of Jay Ltd and will continue to work for the company until he sells the shares.

- Pat intends to sell the shares in January 2015 and expects to receive £170,000.

- He will use the funds to finance a business venture.

Morrison

Gift of a painting on 1 September 2013:

- To be made to Morrison's daughter, Sula, on her wedding day.

- This will be Morrison's first gift since 1 May 2006.

- The painting is one of a set of three.

- Each of the individual paintings is expected to be worth £25,000 on 1 September 2013; a pair of paintings is expected to be worth £70,000 on that date.

The set of paintings:

- Morrison purchased the set of three paintings in April 2005.

- Each of the paintings has a base cost for capital gains tax purposes of £8,300.

- He gave one of the paintings to his wife on 1 May 2006.

- The complete set of three paintings is expected to be worth £120,000 on 1 September 2013.

Required:

(a)   In respect of the gift of the shares by Fitzgerald and their subsequent sale by Pat:

  (i)   Explain whether or not capital gains tax gift relief will be available on the gift, noting any additional information required. State the latest date for submission of a claim and identify who must sign it;   **(4 marks)**

  (ii)   Calculate the effect of submitting a valid claim for gift relief on the total capital gains tax liability of Fitzgerald and Pat on the assumption that the gift by Fitzgerald and the sale by Pat take place as planned;   **(7 marks)**

  (iii)   Explain whether or not business property relief will be available if Fitzgerald dies within seven years of making the gift.   **(4 marks)**

(b)   In respect of the gift of the painting by Morrison:

  (i)   Calculate the value of the potentially exempt transfer, after deduction of all exemptions, for the purposes of inheritance tax;   **(3 marks)**

  (ii)   Calculate the capital gain arising on the gift and comment on the availability of gift relief.   **(2 marks)**

                                                    (Total: 20 marks)

23   AVA (ADAPTED) *Walk in the footsteps of a top tutor*

Ava has not yet submitted her income tax return for the tax year 2011/12. She also requires advice on the capital gains tax and inheritance tax implications of making a gift of a farm to her nephew.

The following information has been obtained from a letter from Ava and from her client file.

Ava's personal circumstances:

–   Ava is 84 years old.

–   Ava's husband, Burt, died on 1 November 2013 after a long and serious illness.

–   Ava has no children.

–   Ava has taxable income of £68,000 during 2012/13.

Ava's income tax reporting:

–   Burt had always looked after Ava's tax affairs as well as his own.

–   Ava has recently realised that her income tax return for the tax year 2011/12 has not been submitted.

–   The notice to file the income tax return for the tax year 2011/12 was sent to Ava on 1 May 2012.

Burt's will and lifetime gifts:

–   Burt made no transfers for the purposes of inheritance tax during his lifetime.

–   Burt left quoted shares worth £293,000 to his sister.

–   Burt left 'Hayworth', a small farm, and the residue of his estate to Ava.

–   Consequently, his chargeable death estate was less than his nil rate band.

Ava's lifetime gifts:

–   Ava made a gift of quoted company shares (all minority holdings) worth £251,000 to her niece on 1 December 2012.

–   Ava intends to gift Hayworth Farm to her nephew on 1 February 2014.

–   Capital gains tax gift relief will not be claimed in respect of the intended gift.

Hayworth Farm:

–   Is situated in the UK.

–   Was purchased by Burt on 1 January 2004 for £330,000.

–   Was leased to tenant farmers on 1 January 2004 and was never farmed by Burt.

–   Will continue to be leased to and farmed by the tenant farmers in the future.

Hayworth Farm – Valuations of farm buildings and surrounding land:

	1 November 2013 £	1 February 2014 £
Market value	494,000	650,000
Agricultural value	300,000	445,000

–   It can be assumed that both values will increase by 5% per year from 1 February 2014.

Required:

(a)   State by when Ava's 2011/12 income tax return should have been submitted and list the consequences of submitting the return, together with Ava's outstanding income tax liability, on 15 December 2013.

Note: you are not required to prepare calculations for part (a) of this question.
(4 marks)

(b)   (i)   Provide a reasoned explanation for the availability or non-availability of agricultural property relief and business property relief in respect of the intended gift of Hayworth Farm by Ava;   (4 marks)

(ii)   Calculate the capital gains tax and the inheritance tax payable in respect of the gift of Hayworth Farm on the assumption that Ava dies on 1 January 2018.

State the due dates for the payment of the tax liabilities (on the assumption that they are not paid in instalments), the date on which any beneficial claim(s) need to be submitted and any assumptions made.   (12 marks)

(Total: 20 marks)

24   SAKURA (ADAPTED)   *Walk in the footsteps of a top tutor*

Sakura requires advice on the receipt of insurance proceeds, the sale of a painting in exchange for a boat and the implications of making an error when preparing his tax return.

The following information has been obtained from a telephone conversation with Sakura.

Sakura:

–   Is a higher rate taxpayer who is resident, ordinarily resident and domiciled in the UK.

- Is finalising his tax return for the tax year 2012/13.

- Has not previously made any gifts or disposals for the purposes of capital gains tax or inheritance tax other than those set out below.

- Does not expect to make any gifts or disposals for the purposes of capital gains tax or inheritance tax in the tax years 2013/14 or 2014/15 other than those set out below.

- Has received insurance proceeds of £67,000.

- Intends to sell a painting to his son, Cashel, in exchange for a boat.

The insurance proceeds of £67,000:

- The insurance proceeds were paid to Sakura on 1 June 2013.

- The insurance proceeds relate to the destruction of an antique china figurine on 1 March 2013.

- Sakura paid £28,000 for the figurine on 1 April 2009.

- The figurine had a market value of £80,000 on 1 March 2013.

- Sakura intends to use the money to purchase a modern glass figurine for £59,000.

Exchange of painting for boat:

- Sakura intends to sell a painting with a market value of £48,000 to his son, Cashel.

- The consideration for the sale will be a boat owned by Cashel that has a market value of £25,000.

- The painting and the boat cost £22,000 and £37,000 respectively.

Sakura's tax return:

- Sakura always prepares his tax returns in an honest manner.

- However, he is aware that he could still make an honest mistake.

Required:

(a) Explain, with supporting calculations where necessary, the capital gains tax and inheritance tax implications for Sakura of the receipt of the insurance proceeds and the sale of the painting in exchange for the boat.

Advise Sakura of the actions he should take in relation to his plans in order to minimise his capital gains tax liability and point out any matter(s) that would need to be resolved with HM Revenue and Customs.

You should clearly identify the tax years relevant to the disposals and the due date of payment of any minimised capital gains tax liability.   **(13 marks)**

(b) State, with reasons, whether there will be any capital gains tax and/or inheritance tax implications for Cashel from the disposal of the boat.   **(2 marks)**

(c) Explain the manner in which a penalty would be calculated if Sakura were to make an honest mistake when completing his tax return.   **(5 marks)**

(Total: 20 marks)

MULTI TAX PERSONAL INCLUDING OVERSEAS

25   MING WONG (ADAPTED) *Walk in the footsteps of a top tutor*

Ming Wong, aged 63, was born in the country of Yanga, but has lived in the UK since 6 April 1998. Ming is resident and ordinarily resident in the UK, but is not domiciled in the UK. Following her marriage to a UK citizen, Ming is planning to become UK domiciled.

Ming is employed by the Yangan National Bank in London, and was paid a salary of £30,100 during 2012/13.

At 5 April 2013 Ming owned the following assets:

(1)   A main residence valued at £260,000. This is situated in the UK, and has an outstanding endowment mortgage of £80,000.

(2)   A house in Yanga worth £60,000, from which rental income of £8,990 (gross) was received during 2012/13. Yangan tax at the rate of 35% was paid on the rental income.

(3)   40,000 shares, representing a 12% holding, in Ganyan Inc., a company quoted on the Yangan Stock Exchange at 308p – 316p. Dividends of £5,950 (net) were received during 2012/13, after the deduction of Yangan tax at the rate of 15%.

(4)   Antiques worth £61,500. These were bought in Yanga many years ago, but are now situated in Ming's UK residence.

(5)   Bank deposits of £58,000 with the Yangan National Bank, of which £38,000 is held at the London branch and £20,000 at the main branch in Yanga. During 2012/13 interest of £1,680 (net) was credited to the account in London, and £1,530 (net of Yangan tax at the rate of 15%) was credited to the account in Yanga.

(6)   An interest-free loan of £15,000 to Ming's brother who is resident in Yanga. The loan was used to purchase property situated in the UK.

None of the income arising in Yanga has been remitted to the UK.

Ming has made no lifetime gifts.

Under the terms of her will, Ming has left all of her assets to her three children. If she were to die, Yangan death duty of £13,600 would be payable in respect of the house situated in Yanga and £34,400 in respect of the 40,000 shares in Ganyan Inc., irrespective of her domicile. No foreign death duty is payable in respect of the Yanga bank account.

There is no double taxation agreement between the UK and Yanga.

All of the above figures are in pounds sterling.

Required:

(a)   **Advise Ming of**

(i)   **when she will be treated as domiciled in the UK for the purposes of IHT, and**

(ii)   **how she could acquire domicile in the UK under general law.**   **(4 marks)**

(b) Advise Ming as to the potential increase in her liability to UK IHT if she were to become domiciled in the UK.

Your answer should include an explanation of why Ming's assets are or are not subject to UK IHT. **(12 marks)**

(c) Explain how Ming may be assessed to income tax in 2012/13. **(5 marks)**

(d) Calculate the UK income tax payable by Ming for 2012/13 under both possible bases of assessment and conclude which basis is preferable for Ming. **(12 marks)**

(Total: 33 marks)

26 JAN (ADAPTED)

Assume that today's date is 1 July 2013.

Jan is aged 45 and single. He is of Danish domicile but has been working for ABC Ltd in the United Kingdom since 1 May 2012 and intends to remain in the UK for the medium to long term. Although Jan worked briefly in the UK in 1993, he has forgotten how UK taxation works and needs some assistance before preparing his UK income tax return.

Jan's salary from 1 May 2012 was £74,967 per annum. During 2012/13 PAYE of £25,148 was deducted. Jan also has a company car – a Jaguar XJ8 with a list price of £42,550 including extras, and CO_2 emissions of 218g/km. The car was available to him from 1 July 2012. Free petrol is provided by the company. Jan has other taxable benefits amounting to £3,780

Jan's other 2012/13 income comprises:

	£
Dividend income from UK companies (cash received)	3,240
Interest received on an ISA account	230
Interest received on a UK bank account	740
Income remitted from a villa in Portugal (net of 45% withholding tax)	4,598

In addition, Jan has not remitted other Portuguese rental income arising in the year, totalling a further £1,500 (gross).

Jan informs you that his employer is thinking of providing him with rented accommodation while he looks for a house to buy. The accommodation would be a two bedroom flat, valued at £155,000 with an annual value of £6,000. It would be made available from 6 August 2013. The company will pay the rent of £600 per month for the first six months. All other bills will be paid by Jan.

Jan also informs you that he has 25,000 ordinary shares in Gilet Ltd ('Gilet'), an unquoted UK trading company which represents a 3% interest. He has held these shares since August 2002 when he bought 2,500 shares at £4.07 per share. In January 2004, a bonus issue gave each shareholder nine shares for each ordinary share held.

In the last week all Gilet's shareholders have received an offer from Jumper plc ('Jumper') who wishes to acquire the shares. Jumper has offered the following:

- 3 shares in Jumper (currently trading at £3.55 per share) for every 5 shares in Gilet, and

- 25p cash per share

Required:

(a) (i) Explain how Jan will be assessed to income tax in 2012/13. **(4 marks)**

    (ii) Calculate Jan's income tax (IT) payable for 2012/13. **(11 marks)**

(b) Calculate the taxable benefit in 2013/14 if Jan were to use the accommodation offered by his employer.

    You may assume that the rules for calculating benefits are the same as in 2012/13. **(3 marks)**

(c) (i) Explain the capital gains tax (CGT) implications of a takeover where the consideration is in the form of shares (a 'paper for paper' transaction) stating any conditions that need to be satisfied. **(4 marks)**

    (ii) Calculate the chargeable gain arising as a consequence of Jan accepting Jumper's offer. **(3 marks)**

    (iii) Define a qualifying corporate bond for the purposes of capital gains tax (CGT) and explain the effect on the chargeable gain calculated in (ii) if the cash element in the offer were replaced with a qualifying corporate bond. **(4 marks)**

(Total: 29 marks)

27 ARTHUR AND CINDY WAKEFIELD (ADAPTED) *Walk in the footsteps of a top tutor*

Your manager has had a meeting with Arthur and Cindy Wakefield and has sent you a copy of the following memorandum.

To	The files
From	Tax manager
Date	1 December 2013
Subject	Arthur and Cindy Wakefield

Background

Arthur and Cindy Wakefield are married with two children aged four and seven years. Cindy has worked for Picture Perfect Ltd, a company that buys, sells and values works of art, for four years. Her annual gross employment income is £45,000. Cindy's only other income arises in respect of the assets inherited from her father as set out below.

Arthur is a self-employed carpenter whose taxable trading profits after deduction of capital allowances are £32,580 each year. He has no other income. He has not yet completed his self-assessment return for 2012/13, which he normally submits in September, and is not sure when he is going to complete it due to busy work commitments, but he does intend to submit it in electronic format.

The investments

On 1 March 2013 Cindy inherited UK quoted shares and an investment property in London on the death of her father. The probate values of the assets together with the taxable income generated by them in a full year are set out below. Cindy intends to give either the quoted shares or the investment property to Arthur with the objective of maximising the family's after tax income.

	Probate value	Annual taxable income
	£	£
Quoted shares	305,000	12,300
Investment property	320,000	14,100

The business

Cindy and Arthur plan to start a business, buying and restoring paintings, on 1 April 2014. They will work on the new business in their spare time; Cindy will continue to work for Picture Perfect Ltd and Arthur will carry on with his carpentry business.

Cindy's forecast of the income and expenditure of the new business for its first three years, including the cost of equipment, is set out below. These figures do not include the cost of employing Cindy and Arthur on annual salaries of £8,500 each. Cindy is planning to set up a company to run the business but would consider using a partnership, with profits and losses shared equally between them, if it was advantageous to do so.

Year ending 31 March	2015	2016	2017
	£	£	£
Sales	18,000	70,000	80,000
Less Cost of materials and overheads	(38,000)	(24,000)	(25,000)
Purchase of equipment	(24,000)		
Profit/(loss) arising	(44,000)	46,000	55,000

Proposed investment in shares

Arthur and Cindy wish to reduce their income tax liability and have heard that it is possible to obtain an income tax deduction for investing in unquoted shares. They do not like the fact that the shares involved are more risky than quoted shares but they are still considering investing £50,000 on 1 January 2014.

Gift to Cindy

Cindy's mother Elsa is concerned about her IHT position following the death of her husband. She has decided to sell the family home and gift the cash to various family members. She is proposing to gift £130,000 to Cindy, who will use the cash to purchase a house for her mother to live in, rent free. The annual rental value of the house is £6,000.

Tax manager

An extract from an email from your manager is set out below.

Please prepare a memorandum for me, incorporating the following:

(a) (i) Advice as to whether Cindy should give Arthur the investment property or the quoted shares in order to achieve her objective.

I would like you to support your recommendation with relevant calculations based on a complete tax year. Please make sure your calculations are clear and logical. You will need to think about the rates of tax that each of the couple will pay on the extra income.

(ii) A computation of the annual income tax saving from your recommendation in (i) above as compared with the situation where Cindy retains both the property and the shares.

I would also like you to identify any other tax implications arising from your recommendation. You should consider all relevant taxes.

(b) An explanation of the advantages from a tax point of view of operating the new business as a partnership rather than as a company whilst it is making losses.

You should calculate the tax adjusted trading loss for the year ending 31 March 2015 for both situations and indicate the years in which the loss relief will be obtained.

I don't need you to prepare any other supporting calculations.

(c) An outline of the ways in which Arthur and Cindy can reduce their income tax liability by investing in unquoted shares and a reasoned recommendation of the most appropriate form of investment, given their personal circumstances.

You don't need to discuss the qualifying conditions applicable to the investment vehicle recommended.

(d) An explanation of the income tax and inheritance tax implications for Elsa of giving the £130,000 cash to Cindy her daughter. I believe that Elsa is a higher rate tax payer.

(e) Advice for Arthur about his responsibilities under self assessment and the consequences of submitting late returns and/or payments.

Required:

Prepare the memorandum requested by your manager.

You should assume today's date is 2 December 2013.

Marks are available for the components of the memorandum as follows:

(a) (i) **Recommendation as to whether Cindy should give Arthur the investment property or the quoted shares in order to achieve her objective, with supporting calculations based on a complete tax year.** **(7 marks)**

(ii) **Computation of the annual income tax saving from your recommendation in (i) above as compared with the situation where Cindy retains both the property and the shares.** **(3 marks)**

(b) **Explanation of the advantages of operating the new business as a partnership rather than as a company.** **(10 marks)**

(c) **Advice regarding the most suitable form of investment in unquoted shares.** **(5 marks)**

(d) **Explanation of the income tax and inheritance tax implications for Elsa of the gift to Cindy.** **(4 marks)**

(e) **Advice for Arthur about his responsibilities under self assessment and the consequences of submitting late returns and/or payments.** **(4 marks)**

Additional marks will be awarded for the appropriateness of the format and presentation of the memorandum and the effectiveness with which the information is communicated.

(2 marks)

You should assume that the income tax rates and allowances for the tax year 2012/13 and the FA2012 apply throughout this question.

(Total: 35 marks)

28   CORAL (ADAPTED)

Coral is the owner and managing director of Reef Ltd. She is considering the manner in which she will make her first pension contributions. In November 2013 she inherited her mother's house in the country of Kalania.

The following information has been extracted from client files and from telephone conversations with Coral.

Coral:

–   1978 – Born in the country of Kalania. Her father, who died in 2008, was domiciled in Kalania.

–   2004 – Moved to the UK and has lived and worked here since then.

–   2007 – Subscribed for 100% of the ordinary share capital of Reef Ltd.

–   Intends to sell Reef Ltd and return to live in the country of Kalania in 2018.

–   No income apart from that received from Reef Ltd.

Reef Ltd:

–   A UK resident trading company with annual taxable total profits of approximately £370,000.

–   Fourteen employees including Coral.

Payments from Reef Ltd to Coral in 2013/14:

–   Director's fees of £950 per month.

–   Dividends paid of £13,500 in June 2013 and £13,500 in September 2013.

Pension contributions:

–   Coral has not so far made any pension contributions in the tax year 2013/14 but wishes to make gross pension contributions of £15,000.

–   The contributions are to be made by Reef Ltd or Coral or a combination of the two in such a way as to minimise the total after tax cost.

–   Any contributions made by Coral will be funded by an additional dividend from Reef Ltd.

House in the country of Kalania:

–   Beachfront property with potential rental income of £550 per month after deduction of allowable expenditure.

–   Coral will use it for holidays for two months each year.

–   The earliest date the property can be rented from is 1 January 2014.

The tax system in the country of Kalania:

–   No capital gains tax or inheritance tax.

–   Income tax at 8% on income arising in the country of Kalania.

–   No double tax treaty with the UK.

Required:

(a) With the objective of minimising the total after tax cost, advise Coral as to whether the gross pension contributions of £15,000 should be made:

    –   wholly by Reef Ltd; or

    –   by Coral to the extent that they are tax allowable with the balance made by Reef Ltd.

    Your answer should include supporting calculations where necessary.   **(10 marks)**

(b) Explain, by reference to Coral's residence, ordinary residence and domicile position, how the rental income arising in respect of the property in the country of Kalania will be taxed in the UK in the tax year 2013/14 and in subsequent years.

    State the strategy that Coral should adopt in 2013/14 in order to minimise the total income tax suffered on the rental income.   **(10 marks)**

    You are not required to prepare calculations for part (b) of this question.

You should assume that the tax rates and allowances for the tax year 2012/13 and for the financial year to 31 March 2013 will continue to apply for the foreseeable future.

    (Total: 20 marks)

29   NUCLEUS RESOURCES (ADAPTED) *Walk in the footsteps of a top tutor*

You have received the following memorandum from your manager.

To	Tax senior
From	Tax manager
Date	28 November 2013
Subject	Maria Copenhagen and Nucleus Resources

I spoke to Maria Copenhagen this morning. We arranged to meet on Thursday 4 December to discuss the following matters.

Nucleus Resources

Maria is planning a major expansion of her business, Nucleus Resources. I attach a schedule, prepared by Maria, showing the budgeted income and expenditure of the business for a full year. Maria wants to know how much additional after tax income the expansion of the business will create depending on whether she employs the two additional employees or uses a sub-contractor, Quantum Ltd.

Quoted shares

In October 2011 Niels, Maria's husband, received a gift of shares with a value of £170,000 from his uncle. The shares are quoted on the Heisenbergia Stock Exchange. The uncle died in November 2013 and Maria wants to know whether there will be any UK inheritance tax in respect of the gift. The uncle had been living in the country of Heisenbergia since moving there from the UK in 1992 and had made substantial gifts to other close relatives in 2010 and 2011. Inheritance tax of £30,600 has been charged in Heisenbergia in respect of the gift to Niels.

According to Maria, Niels is considering transferring the shares to a trust for the benefit of their two sons.

Please prepare the following:

(a) In respect of Nucleus Resources:

Calculations of the additional annual after tax income that would be generated by the expansion of the business under the two alternatives i.e. the recruitment of the additional employees and the use of the sub-contractor. You should check to see if Maria is currently an additional rate taxpayer. If she is, you can simply deduct tax and national insurance at the marginal rates from the additional profits.

Don't worry about the precise timing of the capital allowances in respect of the car, just spread the total allowances available for the car equally over the period of ownership. Also, watch out for the VAT implications of the expansion; there is bound to be an effect on the recoverability of input tax due to the business being partially exempt.

(b) In respect of the quoted shares:

(i) A list of the issues to be considered in order to determine whether or not the gift from the uncle is within the scope of UK inheritance tax and the treatment of any inheritance tax suffered in the country of Heisenbergia.

(ii) A brief outline of the tax implications of transferring the shares to the trust and the taxation of the trust income paid to the beneficiaries. The shares are currently worth £210,000.

(iii) Notes on the extent to which it is professionally acceptable for me to discuss issues relating to the shares with Maria.

I want to be able to use the calculations and notes in my meeting with Maria (or in a subsequent meeting with Niels) and I may not have much time to study them beforehand so please make sure that they are clear, concise and that I can find my way around them easily.

Thank you

Tax manager

The schedule prepared by Maria is set out below.

Nucleus Resources – Estimated income and expenditure for a full year

Notes

1. The figures in the 'expansion' column relate to the expansion only and will be in addition to the existing business.

2. Nucleus Resources is registered for VAT.

3. All amounts are stated exclusive of VAT.

4. Materials and overheads are subject to VAT at 20%. The expenditure cannot be attributed to particular supplies.

		Existing business £	Expansion £
Turnover:	Standard rated	40,000	190,000
	Exempt	90,000	–
Expenditure:			
Materials and overheads		37,000	See
Wages		35,000	below

Costs relating to the expansion

In order to expand the business I will either recruit two additional employees or sub-contract the work to Quantum Ltd, an unconnected company. Details of the expenditure relating to these two possibilities are set out below.

Employees

Employee 1 would be paid a salary of £55,000. He would also be provided with a petrol driven car with a list price when new of £12,800 (including VAT) and a CO_2 emission rate of 129 grams per kilometre. It can be assumed that the car will be sold in five years time for £2,000. Employee 2 would be paid a salary of £40,000 and would not be provided with a car.

There would also be additional materials and overheads, net of VAT at 20%, of £20,000.

Quantum Ltd

Quantum Ltd would charge an annual fee of £140,000 plus VAT.

There would be no additional materials or overheads.

Niels and Maria Copenhagen are both clients of your firm. The following information has been obtained from their files.

Niels Copenhagen

– Resident, ordinarily resident and domiciled in the UK.

– Niels has not made any previous transfers for the purposes of inheritance tax.

– Married to Maria. They have two children; Hans (11 years old) and Erik (8 years old).

Maria Copenhagen

– Resident, ordinarily resident and domiciled in the UK.

– Trades as 'Nucleus Resources', an unincorporated business.

– Receives annual gross rental income from an interest in possession trust of £110,000.

Required:

Prepare the meeting notes requested by your manager. The following marks are available.

(a) Calculations of the annual additional after tax income generated by the expansion of Maria's business under each of the two alternatives. **(14 marks)**

(b) (i) The issues to be considered in order to determine whether or not the gift from the uncle is within the scope of UK inheritance tax and the treatment of any inheritance tax suffered in the country of Heisenbergia. **(6 marks)**

(ii) The tax implications of transferring the shares to the trust and the taxation of any trust income paid to the beneficiaries, Hans and Erik. **(7 marks)**

(iii) The extent to which it is professionally acceptable to discuss issues relating to the shares with Maria. **(4 marks)**

Appropriateness of the format and presentation of the notes and the effectiveness with which the information is communicated. **(4 marks)**

You should assume that today's date is 1 December 2013 and that the rates and allowances for the tax year 2012/13 apply throughout the question.

(Total: 35 marks)

 Online question assistance

30   **BOSON (ADAPTED)** *Walk in the footsteps of a top tutor*

Boson has been working overseas and is about to return to the UK. He requires advice on his capital gains tax position and on whether to retain an overseas investment property or to sell it and invest the funds in the UK.

The following information has been obtained from telephone conversations with Boson.

Boson's current position:

- He is UK domiciled.

- He had lived in the UK all of his life until he moved to the country of Higgsia on 1 January 2009.

- He sold shares in Meson plc whilst living in Higgsia.

- He purchased a house in Higgsia but retained his principal private residence in the UK.

Boson's future:

- Boson plans to return permanently to his home in the UK on 20 January 2014.

- He has signed an employment contract with Graviton Ltd, which commences on 15 April 2014.

- He is considering selling the house in Higgsia and investing the after tax proceeds in a portfolio of quoted shares in UK companies or, alternatively, retaining the house and renting it out.

Sales of shares in Meson plc:

- Meson plc is a UK resident quoted company.

- Boson inherited 19,500 shares on 1 August 2002 when they were worth £2 each.

- Boson sold 10,000 shares on 1 May 2009 for £11 each.

- Boson sold the remaining shares on 1 November 2013 for £15 each.

House in the country of Higgsia:

- Purchased by Boson on 1 May 2009 for £105,000.

- Could be rented out for £11,000 per year after deduction of allowable expenses.

- Is currently worth and could be sold for £200,000.

The tax system in the country of Higgsia:

– Non-residents of Higgsia are charged income tax at 30% on income arising in the country of Higgsia.

– No capital gains tax.

– No double tax treaty with the UK.

Employment contract with Graviton Ltd:

– Boson will be paid an annual salary of £35,590.

Portfolio of quoted shares:

– The portfolio would be expected to generate annual dividends at the rate of approximately 4·3% of the capital invested.

Required:

(a) Advise Boson, by reference to his residence and ordinary residence position, as to whether or not the sales of the shares in Meson plc on 1 May 2009 and 1 November 2013 and the possible sale of the house in the country of Higgsia will be subject to capital gains tax.

State what he should do in order to ensure that any gains arising are not subject to capital gains tax.

You are not required to prepare calculations for part (a) of this question. **(10 marks)**

(b) (i) Calculate Boson's annual rental income after deduction of all taxes in respect of the house in Higgsia. **(4 marks)**

(ii) On the assumption that the house in Higgsia is sold for £200,000, with no capital gains tax payable, calculate the annual after tax income generated if the whole amount is invested in the portfolio of quoted shares. **(3 marks)**

(iii) Calculate the maximum by which the rate of return on the portfolio of quoted shares could fall before the after tax income generated would cease to exceed the return from renting out the house in Higgsia. **(3 marks)**

You should assume that today's date is 1 December 2013 and that the rates and allowances for the tax year 2012/13 apply throughout the question.

(Total: 20 marks)

---

31 **CHARLESTON DANCE (ADAPTED)**   *Walk in the footsteps of a top tutor*

 Timed question with Online tutor debrief

An extract from an e-mail from your manager following a meeting he has had with Charleston Dance is set out below.

> I attach a memorandum summarising the matters discussed in a meeting I had yesterday with Charleston. I also attach a calculation of the inheritance tax due on his father's death as prepared by his friend, Lindy. I have not had the chance to look at this in detail but I can confirm that the annual exemptions and the taper relief have been applied correctly and that there are no arithmetical errors; please review it with care.

I want you to write a letter from me to Charleston covering the following issues.

(i)   Inheritance tax

–   Brief explanations of any errors you find when you review Lindy's calculation of the inheritance tax due on Charleston's father's death and the effect of correcting the errors on the total inheritance tax due.

(ii)   Investments and pensions

–   The suitability of investing in venture capital trusts and a summary of the tax reliefs available in respect of such an investment.

–   The maximum tax allowable pension contributions that can be made by Charleston and Betty and the effect on this, if any, of purchasing further rental properties.

(iii) Income tax planning

–   Calculations, with supporting explanations to show that the total tax payable would increase (rather than decrease!) if he were to transfer all of the quoted shares and government stocks to a company wholly owned by him. Use the income figures from Lindy's inheritance tax calculation for these purposes and assume that the whole of the new company's post-tax income would be paid as a dividend to Charleston.

–   The income tax advantages of Charleston transferring investments to Betty or their children.

–   The points that Charleston needs to be aware of in connection with tax avoidance schemes and the taxation of the Balboan properties.

Thank you

The memorandum prepared by your manager is set out below.

To	The files
From	Tax manager
Date	29 May 2013
Subject	Charleston Dance

I met Charleston and his wife Betty on 28 May 2013. The couple have two children who are both at university.

Charleston's father died on 1 April 2013 leaving Charleston the whole of his estate. Charleston and Betty immediately resigned from their jobs and now have no income other than that generated from Charleston's inherited investments.

Charleston agreed to send me a schedule of the assets he inherited from his father together with a calculation that a friend of his, Lindy, has done of the inheritance tax due. The schedule will also include details of gifts made by his father whilst he was alive and the income generated by the inherited investments.

Charleston has asked me to comment on the following ideas.

Charleston's investment ideas

1.   Charleston and Betty intend to make the maximum possible tax allowable personal pension contributions.

2. Charleston will sell his father's home and invest much of the proceeds in further rental property situated either in the UK or in the country of Balboa.

3. Charleston wants to invest in unquoted trading companies but does not want to invest in enterprise investment scheme shares due to the level of risk involved.

Charleston's tax planning ideas

1. Lindy has convinced him that he would save income tax if he formed a company and transferred the quoted shares and government stocks inherited from his father into it. Charleston would own the whole of the company.

2. A London based financial institution has sent Charleston details of a number of tax avoidance schemes that they are promoting. Lindy has assured Charleston that there is no need to disclose the income from the Balboan properties to HM Revenue and Customs (HMRC) because the income is taxed in the country of Balboa. Charleston is concerned about the legality of the tax avoidance schemes and the accuracy of Lindy's suggestion.

Our input

I told Charleston that I would suggest an alternative to enterprise investment scheme shares as well as other tax planning opportunities. I also suggested that it may be possible to increase his tax allowable pension contributions depending on the property he buys.

Charleston, Betty and the children are resident, ordinarily resident and domiciled in the UK. Charleston's father was also resident, ordinarily resident and domiciled in the UK.

Tax manager

Lindy's calculation of the inheritance tax due and the income generated by the inherited investments is set out below.

Inheritance tax computation		
Father's lifetime gifts	£	£
1 November 2003 – Gift of cash to Charleston – more than seven years prior to death		200,000
1 July 2006 – Gift of cash to Charleston		370,000
Annual exemptions		(6,000)
		364,000
Nil band	325,000	
Gifts in last seven years (£200,000 – £6,000 (Two AEs))	(194,000)	
		(131,000)
		233,000
Inheritance tax at 40%		93,200
Taper relief (£93,200 x 80%)		(74,560)
		18,640

Father's death estate			Annual income received
	£	£	£
UK assets:			
Father's home		1,300,000	
UK quoted shares and related dividends		500,000	21,000
UK Government stocks and related interest		600,000	27,000
Bank accounts and related interest,			
- furniture and paintings		410,000	8,000
- Cars		34,000	
Investment properties in the country			
of Balboa and related rental income	800,000		72,000
Less: Balboan inheritance tax	(160,000)		
ERROR			
		640,000	
Chargeable estate		3,484,000	Ignore
Inheritance tax at 40% (no nil band available)		1,393,600	
Total tax due (£18,640 + £1,393,600)		1,412,240	

Required:

Prepare the letter requested in the e-mail from your manager. Marks are available for the three sections of the letter as follows:

(i)   Inheritance tax;   **(8 marks)**

(ii)   Investments and pensions;   **(9 marks)**

(iii) Income tax planning.   **(14 marks)**

Professional marks will be awarded for the appropriateness of the format and presentation of the letter and the effectiveness with which the information is communicated.   **(4 marks)**

(Total: 35 marks)

 Calculate your allowed time, allocate the time to the separate parts...................

32   GRIFTER (ADAPTED) *Walk in the footsteps of a top tutor*

An extract from an e-mail from your manager detailing two tasks for you to perform is set out below.

(a)   You will find a letter on your desk from a new client, Grifter, who is a self-employed information technology consultant. I need you to write a memorandum for the files addressing the matters regarding Grifter set out below. Keep any narrative to a minimum unless I have specifically asked for it.

Rental income (i)
40%
Penalty 100%
No DTR

01/11/13 died
01/02/08 gift
No A/E + NRB
No DTR

(i) Property in the country of Shadowsia

Calculate the income tax on the rental income in respect of the property in Shadowsia on the basis that Grifter is a higher rate taxpayer for all of the relevant years and the rent does not take his income over £100,000. Grifter has asked us to assume that there will be interest and penalties payable equal to 100% of the tax due. There is no double tax treaty between the UK and the country of Shadowsia.

Unfortunately, Grifter's uncle died in November of this year so you will need to include a calculation of Grifter's inheritance tax liability, after any available reliefs, on the gift of the property. Grifter has informed me that his uncle was domiciled in the UK and that, due to gifts made in February 2008, there is no annual exemption or nil rate band available in respect of the gift. There was no inheritance tax liability in Shadowsia in respect of the property.

You should also include your assessment of Grifter's view of the tax repayment he has received.

(ii) Reduction in mortgage

Calculate the amount by which Grifter could reduce his mortgage if he were to sell the cars. This will be the after tax proceeds from the sale of the cars less any amounts due under (i) above.

Please include a detailed explanation of your tax treatment of the sale of the cars based on our knowledge of Grifter's circumstances. I understand from Grifter that he has not previously sold any cars from his collection.

Proceeds 20,050
fee (6,400)

Calculate the maximum price that Grifter could pay for a new house if he were to sell his existing house. Assume that his existing house will be sold on 28 February 2014 for £1,200,000 and that there will be professional fees of £6,400.

new purchase
Fee (400)
No A/E on CGT

In calculating the amount available to buy a new house you should assume that Grifter will reduce his mortgage by the same amount as the figure you have computed in respect of the sale of the cars and that there will be professional fees in respect of the purchase of the new house of £4,000.

When carrying out these calculations you should assume that Grifter's capital gains tax annual exempt amount is not available.

(b) I want you to write a briefing note on the remittance basis of taxation for individuals in respect of both investment income and capital gains. The note will be sent to all of our staff to provide them with a summary of the basic rules so that they will know when there is a need to consider the matter in more detail. I suggest you use the following headings: Non UK domicile living UK.

– Who is entitled to be taxed on the remittance basis?

– Is a claim required?

– How does the remittance basis affect an individual's UK tax liability?

Thanks

Bob

The letter from Grifter is set out below.

1 Dark Lane
London

Mr B Mitchum
M & M Co
London

1 December 2013

Dear Mr Mitchum

I shall be grateful if you will advise me on the following matters.

Property in the country of Shadowsia

On 1 April 2008 my uncle gave me a small investment property in the country of Shadowsia. The property is only worth £48,000 now but was worth £94,000 at the time of the gift. Rental income in respect of the property of £484 per month has been paid into my UK bank account since I acquired the property.

My understanding has always been that, because I am not domiciled in the UK, the rental income was not taxable in the UK and so I have not reported it on my income tax returns. However, I now realise from talking to you that I should have paid UK tax on the income (despite 12% Shadowsian tax being deducted from the payments made to me). Accordingly, please let me know how much in total I owe to the tax authorities in respect of this income up to and including the tax year 2012/13.

Hopefully the amount payable in respect of the rental income will be less than the tax refund of £14,600 that I received earlier this year. I'm quite sure that HM Revenue and Customs did not owe me this money but, whilst I'm happy to admit to my mistake over the rental income, I don't see any need to point out their mistakes. I have already spent the tax refund so I will need to use the funds generated by the sale of my cars or my house to pay any liabilities due in respect of the rental income.

Reduction in mortgage

I have not had a particularly successful year in 2013 and I have decided to repay some of my mortgage (current balance of approximately £350,000) in order to reduce my outgoings. I am considering two options.

1   Sell three of my cars and use the net proceeds to reduce my mortgage.

2   Sell my house and buy a smaller one with a smaller mortgage. I would want to reduce my mortgage by the same amount as in option 1, so the two options are comparable. My preference would be option 2 provided I could still afford a house of a sufficient size in a suitable location.

1   **My cars**

I have a collection of four cars that I drive regularly and race against other collectors. I would be very sad to have to sell any of them although, despite doing most of the repairs and maintenance myself, it is a very expensive hobby.

I set out below the details of the three cars that would be sold. I would have to pay a fee of 8% of the selling price to the auction house.

	Mercedes	Bugatti	Porsche
Date of purchase	1 June 2001	1 March 2003	1 October 2007
Cost	£42,000	£89,000	£77,000
Current valuation	£84,000	£127,000	£68,000

2 **My house**

I bought the house on 1 March 2003 for £500,000. However, I did not move into it until 1 September 2007 as I'd also bought a boat and I was sailing around the Mediterranean Sea. I've been told that I should be able to sell the house for £1,200,000.

Yours sincerely

Grifter

[handwritten margin notes] 1/ 3/ 83 - 5000 PPR Proceeds 1200000

Required:

(a) **Prepare the memorandum requested by your manager in his e-mail.**

Marks are available for the sections of the memorandum as follows:

(i) **Property in the country of Shadowsia;** **(9 marks)**

(ii) **Reduction in mortgage.** **(13 marks)**

Professional marks will be awarded in part (a) for the appropriateness of the format and presentation of the memorandum and the effectiveness with which the information is communicated. **(4 marks)**

(b) **Prepare the briefing note on the remittance basis of taxation for individuals as requested by your manager in his e-mail.** **(9 marks)**

(Total: 35 marks)

33 **POBLANO (ADAPTED)** *Walk in the footsteps of a top tutor*

 Timed question with Online tutor debrief

Your manager has had a meeting with Poblano. Poblano is the Finance Director of Capsicum Ltd, a subsidiary of Scoville plc. He is a higher rate taxpayer earning £60,000 per year and currently has no other income. Scoville plc together with its subsidiaries and its directors have been clients of your firm for many years.

The memorandum recording the matters discussed at the meeting and an extract from an email from your manager detailing the tasks for you to perform are set out below.

Memorandum recording matters discussed at meeting with Poblano

To The files
From Tax manager
Date 4 June 2013
Subject Poblano

I had a meeting with Poblano on 3 June 2013.

(i)   **Working in Manchester**

Poblano currently lives and works in Birmingham. However, Capsicum Ltd has recently acquired the Manchester operations of the group from a fellow subsidiary of Scoville plc. As a result of this, Poblano is going to be based in Manchester from 1 August 2013 for a period of at least five years. He will be paid an additional £15,000 per year during this period.

Poblano does not want to relocate his family to Manchester for personal reasons. He has been offered the use of a furnished flat in Manchester belonging to Capsicum Ltd to live in during the week. He will drive home each weekend.

Details of the company's flat are set out below.

	£
Current market value	490,000
Purchase price (1 June 2010)	350,000
Annual value	8,500
Monthly contribution required from Poblano	200

Alternatively, if he does not live in the flat, Capsicum Ltd will pay him a mileage allowance of 50 pence per mile to cover the cost of travelling to Manchester every Monday and returning home every Friday. During the week, whilst he is in Manchester, Poblano will stay with his aunt, paying her rent of £325 per month.

Poblano estimates that he will drive 9,200 miles per year travelling to Manchester each week and that he will spend £1,400 per year on petrol. There would also be additional depreciation in respect of his car of approximately £1,500 per year. Capsicum Ltd has a policy of not providing its employees with company cars.

Poblano expects to be better off due to the increase in his salary. He wants to know how much better off he will be depending on whether he lives in the company flat or receives the mileage allowance and stays with his aunt.

(ii)   **Senior accounting officer rules**

Poblano is aware that there are some relatively new rules affecting senior accounting officers. He asked me for a brief summary of the rules and whether or not they could apply to him.

iii)   **Father's property in the country of Chilaca**

Paprikash (Poblano's father) owns a property in the country of Chilaca that he uses for holidays. It has always been intended that the property would be left to Poblano in his father's will. However, Paprikash has recently agreed to give the property to Poblano now, if to do so would make sense from a tax point of view. Paprikash may still wish to use the property occasionally in the future.

The property is currently worth £600,000. However, due to the economic situation in the country of Chilaca, it is possible that this figure could either rise or fall over the next few years.

Paprikash is domiciled in the UK. He is in poor health and is not expected to live for more than a further five years. His total assets, including the property in the country of Chilaca, are worth £2 million.

Paprikash makes gifts on 1 May each year in order to use his annual exemption. His only other gift in the last seven years was to a trust on 1 June 2012. The gift consisted of a number of minority holdings of quoted shares valued at £290,000 in total. The trust is for the benefit of Poblano's daughter, Piri. It can be assumed that Paprikash will not make any further lifetime gifts.

There is no capital gains tax or inheritance tax in the country of Chilaca.

(iv) **Trust created for the benefit of Poblano's daughter**

The trust was created on 1 June 2012 as noted above. Poblano's daughter, Piri, received income from the trust for the first time in March 2013. Poblano did not have any further information on the trust and agreed to bring the relevant documentation to our next meeting. Piri's only other income is an annual salary of approximately £35,000.

Tax manager

E-mail from your manager

I want you to prepare notes for a meeting that we will both attend with Poblano. You will be leading the meeting.

Set out the information so that it is easy for you to find what you need as we go through the various issues. Include the briefest possible notes where the numbers are not self-explanatory.

The meeting notes need to include:

(i) **Working in Manchester**

- Calculations showing how much better (or worse) off Poblano will be under each of the alternatives as compared to his current position. If he is worse off under either of the alternatives, include a calculation of the amount of salary he would have to be paid, in addition to the £15,000, so that he is not out of pocket.

- An explanation of the tax treatment for the recipients of the mileage allowance to be paid to Poblano and the rent to be paid to his aunt.

- Any further information required and the effect it could have on the calculations you have prepared.

(ii) **Senior accounting officer rules**

- The information requested by Poblano.

(iii) **Father's property in the country of Chilaca**

- Calculations of the inheritance tax liability that will become due in respect of the property in the country of Chilaca depending on whether the property is gifted to Poblano on 1 August 2013 or via his father's will.

You should assume the following:

- His father, Paprikash, will die on either 31 December 2015 or 31 December 2017.

- The property will be worth £600,000 on 1 August 2013.

- Three possible values of the property at the date of Paprikash's death: £450,000, £600,000 and £900,000.

You should calculate the inheritance tax for each of the 12 possible situations on the property only, assuming that Paprikash does not use the property after the date of the gift.

You should start by calculating the tax on a lifetime gift with Paprikash's death on 31 December 2015. If you then think about the relationships between the different situations you should find that the calculations do not take too long.

In order for the calculations to be comparable, when calculating the tax on the gift via Paprikash's will, you should assume that any available nil band is deductible from the property.

– Conclusions drawn from the calculations.

– Any other issues that we should draw to Poblano's attention.

(iv) **Trust created for the benefit of Poblano's daughter**

– A summary of the tax treatment of the income received by Poblano's daughter Piri, as beneficiary, depending on the nature of the trust.

I understand from Poblano that the only income of the trust is dividend income.

Required:

Prepare the meeting notes requested in the email from your manager.

The following marks are available.

(i)	Working in Manchester;	**(10 marks)**
(ii)	Senior accounting officer rules;	**(3 marks)**
(iii)	Father's property in the country of Chilaca;	**(12 marks)**
(iv)	Trust created for the benefit of Poblano's daughter.	**(6 marks)**

Professional marks will be awarded for the appropriateness of the format and presentation of the notes and the effectiveness with which the information is communicated. **(4 marks)**

(Total: 35 marks)

 Calculate your allowed time, allocate the time to the separate parts....................

34   SUSHI (ADAPTED) *Walk in the footsteps of a top tutor*

An extract from an e-mail from your manager regarding a meeting with a client, Sushi, together with an e-mail from Sushi are set out below.

E-mail from your manager

I have just had a meeting with Sushi who has been a client of the firm since she moved to the UK from the country of Zakuskia in May 1999. Sushi is 57 years old and was born in the country of Zakuskia. Her father died in 2006 and, as you will see from her e-mail, her mother died in October 2013. Her father and mother were both domiciled and resident in the country of Zakuskia throughout their lives. Zakuskian inheritance tax is charged at the rate of 24% on all land and buildings situated within the country that are owned by an individual at the time of death. There is no capital gains tax in the country of Zakuskia. There is no double tax treaty between the UK and the country of Zakuskia.

Until the death of her mother, Sushi's only assets consisted of her house in the UK, a number of investment properties also situated in the UK, and cash in UK bank accounts. Her total UK assets are worth approximately £3 million. Sushi is an additional rate taxpayer and realises taxable capital gains of more than £20,000 each year. She has made significant cash gifts to her son in the past and, therefore, does not require an explanation of the taxation of potentially exempt transfers or the accumulation principle. Sushi is resident and ordinarily resident in the UK.

I want you to write notes addressing the points below:

(i)   **UK inheritance tax and the statue**

An explanation of:

–   The UK inheritance tax implications of the death of Sushi's mother.

–   Which of Sushi's assets will be subject to UK inheritance tax when she dies. This will require some careful and detailed consideration of her domicile position both now and in the future.

–   The manner in which UK inheritance tax would be calculated, if due, on any land and buildings situated in the country of Zakuskia that are owned by Sushi when she dies.

–   Why the gift of the statue to her son, as referred to in her e-mail, will be a potentially exempt transfer, and how this treatment could be avoided.

The statue has not increased in value since the death of Sushi's mother. Accordingly, the proposed gift of the statue to Sushi's son will not give rise to a capital gain.

(ii)   **The Zakuskian income**

The Zakuskian income will be subject to tax in the UK because Sushi is UK resident and ordinarily resident. Accordingly, we need to think about whether or not Sushi should claim the remittance basis. In order to do this I want you to prepare calculations of the increase in her UK tax liability due to the Zakuskian income on the assumption that the remittance basis **is not** available and then on the assumption that it **is** available. You should assume that Sushi remits £100,000 (gross) to the UK each year in accordance with her plans.

In relation to the taxation of the Zakuskian income, your notes should include explanations of the meaning of the terms 'remittance basis' and 'remittance', and whether or not the remittance basis is available to Sushi, together with your conclusions based on your calculations but no other narrative. You should include brief footnotes to your calculations where necessary to aid understanding of the figures.

There is no need to consider the implication of capital gains on overseas assets as Sushi does not intend to dispose of any of her Zakuskian assets, apart from the statue, for the time being.

Thank you

Tax manager

E-mail from Sushi

My mother died on 1 October 2013 and left me the whole of her estate. I inherited the following assets.

The family home in the country of Zakuskia
Investment properties in the country of Zakuskia
Cash in Zakuskian bank accounts
Paintings and other works of art in the country of Zakuskia

The works of art include a statue that has been owned by my family for many years. I intend to bring the statue to the UK in December 2013 and give it to my son on his birthday on 1 July 2014. The statue was valued recently at £390,000.

The assets inherited from my mother will generate gross annual income of approximately £200,000 before tax, all of which is subject to 10% Zakuskian income tax. I intend to bring half of this income into the UK each year. The balance will remain in a bank account in Zakuskia.

I would like to meet with you to discuss these matters.

Thank you for your help.

Sushi

Required:

Prepare the notes requested in the e-mail from your manager. The following marks are available.

(i)   UK inheritance tax and the statue;   (12 marks)

(ii)   The Zakuskian income.   (13 marks)

You should assume that today's date is 6 December 2013 and that the rates and allowances for 2012/13 continue for the foreseeable future.

(Total: 25 marks)

35 JOHN AND MAUREEN ROBINSON (ADAPTED) *Walk in the footsteps of a top tutor*

You have received the following memorandum from your manager, Irwin Allen.

To	Tax senior
From	Irwin Allen
Date	2 June 2013
Subject	John and Maureen Robinson

I had a meeting with John Robinson and his wife Maureen yesterday. They have two children; Will, aged seven and Penny, aged nine. John and Maureen have made a number of errors in their income tax returns and Maureen requires advice in connection with her business.

Errors in income tax returns

John inherited a portfolio of quoted shares, an investment property and a large sum of cash in May 2010. Whilst completing his tax return for 2010/11 he decided to 'give' all of the income arising from the shares, property and cash deposits to his wife for tax purposes. Accordingly, he omitted the income from his own tax return and included it in that of his wife. He did the same thing in 2011/12.

John has since realised that such a 'gift' has no effect for tax purposes and has decided to notify HM Revenue and Customs (HMRC) of his mistake.

In January 2011 John gave the investment property to Maureen who sold it a week later. The gift to Maureen was the subject of a legitimate legal conveyance but, after the sale, Maureen gave the sales proceeds to John in accordance with an agreement they had made prior to the gift. Maureen declared the capital gain of £13,470 in her 2010/11 income tax return.

John has asked us to calculate the additional tax payable as a result of his mistaken declarations to HMRC. A schedule prepared by John summarising the family's income for the two tax years 2010/11 and 2011/12 together with details of the investment property is on your desk. The gain on the sale of the investment property was the couple's only capital gain in the last four years.

Maureen's business

Maureen began trading as Robinson Mapping on 1 November 2010. She registered for value added tax (VAT) immediately and prepared her first accounts to 30 September 2011. A schedule prepared by Maureen summarising the results of the business is also on your desk.

Maureen supplies specialised maps to businesses in the leisure industry. All of her customers are registered for VAT. The business has recoverable input tax of approximately £300 per quarter. Despite accounting for VAT on an annual basis, Maureen is finding the administration of the tax very time consuming and is considering deregistering unless the amount of administration can be reduced.

Please prepare the following for me.

(a)   A calculation of the additional taxes payable by John Robinson in respect of the tax years 2010/11 and 2011/12 as a result of disclosing to HMRC the errors in his tax returns.

There's quite a bit to do here; please ensure that your calculations are clear and logical so that they are easy to follow.

You'll need to work out the extra tax payable by John on the investment income and compare it with the tax paid by Maureen (probably a fairly small amount as most if not all of the income will have fallen into her basic rate band).

Please **do not** address the issue of interest and penalties for the moment.

(b)   Advice for Maureen on her ability to deregister for the purposes of VAT together with the procedure she should follow and the implications of deregistration.

Include details of any alternative strategy that might solve her problem.

I do not want you to write a letter or to prepare illustrative calculations; just write the necessary paragraphs for me to incorporate in a letter that will cover a number of other issues.

Thank you

Irwin

The schedule summarising all of the family's income, with the exception of that relating to Maureen's business, is set out below.

Robinson Family – Income received in tax years 2010/11 and 2011/12			
	Notes	2010/11 £	2011/12 £
Income arising on inherited assets:			
Dividend income received in respect of share portfolio		8,856	9,108
Rental income in respect of investment property		2,550	–
Bank interest income received in respect of cash deposits		2,424	2,576
John			
Other income:			
Salary		32,040	31,362
Company car	1		
Trust income received	2	600	650

	Notes	2010/11 £	2011/12 £
Maureen			
Other income:			
Unincorporated business	3		
Will – bank deposit interest received	4	Nil	88
Penny – bank deposit interest received	4	Nil	144

Notes

1. I have had use of the car since 1 August 2010 for both business and private use. I also receive free petrol in respect of all of my mileage. The car had a list price when new of £17,400 and has a CO_2 emission rate of 166 grams per kilometre.

2. The trust is a discretionary trust established by my uncle.

3. Maureen will provide you with a summary of the results of her business.

4. I transferred cash from my bank account to two new accounts for the children on 1 June 2011. The interest is credited gross as there is no tax liability on the children's income.

The schedule summarising the results of Maureen's business is set out below.

Maureen Robinson – Robinson Mapping

–   Began trading on 1 November 2010

–   Tax adjusted trading profits, after the deduction of capital allowances:

Period ended 30 September 2011	£29,100
Year ended 30 September 2012	£30,360

Required:

(a) Prepare a calculation of the additional taxes payable by John and Maureen Robinson in respect of the tax years 2010/11 and 2011/12 as a result of disclosing to HMRC the errors in their tax returns. **(24 marks)**

Additional marks will be awarded for the clarity with which the information is presented and the extent to which the calculations are structured in a logical manner. **(3 marks)**

(b) Advise Maureen on deregistration for the purposes of value added tax (VAT) and any possible alternative strategy. **(7 marks)**

An additional mark will be awarded for the effectiveness with which the information is communicated. **(1 mark)**

You should assume that the tax rates and allowances for the tax year 2012/13 apply throughout the question.

(Total: 35 marks)

36   ALICE AND ZARA (ADAPTED)

You should assume that today's date is 15 February 2013.

Alice and Zara Sibling are two sisters who have recently inherited £75,000 each.

They have asked for your advice regarding the following proposals concerning the investment of their inheritance:

(1)   Alice and Zara will both invest the maximum amount possible in Individual Savings Accounts (ISAs). Alice wants to invest in a cash ISA, with the balance of the maximum investment being put in low risk investments within a stocks and shares ISA. Zara wants to invest solely in a stocks and shares ISA, with investments being made in ordinary shares.

(2)   Alice and Zara will both invest the maximum tax-deductible amount into pension schemes. Alice was born on 15 June 1962, and earns a salary of £55,000 pa. She contributes 6% of her salary into her employer's HMRC registered occupational pension scheme, with the employer contributing a further 5%. Her pensionable income for 2010/11 was £45,000 and 2011/12 £52,000.

Zara was born on 4 November 1974, and is self-employed. She has not previously made any provision for retirement. Zara's taxable trading profit for 2012/13 is expected to be £47,400.

(3)   Alice is to invest the balance of her inheritance in an open-ended investment company aimed at capital growth. Zara is to use the balance of her inheritance to subscribe for new ordinary shares in a Venture Capital Trust that invests in unquoted high technology companies.

Alice already has investments worth £140,000, and receives investment income of £10,000 pa.

Her investment criteria are:

(1)   capital growth is more important than additional income,

(2)   she is prepared to take a moderate amount of risk, and

(3)   the capital is not needed for at least ten years.

Zara currently has no investments, and does not have any other income.

Her investment criteria are:

(1)   income is more important than capital growth,

(2)   she is prepared to accept a high level of risk, and

(3)   the capital will be needed in five years' time when Zara plans to buy a new house.

Required:

For each of the proposed investments:

(i) Explain the potential income tax and CGT implications.

Your answer should include details of the maximum amount that can be invested in each case, and be confined to the implications for 2012/13.

(ii) Advise Alice and Zara as to the suitability of each investment in relation to their investment criteria. **(18 marks)**

37 ANDREW

Andrew is aged 38 and is single. He is employed as a consultant by Bestadvice & Co and pays income tax at the higher rate.

Andrew is considering investing in a new business, and to provide funds for this investment he has recently disposed of the following assets:

(1) A short leasehold interest in a residential property. Andrew originally paid £50,000 for a 47 year lease of the property in May 2001, and assigned the lease in May 2013 for £90,000.

(2) His holding of £10,000 7% Government Stock, on which interest is payable half-yearly on 20 April and 20 October. Andrew originally purchased this holding on 1 June 2004 for £9,980 and he sold it for £11,250 on 14 March 2012.

Andrew intends to subscribe for ordinary shares in a new company, Scalar Limited, which will be a UK based manufacturing company. Three investors (including Andrew) have been identified, but a fourth investor may also be invited to subscribe for shares. The investors are all unconnected, and would subscribe for shares in equal measure.

The intention is to raise £450,000 in this manner. The company will also raise a further £50,000 from the investors in the form of loans. Andrew has been told that he can take advantage of some tax reliefs on his investment in Scalar Limited, but does not know anything about the details of these reliefs

Andrew's employer, Bestadvice & Co, is proposing to change the staff pension scheme from a defined benefit scheme to which the firm and the employees each contribute 6% of their annual salary, to a defined contribution scheme, to which the employees will continue to contribute 6%, but the firm will contribute 8% of their annual salary.

The majority of Andrew's colleagues are opposed to this move, but, given the increase in the firm's contribution rate Andrew himself is less sure that the proposal is without merit.

Required:

(a) **(i)** Calculate the capital gain arising on the assignment of the residential property lease in May 2013. **(2 marks)**

(ii) Advise Andrew of the tax implications arising from the disposal of the 7% Government Stock, clearly identifying the tax year in which any liability will arise and how it will be paid. **(3 marks)**

(b) **(i)** Advise Andrew of the income tax (IT) and capital gains tax (CGT) reliefs available on his investment in the ordinary share capital of Scalar Limited, together with any conditions which need to be satisfied.

Your answer should clearly identify any steps that should be taken by Andrew and the other investors to obtain the maximum relief. **(14 marks)**

(ii) State the taxation implications of both equity and loan finance from the point of view of a company. **(3 marks)**

(c) State the key characteristics of a defined benefit and a defined contribution pension scheme, explaining why the employer and the employees might have differing views as to the merits of each. **(4 marks)**

You should assume that the rates and allowances for the tax year 2012/13 apply throughout this question.

(Total: 26 marks)

Relevant extracts from the leasehold depreciation tables are as follows:

35 years	**91.981**
47 years	**98.902**

38 SERGIO AND GERARD

Sergio and Gerard each inherited a half interest in a property, 'Hilltop', in October 2011. 'Hilltop' had a probate value of £124,000, but in November 2011 it was badly damaged by fire. In January 2012 the insurance company made a payment of £81,700 each to Sergio and Gerard. In February 2012 Sergio and Gerard each spent £55,500 of the insurance proceeds on restoring the property. 'Hilltop' was worth £269,000 following the restoration work. In July 2012, Sergio and Gerard sold 'Hilltop' for £310,000.

Sergio is 69 years old and a widower with three adult children and seven grandchildren. His annual income consists of a pension of £9,900 and interest of £300 on savings of £7,600 in a bank deposit account. Sergio owns his home but no other significant assets. He plans to buy a domestic rental property with the proceeds from the sale of 'Hilltop', such that on his death he will have a significant asset which can be sold and divided between the members of his family.

Gerard is 34 years old. He is employed by Fizz plc on a salary of £70,500 per year together with a performance related bonus. Gerard estimates that he will receive a bonus in December 2013 of £4,500, in line with previous years, and that his taxable benefits in the tax year 2013/14 will amount to £7,180.

He also expects to receive dividends from UK companies of £1,935 and bank interest of £648 in the tax year 2013/14. Gerard intends to set up a personal pension plan in August 2013. He has not made any pension contributions in the past and proposes to use part of the proceeds from the sale of 'Hilltop' to make the maximum possible tax allowable contribution.

Fizz plc has announced that it intends to replace the performance related bonus scheme with a share incentive plan, also linked to performance, with effect from 6 April 2014. Gerard estimates that Fizz plc will award him free shares worth £2,100 each year. He will also purchase partnership shares worth £700 each year and, as a result, will be awarded matching shares (further free shares) worth £1,400.

Required:

(a) Calculate the chargeable gains arising on the receipt of the insurance proceeds in January 2012 and the sale of 'Hilltop' in July 2012.

You should assume that any elections necessary to minimise the gain on the receipt of the insurance proceeds have been submitted. **(4 marks)**

(b) Advise Sergio on the appropriateness of investing in a domestic rental property in view of his personal circumstances and recommend suitable alternative investments giving reasons for your advice. **(4 marks)**

(c) Calculate and explain the amount of income tax relief that Gerard will obtain in respect of the pension contributions he proposes to make in the tax year 2013/14 and contrast this with how his position could be improved by delaying some of the contributions that he could have made in 2013/14 until 2014/15.

You should include relevant supporting calculations and quantify the additional tax savings arising as a result of your advice.

You should ignore the proposed changes to the bonus scheme for this part of this question and assume that Gerard's income will not change in 2014/15. **(12 marks)**

(d) Evaluate the effect on Gerard of the changes to be made by Fizz plc to its performance related bonus scheme.

You should ignore the effect of any pension contributions to be made by Gerard in the future, consider both the value and timing of amounts received by Gerard and include relevant supporting calculations. **(5 marks)**

You should assume that the income tax rates and allowances for the tax year 2012/13 apply throughout this question.

(Total: 25 marks)

 Online question assistance

---

39   ADAM SNOOK (ADAPTED) *Walk in the footsteps of a top tutor*

Your manager has had a meeting with Adam Snook and has sent you a copy of the following memorandum.

To	The files
From	Tax manager
Date	1 December 2013
Subject	Adam Snook

Adam Snook (AS) has been entertaining children at parties as a hobby for the last two years. On 1 June 2013 his aunt gave him shares in Brill plc, a quoted company, worth £88,040. As a result, AS intends to give up his job on 31 December 2013 (he is a regional sales manager with Rheims Ltd) and purchase a small theatre from which he will carry on a business of providing entertainment for children's parties.

The business

AS will begin advertising and charging for attending children's parties on 1 January 2014. He estimates that his net profit for the first five months (until the theatre opens) will only be £400 per month. Accordingly, he has agreed to work part-time for his existing employer from 1 January 2014 until 31 May 2014 for a salary of £1,050 per month.

AS will purchase the theatre on 1 April 2014. He estimates that it will take six weeks or so to renovate the theatre such that it should be ready for business by 1 June 2014 at the latest. AS will seek to rent out the theatre for the days when it is not required for his business.

We agreed that the business should prepare accounts to 31 March each year. AS does not wish to form a limited company.

The supply of entertainment at the theatre will be standard rated for the purposes of value added tax (VAT) and AS will register for VAT on 1 June 2014.

The finance required

The costs of establishing the business, exclusive of recoverable VAT, are set out below.

	£
Purchase price of the theatre	215,000
Renovation of the theatre	45,000
Equipment and other costs	50,000
	———
Finance required	310,000
	———

The finance available

AS sold 42,600 shares in Snapper plc for £104,370 on 1 December 2013 and intends to sell £25,000 6% Snapper plc non-convertible loan stock next week for £29,900. He will use the net proceeds of these sales to finance the business and obtain the balance of the funds required via a bank overdraft at an annual interest rate of 10%. The shares and loan stock in Snapper plc were acquired as follows:

- AS was given 14,200 shares in Brill plc by his aunt on 1 June 2013. At that time the shares were worth £88,040.

- On 1 November 2013 Brill plc was acquired by Snapper plc. Both Brill plc and Snapper plc are UK resident trading companies.

- AS received 42,600 shares in Snapper plc together with £25,000 6% Snapper plc non-convertible loan stock (a qualifying corporate bond) in exchange for his shares in Brill plc.

- The shares and the loan stock were worth £97,980 and £28,400 respectively as at 1 November 2013.

Other background information

AS is 35 years old. His full time salary with Rheims Ltd is £25,200 per annum. He is provided with a diesel company car which had a list price when new of £13,950 and a CO_2 emission rate of 162 grams per kilometre. He is not provided with free fuel. He will return the car to the company on 31 December 2013.

AS's aunt is 71 years old and is domiciled in the UK. This is the first substantial gift that she has made to AS although he suspects that she has made similar gifts to other relatives in the past. He is also drafting his will and wants to understand how any amounts left to charity would affect the inheritance position on his death.

Tax manager

An extract from an email from your manager is set out below.

Please prepare a memorandum for me, incorporating the following:

(a) (i) Calculations to support the amount of external finance required by Adam including a note of any assumptions made.

Don't forget to take his capital gains tax liability into account but ignore any possible inheritance tax liability.

(ii) A proposal which will increase the after tax proceeds from the sale of the Snapper plc loan stock together with the amount of the increase.

A reasoned recommendation of a more appropriate form of external finance for the business.

(b) Explanations of the following matters:

(i) Adam's liability to Class 2 and Class 4 national insurance contributions in 2013/14.

(ii) The income tax relief available in respect of both the cost of purchasing and renovating the theatre.

(iii) For value added tax (VAT) purposes: the effect of renting out the theatre on Adam's ability to recover input tax, the implications of opting to tax the theatre and the factors affecting the decision to opt to tax.

(c) An explanation of the inheritance tax payable by Adam in respect of the gift from his aunt depending on when his aunt dies and an explanation of the consequences of charitable bequests.

We will be under significant fee pressure on this job so please don't do any unnecessary work – I'm sure that time spent thinking about what needs to be done before you start will save you time in the long run.

Tax manager

Required:

Prepare the memorandum requested by your manager.

You should assume that today's date is 3 December 2013.

Marks are available for the components of the memorandum as follows:

(a) (i) Calculations to support the amount of external finance required.

You should state any assumptions you have made in preparing the calculations. **(10 marks)**

(ii) A proposal which will increase the after tax proceeds from the sale of the Snapper plc loan stock and a reasoned recommendation of a more appropriate form of external finance. **(3 marks)**

(b) Explanations of the various matters. **(11 marks)**

(c)   The inheritance tax payable by Adam in respect of the gift from his aunt and an explanation of the consequences of charitable bequests.   **(7 marks)**

Additional marks will be awarded for the appropriateness of the format and presentation of the memorandum and the effectiveness with which the information is communicated.
(4 marks)

You should assume that the tax rates and allowances for the tax year 2012/13 will continue to apply for the foreseeable future.

(Total: 35 marks)

40   GAGARIN (ADAPTED)

Gagarin wishes to persuade a number of wealthy individuals who are business contacts to invest in his company, Vostok Ltd. He also requires advice on the recoverability of input tax relating to the purchase of new business premises.

The following information has been obtained from a meeting with Gagarin.

Vostok Ltd:

−   An unquoted UK resident company, set up in 2007.

−   Gagarin owns 100% of the company's ordinary share capital.

−   Has 18 employees.

−   Provides computer based services to commercial companies.

−   Requires additional funds to finance its expansion.

Funds required by Vostok Ltd:

−   Vostok Ltd needs to raise £420,000.

−   Vostok Ltd will issue 20,000 shares at £21 per share on 31 August 2013.

−   The new shareholder(s) will own 40% of the company.

−   Part of the money raised will contribute towards the purchase of new premises for use by Vostok Ltd.

Gagarin's initial thoughts:

−   The minimum investment will be 5,000 shares and payment will be made in full on subscription.

−   Gagarin has a number of wealthy business contacts who may be interested in investing.

−   Gagarin has heard that it may be possible to obtain tax relief for up to 58% of the investment via the Enterprise Investment Scheme.

Wealthy business contacts:

−   Are all UK resident higher rate and additional rate taxpayers.

−   May wish to borrow the funds to invest in Vostok Ltd if there is a tax incentive to do so.

New premises:

−   Will cost £456,000 including value added tax (VAT).

−   Will be used in connection with all aspects of Vostok Ltd's business.

- Will be sold for £600,000 plus VAT in six years time.

- Vostok Ltd will waive the VAT exemption on the sale of the building.

The VAT position of Vostok Ltd:

- In the year ending 31 March 2014, 28% of Vostok Ltd's supplies will be exempt for the purposes of VAT.

- This percentage is expected to reduce over the next few years.

- Irrecoverable input tax due to the company's partially exempt status exceeds the *de minimis* limits.

Required:

(a) **Prepare notes for Gagarin to use when speaking to potential investors.**

The notes should include:

(i) **The tax incentives immediately available in respect of the amount invested in shares issued in accordance with the Enterprise Investment Scheme;**

(5 marks)

(ii) **The answers to any questions that the potential investors may raise in connection with the maximum possible investment, borrowing to finance the subscription and the implications of selling the shares.** **(9 marks)**

You should assume that Vostok Ltd and its trade qualify for the purposes of the Enterprise Investment Scheme and you are not required to list the conditions that need to be satisfied by the company, its shares or its business activities.

(b) **Calculate the amount of input tax that will be recovered by Vostok Ltd in respect of the new premises in the year ending 31 March 2014 and explain, using illustrative calculations, how any additional recoverable input tax will be calculated in future years.** **(6 marks)**

(Total: 20 marks)

TAXATION OF CORPORATE BUSINESSES

FAMILY COMPANY ISSUES

41 JAMES & MELVIN (ADAPTED)

Assume today's date is 1 January 2013.

Your have recently held a meeting with James and Melvin who are both UK resident. They each own 50% of the issued ordinary share capital of JM Limited, an unquoted trading company which prepares its accounts to 31 March each year.

JM Limited is a close company and was formed on 1 May 2008 with 1,000 £1 ordinary shares being issued at par value. James is both a director of and employed by JM Limited whereas Melvin is neither employed nor a director of this company. Both James and Melvin are higher rate taxpayers with incomes of £45,000.

JM Limited has been reasonably successful and James now wishes to partially realise some of his investment in the company either by a direct sale to Melvin or via a company purchase of its own shares. He is, however, currently undecided as to how many of his ordinary shares he will sell although this will be no less than 100 and no more than 350.

Each JM Limited share currently has a market value of £500 which will be the price paid for each share in any sale. It is anticipated that the share sale will occur on 31 March 2013 but it could be deferred until 31 May 2013.

Your further ascertain the following

(1)   Throughout 2012/13 both James and Melvin were provided with new cars by JM Limited. Both cars use petrol and have a CO_2 emission level of 136 grams per kilometre and a list price of £20,000. In addition both James and Melvin are provided with fuel for private purposes.

(2)   On 6 July 2012 JM Limited paid some personal bills for Melvin amounting to £20,000. It is probable that this amount will be written off by JM Limited at some point in the future.

Required:

Write a letter to James and Melvin which is supported by relevant calculations:

(a)   Advising them of the tax and national insurance implications for both themselves individually and for JM Limited arising from the provision of cars to James and Melvin and the settling of some of Melvin's personal bills by the company.

(11 marks)

(b)   Advising them of the tax implications arising from the proposed sale of shares by James either directly to Melvin or via a company purchase of own shares.

(14 marks)

Marks will be awarded for presentation, structure and format.

(Total: 25 marks)

42   CHARLES AND JANE MIRO (ADAPTED)

Charles and Jane Miro, aged 31 and 34 years respectively, have been married for ten years and have two children aged six and eight years. Charles is a teacher but for the last five years he has stayed at home to look after their children. Jane works as a translator for Speak Write Ltd.

Speak Write Ltd was formed and began trading on 6 April 2013. It provides translation services to universities. Jane, who ceased employment with Barnham University to found the company, owns 100% of its ordinary share capital and is its only employee.

Speak Write Ltd has translated documents for four different universities since it began trading. Its biggest client is Barnham University which represents 70% of the company's gross income. It is estimated that the company's gross fee income for its first 12 months of trading will be £110,000. Speak Write Ltd usually agrees fixed fees in advance with its clients although it charges for some projects by reference to the number of days taken to do the work. None of the universities makes any payment to Speak Write Ltd in respect of Jane being on holiday or sick.

All of the universities insist that Jane does the work herself. Jane carries out the work for three of the universities in her office at home using a computer and specialised software owned by Speak Write Ltd. The work she does for Barnham University is done in the university's library on one of its computers as the documents concerned are too delicate to move.

The first set of accounts for Speak Write Ltd will be drawn up for the year ending 5 April 2014. It is estimated that the company's tax adjusted trading profit for this period will be £52,500. This figure is after deducting Jane's salary of £4,000 per month and the related national insurance contributions but before any adjustments required by the application of the personal service companies (IR 35) legislation. The company has no other sources of income or capital gains.

Jane has not entered into any communication with HM Revenue and Customs (HMRC) with respect to the company and wants to know:

–   When the corporation tax return should be submitted and when the tax is due.

–   When the corporation tax return can be regarded as having been agreed by HMRC.

Required:

(a)   **Write a letter to Jane as at 6 September 2013 setting out:**

   (i)   **the arguments that HMRC could put forward, based only on the facts set out above, in support of applying the IR 35 legislation to Speak Write Ltd; and**

   (ii)   **the additional income tax and national insurance contributions that would be payable, together with their due date of payment, if HMRC applied the IR 35 legislation to all of the company's income in 2013/14.** **(11 marks)**

(b)   (i)   **Compute the corporation tax liability of Speak Write Ltd for its first trading period on the assumption that the IR 35 legislation applies to all of its income.** **(2 marks)**

   (ii)   **Set out the information required by Jane in connection with the administration of the company's tax affairs and identify any penalties that may already be payable.** **(3 marks)**

You should assume that the income tax rates and allowances for the tax year 2012/13 and the corporation tax rates for the Financial Year 2012 apply throughout this question.

(Total: 16 marks)

43   CARVER LTD

(a)   Carver Ltd was incorporated and began trading in August 2008. It is a close company with no associated companies. It has always prepared accounts to 31 December and will continue to do so in the future.

It has been decided that Carver Ltd will sell its business as a going concern to Blade Ltd, an unconnected company, on 31 July 2013. Its premises and goodwill will be sold for £2,165,000 and £290,000 respectively and its machinery and equipment for £187,000. The premises were acquired on 1 August 2008 for £1,708,000 and the goodwill has been generated internally by the company. The machinery and equipment cost £294,000; no one item will be sold for more than its original cost.

The tax adjusted trading profit of Carver Ltd in 2013, before taking account of both capital allowances and the sale of the business assets, is expected to be £81,000. The balance on the plant and machinery pool for the purposes of capital allowances as at 31 December 2012 was £231,500. Machinery costing £38,000 was purchased on 1 March 2013.

On 1 August 2013, the proceeds from the sale of the business will be invested in either an office building or a portfolio of UK quoted company shares, as follows:

Office building

The office building would be acquired for £3,100,000; the vendor is not registered for value added tax (VAT). Carver Ltd would borrow the additional funds required from a UK bank. The building is let to a number of commercial tenants who are not connected with Carver Ltd and will pay rent, in total, of £54,000 per calendar quarter, in advance, commencing on 1 August 2013.

The company's expenditure for the period from 1 August 2013 to 31 December 2013 is expected to be:

	£
Loan interest payable to UK bank	16,000
Building maintenance costs	7,500

Share portfolio

Shares would be purchased for the amount of the proceeds from the sale of the business with no need for further loan finance. It is estimated that the share portfolio would generate dividends of £36,000 and capital gains, after indexation allowance, of £10,000 in the period from 1 August 2013 to 31 December 2013.

All figures are stated exclusive of value added tax (VAT).

Required:

(i) **Taking account of the proposed sale of the business on 31 July 2013, state with reasons the date(s) on which Carver Ltd must submit its corporation tax return(s) for the year ending 31 December 2013.** **(2 marks)**

(ii) **Explain whether or not Carver Ltd will become a close investment-holding company as a result of acquiring either the office building or the share portfolio and state the relevance of becoming such a company.** **(2 marks)**

(iii) **Calculate the corporation tax liability of Carver Ltd for the year ending 31 December 2013 based on its anticipated results under each of the investment strategies, on the assumption that all beneficial elections are made.**

You should support your calculations with an explanation of whether or not rollover relief is available on the sale of the business' premises in respect of both investment strategies and the treatment of the interest payable to the UK bank if Carver Ltd were to buy the office building. **(11 marks)**

You should assume that the corporation tax rates and allowances for the financial year 2012 will continue to apply for the foreseeable future.

You should ignore value added tax (VAT).

The relevant retail price index figures are:
August 2008 217.2
July 2013 251.0 (estimated)

(b) The directors of Carver Ltd are aware that some of the company's shareholders want to realise the value in their shares immediately. Accordingly, instead of investing in the office building or the share portfolio they are considering two alternative strategies whereby, following the sale of the company's business, a payment will be made to the company's shareholders.

(i) Liquidate the company. The payment by the liquidator would be £126 per share.

(ii) The payment of a dividend of £125 per share following which a liquidator will be appointed. The payment by the liquidator to the shareholders would then be £1 per share.

The company originally issued 20,000 £1 ordinary shares at par value to 19 members of the Cutler family. Following a number of gifts and inheritances there are now 41 shareholders, all of whom are family members.

The directors have asked you to attend a meeting to set out the tax implications of these two alternative strategies for each of the two main groups of shareholders: adults with shareholdings of more than 500 shares and children with shareholdings of 200 shares or less.

Required:

Prepare notes explaining:

– **the amount chargeable to tax; and**

– **the rates of tax that will apply**

in respect of each of the two strategies for each of the two groups of shareholders ready for your meeting with the directors of Carver Ltd.

You should assume that none of the shareholders will have any capital losses either in the tax year 2013/14 or brought forward as at 5 April 2013. **(10 marks)**

You should assume that the rates and allowances for the tax year 2012/13 will continue to apply for the foreseeable future.

(Total: 25 marks)

44 BANDA ROSS (ADAPTED) *Walk in the footsteps of a top tutor*

You have received the following email from your manager, Kara Weddell.

From	Kara Weddell
Date	3 December 2013
To	Tax senior
Subject	Banda Ross

I've put a copy of a letter from a potential new client, Banda Ross, on your desk. I've arranged a meeting with Banda for Friday this week to discuss the most appropriate structure for her new business, 'Aral'.

I spoke to Banda yesterday and obtained the following additional information.

• Banda has owned the whole of the ordinary share capital of Flores Ltd since 1 January 2010.

- Flores Ltd pays Banda a salary of £13,140 per annum and pays dividends to her of £20,250 on 31 July each year.
- Banda does not intend to take any income from Aral until the tax year 2016/17 at the earliest.
- Flores Ltd is Banda's only source of income.

Banda also mentioned that Flores Ltd made some sort of 'informal loan' to her in 2010 of £21,000 to pay for improvements to her house. I decided not to press her about this over the phone but I need to discuss with her what she meant by 'informal' and whether or not the loan has been disclosed to HM Revenue and Customs.

Please prepare the following schedules for me to use as a basis for our discussions. I will give Banda copies of schedules (a) and (b) but not schedule (c), as some of its contents may be sensitive.

(a)   Calculations of the anticipated tax adjusted trading profit/loss of Aral for its first three trading periods.

(b)   Explanations, together with relevant supporting calculations, of the tax relief available in respect of the anticipated trading losses depending on whether the business is run as a sole trader or a limited company. When considering the use of a limited company, don't forget that it could be owned by Banda or by Flores Ltd.

Please include a recommendation based on your figures but do not address any other issues regarding the differences between trading as a sole trader and as a company; I just want to focus on the losses for the moment.

(c)   Explanatory notes of the tax implications of there being a loan from Flores Ltd to Banda and whether or not such a loan might affect our willingness to provide her with tax advice.

Take some time to think about your approach to this before you start; I want you to avoid preparing any unnecessary calculations and to keep the schedules brief.

Thank you

Kara

The letter referred to in Kara's email is set out below.

Dear Kara

Aral business

I am the managing director of Flores Ltd, a company that manufactures waterskiing equipment. I am looking for a tax adviser to help me with my next business venture.

When I began the Flores business in 2008 it was expected to make losses for the first year or so. I was advised not to form a company but to trade as a sole trader and to offset the losses against my income of earlier years. I followed that advice and transferred the business to Flores Ltd on 1 January 2010, once it had become profitable. Flores Ltd has made taxable trading profits of approximately £120,000 each year since it was formed. It prepares accounts to 30 June each year.

For the past few months I have been researching the windsurfing market. I must have spent at least £6,000 travelling around the UK visiting retailers and windsurfing clubs (half of which was spent on buying people lunch!). However, it was all worthwhile as on 1 January 2014 I intend to start a new business, 'Aral', manufacturing windsurfing equipment.

The budgeted results for the first three trading periods of the Aral business are set out below:

		£
6 months ending 30 June 2014	Trading loss	(25,000)
Year ending 30 June 2015	Trading loss	(13,000)
Year ending 30 June 2016	Trading profit	77,000

The figures above have been adjusted for tax purposes but take no account of the tax relief available in respect of the equipment and car to be acquired on 2 January 2014.

The business will rent its premises but will purchase equipment (machinery, computers, shelving etc) at a cost of £13,500. The equipment should last approximately three years so there will be no further acquisitions of equipment until the year ending 30 June 2017. The business will also buy a second hand car with CO_2 emissions of 155 g/km for £9,875. The car will be available for general staff use on business trips and will be left at the work premises every night.

The next decision I need to make is whether the new business should trade as a company or as an unincorporated entity. It would make more sense commercially to form a company immediately but I would be willing to use the same approach as I used when establishing the Flores business if this maximises the relief obtained in respect of the trading losses. I want to obtain relief for the losses now; I do not want the losses carried forward for relief in the future unless there are no other options available.

Yours sincerely

Banda

Required:

Prepare the schedules requested by Kara.

Marks are available for the three schedules as follows:

(a) Tax adjusted trading profit/loss of the new business (Aral) for its first three trading periods. **(5 marks)**

(b) The tax relief available in respect of the anticipated trading losses, together with supporting calculations and a recommended structure for the business. **(18 marks)**

(c) Explanatory notes, together with relevant supporting calculations, in connection with the loan. **(8 marks)**

Additional marks will be awarded for the appropriateness of the format and presentation of the schedules, the effectiveness with which the information is communicated and the extent to which the schedules are structured in a logical manner. **(4 marks)**

You should assume that the tax rates and allowances for the tax year 2012/13 and for the financial year to 31 March 2013 apply throughout the question.

You should ignore value added tax (VAT). **(Total: 35 marks)**

45   SPICA (ADAPTED)

Spica, one of the director shareholders of Acrux Ltd, has been in dispute with the other shareholders over plans to expand the company's activities overseas. In order to resolve the position it has been agreed that Spica will sell her shares back to the company.

The following information has been obtained from client files and meetings with the parties involved.

Acrux Ltd:

–   An unquoted UK resident trading company.

–   Share capital consists of 50,000 ordinary shares issued at £1·25 per share in July 2004.

–   None of the other shareholders has any connection with Spica.

The purchase of own shares:

–   The company will purchase all of Spica's shares for £8 per share.

–   The transaction will take place by the end of 2013.

Spica:

–   Purchased 8,000 shares in Acrux Ltd for £3.95 per share on 30 September 2008.

–   Has no income in the tax year 2013/14.

–   Has chargeable capital gains in the tax year 2013/14 of £2,300, but does not anticipate making any capital gains in the foreseeable future.

–   Has houses in the UK and the country of Solaris and divides her time between them.

Required:

(i)   **Prepare detailed calculations to determine the most beneficial tax treatment of the payment Spica will receive for her shares;**   **(7 marks)**

(ii) **Identify the points that must be confirmed and any action necessary in order for capital treatment to apply to the transaction.**   **(4 marks)**

(Total: 11 marks)

Part (b) of this question has been deleted as it is no longer applicable following changes to the tax legislation.

46   JAMES (ADAPTED)   *Walk in the footsteps of a top tutor*

James is about to be made redundant by Quark Ltd. He is seeking advice on the taxation of his redundancy payment and on the sale of shares acquired via an approved share incentive plan. He intends to form Proton Ltd, which is expected to be treated as a personal service company, and wants to know how much better or worse off he will be as compared to the job he is about to lose.

The following information has been obtained from a meeting with James.

James – Income, national insurance and capital gains tax position:

–   James is paid a salary of £70,000 per year by Quark Ltd.

- He is not contracted out of the State Second Pension.

- He has no income other than that from Quark Ltd and Proton Ltd in the tax year 2013/14.

- He withdrew shares from the Quark Ltd approved share incentive plan on 1 September 2013.

- His disposal of the shares in Quark Ltd is his only disposal for the purposes of capital gains tax in the tax year 2013/14.

Withdrawal and sale of shares from the Quark Ltd approved share incentive plan:

- James has been awarded free shares on 1 June every year since 2009.

- James withdrew all of the shares in the plan on 1 September 2013 and immediately sold them.

Redundancy and future plans:

- Quark Ltd will make James redundant on 31 January 2014.

- The company will make a redundancy payment to James of £38,500.

- In accordance with its usual policy, the company will also pay James £17,500 in lieu of notice.

- James will form a new company, Proton Ltd.

Proton Ltd – Activities:

- Proton Ltd will provide services to Quark Ltd and to other companies.

- The services will be carried out by James personally.

- All of Proton Ltd's income will be in respect of relevant engagements and therefore subject to the personal service company (IR 35) legislation.

Proton Ltd – Estimated income and outgoings for a full year:

	£
Gross fee income	80,000
Salary paid to James	48,000
Administrative expenses	3,000
Travel expenses reimbursed to James	1,500
Dividends paid to James	18,000

Notes:

1. Where applicable, the above amounts are stated excluding value added tax (VAT).

2. The travel expenses are those which will be necessarily incurred by James in performing the work for Quark Ltd and the other customers of Proton Ltd. These expenses were not incurred by James as an employee of Quark Ltd.

Required:

(a) Identify the income tax, national insurance contribution and capital gains tax implications, if any, of the withdrawal and subsequent sale of the shares in Quark Ltd, the redundancy payment and the payment in lieu of notice. **(7 marks)**

(b) (i) Prepare calculations to determine the effect on James's annual income, after deduction of all taxes, of working for Proton Ltd rather than Quark Ltd.

(8 marks)

     (ii)   Calculate the effect on James's annual income, after deduction of all taxes, if the income of Proton Ltd were not regarded as being in respect of relevant engagements. **(2 marks)**

(c)   Give three examples of specific contractual arrangements that would assist in arguing that the relationships between Proton Ltd and its customers do not amount to relevant engagements such that they would no longer be covered by the personal service company (IR 35) legislation. **(3 marks)**

You should assume that today's date is 1 December 2013 and that the rates and allowances for the tax year 2012/13 apply throughout the question.

(Total: 20 marks)

---

47   FEDORA AND SMOKE LTD (ADAPTED)   *Walk in the footsteps of a top tutor*

Fedora wants to improve the overall financial position of his family and his company, Smoke Ltd. He is considering three possibilities: repaying a loan to the company, employing his wife, Wanda, in the business, and selling a piece of land owned by the company.

The following information has been obtained from a telephone conversation with Fedora and from client files.

Fedora:

–   Fedora's only income is his annual salary of £80,000 from Smoke Ltd together with annual taxable benefits of £6,600.

–   Fedora is aged 49.

Smoke Ltd:

–   Is wholly owned by Fedora.

–   Manufactures precision engineering tools.

–   Has a year end of 31 March and pays corporation tax at the small profits rate.

Fedora's plans:

–   Repay an interest-free loan of £18,400 made to him by Smoke Ltd in February 2008.

–   Smoke Ltd to employ Wanda.

–   Smoke Ltd to sell part of the land surrounding its factory.

Smoke Ltd to employ Wanda:

–   Wanda would carry out duties currently performed by Fedora and would be paid an annual salary of £20,000.

–   Wanda's salary would represent an arm's length price for the work that she would perform.

–   Fedora's salary would be reduced by £20,000 to reflect the reduction in the level of his duties.

–   Wanda's only income is bank interest of £470 per year. She has notified the bank that she is a non-taxpayer.

–   Wanda is aged 43.

Smoke Ltd to sell land:

–   The land is currently used by Smoke Ltd for parking vehicles.

–   The land was purchased together with the factory on 1 April 1995 for £174,000.

– The land would be sold on 1 February 2014 for £22,000.

– The value of the factory together with the remaining unsold land on 1 February 2014 will be £491,000.

– Smoke Ltd will use £19,000 of the sales proceeds to acquire engineering machinery in March 2014.

Required:

(a) **Explain, with the aid of supporting calculations, the tax implications for both Fedora and Smoke Ltd of the proposed repayment by Fedora of the loan from Smoke Ltd.** **(5 marks)**

(b) **Calculate the annual net effect on the total of the tax liabilities of Fedora, Wanda and Smoke Ltd of Smoke Ltd employing Wanda under the arrangements set out above.** **(7 marks)**

(c) **Calculate the taxable gain arising on the sale of the land in the year ending 31 March 2014 on the assumption that any beneficial claim available is made.**

Explain in detail the beneficial claim available, state the amount of the gain relieved and the manner in which any deferred part of the gain will be charged in the future. **(8 marks)**

Note: The following figures from the Retail Prices Index should be used.

April 1995   149.0
February 2014   256.2 (assumed)

(Total: 20 marks)

48 TRIFLES LTD, VICTORIA AND MELBA (ADAPTED) *Walk in the footsteps of a top tutor*

Trifles Ltd intends to carry out a purchase of its own shares. The shareholders from whom the shares are to be purchased require advice on their tax position. Trifles Ltd also intends to loan a motorcycle to one of the shareholders.

The following information has been obtained from the shareholders in Trifles Ltd.

Trifles Ltd:

– Is an unquoted company specialising in the delivery of small, high value items.

– Was incorporated and began trading on 1 February 2006.

– Has an issued share capital of 10,000 ordinary shares subscribed for at £2 per share.

– Has four unrelated shareholders: Torte, Baklava, Victoria and Melba.

– Intends to purchase some of its own shares from Victoria and Melba.

– Victoria and Melba have been directors of the company since they acquired their shares but will resign immediately after the purchase of their shares.

The purchase by Trifles Ltd of its own shares:

– Will take place on 28 February 2014 for Victoria's shares, and on 31 March 2014 for Melba's shares at an agreed price of £30 per share.

– Will consist of the purchase of all of Victoria's shares and 450 shares from Melba.

Victoria:

– Is resident and ordinarily resident in the UK.

– Is a higher rate taxpayer with taxable income of £50,000 who will make no other capital disposals in the tax year 2013/14.

– Has a capital loss carried forward as at 5 April 2013 of £4,300.

– Will have no link with Trifles Ltd following the purchase of her shares.

– Inherited her holding of 1,500 ordinary shares on the death of her husband, Brownie, on 1 February 2012.

– Brownie paid £16,500 for the shares on 1 February 2010.

– The probate value of the 1,500 ordinary shares was £16,000 on 1 February 2012.

Melba:

– Is resident and ordinarily resident in the UK.

– Is a higher rate taxpayer.

– Acquired her holding of 1,700 ordinary shares when Trifles Ltd was incorporated.

– Following the purchase of her shares Melba's only link with Trifles Ltd will be her remaining ordinary shareholding and the use of a motorcycle belonging to the company.

The motorcycle:

– Will be purchased by Trifles Ltd for £9,000 on 1 April 2014.

– Will be made available on loan to Melba for the whole of the tax year 2014/15.

– Melba will pay Trifles Ltd £30 per month for the use of the motorcycle.

Required:

(a) **Explain whether or not Victoria and/or Melba satisfy the conditions relating to period of ownership and reduction in level of shareholding such that the amount received from Trifles Ltd on the purchase of own shares may be treated as a capital event.** **(7 marks)**

(b) **Calculate Victoria's after tax proceeds from the purchase of her shares:**

– **if the amount received is treated as capital; and**

– **if the amount received is treated as income.** **(7 marks)**

(c) **Explain, with supporting calculations where necessary, the tax implications of the purchase and loan of the motorcycle for both Melba and Trifles Ltd.** **(6 marks)**

Ignore value added tax (VAT).

(Total: 20 marks)

49 ROBUSTO LTD (ADAPTED) *Walk in the footsteps of a top tutor*

Robusto Ltd, a partially exempt company for the purposes of value added tax (VAT), requires advice on the cost of purchasing services from various suppliers and an explanation of the implications if the relationship between the company and the person providing the services is one of employer and employee.

The following information was obtained during a meeting with the managing director of Robusto Ltd.

Robusto Ltd – Budgeted results for the year ending 31 March 2014:

	£
– Turnover (exclusive of VAT):	
Standard rated	850,000
Exempt	330,000
Zero rated	120,000

- The irrecoverable VAT for the year will exceed the *de minimis* limits.

- Robusto Ltd is growing quickly and intends to purchase market analysis services relating to all aspects of its business.

Potential providers of market analysis services:

- There are three potential service providers: Cognac Ltd, Fonseca Inc and Pisco.

- Robusto Ltd will use the provider that results in the lowest cost to the company.

- Alternatively, Robusto Ltd will take on a new employee to carry out the market analysis.

Cognac Ltd:

- Cognac Ltd is a UK resident company wholly owned by Offley, a UK resident individual.

- Offley is the company's only employee.

- Offley would be contractually obliged to perform all of the market analysis services provided by Cognac Ltd.

- Cognac Ltd would charge a fixed fee of £28,500 plus VAT.

Fonseca Inc:

- Fonseca Inc is a company resident in the country of Parejo.

- The country of Parejo is not a member of the European Union.

- Fonseca Inc would charge a fixed fee of £29,000.

Pisco:

- Pisco is a UK resident unincorporated sole trader who is not registered for VAT.

- Pisco would charge a fixed fee of £29,500.

Required:

(a) **In respect of the market analysis services:**

- **explain, with the aid of supporting calculations, which service provider would result in the lowest cost to Robusto Ltd; and**

      –   calculate the maximum salary that could be paid by Robusto Ltd to an employee such that the total cost would be no more than that of the cheapest service provider.   **(10 marks)**

(b)   On the assumption that the services are purchased from Pisco, give FOUR examples of specific contractual arrangements that would assist HM Revenue and Customs in arguing that the relationship between Robusto Ltd and Pisco is that of employer and employee.   **(4 marks)**

(c)   On the assumption that HM Revenue and Customs could successfully argue that the relationship between Robusto Ltd and the individual carrying out the market analysis services, Offley or Pisco, is one of employer and employee:

      –   explain the tax implications for Robusto Ltd and Cognac Ltd if the services are purchased from Cognac Ltd; and

      –   explain why Robusto Ltd might prefer to offer the contract to Cognac Ltd rather than to Pisco.

   You are not required to prepare any calculations for part (c) of this question or to describe in detail how any deemed salary payment would be calculated.   **(6 marks)**

   (Total: 20 marks)

GROUPS, CONSORTIA AND OVERSEAS COMPANY ASPECTS

50   JUGLANS LTD AND LARIX LTD (ADAPTED)

Bob has owned all of the issued share capital of two UK resident companies, Juglans Limited and Larix Limited, for a number of years.

You have extracted the following information from client files and meetings with the parties involved.

Juglans Ltd

–   Has always had an accounting date of 31 December.

–   Most recent accounts have been prepared to 31 December 2012.

–   Now planning to prepare its accounts to 31 March and is considering whether it should:

      –   prepare two sets of accounts, one to 31 March 2013 and the other to 31 March 2014, or

      –   prepare a single set of accounts for the fifteen month period ended 31 March 2014

–   Taxable trading profits (before capital allowances) are expected to accrue as follows:

      –   £25,000 per calendar month for the 12 months to 31 December 2013

      –   £40,000 per calendar month for the 3 months to 31 March 2014

–   Tax written down value of the capital allowance pool as at 31 December 2012 is £72,000.

–   Bought some additional equipment on 30 April 2013 costing £81,000.

– Sold two properties, one on 15 February 2013 realising a chargeable gain (after indexation) of £92,000 and the other on 30 June 2013 realising a capital loss of £29,000.

Larix Ltd

– Expects to make a tax adjusted trading loss of £45,000 and a capital loss of £30,000 for its twelve month accounting period ended 31 March 2014.

VAT

– Juglans Limited makes only taxable supplies for the purposes of VAT

– 90% of the supplies made by Larix Limited are exempt for VAT purposes.

– The following information is relevant for the 12 month period ended 31 March 2014.

		£
Juglans Limited	Total supplies (excluding VAT)	1,100,000
	Input tax	125,000
Larix Limited	Total supplies (excluding VAT)	1,550,000
	Input tax	
	Relating to exempt supplies	134,000
	Relating to taxable supplies	12,000
	Unattributed	20,000

– There is no trading between Juglans Limited and Larix Limited.

– £123,000 of the total input tax for Juglans Limited is directly attributed to making its taxable supplies. The other £2,000 relates to group overheads.

Required:

(a) Advise Juglans Limited whether it would be beneficial to:

(i) prepare two sets of accounts, one to 31 March 2013 and the other to 31 March 2014; or

(ii) one set of accounts for the fifteen month period to 31 March 2014.

Your answer should explain how the various items are allocated where there is a long period of account and also include a calculation of the corporation tax liabilities payable under both options.

You should assume that the tax rates and allowances applicable to the Financial Year 2012 only apply throughout. **(12 marks)**

(b) (i) Having specific regard to the trading and capital losses made by Larix Limited in its accounting period ended 31 March 2014 advise Bob of the reliefs available to groups of companies and explain whether Juglans Limited is able to benefit from these reliefs. **(4 marks)**

(ii) Advise Bob whether Juglans Limited and Larix Limited can be group registered for VAT purposes and explain whether a group VAT registration is likely to be beneficial. **(4 marks)**

(Total: 20 marks)

 Online question assistance

51   A, B, C AND D (ADAPTED)

The following diagram illustrates a group of companies:

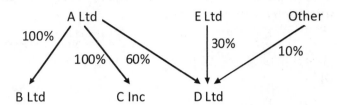

Additional information:

1.   All the companies are trading companies and all are resident in the UK with the exception of C Inc, which is resident overseas.

2.   All the companies prepare their accounts to 31 March with the exception of B Ltd, which prepares its accounts to 31 December.

3.   The group structure and related shareholdings have been unchanged for several years.

The most recent results of the four group companies, A Ltd, B Ltd, C Inc and D Ltd are as follows:

	A Ltd Year ended 31.3.2013 £	B Ltd Year ended 31.12.2012 £	C Inc Year ended 31.3.2013 £	D Ltd Year ended 31.3.2013 £
Trading profit/(loss)	234,500	(202,000)	100,000	(120,000)
Property income	41,650	25,000		
Chargeable gain	50,000			20,000
Dividends paid	40,000		35,000	

The property income received by A Ltd is from C Inc, and is shown net of 15% withholding tax.

The dividend paid by C Inc is stated before the deduction of 15% withholding tax.

B Ltd had a capital loss brought forward of £20,000 as at 1 January 2012.

Required:

(a)   Calculate the corporation tax (CT) payable by A Ltd, B Ltd and D Ltd, clearly identifying the beneficial reliefs that should be claimed/elections to be made.

Assume that all three companies wish to take relief for losses as early as possible.

(8 marks)

(b)   The managing director of A Ltd intends to sell the trade of B Ltd, as the company has been loss making for several years.

Prepare a report advising him of the corporation tax (CT) (including capital gains), value added tax (VAT) and stamp duty/stamp duty land tax (SD/SDLT) consequences resulting from:

(1)   selling all of the shares in B Ltd to a third party; or

(2)   selling the assets of B Ltd to a third party, but retaining the shares in B Ltd.

> Assume that any sale will take place in December 2013 and that B Ltd is not part of a VAT group, and that today's date is 1 May 2013. **(18 marks)**
>
> Appropriateness of the format and presentation of the report and effectiveness with which the information is communicated. **(2 marks)**
>
> **(Total: 28 marks)**

52 GLOBAL PLC (ADAPTED)

Global plc is a large UK resident manufacturing company whose taxable trading profits for the year ended 30 September 2013 are forecast to be £2,250,000. The company has asked for your advice regarding transactions taking place during the year ended 30 September 2013.

You should assume that today's date is 15 March 2013.

(1) On 1 November 2012 Global plc purchased a 90% shareholding in Nouveau Inc., a manufacturing company resident in and controlled from the country of Northia.

Its forecast profits for the year ended 31 March 2013 are £700,000, and these will be subject to corporation tax at the rate of 20% in Northia.

On 15 April 2013 Nouveau Inc. is planning to pay a dividend of £300,000, and this will be subject to withholding tax at the rate of 5%.

(2) During May 2013 Global plc is planning to sell 10,000 units of a product to Nouveau Inc. at a price of £12.75 per unit. This is 25% less than the trade-selling price given to other customers. $10,000 \text{ units} \times 12.75 \times \frac{25}{75} = 42510$

(3) On 1 November 2012 Global plc set up a branch in the country of Eastina. The branch is controlled from Eastina, and its forecast profits for the period to 30 September 2013 are £175,000. These are subject to tax at the rate of 40% in Eastina. 50% of the after tax profits will be remitted to the UK.

(4) On 31 March 2013 Global plc is planning to sell its 80% shareholding in Surplus Ltd, a trading company resident in the UK, for £1,750,000. The shares were purchased on 15 May 2003 for £760,000, and the indexation allowance from May 2003 to March 2013 is £282,226

Global plc transferred a factory to Surplus Ltd on 20 June 2007, when the factory was valued at £630,000. The factory originally cost Global plc £260,000 on 17 May 1998. It is still owned by Surplus Ltd, and is currently valued at £720,000. The indexation allowance from May 1998 to June 2007 is £69,680, and from May 1998 to March 2013 it is £135,720. Surplus Ltd prepares its accounts to 30 September and pays corporation tax at the main rate.

(5) On 1 February 2013 Global plc purchased an 85% shareholding in Wanted Ltd, a UK resident company. The company is forecast to make a tax adjusted trading loss of £240,000 for the year ended 30 September 2013. On 20 December 2012 Wanted Ltd sold investments for £425,000, resulting in a capital loss of £170,000.

In all cases, the overseas forecast profits are the same for accounting and taxation purposes. The double taxation treaties between the UK and Northia and Eastina provide that overseas taxes are relieved as a tax credit against UK corporation tax. Nouveau Inc is not a controlled foreign company.

Required:

(a)   Advise Global plc of the corporation tax implications of each of the transactions during the year ended 30 September 2013.   **(18 marks)**

(b)   Explain how Global plc will be affected by the requirement to make quarterly instalment payments in respect of its corporation tax liability for the year ended 30 September 2013.   **(4 marks)**

You are *not expected* to calculate Global plc's corporation tax liability for the year ended 30 September 2013.

(Total: 22 marks)

53   TAY LIMITED (ADAPTED)

An extract from an email from your manager is set out below

I recently had a telephone conversation with Laura Foxcroft, the managing director of Tay Limited (Tay).   She would like to meet with me next week to run through the tax implications of various issues.   All the relevant details are disclosed in the attached memorandum.

I need you to prepare notes covering the following for me to take to the meeting:

(a)   (i)   A statement, with reasons, indicating whether or not Tay is entitled to claim a tax allowance in respect of the purchased intellectual property.

      (ii)   A calculation of the corporation tax payable by Tay for the year ended 31 March 2013, taking advantage of all available reliefs.

      (iii) An explanation of the potential corporation tax implications of Tay transferring work to Trent Limited (Trent).

             I would also like you to make suggestions as to how these can be minimised or eliminated.

      (iv)   Advice on the capital gains implications of the proposed sale of Trent's building with supporting calculations.

(b)   I also need a brief memorandum to the management board outlining the corporation tax issues that Tay should consider when deciding whether to acquire the shares or the assets of Tagus LDA (Tagus).

      I don't need you to discuss issues relating to transfer pricing.

(c)   Could you also draft some notes about the consequences arising from the submission of the incorrect VAT return by Trent. I'm sure it was not a deliberate mistake, just an oversight on the part of the company.

The memorandum attached to the email is set out below.

To	Internal filing
From	Tax Manager
Date	1 May 2013
Subject	Tay Limited

Background – Tay Limited

–   Unquoted trading company with a 31 March year end.

- Acquired 100% of the shares of another company, Trent Limited, on 1 September 2012.

- Both companies manufacture engine components.

Proposed transfer of work

Trent Limited has been incurring trading losses for some time, and at 1 January 2012 had tax losses of £300,000 (including £60,000 relating to the year ended 31 December 2011).

Tay Limited lacks the capacity to take on more work, so intends to transfer several of its orders to Trent Limited.

By doing this, it is anticipated that Trent Limited will make small profits in the year to 31 December 2013, and even greater profits in subsequent years, thereby utilising its existing corporation tax losses.

Trading results

The trading results of the two companies (actual and estimated) are as follows:

Company	Year ended	Taxable profits/ (losses) £
Tay Limited	31 March 2013	250,000
Trent Limited	31 December 2012	(120,000)
	31 December 2013	50,000

Intellectual property

On 1 January 2013, Tay Limited incurred expenditure of £250,000 on intellectual property. It does not depreciate this amount and so has not claimed any tax relief for the expenditure.

Proposed sale of building

Trent Limited owns an old building, which was purchased in September 2003. This building has always been used for the purposes of Trent Limited's trade. The building cost Trent Limited £400,000, and was valued at £300,000 when Trent Limited was acquired by Tay Limited. The building is currently worth £250,000. Tay Limited is planning to sell a capital asset in September 2013, which will realise a capital gain of £75,000 and has recently suggested that Trent Limited sell the old building at the same time in order to take advantage of the capital loss that would arise.

Acquisition of Tagus LDA

Tay Limited has recently identified an opportunity to purchase either the shares or the assets of Tagus LDA, an engineering company based in Portugal, an EEA country. It is considered that the business of Tagus LDA will remain Portuguese resident irrespective of which acquisition route is taken. Portuguese companies and businesses pay tax on profits at the rate of 23·5%.

VAT error

A recent investigation by Trent Limited of their accounting records has revealed an error in the value added tax (VAT) return submitted for the quarter to 31 March 2013. Although input VAT has been correctly calculated at £40,000, the output VAT stated as £87,500, has been under declared by £55,000. The additional VAT due has not yet been paid.

Required:

Prepare the notes requested by your manager.

You should assume today's date is 3 May 2013.

(a)   Marks will be given for the four different components as follows:

    (i)   The tax allowance available in respect of the purchased intellectual property.

                                                      (2 marks)

    (ii)   Calculation of corporation tax (CT) payable by Tay Limited for the year ended 31 March 2013   **(3 marks)**

    (iii)   Explanation of the potential corporation tax (CT) implications of Tay Limited transferring work to Trent Limited   **(3 marks)**

    (iv)   Advice on the capital gains implications of the sale of Trent Limited's old building   **(4 marks)**

(b)   Draft the memorandum to the board regarding the acquisition of the shares or the assets of Tagus LDA.   **(10 marks)**

(c)   Prepare the notes setting out the tax consequences arising from the submission of the incorrect value added tax (VAT) return.   **(8 marks)**

Additional marks will be awarded for the appropriateness of the format and presentation of the notes and memorandum and the effectiveness with which the information is communicated.   **(2 marks)**

You should assume that the tax rates and allowances for Financial Year 2012 will continue to apply for the foreseeable future.

(Total: 32 marks)

54   PALM PLC (ADAPTED)

Palm plc recently acquired 100% of the ordinary share capital of Nikau Ltd from Facet Ltd. Palm plc intends to use Nikau Ltd to develop a new product range, under the name 'Project Sabal'. Nikau Ltd owns shares in a non-UK resident company, Date Inc.

The following information has been extracted from client files and from a meeting with the Finance Director of Palm plc.

Palm plc:

–   Has more than 40 wholly owned subsidiaries such that all group companies pay corporation tax at 24%.

–   All group companies prepare accounts to 31 March.

–   Acquired Nikau Ltd on 1 November 2013 from Facet Ltd, an unrelated company.

Nikau Ltd:

–   UK resident company that manufactures domestic electronic appliances for sale in the European Union (EU).

–   Large enterprise for the purposes of the enhanced relief available for research and development expenditure.

–   Trading losses brought forward as at 1 April 2013 of £195,700.

- Budgeted taxable trading profit of £360,000 for the year ending 31 March 2014 before taking account of 'Project Sabal'.

- Nikau owns 35% of the shares in Date Inc and received dividend income of £38,200 in the year ending 31 March 2014 in respect of these shares.

'Project Sabal':

- Development of a range of electronic appliances, for sale in North America and to VAT registered customers in the European Union.

- Project Sabal will represent a significant advance in the technology of domestic appliances.

- Nikau Ltd will spend £70,000 on staffing costs and consumables researching and developing the necessary technology between now and 31 March 2014. Further costs will be incurred in the following year.

- Sales to North America will commence in 2015 and are expected to generate significant profits from that year.

Shares in Olive Ltd:

- In order to finance the purchase of Nikau Ltd Palm plc sold its shares in another 100% subsidiary Olive Ltd.

- The shares in Olive Ltd were purchased on 1 June 1999 for £338,000, and sold on 1 November 2013 for £1,400,000

- Olive Ltd is a property investment company.

- On 2 May 2009 Spring Ltd, another 100% subsidiary of Palm plc, transferred a property to Olive Ltd for its then market value £900,000. The building had cost Spring Ltd £380,000 in October 1999.

Date Inc:

- A controlled foreign company resident in the country of Palladia.

- Annual chargeable profits arising out of property investment activities are approximately £120,000, of which approximately £115,000 is distributed to its shareholders each year.

The tax system in Palladia:

- No taxes on income or capital profits.

- 4% withholding tax on dividends paid to shareholders resident outside Palladia.

Required:

(a) Prepare detailed explanatory notes, including relevant supporting calculations, on the effect of the following issues on the amount of corporation tax payable by Nikau Ltd and Palm plc for the year ending 31 March 2014.

(i) The costs of developing 'Project Sabal' and the significant commercial changes to the company's activities arising out of its implementation. **(10 marks)**

(ii) The shares held in Date Inc and the dividend income received from that company. **(2 marks)**

(iii) The sale of shares in Olive Ltd **(3 marks)**

(b)   Explain why making sales of Sabals in North America will have no effect on Nikau Ltd's ability to recover its input tax.   **(5 marks)**

You should assume that the corporation tax rates and allowances for the financial year to 31 March 2013 will continue to apply for the foreseeable future.

You should ignore indexation allowance.   **(Total: 20 marks)**

---

55   SATURN LTD (ADAPTED)   *Walk in the footsteps of a top tutor*

An extract from an email from your manager is set out below.

I had a telephone conversation with Daniel Dare (DD), the managing director of Saturn Ltd, first thing this morning. We discussed the anticipated results of the Saturn Ltd group of companies and the proposed acquisition of a majority holding in Tethys Ltd. All the relevant details are included in the attached memorandum.

DD has asked me to call him later this afternoon to go through the tax implications of the various issues. The Saturn Ltd group is not a client; I think DD is just testing us to see whether he would like to use us for tax advice.

I need the following:

(i)   A memorandum that I can use to prepare for my telephone call to DD. I realise that DD did not give me all of the information we need so please identify any additional information that you think could have an effect on our advice.

       It is important that you cover all of the points raised by DD; I don't want to end up with detailed answers to some of his questions and no answers to the others. Also, clients often forget about stamp duty and stamp duty land tax so please highlight any such amounts payable by the Saturn Ltd group in respect of the proposed transactions.

(ii)   A summary of the information we need and any action we should take before agreeing to become tax advisers to the Saturn Ltd group.

Tax manager

The memorandum attached to the email is set out below.

To	Internal filing
From	Tax manager
Date	2 June 2013
Subject	Saturn Ltd group of companies

This memorandum sets out the matters discussed with Daniel Dare (DD), the managing director of Saturn Ltd, earlier today.

Group structure

Saturn Ltd has three wholly-owned subsidiaries; Dione Ltd, Rhea Ltd and Titan Inc. Titan Inc trades in and is resident in the country of Galactica. The other three group companies are resident in the UK. Saturn Ltd has owned all three subsidiary companies for many years.

Budgeted results for the year ending 30 June 2013

It is estimated that Dione Ltd will make a tax adjusted trading loss of £187,000 in the year ending 30 June 2013; it will have no other income or capital gains in the period. The budgeted taxable total profits of the other companies in the group are set out below.

	£
Saturn Ltd	385,000
Rhea Ltd	590,000
Titan Inc	265,000

Rhea Ltd paid a dividend of £240,000 to Saturn Ltd on 1 May 2013.

Proposed acquisition of 65% of Tethys Ltd

On 1 August 2013, Saturn Ltd will purchase 65% of the ordinary share capital of Tethys Ltd for £235,000 from the personal representatives of George Jetson. The whole of the balance of the company's share capital is owned either by Edith Clanger or by her family company, Clangers Ltd; DD cannot remember which.

It is anticipated that Tethys Ltd will make a tax adjusted trading loss of approximately £80,000 in the year ending 31 December 2013.

In early 2014, Tethys Ltd will sell its manufacturing premises for £240,000 and move to a rented factory. The premises were acquired new on 1 May 2002 for £112,000. We agreed that the indexation factor on the disposal can be assumed to be 27%.

Information requested by DD

(i) The maximum amount of tax that can be saved via the use of the loss of Dione Ltd assuming it is not carried forward and the date by which the necessary claims must be submitted.

(ii) The amount of the trading loss of Tethys Ltd for the year ending 31 December 2013 that can be used by Saturn Ltd and the ability of Tethys Ltd to use this loss in the future.

(iii) In respect of the sale of the manufacturing premises:

– Whether or not Tethys Ltd should charge value added tax (VAT) on the sale of the property.

– The taxable profit arising in respect of the sale.

– The amount of the gain that could be rolled over if Tethys Ltd or any of the other Saturn Ltd group companies acquired assets costing £200,000, the types of asset that would have to be purchased and the period during which the assets would need to be acquired.

(iv) Any stamp duty and/or stamp duty land tax payable by the Saturn Ltd group in respect of the proposed transactions.

Tax manager

Required:

(a)   **Prepare the memorandum requested by your manager.**

The memorandum should include explanations together with supporting calculations and should identify any further information that you think is required.

The following marks are available for the four components of the memorandum:

(i)   The amount of tax that can be saved via the use of the loss of Dione Ltd;

(8 marks)

(ii)   The use of the trading loss of Tethys Ltd for the year ending 31 December 2013;

(7 marks)

(iii) Advice in connection with the sale of the manufacturing premises by Tethys Ltd;

(9 marks)

(iv)   The stamp duty and/or stamp duty land tax payable by the Saturn Ltd group;

(2 marks)

Additional marks will be awarded for the appropriateness of the format and presentation of the memorandum and the effectiveness with which the information is communicated.

(4 marks)

(b)   **A summary of the information needed to satisfy our obligations under the money laundering legislation and any action that should be taken before agreeing to become tax advisers to the Saturn Ltd group.**

(5 marks)

You should assume that the tax rates and allowances for the tax year 2012/13 and for the financial year to 31 March 2013 apply throughout the question.

(Total: 35 marks)

---

56   PARTICLE LTD GROUP (ADAPTED) *Walk in the footsteps of a top tutor*

An extract from an e-mail from your manager is set out below.

> I attach a schedule I received this morning from Max Constant, the new managing director of the Particle Ltd group of companies. With Max in charge this client has recently become a lot more lively!
>
> This e-mail will make more sense when you have read Max's schedule so I suggest you read that first.
>
> **Report**
>
> Please prepare a report to the management of Particle Ltd addressing the three areas of advice requested by Max. The report should also cover the following additional points.
>
> Sale of Kaon Ltd – the value added tax (VAT) implications of selling the trade and assets of the business.
>
> Muon Inc – any tax problems in connection with the loan.
>
> Payment of corporation tax – the advantage of group payment arrangements.

Further information

The information in Max's schedule is pretty clear but you will see that there are two question marks in connection with the assets of Kaon Ltd. I've spoken to him about this and to check on a couple of other things and I set out below some additional information that you will need.

– All of the companies are UK resident with the exception of Muon Inc, which is resident in the country of Newtonia. Newtonia is not in the European Union (EU) and there is no double tax treaty between Newtonia and the UK.

– Shortly after its acquisition, Muon Inc approached a number of financial institutions for a loan. However, the interest rates demanded were so high that Particle Ltd has made the loan to Muon Inc instead. Particle Ltd is charging 4% interest on the loan. By the way, Muon Inc is not a controlled foreign company.

– The goodwill of Kaon Ltd has been created within the company since its formation on 1 May 2004.

– Kaon Ltd purchased its premises (Atom House) from Baryon Ltd on 1 March 2006 for its market value at that time of £490,000. Baryon Ltd purchased Atom House on 1 July 2002 for £272,000. Three months later, on 1 October 2002, Baryon Ltd sold another building (Bohr Square) for £309,400 making a capital gain of £89,000 and claimed rollover relief in respect of the purchase of Atom House. No option to tax for VAT purposes has been made in respect of Atom House.

Max has a reasonable knowledge of the UK tax system so keep the narrative in the report brief. As always, assume that all beneficial claims will be made and include a reference to them in the report.

A final thought; watch out for the impact of the sale of the business on the rate of corporation tax payable by Kaon Ltd.

Tax manager

The schedule from Max Constant is set out below.

Particle Ltd Group – Situation as at 1 December 2013

Background information

– Particle Ltd owns 100% of its five subsidiaries. All six companies are trading companies preparing accounts to 31 March.

– Their approximate annual taxable profits are included in the group structure below.

– None of the companies receive any franked investment income and there are no unused trading losses within the group.

– Baryon Ltd has a capital loss of £37,100 brought forward in respect of a disposal on 1 May 2007.

– Particle Ltd, Baryon Ltd and Kaon Ltd have a group VAT registration.

Group structure

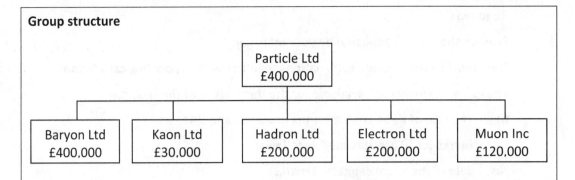

Notes

1. Baryon Ltd has been a subsidiary since 1998.

2. Kaon Ltd was incorporated by Particle Ltd on 1 May 2004. This company is to be sold – see below.

3. Hadron Ltd, Electron Ltd and Muon Inc were all purchased on 1 August 2013 from three unrelated individual vendors.

The sale of Kaon Ltd

The sale will take place on 31 January 2014. We have received offers from two separate purchasers.

Offer 1 – Sale of shares

We have been offered £650,000 for the whole of the company's share capital.

Offer 2 – Sale of trade and assets of the business

We have been offered £770,000 for the company's trade and assets as follows:

	Offer	Cost	Tax written down value
	£	£	£
Office premises (Atom House)	604,000	490,000?	N/A
Machinery and equipment	46,000	80,000	65,000
Goodwill	120,000	Nil	?
	770,000		

This will leave Kaon Ltd with net current liabilities of £25,000, which it will pay out of the sale proceeds of the business.

Advice required

(a) Sale of Kaon Ltd – the after tax proceeds in respect of each of the two offers.

(b) Muon Inc – the possibility of avoiding any VAT problems on the future sale of components by Baryon Ltd to Muon Inc by bringing Muon Inc into the Particle Ltd VAT group with Baryon Ltd.

(c) Payment of corporation tax – whether the recent corporate acquisitions will change the dates on which the group companies are required to pay corporation tax.

Required:

Prepare the report requested by your manager.

The report should include explanations together with supporting calculations.

The following marks are available for the three areas of the report.

(i)   The sale of Kaon Ltd – after tax proceeds and VAT.

       Marks for (i) are allocated as follows:

       Sale of the share capital – 2 marks,

       Sale of the trade and assets of the business – 15 marks.   **(17 marks)**

(ii)   Muon Inc – VAT and issues in connection with the loan.   **(6 marks)**

(iii)   Payment of corporation tax – payment dates and group payment arrangements.

       (8 marks)

Appropriateness of the format and presentation of the report and the effectiveness with which the information is communicated.   **(4 marks)**

The following indexation factors should be used.

July 2002 to March 2006	0.109
July 2002 to January 2014	0.443
May 2004 to January 2014	0.377
March 2006 to January 2014	0.312

You should assume that today's date is 1 December 2013 and that the rates and allowances for the financial year to 31 March 2013 apply throughout the question.

(Total: 35 marks)

57   BAND PLC GROUP (ADAPTED) *Walk in the footsteps of a top tutor*

 Timed question with Online tutor debrief

The management of Band plc intend to acquire Trumpet Ltd. They require advice on the post tax profits of Trumpet Ltd, a company which will receive dividends from two subsidiaries, one of which is non-UK resident, and is also paying interest to Trumpet Ltd. They are also considering whether to use a branch or a subsidiary in order to establish a trading operation overseas.

The following information has been obtained from telephone conversations with the management of Band plc and from client files.

Band plc's plans:

–   Band plc will acquire the whole of the Trumpet Ltd group on 1 August 2013.

–   Band plc intends to establish a trading operation in the country of Swingerra.

Trumpet Ltd:

–   Is a UK resident company with budgeted taxable trading profits for the year ending 31 July 2014 of £40,000.

- Will have a deficit in respect of non-trading loan relationships of £174,000 to carry forward as at 31 July 2013.

- Has two wholly owned subsidiaries; Clarinet Ltd and Flugel Inc.

- Will pay a dividend to Band plc equal to its taxable trading profit plus the dividends and interest received from Clarinet Ltd and Flugel Inc less its corporation tax liability.

- It can be assumed that Trumpet Ltd and Clarinet Ltd will pay corporation tax at the main rate due to the number of companies in the Band plc group.

Clarinet Ltd:

- Is a UK resident company with budgeted taxable trading profits for the year ending 31 July 2014 of £107,000.

- Will have a trading loss for tax purposes of £32,000 to carry forward as at 31 July 2013.

- Will pay a dividend to Trumpet Ltd equal to its taxable trading profit of £107,000 less its corporation tax liability.

Flugel Inc:

- Is resident in the country of Jazzerra.

- Is not a controlled foreign company.

- Has budgeted taxable trading profits for the year ending 31 July 2014 of £182,500.

- Pays interest on a loan of £3,000,000 from Trumpet Ltd at 6% per annum (this is approximately the market rate). Withholding tax is deducted from this interest at 20%. The money was borrowed for trading purposes and the interest payable has been deducted correctly in calculating the trading profit figure of £182,500.

- Will pay a dividend to Trumpet Ltd equal to its current year taxable trading profit less its corporation tax liability.

- The rate of corporation tax in the country of Jazzerra is 20%.

- Jazzerra levies withholding tax at 8% on dividends paid overseas.

Planned trading operation in the country of Swingerra:

- Will be operated via a branch of Band plc or via a new subsidiary incorporated and resident in Swingerra.

- Is expected to make a loss in its first year of trading of £90,000.

- Is expected to make profits in excess of £125,000 per year in future years.

The tax system in the country of Swingerra:

- Is broadly the same as that in the UK.

- The rate of corporation tax is 34%.

- Trading losses may only be utilised by companies resident in Swingerra.

- Swingerra is not a member of the European Union and there is no double tax treaty between the UK and Swingerra.

Required:

(a) (i) Explain precisely the ways in which the brought forward trading loss in Clarinet Ltd and the brought forward non-trading loan relationships deficit in Trumpet Ltd can be relieved; **(3 marks)**

(ii) On the assumption that Trumpet Ltd, Clarinet Ltd and Flugel Inc pay dividends as set out above, and that the non-trading loan relationships deficit is used in the most tax efficient manner, calculate the dividend that will be paid by Trumpet Ltd to Band plc in respect of the year ending 31 July 2014. **(9 marks)**

(b) Provide a detailed explanation of the relief available in respect of the anticipated loss to be made by the planned trading operation in the country of Swingerra depending on whether a branch or a subsidiary company is used and advise the management of Band plc on the choice available to them. **(8 marks)**

(Total: 20 marks)

 Calculate your allowed time, allocate the time to the separate parts....................

58 AUTOMATIC LTD (ADAPTED) *Walk in the footsteps of a top tutor*

An extract from an e-mail from your manager is set out below.

I have forwarded to you an e-mail I received from Sirene yesterday.

Automatic Ltd, the manufacturing company that Sirene incorporated in 2011, is doing well and she is now finalising the purchase of the trade and assets of Chase Ltd, another profitable company. This acquisition, referred to by Sirene as the 'Chase deal', will be carried out in January 2014 by a new company, Falcon Ltd, which she will incorporate for this purpose. There are likely to be further acquisitions of shares and/or businesses in the future.

I want you to write paragraphs, for inclusion in a letter that I will write later this week, addressing each of the matters raised in Sirene's e-mail. Please include an amended calculation of the budgeted corporation tax payable by Automatic Ltd for the year ending 31 March 2014 together with brief explanations where necessary. This calculation should begin with Sirene's figure for taxable total profits of £280,000 and incorporate any adjustments that need to be made.

Sirene is reasonably knowledgeable about corporation tax and I am happy to assume that her figures for the income and the capital gain are correct. However, I believe that it would be advantageous for Falcon Ltd to be owned by Automatic Ltd rather than Sirene. Accordingly, please include the corporation tax advantages (and any disadvantages) of Automatic Ltd owning Falcon Ltd and amend the budgeted corporation tax computation on the assumption that the deal is structured in this manner and that all beneficial claims are made.

Thank you

Bogard

An extract from the e-mail from Sirene is set out below.

The Chase deal

I have decided to set up a new company, Falcon Ltd, because I want to keep the Chase business separate from Automatic Ltd. I will own the whole of Falcon Ltd personally (just as I do Automatic Ltd) so that the Chase deal does not affect the rate of corporation tax paid by Automatic Ltd. Please confirm that this approach is effective from a corporation tax point of view.

As part of the deal, Falcon Ltd will pay Chase Ltd £320,000 for the purchase of the building it uses for its administrative head office. Am I correct in thinking that this cost will not give rise to tax deductions from trading income?

Degrouping charges

It is my understanding that on the sale of a company or a business it is possible for certain assets to be regarded as having been sold such that chargeable gains, often called degrouping charges, arise. However, I'm not sure how to determine whether or not the Chase deal, or any future deals, will result in such a charge. Please let me have a summary of the circumstances giving rise to such a charge and an explanation of how the charge is calculated and taxed.

VAT (Value added tax)

The management of Chase Ltd have told me that they must charge VAT on the sale of the building, machinery and equipment. Are they correct?

Automatic Ltd – budgeted corporation tax computation
for the year ending 31 March 2014

	£
Tax adjusted trading profit	240,000
Chargeable gain (Note 1)	34,000
Bank interest	6,000
Taxable total profits (Note 2)	280,000
Corporation tax at 20% (Note 3)	56,000

Notes

1   The chargeable gain will arise on the sale of a small building in March 2014 for £138,000. Automatic Ltd uses the building for storage purposes and will rent storage space in the future. I do not anticipate the company buying any assets qualifying for rollover relief within the qualifying period.

2   Automatic Ltd subscribed for 12,000 shares (a 6% shareholding) in Rye Ltd in September 2013 for £19,000. Rye Ltd is a very small unquoted engineering company that is run by two brothers who own 60% of its ordinary share capital. The remainder of its share capital is owned by a number of unrelated individuals, none of whom is connected with Automatic Ltd. Automatic Ltd has subsequently received a dividend of £2,160 in respect of these shares. I have excluded these dividends when calculating the taxable profits of Automatic Ltd. Please confirm that this treatment is correct.

3   Automatic Ltd has no associated companies.

Required:

Prepare the paragraphs for inclusion in your manager's letter as requested in his e-mail, together with the amended corporation tax computation. The following marks are available.

(i)	The Chase deal;	(8 marks)
(ii)	Degrouping charges;	(6 marks)
(iii)	VAT (value added tax);	(6 marks)
(iv)	Automatic Ltd – amended budgeted corporation tax computation, together with brief explanations, for the year ending 31 March 2013.	(5 marks)

(Total: 25 marks)

59 CACAO LTD GROUP (ADAPTED) *Walk in the footsteps of a top tutor*

 Timed question with Online tutor debrief

Extracts from e-mails from your manager and a client, Maya, together with information obtained from client files are set out below.

Email from your manager

I have forwarded an e-mail to you from Maya who owns The Cacao Ltd group of companies. Maya is a scientist and relies on us for all of her tax advice.

Please write a memorandum addressing the matters raised by Maya whilst taking into account the following instructions and additional information.

(i) **The corporation tax liability for the year ending 30 September 2014**

Last week, Maya and I prepared a budget for the group for the year ending 30 September 2014 and arrived at the figures set out below for the three subsidiaries.

	Ganache Ltd	Truffle Ltd	Fondant Ltd
	£	£	£
Taxable trading profit	45,000	168,000	55,000
Chargeable gain (does not qualify for rollover relief)	Nil	42,000	Nil

These figures do not take into account the additional expenditure identified by Maya as set out in her e-mail below or the capital allowances available in respect of any capital expenditure in the year.

When calculating the total corporation tax liability of the three subsidiaries as requested by Maya I want you to:

– calculate the corporation tax liabilities based on the above figures on the assumption that the purchase of Praline Inc, as described in Maya's e-mail, will take place as planned;

–   explain, with supporting calculations, the potential effects of the additional expenditure identified by Maya on the total of the liabilities you have calculated.

When preparing these calculations you should take advantage of any opportunities available to reduce the total corporation tax liability of the companies. We do not have sufficient information regarding the financial position of Cacao Ltd at present so you should ignore any effect of that company's results on the tax position of the subsidiaries.

(ii)   **Praline Inc**

It is possible that Praline Inc will be a controlled foreign company.

Accordingly, in addition to addressing Maya's point about the interest, the memorandum should include the following:

–   a detailed analysis of the information we have and any further information we require in order to determine whether or not Praline Inc will be a controlled foreign company when it is purchased by Cacao Ltd or could become one at some time in the future;

–   the implications of Praline Inc being a controlled foreign company;

–   a summary of your findings so that Maya will understand the likely ways in which Praline Inc's profits will be taxed.

You should assume that Praline Inc will retain its profits in the country of Noka and will not pay any dividends to Cacao Ltd.

(iii)   **Fondant Ltd**

You will need to include a brief outline of the capital goods scheme in order to address Maya's query. I would also like you to draw her attention to the partial exemption percentage used by Fondant Ltd when preparing its VAT returns. It may be advantageous for the company to use the partial exemption percentage for the previous year rather than calculating it for each particular quarter as it appears to be doing at the moment.

Tax manager

① staff cost ② software ③ materials)

E-mail from Maya

The corporation tax liability for the year ending 30 September 2014

Following on from our discussion of the subsidiaries' budgeted profits for the year ending 30 September 2014, I have now identified some additional expenditure. Ganache Ltd will spend £11,000 on hiring temporary staff to carry out scientific research in connection with its business activities.

In addition, I have finalised the capital expenditure budget. Truffle Ltd and Ganache Ltd will purchase manufacturing equipment at a cost of £16,000 and £29,000 respectively.

Most of this additional expenditure will need to be borrowed. Please let me know the budgeted total corporation tax liability for the three subsidiaries, after taking account of the proposed expenditure, so that I can estimate the group's total borrowing requirements.

Praline Inc

I am hopeful that Cacao Ltd will be able to purchase the whole of the share capital of Praline Inc, probably towards the end of 2013. Praline Inc is incorporated in the country of Noka. The company's main source of income is the receipt of royalties in respect of various licences and patents. The great thing is that the rate of corporation tax in the country of Noka is only 12%. At the moment Praline Inc's annual profit is in the region of £36,000 but I intend to transfer additional intellectual property to it in the future in order to take advantage of the low rate of tax.

I have not agreed a price for Praline Inc yet. However, I am conscious that the necessary funds will be borrowed by Cacao Ltd resulting in costs in that company in respect of arrangement fees and interest. Bearing in mind that Cacao Ltd's taxable profits are very small, does that mean that these costs will not give rise to a tax deduction?

Fondant Ltd

As you know, Fondant Ltd rents the premises from which it runs all of its activities. It has recently been offered the chance to buy the building (for a price likely to be in the region of £450,000) rather than renewing the lease.

In the quarter ended 31 March 2013 the company was only able to recover 62% of the VAT charged on the rent and I expect this percentage to fall over the next year or two. I wondered if the irrecoverable VAT problem could be solved if Fondant Ltd were to purchase the building.

Regards Maya

Extracts from the client files for the Cacao Ltd group of companies.

	Cacao Ltd	Ganache Ltd	Truffle Ltd	Fondant Ltd
Shareholders	Maya (100%)	Cacao Ltd (100%)	Cacao Ltd (100%)	Cacao Ltd (100%)
Residency	UK	UK	UK	UK
Trading company?	Yes	Yes	Yes	Yes
As at 1 October 2012:				
Trading loss brought forward	–	–	–	–
Capital loss brought forward	–	–	–	£23,000
VAT partially exempt?	No	No	No	Yes

Notes

1. The subsidiaries have always been owned by Cacao Ltd.
2. The group is small for the purposes of research and development expenditure.

Required:

Prepare the memorandum requested in the email from your manager.

The following marks are available.

(i) The corporation tax liability for the year ending 30 September 2013; **(12 marks)**

(ii) Praline Inc; **(13 marks)**

(iii) Fondant Ltd. **(6 marks)**

Professional marks will be awarded for the appropriateness of the format and presentation of the memorandum and the effectiveness with which the information is communicated.　　　　　　　　　　　　　　　　　　　　　　　　　　　　**(4 marks)**

You should assume that today's date is 7 June 2013 and that the rates and allowances for the financial year to 31 March 2013 continue to apply for the foreseeable future.

(Total: 35 marks)

 Calculate your allowed time, allocate the time to the separate parts....................

60　DAUBE GROUP (ADAPTED) *Walk in the footsteps of a top tutor*

Your manager has had a meeting with Mr Daube, a potential new client. The memorandum recording the matters discussed at the meeting and an extract from an e-mail from your manager detailing the tasks for you to perform are set out below.

Memorandum recording matters discussed at meeting with Mr Daube

To:	The files
From:	Tax manager
Date:	3 December 2013
Subject:	Mr Daube – Corporate matters

I had a meeting with Mr Daube on 2 December 2013. He wants us to advise him on the sale of Shank Ltd, one of his companies, and on the sale of a number of buildings.

Mr Daube owns the Hock Ltd group of companies and Knuckle Ltd as set out below. The dates in brackets are the dates on which the companies were purchased. Neither Mr Daube nor his companies are associated with any other companies.

All five companies are UK resident trading companies with a 31 March year end. All of the companies, with the exception of Shank Ltd, are profitable.

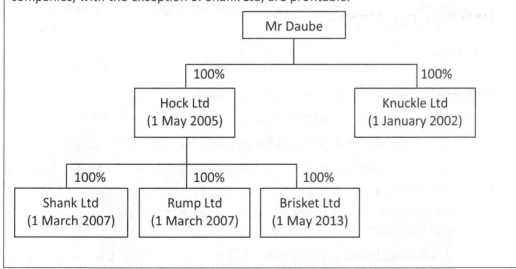

(i) **Sale of Shank Ltd**

Shank Ltd has made trading losses for a number of years and, despite surrendering the maximum possible losses to group companies, it has trading losses to carry forward as at 31 March 2013 of £35,000. Shank Ltd is expected to make a further trading loss of £54,000 in the year ending 31 March 2014 and has no other sources of income.

Mr Daube is of the opinion that the company will only become profitable following significant financial investment, which the group cannot afford, together with fundamental changes to its commercial operations.

Accordingly, Hock Ltd entered into a contract on 1 November 2013 to sell the whole of the ordinary share capital of Shank Ltd to Raymond Ltd (an independent third party) on 1 February 2014 for £270,000; an amount that is considerably less than the group paid for it.

(ii) **Sales of buildings**

The following buildings are to be sold during the year ending 31 March 2014, with the exception of the Monk building which was sold on 1 March 2013. Rollover relief will not be claimed in respect of any of the gains arising

	Gar building	Cray building	Monk building	Sword building
Owned by:	Shank Ltd	Rump Ltd	Brisket Ltd	Knuckle Ltd
Cost:	£210,000	£240,000	£380,000	See below
Estimated indexation allowance factors:	0.350	0.250	0.070	0.480
Date of sale:	1 January 2014	1 February 2014	1 March 2013	1 February 2014
Purchaser:	Hock Ltd	Quail plc	Hare plc	Pheasant plc
Estimated proceeds:	£370,000	£420,000	£290,000	£460,000

On 30 June 2003 Knuckle Ltd sold its original premises, the Pilot building, for £270,000 resulting in a chargeable gain of £60,000. On 1 January 2004 it purchased the Sword building for £255,000 and claimed rollover relief in respect of the gain on the Pilot building.

Tax manager

Email from your manager

I have just had a further conversation with Mr Daube. He informed me that:

– Brisket Ltd acquired the Monk building on 1 January 2010.

– Quail plc, Hare plc and Pheasant plc are all unrelated to Mr Daube and his companies.

– None of the companies will make any other chargeable gains or allowable losses in the year ending 31 March 2014.

– Knuckle Ltd has identified a number of potential overseas customers and expects to begin selling its products to them in 2014. At the moment, all of Knuckle Ltd's supplies are standard rated for the purposes of value added tax (VAT).

I want you to draft a report for Mr Daube dealing with the matters set out below.

(i) **Sale of Shank Ltd**

— The alternative ways in which the company's trading losses can be relieved. I want some precise detail here so please try to consider all of the possibilities and any anti-avoidance legislation that may restrict the use of the losses.

— The tax treatment of the loss arising on the sale of Shank Ltd.

— An explanation of the upper and lower limits for all of the companies for the purposes of calculating the rate of corporation tax for the year ending 31 March 2014.

(ii) **Sales of buildings**

On the assumption that the three future building sales go ahead as planned:

— Calculations of the chargeable gain/allowable loss arising on the sale of each of the four buildings.

— The alternative ways in which any capital losses arising can be relieved. I need a detailed explanation of the options available together with any restrictions that will apply. Watch out for the Monk building because the loss was incurred prior to the purchase of Brisket Ltd.

— The need to charge VAT on the sales of the buildings.

— The stamp duty land tax implications of the sales of the buildings.

(iii) **Potential sales by Knuckle Ltd to overseas customers**

— The VAT implications.

Tax manager

Required:

(a) **Prepare the report as set out in the e-mail from your manager.**

The following marks are available.

(i) Sale of Shank Ltd; (12 marks)

(ii) Sales of buildings; (10 marks)

(iii) Potential sales by Knuckle Ltd to overseas customers. (4 marks)

Professional marks will be awarded in part (a) of question 1 for the appropriateness of the format of the report and the effectiveness with which the information is communicated. (4 marks)

(b) Prepare a summary of the information required and any action that should be taken before the firm agrees to become tax advisers to Mr Daube and his companies. (5 marks)

(Total: 35 marks)

Section 2

ANSWERS TO PRACTICE QUESTIONS

TAXATION OF INDIVIDUALS

EMPLOYMENT

1   BENNY KORERE

Key answer tips

This question has five small requirements which relate to specific sections of the question. When reading through the question make sure you highlight which paragraph or paragraphs relate to each requirement.

When sections only have a few marks make sure you still give enough detail in your answers.

(a)   **Employment income – 2013/14**

	£
Salary (£32,000 x 11/12)	29,333
Payment in lieu of notice (see Tutorial note)	8,000
Payment for agreeing not to work for competitors	17,500
Car benefit (W1)	3,621
	———
Employment income	58,454
	———

Tutorial note

As the payment in lieu of notice is made in accordance with Benny's contractual arrangements with Golden Tan plc, it will be treated as a payment in respect of services provided and will be taxable in 2013/14, the year in which it is received.

The payment for agreeing not to work for competitors is a restrictive covenant payment and is specifically taxable as earnings in the year received.

Working: Car benefit

CO_2 emissions 167 g/km, available for 11 months in 2013/14

	%
Petrol	11
Plus $(165 - 100) \times {}^1/_5$	13
	——
Appropriate percentage	24
	——

	£
List price (£22,360 – £5,000)	17,360
	——
Car benefit $(£17,360 \times 24\% \times {}^{11}/_{12})$	3,819
Less Contributions for private use (£18 × 11)	(198)
	——
Assessable benefits	3,621
	——

(b)   (i)   **The share options**

There are no income tax implications on the grant of the share options.

In the tax year in which Benny exercises the options and acquires the shares, the excess of the market value of the shares over the price paid, i.e. £11,500 ((£3.35 – £2.20) x 10,000) will be subject to income tax.

Benny's financial exposure is caused by the rule within the share option scheme obliging him to hold the shares for a year before he can sell them.

If the company's expansion into Eastern Europe fails, such that its share price subsequently falls to less than £2.20 before Benny has the chance to sell the shares, Benny's financial position may be summarised as follows:

– Benny will have paid £22,000 (£2.20 x 10,000) for shares which are now worth less than that.

– He will also have paid income tax of £4,600 (£11,500 × 40%).

(ii)   **The flat**

The following additional information is required in order to calculate the employment income benefit in respect of the flat.

– The flat's annual value.

– The cost of any improvements made to the flat prior to 6 April 2014.

– The cost of power, water, repairs and maintenance etc borne by Summer Glow plc.

– The cost of the furniture provided by Summer Glow plc.

– Any use of the flat by Benny wholly, exclusively and necessarily for the purposes of his employment.

Tutorial note

The market value of the flat is not required as Summer Glow plc has owned it for less than six years.

Income tax consequences of requesting a more centrally located flat

One element of the employment income benefit in respect of the flat is calculated by reference to its original cost plus the cost of any capital improvements prior to 6 April 2014.

If Benny requests a flat in a different location, this element of the benefit will be computed instead by reference to the cost of the new flat, which in turn equals the proceeds of sale of the old flat.

Accordingly, if, as is likely, the value of the flat has increased since it was purchased, Benny's employment income benefit will also increase. The increase in the employment income benefit will be the flat's sales proceeds less its original cost less the cost of any capital improvements prior to 6 April 2014 multiplied by 4%.

(c)   (i)   **Capital gains tax liability – Sale of shares in Mahana plc**

As there are no same day acquisitions or acquisitions within the next 30 days, the shares sold are matched with the shares in the share pool which are disposed of at their average cost.

	£
Disposal proceeds	24,608
Less: Deemed cost (W)	(7,122)
Capital gain	17,486
Less: Annual exempt amount	(10,600)
Taxable gains	6,886
Capital gains tax (£6,886 × 28%)	1,928

Tutorial note

Entrepreneurs' relief is not available as Benny holds less than 5% of the shares and does not work for the company.

Working: Share Pool

		Number of shares	Cost £
June 2003	Purchase	8,400	10,240
February 2006	Sale of rights nil paid (see Tutorial note)		(610)
			9,630
January 2011	Purchase	1,300	2,281
		9,700	11,911
March 2014	Sale (£11,911 x 5,800/9,700)	(5,800)	(7,122)
Balance c/f		3,900	4,789

Tutorial note

The proceeds from the sale of the rights are regarded as small because they are less than £3,000. Accordingly, there is no part disposal and the treatment is to deduct the proceeds received from the cost in the share pool.

(d)　**Submission of 2012/13 tax return**

Late filing

The final date for filing the 2012/13 tax return in paper format is 31 October 2013.

Alternatively he could file electronically by 31 January 2014. However he does not intend to do this so he will incur a fixed filing penalty of £100 at 31 January 2014, unless he can claim to have a reasonable excuse.

Reasonable excuses accepted by HMRC include a serious illness or the destruction of the taxpayer's records by fire. HMRC would not accept being too busy to submit the return on time as a reasonable excuse.

Tax payments

The deadline for final payment of tax under self-assessment is 31 January 2014.

If Benny has not prepared his tax return he may not have sufficient information to make the payments on time.

As the balance of Benny's income tax payable for 2012/13 is due on 31 January 2014, interest will be charged on the amount due from 31 January 2014 until the day before the tax is paid.

In addition, a penalty of 5% of the tax due will be charged if it is not paid within one month of 31 January 2014.

If Benny is due to make payments on account for 2013/14 in respect of his rental income, the first payment is due on 31 January 2014. Again, interest will be charged on the amount due from 31 January 2014 until the day before the tax is paid.

There is no 5% penalty in respect of payments on account.

2　CLIFFORD AND AMANDA (ADAPTED)

Key answer tips

This is a very long question to read through. It is important to be clear as to the requirements of the question as you read through it. Break the information in the question down into the different parts of the requirements. The requirements are all separate so that the answer to one part does not affect the answer to another. Once you have identified which bit of the question relates to which bit of the requirement, you should be able to set down your answer.

Part (b) is a short section dealing with a potential conflict of interest. You must be prepared to write about ethical and professional issues.

(a)   **Notes to Manager**

To: Tax Manager
Date: 13 July 2013
From: Tax Senior
Subject : Notes for Meeting with Clifford and Amanda Johnson

(i)   **Clifford – Capital gains tax liability on sale of house in 2013/14**

	£
Proceeds	284,950
Less: Cost	(129,400)
Capital gain	155,550
Less: PPR exemption (£155,550 x 54/144) (W)	(58,331)
Chargeable gain	97,219
Capital gains tax (£97,219 × 28%)	27,221

Size of the garden

It has been assumed that the garden is no more than half a hectare or, if larger, is required for the reasonable enjoyment of the house.

If this is not the case, there will be no principal private residence relief in respect of the gain on the excess land.

Working: PPR relief

		Months
Period of ownership	(1 August 2001 – 31 July 2013)	144
Actual occupation	(1 August – 31 January 2003)	18
Deemed occupation	(last three years)	36
		54

Tutorial note

The last three years of ownership of any property that has been the taxpayer's principal private residence at any time, is exempt.

(ii)   **The implications of selling the Oxford house and garden in two separate disposals**

- The additional sales proceeds would result in an increase in Clifford's capital gains and consequently his tax liability.

- When computing the gain on the sale of the house together with a small part of the garden, the allowable cost would be a proportion of the original cost as the part disposal rules would need to be used.

- That proportion would be A/A + B where A is the value of the house and garden that has been sold and B is the value of the part of the garden that has been retained.

- Principal private residence relief would be available in the same way as in (i) above.
- When computing the gain on the sale of the remainder of the garden, the cost would be the original cost of the property less the amount used in computing the gain on the earlier disposal.
- Principal private residence relief would not be available as the land sold is not a dwelling house or part of one.

Tutorial note

Principal private residence relief should be available if the parcel of land was sold <u>before</u> the house and the rest of the garden rather than afterwards.

(iii)   **Amanda – Income tax payable for 2012/13**

	£
Salary (£136,600 x 10/12)	113,833
Bonus on joining the company	15,750
Car benefit (W1)	3,568
Fuel benefit (W1)	3,232
Claim in respect of business mileage (720 x (45p – 34p))	(79)
Employment income	136,304
Excess pension contribution (£60,000 – £50,000)	10,000
Property income (W2)	8,611
Dividends – REIT (£485 x 100/80)	606
Dividends – Quoted shares (£1,395 x 100/90)	1,550
Total income	157,071
Less: PA (reduced to £nil as total income > £116,210)	
(£100,000 + (2 x £8,105))	(nil)
Taxable income	157,071

Analysis of income (see Tutorial note)
Excess pension £10,000   Dividends £1,550   Other income £145,521

Income tax payable

£		£
34,370	x 20% (Other income)	6,874
111,151	x 40% (Other income)	44,460
———		
145,521		
1,550	x 32.5% (Dividends)	504
2,929	x 40% (Pension annual allowance charge)	1,172
———		
150,000		
7,071	x 50% (Pension annual allowance charge)	3,535
———		———
157,071		

Income tax liability		56,545
Less	Tax credits	
	On dividends (£1,550 x 10%)	(155)
	On REIT (£606 x 20%)	(121)
	PAYE	(47,785)
		———
Income tax payable		8,484

Tutorial note

Dividends from REITs are treated as 'other property income' and are taxed at 20%/40%/50% not 10%/32.5%/42.5%.

The annual allowance for pension contributions is £50,000. Where an employer pays over this amount the individual becomes taxable on the excess – in this case £10,000.

Amanda has no unused relief from earlier years as she was not a member of a registered scheme in the preceding 3 years.

Workings

(W1) Car and fuel benefits

CO_2 emissions 169 g/km, car and fuel available for 8 months in 2012/13

	%
Petrol	11
Plus (165 – 100) × $^1/_5$	9
	—
Appropriate percentage	24
	—

	£
Car benefit (£23,400 x 24% x 8/12)	3,744
Less Contributions for private use (£22 × 8)	(176)
	———
	3,568
	———
Fuel benefit (£20,200 x 24% x 8/12)	3,232
	———

(W2) Property income

	£
Rent receivable (£2,100 x 10)	21,000
Assessment – granting of a 9 year sub-lease (W3)	10,711
	31,711
Less: Rent payable (£2,100 x 11)	(23,100)
Property income	8,611

(W3) Assessment on granting of 9 year sub-lease

	£	£
Premium received on granting 9 year sub-lease		14,700
Assessable as property income £14,700 × (51 – 9)/50		12,348
Less: Allowance for premium paid on granting of a 22 year head lease: Premium paid	6,900	
Assessed on landlord £6,900 × (51 – 22)/50	4,002	
Relief for 9 years (£4,002 x 9/22)		(1,637)
Assessment on granting of 9 year sub-lease		10,711

(iv) **Income tax implications of the additional benefits**

- Amanda is an employee earning more than £8,500. Accordingly, the purchase of shares at a discount, the provision of a low interest loan and the free use of a company asset may give rise to taxable benefits.

- Amanda will pay income tax at 40% on the taxable amount in respect of each of the benefits, increasing to 50% (42.5% for dividends) if her income exceeds £150,000.

Shares

- Amanda does not appear to be acquiring the shares under an approved share incentive scheme. Therefore, a taxable benefit will arise, equal to the excess of the market value of the shares over the price paid by Amanda.

- No taxable benefit will arise if the loan does not exceed £5,000.

- Where the loan is for more than £5,000, the taxable benefit is the value of the loan multiplied by the official rate of interest of 4% multiplied by the proportion of the year for which it is outstanding (i.e. 9/12 for 2013/14).

- Any interest paid by Amanda in respect of the loan will reduce the taxable benefit.

Use of the sailing boat

- Where an asset is made available for the use of an employee earning more than £8,500 per annum or a director, the annual taxable benefit is 20% of the value of the asset when it is first made available for any employee.

- The annual benefit is apportioned where, as here, the asset is not available for the whole year.

- There will also be a taxable benefit of £1,400 in respect of the weekly running expenses.

(b) **Paragraph to insert in e-mail to Clifford**

Acting for Amanda

Thank you for supplying the information about Amanda's affairs and for informing us that she would like us to act on her behalf as well as on behalf of yourself.

We will however need to talk with Amanda directly to verify the information supplied and she will need to instruct us herself as to her requirements of the firm.

However, at this stage we are bound to inform you that acting on behalf of both parties of a husband and wife relationship may, at times, present us with a potential conflict of interest.

We therefore will need agreement from both of you that you understand and agree to us acting for both of you. It may be advisable for you to seek independent advice as to whether this is appropriate.

We can however assure you that different personnel within the firm will deal with your separate affairs, but they will work together where there are mutually beneficial reasons for doing so. However, if there is ever any cause for concern that there is a potential conflict of interest, all facts will be disclosed to both parties.

3 DOKHAM (ADAPTED) *Walk in the footsteps of a top tutor*

Key answer tips

This question is really two separate questions, which could be answered in any order.

Part (a) covers pensions and EMI schemes – neither of which are generally liked by students.

Part (b) covers the frequently tested area of IHT vs CGT for lifetime gifts, but this was perhaps not obvious from the requirement.

The highlighted words in the written sections are key phrases that markers are looking for.

(a)   **The information requested by Dokham**

Tutor's top tips

This part of the question is tricky, and you need to think carefully before you answer.

There are several specific questions to address, and you need to make sure that you leave enough time to cover all of them to increase your chance of passing.

Additional salary instead of pension contributions

Tutor's top tips

Think about what you are comparing here:

1.   Dokham receives an employer's pension contribution, which is a tax free benefit, or

2.   Dokham receives extra salary, which is subject to income tax and NICs, and pays his own personal pension contribution, which saves income tax.

There is no need to prepare full tax computations. Dokham has a salary of £70,000, so is clearly a higher rate tax payer and is above the NIC limit. Any extra income tax will therefore be at 40%, and extra NICs at 2%.

Employer pension contributions:

There are no tax implications for you when Criollo plc makes contributions into your personal pension scheme.

If you received additional salary instead:

- Your taxable income would increase by £8,000 resulting in additional tax of £3,200 (£8,000 × 40%).

- However, you would pay the additional pension contributions net of 20% income tax (saving you £1,600) and, as a result of the pension contributions, £8,000 of your taxable income would be taxed at 20% rather than 40% (saving you a further £1,600).

- Accordingly, the effective income tax implications of the two alternatives are the same.

- However, you would have to pay additional national insurance contributions of £160 (£8,000 × 2%) if Criollo plc paid you additional salary of £8,000.

Benefits from the pension scheme

Tutor's top tips

Even if you do not know the detailed rules here, you should be aware that pension income is taxable, and that part of the pension fund can be taken as a tax free lump sum.

You cannot receive any benefits from the pension scheme until you are 55 (unless you are incapacitated by ill health).

Once you are 55, you can receive up to a quarter of the value of the fund as a tax free one-off payment.

The balance of the fund can be used to purchase an annuity, which will provide a fixed pension income for the remainder of your life.

Alternatively you may draw an income from the fund, subject to limits, leaving the remainder of the funds in the pension scheme until you decide you need further income.

Pension income is subject to income tax as and when it is received.

The number of shares within the Enterprise Management Incentive (EMI) scheme

Tutor's top tips

To score well on this section you needed a good knowledge of the conditions and operation of the EMI scheme.

The value of shares over which you can be granted options within the EMI scheme rules is restricted to £250,000.

This rule results in a maximum number of shares of 26,232 (£250,000/£9.53) at the current share price of £9.53.

Accordingly, it appears that Criollo plc is intending to grant you an option in respect of the maximum possible number of shares whilst allowing for a small increase in the company's share price between now and when the option is granted to you.

Exercise of option and sale of shares

When you exercise the option and purchase shares in Criollo plc:

- You will be liable to income tax and national insurance on the amount by which the value of the shares at the time the option is granted exceeds the price you pay for the shares, i.e. £13,886 (26,200 × (£9.53 − £9)).

When you sell the shares:

- The excess of the sale proceeds over the amount paid for them plus the amount charged to income tax, i.e. £249,686 ((26,200 × £9) + £13,686) less your capital gains tax annual exempt amount (currently £10,600) if available, will be subject to capital gains tax. As you are a higher rate taxpayer the rate of tax will be 28%.

Tutorial note

*Usually, there are no income tax implications on the exercise of options under an approved EMI scheme. However, if the exercise price is less than the value at **grant**, then the shortfall will be subject to income tax and NICs when the option is exercised.*

(b)   **The tax implications of Virginia contributing towards the children's school fees**

Tutor's top tips

This section is similar to those seen in previous exams, but the wording of the question which refers to 'contributions towards school fees' may have confused some students.

It is really just a question about three lifetime gifts, and the 'possible tax liabilities' here are CGT and IHT.

One-off gift to Dokham of cash of £54,000

Inheritance tax

- The gift will be a potentially exempt transfer for the purposes of inheritance tax.

- There will be no inheritance tax liability if Virginia survives the gift for seven years.

- If Virginia were to die within seven years of the gift:

    - Inheritance tax would be charged at 40% on the excess of the gift over the available nil rate band.

        The available nil rate band is the nil rate band (currently £325,000) as reduced by chargeable transfers in the seven years prior to the gift.

        Chargeable transfers include, broadly, transfers into trust in the seven years prior to the gift and transfers to individuals prior to the gift that take place within the seven years prior to death.

    - Any inheritance tax due in respect of the gift will be reduced by 20% if Virginia survives the gift for three years and by a further 20% for each additional year she survives.

- Any tax due will be payable by Dokham within six months of the end of the month of death.

Capital gains tax

- There is no liability to capital gains tax on a gift of cash.

One-off gift to Dokham of quoted shares worth £54,000

Inheritance tax

- The inheritance tax implications are the same as for the one-off cash gift of £54,000.

Capital gains tax

- Virginia will be subject to capital gains tax at 28% on the excess of the value of the shares over the price she paid for them.

Tutorial note

Gift relief would not be available on the gift of the shares as Panatella plc is a quoted company and Virginia owns less than 5% of the company.

Gift to Dokham of cash of £8,000 every year for the next seven years

Inheritance tax

- Virginia should argue that this series of gifts represents normal expenditure out of her income such that each gift is an exempt transfer for the purposes of inheritance tax.

  For this exemption to be available, Virginia would have to show that:
  - Each gift is part of her normal expenditure.
  - The gifts are made out of income rather than capital.
  - Having made the gifts, she still has sufficient income to maintain her usual standard of living.

  Virginia's taxable income of more than £120,000 per year would help to support this argument.

- If the exemption in respect of normal expenditure out of income is not available, each gift of £8,000 would be a potentially exempt transfer and the inheritance tax implications of each gift would be the same as for the one-off cash gift of £54,000.

Capital gains tax

- Again, there will be no liability to capital gains tax on these cash gifts.

Examiner's comments

This question required candidates to provide advice on pensions, the enterprise management incentive scheme and the tax implications of the funding of school fees by a grandparent. The question was in two parts.

The pension scheme element of part (a) was not done particularly well. Candidates struggled in an attempt to produce detailed calculations when a few well chosen sentences would have been much more efficient. Many candidates failed to consider national insurance contributions and there was particular confusion in relation to the employer's contributions to the pension scheme with many candidates deducting the contributions from the employee's salary.

The main problem here was an inability to set down a clear explanation of the rules. Before starting to write an answer, candidates should be willing to stop and think in order to plan what they want to say. Also, as, part of their preparation for the exam, candidates should practise explaining the tax implications of transactions in writing in order to improve their ability to get to the point in a clear and precise manner.

A small minority of candidates failed to address the three additional questions raised by the client in respect of pension scheme benefits. This was a shame as there were some relatively straightforward marks available here.

The enterprise management incentive scheme element of part (a) again required candidates to address particular points as opposed to writing generally. Although many candidates were aware that there was a maximum value to the options granted under such a scheme, not all of them applied the rule to the facts of the question in terms of the restriction on the number of share options granted by the company. A significant number of candidates confused the enterprise management incentive scheme with the enterprise investment scheme.

Part (b) concerned a grandmother who wished to help finance the school fees of her grandchildren. It was done well by many candidates. Those who did not do so well were often too superficial in their explanations; the question required candidates to 'explain in detail'. Also, weaker candidates failed to consider the capital gains tax implications of the gifts and/or the possibility of the exemption in respect of normal expenditure out of income being available in relation to inheritance tax. Of those who did address capital gains tax, many thought, incorrectly, that gift relief would be available in respect of the proposed gift of quoted shares.

ACCA marking scheme		
		Marks
(a)	Additional pension contributions	
	Income tax	2·5
	National insurance contributions	1.0
	Benefits from the pension scheme	2.0
	Enterprise management incentive scheme	
	Maximum number of shares	1·5
	Exercise of option	1·5
	Sale of shares	1·5
		10.0
	Maximum	9.0
(b)	One-off gift of cash	
	Potentially exempt transfer	1.0
	Death within seven years	2.0
	Taper relief	1.0
	Payment of tax	1.0
	Capital gains tax	0·5
	One-off gift of shares	
	Inheritance tax	0·5
	Capital gains tax	1.0
	Series of gifts	
	Exemption for normal expenditure identified	1.0
	From income	1.0
	Normal/regular expenditure	1.0
	Able to maintain standard of living	1.0
	Consideration of Virginia's income	1.0
	If exemption not available	0·5
		12·5
	Maximum	11.0
Total		20

UNINCORPORATED BUSINESSES

4   BOB

Key answer tips

When writing about the 'badges of trade' in part (a), make sure that you link each one to relevant facts in the question. Note that you are asked to advise Bob on whether his car sales are taxable income, so you must reach a conclusion.

In part (b) it is important to explain all the loss reliefs available and not just the one selected.

Part (c) has only a few marks so do not worry if you were not sure of the technical points.

(a)   Evidence of trading

Letter to client

[Client address]

[Own address]
[Date]

Dear Bob,

Sale of Classic Cars

I note that you have been selling some cars from your collection in order to raise some extra cash for your business.

While you believe that the sums are not taxable, I believe that there may be a risk of the car sales being treated as a trade, and therefore subject to income tax as trading income.

To be sure, we need to refer to guidance in the form of a set of principles established by HMRC, known as the 'badges of trade'. These help determine whether or not a trade exists, and need to be looked at in their entirety.

The badges of trade are as follows:

1   *The subject matter*

Some assets can be enjoyed by themselves, some purchased as an investment, while others (such as large amounts of aircraft linen) are clearly neither. Cars are frequently assets acquired as trading inventory, and therefore the resale may be a sign of trading. However, vintage and classic cars can also be purchased as an investment, or for enjoyment of the asset and so this test is not conclusive.

2   *Frequency of transactions*

Where transactions are frequent (not one-offs), this suggests trading. You have sold several cars, which might suggest trading, although you have only done this for a short period in this tax year.

3   *Length of ownership*

Where items are bought and sold soon afterwards, this indicates trading. You have acquired your cars over a significant time period and the length of time between acquisition and sale would not suggest trading.

4   *Supplementary work and marketing*

You are actively marketing the cars on your internet website, which is an indication of trading.

5   *Profit motive*

A motive to make profit suggests trading activity. You sold the cars to raise funds for your property business, and not to make a profit as such, which suggests that your motive was to raise cash, and not make profits.

6   *The way in which the asset sold was acquired*

Selling assets which were acquired by way of gift/inheritance is not usually seen as trading, whereas selling assets you have purchased could be viewed as trading. In this case some of the cars were acquired through inheritance and others purchased for personal pleasure over a significant period. Both of these facts would not suggest that there is a trading activity.

HMRC will look at all of the factors and decide, no one factor is conclusive.

By applying all of these tests, I believe it should be possible to argue that you were not trading, merely selling some assets in order to generate short-term cash for your business. However, you should be aware of the degree of ambiguity in this.

If they are not treated as trading, the asset disposals will be taxed under the capital gain tax rules, but as they are cars , they will be exempt from capital gains tax.

Yours sincerely

A N. Accountant

(b)   **Calculation of taxable income and gains**

The trading income assessments are based on the rules relating to the commencement of trade, and are as follows (before loss utilisation);

	Tax adjusted trading profit/loss		*Trading income assessment*
	£	£	£
2009/10 (basis period 1.10.09 – 5.4.10)			
£3,500 × 6/7 Profit		3,000	3,000
2010/11 (basis period: first 12 months)			
£3,500 × 7/7 Profit	3,500		
(£18,000) × 5/12 Loss	(7,500)	(4,000)	Nil
	———		
2011/12 (basis period: year to 30 April 2011)			
Loss	(18,000)		
Less 5/12 × (£18,000) utilised in 2010/11	7,500	(10,500)	Nil
	———		
2012/13 (basis period: year to 30 April 2012)		41,040	41,040

Bob has two losses available for relief: £4,000 in 2010/11 and £10,500 in 2011/12.

Loss relief options

The loss relief options available are as follows:

- Losses can be relieved against total income of the year of loss and/or the total income of the prior year. Unused losses can be carried forward against the first available future trading profits from the same trade.
- A loss relief claim against total income can also be extended to include set-off against capital gains in either the year of loss or the previous year. However, Bob has no chargeable gains until 2012/13, which is after the years of the loss.
- As this is a new business, relief is also available against income in the three years prior to the year of first loss under, but Bob has not earned any income in the three years prior to the start of his business, and his 2009/10 trading profits are covered by his personal allowance.

Conclusion

The most beneficial way for Bob to use the losses incurred is to carry them forward to 2012/13 as this will relieve tax at the highest rate and will not result in wasted use of personal allowances.

Bob's marginal rate of income tax is 40%, but not all £14,500 of loss is relieved at 40%.

The tax saving will be £5,171 ((£11,355 (W) × 40%) + (£3,145 (W) × 20%)).

His taxable income and gains for the years in question will therefore be as follows:

Taxable income and gains	2009/10	2010/11	2011/12	2012/13
	£	£	£	£
Trading income	3,000	Nil	Nil	41,040
Less: Relief for losses b/f	Nil	Nil	Nil	(14,500)
	3,000	Nil	Nil	26,540
Employment income	Nil	3,198	12,790	12,790
Net income	3,000	3,198	12,790	39,330
Less: Personal allowance	(8,105)	(8,105)	(8,105)	(8,105)
Taxable income	Nil	Nil	4,685	31,225
Taxable gains (£24,120 − £10,600)				13,520

Loss memorandum	2010/11	2011/12	2012/13
	£	£	£
Losses brought forward	Nil	4,000	14,500
Utilised	–	–	(14,500)
Losses arising in the year	4,000	10,500	
Losses carried forward	4,000	14,500	Nil

Working: Tax saving

	£
Taxable income with no loss relief (£41,040 + £12,790 − £8,105)	45,725
Income falling above the basic rate band and taxable at 40% (£45,725 − £34,370)	11,355
Amount of loss relieved against income in the basic rate band (£14,500 − £11,355), or alternatively (£34,370 − £31,225)	3,145

(c) **Claims for capital losses**

Where the value of shares (a chargeable asset) has become negligible (defined as < 5% of the original cost), a claim can be made to treat the asset as though it was sold and then immediately reacquired for its current market value. This is known as a negligible value claim.

The sale and reacquisition is treated as taking place at the time that the claim is made or at a specified time (up to 2 years before the start of the tax year in which the claim was made) if the asset was of negligible value at that time.

As the loss is on unquoted shares, a special relief allows the loss to be relieved against the total income of the taxpayer for the year in which the loss arose, and/or against the total income of the previous year.

Losses are first relieved against current year income, with any excess being available for offset against the prior year's income.

Bob can therefore make a negligible value claim as at 1 December 2012. This will give rise to a loss of £14,500 (£500 – £15,000) which will be deemed to arise in the year 2012/13. By doing so, his taxable income and gains for that year will be reduced.

Tutorial note

These shares would probably have been eligible for Enterprise Investment Scheme income tax relief, however as Bob had no income in 2008/09 when he made the investment (or in 2007/08), no income tax relief can have been claimed.

There would have been no clawback of income tax relief, as Bob owned the shares for more than three years. However, had Bob claimed income tax relief, the capital loss would have been reduced by the amount of relief claimed.

5   GLORIA SEAFORD (ADAPTED)   *Online question assistance*

Key answer tips

Parts (a) to (c) of this question are reasonably straightforward sections dealing with the income tax, VAT and capital gain implications of a trader who is giving up business.

Whenever a question refers to an individual's residence, ordinary residence and domicile status, you should be on the lookout for income and assets whose tax treatment may be affected. In this question it was part (d) where this information was relevant.

(a)   **Value added tax (VAT) implications of the sale by Gloria of the business assets**

- The sale of the premises is an exempt supply for VAT purposes because they are more than three years old. Accordingly, Gloria cannot recover any VAT incurred on any costs relating to the sale.

- Gloria must charge VAT on the shelving, shop fittings and the inventory of cards and small gifts.

- The sale of the inventory of books will be zero-rated.

- Gloria is making a taxable supply to herself of the van. However, there is no need to account for VAT as the amount due of £940 (£4,700 x 20%) is less than £1,000.

- Gloria must inform HMRC by 30 March 2014 that she has ceased to trade. Her VAT registration will be cancelled with effect from 28 February 2014.

Tutorial note

This is not a transfer of a going concern: the assets are being sold to different purchasers and the building is to be used for a different purpose.

(b) **Income tax and national insurance liability for 2013/14**

Tutorial note

An individual's tax status is only important for income tax in determining their liability to UK tax on overseas income and the availability of the personal allowance.

The question says that Gloria is resident and ordinarily resident in the UK, but not UK domiciled.

As she is UK resident in 2013/14, Gloria is liable to tax on all of her UK income and is entitled to a full personal allowance.

Her ordinary residence status and domicile are not important in this part as she has no source of overseas income.

Income tax liability

	£
Trading income (W1)	32,434
Retirement pension	5,312
Bank interest (£13,500 × 100/80)	16,875
Total income	54,621
Less Personal age allowance (Note)	(8,105)
Taxable income	46,516

Analysis of income:
Savings income £16,875, Other income £29,641

£	£
29,641 × 20% (other income)	5,928
4,729 × 20% (savings income)	946
34,370	
12,146 × 40% (savings income)	4,858
46,516	
Income tax liability	11,732

Note

The personal age allowance is abated to the standard personal allowance due to the level of Gloria's total income.

National insurance liability

Gloria has no Class 2 or Class 4 National Insurance Contributions liability as she was over the state pensionable age on 6 April 2012.

Workings

(1) **Trading income**

Closing year rules apply:

Year of cessation	2013/14
Penultimate year	2012/13

Accounts assessed in penultimate year (CYB) = y/e 31 October 2012

The year of cessation will assess all profits not yet assessed less overlap relief.

	£	£
Year ended 31 October 2013		39,245
Period ending 28 February 2014	11,500	
Profit on closing inventory (£8,300 × 5/105)	395	
Capital allowances (W2)	(2,986)	
	———	
		8,909
		———
		48,154
Less: Overlap profits		(15,720)
		———
Trading income		32,434
		———

(2) **Capital allowances**

	Pool	Van	B.U.	Allowances
	£	£	%	£
TWDV b/f	4,050	4,130		
Addition	820	–		
Less: Proceeds	(1,400)	(4,700)		
	———	———		
	3,470	570		
Balancing allowance	(3,470)	–		3,470
Balancing charge	–	(570)	x 85%	(484)
	———	———		
	Nil	Nil		
	———	———		———
Total Allowances				2,986
				———

(c)   (i)   **Capital gains tax liability for 2013/14**

Tutorial note

The question says that Gloria is resident and ordinarily resident in the UK, but not UK domiciled.

Her non-UK domicile status is however not important in this part as she has not disposed of any overseas assets.

Accordingly, in 2013/14, Gloria is liable to capital gains tax on the net taxable gains arising on all of her UK asset disposals with a full annual exempt amount.

	£	£
Gains not qualifying for Entrepreneurs' relief		
Gain on painting	7,100	
Gains qualifying for Entrepreneurs' relief		
Gain on shop (£335,000 – £267,000)		68,000
Less: Capital losses b/f (Note)	(7,100)	(24,300)
Less: Annual exempt amount	–	(10,600)
	———	———
	–	33,100
	———	———
Capital gains tax: qualifying gains		
(£33,100 × 10%)		3,310
		———

Tutorial note

Entrepreneurs' relief is available on the disposal of the shop as although Gloria is not disposing of the whole or part of the business as a going concern, the relief is available on the disposal of assets of an individual's trading business that has now ceased.

Furthermore, the assets have been held at least 12 months prior to the disposal and the disposal of assets is to take place within three years of the cessation of trade.

Capital losses and the AEA are set against non-qualifying gains first, as these would otherwise be taxed at 28% (as Gloria is a higher rate taxpayer).

The rate of CGT on a gain qualifying for Entrepreneurs'Relief is 10%.

(ii)   **Relief in respect of the fall in value of the shares in All Over plc**

The shares in All Over plc are worth three pence each and are of negligible value. Gloria can make a negligible value claim in order to realise the loss on the shares without selling them.

	£
Value (17,500 x 3p)	525
Cost (probate value)	(11,400)
	———
Capital loss on making the claim	(10,875)
	———

Gloria can claim the loss in any year in which the shares are of negligible value provided she notifies HMRC within two years of the end of that year.

Accordingly, she can claim to realise the loss in 2012/13 or even in 2011/12 if she can show that the shares were of negligible value in that year.

Alternatively, she can claim the loss in 2013/14 or a later year if that would give rise to a greater tax saving.

(d) **UK tax implications of shares in Bubble Inc**

If Gloria invests in Bubble Inc shares, she will own an overseas asset and will be in receipt of overseas income. Her tax status is therefore important in determining how she will be assessed to UK taxes.

The important factors in determining Gloria's liability to tax are as follows:

- She is resident and ordinarily resident in the UK, but not UK domiciled
- Her unremitted dividends from Bubble Inc will be > £2,000.

Accordingly, she will be taxed as follows:

Income tax

- She will be assessed on the dividends on an arising basis with full personal allowance available **unless** a claim for the remittance basis is made
- If a claim for the remittance basis is made:
  - The dividends arising in that year will only be assessed in the UK if they are remitted into the UK
  - As Gloria plans to leave the dividends in her overseas bank account, they will not be taxed in the UK
  - Note that they will be taxed even if remitted in a later year when the remittance basis is not claimed
  - No personal allowance available in the year the remittance basis is claimed
  - In addition, Gloria will be liable to a £50,000 annual tax charge as she has been UK resident and ordinarily resident for more than 12 out of the previous 14 tax years.

Income tax liability: Arising basis

	£
Retirement pension	5,312
Bank interest (£13,500 × 100/80)	16,875
Dividends from Bubble Inc (£12,000 x 100/90)	13,333
Total income	35,520
Less Personal age allowance (abated due to level of income)	(8,105)
Taxable income	27,415

Analysis of income:
Dividend income £13,333, Savings income £14,082

	£	£
2,710 × 10% (savings income)		271
11,372 × 20% (savings income)		2,274
	14,082	
13,333 × 10% (dividend income)		1,333
	27,415	
Income tax liability		3,878
Less: Tax deducted at source		
Dividends (£13,333 x 10%)		(1,333)
Bank interest (£16,875 x 20%)		(3,375)
Income tax repayable		(830)

Tutorial note

The overseas dividends are treated like UK dividends in that they are grossed up at 100/90 and have a deemed tax credit of 10%.

This tax credit is not repayable, and should be deducted before the tax credit on the bank interest, which can be repaid.

If the dividends had foreign tax withheld, they would be grossed up for the foreign tax first, and then for the 10% notional credit. Double tax relief would then be available for the foreign tax in the normal way.

Income tax liability: Remittance basis claimed

	£
Retirement pension	5,312
Bank interest (£13,500 × 100/80)	16,875
Dividends from Bubble Inc (None remitted)	–
Total income	22,187
Less Personal age allowance	–
Taxable income	22,187

Analysis of income:
Savings income £16,875, Other income £5,312

	£		£
5,312 × 20% (other income)			1,062
16,875 × 20% (savings income)			3,375

22,187

Add Remittance basis charge	50,000

Income tax liability	54,437
Less: Tax deducted at source	
Bank interest (£16,875 x 20%)	(3,375)

Income tax payable	51,062

- **Gloria should clearly not claim the remittance basis in 2014/15**
- Note that the remittance basis claim is made on a year by year basis

Capital gains tax

- Individuals are subject to capital gains tax on worldwide assets if they are resident or ordinarily resident in the UK.
- However, because Gloria is non-UK domiciled and the shares are situated abroad, the treatment of gains and losses on the disposal of overseas assets depends on whether Gloria's unremitted overseas income and gains in the tax year that the shares are sold exceed £2,000 as follows:

If unremitted overseas income and gains:	Treatment:
≤ £2,000	<ul><li>Only assessed on gains if proceeds are remitted to the UK</li><li>Overseas losses will be allowable</li><li>The annual exempt amount is available</li></ul>

> £2,000	<ul><li>Assessed on gains on all overseas disposals on an arising basis **unless** an election is made for the remittance basis to apply</li><li>If the election is not made (i.e. arising basis applies)
	   – all gains assessed
	   – annual exempt amount available
	   – overseas losses are allowable</li><li>If the election is made (i.e. remittance basis applies)
	   – only assessed to gains if proceeds are remitted into the UK
	   – annual exempt amount is not available
	   – overseas losses are not allowable unless a further election is made
	   – the election will apply to both income and gains
	   – Gloria cannot elect for it to apply to just one or the other</li></ul>

Tutorial note

The remittance basis election applies to both income and gains.

As Gloria has been resident in the UK for 12 out of the last 14 tax years she will have to pay the remittance basis charge of £50,000 in any tax year where her unremitted income and gains exceed £2,000 and she claims the remittance basis

- Any tax suffered in Oceania in respect of the gain is available for offset against the UK capital gains tax liability arising on the shares.

Investment advice costs

In computing a capital gain or allowable loss, a deduction is available for the incidental costs of acquisition. However, to be allowable, such costs must be incurred wholly and exclusively for the purposes of acquiring the asset.

The fee paid to Eric related to general investment advice and not to the acquisition of the shares and therefore, would not be deductible in computing the gain.

Inheritance tax

For IHT, Gloria's domicile status is important in deciding how she will be taxed.

Assets situated abroad owned by non-UK domiciled individuals are excluded property for the purposes of inheritance tax.

However, Gloria will be deemed to be UK domiciled (for the purposes of inheritance tax only) if she has been resident in the UK for 17 out of the 20 tax years ending with the year in which the disposal occurs.

Gloria has been running a business in the UK since June 1999 and would therefore, appear to have been resident for at least 15 tax years (1999/00 to 2013/14 inclusive).

If Gloria is deemed to be UK domiciled such that the shares in Bubble Inc are not excluded property, business property relief will not be available because Bubble Inc is an investment company.

6 SIMONE (ADAPTED) *Walk in the footsteps of a top tutor*

Key answer tips

This question covers capital allowances, partnership apportionment of profits, use of trading losses and VAT registration. Most of this is F6 level technical knowledge and therefore fairly straightforward, IF you have the knowledge! It may be some time since you sat your F6 exam (or equivalent) but this brought forward knowledge is important and you must make sure you include it in your revision.

The highlighted words in the written sections are key phrases that markers are looking for.

Tutor's top tips

Apportionment of partnership profits is a straightforward calculation, as long as you work through it in the correct order:

(1)   Adjust the profits and deduct capital allowances for the accounting period

(2)   Allocate the profits between the partners – first any salaries, then interest on capital and the balance based on the partnership profit sharing agreement

(3)   It may be necessary to split the profits into shorter periods if there have been any changes in the profit sharing agreement during the period

(4)   Allocate each partner's share of the profits to the relevant tax year

(5)   If the partnership has made a loss, each partner can individually choose how that loss should be relieved.

(a)   (i)   **Share of the taxable trading loss for the year ended 5 April 2013**

			Ellington	Simone	Basie
	£		£	£	£
Tax adjusted trading loss	90,000				
Capital allowances					
Additions within AIA limit	21,200				
Writing down allowance	700				
	111,900				
6 April 2012 – 28 February 2013					
Tax adjusted trading loss					
(£111,900 x 11/12)	(102,575)				
Salaries					
(£15,000/£11,500/£13,000					
x 11/12)	(36,209)		13,750	10,542	11,917
Balance (3:2:2)	(138,784)		(59,478)	(39,653)	(39,653)
1 March 2013 – 5 April 2013					
Tax adjusted trading loss					
(£111,900 x 1/12)	(9,325)				
Salaries (£14,000 x 1/12)	(2,334)		1,167	1,167	
Balance (1:1)	(11,659)		(5,830)	(5,829)	
	(111,900)		(50,391)	(33,773)	(27,736)

Tutorial note

The unrelieved expenditure on the general pool is less than £1,000 and can therefore be claimed in full. This is the new 'small pools WDA' and is easy to miss. Be careful to look out for this.

When apportioning partnership profits where there has been a change in the profit sharing agreement don't forget to time apportion salaries and any interest on capital as well as the partnership profits.

(ii) **Alternative strategies**

Tutor's top tips

Three marks are available here for simply stating the different options available for use of the loss before doing any calculations.

Loss relief is a key planning area, and it is important to be very comfortable with the different options.

The following alternative strategies are available to Simone in respect of her share of the taxable trading loss.

Offset against her general income for the current year (2012/13) and/or the previous year (2011/12).

Following a claim against her general income in 2012/13, the remaining loss could be offset against her capital gains of that year.

Any losses not used as set out above will be carried forward for offset against her share of the taxable trading profits of Ellington & Co in the future.

(iii) **Advice**

 Tutor's top tips

The calculations are time consuming, but not especially technically difficult.

It is important to make clear what you are doing, as the examiner has asked you to 'explain' which of the strategies will save the most tax.

Simply doing the calculations cannot get you full marks.

Offset against future profits of the same trade

Assuming an annual taxable trading profit of £25,000, Simone's share of the budgeted profit of Ellington and Co in 2013/14 and future years will be £12,500 (£25,000 x 1/2). The profit from her new business is budgeted to be £10,500 (£1,500 x 7) in 2013/14 and £18,000 (£1,500 x 12) in future years. Accordingly, Simone will be a basic rate taxpayer and the tax saved via the offset of the loss will be £6,755 (£33,773 x 20%) (Note).

Note: the tax saved will be £2,500 (£12,500 x 20%) in 2013/14 and in 2014/15 and the balance of £1,755 (£6,755 – (2 x £2,500)) in 2015/16.

Offset against total income and capital gains in 2012/13

Simone's only income in 2012/13 is dividend income of £10,800. Offsetting her loss against this income will not save any tax as the dividend tax credit is not repayable in cash. However, having offset the loss against her net income in 2012/13, Simone would then be able to offset the remaining loss of £21,773 (£33,773 – (£10,800 x 100/90)) against her capital gain. The capital gains tax saved would be £6,096 (£21,773 x 28%), as the top part of the gain currently falls into the higher rate tax band.

Offset against income in 2011/12

Simone's original income tax liability in 2011/12 is set out below.

	Total £	Trading £	Dividend £
Trading income	48,200	48,200	
Dividend income			
(£12,600 x 100/90)	14,000		14,000
Less: Personal allowance	(8,105)	(8,105)	
Taxable income	54,095	40,095	14,000

	£
34,370 x 20% (Trading income)	6,874
5,725 x 40% (Trading income)	2,290
40,095	
14,000 x 32.5% (Dividend income)	4,550
54,095	
Income tax liability	13,714

Simone's liability in 2011/12 following the offset of the trading loss is set out below.

	Total £	Trading £	Dividend £
Trading income	48,200	48,200	
Dividend income (£12,600 x 100/90)	14,000		14,000
Less: Trading loss	(33,773)	(33,773)	
Less: Personal allowance	(8,105)	(8,105)	
Taxable income	20,322	6,322	14,000

Income tax

	£	£
6,322 x 20% (Trading income)		1,264
14,000 x 10% (Dividend income)		1,400
20,322		
Income tax liability		2,664

The tax saved via the offset of the trading loss would be £11,050 (£13,714 – £2,664).

Conclusion

Simone will save the most tax by offsetting the loss against her income of 2011/12.

Tutorial note

It is not simple to work out the tax saving by using just marginal rates of tax, as the loss relief will take Simone from being a higher rate to a basic rate taxpayer.

It is therefore easiest and clearest to calculate the tax saving by doing two full income tax computations.

The offset of the losses would also have implications for Simone's liability to Class 4 National Insurance Contributions. Credit was available for reference to this point.

(b)   **VAT registration**

Tutor's top tips

Again, this part of the question relies on retention of F6 knowledge regarding compulsory registration for VAT.

You are told that you are not required to prepare calculations, therefore the examiner is looking for a clear written explanation of the rules.

Being able to describe how the rules work, rather than simply applying them to the numbers in the question is a key skill at P6.

Simone is required to register for VAT when her cumulative taxable supplies (standard and zero rated), excluding supplies of capital assets, exceed £77,000 in the previous 12 months. She must notify HM Revenue and Customs (HMRC) within 30 days of the end of the period in which the limit is exceeded. She will be registered and must charge VAT from the first day of the month beginning one month after the end of the period in which the limit is exceeded.

The fact that Ellington and Co is VAT registered is irrelevant when considering Simone's position, as Simone and Ellington and Co are separate taxable persons.

Examiner's comments

Part (a) required calculations of a partner's share of a loss arising in a partnership and the most beneficial use of that loss. The calculation of the capital allowances was done well. However, the allocation of the loss between the partners was done poorly with the majority of candidates treating the salaries as employment income rather than as a share of the trading loss.

The use of the loss was also problematic. Weaker candidates were confused as to corporate and personal loss offset rules. Even many stronger candidates lacked the precise knowledge required to score well; a statement of how losses can be used must describe precisely the income against which the loss can be offset, for example, 'against future profits of the same trade' in order to earn all of the marks available.

The calculations were not done particularly well and many answers were very difficult to follow. Many candidates ignored the requirement to calculate the total tax saved and simply prepared various income tax computations.

Part (b) required an explanation of the rules relating to registration for VAT. Weaker candidates wasted time describing the future test in detail despite it not being relevant to this particular question. In addition, many candidates lacked precise knowledge (for example in relation to the date registration comes into effect) such that they did not score as well as would have been expected.

				Marks
		ACCA marking scheme		
(a)	(i)	Capital allowances		1.5
		6 April 2012 to 28 February 2013		2.0
		1 March 2013 to 5 April 2013		2.0
				5.5
			Maximum	5.0
	(ii)	Against net income of 2012/13 and/or 2011/12		1.0
		Against capital gain in 2012/13		1.0
		Against future profits of the same trade		1.0
				3.0
			Maximum	3.0
	(iii)	Evaluation of offset in 2012/13		2.0
		Evaluation of offset in 2011/12		4.0
		Evaluation of offset against future profits of the same trade		2.5
		Calculation of maximum tax saving		0.5
				9.0
			Maximum	8.0
(b)		Taxable supplies exceed £77,000 in the previous 12 months		1.0
		Exclude capital assets		0.5
		Notify within 30 days		0.5
		Date of effective registration		1.0
		Relevance of Ellington and Co being VAT registered		1.0
				4.0
Total				20

7   ELLROY (ADAPTED) *Walk in the footsteps of a top tutor*

Key answer tips

This optional question is based on F6 level knowledge of opening year rules for sole traders, change of accounting date and the flat rate scheme for VAT.

You should know the opening year rules for assessment of trading profits, as these are still regularly tested in the P6 exam.

However, change of accounting date and the flat rate scheme for VAT are less mainstream areas, and if you had forgotten the rules for these you would be advised not to choose this question in the exam!

The highlighted words in the written sections are key phrases that markers are looking for.

(a)   (i)   Difference in Ellroy's total tax liability depending on his choice of year end

Tutor's top tips

You could potentially spend a very long time on this part of the question if you calculated the total income tax and NIC for three different tax years with two different year ends!

As Ellroy already has partnership profits of more than £165,000, you know that he must already be an additional rate taxpayer, and is above the upper limit for Class 4 NICs.

This means that you just need to calculate the taxable profits for the new business for each tax year, then multiply the difference by 52% to calculate the extra tax/tax saving.

The order to approach the calculation of taxable profits is as follows:

1.   Calculate trading profits for each accounting period (already done for the March year end).

2.   Deduct capital allowances for each accounting period (just the annual investment allowance for the accounting period in which the vans are purchased).

3.   Apply the opening year rules to match the profits to the tax years.

This answer shows the examiner's model answer, although there are alternative ways of presenting the answer – see the end of the answer for an alternative.

	2013/14 £	2014/15 £	2015/16 £
March year end:			
Six months ending 31 March 2014	13,100		
Year ending 31 March 2015			
(£87,200 – £22,000)		65,200	
Year ending 31 March 2016			74,400
	___	___	___
September year end:			
1 October 2013 to 5 April 2014			
(£34,700 (W1) × 6/12)	17,350		
Year ending 30 September 2014 (W1)		34,700	
Year ending 30 September 2015 (W1)			80,800
	___	___	___
Increase/(fall) in profit due to adopting a September year end	4,250	(30,500)	6,400
	___	___	___
Income tax and Class 4 National insurance contributions at 52%	2,210	(15,860)	3,328
	___	___	___
Reduction in total tax liability over the three years			10,322
			___

Tutorial note

The income tax and Class 4 national insurance contributions on the change in the level of profits will be at 50% and 2% respectively due to the level of Ellroy's partnership income.

Working: Tax adjusted profits – 30 September year end

	£
Year ending 30 September 2014	
Adjusted trading profit	
Six months ending 31 March 2014	13,100
Six months ending 30 September 2014 (£87,200 × 6/12)	43,600
Less: Capital allowances (AIA)	(22,000)
	___
	34,700
	___
Year ending 30 September 2015	
Adjusted trading profit	
Six months ending 31 March 2015 (£87,200 × 6/12)	43,600
Six months ending 30 September 2015 (£74,400 × 6/12)	37,200
	___
	80,800
	___

Alternative calculation of reduction in total tax liability

	March year end £	Sept year end £
2013/14	13,100	17,350
2014/15	65,200	34,700
2015/16	74,400	80,800
	152,700	132,850

Reduction in assessable profits if Sept year end (£152,700 – £132,850)	£19,850
Income tax and NIC saving @ 52%	£10,322

(ii)   **The effect on Ellroy's total taxable profits of changing his year end**

Tutor's top tips

Even if you could not remember the rules on change of accounting date, you could have made a few sensible points to score some marks here.

Remember that overlap profits are dependent on the date chosen as the year end. If the year end is changed, we either create more, or use up existing, overlap profits.

*Under the current year basis we always try to tax the 12 month accounting period ended in the tax year. If we have a short accounting period ended in the tax year, as will happen here, we need to make this up to 12 months by taxing the **12 months** to the new accounting date.*

Remember to address the specific requirement and consider what will happen if profitability increases and is profitability decreases.

With a 31 March year end, Ellroy's basis period for the tax year 2016/17 will be the year ending 31 March 2017.

If Ellroy were to change his year end to 30 September and prepare accounts for the six months ending 30 September 2016, he would have a six-month trading period ending in the tax year 2016/17.

His basis period for 2016/17 would be the 12 months ending 30 September 2016, such that the profits for the six months ending 31 March 2016 would be taxed again in 2016/17 having already been taxed in 2015/16.

The profits taxed twice would be classified as overlap profits and would be relieved when the trade ceases or, potentially, on a future change of accounting date.

Accordingly, by changing his year end, in the tax year 2016/17 Ellroy would be taxed on the profits arising in the six months ending 31 March 2016 rather than those arising in the six months ending 31 March 2017.

If Ellroy's profits are rising, the change in accounting date will reduce his taxable profits for 2016/17.

If Ellroy's profits are falling, the change in accounting date will cause his taxable profits for 2016/17 to increase.

Ellroy would need to notify HM Revenue and Customs of the change in accounting date by 31 January 2018 in order for the change to be valid in 2016/17.

(b)   **Maximum flat rate percentage**

Tutor's top tips

This is a tricky little section requiring application of your knowledge of the VAT flat rate scheme.

The key here is to work out the VAT currently paid by Ellroy, and then calculate this as a % of VAT inclusive turnover.

If the flat rate % is less than this, it would be beneficial for Ellroy to join the flat rate scheme. If it is more than this, then the scheme is not worthwhile.

The annual VAT payable by the business when calculated in the normal way is set out below.

	£
Output tax (£100,000 × 20%)	20,000
Input tax (£21,000 × 20%)	(4,200)
Payable to HMRC	15,800

Under the flat rate scheme a business continues to charge its customers output tax in the normal way but pays a fixed percentage of its VAT inclusive turnover to HMRC rather than calculating output tax minus input tax.

The VAT due under the flat rate scheme in respect of Ellroy's business would be £120,000 (£100,000 × 1.20) multiplied by the flat rate percentage.

The percentage necessary to result in VAT payable of £15,800 is 13.167% (£15,800/ £120,000).

Accordingly, the scheme will be financially beneficial if the flat rate percentage for Ellroy's business is no more than 13%.

Tutorial note

Flat rate scheme percentages increase in increments of either a half or a whole percentage point. Accordingly, the scheme would be financially beneficial if the relevant percentage is 13% but not if it is 13.5%.

Examiner's comments

This question required advice to a sole trader on his choice of accounting date and a possible change of accounting date together with explanations of certain aspects of the flat rate scheme. It was in two parts.

Part (a) concerned the various aspects of the trader's year end and was in two parts.

Part (i) required calculations of the difference in the trader's tax liability depending on the year end adopted. This was not hard but it was not done particularly well. Many candidates failed to give the annual investment allowance on the vans and were also unable to apply the opening year rules to the facts of the question. In addition, many candidates would have benefited by thinking before they started calculating. The trader was an additional rate taxpayer so it was not necessary to prepare any income tax computations; it was merely necessary to calculate the difference in the taxable profits by reference to each of the two year ends and then to multiply by 52%.

Part (ii) required explanations of the tax implications of a change of accounting date. This was the more difficult part of the question and was not done well. In particular, candidates needed to think rather than write in order to come up with sensible points to say but most were unable to explain the implications well.

Part (b) concerned VAT and the flat rate scheme and was done reasonably well. Again, however, it required some thought in order to solve the problem and many candidates chose to write down everything they knew about the scheme, most of which did not earn marks, rather than trying to answer the question set.

		ACCA marking scheme		
				Marks
(a)	(i)	Taxable profits with a 31 March year end		2.0
		30 September year end		
		Tax adjusted profits for the trading periods		2.5
		Assessable profits		2.0
		Effect on total tax and national insurance liability		2.0
				8.5
			Maximum	8.0
	(ii)	Basis periods		1.5
		Profits taxed twice		2.0
		Effect on taxable profits		2.5
		Requirement to notify HMRC		1.0
				7.0
(b)		VAT payable in the normal way		1.5
		Basis of flat rate scheme		2.0
		Calculation of maximum percentage		2.0
		Conclusion		0.5
				6.0
			Maximum	5.0
	Total			20

CHANGING BUSINESS SCENARIOS

8 DELIA JONES

Key answer tips

This question deals with the important topic of transfer of a business to a company. This question is clearly set out and has no real traps.

The trickiest part is (b)(ii) which needs a good understanding of incorporation and Entrepreneurs' reliefs. You need to remember that incorporation relief applies automatically to roll over gains when a business is transferred to a company in return for shares, but can be disclaimed in favour of realising an immediate gain which qualifies for Entrepreneurs' relief. This will result in lower tax payable overall if the future disposal of their shares will not be eligible for Entrepreneurs' relief.

Be careful to answer the question set when it asks you to <u>advise</u> Delia. This requires comments not just calculations.

(a) **Disposal 31 March 2013**

(i) **Trading income assessment for 2012/13**

Closing year rules apply:

Year of cessation	2012/13
Penultimate year	2011/12

Accounts assessed in penultimate year (CYB) = y/e 31 August 2011

Therefore year of cessation, 2012/13, will assess all profits not yet assessed less overlap relief as follows:

	£	£
Year ended 31 August 2012		77,200
Period ended 31 March 2013	58,500	
Balancing charge (W)	95,000	
	———	153,500
		230,700
Relief for overlap profits		(24,200)
		———
Trading income assessment		206,500

Delia's total income will be £206,500 meaning no personal allowance will be available, and £56,500 (£206,500 – £150,000) will be taxed at 50% in 2012/13.

Working: Capital Allowances

The disposal of the fixtures and fittings will result in a balancing charge of £95,000 as follows:

	£
TWDV b/f at 31 August 2012	114,000
Additions – December 2012	31,000
	145,000
Disposal proceeds	(240,000)
Balancing charge	(95,000)

Delia and Fastfood Ltd are not connected persons, and so they cannot elect to transfer the fixtures and fittings at their written down value.

(ii) **Capital gains tax liability for 2012/13**

Delia's disposal of her business on 31 March 2013 will result in a CGT liability as follows:

Gains qualifying for Entrepreneurs' relief	£
Goodwill (£125,000 – Nil cost)	125,000
Freehold property (A) (£462,000 – £230,000)	232,000
Freehold property (B) (£118,000 – £94,000)	24,000
	381,000
Less: Capital losses b/f	(12,400)
Net chargeable gains	368,600
Less: Annual exempt amount	(10,600)
Taxable gains	358,000
Capital gains tax (£358,000 × 10%)	35,800

Tutorial note

Entrepreneurs' relief is available as Delia is disposing of her whole business and she has owned the business assets for the 12 months prior to the disposal. The gains are therefore taxed at 10%.

(iii) **Value added tax implications of sale**

Output VAT will not have to be charged on the value of inventory and other assets on which VAT has been claimed, since Delia's business is being transferred as a going concern.

Delia will have to inform HMRC by 30 April 2013 that she has ceased to make taxable supplies. They will then cancel her VAT registration as from 31 March 2013.

Tutorial note

The sale of Delia's business qualifies as the transfer of a going concern if it is the transfer of a complete business, there is no significant break in trading, the same type of trade is carried on and the new owner is VAT registered.

(b) (i) **Disposal on 30 April 2013**

Income tax implications

Year of cessation now becomes 2013/14, and penultimate year becomes 2012/13, which assesses the accounts for the year ended 31 August 2012.

Delia's trading income assessments will therefore be as follows:

		£	£
2012/13	Year ended 31 August 2012		77,200
2013/14	Period ended 30 April 2013		
	(£58,500 + £9,000)	67,500	
	Balancing charge	95,000	
		———	
		162,500	
	Relief for overlap profits	(24,200)	
		———	138,300

The balancing payment of the related income tax liability will be due on 31 January 2015 rather than on 31 January 2014, although payments on account will be required on 31 January and 31 July 2014 based on the 2012/13 assessment.

The personal allowance will be reduced to £Nil for 2013/14, as the adjusted net income will be greater than £116,210 in that year. The income for 2012/13 will be taxed at 20% and 40%. In 2013/14 only £33,300 (£138,300 + £45,000 – £150,000) will be taxed at 50%.

Therefore the overall liability will be lower if the cessation occurs in 2013/14 rather than 2012/13.

National insurance implications

Delia will have to pay the higher rate (9%) of Class 4 NIC contributions on profits between £7,605 and £42,475 for 2012/13 and 2013/14 rather than just for 2012/13. However, she will also save £7,605 at 2% as the primary threshold of £7,605 will be available again in 2013/14.

This is an additional cost of £2,441 ((£42,475 – £7,605) at 7% (9% – 2%)).

Delia will also be liable to another 4 weeks of Class 2 NICs.

Capital gains tax implications

There would be no difference in the CGT payable.

The CGT liability will be due on 31 January 2015 rather than on 31 January 2014.

Conclusion

A disposal date of 30 April 2013 is likely overall to be beneficial because of the postponement of the payment of a substantial proportion of the tax by one year.

(ii) **Consideration as ordinary shares in Fastfood Ltd**

If the consideration is in the form of ordinary shares then the total capital gains of £381,000 will automatically be rolled over against the base cost of the shares in Fastfood Ltd.

This is because Delia's business is transferred as a going concern, and all of the business assets are being transferred and accordingly incorporation relief applies. The fact that Delia does not become an employee or director of Fastfood Ltd is irrelevant for the purposes of incorporation relief.

The base cost of her shares in Fastfood Ltd will be £469,000 (£850,000 – £381,000).

If Delia plans to make regular disposals of the shares over the next ten years, she needs to be aware that on the subsequent disposals of the shares in Fastfood Ltd, Entrepreneurs' relief will not be available. This is because although she has a shareholding of ≥ 5%, she is not an employee of the company.

She will however be able to minimise the CGT impact if she ensures she utilises her annual exempt amount each year. However, gains overall would be significantly lower if Delia elects to disapply incorporation relief. She would then benefit from Entrepreneurs' relief on all of the gains arising on the disposal of the business as in paragraph (a)(ii).

However, Delia should also consider the commercial aspects of the transaction and balance the chance of cash now against the relatively risky nature of holding an investment quoted on the AIM.

Key answer tips

Remember to take commercial and investment factors into account when giving advice.

9 DAVID AND PATRICIA

Key answer tips

This question is based on the common scenario of a sole trader wanting to bring his wife into business with him either as an employee or as a partner.

They key tax planning point in part (a) is that David is a higher rate taxpayer, whereas his wife is a basic rate taxpayer and has no other income. If profits can be transferred from David to Patricia, then there will be an income tax saving.

Remember that partners can choose how to split their profits, so David would not have to take on his wife as an equal partner.

Remember also that if David employs his wife, she will be subject to Class 1 NICs and David, as her employer, will have to pay Class 1 employers' NICs. However, partners in a partnership are taxed in the same way as sole traders, so each will pay Class 2 and 4 NICs – with no employers' NICs - which should also result in a tax saving.

Make sure you know the key dates for self assessment – these were worth 4 easy marks in part (a) (ii).

Part (b) covers some fairly basic loss relief planning.

(a)   (i)   **Taxation implications for David of involving his wife in the business**

Employing Patricia

If David employs his wife, he is only able to claim a tax deduction for the salary paid if he pays her the market rate. As she was earning £13,200 (£1,100 × 12) as a bookkeeper previously, this would appear to be the market rate.

The business must pay employers' National Insurance Contributions (NIC) at 13.8% on her gross salary in excess of £7,488 per annum.

The salary and NICs will both be tax deductible expenses for the business.

Patricia will have to pay NICs at 12% as an employee on her salary in excess of £7,605, and will be taxed on her salary under PAYE.

Setting up a partnership

If David and Patricia are in partnership, then the profit sharing ratios can be in any proportion they decide. The ratio does not have to reflect their respective input to the business provided there is a proper partnership agreement and Patricia takes an active part in the business.

The ratio can therefore be chosen so as to reduce their overall tax liability, and may even be changed at a later date if their circumstances change.

David has property business income of £45,000 from 2013/14 onwards and so he will be a higher rate taxpayer. Patricia has no other income. The maximum income tax saving will therefore be generated where Patricia's share equates to £42,475 (that is, equivalent to the personal allowance £8,105 plus the basic rate band of £34,370).

This would imply a profit sharing ratio of 3:7 (David:Patricia) as £42,475 is approximately 70% of £60,600.

In addition, Patricia will pay NIC at a maximum rate of 9%, compared to 12% for her and 13.8% by the business, as an employee.

Calculation of income tax and NICs under each option

1   **Patricia as an employee**

Employment costs relating to Patricia

	£
Salary	13,200
Employers' NIC (£13,200 – £7,488) × 13.8%	788
Employment costs	13,988

This amount is tax deductible for the business.

Income tax and NIC payable by David

	£	£
Trading income (£60,600 − £13,988)		46,612
Income tax (£46,612 × 40%)		18,645
Class 2 NIC (52 × £2.65)		138
Class 4 NIC (£42,475 − £7,605) × 9%	3,138	
(£46,612 − £42,475) × 2%	83	
		3,221
Total income tax and NIC		22,004

Income tax and NIC payable by Patricia

	£
Salary	13,200
Less: Personal allowance	(8,105)
Taxable income	5,095
Income tax (£5,095 × 20%)	1,019
Class 1 NICs (£13,200 − £7,605) × 12%	671
Total income tax and NIC	1,690
Total tax payable by the couple (£22,004 + £1,690 + £788)	24,482

2   **Patricia as a partner, sharing profits 3:7 (David:Patricia)**

The profits for a full year will be allocated £18,180 (£60,600 × 30%) to David and £42,420 (£60,600 × 70%) to Patricia.

Income tax and NIC payable by David

	£
Income tax (£18,180 × 40%)	7,272
Class 2 NIC (52 × £2.65)	138
Class 4 NIC (£18,180 − £7,605) × 9%	952
Total income tax and NIC	8,362

Income tax and NIC payable by Patricia

	£
Trading income	42,420
Less: Personal allowance	(8,105)
Taxable income	34,315

	£
Income tax (£34,315 × 20%)	6,863
Class 2 NIC (52 × £2.65)	138
Class 4 NIC (£42,420 − £7,605) × 9%	3,133
Total income tax and NIC	10,134
Total tax payable by the couple (£8,362 + £10,134)	18,496

Conclusion

By operating as a partnership the couple can achieve a tax saving of £5,986 (£24,482 − £18,496).

Tutorial note

The profit sharing ratio of 3:7 is not the only answer that would have been acceptable.

You may have assumed that David and Patricia would just split profits equally, which would score the same number of marks for the calculations.

However, you will be given credit for the recognition that an unequal split of profits between David and Patricia would reduce the income tax payable by the couple (using Patricia's lower rate bands).

(ii) **Tax administration**

Notification of new source of income in 2012/13

For income tax purposes HMRC should be notified by 6 October 2013 (i.e. within six months from the end of the tax year in which the liability on the new source of income arises).

Submission of tax return

David's self assessment return due filing date for 2012/13 depends upon whether he intends to file electronically or in paper format.

If he decides to file in paper format it is due on the later of:

(1) 31 October 2013

(2) 3 months after the notice to file the return is issued.

If he files electronically it is due on the later of:

(1) 31 January 2014

(2) 3 months after the notice to file the return is issued.

Payment dates

Income tax is normally payable as follows:

31 January in the tax year

31 July following the tax year

$\Big\}$ Payments on account

31 January following the tax year   Balancing payment

However, as the payments on account are each based on 50% of the previous year's income tax and NIC liability, this is not possible in the first tax year.

Thus, if the business starts to trade on 1 January 2013, the first payment on account is due on 31 January 2013, but no payment will be made, as trade has just commenced. The second payment on account is due on 31 July 2013, but again, it is unlikely that any payments will be made as there was no liability in the prior year. The balancing payment is due on 31 January 2014, and the total liability will be paid on that date.

(b)   **Loss reliefs available to David**

The loss relief options available to David are as follows:

(1)   Relief against total income of the previous three tax years on a first in first out (FIFO) basis.

(2)   Relief against total income (and gains, if required) of the current tax year and/or the previous tax year.

(3)   Relief by carrying forward against future trading profits of the same trade.

When deciding which loss relief to take, consideration should be given to the rate of tax saved, to the timing of any relief/repayment and to avoiding the loss of personal allowances.

The profit sharing ratio is 50:50, so the loss arising to David (and Patricia) in 2012/13 is £20,000 each.

David – the most beneficial claim

David has had employment income of £45,000 per annum since 2002, with £33,750 (£3,750 × 9 months) in 2012/13. David will also have total income of £75,300 (£45,000 property income + £30,300 equal share of trading profits) from 2013/14 onwards.

The tax savings achieved under each option is as follows:

(1)   Carry the loss back to the tax year 2009/10 and receive a repayment of income tax of £4,505 (W1)

(2)   Use the loss against total income in 2012/13 resulting in a tax saving of £4,000 (W2) or against total income in 2011/12 resulting in a tax saving of £4,505 (W1); or

(3)   carry forward the loss against trading profits in 2013/14 saving tax of £8,000 (W3).

Ignoring the timing of tax saving, the greatest tax is saved if the loss is carried forward to 2013/14.

Key answer tips

When explaining the reliefs available, make sure you are very specific about exactly what type(s) of income the loss can be set against, and in which tax years. Remember that the two key objectives are to save as much tax as possible, but also to get relief as soon as possible.

The tax savings could be calculated by doing full income tax computations with and without the loss, but it is quicker to just compare the taxable income with and without the loss to see what rate of tax the loss would save in each case.

Workings

(W1)　**Using the loss in 2009/10 or 2011/12**

	Before loss relief £	After loss relief £
Employment income	45,000	45,000
Less: Loss relief	–	(20,000)
Net income	45,000	25,000
Less: Personal allowance	(8,105)	(8,105)
Taxable income	36,895	16,895
(£36,895 – £34,370)	2,525 × 40%	1,010
(£20,000 – £2,525)	17,475 × 20%	3,495
Tax saved	20,000	4,505

Tutorial note

The basic rate of tax saved by carrying the loss back would actually be higher, but the question says assume that the rates and allowances for 2011/12 apply throughout.

(W2)　**Using the loss in 2012/13**

	Before loss relief £	After loss relief £
Employment income (9 × £3,750)	33,750	33,750
Trading profit	Nil	Nil
	33,750	33,750
Less: Loss relief	–	(20,000)
Net income	33,750	13,750
Less: Personal allowance	(8,105)	(8,105)
Taxable income	25,645	5,645
Tax saved: (£20,000 × 20%)		4,000

(W3)   **Using the loss in 2013/14**

	Before loss relief £	After loss relief £
Trading profit (£60,600 × 50%)	30,300	30,300
Less: Loss relief	–	(20,000)
	30,300	10,300
Property income	45,000	45,000
Net income	75,300	55,300
Less: Personal allowance	(8,105)	(8,105)
Taxable income	67,195	47,195
Tax saved: (£20,000 × 40%)		8,000

10   THE STILETTO PARTNERSHIP (ADAPTED)

Key answer tips

This question is really two separate questions.

The first part is about incorporation of a partnership, but this time deals with the income tax and national insurance implications instead of the more common CGT implications.

This section is really just asking you to look at the effect of delaying cessation of trade until the following tax year, and tests your basic F6 knowledge of closing year assessments. There is a slight twist in that Clint reaches the age of 65 during 2012/13 – you need to think about how this will impact on his income tax and NICs.

The second part is a written section on various overseas aspects of tax for companies and individuals. Overseas aspects of tax are very popular in P6, so you must make sure you learn the rules.

There were 2 easy marks available here for structuring your answer as a report.

(a)   (i)   **Clint's assessable trading income**

Selling the business on 30 April 2013 rather than 28 February 2013 would mean that the final year of trading would be 2013/14 rather than 2012/13.

Clint's taxable trading income under each of the alternative cessation dates is as follows:

	2012/13 £	2013/14 £
Sale of business on 28 February (W)	53,723	–
Sale of business on 30 April (W)	35,708	24,935

(ii)   **The implications of delaying the sale of the business**

The implications of delaying the sale of the business until 30 April would have been as follows:

- Clint would have received an additional two months of profits amounting to £6,920 (£20,760 x 1/3)
- Clint's trading income in 2012/13 would have been reduced by £18,015 (£53,723 – £35,708), much of which would have been subject to income tax at 40%. His additional trading income in 2013/14 of £24,935 would all have been taxed at 20%.
- Clint is entitled to the personal age allowance of £10,500 in both years. However, it is abated by £1 for every £2 by which his total income exceeds £25,400.
- Once Clint's total income exceeds £30,190 (£25,400 + ((£10,500 – £8,105) x 2)), his personal allowance will be reduced to the standard amount of £8,105.

    Accordingly, the increased personal allowance would not be available in 2012/13 regardless of the year in which the business was sold. It is available in 2013/14 although part would have been wasted if the sale of the business had been delayed.

- Clint's Class 4 national insurance contributions in 2012/13 would have been reduced due to the fall in the level of his trading income. However, much of the saving would be at 2% only. Clint is not liable to Class 4 national insurance contribuions in 2013/14 as he is 65 at the start of the year.
- Changing the date on which the business was sold would have had no effect on Clint's Class 2 liability as he is not required to make class 2 contributions once he is 65 years old.

Working: Trading income assessments

Cessation on 28 February 2013

Business ceases in 2012/13.

Penultimate year is 2011/12 and would have assessed y/e 30 June 2011 profits.

Final assessment in 2012/13 therefore assesses profits from 1 July 2011 to the date of cessation, less overlap profits.

2012/13	Total £		Clint's share £
Year ended 30 June 2012	107,124		
1 July 2012 to 28 February 2013	96,795		
	203,919	x 1/3	67,973
Less: Overlap profits			(14,250)
Trading income assessment			53,723

Cessation on 30 April 2013

Business ceases in 2013/14

Penultimate year is 2012/13 and would assess y/e 30 June 2012 profits.

Final assessment in 2013/14 will assess profits from 1 July 2012 to the date of cessation, less overlap profits.

2012/13	Total £		Clint's share £
Year ended 30 June 2012	107,124	x 1/3	35,708
2013/14			
1 July 2012 to 28 February 2013	96,795		
1 March to 30 April 2013	20,760		
	117,555	x 1/3	39,185
Less: Overlap profits			(14,250)
Trading income assessment			24,935

(b) **Report to the management of Razor Ltd**

To	The management of Razor Ltd
From	Tax advisers
Date	6 June 2013
Subject	The proposed activities of Cutlass Inc

(i) **Rate of tax on profits of Cutlass Inc**

When considering the manner in which the profits of Cutlass Inc will be taxed it must be recognised that the system of corporation tax in Sharpenia is the same as that in the UK.

The profits of Cutlass Inc will be subject to corporation tax in the country in which it is resident or where it has a permanent establishment. It is desirable for the profits of Cutlass Inc to be taxed in the UK rather than in Sharpenia as the rate of corporation tax in the UK on annual profits of £120,000 will be 20% whereas in Sharpenia the rate of tax would be 38%.

Residency of Cutlass Inc

Cutlass Inc will be resident in Sharpenia, because it is incorporated there. However, it will also be resident in the UK if it is centrally managed and controlled from the UK. For this to be the case, Amy and Ben should hold the company's board meetings in the UK.

Under the double tax treaty between the UK and Sharpenia, a company resident in both countries is treated as being resident in the country where it is effectively managed and controlled. For Cutlass Inc to be treated as UK resident under the treaty, Amy and Ben would need to ensure that all key management and commercial decisions are made in the UK and not in Sharpenia.

Permanent establishment

A permanent establishment is a fixed place of business, including an office, factory or workshop, through which the business of an enterprise is carried on. A permanent establishment will also exist in a country if contracts in the company's name are habitually concluded there.

The trading profits of Cutlass Inc will normally be taxable in Sharpenia if they are derived from a permanent establishment in Sharpenia even if it can be established that Cutlass Inc is UK resident under the double tax treaty.

Double taxation

If Cutlass Inc is UK resident but has a permanent establishment in Sharpenia, its trading profits will be subject to corporation tax in both the UK and Sharpenia with double tax relief available in the UK. The double tax relief will be the lower of the UK tax and the Sharpenian tax on the trading profits. Accordingly, as the rate of tax is higher in Sharpenia than it is in the UK, there will be no UK tax to pay on the company's trading profits and the rate of tax on the profits would be the rate in Sharpenia (i.e. 38%).

Alternatively, Cutlass Inc could make an election for the profits from the overseas permanent establishment to be exempt in the UK. However, this would not affect the tax position as the double tax relief means that there is no tax to pay in the UK in any case (as explained above). Again, the rate of tax on the profits would be the rate in Sharpenia (i.e. 38%).

If Cutlass Inc is UK resident and does **not** have a permanent establishment in Sharpenia, its profits will be taxable in the UK at the rate of 20% and not in Sharpenia.

(ii) **Value added tax (VAT)**

Goods exported are zero-rated. Razor Ltd must retain appropriate documentary evidence that the export has taken place.

Razor Ltd must account for VAT on the value of the goods purchased from Cutlass Inc at the time the goods are brought into the UK. The VAT payable should be included as deductible input tax on the company's VAT return.

(iii) **Amy's UK income tax position**

Amy will remain UK resident and ordinarily resident as she is not leaving the UK permanently or for a complete tax year under a full time contract of employment and she is UK domiciled.

Accordingly, she will continue to be subject to UK tax on her worldwide income including her earnings in respect of the duties she performs for Cutlass Inc. The earnings from these duties will also be taxable in Sharpenia as the income arises in that country.

The double tax treaty between the UK and Sharpenia will either exempt the employment income in one of the two countries or give double tax relief for the tax paid in Sharpenia. The double tax relief will be the lower of the UK tax and the Sharpenian tax on the income from Cutlass Inc.

Amy will not be subject to UK income tax on the expenses borne by Cutlass Inc in respect of her flights to and from Sharpenia provided her journeys are wholly and exclusively for the purposes of performing her duties in Sharpenia.

The amounts paid by Cutlass Inc in respect of Amy's family travelling to Sharpenia will be subject to UK income tax as Amy will not be absent from the UK for a continuous period of at least 60 days.

Key answer tips

You should use headings in your report, particularly in part (i), to make it easier for the marker to follow. You must also make sure that you apply your knowledge to the scenario, which you can show by using the names of the people and companies involved in your answer. If you just write out the rules you will not score many marks.

11   FRANK COLTRANE (ADAPTED) *Walk in the footsteps of a top tutor*

Key answer tips

This question is really three unconnected questions. It is therefore important to make sure you are clear about which information is relevant to which part of the question.

The first part involves the capital gains tax implications of the disposal of a business in exchange for a mixture of cash and shares (applying Entrepreneurs' relief), and disposal of those shares. There is also a possible gift of shares to Frank's wife prior to disposal to consider and advise on.

The second part covers corporation tax self assessment, and is largely just F6 level knowledge. There were 11 marks available here, which shows how important it is to revise all of the F6 level information as well as learning the new areas covered at P6.

The final part was more F6 level detail on VAT, covering VAT groups, zero-rated companies and overseas aspects.

The highlighted words in the written sections are key phrases that markers are looking for.

Tutor's top tips

Read the email in the question carefully. The examiner gives you some helpful tips on how to approach this part of the question. You are told that they have already agreed to disclaim incorporation relief, which means you do not have to consider that in your answer, and makes the calculations a lot simpler!

Be careful to answer the questions being asked. For example, in terms of the potential gift to his wife, you are asked for all the tax implications, not just the capital gains tax. Also, you are only asked for the maximum potential tax saving, not to advise how many shares should be transferred to her.

Remember you are acting for Frank Coltrane, and you are not concerned with the tax position of Tenor plc.

Make sure that you show your workings clearly, so that if you do make some mistakes you can still gain marks for consistency.

Notes for meeting with Frank Coltrane

(i)   **Capital gains tax liability**

Sale of the Alto business (2013/14)

	£
Gains qualifying for Entrepreneurs' relief	
Capital gains	420,000
Less: Capital losses	(155,000)
Net gains	265,000
Less: Annual exempt amount	(10,600)
Taxable gains	254,400
Capital gains tax (£254,400 x 10%) due on 31 January 2015	25,440

Sale of the Tenor plc shares (2016/17)

	£
Gains not qualifying for Entrepreneurs' relief	
Proceeds (assumed)	1,400,000
Less: Cost (£1,350,000 – £200,000)	(1,150,000)
Chargeable gain	250,000
Less: Annual exempt amount	(10,600)
Taxable gains	239,400
Capital gains tax (£239,400 x 28% (Note)) due on 31 January 2018	67,032

Tutorial note

Due to the level of Frank's salary, he is a higher rate taxpayer and will pay CGT at 28%.

Gift of shares in Tenor plc to wife

No gain or loss would arise for the purposes of capital gains tax.

The gift would be exempt for the purposes of inheritance tax.

The gift would not be subject to stamp duty.

When the shares are sold on 31 July 2016, the total gains of Coltrane and his wife would still be £250,000 (as above). This is because Mrs Coltrane will hold the shares with a base cost equal to Coltrane's base cost.

If Mrs Coltrane has not used her annual exempt amount, the total capital gains tax due would fall by £2,968 (£10,600 x 28%). A further saving may be made if Mrs Coltrane is a basic rate taxpayer, as some of the gain would then be taxed at 18% instead of 28%.

This strategy will only work if the gift of shares is absolute with no requirement for Mrs Coltrane to pay the sales proceeds to her husband.

Tutorial note

It may not seem initially obvious what the examiner is looking for in terms of the potential transfer to Frank's wife, however there were potentially 5 marks available here, and most can be easily attained.

It is worth considering the implications of the gift in terms of each tax, (i.e. CGT, IHT and stamp duty) and making any relevant comments. Make sure you do not limit your answer to the capital gains tax implications.

Nil gain nil loss transfers between husband and wife are a common planning tool and regularly examined, therefore you should be comfortable in commenting on these.

(ii) **Taxation position of Soprano Ltd**

Tutor's top tips

The information you are being asked for here is quite straightforward, however as there are 11 marks available it is important that you plan and structure your answer to ensure you have dealt with everything asked, and to make it easy for the examiner to give you credit.

Using headings and bullet points can help to make your answer easier to read, and therefore award marks. It is also important to apply what you say to the facts in the question and not just state the rules.

Taxable period

Soprano Ltd will pay corporation tax in respect of its accounting period.

This will normally be the same as the period for which it prepares its accounts (known as a period of account), i.e. the 12 months ending on 31 July each year, unless the company changes its accounting date.

If a set of accounts is prepared for a period of more than 12 months, it will be necessary to prepare two corporation tax computations; one for the first 12 months and one for the balance of the period of account.

Rate of corporation tax

The rate of corporation tax payable by Soprano Ltd depends on the level of its taxable profits.

The trading profits of Soprano Ltd for the year ending 31 July 2013, as reduced by trading losses brought forward, are expected to be between £15,000 (£80,000 – £65,000) and £45,000 (£110,000 – £65,000).

The rate of tax payable on its taxable profits by Soprano Ltd will be:

–   The main rate of 24% if its taxable profits exceed £42,857 (£1,500,000/35).

–   The main rate less marginal relief if its taxable profits are between £8,571 and £42,857. Marginal relief will be 1/100 x (£42,857 – taxable profits).

Tutorial note

Do not be caught out by the comment that 'the group is large for all aspects of corporation tax' – this does not mean that the company is automatically paying tax at the main rate (although it is a little misleading).

This comment was aimed at the potential transfer pricing issue (see below), not the tax rate.

Sufficient information is given in Frank's letter to calculate the maximum and minimum level of profits, and therefore determine the potential rate of tax.

Due date for payment of corporation tax

The due date depends on the rate of tax paid by Soprano Ltd.

If Soprano Ltd pays corporation tax at the main rate in both this year and the previous year, its liability will be payable quarterly.

One quarter of its corporation tax liability for the year ending 31 July 2013 will be due on each of the following dates.

–   14 February 2013
–   14 May 2013
–   14 August 2013
–   14 November 2013

Interest will be charged on any amounts paid late and will be credited in respect of any overpayments.

If Soprano Ltd does not pay corporation tax at the main rate (in either this year or the previous year), its liability will be payable on 1 May 2014 (nine months and one day after the end of the accounting period).

Pricing of services

Rules exist to prevent companies under common control using non-arm's length transfer prices to obtain a tax advantage. The rules apply to companies in the Tenor plc group because the group is large. If the prices charged to Soprano Ltd were to be increased in the manner proposed, the company would have to adjust the prices back to arm's length amounts in its corporation tax computation. Accordingly, the strategy would not succeed.

(iii) **Value added tax (VAT)**

Tutor's top tips

There are various aspects of VAT to deal with here, and again headings to break up your answer are very useful.

You need to connect the information that Soprano Ltd makes and sells baby clothes (per the letter) and the fact that baby clothes are zero-rated (per the email), to spot that the company will be in a net-recovery position for VAT purposes. Remember that zero-rated does not mean exempt, and you do not need to mention partial-exemption here.

Do not get caught up discussing the cash basis in detail – this is how Frank's existing business operates, not Soprano Ltd.

Accounting for VAT

Soprano Ltd makes zero rated supplies. This means that it does not charge VAT on its sales but can recover its input tax. It will therefore always be in a repayment situation.

It is accounting for VAT monthly (rather than quarterly or annually) in order to obtain the repayments of its input tax as fast as possible.

It would not be beneficial for it to account for VAT on a cash basis as this would delay the recovery of its input tax until it paid its creditors.

Group position

A group of companies is not automatically treated as a single entity for the purposes of VAT.

A decision must have been made not to include Soprano Ltd in a VAT group with other Tenor plc group companies.

This may be because Soprano Ltd makes zero rated supplies and therefore accounts for VAT monthly whilst the other group companies account for VAT quarterly.

Purchase of raw materials from South America

Soprano Ltd will have to pay output tax at the standard VAT rate when it brings the raw materials into the UK.

It will then reclaim the same amount as allowable input tax on its next VAT return.

Examiners comment's

Although the meeting notes were for the candidate's manager many candidates provided unnecessary detailed descriptions of the operation of the various taxes rather than simply addressing the particular issues in the question.

Part (i) required calculations of the capital gains tax on the sale of an unincorporated business and on a subsequent sale of shares together with advice on the tax implications of making a gift of shares to the spouse prior to the sale.

Candidates' performance on this part of the question was good. Most problems that arose were self-inflicted in that the question stated that incorporation relief would not be claimed but many candidates insisted on carrying out various calculations in relation to that relief. Also, a minority of candidates treated the sale of the unincorporated business as a sale of shares.

Most candidates handled the Entrepreneurs' relief and the inter-spouse transfer correctly.

Part (ii) was a test of the ability of candidates to identify their relevant knowledge of the basics of corporation tax and to summarise it in an appropriate manner.

This should have been a straightforward requirement and for many candidates it was. However, some candidates failed to stick to the point and so addressed unnecessary areas (for example group losses) whilst failing to cover all of the required issues.

There was also a failure to use the information in the question (for example, the predicted profit levels) in order to ensure that the comments made were specific to this particular company.

The transfer pricing aspect of this part was handled well.

Part (iii) required the consideration of a number of aspects of VAT and was done well. As always, weaker candidates could not resist writing down everything they knew rather than simply answering the question, particularly in connection with group registration.

ACCA marking scheme		
		Marks
(i)	Alto business	
	Capital losses and annual exempt amount	1.0
	Entrepreneurs' relief: tax at 10%	1.0
	Due date	0.5
	Tenor plc	
	Cost	1.0
	Annual exempt amount	0.5
	Tax and due date	1.0
	Potential gift to wife	
	Capital gains tax	1.0
	Inheritance tax	1.0
	Stamp duty	1.0
	Tax saving	1.0
	Gift must be absolute	1.0
		——
		10.0
	Maximum	8.0
		——

			Marks
(ii)	Taxable period		
	Basic rule		1.0
	Period of account of more than 12 months		1·5
	Rate of corporation tax		
	Taxable profits		1·5
	Main rate company		1.0
	Marginal company		1.5
	Due date for payment of corporation tax		
	Quarterly if large company		1.0
	The dates		1.0
	Interest		1.0
	Marginal company		1.0
	Transfer pricing		
	Rules apply with reason		2.0
	Evaluation of proposed strategy		0.5
			———
			13.0
		Maximum	11.0
			———
(iii)	Accounting for VAT		
	Repayment position		1.0
	Reason for monthly accounting		1.0
	Reason for accruals basis		1.0
	Group position		
	VAT group is not automatic		1.0
	Reason for excluding Soprano Ltd		1.0
	Purchase of raw materials from overseas		
	Account for output VAT		1.0
	Recover as input VAT		1.0
			———
			7.0
		Maximum	6.0
			———
Total			25
			———

12 DESIREE (ADAPTED) *Walk in the footsteps of a top tutor*

Key answer tips

This question covers the familiar scenario of sole trader versus company, with some easy marks on voluntary VAT registration.

Part (a) requires calculation of taxable profits or losses for the first three periods, and was almost identical to a requirement set in one of the compulsory questions in a previous exam.

Part (a)(ii) requires discussion of the use of losses for a sole trader compared to a company. This is a typical textbook scenario with no tricks, and you should score well here as long as you have learnt the rules.

Part (b) requires discussion of voluntary VAT registration – an F6 topic, but one which most students are likely to be happy with. There are also marks for discussing imports – a popular P6 topic. The danger here is not applying the discussion to the specific scenario.

The highlighted words in the written sections are key phrases that markers are looking for.

(a) (i) **Taxable profit/allowable loss for each of the first three taxable periods**

Tutor's top tips

Think carefully before attempting this section.

If the business is unincorporated, the losses must be matched to tax years before reliefs can be claimed.

However, if the business is set up as a company, the loss reliefs will be for chargeable accounting periods, so no further adjustments will be needed.

Make sure that your answer is clearly labelled!

Business is unincorporated

	Loss	Assessable profit
	£	£
2013/14 – Actual basis (1 September 2013 to 5 April 2014) (£46,000 × 7/10)	(32,200)	Nil
2014/15 – First 12 months (1 September 2013 to 31 August 2014)		
1 September 2013 to 30 June 2014 – Loss	(46,000)	
Loss allocated to 2013/14	32,200	
1 July 2014 to 31 August 2014 – Profit (£22,000 × 2/12)	3,667	
	(10,133)	Nil
2015/16 – Current year basis (Year ending 30 June 2015)		22,000

Tutorial note

Remember that when you apply the opening year rules to losses there is no overlap!

Losses can only be relieved once, and if they are matched with two tax years in the assessments, they must be removed from the later year.

Business is operated via a company

	Loss	Assessable profit
	£	£
Ten months ending 30 June 2014	(46,000)	Nil
Year ending 30 June 2015		22,000
Year ending 30 June 2016		64,000

(ii) **Advice on whether or not the business should be incorporated**

Tutor's top tips

You must learn the loss reliefs available to individuals and companies, as these often feature in exam questions.

Don't write about all the loss reliefs available; just pick the ones that are relevant. For example, in this question, there is no point in talking about reliefs on cessation of trade.

When writing about loss reliefs, make sure that you use very specific language. For example, don't just say 'losses can be carried forward'; say that 'losses can be carried forward against the first available future trading profits from the same trade'.

You must also apply the reliefs to the scenario.

The two key considerations for both the unincorporated business and the company are:

– Amount of tax saved, and
– Timing of the relief

There is no point in preparing full computations of the tax saved, as the question states that detailed calculations are not required.

Business is operated via a company

If the business is operated via a company, the loss of the ten month period ending 30 June 2014 will be carried forward for offset against future trading profits of the same trade.

The earliest that any of the company's losses will be relieved is the year ending 30 June 2015 thus reducing the corporation tax payable on 1 April 2016.

However, the tax savings will only arise if the budgeted profits are achieved. If the business does not achieve profitability the losses will be wasted.

Business is unincorporated

If the business is unincorporated, the loss in each of the two tax years can be offset against:

- The total income of the year of loss and/or the previous year
- The total income of the three years prior to the year of loss starting with the earliest of the three years.

This enables Desiree to obtain immediate relief for the losses.

Desiree has employment income in 2013/14 of only £10,000 (£60,000 × 2/12) together with bank interest of less than £1,000. Most of this income will be covered by her personal allowance.

Her total income in earlier years is her salary of £60,000 and the bank interest. Accordingly, she should offset the losses against the income of 2012/13 and earlier years rather than the income of 2013/14.

The loss of 2013/14 could be offset against the total income of 2012/13 (the previous year) or 2010/11 (the first of the three years prior to 2013/14).

The loss of 2014/15 could be offset against the total income of 2011/12 (the first of the three years prior to 2014/15).

This will obtain full relief for the losses at a mixture of basic and higher rates of tax.

Conclusion

Desiree's primary objective is the most beneficial use of the loss.

She should therefore run the business as an unincorporated sole trader in order to obtain relief for the losses as soon as possible.

Tutor's top tips

Make sure that you state your conclusion. As long as it is consistent with your analysis, you will be given credit.

(b)   **Financial advantages and disadvantages of Desiree registering voluntarily for VAT**

Tutor's top tips

This section of the question is mainly based on F6 knowledge and is very straightforward.

You could attempt this part of the question first, just in case you run out of time on part (a).

Advantages

- Registering for VAT will enable the business to recover input tax, where possible, on expenses and capital expenditure.

This will reduce the costs incurred by the business thus reducing its losses and its capital allowances.

- The VAT incurred on the fees paid to the market research consultants in March 2013 can be recovered as pre-registration input tax.

  The payment in November 2012 is more than six months prior to registration and therefore the input tax in relation to it cannot be recovered.

Disadvantages

- The business will have to charge its customers VAT at 20%.

  This will represent an increase in the prices charged to those customers who are unable to recover VAT, i.e. domestic customers and non-registered business customers.

  Desiree may need to consider reducing prices in order to reduce the impact of the additional VAT on these customers.

Treatment of non-EU imports

- VAT will be payable by Desireer at the place of importation.

- If the goods are kept in a bonded warehouse or free zone, then the payment of VAT is delayed until they are removed from the warehouse/zone.

- Desiree can then reclaim the VAT as input tax on the VAT return for the period during which the goods were imported.

Examiner's comments

This question concerned the choice of business vehicle for a new business that was anticipating initial trading losses and the implications of registering voluntarily for VAT. It was in three parts.

Part (a) (i) required candidates to calculate the taxable trading profit or allowable trading loss depending onwhether the business vehicle was a company or an unincorporated business. The majority of candidates scored high marks here although some had difficulty calculating the figure for the second tax year of an unincorporated business based on the first 12 months of trading. Those who did not do so well simply did not know the basic mechanical rules and either missed out this part of the question or tried to make it up. The opening and closing years rules for unincorporated traders are examined regularly and candidates preparing for future sittings are likely to benefit from being able to handle them.

Part (a) (ii) required candidates to provide a 'thorough and detailed explanation' of the manner in which the losses could be used depending on the choice of business vehicle. This part of the question was done well by almost all of the candidates who attempted it. In order to maximise marks here it was necessary to be precise in terms of language used. For example, it was not sufficient to state that losses can be carried forward against future profits. Instead, candidates needed to state that losses could be carried forward for offset against future profits of *the same trade*.

There was also a requirement to state which business structure would best satisfy the client's objectives. The mark available for this was missed by those candidates who had stopped thinking and were simply writing down everything they knew about loss relief.

The other difficulty which candidates had with this part of the question was a failure to recognise that not all possible loss reliefs were available due to the particular facts of the question. Candidates should ensure that they do not write at length about matters which are irrelevant.

The final part of the question concerned the 'financial' advantages and disadvantages of registering voluntarily for VAT. Many candidates let themselves down by not reading the question carefully such that they simply listed all the advantages and disadvantages they could think of without focusing on the word financial or the particular facts surrounding the client. This meant that they missed the possibility of recovering pre-registration VAT, which was often the difference between an OK mark and a good mark.

ACCA marking scheme					Marks
(a)	(i)	Business is unincorporated			
			Application of opening year rules		2·5
			Losses counted once only		1.0
		Business is operated via a company			1.0
					4·5
				Maximum	4.0
	(ii)	Business is operated via a company			2·5
		Business is unincorporated			
			Reliefs available		2·5
			Application to Desiree's position		3.0
		Conclusion			1.0
					9.0
				Maximum	9.0
(b)		Advantages			
			Recovery of input tax		1·5
			Pre registration input tax		1·5
		Disadvantages			1·5
		VAT treatment of non-EU imports			3.0
					7·5
				Maximum	7.0
Total					20

13 VINE (ADAPTED) *Walk in the footsteps of a top tutor*

Key answer tips

This question mainly covers incorporation, a popular exam scenario.

Part (a) covers capital allowances, and is very straightforward.

Part (b) deals with the disposal of shares after incorporation, and requires calculation of the gain at incorporation first. This section is very similar to the first part of question 3 of the pilot paper.

Part (c) covers the tax implications of company bicycles, child care vouchers and free breakfasts. These are not areas that are tested regularly, but are only worth four marks.

The highlighted words in the written sections are key phrases that markers are looking for.

(a) **Capital allowances**

The transfer of the equipment to Passata Ltd

The market value of the equipment exceeds its tax written down value such that a sale would normally result in additional taxable income for Vine in the form of a balancing charge.

However, because Vine and Passata Ltd will be connected persons (Vine will control Passata Ltd), an election is available to transfer the equipment at tax written down value, rather than market value, such that no balancing charge will arise.

Tutorial note

To be eligible to transfer assets at TWDV (Tax written down value), the owner of the business must be 'connected' to the new company, which means that they must control the shares in the new company.

A claim must be made for this treatment within two years of the incorporation.

The false ceiling to be installed in the supermarket premises

For the purposes of capital allowances, the meaning of the term machinery is taken to be its ordinary, everyday meaning. The meaning of the term plant has been considered in many cases and certain items are dealt with by statute.

Case law tends to draw a distinction between items that perform a function in the operation of the business, and may therefore be plant, and those which comprise the setting in which the business is carried on, which are not plant.

It has been held that a false ceiling does not perform a function but is merely part of the setting in which the business is carried on. Accordingly, the false ceiling will not qualify as plant and machinery.

Tutorial note

You are not expected to know details of specific tax cases in the exam, but you are expected to be aware of some of the key decisions made.

Even if you had not come across false ceilings before, you could have scored the marks here by applying basic tax principles.

(b) **The proposed sale of the shares to the store manager**

Tutor's top tips

Before calculating the chargeable gain on the sale of the shares, you need to work out the base cost of the shares.

The base cost of the shares will be the market value of the assets exchanged for shares, less any gains deferred on incorporation.

The gains deferred on incorporation will be the total net chargeable gains arising multiplied by the value of shares acquired, then divided by the total value of the consideration received.

You need to approach the calculations in the following order:

1.   *Calculate the net chargeable gains on the incorporation of the business.*

2.   *Calculate the gains deferred, i.e. the incorporation relief.*

   This is tricky – the question states that the consideration will be a mixture of shares and cash/loans, such that there is no capital gains tax liability.

   A gain equal to the capital losses plus the annual exempt amount should therefore remain chargeable, and the rest will be deferred.

3.   *Once the deferred gain has been calculated, the value of the shares can be calculated from the following formula:*

   Value of shares/total value = incorporation relief

4.   *The final step is to deduct the incorporation relief from the value of the shares, to give the CGT base cost of the shares.*

Chargeable gain on the disposal of shares

	£
Proceeds	64,000
Less: Cost (20% × £187,614 (W1))	(37,523)
Chargeable gain	26,477

Tutor's top tips

Even if you did not manage to correctly calculate the base cost of the shares, you will score marks for consistency here!

Entrepreneurs' relief

Entrepreneurs' relief would reduce the tax rate on the gain to 10%.

However, it is only available if the shares have been owned for at least a year.

Accordingly, Vine should delay the sale until August in order to qualify for the relief.

Tutor's top tips

There is a clue in the question that Entrepreneurs' relief is not currently available: the examiner asks you to suggest a minor change that would reduce the chargeable gain.

The timing of a sale is often relevant for CGT, and may affect the availability of reliefs, annual exemption, and also the payment date.

Workings

(W1) **Base cost of the shares**

	£
Value of the business transferred	320,000
Amount left on loan account (W2)	(70,886)
Market value of the shares received	249,114
Less: Incorporation relief (W3)	(61,500)
Base cost of shares	187,614

(W2) **Loan account**

	£
Value of the business transferred	320,000
Market value of shares received (W3)	(249,114)
Loan account required	70,886

(W3) **Incorporation relief**

	£
Gains on assets transferred:	
Premises (£260,000 – £205,000)	55,000
Goodwill	24,000
Total net chargeable gains	79,000
Less: Capital loss available	(6,900)
Annual exempt amount	(10,600)
Incorporation relief	61,500

Therefore to calculate the market value of the shares to be received to achieve incorporation relief of £61,500:

Incorporation relief =

(MV of shares / MV of business) × Total net chargeable gains

£61,500 = (MV of shares / £320,000) × £79,000

MV of shares = £249,114

Tutorial note

Entrepreneurs' relief is not relevant on the incorporation of the business as Vine will not have any gains remaining taxable.

(c) **The tax implications of the active supermarket marketing strategy**

Tutor's top tips

Some of the benefits covered here are rather obscure, and have not been tested in the past.

However, even if you did not know the rules, you could still score some marks by applying basic principles:

- *bicycles are plant and machinery, so would qualify for capital allowances;*
- *staff costs are generally allowable deductions for the employer;*
- *there is a tax free mileage allowance for bicycles just like there is for cars.*

Passata Ltd

The cost of the bicycles will qualify for capital allowances.

The mileage allowance paid to employees, the cost of the child care vouchers and the cost of the breakfasts will be tax allowable expenses.

Employees

Bicycles

The loan of the bicycles will not give rise to a taxable benefit provided they are used mainly for travel to and from work and for business purposes.

Mileage allowance

A tax-free mileage allowance of up to 20 pence per mile can be paid to employees who use their own bicycles for business purposes.

The employees of Passata Ltd will be entitled to a tax deduction from their employment income if the company pays them less than this amount.

Accordingly, with the mileage rate set at 15 pence per mile, they will be entitled to a tax deduction of five pence per business mile cycled.

Child care vouchers

The child care vouchers are less than £55 per week, so will be tax free for any employees who are basic rate taxpayers.

However, higher rate taxpayers are only entitled to £28 per week tax free and thus would be taxed on a benefit of £12 (£40 – £28) per week.

The tax free allowance for additional rate taxpayers is lower still at £22 per week, so any employees in this category would have a taxable benefit of £18 (£40 – £22) per week.

Breakfasts

The provision of free breakfasts on designated cycle to work days does not give rise to a taxable benefit.

Examiner's comments

This question concerned the incorporation of a business and the provision of a number of employee benefits. It was in three parts.

Part (a) concerned the capital allowances implications of incorporating the business and the allowances available in respect of a false ceiling to be installed in a supermarket. It was not done particularly well. Many candidates thought that on incorporation the assets would be transferred to the company at tax written down value whereas the correct position is that a balancing charge would arise unless a succession election were entered into. A number of candidates wrote that a balancing charge or a balancing allowance would arise when it was clear from the facts that it would be a balancing charge.

Part (b) required candidates to prepare calculations in order to determine the base cost of the shares received on incorporation and the subsequent gain on the sale of some of the shares. Common errors here included calculating a capital loss on the equipment (not available due to the availability of capital allowances) and giving entrepreneurs' relief on the incorporation (not available as the business had not been owned for a year). The quality of the answers to this part of the question depended on the clarity of the candidates' knowledge. There were many candidates who knew how to perform the necessary calculations and whose only common error was the failure to deduct the gain relieved on incorporation from the base cost of the shares. There was then another group of candidates who had no clear knowledge of the rules and consequently did not score well.

Candidates were asked to suggest a minor change in relation to the sale of shares that would reduce the chargeable gain. Suggestions needed to be sensible and commercial and not, as put forward by a number of candidates, 'reduce the selling price of the shares'.

The final part of the question concerned the provision of bicycles and other related benefits to employees.

Candidates were asked to outline the tax implications for the company and its employees of the various benefits. There were four benefits, so all answers should have consisted of eight brief elements. Unfortunately, most answers were not that well organised with candidates addressing the issues in what was often a haphazard manner such that they did not score as well as they could have done.

	ACCA marking scheme		Marks
(a)	Transfer of the equipment		2.5
	False ceiling		2.0
			———
			4.5
		Maximum	4.0
			———
(b)	Incorporation:		
	Gains arising		2.0
	Calculation of the loan account		3.0
	Gain on the sale of the shares		2.0
	Entrepreneurs' relief		2.0
			———
			9.0
			———
(c)	Passata Ltd		2.0
	Employees		
	Use of bicycles		1.0
	Mileage allowance		1·5
	Child care vouchers		2.0
	Free breakfasts		1.0
			———
			7.5
		Maximum	7.0
			———
Total			20
			———

CAPITAL TAXES

14 JOAN ARK

Key answer tips

This is a good practice question covering the IHT and CGT implications of lifetime gifts in part (a), with a written requirement on general IHT planning points in part (b).

The style of question is more like the Section B optional questions, although it is much longer than the Section B questions you will see under the current exam format.

When attempting part (a), the best approach is to run through each disposal twice: once to deal with the IHT implications, then again to deal with the CGT implications.

If you try to cover both taxes at once, it is very easy to get them confused! You must also make sure that your answer is clearly labelled so that the marker knows exactly which tax and which gift you are discussing.

(i) **IHT and CGT implications of gifts made in 2012/13**

(a) **Ordinary shares in Orleans plc**

IHT implications

For IHT purposes, a discretionary trust is a 'relevant property trust' and lifetime gifts into trusts are chargeable lifetime transfers.

BPR is not available as the shares are quoted and Joan does not have a controlling interest.

There would be two annual exemptions available against this gift, however, the question says to ignore the effect of the annual exemption.

The shares are valued at the lower of:

– Quarter up method = 147p (146 + ¼ × (150 −146)) per share, or

– Average of the marked bargains = 147.5p ((140 + 155) ÷ 2).

As Joan is to pay any IHT, the gift is a net gift and will be taxed at 25%.

	£
Transfer of value (£250,000 x 147p)	367,500
Less: BPR	(Nil)
Exemptions	(Nil)
Net chargeable transfer	367,500
Less: NRB	(325,000)
Taxable amount	42,500
IHT payable (£42,500 x 25%)	10,625

The tax payable by Joan is due by 30 April 2013.

Gross gift to c/f = (£367,500 + £10,625) = £378,125

If Joan dies within seven years, before 30 July 2019, a further IHT liability may arise.

CGT implications

There are no acquisitions on the same day or in the next 30 days, therefore, the disposal of shares is from the share pool as follows:

	Number	Cost
		£
1997 – Purchase	200,000	149,000
August 2010 – Purchase	75,000	69,375
July 2011 – Purchase	10,000	14,800
	————	————
	285,000	233,175
July 2012 – Gift	(250,000)	(204,539)
	————	————
	35,000	28,636
	————	————

The chargeable gain is calculated as follows:

	£
Market value	367,500
Less: Cost	(204,539)
	————
Chargeable gain	162,961
	————

Joan does not have a 5% interest in the company and therefore the shares are not qualifying business assets for gift relief purposes.

However, Joan can elect to defer all of the gain with a gift relief claim as there is an immediate charge to IHT.

Tutorial note

The full gain is deferred, therefore Entrepreneurs' relief is not a consideration here.

However, even if gift relief were not available, Entrepreneurs' relief would not be available as Joan is not an employee and does not own a 5% interest. The gain would therefore be taxed at 28% (as Joan is a higher rate taxpayer), not 10%.

(b) **Ordinary shares in Rouen Ltd**

IHT implications

Joan's gift of shares in Rouen Ltd in July 2012 to her son will be a PET, calculated as follows:

	£
Value of shares held before the transfer (see Tutorial note)	
40,000 × £17.10 (part of a 80% holding)	684,000
Value of shares held after the transfer	
20,000 × £14.50 (part of a 60% holding)	(290,000)
Value transferred	394,000
Less: BPR (100%) (see Tutorial note)	(394,000)
Chargeable amount	Nil

As a PET there is no lifetime IHT payable.

If Michael still owns the shares at the date of Joan's death, 100% BPR is still available and there will be nil taxable amount.

An IHT liability will arise if Joan dies before 15 July 2019 and Michael has disposed of the shares before that date.

Tutorial note

When valuing the shares for IHT purposes, the related property provisions must be taken into account. Joan is therefore disposing of 20,000 shares out of a combined 80% holding of shares held by her husband.

Business property relief at the rate of 100% will be available as the shares are unquoted trading company shares held for more than two years.

CGT implications

A capital gain will arise as follows:

	£
MV of 20% holding (20,000 × £7.90)	158,000
Less: Cost £96,400 × (20,000/40,000)	(48,200)
Chargeable gain	109,800

Provided Joan and her son jointly elect, the gain can be held over as a gift of business assets, since Rouen Ltd is an unquoted trading company.

Tutorial note

Entrepreneurs' relief is not a consideration as the full gain is deferred with a gift relief claim.

However, even if gift relief were not available, Entrepreneurs' relief would not be available as Joan does not work for Rouen Ltd. The gain would therefore be taxed at 28%.

Key answer tips

For IHT purposes, the diminution in the value of Joan's estate is the starting point.

For CGT purposes, the deemed proceeds is the market value of the asset gifted (i.e. a 20% holding).

Note that the diminution in value concept does not apply to CGT and the related property provisions do not apply to CGT.

(c) **Antique vase**

IHT implications

The gift of the vase is in consideration of marriage, and will therefore qualify for an exemption of £2,500 as it is a gift from a grandparent to grandchild.

The balance of the gift of £16,000 (£18,500 – £2,500) will be a PET made on 4 November 2012, with no tax unless Joan dies within seven years.

CGT implications

The gift of the vase is a disposal of a non-wasting chattel. The gain is calculated as £4,350 (£18,500 – £14,150).

Gift relief is not available as a vase is not a qualifying business asset and there is no immediate charge to IHT.

The CGT liability due on 31 January 2014 is therefore £1,218 (£4,350 × 28%) (ignoring the annual exempt amount).

(d) **Agricultural land**

IHT implications

The gift of the agricultural land will be a PET for £300,000 on 15 January 2013 and will not become chargeable unless Joan dies within seven years.

The increase in the value of her son Charles' property is irrelevant in valuing the PET. Only the diminution in the value of Joan's estate as a result of the gift is relevant.

If the PET becomes chargeable as a result of Joan dying before 15 January 2020, agricultural property relief at the rate of 100% based on the agricultural value of £175,000 will be available. This is because the land is let out for the purposes of agriculture and has been owned for at least seven years.

However, relief will only be available if, at the date of Joan's death, Charles still owns the land and it still qualifies as agricultural property.

CGT implications

The gift of agricultural land to Charles will be valued at its open market value on the date of the gift of £300,000.

Since the land qualifies for agricultural property relief it is also eligible for gift relief for CGT purposes. Joan and Charles can therefore jointly elect that the gain of £208,000 (£300,000 – £92,000) is held over as a gift of business assets.

Tutorial note

Entrepreneurs' relief is not a consideration as the full gain is deferred with a gift relief claim. However, even if gift relief were not available, Entrepreneurs' relief would not be available for the disposal of investment assets. The gain would therefore be taxed at 28%.

(e)   **Main residence**

IHT implications

The gift of the main residence is a gift with reservation because although Joan has gifted the freehold interest, she retains an interest in the property as she has continued to live rent free in the property.

The gift will be treated as a PET for £265,000 as normal on 31 March 2013, but Joan will still be treated as beneficially entitled to the property.

It will therefore be included in her estate when she dies at its market value at that date, although relief will be given should there be a double charge to IHT.

Joan could avoid these provisions by paying full consideration for the use of the property.

CGT implications

The gift of the main residence is a chargeable disposal for CGT purposes and the time of the disposal is when the ownership of the asset passes to the donee.

The reservation of benefit is therefore not relevant for CGT, and a normal CGT computation is required on 31 March 2013.

	£
Deemed consideration	265,000
Less: Cost	(67,000)
	198,000
Less: PPR exemption (W1)	(95,586)
Letting relief (W2)	(40,000)
Chargeable gain	62,414
Capital gains tax (£62,414 × 28%)	17,476

Workings

(W1) Principal private residence exemption

		Notes	Months	Exempt	Chargeable
1.7.91 – 31.12.95	Owner occupied		54	54	
1.1.96 – 31.12.99	Unoccupied	1	48	36	12
1.1.00 – 31.12.10	Rented out	2	132	9	123
1.1.11 – 31.03.13	Owner occupied		27	27	
			261	126	135

PPR exemption = (126/261) × £198,000 = £95,586

Notes

1   Three years allowed for no reason provided the property is owner occupied at some time before and some time after the period of absence.

2   The last 36 months are always exempt. They fall partly into the final period of owner occupation but partly in the period when the property was rented out.

(W2) Letting relief

Lower of:

		£
(a)	PPR exemption	95,586
(b)	Maximum	40,000
(c)	Period not exempted by PPR but the property is let	
	$(123/261) \times £198,000$	93,310

(ii)   Main advantages in lifetime giving for IHT purposes

Possible advantages of lifetime giving include:

- Making use of lifetime IHT exemptions in reducing a taxpayer's chargeable estate at death. In particular gifts between individuals will not become liable to IHT unless the donor dies within seven years of making the gift.

- If the donor does die prematurely there may still be an IHT advantage in lifetime giving because usually:

    −   The value of the asset for calculating any additional IHT arising upon death is fixed at the time the gift is made.

    −   The availability of tapering relief (providing the donor survives at least three years) may help reduce the effective IHT rate.

Main factors to consider in choosing assets to gift

The main factors to consider include:

(i)   Whether or not a significant CGT liability will arise upon making the gift.

Lifetime gifting may give rise to CGT. This therefore needs to be balanced against the fact that no CGT liability will arise upon death (i.e. if the assets are left in the estate and gifted in a will). Death results in the 'tax free' uplift of the chargeable assets included in the deceased's estate to market value.

The availability of CGT reliefs (primarily gift relief for business assets or if there is an immediate charge to IHT) and CGT exemptions (e.g. annual exempt amount) to ensure there is no CGT liability on the lifetime gift is therefore relevant in selecting assets.

(ii)   Whether an asset is appreciating in value.

Because any additional IHT arising as a result of death will be based on the (lower) value of the asset at the date of gift it may be advantageous to select assets that are likely to significantly appreciate in value.

(iii)   Whether the donor can afford to make the gift.

Whilst lifetime gifting can result in significant IHT savings this should not be at the expense of the taxpayer's ability to live comfortably, particularly in old age.

(iv)   The availability of significant IHT reliefs, particularly BPR.

There may be little point in selecting an asset that already qualifies for 100% relief.

15   DEE LIMITED (ADAPTED)

Key answer tips

This question tests your IHT knowledge. It has been adapted to reflect the style of questions you are likely to see in Part A of the exam, although the current examiner is unlikely to set a question of this length purely on IHT. Read the question carefully so that you know which gifts were made by which individuals, and the relationship between the individuals in the question.

In part (a) you should work through the calculations twice: once to calculate the lifetime tax, gift by gift, then again to calculate the death tax. Make sure that you explain any reliefs given, as the question specifically asks you to do this.

There are some easy marks in part (b) for stating the due dates for payment and who is to pay the tax.

In part (c) you can maximise your marks applying your knowledge to the scenario. Don't just list all the IHT planning points you know – think about whether or not they are relevant. For example, Debbie will die within less than seven years, but will live for more than three years, so there will be some taper relief available.

Notes for meeting

From   Tax senior
Date   8 June 2013
To   Lucy Sawry
Subject David and Debbie Dee

The following notes cover the IHT implications of David's death and IHT planning for Debbie as requested.

(a)   **IHT payable as a result of David's death**

Lifetime transfers

February 2006 – Gift of cottage

- The gift of the cottage is a PET and therefore no lifetime IHT is payable.

- The PET is more than seven years before the date of David's death and therefore does not become chargeable on death.

- However, David's continued use of the cottage for 2 months a year means that this represents a gift with reservation as the property is not occupied to the exclusion of the donor (David).

- As a result, the property will remain in David's estate at the time of his death, at the market value at the date of death of £150,000.

June 2007 – Gift into a discretionary trust

- David's gift into a relevant property trust is a chargeable lifetime transfer (CLT) and therefore lifetime IHT is payable.

- As David paid the tax in lifetime himself, the gift is a net gift.

- Two annual exemptions of £3,000 for 2007/08 and 2006/07 reduce the taxable gift as follows:

	£
Transfer of value	333,000
Less: Annual exemptions	(6,000)
Net chargeable amount	327,000

- As there are no other chargeable lifetime transfers in the previous seven years, the lifetime IHT tax payable is:

(£327,000 – £300,000) × 25%   6,750

 • The gross gift is therefore £333,750 (£327,000 + £6,750).

- Further IHT is payable on this gift when David dies (see below).

February 2008 – Gift of shares to children

- The gift of the shares to his children is a PET, therefore no lifetime IHT is due.

- However David dies within 7 years and therefore the PET becomes chargeable.

- The value of the PET is based on the diminution in David's estate after taking account of the related property rules as follows:

	Before the transfer		After the transfer	
	Number	*%*	*Number*	*%*
David's holding	4,500	90	3,000	60
Debbie's holding (Wife)	500	10	500	10
	5,000	100	3,500	70

Key answer tips

Remember that related property does not include property held by other relatives, just a spouse or civil partner.

Although this gift will be covered by BPR, you must still show your workings as the requirement asks you to explain the IHT implications.

	£
Value of David's holding before the gift	
£900,000 × (4,500/5,000)	810,000
Value of David's holding after the gift	
£475,000 × (3,000/3,500)	(407,143)
Diminution in value of estate	402,857
Less: BPR (100%)	(402,857)
PET	Nil

- As the shares are unquoted trading company shares they are relevant business property for BPR purposes and have been held for more than two years. 100% relief will therefore be available on the lifetime transfer.

- Assuming both children still hold the shares on David's death, business property relief will continue to be available.

- Therefore no further IHT will be payable on David's death.

Additional IHT arising on death re June 2007 gift

- The gross CLT of £333,750 becomes chargeable on death as follows:

	£
(£333,750 − £325,000) × 40%	3,500
Less: Taper relief (60%) (5 − 6 years)	(2,100)
	1,400
Less: Lifetime tax paid	(6,750)
Additional IHT payable (see Tutorial note)	Nil

Tutorial note

The lifetime tax paid is never repaid.

Estate on death

	£	£
Residence		275,000
Shares in Dee Ltd (W)	570,000	
Less: Business property relief (100%)	(570,000)	
		Nil
Cash deposits		60,000
Paintings		12,000
Death in service		200,000
Quoted shares		125,000
		672,000
Less: Exempt legacy to spouse		(672,000)
		Nil
GWR: Holiday cottage (Note)		150,000
Gross chargeable estate		150,000
IHT (£150,000 × 40%) (Note)		60,000

(handwritten: Gift with reservation)

Working: Shares in Dee Ltd

Value of 60% holding on death (taking account of related property of a 10% interest)

£665,000 × (3,000/3,500) = £570,000

The shares are eligible for 100% BPR as they are unquoted trading company shares held for more than two years.

Gift with reservation

The house which is a gift with reservation (GWR) is included in the donor's estate using the value at death, but is then charged at 40%.

There is no nil rate band remaining as it has been fully utilised against gifts in the previous years.

This is the position because it results in a higher tax charge compared to the lifetime gift which has become exempt. The tax is due from Andrew (i.e. the lifetime donee), not the estate.

Tutorial note

This is not a single grossing up scenario as the chargeable amount is a gift with reservation, which is a tax-bearing gift (i.e. the IHT on a gift with reservation is chargeable on the donee and is not directly borne by the estate).

(b) **IHT payable if Debbie's death is in June 2013**

Lifetime transfers

June 2011 – Gift of villa

- This gift is a PET.

- No IHT payable at the time of the gift.

- It would become chargeable on Debbie's death in June 2013 as the transfer was within seven years.

			£
Value of transfer			205,000
Less: Annual exemption	–	2011/12	(3,000)
	–	2010/11	(3,000)
			————
PET			199,000
			————

- No IHT is payable on death as the gift is covered by Debbie's nil rate band.

- Debbie will still have £126,000 (£325,000 – £199,000) of her nil rate band left at death.

- As Allison still owns the villa on Debbie's death, the fall in value of £92,000 (£205,000 – £113,000) is taken account of when calculating any tax payable on the PET when (if) it becomes chargeable on Debbie's death.

- In this case, however, this will have no effect because the gift falls entirely within Debbie's nil tax band.

- Fall in value relief also has no effect on subsequent gifts and the estate computation. Therefore the £126,000 nil rate band remaining is used in the estate computation.

Tutorial note

Despite leaving all his assets to Debbie, David has utilised his nil rate band against his lifetime gifts and therefore there is no unused nil rate band to transfer to Debbie.

Estate at death

	£	£
Residence		550,000
Shares in Dee Ltd (70% holding)	665,000	
Less: Business property relief (100%)	(665,000)	
	———	Nil
Cash deposits		100,000
Paintings		18,300
Cash (Death in service)		200,000
Quoted shares		150,000
		———
Chargeable estate		1,018,300
		———
IHT (£1,018,300 − £126,000 see above) × 40%		356,920

Tutorial note

Although Debbie has owned some of the shares for less than two years, her husband's ownership can also be included when calculating BPR.

Inheritance tax administration

- The tax on Debbie's estate would be paid by the personal representatives, usually an executor.

- Inheritance tax would be payable by 31 December 2013 (i.e. within six months of the end of the month in which death occurred) or the date on which probate is obtained (if earlier).

- However, an instalment option is available for certain assets, which includes land and buildings (i.e. the residence), whereby the tax can be paid in 10 equal annual instalments starting on the normal due date.

(c)   **Debbie survives until July 2017 – Tax planning recommendations**

Lifetime gifts to children

- Debbie should consider giving away some of her assets to her children, while ensuring that she still has enough to live on.

- Such lifetime gifts would be PETs.

- The PETs will become chargeable on Debbie's death as she will not survive seven years.

- However, taper relief will reduce the amount chargeable to IHT provided the gifts were made prior to July 2014.

- Note that it does not make sense for Debbie to gift shares in Dee Limited, as these qualify for full business property relief and therefore are not subject to IHT.

Use of lifetime exemptions

- It is important to remember that Debbie's annual exemptions will reduce the value of any PET when assets are gifted.

- Debbie has not used her annual exemption for the last two years, and so she can gift £6,000 (2 × £3,000) in the current tax year as well as £3,000 per year in future tax years.

- Debbie could therefore give away £18,000 (£6,000 in 2013/14 and £3,000 in the next four years), saving tax of £7,200 (£18,000 × 40%).

- Debbie can also make use of the small gifts exemption of up to £250 per donee per year.

- As Andrew is shortly to be married, Debbie could give up to £5,000 in consideration of his marriage. This would save £2,000 (£5,000 x 40%) in IHT.

- Expenditure out of normal income is also exempt from IHT. This is where the transferor is left with sufficient income to maintain his/her usual standard of living. Broadly, you need to demonstrate evidence of a prior commitment, or a settled pattern of expenditure.

Lifetime gifts to grandchildren

- Debbie should consider making gifts to Allison's children instead of Allison.

- This would not save any IHT now, but the gifts skip a generation and this action would ensure that the assets are not included in Allison's death estate should she die.

Insurance policies

- If substantial gifts are made, the donees would be advised to consider taking out insurance policies on Debbie's life to cover the potential tax liabilities that may arise on PETs in the event of her early death.

16   ALEX (ADAPTED)

Key answer tips

This question includes some nice easy marks for basic income tax and inheritance tax computations, with a written section on the use of trusts.

There are a few tricky points in part (b) – make sure that you calculate the lifetime tax before trying to calculate the death tax on lifetime transfers, as the PET uses the nil band on death but does not affect the nil band when calculating the lifetime tax on the CLT.

Where shares are quoted "ex div" you must add the dividend to the estate too. Don't forget to include the income tax from part (a) – this will be a mark for consistency, even if your figure is wrong.

Trusts are only likely to feature as part of a question in the exam, as in part (c).

(a)   **Income tax payable/repayable – 2012/13**

	Total	Other income	Savings income	Dividends
	£	£	£	£
Pension	11,740	11,740		
B.Soc interest (£1,280 x 100/80)	1,600		1,600	
NS & I EASA interest (received gross)	370		370	
Dividends – other (£8,100 x 100/90)	9,000	–		9,000
– Nacional plc (Note 1)	4,000			4,000
Total income	26,710	11,740	1,970	13,000
Less: PAA (W)	(10,005)	(10,005)		
Taxable income	16,705	1,735	1,970	13,000

Income tax

£		
		£
1,735	@ 20% (Other income)	347
975	@ 10% (Savings income) (Note 2)	97
2,710		
995	@ 20% (Savings income)	199
13,000	@ 10% (Dividends)	1,300
16,705		

Income tax liability		1,943
Less: Tax at source		
On dividends (£13,000 x 10%)		(1,300)
On savings (£1,600 x 20%)		(320)
PAYE		(1,184)
Income tax repayable		(861)

Tutorial note

1.   *Alex will be taxed on his income due and payable up to the date of death. He will have a full (non-apportioned) personal allowance for 2012/13, the tax year of death.*

   Re-the Nacional plc dividends:

   –   *The dividends are declared before Alex's death and are therefore included in Alex's last income tax computation even though they are received post death.*

   –   *Gross dividends to include = (20,000 ×18p ×100/90) = £4,000*

   The ACCA have confirmed that this is the treatment they expect for dividends declared pre-death, received post death.

2.   *Note that where savings income falls in the first £2,710 of taxable income, it is taxed at 10%.*

Working: Personal age allowance (PAA)

	£	£
PAA, aged 85		10,660
Total income	26,710	
Less Abatement limit	(25,400)	
Abatement	1,310 × ½	(655)
Reduced PAA		10,005

(b)   **Inheritance tax liability on Alex's death**

   Lifetime inheritance tax

   July 2007 – PET

   •   The gift in July 2007 was a potentially exempt transfer (PET).

   •   No IHT is payable at the time of the gift.

   •   IHT only becomes payable when Alex dies within seven years.

   March 2008 – CLT

   •   The transfer into the discretionary trust in March 2008 was a chargeable lifetime transfer (CLT).

   •   Lifetime IHT is due when the gift is made and additional tax is due as Alex dies within seven years of the gift.

   •   The value of the CLT was £338,000.

   •   No annual exemptions were available, as these are allocated in date order against the PET in July 2007.

   •   The lifetime tax on the CLT was as follows:
       (£338,000 – £300,000 nil rate band) × 25% = £9,500

   •   The gross gift was therefore £347,500 (£338,000 + £9,500).

Tutorial note

1. *The question tells you that when Alex's wife died, she had utilised all of her nil rate band. As a result, only Alex's nil rate band is available.*

    Had his wife not utilised her nil rate band, the proportion of unused nil rate band could be transferred to Alex on his death.

2. *Where the donor suffers the lifetime tax due, the tax rate used to calculate lifetime tax is 25% (i.e. 20/80).*

    All of the nil rate band is available against this lifetime gift; the PET is ignored as it is not chargeable during Alex's lifetime, although it does use the annual exemptions.

Additional inheritance tax due at death

IHT on PET in July 2007

The PET becomes chargeable on death, as Alex died within seven years of making the gift. As there are no lifetime transfers in the previous seven years, all of the nil rate band is available.

		£
Value transferred		338,000
Less: Annual exemptions:	2007/08	(3,000)
	2006/07	(3,000)
PET		332,000
IHT due (£332,000 – £325,000) × 40%		2,800
Less: Taper relief (5 – 6 years) (60%)		(1,680)
IHT due on death		1,120

This additional tax is paid by Brian (see Tutorial note).

IHT on CLT in March 2008

The PET has used up the nil rate band, so the CLT in March 2008 is fully taxable as follows:

	£
IHT due on gross gift (£347,500 × 40%)	139,000
Less: Taper relief (4 – 5 years) (40%)	(55,600)
	83,400
Less IHT paid during lifetime	(9,500)
IHT due on death	73,900

This additional tax is paid by the trustees of the discretionary trust (see Tutorial note below).

Tutorial note

The additional tax on PETs and CLTs as a result of death is always paid by the donee.

Estate at death

	£	£
Residence		475,000
Touriga shares (W1)	26,950	
Less: Business property relief	(26,950)	
	———	Nil
Nacional shares (W2)		128,800
Building society account		15,000
NS & I EASA		55,000
NS & I savings certificates		180,000
Chattels		40,000
Other quoted investments		115,000
Income tax repayment (part (a))		861
		———
		1,009,661
Less: Exempt charitable legacy		(150,000)
		———
Gross chargeable estate = taxable estate		859,661
		———

The nil band has already been used against gifts made in the seven years prior to death.

IHT on estate (£859,661 × 36%) (W3)	309,478
	———

The inheritance due to each of Brian and Beatrice is £288,566 (W4).

Workings

(W1) **Touriga Ltd**

The total value of Touriga Ltd shares at death = (£11.00 x 2,450) = £26,950.

As these shares are unquoted trading company shares and have been held for more than two years, 100% business property relief applies.

(W2) **Nacional plc**

The Nacional plc shares are valued at the lower of:

(i)   Quarter up method (624p + (632p − 624p) × 1/4) = 626p

(ii)   Average of highest and lowest marked bargains = (625p + 630p) × ½ = 627.5p

Value of 20,000 shares = (626p × 20,000) = £125,200

As the shares are quoted ex-div at the date of death, the value of the shares in the death estate, needs to include the value of the next net dividend (18p x 20,000 = £3,600).

The total value of the shares is therefore £128,800 (£3,600 + £125,200).

(W3) **Rate of tax**

	£
Taxable estate	859,661
Add: exempt legacy to charity	150,000
Baseline amount	1,009,661
Apply 10% test	
£1,009,661 x 10%	100,966

As the exempt charitable legacy exceeds £100,966, the estate is taxed at 36% instead of 40%.

(W4) **Share of inheritance**

	£
Value of estate	859,661
Value of Touriga shares	26,950
	886,611
IHT payable from estate	(309,478)
Estate value to share	577,133

Half share to each of Brian and Beatrice (£577,133 ÷ 2) = £288,566.

(c) **(i)** **Use of a trust**

Relevant property trusts

Brian has the choice of setting up an interest in possession trust or a discretionary trust.

However, regardless of the type of trust set up, if the trust is set up by Brian during his lifetime it will be a 'relevant property trust' for IHT purposes.

A relevant property trust is taxed as follows:

- Gifts into a relevant property trust are chargeable lifetime transfers (CLTs). They attract IHT at half the death rate to the extent that the cumulative lifetime transfers in the last seven years of the settlor (Brian) exceed the nil rate band (£325,000).

- The tax can be paid by the trustees out of the settled assets (i.e. borne by the trust).

- Once the assets are settled in a relevant property trust, the trust will suffer a 10 year charge (the 'principal charge') based on the value of the trust at the 10 year anniversary, cumulated with the previous chargeable transfers of the settlor at the time the trust was created.

- The charge is 6%, based on 30% of the lifetime rate (20%).

- If capital assets are removed from the trust (i.e. distributed to the beneficiaries), an exit charge is also levied at a rate based on 30% of the tax charged on the creation of the trust or the periodic charge at the last 10 year anniversary (if later), and the length of time that has elapsed since.

Type of trust

Given Brian's desire to retain control over the assets, it would appear that a discretionary trust would be advisable, rather than an interest in possession trust.

This is because:

- The trustees of a discretionary trust have the discretion (hence the name) over how the funds will be used.

- They can thus control the assets comprising the inheritance, while allowing Colin or Charlotte access to some or all of the income.

- It is likely that Brian himself would wish to be a trustee and he could therefore control how his children accessed the money, both the income and capital.

- In contrast, if an interest in possession trust is set up, the beneficiaries Colin and Charlotte would be legally entitled to the income generated by the trust each year and it must be paid to them.

- In the trust deed the capital must be directed to pass at a set future date or as a consequence of a future event.

(ii) **Inheritance tax planning**

If Brian creates a discretionary trust by making a lifetime gift of the inherited assets, this will be a CLT and will give rise to a charge to IHT with a further liability arising if Brian dies within seven years.

Therefore, Brian should be advised to pass his inheritance directly to his children by using a deed of variation to alter the disposition of Alex's estate.

Provided the deed includes a statement that the deed is effective for inheritance tax purposes, the transfer into the trust will be treated as a legacy under the will.

There will be no alteration in the tax payable on Alex's estate but Brian will not have a CLT, there will be no lifetime tax on setting up the trust and Brian will have preserved his own nil rate band for use against future lifetime gifts or the value of his own estate on death.

Tutorial note

If Brian had chosen to set up an interest in possession trust, if set up on death (under a Deed of Variation of Alex's will), it will be an Immediate Post Death Interest trust (IPDI) and not a 'relevant property trust'. As a result, different rules apply to the taxation of trust.

Note that it is not possible to change Alex's will with a Deed of Variation to set up a special privileged children's trust as the new children's trusts can only be set up on the death of the parent, not the grandparent.

---

17 MABEL PORTER *Online question assistance*

Key answer tips

This question covers the popular area of CGT versus IHT for lifetime gifts, with IHT calculations on death and further IHT planning.

You must make sure that your answer is well structured and well labelled in part (a) – you are looking at four gifts in total, and need to consider CGT and IHT. The best way to approach this is to deal with one tax at a time. Think about all the CGT implications, remembering to state which reliefs are not available, as well as those that are; then deal with the IHT implications in the same way.

As long as your advice and calculation of the tax saving in (b) is consistent with your analysis in part (a), you could still score full marks here.

(a)   **Tax implications of the four possible gifts**

All four possible gifts would be potentially exempt transfers (PETs) such that no inheritance tax would be due at the time of the gift.

The capital gain or allowable loss arising on each gift will be computed by reference to the market value of the asset as at the date of the gift.

Gift to Bruce of shares in BOZ plc

Capital gains tax

The gift will result in a capital gain of £32,500 (£77,000 – £44,500).

BOZ plc is Mabel's personal company as she is able to exercise at least 5% of the voting rights. Accordingly, the shares qualify for gift relief.

However, gift relief would only be available if Bruce (the recipient of the gift) were UK resident or UK ordinarily resident. This is unlikely to be the case as he emigrated to South Africa in January 2010, therefore gift relief is not available.

Entrepreneurs' relief is not available as although BOZ plc is Mabel's personal company and she has owned the shares for more than a year, she does not work for BOZ plc.

Key answer tips

Where an individual owns shares in a plc, you should generally assume that they hold less than a 5% interest and that they don't work for the company, unless clearly told otherwise.

Inheritance tax

The value transferred will be reduced by business property relief at the rate of 50% because Mabel owns a controlling shareholding in the company.

Luke's period of ownership can be taken into account in order to satisfy the two-year period of ownership requirement.

The relief is restricted because the company owns excepted assets.

	£
Value transferred	77,000
Less: BPR (£77,000 x 92% x 50%)	(35,420)
Annual exemptions – 2013/14 and 2012/13 (£3,000 $\times$ 2)	(6,000)
PET	35,580

Gift to Bruce of the land in Utopia

Capital gains tax

The gift will result in a capital loss of £24,000 (£99,000 – £75,000).

This loss is available for relief against capital gains made by Mabel in 2013/14 or future years.

Mabel and Bruce (aunt and nephew) are not connected persons for the purposes of capital gains tax and therefore, there is no restriction on Mabel's use of the losses.

Inheritance tax

Agricultural property relief is not available because the land is not situated in the UK or the EEA.

Business property relief is also not available because the farm is an investment asset, not a business asset.

The value of the PET will therefore be:	£
Value transferred	75,000
Less: Annual exemptions – 2013/14 and 2012/13 (£3,000 $\times$ 2)	(6,000)
PET	69,000

Tutorial note

BPR is available on worldwide business property, whereas APR is only available on farm land and buildings situated in the UK or the EEA.

The minimum period of ownership rules also have to be satisfied. Even if the farm had been in the UK or EEA, APR would not be available as a tenanted farm must be owned by the donor and occupied and farmed by the tenant for at least 7 years prior to the transfer.

Gift to Padma of the Rolls Royce motor car

Capital gains tax

No gain or loss will arise as cars are exempt assets for the purposes of capital gains tax.

Inheritance tax

The PET will equal the market value of the car of £71,000.

There are no annual exemptions available as they have already been used against the gift to Bruce.

Gift to Padma of the necklace

Capital gains tax

The gift will result in the following chargeable gain.

	£
Deemed proceeds (market value)	70,000
Less: Cost (probate value when inherited)	(21,500)
	————
Chargeable gain	48,500
	————

Gift relief is not available as the necklace is not a business asset.

Inheritance tax

The value of the PET will equal the market value of the necklace of £70,000.

There are no annual exemptions available as they have already been used against the gift to Bruce.

Key answer tips

Watch out for the dates here – the gift to Padma will be made after the gift to Bruce.

(b) **Recommendation of gifts to make**

Mabel's criteria in deciding which assets to give are:

– The gifts must not give rise to any tax liabilities prior to her death.

   The gifts will not give rise to inheritance tax prior to Mabel's death because they are potentially exempt transfers. Accordingly, in satisfying this criterion, it is only necessary to consider capital gains tax.

– If possible, the gifts should reduce the inheritance tax due on her death.

Bruce

A gift of the shares in BOZ plc would result in a capital gain of £32,500.

This exceeds Mabel's capital losses brought forward of £15,100 and the annual exempt amount of £10,600, such that a capital gains tax liability would arise.

Accordingly, she should give Bruce the land in Utopia. This will result in a capital loss of £24,000.

Padma

There would be no capital gains tax on either of the proposed gifts to Padma.

The car is an exempt asset and the capital gain arising on the necklace would be relieved by Mabel's capital losses and the annual exempt amount as follows:

	£
Capital gain	48,500
Less: Capital loss on the gift to Bruce of the land	(24,000)
Capital losses brought forward (restricted)	(13,900)
	10,600
Less: Annual exempt amount	(10,600)
Taxable gain	Nil

Accordingly, the gift to be made to Padma should be chosen by reference to the amount of inheritance tax saved.

Mabel should give Padma the necklace as its value is expected to increase.

Key answer tips

Don't worry if you made some mistakes in part (a) – as long as you have provided clear, consistent advice with reasons, you should still score full marks here.

IHT payable if the lifetime gifts to Bruce and Padma are not made

IHT payable on Mabel's lifetime gift – during her lifetime

1 May 2007 – Gift into discretionary trust

		£
Transfer of value		210,000
Less: Annual exemptions	– 2007/08	(3,000)
	– 2006/07 b/f	(3,000)
Net chargeable amount		204,000

The gift is covered by the NRB and therefore no IHT was paid.

Gross chargeable amount	204,000

IHT payable on Mabel's lifetime gift – due to her death

If Mabel dies on 30 June 2018, this gift is more than 7 years before death and therefore no IHT payable.

As there are no other lifetime gifts, the full NRB is available against the death estate.

Death Estate

	£	£
House and furniture		450,000
Rolls Royce car		55,000
Diamond necklace		84,000
Cash and investments		150,000
Shares in BOZ plc	95,000	
Less: BPR (50% × £95,000 × 92%)	(43,700)	
		51,300
Land in Utopia		75,000
Chargeable Estate		**865,300**
IHT payable (£865,300 – £325,000) × 40%		216,120

Tutorial note

Luke has fully utilised his nil rate band, so there is no unused proportion to transfer to Mabel.

IHT payable if Mabel makes the lifetime gifts to Bruce and Padma

IHT payable on Mabel's lifetime gifts - during her lifetime

1 May 2007 – Gift into discretionary trust

As before, the IHT payable will be £Nil as the gift of £204,000 is covered by the NRB.

1 February 2014 – Gift to Bruce – Land in Utopia

		£
Transfer of value		75,000
Less Annual exemption	– 2013/14	(3,000)
	– 2012/13 b/f	(3,000)
PET – chargeable amount		69,000

No IHT payable during lifetime as the gift is a PET.

1 March 2014 – Gift to Padma – Diamond necklace

	£
Transfer of value	70,000
Less: Annual exemptions (already used)	(Nil)
PET – chargeable amount	70,000

No IHT payable during lifetime as the gift is a PET.

IHT payable on Mabel's lifetime gifts – due to her death

1 May 2007 – Gift into discretionary trust

As before, if Mabel dies on 30 June 2018, this gift is more than 7 years before death and therefore no IHT payable

1 February 2014 – Gift to Bruce – Land in Utopia

	£	£
Chargeable amount		69,000
NRB at death	325,000	
Less: Gross transfers in last 7 years (1.2.07 – 1.2.14)	(204,000)	
	————	(121,000)
Taxable amount		Nil

No IHT payable as the gift is covered by the NRB.

1 March 2014 – Gift to Padma – Diamond necklace

	£	£
Chargeable amount		70,000
NRB at death	325,000	
Less: Gross transfers in last 7 years (1.3.07 – 1.3.14) (£204,000 + £69,000)	(273,000)	
	————	(52,000)
Taxable amount		18,000
IHT payable (£18,000 × 40%)		7,200
Less: Taper Relief (1.03.14 to 30.06.18) (4 – 5 years) (40%)		(2,880)
		4,320
Less: IHT paid in lifetime (PET)		(Nil)
IHT due on death		4,320

Death Estate

	£	£
House and furniture		450,000
Rolls Royce car		55,000
Cash and investments		150,000
BOZ plc shares (as before)		51,300
Chargeable Estate		706,300
NRB at death	325,000	
Less: Gross transfers in last 7 years (30.6.11 – 30.6.18) (£69,000 + £70,000)	(139,000)	
	————	(186,000)
Taxable estate		520,300
IHT payable (£520,300 x 40%)		208,120

Quantifying the IHT saving as a result of making the lifetime gifts

	£
Total IHT payable if the gifts are not made	216,120
Total IHT payable if the gifts are made (£4,320 + 208,120)	(212,440)
Total IHT saved	3,680

Key answer tips

Even if you recommended different gifts, you could still score full marks for calculating the tax saving by comparing the tax payable without the gifts and the tax payable with the gifts (remembering that the assets given would no longer be in the death estate!).

(c) **Further advice**

Mabel should consider delaying one of the gifts until after 1 May 2014 such that it is made more than seven years after the gift to the discretionary trust.

Both PETs would then be covered by the nil rate band resulting in a saving of inheritance tax of £4,320 (from (b)).

Mabel should ensure that she uses her inheritance tax annual exemption of £3,000 every year by, say, making gifts of £1,500 each year to both Bruce and Padma. The effect of this will be to save inheritance tax of £1,200 (£3,000 × 40%) every year.

18 ALVARO PELORUS (ADAPTED) *Walk in the footsteps of a top tutor*

Key answer tips

This question is all about the capital taxes (IHT and CGT), with the added complication that Alvaro and his wife are not UK domiciled.

This question has been altered to reflect the extensive changes to the rules governing the taxation of non domiciled individuals which were introduced in the Finance Act 2008.

The highlighted words in the written sections are key phrases that markers are looking for.

Tutor's top tips

Make sure you read the question carefully and identify the relationship between the individuals involved. Part (a) is all about the IHT payable on Ray's death; parts (b) and (c) relate to his son, Alvaro, who is disposing of assets whilst still alive.

The best way to approach the calculations in part (a) is to deal with each transfer separately, starting with the earliest gift. Note that the requirement specifically asks you to explain the availability or otherwise of APR and BPR, so make sure that you do this. The words "or otherwise" are a hint that perhaps these reliefs may not both be available!

As Ray is UK domiciled, he will be subject to IHT on his UK and overseas assets, with double tax relief available for any overseas tax suffered

(a)   **Inheritance tax (IHT) payable as a result of the death of Ray Pelorus**

Lifetime gifts

IHT is payable in respect of the potentially exempt transfers (PETs) made in the seven years prior to Ray's death and on the death estate.

PET on 1 May 2009 – Gift of farm land

	£
Value transferred	273,000
Less: Agricultural property relief (100% of agricultural value)	(120,000)
Annual exemptions – 2009/10 and 2008/09 (£3,000 x 2)	(6,000)
PET – gross chargeable amount	147,000

No IHT is due during lifetime. There is no IHT on death as the PET is less than the available nil rate band of £325,000.

Availability of agricultural property and business property relief

Agricultural property relief is available on the agricultural value of the land on Ray's death because:

–   Ray owned the tenanted land for at least seven years prior to the gift to Alvaro, and

–   Alvaro still owned the land when Ray died.

Business property relief (BPR) is not available on the excess of the market value over the agricultural value because the land was held by Ray as an investment and not a business asset.

Tutorial note

Another condition for the availability of APR is that the farm must be occupied and farmed by the tenant throughout Ray's ownership. This condition was not however included in the examiner's model answer, but would have been a mark earning point.

PET on 1 August 2012 – Gift of shares in Pinger Ltd

	£
Transfer of value	195,000
Less: BPR (100%)	(195,000)
PET – gross chargeable amount	Nil

No IHT payable during lifetime as the gift is a PET and has Nil chargeable value

IHT payable on death:

	£	£
Chargeable amount (as above)		Nil
Add BPR (see below)		195,000
Less Annual exemptions (see Tutorial Note)		
– 2012/13 and 2011/12 (£3,000 x 2)		(6,000)
PET – chargeable amount on death		189,000
NRB at death	325,000	
Gross transfers in the previous 7 years (1.8.05 – 1.8.12)	(147,000)	
NRB available		(178,000)
Taxable amount		11,000
IHT payable on death (£11,000 x 40%)		4,400

Availability of business property relief

Although the shares qualified for BPR at the time the PET was made, BPR is not available when the PET becomes chargeable because Alvaro did not own the shares at the date of Ray's death.

Tutorial note

BPR is clawed back if the asset is not owned by the donee at the date of the donor's death, unless the sale proceeds have been reinvested in qualifying replacement assets.

There is nothing in the question to suggest that Alvaro invested the proceeds from the sale of the shares in replacement business property, therefore BPR is not available in the death calculation.

To calculate the chargeable amount on death, the BPR must be added back. However, provided they have not been used against a CLT during his lifetime, the annual exemptions are still available against this PET when calculating the chargeable amount.

Death estate

	£	£
UK assets		870,000
House in Pacifica (W)		89,300
Chargeable estate		959,300
NRB at death (Note 1)	325,000	
Gross transfers in the previous 7 years (1.2.06 – 1.2.13) (£147,000 + £189,000)	(336,000)	
NRB available		(Nil)
Taxable estate		959,300
IHT (£959,300 x 40%)		383,720
Less: Double tax relief – the lower of:		
Overseas tax suffered	1,800	(1,800)
UK IHT on the house (£89,300 x 40%) (Note 2)	35,720	
IHT payable		381,920

Working: House in Pacifica

	£	£
Value as at 1 February 2013		94,000
Less: Legal fees – the lower of:		
The fees incurred	7,700	
Maximum (5% x £94,000)	4,700	(4,700)
Value to include in the estate		89,300

Tutor's top tips

1.   *There is no mention of Ray's wife, whether she is still alive or predeceased him. Without further information in the question you should assume there is no unutilised spouse nil rate band available.*

2.   *As there is no nil band available to set against the death estate, the rate of UK tax suffered is simply 40%.*

     Remember that if there is some nil band remaining, the estate rate will be less than 40%, and is calculated by dividing the tax by the chargeable estate.

     The UK rate of tax on foreign property can then be calculated and compared with the overseas tax suffered.

(b) (i) **Alvaro Pelorus**

Assessment to capital gains tax – 2012/13

Tutor's top tips

This section requires you to know about the complex rules for non UK domiciled individuals. You must make sure that you learn these rules, as overseas aspects of tax are very popular in the exam.

In 2012/13 Alvaro is resident, but not ordinarily resident in the UK and not UK domiciled.

Accordingly, he is assessed to UK CGT in the normal way on all of his disposals of UK assets.

However, the treatment of his capital gains and losses on his disposals of overseas assets depends on whether the amount of his unremitted overseas income and gains exceeds £2,000 as follows:

If unremitted overseas income and gains:	Treatment:
≤ £2,000	• Only assessed on overseas gains if proceeds are remitted to the UK • Overseas losses will be allowable • The annual exempt amount is available
> £2,000	• Assessed on gains on all overseas disposals on an arising basis **unless** an election is made for the remittance basis to apply

> £2,000 (continued)	• If the election is not made (i.e. arising basis applies)
	  – all gains assessed
	  – annual exempt amount available
	  – overseas losses are allowable
	
	• If the election is made (i.e. remittance basis applies)
	  – only assessed to overseas gains if proceeds are remitted into the UK
	  – annual exempt amount is not available
	  – overseas losses are not allowable unless a further election is made

Tutorial note

If the election for the remittance basis is made, it applies to both income and gains – it cannot just be made for one tax or the other.

The £30,000/£50,000 remittance basis charge is not applicable here, as Alvaro has only been resident in the UK since 2011/12.

Note that the status of the individual in the current year determines the tax treatment. Checking the residence status in the last 9/14 tax years is only relevant in determining whether or not the remittance basis charge of £30,000 or £50,000 applies.

(b) (ii) **Alvaro Pelorus**

Capital gains tax (CGT) liability – 2012/13

Tutor's top tips

As Alvaro is UK resident, he must pay tax on his UK gains. You must then apply the non domicile rules to decide on the tax treatment of any overseas gains or losses, and the availability of the annual exempt amount.

Alvaro only disposes of one overseas asset in 2012/13 which gives rise to a capital loss.

As he has no unremitted income (per the question): his total unremitted gains and income is therefore less than £2,000, so:

–   There is no need to make an election

–   He will automatically be assessed on all of his UK gains with a full annual exempt amount available, and

–   His overseas loss is allowable.

	£
Shares in Pinger Ltd (W1)	200,200
Shares in Lapis Inc (W4)	(2,818)
Shares in Quad plc (W5)	Nil
Net chargeable gains	197,382
Less: Annual exempt amount	(10,600)
Taxable gains	186,782
Capital gains tax (£186,782 x 28%)	52,299

Workings

(W1) Shares in Pinger Ltd – UK asset

	£
Proceeds (September 2012)	228,000
Less: Base cost (W2)	(23,400)
IHT payable by Alvaro on the PET (Note 1)	(4,400)
Chargeable gain (Note 2)	200,200

Tutorial note

1. Relief is available in respect of any inheritance tax payable on the gift of the shares on 1 August 2012.

    Although IHT will not have been paid at the time of this gift (as it was a PET for IHT purposes), following the death of Ray Pelorus, the PET becomes chargeable and IHT is paid in respect of this gift.

    As a result, the capital gains tax due in respect of the disposal of the shares in Pinger Ltd will be re-computed in order to take account of the IHT relief.

2. Alvaro is not entitled to Entrepreneurs' relief as the shares are not shares in his personal trading company (he owns < 5% interest) and he does not appear to work for the company. The gain will therefore be taxed at 28%, not 10%.

(W2) Base cost of shares in Pinger Ltd

	£
Market value (1 August 2012)	195,000
Less: Gift relief on gift by Ray (W3)	(171,600)
Alvaro's base cost in the shares	23,400

(W3) Gift relief on gift by Ray to Alvaro

	£
Market value as at 1 August 2012	195,000
Less: Cost (£54,600 x 6,000/14,000)	(23,400)
Gift relief claimed (see Tutorial note)	171,600

Tutorial note

Gift relief is optional, therefore at the time of the gift by Ray, he should have considered whether or not it would be beneficial to claim gift relief.

> *It may not be beneficial to claim gift relief if Ray is entitled to Entrepreneurs' relief on the disposal and Alvaro is not entitled to claim Entrepreneurs' relief on his later disposal.*
>
> *However, neither Ray nor Alvaro are entitled to Entrepreneurs' relief in this question as they own < 5% interest and do not appear to work for the company.*
>
> *Therefore, it is advantageous to claim gift relief and the question states that you should assume that all available reliefs are claimed.*

(W4) **Shares in Lapis Inc – Overseas asset**

	£
Proceeds	8,270
Less: Cost (£25,950 x 2,350/5,500)	(11,088)
Capital Loss	(2,818)

The overseas capital loss is available for relief because although Alvaro is domiciled outside the UK, he has unremitted overseas gains of ≤ £2,000 (see part (b)(i)).

(W5) **Shares in Quad plc**

	£
Deemed proceeds	74,000
Less: Cost	(59,500)
	14,500
Less: Gift relief (see Tutorial note)	(14,500)
Chargeable gain	Nil

Tutorial note

Gift relief is available on the transfer of any asset to a discretionary trust because the transfer is subject to an immediate charge to inheritance tax.

Gift relief is optional and is given before considering Entrepreneurs' relief.

Therefore Alvaro should consider whether or not he wants to make the gift relief claim or leave the gains to be chargeable and claim Entrepreneurs' relief instead, if the conditions are satisfied.

However, the Quad plc shares do not qualify as the company is a plc and unless the question clearly states otherwise, it is assumed that:

– *he will have a less than 5% interest*

– *he does not work for the company, and*

– *he has held the shares for less than a year.*

He will therefore claim gift relief to defer the gain. The question states that you should assume that all available reliefs are claimed.

(c) (i) **Variation of Ray's will**

Tutor's top tips

Don't forget that it is possible to change a person's will after they have died, as long as all beneficiaries agree. This can be a useful tax planning tool.

The variation by Alvaro of Ray's will, such that assets are left to Vito and Sophie, will not be regarded as a gift by Alvaro. Instead, provided the deed states that it is intended to be effective for IHT purposes, it will be as if Ray had left the assets to the children in his will.

This strategy, known as skipping a generation, will have no effect on the IHT due on Ray's death but will reduce the assets owned by Alvaro and thus his potential UK IHT liability.

A deed of variation is more tax efficient than Alvaro making gifts to the children as such gifts would be PETs and IHT may be due if Alvaro were to die within seven years.

The deed of variation must be entered into by 31 January 2015 (i.e. within two years of the date of Ray's death).

(ii) **IHT planning opportunities**

Tutor's top tips

Read the question carefully – it says that Alvaro does not wish to make any lifetime gifts other than to his wife. This means that there will be no marks available for discussion of lifetime gifts to people other than Maria!

The key point here is that Alvaro is not UK domiciled, and therefore will be taxed on his UK assets, but not overseas assets. If he can divest himself of UK assets, he will reduce the IHT due when he dies.

Alvaro will be subject to UK IHT on his UK assets only (e.g. land and chattels situated in the UK, shares registered in the UK and cash held in UK branches of banks) as he is domiciled in Koruba.

UK IHT will be charged on the excess of the value of these assets over Alvaro's available nil rate band.

Until 30 November 2019, Alvaro's available nil rate band is £257,000 (£325,000 – (£74,000 – £6,000)) due to the gift to the discretionary trust.

In order to minimise his UK IHT liability Alvaro should reduce the value of his UK assets by making gifts to Maria or selling the UK assets to third parties and acquiring foreign assets.

Maria can own UK assets equal to her available nil rate band of £325,000 without incurring a UK IHT liability on death.

There will be no CGT on the gifts even if Alvaro is UK resident or ordinarily resident, because transfers between spouses take place at no gain, no loss.

For the purposes of IHT, the gifts will be covered by the spouse exemption. The £55,000 limit on transfers to a non-UK domiciled spouse does not apply where the donor spouse is also non-UK domiciled.

Accordingly, Alvaro can gift assets to Maria with no UK tax consequences.

Alternatively, Alvaro can leave all of his UK assets to Maria on his death. There will be no IHT payable on Alvaro's death due to the spouse exemption. On Maria's death, Alvaro's unused nil rate band can be claimed against her estate, along with her nil rate band.

Alvaro should not sell any UK assets to third parties until he is both non-resident and non-ordinarily resident otherwise he will be subject to UK CGT. Once he is both non-resident and non-ordinarily resident the disposals will not have any UK tax consequences.

Tutorial note

The nil rate band unused on the death of a spouse (or civil partner) can be used to reduce the inheritance tax payable on the death of the surviving spouse (or civil partner).

19 CRUSOE (ADAPTED)

Key answer tips

This is a capital taxes question which is relatively straightforward.

In part (a) it is important to note the instructions to quantify the tax relief. Even if you did not know that capital losses in the year of death could be carried back, it seems likely that for 4 marks you have to do more than just net off the gains and losses in the year of death.

Part (b) concerns a gift of quoted shares. The examiner asks for immediate tax implications so it is important to consider all relevant taxes and not to consider future events, except in relation to the alternative strategy proposed.

In part (c) there are some tricky points involving a gift with reservation. However, provided you understand that the examiner is essentially asking for a calculation of inheritance tax due on death, you should be able to pick up a good mark.

(a) **The potential tax relief available in respect of the capital losses realised in 2013/14**

The capital losses must first be offset against the chargeable gains of £7,100 in 2013/14. This will not save any capital gains tax as the gains would have been relieved by the annual exempt amount.

Unrelieved capital losses can then normally only be carried forward and set against future net capital gains. However, capital losses in the year of death can be carried back against net chargeable gains of the three years prior to the year of death

The remaining capital losses of £10,700 (£17,800 – £7,100) may be offset against the chargeable gains of the previous three years on a last in, first out basis. The losses will reduce the chargeable gains of each year down to the level of the annual exempt amount.

The personal representatives of Noland's estate will receive a refund of capital gains tax calculated as follows:

	Losses		Tax relief
	£		£
Available capital losses	10,700		
2012/13 (£14,500 – £10,600)	(3,900)	× 18%	702
2011/12 (£14,500 – £10,600)	(3,900)	× 18%	702
	2,900		
2010/11 the remainder	(2,900)	× 18%	522
Refund due			1,926

Tutorial note

Capital gains and losses incurred in the same tax year must be netted off in full without considering the annual exempt amount. When net losses are carried back (in year of death) or forward (all other times) they only have to reduce the net gains down to a figure equal to the annual exempt amount.

The gains for 2010/11 – 2012/13 will have been taxed at 18% as the question states that Noland has taxable income of £20,000 p.a.

(b)   **Gift of the share portfolio to Avril**

Inheritance tax

The gift would be a potentially exempt transfer at market value. No inheritance tax would be due at the time of the gift.

Tutorial note

Because the shares are quoted, there is no business property relief unless Crusoe controls the company.

Capital gains tax

The gift would be a disposal by Crusoe deemed to be made at market value for the purposes of capital gains tax. No gain would arise as the deemed proceeds will equal Crusoe's base cost of probate value.

Stamp duty

There is no stamp duty on a gift of shares for no consideration.

Strategy to avoid a possible tax liability in the future

Crusoe should enter into a deed of variation directing the administrators to transfer the shares to Avril rather than to him. This will not be regarded as a gift by Crusoe. Instead, provided the deed states that it is intended to be effective for inheritance tax purposes, it will be as if Noland had left the shares to Avril in a will.

This strategy is more tax efficient than Crusoe gifting the shares to Avril as such a gift would be a potentially exempt transfer and inheritance tax may be due if Crusoe were to die within seven years.

The deed of variation must be in writing, signed by Crusoe, and entered into by 1 October 2015, (i.e. within two years of the date of Noland's death).

Tutorial note

Deeds of variation are very useful tax planning tools. They can be used to 'rewrite' a will or, as in this case, change an inheritance under the intestacy rules.

(c) **Value of quoted shares that can be transferred to Avril**

The administrators will sell the quoted shares to fund the IHT due as a result of Noland's death.

The value of shares to be transferred to Avril will therefore be equal to £370,000 less the inheritance tax due by the estate excluding the gift with reservation (see below).

Death estate

	£	£
Quoted shares		370,000
House – Gift with reservation (Note 1)		310,000
Shares in Kurb Ltd (Note 2)		38,400
Chattels and cash		22,300
Capital gains tax refund due (part (a))		1,926
Less: Liabilities due		(1,900)
		———
Gross chargeable estate		740,726
Nil rate band	325,000	
Gross chargeable transfers in last 7 years (W)	(254,000)	
	———	
Nil rate band available		(71,000)
		———
Taxable estate		669,726
		———

	£
Inheritance tax (40% × £669,726)	267,890

Estate rate (£267,890/£740,726) = 36.166%

	£
Inheritance tax payable by administrators (Note 1) ((£740,726 – £310,000) × 36.166%)	155,776

	£
Value that can be transferred to Avril (£370,000 – £155,776)	214,224

Notes

(1)   The gift of the house was a potentially exempt transfer made more than seven years prior to 1 October 2013. However, as Noland has continued to live in the house and is not paying a full commercial rent, the gift will be treated as a gift with reservation. Accordingly, the house will be included in Noland's death estate at its market value as at the date of death.

The inheritance tax due in respect of the gift with reservation will be paid by Crusoe as the owner of the property, not from the estate funds.

(2)   Business property relief is not available in respect of the shares in Kurb Ltd as the shares were not owned by Noland for the necessary two years.

Working: Gross chargeable transfers in the 7 years prior to death

	1 Nov 2010 £
Transfer of value	260,000
Annual exemption 2010/11	(3,000)
Annual exemption 2009/10 b/f	(3,000)
CLT	254,000

No lifetime tax and no death tax is due as covered by nil rate band, but the gross amount reduces NRB available on death estate.

Key answer tips

Always look out for an annual exemption brought forward from the previous year.

Examiner's comments

This question concerned the capital gains tax and inheritance tax position of a recently deceased individual. It was the most accessible of the optional questions and gave rise to the best answers.

Part (a) was done well by many candidates. Those who did not perform well were either not aware of the ability to carry back capital losses arising in the year of death or lacked precision in their application of the rules.

Part (b) required candidates to identify the *immediate tax implications* of a gift of shares. Answers to this part were relatively disappointing given the simplicity of the situation. It was particularly surprising to note how few candidates recognised that there would be no capital gain as the deemed proceeds would be equal to the donor's base cost. In addition, the word 'immediate' in the requirement meant that candidates should only have concerned themselves with what was going to happen now as opposed to what would happen in the future.

ACCA marking scheme		
		Marks
(a)	Current year offset	1.0
	Availability of carryback	0.5
	Three years – last in, first out	1.0
	Calculation:	
	Approach and layout	1.0
	Reduce chargeable gains to level of the AEA	0.5
	Rate of tax	0.5
		――
		4.5
	Maximum	4.0
		――
(b)	No IHT with reason	1.0
	No CGT with reason	1.0
	No stamp duty with reason	1.0
	Identification of use of deed of variation	1.0
	Advantage of this strategy	1.0
	Deadline	1.0
		――
		6.0
(c)	Transfer value of shares less the IHT due	1.0
	Gift within seven years of death	1.0
	Death estate	
	Quoted shares, house, Kurb Ltd, chattels/cash	2.0
	Refund of CGT	1.0
	Liabilities	0.5
	Nil band	1.0
	IHT at 40%	0.5
	Payable by administrators	1.0
	Treatment of house:	
	Identified as gift with reservation	0.5
	Reason	1.0
	Implication	1.0
	No BPR on shares in Kurb Ltd with reason	1.0
		――
		11.5
	Maximum	10.0
		――
Total		20
		――

20   KEPLER (ADAPTED)

Key answer tips

This is a reasonable capital taxes question but with some complications. The calculation of inheritance tax on the lifetime gift of shares is something a well prepared student should have no problems with. You might have been puzzled when asked to calculate Galileo's inheritance tax payable on his inheritance when there is none. The examiner did give a clue by saying tax payable (if any).

Payment by instalments is important in practice and the rules should be learnt.

You must also make sure that you are happy with the overseas aspects of personal tax, as these are very popular in the exam.

There are some easy marks in the last sections asking for advice about employment benefits.

(a)   (i)   **Galileo – Inheritance tax payable**

(1)   **Gift of shares in June 2009**

The gift of shares to Galileo was a potentially exempt transfer. It has become chargeable due to Kepler's death within seven years of the gift.

Any tax arising on a PET which becomes chargeable on death is payable by the donee (i.e. Galileo).

	£	£
Value of Kepler's holding prior to the gift to Galileo (2,000 × £485)		970,000
Less: Value of Kepler's holding after the gift (1,400 × £310)		(434,000)
Transfer of value		536,000
Less: Business property relief (W1)		(367,843)
Less: Annual exemption – 2009/10		(3,000)
– 2008/09 (W2)		(1,200)
Chargeable amount		163,957
Nil rate band at death	325,000	
Gross chargeable transfers in last 7 years (W2)	(305,000)	
Nil rate band available		(20,000)
Taxable amount		143,957
		£
Inheritance tax (£143,957 x 40%)		57,583
Less: Taper relief (3–4 years) (£57,583 × 20%)		(11,517)
Inheritance tax payable by Galileo		46,066

(2)   **Inheritance of shares in May 2013**

The inheritance tax payable in respect of the shares in the death estate will be paid by the executors and borne by Herschel, the residuary legatee.

None of the tax will be payable by Galileo.

Workings

(W1) **Business property relief**

BPR at 100% is available on unquoted trading company shares held for at least two years. However, BPR is restricted if the company has excepted assets.

Excepted assets and total assets

	Total assets	Excluding excepted assets
	£	£
Premises	900,000	900,000
Surplus land	480,000	–
Vehicles	100,000	100,000
Current assets	50,000	50,000
	1,530,000	1,050,000
BPR		
(£536,000 × 100% × (£1,050,000/£1,530,000))		367,843

Tutorial note

Excepted assets are those which have not been used wholly or mainly for business in the last two years and are not likely to be required for future use in the business.

(W2) **Lifetime gifts in the 7 years before 1 June 2009**

	1 Feb 2008	1 July 2008
	£	£
Transfer of value	311,000	1,800
(2 × £900)		
Less Annual exemptions		
- 2007/08	(3,000)	
- 2006/07 b/f	(3,000)	
- 2008/09		(1,800)
	305,000	Nil

–   No tax is due at the time of the gifts as they are PETs.

–   The NRBs at the time of the gifts, given in the question, are therefore not relevant.

–   Both gifts fall within 7 years of Kepler's death and therefore become chargeable on death.

–   Therefore, the GCTs in the 7 years before the gift in June 2009 are £305,000.

(ii)   **Payment by instalments**

The inheritance tax can be paid by instalments because Messier Ltd is an unquoted company controlled by Kepler at the time of the gift, and is still unquoted at the time of his death.

The tax is due in ten equal annual instalments starting on 30 November 2013.

Interest will be charged on any instalments paid late; otherwise the instalments will be interest free because Messier is a trading company that does not deal in property or financial assets.

All of the outstanding inheritance tax will become payable if Galileo sells the shares in Messier Ltd.

Tutorial note

Candidates were also given credit for stating that payment by instalments is available because the shares represent at least 10% of the company's share capital and are valued at £20,000 or more.

(b)   **Minimising capital gains tax on the sale of the paintings**

Galileo will become resident and ordinarily resident from the date he arrives in the UK as he intends to stay for more than three years. Prior to that date he will be neither resident nor ordinarily resident such that he will not be subject to UK capital gains tax.

Galileo should sell the paintings before he leaves Astronomeria; this will avoid UK capital gains tax completely.

Tutorial note

If Galileo sells the paintings after arriving in the UK, then as a non domiciled individual, the taxation of his gains depends on how much of them he remits to the UK.

If his unremitted gains exceed £2,000 then Galileo must choose whether to be taxed on all his gains (arising basis) but keep his entitlement to the capital gains annual exempt amount, or to be taxed only on the gains remitted to the UK (remittance basis) and lose the annual exempt amount.

> *If he chooses the remittance basis then he will not have to pay the £30,000/£50,000 annual charge as he has not been resident in the UK for 7 out of the last 9/12 out of the last 14 tax years.*
>
> *If his unremitted gains are less than £2,000, then the remittance basis of taxation applies automatically and he will be entitled to a capital gains annual exempt amount.*
>
> *However, since he wants to use the proceeds of selling his paintings to help buy a house, it is likely he will bring in all the money raised from the sale and consequently will automatically be taxed on the whole of his gains under the remittance basis, with the capital gains annual exempt amount.*

(c) (i) **Relocation costs**

Direct assistance

Messier Ltd can bear the cost of certain qualifying relocation costs of Galileo up to a maximum of £8,000 without increasing his UK income tax liability.

Qualifying costs include the legal, professional and other fees in relation to the purchase of a house, the costs of travelling to the UK and the cost of transporting his belongings. The costs must be incurred before the end of the tax year following the year of the relocation, (i.e. by 5 April 2015).

Assistance in the form of a loan

Messier Ltd can provide Galileo with an interest-free loan of up to £5,000 without giving rise to any UK income tax.

(ii) **Tax-free accommodation**

It is not possible for Messier Ltd to provide Galileo with tax-free accommodation.

The provision of accommodation by an employer to an employee will give rise to a taxable benefit unless it is:

– necessary for the proper performance of the employee's duties (e.g. a caretaker); or

– for the better performance of the employee's duties and customary (e.g. a hotel manager); or

– part of arrangements arising out of threats to the employee's security (e.g. a government minister).

As a manager of Messier Ltd, Galileo is unable to satisfy any of the above conditions.

Examiner's comments

This question was the most popular of the optional questions. It concerned inheritance tax, capital gains tax and income tax together with certain implications of moving to the UK from overseas. There were five separate parts to this question, all of which had to be addressed in the time. A number of candidates failed to tailor their answers to the number of marks available and wasted time producing inappropriately long answers.

Part (a) required candidates to calculate the inheritance tax payable by the donee of a potentially exempt transfer following the death of the donor. This was done well by many candidates although a minority did not consider business property relief, which was an important element of the question. Those who did consider business property relief often failed to recognise the existence of excepted assets in the company. Candidates were also asked to explain why the tax could be paid in instalments and to state when the instalments were due. This was not handled particularly well; many candidates did not know the circumstances in which payment by instalments is available and the payment dates given often lacked precision.

Part (b) concerned the liability to capital gains tax of an individual coming to the UK. It was only for two marks but it illustrated continued confusion on the part of many as to the treatment of someone who is not resident or ordinarily resident. Such a person is not subject to UK capital gains tax on personal investment assets and the remittance or otherwise of the proceeds is irrelevant. Candidates preparing for future exams should ensure that they fully understand the rules.

Part (c) involved the desire to assist an employee's relocation to the UK without giving rise to an income tax liability. This was done rather well with many candidates identifying the possibility of a tax free loan and relocation assistance.

		ACCA marking scheme	
			Marks
(a)	(i)	Fall in value	1
		Business property relief	1·5
		Annual exemptions	1·5
		Available nil band	1·5
		Inheritance tax at 40%	0·5
		Taper relief	1.0
		Tax due in respect of shares in death estate	1.0
			8.0
	(ii)	Valid reason for payment by instalments being available	1.0
		When due	1.0
		Interest on instalments	1·5
		Implication of Galileo selling the shares	1.0
			4·5
		Maximum	4.0
(b)		Residence and ordinary residence position	1.0
		Advice	1.0
			2.0

				Marks
(c)	(i)	Relocation costs		
		Tax free with maximum		1.0
		Examples of qualifying costs (0·5 each, maximum 1)		1.0
		Deadline		0·5
		Interest-free loan		
		Maximum tax-free amount		1.0
				———
				3·5
			Maximum	3.0
				———
	(ii)	Provision of accommodation will be taxed		1.0
		Reasons why not exempt		2.0
				———
				3.0
				———
Total				20
				———

21   ERNEST AND GEORGINA (ADAPTED)   *Walk in the footsteps of a top tutor*

Key answer tips

This question is in two separate parts. Part (a) is purely computational, and involves some fairly straightforward CGT computations.

Part (b) is purely written, and requires you to give advice about IHT and CGT.

The highlighted words in the written sections are key phrases that markers are looking for.

(a)   Ernest – Maximisation of after tax sales proceeds

Tutor's top tips

Make sure that you answer the specific question here. If you just calculate the gains and capital gains tax, you will not score full marks. You must also calculate the after tax proceeds (i.e. the cash proceeds less the tax), not the (gains less the tax).

If the examiner just asks you to 'calculate', there is no point in providing a detailed narrative to your answer, although you must label your calculations sufficiently so that the marker can see what you are calculating.

Sale of painting

	£	£
Proceeds	47,000	47,000
Less: Cost (probate value)	(23,800)	
Capital gain	23,200	
Less: Annual exempt amount	(10,600)	
Taxable gain	12,600	
Less: Capital gains tax (£12,600 × 28%)		(3,528)
After tax sales proceeds		43,472

Sale of shares

	£	£
Proceeds (£7,700 × £5)	38,500	38,500
Less: Cost (W1)	(52,780)	
Allowable loss	(14,280)	
Less: Capital gains tax		(Nil)
Plus: Income tax refund (see Tutorial note) (£14,280 × 40%)		5,712
After tax sales proceeds		44,212

Tutorial note

The capital loss on the sale of the shares in Neutron Ltd can be offset against Ernest's income in the year of disposal and/or the previous year.

This is because Ernest subscribed for the shares and, as they qualified for relief under the Enterprise Investment Scheme (EIS), Neutron Ltd satisfies the conditions necessary to qualify as a trading company for the purposes of offsetting any capital loss on disposal against income.

As the examiner just asks you to 'prepare calculations', you do not need to provide explanations of the elections claimed.

Working: Neutron Ltd – Cost of shares sold

		Number		£
1 April 2006	Purchase	18,600	@ £8.90	165,540
1 March 2008	Bonus issue – 1 for 4	4,650	@ Nil	Nil
		23,250		
1 July 2011	Rights issue – 1 for 10	2,325	@ £4.20	9,765
		25,575		175,305
1 February 2014	Proposed sale			
	(7,700/25,575 × £175,305)	(7,700)		(52,780)
Balance c/f		17,875		122,525

(b)   **Planning for inheritance tax**

Tutor's top tips

Read the information carefully!

It is easy to miss the fact that Ernest and Georgina are not married, and will not therefore benefit from the inter-spouse exemption for IHT purposes and will not benefit from the no gain, no loss transfers rule for CGT purposes.

The examiner has stated that credit was available for pointing this out, or for identifying the advantage of the couple getting married.

Do not confuse two people living together with a civil partnership. A civil partnership is where two people of the same sex officially register their partnership, and thereafter the couple are treated exactly the same as a married couple.

The examiner does not state who will die first, so you need to consider both alternatives: Ernest dying first and Georgina dying first.

There is no point in talking about making lifetime gifts to Eileen, as the information says that Ernest and George are only willing to make gifts to each other.

Note also that the examiner does not require you to prepare calculations.

Current position

– The shares in Neutron Ltd will be fully relieved via business property relief and therefore will not give rise to any inheritance tax either on Ernest's death or in the case of their subsequent disposal (on death or by lifetime gift) by whoever inherits them.

Tutorial note

The minimum two years ownership period does not apply to inherited assets that qualified for business property relief at the time of the previous death.

If Ernest dies before Georgina

– Ernest's estate, as reduced by the nil band of £325,000, will be taxed at 40%.

– When Georgina dies, her estate (including those assets inherited from Ernest), as reduced by the nil band of £325,000, will be taxed at 40%.

– Problem:

Some of Ernest's assets will be taxed twice, once on his death and again on the death of Georgina.

Quick succession relief will mitigate the double taxation if the deaths occur within five years of each other but only to a limited extent.

If Georgina dies before Ernest

– Georgina's estate of £60,000 will be covered by the nil rate band such that there will be no inheritance tax liability.

– When Ernest dies, his estate, as reduced by the nil band of £325,000, will be taxed at 40% (as above).

– Problem:

Georgina is wasting most of her nil rate band due to an insufficiency of assets.

Advice to Ernest

1. Ernest should give assets worth £265,000 to Georgina.

   This gift will be a potentially exempt transfer but will become a chargeable transfer if Ernest dies within seven years.

   Even so, the gift must improve Ernest's inheritance tax position. This is because:

   – the value of the assets given will be frozen at the time of the gift

   – the gift will be reduced by the annual exemption, and

   – taper relief will be available if Ernest survives the gift by at least three years.

   On Georgina's death, £325,000 of her estate, i.e. £265,000 more than before, will not give rise to any inheritance tax as it will be covered by her nil rate band.

   Accordingly, there will be no inheritance tax liability in respect of the value of the gift if Ernest survives the gift by seven years. This will save inheritance tax of £106,000 (£265,000 at 40%).

   The gift will be a disposal at market value for the purposes of capital gains tax. However, if any of the antiques or works of art have a cost and current market value of less than £6,000, these will be exempt from capital gains tax. The family home will also be exempted by principal private residence relief provided Ernest has not been absent from the home for substantial periods. Ernest should take advantage of his CGT annual exempt amount each year in making gifts.

   The gift should not be made out of the Neutron Ltd shares because of the availability of the 100% business property relief.

2.   Ernest should change his will and leave some assets directly to Eileen. These assets will then be subject to inheritance tax once only rather than potentially twice saving inheritance tax up to a maximum of 40%.

Tutor's top tips

Don't panic if you missed the fact that Ernest and Georgina are not married.

You could still score a pass mark here for demonstrating knowledge of business property relief, the nil band, rates of tax, the effect of lifetime giving on IHT and CGT and general planning points.

Examiner's comments

This question concerned capital gains tax and inheritance tax and was the most popular of the Section B questions. It was in two parts.

Part (a) required calculations of the after tax sales proceeds on the sale of a painting and some shares. Almost all candidates scored high marks for this part.

However, a significant minority merely calculated tax liabilities and not the after tax proceeds. This was important as the sale of the shares resulted in a loss such that, before taking account of the relief available in respect of the loss, the after tax sales proceeds was simply the proceeds and not zero as many candidates wrote.

There was also a common technical error in the answers to this question in that many candidates incorrectly treated the rights issue shares as a separate identifiable acquisition rather than as part of the original purchase.

The ability to offset the loss on the shares against income was a tricky point that was missed by the majority of candidates.

Part (b) required candidates to consider the inheritance tax position of an unmarried couple with unequal estates.

This part of the question was done well by the majority of those who attempted it and there was clearly a good knowledge of the subject. However, many candidates would have scored more marks if they had slowed down, written less and thought more. For example, it was relatively common for candidates to omit any reference to business property relief even though they were probably well aware of the existence of the relief.

The candidates who did best worked their way through the question logically and addressed specifics. They considered what would happen on the death of Ernest followed by the death of Georgina and then what would happen if the deaths occurred the other way around. They then explained, in a clear and succinct manner, the need to transfer assets to Georgina.

			Marks
ACCA marking scheme			
(a)	Sale of painting		
		Capital gain	1.0
		Annual exempt amount	0.5
		Capital gains tax payable	0.5
		After tax sales proceeds	0.5
	Sale of shares		
		Cost of shares sold	2.0
		Capital loss	0.5
		Tax saving in respect of losses	1.5
	After tax sales proceeds		0.5
			────
			7.0
			────
(b)	Current position		
		Business property relief on the shares in Neutron Ltd	1.5
	Ernest dies before Georgina		
		Tax on Ernest's death estate	1.0
		Tax on Georgina's death estate	1.0
		Identification of problem	1.0
		Quick succession relief	1.0
	Georgina dies before Ernest		
		Tax on Georgina's death estate	0.5
		Tax on Ernest's death estate	0.5
		Identification of problem	1.0
	Advice		
		Gift assets to Georgina	1.0
		Inheritance tax implications	1.5
		Potential inheritance tax saving	1.0
		Capital gains tax implications	2.0
		Should not gift shares in Neutron Ltd	0.5
		Change will and leave assets to Eileen	1.0
		Potential inheritance tax saving	0.5
			────
			15.0
		Maximum	13.0
			────
	Total		20
			────

22 FITZGERALD AND MORRISON (ADAPTED) *Walk in the footsteps of a top tutor*

Key answer tips

This is a classic question on IHT and CGT on lifetime gifts, covering gift relief, Entrepreneurs' relief, business property relief and related property.

It is a typical exam question and the interaction of IHT and CGT on lifetime gifts is an important part of the syllabus. It would be a good choice of question in the exam as there are easy marks to be had, and there are no obscure areas of the syllabus.

The highlighted words in the written sections are key phrases that markers are looking for.

(a) **Fitzgerald – gift of shares**

(i) **Availability of gift relief**

Tutor's top tips

Being able to list the conditions for reliefs such as gift relief, rollover relief, Entrepreneurs' relief, incorporation relief, etc, is a valuable skill for the exam.

You may need to provide a written answer, as here, rather than simply applying the rules to the numbers in the question.

The shares qualify for gift relief because Jay Ltd is an unquoted trading company.

For gift relief to be available, Pat must be either resident or ordinarily resident in the UK.

A claim for gift relief would have to be submitted by 5 April 2018.

The claim must be signed by Fitzgerald and Pat.

(ii) **Capital gains tax saved**

Tutor's top tips

Here gift relief is applied to shares, and it is therefore important to consider, as this is the donor's personal company, whether the company holds any chargeable assets which are not business assets, i.e. investments such as quoted company shares.

When comparing the chargeable business assets with the chargeable assets, remember that current assets, cars and non-wasting chattels with cost and proceeds of less than £6,000 are not chargeable.

Fitzgerald's chargeable gain

	£
Gain not qualifying for Entrepreneurs' relief	
Deemed proceeds – market value	127,500
Less: Cost	(32,000)
	95,500
Less: Gift relief (£95,500 x £900,000/£1,150,000 (W))	(74,739)
Chargeable gain	20,761

If a gift relief claim is not made, Fitzgerald's gain would increase by the amount of the gift relief and his capital gains tax liability would increase by £20,927 (£74,739 x 28%).

Working

	Chargeable assets	Chargeable business assets
	£	£
Premises	740,000	740,000
Plant and machinery	160,000	160,000
Quoted company shares	250,000	–
Motor cars	–	–
Net current assets	–	–
	1,150,000	900,000

Tutorial note

Entrepreneurs' relief will not be available as Fitzgerald has not owned the shares for 12 months. It is therefore not necessary to consider any wastage of Entrepreneurs' relief by making a gift relief claim.

Pat's chargeable gain

Gain qualifying for Entrepreneurs' relief	£
Proceeds	170,000
Less: Cost (£127,500 – £74,739)	(52,761)
Chargeable gain	117,239

If a gift relief claim is not made, Pat's gain would fall by the amount of the gift relief and his capital gains tax liability would reduce by £7,474 (£74,739 x 10%) due to the availability of Entrepreneur's relief.

The tax saved as a result of the claim is £13,453 (£20,927 – £7,474).

Tutorial note

Proof of the tax saving

	Claim £	No claim £
Fitzgerald's gain	20,761	95,500
Less: Annual exempt amount	(10,600)	(10,600)
Taxable gain	10,161	84,900
Capital gains tax at 28%	2,845	23,772
	£	£
Pat's gain – gift relief claimed	117,239	
Pat's gain – no gift relief claimed ((£170,000 – £127,500))		42,500
Less: Annual exempt amount	(10,600)	(10,600)
Taxable gain	106,639	31,900
Capital gains tax at 10%	10,664	3,190
Total capital gains tax	13,509	26,962

The capital gains tax saved as a result of making the claim is £13,453 (£26,962 – £13,509).

Candidates who recognised that the tax saving could be calculated by reference to the gift relief as £74,739 x (28% – 10%) = £13,453 received full marks.

   (iii)   **Availability of business property relief**

 Tutor's top tips

Like the capital gains tax reliefs mentioned above, it is important to be able to list the conditions for inheritance tax reliefs such as business property relief, agricultural property relief, quick succession relief, etc.

The shares qualify for business property relief because Jay Ltd is an unquoted company.

There is no need for Fitzgerald to have owned the shares for two years prior to the gift to Pat provided the shares were eligible for business property relief when he inherited them from his mother.

However, for business property relief to be available, Pat must either still own the shares when Fitzgerald dies or must have reinvested all of the sales proceeds in qualifying business property within three years of any sale.

(b) (i) **Potentially exempt transfer**

 Tutor's top tips

You need to be clear on the different valuation rules between capital gains tax and inheritance tax.

For CGT purposes, assets are transferred at market value, but for IHT the valuation is based on the diminution in value of the donor's estate, taking into account related property rules.

When looking at a question which involves both taxes, don't fall into the trap of automatically using the same values for both calculations (although in many instances the values will be the same).

The potentially exempt transfer is calculated by reference to the fall in value of Morrison's estate.

	£
Value before the gift	
– two paintings (£70,000/(£70,000 + £25,000) x £120,000)	88,421
Value after the gift	
– one painting (£25,000/(£25,000 + £25,000) x £70,000)	(35,000)
Transfer of value	53,421
Less: Marriage exemption	(5,000)
Annual exemption (current and brought forward)	(6,000)
Potentially exempt transfer	42,421

Tutorial note

The painting owned by Morrison's wife is related property. Accordingly, for the purposes of inheritance tax Morrison's painting(s) must be valued as a proportion of the value of the whole of the related property when determining the fall in value of his estate as a result of the gift.

The related property formula needs to be learnt to deal with this kind of calculation. It is as follows:

$$\frac{\text{Value of donor's property}}{\text{Value of donor's property} + \text{value of related property}} \times \text{Value of combined property}$$

Before the gift Morrison owned two paintings (worth £70,000) and his wife owned one (worth £25,000). The combined value of their related property was £120,000.

Following the gift Morrison owned only one painting (worth £25,000) and his wife still owned one painting (worth £25,000). The combined value of their related property was £70,000.

It is the fall in the related property value of Morrison's property which is used for inheritance tax purposes.

(ii)   **Capital gain and gift relief**

Tutor's top tips

It is easy to gain two marks here, as the capital gain calculation is simply the market value less the cost (although it is a non-wasting chattel it was bought and 'sold' for more than £6,000).

Gift relief is not available on non-business assets, therefore there is no need to discuss it any further.

The gain, computed by reference to the market value of the painting, will be £16,700 (£25,000 – £8,300).

A painting is not a qualifying asset for the purposes of gift relief.

Tutorial note

The gifts by Morrison to his wife and daughter are not linked transactions for the purposes of capital gains tax because they did not occur within six years of each other.

Examiner's comments

This question concerned inheritance tax and capital gains tax in respect of two proposed gifts. The question was in two parts.

The first part concerned the availability of gift relief and business property relief and required calculations of the effect of submitting a valid claim for gift relief. The calculations were done reasonably well with many candidates identifying the need to restrict the gift relief due to the existence of chargeable assets that were not business assets. The explanations of the availability of the reliefs were not done so well. The majority of candidates knew that an election for gift relief needed to be signed by both the donor and the donee but there was a general lack of precise knowledge as to which assets qualify for which reliefs. In relation to business property relief, many candidates thought the ownership requirements related to the donee rather than the donor.

The second part required calculations of a potentially exempt transfer and the capital gain arising in respect of a gift of a painting. The inheritance tax aspects of this part were difficult and were not done particularly well with the exception of the available exemptions. The capital gains tax aspects were more straightforward and were done well with the exception of weaker candidates who did not know which assets qualify for gift relief.

This question highlighted confusion between capital gains tax and inheritance tax and between gift relief and business property relief; candidates must learn these rules if they are to be successful in this exam.

		ACCA marking scheme			
					Marks
(a)	(i)	Unquoted trading company			1.0
		Need to determine status of donee			1.0
		Date			1.0
		Signatories			1.0
					4.0
	(ii)	Tax saved by Fitzgerald			
		Gain before gift relief			0.5
		Gift relief			1.5
		No Entrepreneurs' relief			0.5
		Capital gains tax saved			1.0
		Additional tax payable by Pat			
		Capital gain			1.0
		Entrepreneurs' relief			1.0
		Additional tax			1.5
		Total tax saved			0.5
					7.5
				Maximum	7.0
	(iii)	Unquoted company			0.5
		Ownership period			2.0
		Pat still owns the shares			2.0
					4.5
				Maximum	4.0
(b)	(i)	Fall in value			2.0
		Exemptions			1.0
					3.0
	(ii)	Capital gain			1.0
		Availability of gift relief			1.0
					2.0
Total					20

23 AVA (ADAPTED) *Walk in the footsteps of a top tutor*

Key answer tips

This is a typical optional question covering both the CGT and IHT implications of lifetime gifts, with a small section on the less frequently tested agricultural property relief.

There is also a requirement covering income tax penalties, which is revision of basic F6 knowledge.

The highlighted words in the written sections are key phrases that markers are looking for.

(a)   **Late submission of the 2011/12 income tax return**

Tutor's top tips

With this part, you either know the self assessment rules or you don't.

You should spend 7 minutes:

- *stating the due submission date*

- *listing the consequences of:*

  (i) late submission, and (ii) late payment.

However, remember that even if you can't remember the rules, you only need two marks to pass this part of the question.

As long as you remember the basic submission dates and penalties, this should be achievable.

Remember that interest is payable on ANY tax paid late, and runs from the due date to the date of payment.

Due date of submission

The latest date for submission of the 2011/12 income tax return was 31 January 2013 provided it was filed online.

Consequences of late submission

A penalty of £100 is charged because the return is late.

Daily penalties of £10 can be imposed for up to 90 days once the return is more than 3 months late.

Finally there will be a further penalty of 5% of the tax unpaid (with a minimum penalty of £300) because the return is between 6 and 12 months late.

Consequences of late payment

A penalty equal to 10% of the outstanding income tax will be levied because the tax will be paid more than six months after 31 January 2013, the date on which it was due.

The penalties in respect of both the late submission of the return and the late payment of the outstanding income tax will be set aside by the Tribunal if they are satisfied that Burt's illness is a reasonable excuse for the late reporting.

Interest will be charged on the outstanding income tax from 31 January 2013 until 14 December 2013 at an annual rate of 3.0 %.

(b)   (i)   **The availability of agricultural property relief and business property relief**

Tutor's top tips

Business property relief (BPR) appears in almost every exam, so you must make sure that you learn the key conditions for it to be available.

The words 'availability or non availability' give you a clue that either APR or BPR may not be available here! Make sure that you apply the rules to the facts given in connection with Hayworth farm.

This section is only worth four marks, so don't spend too much time here, no more than 7 minutes. Again, you only need two marks to pass!

Agricultural property relief

Hayworth Farm is agricultural property situated in the UK (or EEA) and therefore qualifies for agricultural property relief. The relief is given on the agricultural value of the property rather than its market value. 100% relief is available because the lease of the farm was granted after 1 September 1995.

Because the farm is farmed by tenants, it must have been owned by Ava and farmed by the tenants for at least seven years prior to the gift. Ava is able to satisfy this condition because she inherited the farm from her husband and therefore his period of ownership, of more than seven years, can be added to hers.

Business property relief

Business property relief is not available in respect of the gift of the farm as it has always been held as an investment and not as a business asset.

(ii)   **Tax payable in respect of the gift of Hayworth Farm**

Tutor's top tips

There are two different taxes to calculate here, so make sure that your answer is clearly labelled.

Don't forget that:

- *BPR and APR are only available when calculating inheritance tax.*

- *Gift relief and Entrepreneurs' relief are the key reliefs for consideration for CGT, however the examiner states that gift relief will not be claimed, so there is no point in discussing gift relief!*

Capital gains tax

	£
Deemed proceeds at market value	650,000
Less: Cost (probate value)	(494,000)
Chargeable gain	156,000
Less: Annual exempt amount (assumed to be available)	(10,600)
Taxable gain	145,400
Capital gains tax at 28%	40,712

The capital gains tax will be payable on 31 January 2015.

Tutorial note

1.   *Gift relief could be claimed here, as the property qualifies for APR however the question says that it will not be claimed.*

2.   *Entrepreneurs' relief is normally available on the disposal of a business; however it is not available here as the farm is rented out. It is therefore an investment asset rather than a business asset from the owner's point of view.*

Tutor's top tips

Make sure that you get the easy mark for stating the due date for payment of the tax, as this is specifically requested.

Inheritance tax

Tutor's top tips

Remember that the inheritance tax on a lifetime gift is usually based on the value at the date of gift, not the date of death, unless the asset falls in value.

The information in the question about the 5% annual increase in value here is totally irrelevant!

	£	£
Market value as at 1 February 2014		650,000
Less: APR (£445,000 × 100%) (Note 1)		(445,000)
Less: Annual exemptions – 2013/14		(3,000)
– 2012/13 (already used) (Note 2)		Nil
Potentially exempt transfer		202,000
Nil rate band available (Note 3)		
Ava's nil rate band	325,000	
Less: Gift on 1 December 2012		
(£251,000 – £6,000 AEs for 2012/13 and 2011/12))	(245,000)	
Ava's NRB available		(80,000)
Burt's nil rate band	325,000	
Less: Legacy to sister	(293,000)	
Burt's unused NRB available to Ava		(32,000)
Amount chargeable to inheritance tax		90,000
Inheritance tax at 40%		36,000
Less: Taper relief (3–4 years)		
(£36,000 × 20%)		(7,200)
Less: Lifetime IHT paid (none as gift = PET)		Nil
Inheritance tax payable		28,800

Tutorial note

1. *APR at 100% is available on this tenanted farm as the conditions explained in part (b)(i) are satisfied at the time of the gift.*

   However, in addition, when a PET becomes chargeable on death, APR is only available provided:

   - *The donee still owns the asset (or a replacement asset) at the date of the donor's death, or if he predeceases the donor, he owned the asset at his death, and*

   - *The gift still qualifies for relief at the date of death.*

   Therefore, to give APR in this calculation it must be assumed that these additional conditions are satisfied.

   Note that the examiner gave a mark for explaining this assumption (see end of answer).

2.   The gift of the farm is in 2013/14. The annual exempt amount for that year is available, however the previous year's annual exempt amount will have already been utilised against the gift of the quoted shares on 1 December 2012.

3.   Remember that when a spouse dies having not used all of their nil rate band, the excess can be transferred to the surviving spouse.

Burt's nil rate band available is reduced by the legacy to his sister which is chargeable on his death.

As this legacy was quoted shares, it is assumed that no BPR was available as he is unlikely to have a controlling interest in quoted shares.

Due date of payment

The inheritance tax will be payable on 31 July 2018 (i.e. six months after the end of the month of death).

Due date for claims

The claim to transfer Burt's unused nil rate band to Ava must be made by 31 January 2020 (i.e. two years from the end of the month of Ava's death).

Assumptions:

Ava's nephew still owns the farm on 1 January 2018 or has died prior to that date whilst owning it.

Tutor's top tips

Make sure that you follow the examiner's instruction to state:

*   The due dates payment

*   The due date for any claims, and

*   Any assumptions you have made.

Even if your assumptions are not the same as the examiner's, you may still be given credit.

Examiner's comments

This question concerned the late submission of an income tax return and the capital gains tax and inheritance tax implications of making a gift of a farm. It was in two parts.

Part (a) required a list of the consequences of the late submission of an income tax return and the late payment of the individual's income tax liability. This was a relatively straightforward requirement and the majority of candidates earned marks for the points they made. However, the list should have included four separate consequences whereas most candidates only included two. In particular, very few candidates considered the availability of a reasonable excuse for the client's behaviour despite the fact that the client's husband had died after a long and serious illness. Candidates would have benefited from thinking about the consequences before they started writing rather than, as it appeared from many of the scripts, writing about one or two points in great detail.

Part (b) concerned the inheritance tax and capital gains tax implications of the gift of a farm and was in two parts.

Part (i) required a reasoned explanation of the availability of both agricultural property relief and business property relief in respect of the gift. This part was answered well with many candidates scoring full marks.

Part (ii) required calculations of the capital gains tax and inheritance tax payable in respect of the gift together with the due dates of payment. Answers to this part varied considerably. Stronger candidates were able to score well with accurate calculations and correct dates. Weaker candidates confused the two taxes and the reliefs and exemptions available by, for example, including agricultural property relief in the capital gains tax computation. They also failed to include the dates asked for. The majority of students missed the fact that a proportion of the husband's nil rate band could be transferred to the widow.

		ACCA marking scheme		Marks
(a)		Submission date for income tax return		1.0
		Penalty for late submission		1.0
		Penalty on overdue tax		1.0
		Reasonable excuse		1.0
		Interest on overdue tax		1.0
				5.0
			Maximum	4.0
(b)	(i)	Agricultural property relief		
		Location		0.5
		Amount of relief		1.0
		Qualifying period		2.0
		Business property relief		1.0
				4.5
			Maximum	4.0
	(ii)	Capital gains tax		
		Amount payable		2.0
		Due date		1.0
		Inheritance tax		
		Transfer less agricultural property relief and annual exemption		2.0
		Nil rate bands		3.0
		Inheritance tax payable		1.5
		Due date		1.0
		Date of claim to transfer unused nil rate band		1.0
		Assumption		1.0
				12.5
			Maximum	12.0
	Total			20

24 SAKURA (ADAPTED) *Walk in the footsteps of a top tutor*

Key answer tips

This question is really two separate questions, which could be answered in any order.

Parts (a) and (b) cover the frequently tested area of IHT vs CGT for lifetime gifts. The twist here is that the 'gift' is actually the exchange of one asset for another asset.

Part (c) covers the new penalty regime for self assessment. This is an area where the rules have changed recently, and is therefore highly topical.

The highlighted words in the written sections are key phrases that markers are looking for.

(a) **Sakura: Capital gains tax and inheritance tax**

Tutor's top tips

There are two different taxes to deal with here and two different assets. Make sure that you clearly label your answer so that the marker can see which tax and which asset you are addressing.

Don't try to deal with both taxes at once or you are likely to become confused!

*You are asked to **explain** with supporting calculations, so you will need to use words as well as numbers in your answer.*

Make sure that you clearly identify the tax years of disposal, as requested, and give the due date for payment of the capital gains tax.

Capital gains tax

(i) *Receipt of insurance proceeds*

The receipt of insurance proceeds is treated as a chargeable disposal for capital gains tax purposes.

The disposal is deemed to occur in 2013/14, the date the insurance proceeds are received.

A chargeable gain on the antique figurine will arise as follows:

	£
Proceeds	67,000
Less: Cost	(28,000)
Chargeable gain	39,000

Action to minimise capital gains tax liability

Relief is available if the proceeds are reinvested in a replacement asset within 12 months of receipt of the insurance (i.e. by 31 May 2014). The gain may be deferred until the replacement asset is sold.

The purchase of a modern glass figurine may qualify as a replacement for an antique figurine, but this would need to be confirmed with HM Revenue and Customs.

As not all of the proceeds will be reinvested, a gain equal to the amount not reinvested will be chargeable immediately. The balance will be rolled over against the cost of the replacement.

Assuming the replacement figurine qualifies, and is purchased within 12 months, there would be no capital gains tax as the gain would be covered by the annual exempt amount of £10,600 as follows:

	£
Gain on figurine (above)	39,000
Less: Rolled over (balance)	(31,000)
	———
Chargeable gain (£67,000 – £59,000)	8,000
Less: Annual exempt amount	(8,000)
	———
Taxable gain	Nil
	———

The revised base cost of the new figurine would be £28,000 (£59,000 – £31,000)

(ii) *Sale of painting*

The sale of the painting to Sakura's son Cashel is deemed to be at market value, as Cashel is a connected person.

The disposal will occur during the tax year in which the sale takes place.

A chargeable gain will arise as follows:

	£
Proceeds (market value)	48,000
Less: Cost	(22,000)
	———
Chargeable gain	26,000
	———

Action to minimise capital gains tax liability

There is no gift relief available, as the painting is not a qualifying business asset.

The disposal of the painting should be deferred until after 6 April 2014, so that the gain is taxable in 2014/15.

This would enable Sakura to use another annual exempt amount of £10,600.

The capital gains tax liability would then be as follows:

	£
Gain on painting (above)	26,000
Less: Annual exemption	(10,600)
Taxable gain	15,400
Capital gains tax (£15,400 × 28%)	4,312
Due date	31 January 2016

Inheritance tax

(i) *Receipt of insurance proceeds*

Although Sakura's estate will fall in value, there is no inheritance tax implication as there was no gratuitous intent.

Tutorial note

Inheritance tax arises whenever there is a transfer of value (i.e. a diminution in the value of an estate as a result of a gift).

There must be an intention to make a gift to be caught under the IHT provisions.

(ii) *Sale of painting*

Tutorial note

A sale at full market value will have no inheritance tax consequences as there is no diminution in value.

However, a sale deliberately at an undervaluation will have inheritance tax implications as there is both a diminution in value, and gratuitous intent.

The exchange of the painting for the boat will cause a fall in value of Sakura's estate.

This will be a potentially exempt transfer for inheritance tax purposes, with the value based on the diminution in value of the estate:

	£
Value before the transfer (painting)	48,000
Less: Value after the transfer (boat)	(25,000)
Diminution in value	23,000
Less: Annual exemption	
Current tax year	(3,000)
Brought forward	(3,000)
Potentially exempt transfer	17,000

The potentially exempt transfer will only become chargeable if Sakura dies within seven years of the transfer, in which case it would be covered by the nil rate band of £325,000.

(b)   Cashel: disposal of boat

Capital gains tax

The disposal is exempt, as the boat is a wasting chattel.

Tutorial note

Remember that wasting chattels are exempt from capital gains tax.

A wasting chattel is tangible, moveable property with an expected life of 50 years or less. Boats are always deemed to be wasting chattels.

Inheritance tax

There will be no inheritance tax implications as Cashel's estate does not fall in value. The boat is exchanged for a more valuable asset.

(c)   Penalty for honest mistake

Tutor's top tips

There are five marks available here, so try to make sure that you have at least five separately identifiable points in your answer.

- The penalty for an honest mistake would be based on a percentage of the lost revenue (i.e. the additional tax due).
- The percentage due depends on the taxpayer's behaviour:
    - If Sakura has taken reasonable care in preparing his tax return, then no penalty will be due.
    - If the error was due to a careless mistake, the maximum penalty charged would be 30% of the tax due.
- The penalty may be reduced if the error is disclosed to HM Revenue and Customs.
    - Unprompted disclosure could lead to the penalty being reduced to 0%.
    - If the disclosure was prompted, a minimum of 15% would be due.

Examiner's comments

Part (a) required candidates to consider both the capital gains tax and inheritance tax implications of the destruction of an asset and the exchange of one asset for another. This required some clear thinking as to who was disposing of what together with the ability not to confuse the two capital taxes. This part of the question was answered reasonably well by many candidates. However, some candidates would have benefited from addressing each of the taxes separately under clear headings as this would have helped them to organise their thoughts and prevent confusion.

The calculations of the capital gains were done well as were the implications of the potentially exempt transfer.

However, the deferral of the gain on the asset destroyed was usually dealt with, incorrectly, by reference to business asset rollover relief. The reliefs available in respect of capital gains involve a fairly tricky bunch of rules and definitions. Candidates would be well advised to learn the conditions that must be satisfied in order for each of the reliefs to be available.

Part (b) was very small but still required thought; it involved the disposal of a boat. For one of the two available marks candidates simply had to state that a boat is an exempt asset for the purposes of capital gains tax.

However, the vast majority did not pause for thought and instead talked about the capital loss that would occur on disposal.

The final part of the question tested candidates' knowledge of the penalties that may be charged in respect of an error in a tax return. This is a current issue as the rules have changed recently but a minority of candidates were not aware of the new rules. Candidates should ensure that they keep up to date with the changes to the tax system and that they read the Finance Act articles published in Student Accountant.

ACCA marking scheme		Marks
(a)	Capital gains tax	
	Insurance proceeds	2.0
	Painting	2.0
	Inheritance tax	
	Figurine	1.0
	Painting	2.0
	Minimisation of liability	
	Availability of relief and conditions	2.5
	Quantification of relief	1.5
	Use of annual exemptions	1.5
	Liability and due date	1.0
		13.5
	Maximum	13.0
(b)	Capital gains tax	1.0
	Inheritance tax	1.0
		2.0
(c)	The penalty	2.0
	Reasonable care	0.5
	Maximum percentage	0.5
	Disclosure	2.0
		5.0
Total		20

MULTI TAX PERSONAL INCLUDING OVERSEAS

25 MING WONG (ADAPTED) *Walk in the footsteps of a top tutor*

Key answer tips

This question looks at the effect of domicile on a person's inheritance tax and income tax liabilities. It has been adapted to reflect the extensive changes to the income tax rules for non domiciled individuals which were introduced after the original question was set.

Without knowledge of these rules, it would be very difficult to answer parts (c) and (d).

The highlighted words in the written sections are key phrases that markers are looking for.

Tutor's top tips

Overseas aspects of personal tax are very popular in the exam, as they are not examined in detail in F6. You must make sure that you understand these areas, as these are very likely to be tested in the exam.

Section (a) is worth 4 marks, so try to make sure you have at least 4 separately identifiable points in your answer.

(a) **Acquiring UK domicile**

Domicile for IHT purposes

Ming will be deemed domiciled in the UK for the purposes of IHT if she is resident in the UK for 17 out of the 20 years of assessment ending with the year of assessment in which a chargeable transfer is made.

Ming has been resident in the UK since 1998/99, and will therefore be subject to UK IHT in respect of her overseas assets as well as her UK assets if she dies or makes a chargeable transfer during 2014/15 or a subsequent year.

Domicile under general law

Ming can only have one place of domicile at any given time denoting the country considered her permanent home.

She can become domiciled in the UK by acquiring a domicile of choice. This will require the severing of all ties with Yanga, and settling in the UK with the intention of staying there indefinitely.

The intention will have to be demonstrated by positive actions, such as making a will under UK law and obtaining British citizenship.

Tutorial note

Remember that the "deemed domicile" rules just apply for IHT purposes, not for IT or CGT.

(b)   **Consequences for IHT of acquiring UK domicile**

Tutor's top tips

*Read the requirement carefully – it asks for an **explanation** of why Ming's assets are or are not subject to UK IHT, as well as a calculation of the increase in her IHT liability.*

You will often be able to score marks more quickly for written sections of answers than for calculations, so it is always a good idea to attempt the written sections first.

Make sure that you apply your knowledge to the assets in the question – don't just list the rules.

Ming will be charged to UK IHT on her worldwide assets if she becomes domiciled in the UK (whether this is under general law or is deemed for IHT purposes). However, if Ming is not domiciled in the UK she will only be charged to UK IHT in respect of her UK assets.

The following rules apply in determining the location of assets:

1   Land and buildings are situated where they are physically located. Therefore, the property in the UK is chargeable regardless of domicile, whilst the property in Yanga is not chargeable if Ming is not UK domiciled.

2   Registered shares and securities are situated where they are registered, or where they would normally be dealt with in the ordinary course of business. Therefore, the shares in Ganyan Inc. are not chargeable if Ming is not UK domiciled.

3   Chattels are situated where they are physically located at the relevant time, so the antiques are chargeable to IHT regardless of domicile.

4   Bank accounts are situated at the branch that maintains the account. Therefore, the deposit at the London branch is chargeable regardless of domicile, whilst the deposit at the Yanga branch is not chargeable if Ming is not UK domiciled.

5   A debt is situated where the debtor resides at the date of the chargeable event (i.e. gift or death). Therefore, the loan is not chargeable if Ming is not UK domiciled.

If Ming were to die owning her current portfolio of assets, the potential IHT liability on her estate can be calculated assuming she is UK domiciled and assuming she is not UK domiciled as follows:

Estate computation	Not domiciled in UK £	Domiciled in UK £
Main residence	260,000	260,000
House in Yanga	Nil	60,000
Shares in Ganyan Inc (W1)	Nil	124,000
Antiques	61,500	61,500
Bank accounts	38,000	58,000
Debtor	Nil	15,000
Chargeable estate	359,500	578,500

As Ming has made no lifetime gifts, all of the nil rate band is available.

	£	£
IHT on the estate		
(£359,500 – £325,000) × 40%	13,800	
(£578,500 – £325,000) × 40%		101,400
Less Double taxation relief (W2)	Nil	(32,252)
IHT liability	13,800	69,148

The potential increase in Ming's liability to UK IHT if she were to become domiciled in the UK is £55,348 (£69,148 – £13,800).

Tutorial note

An endowment mortgage is repaid upon death by the related life assurance contract, and is not therefore deductible as a debt from the estate computation.

Workings

(W1) **Valuation of shares in Ganyan Inc**

¼ up valuation:

(308p + ¼ (316p – 308p)) = 310p x 40,000 shares

(W2) **Double taxation relief**

DTR is the lower of the overseas tax and the UK tax calculated at the average estate rate.

$$\text{Estate rate} = \frac{£101,400}{£578,500} \times 100 = 17.528\%$$

				£	£
Yanga house					
Lower of	(1)		Overseas tax suffered	13,600	
	(2)		UK IHT		
			(17.528% × £60,000)	10,517	10,517
Shares in Yanga					
Lower of	(1)		Overseas tax suffered	34,400	
	(2)		UK IHT		
			(17.528% × £124,000)	21,735	21,735
					32,252

Tutor's top tips

Don't worry if you have made a mistake in the death estate calculation. As long as your calculation of the estate rate and double tax relief is consistent with your figures, you will still score full marks here.

Make sure you compare the two IHT liabilities you have calculated to show the potential increase. Again, you will be awarded the mark here for consistency.

(c) **Income tax computation – 2012/13 (not domiciled in the UK)**

For 2012/13 Ming is resident and ordinarily resident in the UK, but not UK domiciled. Her unremitted overseas income exceeds £2,000, therefore she is assessed to income tax as follows:

- All UK income on an arising basis.

- Overseas income on an arising basis with full personal allowances available unless a claim for the remittance basis is made.

- If a claim for the remittance basis is made, she will be assessed on her overseas income remitted into the UK and no personal allowance is available.

- However, as Ming has made no remittances in 2012/13, she will be assessed on her UK income only.

- She will also be liable to the £50,000 remittance basis tax charge as she has been resident and ordinarily resident for more than 12 out of the previous 14 tax years.

- The claim for the remittance basis can be made on a year by year basis.

Tutorial note

Where an individual has less than £2,000 of unremitted overseas income and gains in a tax year, the remittance basis applies by default, without making any claim. The full personal allowance is available, and there is no £50,000 remittance basis charge.

(d)   **Income tax payable under both bases of assessment**

Tutor's top tips

There are lots of easy marks available here for basic income tax computations, but the calculation of DTR for the arising basis is tricky as there is more than one source of overseas income.

Try not to get too bogged down with this, and remember that you will score some marks if your answer is partly correct.

Make sure that you conclude which basis is preferable based on your calculations.

If Ming claims the remittance basis

As she has not remitted any of her Yangan income, her income tax liability will be:

	£
Employment income	30,100
Bank interest (£1,680 × 100/80)	2,100
Total income	32,200
Less: Personal allowance (Note 1)	(Nil)
Taxable income	32,200

Analysis of income: Savings £2,100, Other income £30,100

Income tax:

£		£
30,100 × 20% (Other income)		6,020
2,100 × 20% (Savings income)		420
32,200		
		6,440
Plus: Remittance basis charge (Note 2)		50,000
		56,440
Less: Tax suffered at source:		
Bank interest (£2,100 × 20%)		(420)
Income tax payable		56,020

Tutorial note

1.   *Remember that there is no personal allowance available if Ming elects for the remittance basis.*

2.   *The remittance basis charge only applies because Ming is a long term resident in the UK, having been resident for 12 out of the last 14 tax years.*

If Ming does not claim the remittance basis

Ming is assessed on an arising basis on her worldwide income. Her income tax liability will be as follows:

	£
Taxable UK income (as above)	32,200
Overseas income:	
Rental income	8,990
Dividends (£5,950 × 100/85 × 100/90)	7,778
Bank interest (£1,530 × 100/85)	1,800
Total income	50,768
Less: Personal allowance	(8,105)
Taxable income	42,663

Analysis of income:
Dividends £7,778, Savings (£2,100 + £1,800) = £3,900,
Other income (£42,663 − £7,778 − £3,900) = £30,985

Income tax:	£
£	
30,985 × 20% (other income)	6,197
3,385 × 20% (savings)	677
34,370	
515 × 40% (savings)	206
7,778 × 32½% (dividends)	2,528
42,663	
	9,608
Less Double taxation relief (W1)	(3,417)
IT liability	6,191
Less: Tax suffered at source:	
Dividends (£7,778 × 10%)	(778)
Bank interest (£2,100 × 20%)	(420)
IT payable	4,993

Conclusion

It is clearly not beneficial for Ming to claim the remittance basis for 2012/13, as this will increase her UK income tax payable by £51,027 (£56,020 − £4,993).

Tutorial note

The overseas dividends from Ganyan Inc are grossed up for the overseas tax suffered, but also have a deemed tax credit of 10% attached to them just like UK dividends.

> This means that you need to gross them up again by 100/90, claim DTR for the overseas tax, then deduct the 10% notional tax credit.
>
> When calculating the UK tax on the overseas income this 10% credit has to be deducted for the purposes of the DTR computation.
>
> Where the foreign dividends are taxed on the arising basis, they are taxed at 32.5% in the higher rate band.
>
> Where foreign dividends are taxed on the remittance basis, they are taxed at 40% in the higher rate band (not applicable here, as Ming did not remit her foreign dividends to the UK).

Workings

(W1) Double taxation relief

		£	£
Rental income			
Lower of			
(i)	Overseas tax (£8,990 x 35%)	3,147	3,147
(ii)	UK income tax (W2)	3,651	
Bank interest			
Lower of			
(i)	Overseas tax (£1,800 x 15%)	270	270
(ii)	UK income tax (£1,800 x 20%)	360	
Dividends			
Lower of			
(i)	Overseas tax (£5,950 x 15/85)	1,050	
(ii)	UK income tax	nil	nil
	(£7,778 x (10% – 10% tax credit))		
			———
Total DTR			3,417
			———

(W2) UK income tax on overseas rental income

Taxable income including rental income (as above) = £42,663

Taxable income excluding rental income = (£42,663 – £8,990) = £33,673

Analysis of income excluding overseas rental income:

Dividends £7,778, Savings £3,900, Other income £21,995 (£30,985 – £8,990)

UK income tax excluding overseas rental income would therefore be:

£	£
21,995 × 20% (other income)	4,399
3,900 × 20% (savings)	780
7,778 × 10% (dividends)	778
———	
33,673	
———	———
Income tax liability	5,957
	———

UK income tax on overseas rental income is therefore:
(£9,608 – £5,957)   3,651

———

Alternative calculation:

	£
Tax on rental income (£8,990 x 20%)	1,798
Plus: Additional tax on income as it moves into the higher rate band when overseas rental income included:	
Savings income (£515 x 20%)	103
Dividends (£7,778 x 22.5%)	1,750
	———
UK income tax on overseas rental income being included	3,651
	———

Tutorial note

Where there is more than one source of foreign income, the tax suffered is found by excluding the foreign sources one by one, starting with the source suffering the highest rate of overseas tax.

Thus the UK tax on the rents could be determined by first excluding the rents and the tax on the foreign interest can next be found by excluding the rents and the interest, and so on.

However, whatever remains in the computation is still subject to the basic rule of dividends as top slice, with interest next and non-savings income as the lowest part.

---

26   JAN (ADAPTED)

Key answer tips

This is a reasonably straightforward question covering income tax with some overseas aspects, and the capital gains tax implications of a takeover. You must make sure you learn the rules regarding non domiciled individuals. There have been extensive changes recently, and these are very likely to be tested in the exam.

Part (b) should be 3 easy marks for discussing how an accommodation benefit is taxed.

Make sure you don't get confused in part (c) between takeovers and incorporation relief.

- A takeover is when shares are exchanged for shares, and the new shares "step into the shoes" of the old

- Incorporation relief applies when assets are exchanged for shares, and the gain is rolled over against the cost of the shares.

(a)   **Income tax computation – 2012/13**

Jan's position for income tax purposes is as follows:

- As he intends to stay in the UK for the medium to long term, he will be resident and ordinarily resident in the UK from 1 May 2012, but not UK domiciled

- His unremitted overseas income in 2012/13 is < £2,000.

Accordingly Jan will be taxed on:

- All of his UK income on an arising basis, and
- His overseas income on remittance basis
- With full personal allowance available.

Tutorial note

1. As Jan's unremitted overseas income is less than £2,000, there is no choice of basis of assessment to make. He will be assessed on the remittance basis on his overseas income.

    Whether or not he is a long term resident (i.e. resident and ordinarily resident in the UK for at least 7 years out of the previous 9 years) is not relevant.

    The remittance basis charge is only an issue if unremitted income and gains exceeds £2,000.

2. Jan intends to stay in the UK for the medium to long term and so will become ordinarily resident in the UK, however his domicile will not change unless he takes steps to change his domicile of origin to the UK.

    His basis of assessment each year will therefore be dependent on his level of unremitted income and gains.

	Total £	Other income £	Savings £	Dividends £
Salary ($\frac{11}{12} \times$ £74,967)	68,720			
Car benefit (W1)	10,850			
Fuel benefit (W1)	5,151			
Other benefits	3,780			
Employment income	88,501	88,501		
Dividends (£3,240 × 100/90)	3,600			3,600
ISA interest (exempt)	Nil			
Bank interest (£740 × 100/80)	925		925	
O/seas property income (W2)	8,360	8,360		
Total Income	101,386	96,861	925	3,600
Less: Personal allowance (W3)	(7,412)	(7,412)		
Taxable income	93,974	89,449	925	3,600

Income tax	£
£	
34,370 × 20% (other income)	6,874
55,079 × 40% (other income)	22,032
_____	
89,449	
925 × 40% (savings)	370
3,600 × 32.5% (dividends)	1,170
_____	
93,974	
_____	_____
	30,446
Less DTR (W4)	(3,621)
	_____
Income tax liability	26,825
Less Tax suffered at source	
On dividend income (£3,600 × 10%)	(360)
On bank interest (£925 × 20%)	(185)
PAYE	(25,148)
	_____
Income tax payable	1,132
	_____

Tutorial note

Remember that the personal allowance is available despite being assessed on the remittance basis in relation to overseas income.

This is because the unremitted overseas income and gains for 2012/13 is less than £2,000.

Workings

(W1) Car and fuel benefits

CO_2 emissions = 218 g/km, available 9 months

	%
Petrol	11
Plus (215 − 100) × $^1/_5$	23
	___
Appropriate percentage	34
	___

	£
Car benefit (£42,550 x 34% x 9/12)	10,850
	_____
Fuel benefit (£20,200 x 34% x 9/12)	5,151
	_____

(W2) Overseas property income

Rental income is received net of 45% overseas tax.

Gross income = (£4,598 × 100/55) = £8,360

(W3) **Personal allowance**

		£
Basic PA		8,105
Reduction (50% × (£101,386 − 100,000))		(693)
Adjusted PA		7,412

(W4) **Double tax relief on rental income**

Lower of

			£
(a)	UK income tax (40% × £8,360)		3,344
	Plus: Restriction of PA (£8,105 − £7,412) × 40%		277
			3,621
(b)	Overseas tax (45% × £8,360)		3,762

Tutorial note

The UK direct income tax reduction from excluding £8,360 of property income is £3,344 (£8,360 × 40%). However, as the total income is now less than £100,000, there is no longer a restriction in the personal allowance.

There is no additional knock on effect on how the savings income and dividend income is taxed as they will still fall above the basic rate band limit and be taxed at 40% and 32.5% respectively.

(b) **Taxable benefit – accommodation**

If Jan accepts the offer, he will occupy the building for a period of eight months in the tax year 2013/14 (from 6 August 2013 – 5 April 2014).

The company will pay the rent for six months and therefore the benefit will only last for six months.

The taxable benefit is the higher of: £

(i)	The rent borne by the company	(£600 × 6)	3,600
(ii)	The annual (rateable) value	(£6,000 × 6/12)	3,000

The benefit is therefore £3,600.

There is no additional 'expensive accommodation' benefit as the company does not own the property.

(c) (i) **Paper for paper exchange rules**

The proposed transaction broadly falls under the 'paper for paper' exchange rules. Where this is the case, chargeable gains do not arise. Instead, the new holding stands in the shoes (and inherits the base cost) of the original holding.

The company issuing the new shares must:

- as a result of the transaction end up with more than 25% of the ordinary share capital (or a majority of the voting power) of the old company, or

- make a general offer to shareholders in the other company with a condition that, if satisfied, would give the acquiring company control of the other company.

The exchange must be for *bona fide* commercial reasons and must not have as its main purpose (or one of its main purposes) the avoidance of CGT or corporation tax. The acquiring company can obtain advance clearance from HMRC that the conditions will be met.

If part of the offer consideration is in the form of cash, a gain must be calculated using the part disposal rules.

If the cash received is not more than the higher of £3,000 or 5% of the total value on takeover, then the amount received in cash can be deducted from the base cost of the securities under the small distribution rules.

(ii) **Capital gain arising on the takeover**

The cost details are as follows:

	Number of shares	Cost £
August 2002: acquisition	2,500	10,175
January 2004: bonus issue	22,500	Nil
Balance at takeover	25,000	10,175

The takeover consideration is forecast to be:

	£
Shares (25,000 × 3/5 × £3.55)	53,250
Cash (25,000 × £0.25)	6,250
Takeover consideration	59,500

The cash of £6,250 exceeds £3,000 and £2,975 (5% × £59,500 takeover value), so there is a part disposal gain to be calculated.

	£
Disposal proceeds = cash received	6,250
Apportioned cost (£10,175 × £6,250/£59,500)	(1,069)
Chargeable gain	5,181

Tutorial note

Entrepreneurs' relief is not available as Gilet Ltd is not Jan's personal trading company and he does not work for the company. The gain would therefore be taxed at 28%, as Jan is a higher rate taxpayer.

(iii) **Qualifying corporate bond**

A qualifying corporate bond ('QCB') is a security that represents a normal commercial loan. This excludes bonds that can be converted into shares. The security cannot carry a right to excessive interest, or interest which depends on the result of the owner's business.

The security must be expressed in sterling. There can be no provision for conversion into or redemption in another currency. The security must have been acquired (by the person disposing of it) after 13 March 1984.

If Jan received a QCB instead of cash, the gain will be apportioned between the shares and the loan stock in the same way as for cash above.

The new shares will inherit the base cost of the old shares, and any gain will only arise on the subsequent disposal of the new shares, as explained above.

However, unlike with cash consideration received, there is no chargeable gain arising at the time of the takeover in respect of receiving the QCB.

Instead, the gain apportioned to the loan stock is calculated as for cash consideration and will be £5,181 as above, however the gain is not taxed, it is 'frozen' and deferred until the loan stock is disposed of. At that time, the 'frozen' gain becomes chargeable.

The increase in value of the QCBs from the takeover to the date of sale is exempt from CGT as QCBs are exempt assets for individuals. Only the 'frozen' deferred gain becomes chargeable.

27 ARTHUR AND CINDY WAKEFIELD (ADAPTED) *Walk in the footsteps of a top tutor*

Key answer tips

This question covers a number of different areas.

Part (a) is about husband and wife income tax planning, where one spouse is a basic rate taxpayer and the other a higher rate taxpayer.

Then part (b) covers setting up a business as a partnership (unincorporated) versus a company, which should be familiar to you.

Part (c) is less obvious, but is actually about investing in VCT or EIS shares - a point which some students may miss.

Part (d) is also not obvious, and is about the pre-owned asset anti-avoidance legislation for inheritance tax. You need to be prepared for some less mainstream areas to appear in questions, but if you don't know the rules you can still get a good pass mark without even answering this section!

Part (e) is a very straightforward section on self assessment administration and penalties.

The highlighted words in the written sections are key phrases that markers are looking for.

Tutor's top tips

There is a lot to do in this question, and some sections are easier than others. In the exam, you need to make sure you leave enough time to attempt all parts of the question.

You don't necessarily have to attempt each part in order, as long as you label your answer clearly. For example, part (e) is very straightforward, and is a completely standalone section, so why not do this first for an easy 4 marks?

Note that the detailed requirements are set out in the manager's email, so you must make sure you cover all the points mentioned. The examiner also gives tips on how to approach the harder areas of the question here too.

Make sure you set out the answer as a memorandum, as there are 2 easy marks available for doing this.

MEMORANDUM

To   Tax manager
From   Tax assistant
Date   2 December 2013
Subject   Arthur and Cindy Wakefield

This memorandum considers the transfer of investments from Cindy to Arthur and various other matters.

(a)   **Gift to Arthur**

        (i)   **Investment property or quoted shares**

Tutor's top tips

You need to make sure your answer is clearly labelled here so that the examiner can see which individual you are dealing with and which investment you are giving them.

It is vital that you think about the type of income each investment will generate, as this will affect the rate of tax paid.

The income from the shares will be dividends, whereas the income from the investment property will be rent.

There are two options:

(i)   Cindy gives Arthur the investment property. This means Arthur will receive the rent and Cindy will receive the dividends from the shares

(ii)   Cindy gives Arthur the shares. This means Arthur will receive the dividends and Cindy will receive the rent.

Then you need to think about how much tax each of them will pay on the extra income.

You could prepare full income tax computations with and without the extra income, which would still score full marks, but would be very time consuming.

> *The quickest way is to look at the level of other income to see into which income tax band the extra income will fall. Cindy is clearly already a higher rate taxpayer, but Arthur still has some of his basic rate band remaining.*

Cindy is a higher rate taxpayer. Arthur is a basic rate taxpayer with taxable income of £24,475 (£32,580 – £8,105).

He has £9,895 (£34,370 – £24,475) of the basic rate band remaining.

The family's after tax income will be maximised if the additional income tax on the inherited assets is minimised.

If Arthur owns the investment property:

Cindy	£
Dividend income	12,300
Income tax (£12,300 at 32½%)	3,997
Less: Tax credit at 10%	(1,230)
	2,767

Arthur	£
Property income	14,100
£9,895 at 20%	1,979
£4,205 at 40%	1,682
Income tax	3,661
Total tax payable (£2,767 + £3,661)	6,428

If Arthur owns the quoted shares:

Cindy	£
Property income	14,100
Income tax (£14,100 at 40%)	5,640

Arthur	£
Dividend income	12,300
£9,895 at 10%	989
£2,405 at 32½%	782
	1,771
Less: Tax credit at 10%	(1,230)
Income tax	541
Total tax payable (£5,640 + £541)	6,181

Tutor's top tips

Once you have calculated the total tax under each option, don't forget to provide your recommendation. Marks will be awarded here for consistency. As long as the advice ties in with your figures, you will be given the mark!

Advice

The family's tax liability will be minimised if Cindy gives the quoted shares to Arthur.

(ii) **Annual income tax saving and other issues**

Tutor's top tips

This part of the question will again be awarded marks for consistency. You are comparing the total tax on the extra income from your recommendation above with the total tax at higher rates if Cindy keeps both assets.

Don't forget to identify the other tax implications, as requested in the email from the manager. This is just straightforward discussion of a gift of an asset from wife to husband. There are three capital taxes to think about, CGT, IHT and stamp duty.

Annual income tax saving

If Cindy owns all of the inherited assets the additional income tax is as follows.

	£
Tax on property income (see (i))	5,640
Tax on dividend income (see (i))	2,767
	8,407

The tax saved following the gift of the quoted shares to Arthur is £2,226 (£8,407 – £6,181).

Other issues

Transfers between spouses take place at no gain, no loss for the purposes of capital gains tax. Arthur's base cost in the quoted shares will equal Cindy's base cost of £305,000.

There are no inheritance tax implications due to the exemption for transfers between spouses.

There are no stamp duties on gifts.

(b)   **The new business**

Tutor's top tips

This section of the question is about the choice between starting to trade as an unincorporated business or as a company.

The key to scoring well is to make sure you don't just list all the differences you have learned, but actually apply your knowledge to the scenario.

*Make sure you answer the question – it asks for the **advantages** of operating as a **partnership** whilst the business is making **losses**.*

There are two tax advantages to operating the business as a partnership.

(i)   **Reduction in taxable income**

Tutorial note

Remember that partners are assessed on ALL their trading profits (or losses), and drawings have no tax effect. However, if a company is set up, the company is a separate legal entity and Cindy and Arthur will be employees of the company.

They will then be subject to tax on salaries taken from the company, and the company will be able to deduct the salaries and employer's NIC from its taxable trading profits.

If the new business is operated as a company, Cindy and Arthur would both be taxed at 40% on their salaries. In addition, employer national insurance contributions would be due on £1,012 (£8,500 – £7,488), and employee national insurance contributions on £895 (£8,500 – 7,605) in respect of each of them.

If the new business is operated as a partnership, the partners would have no taxable trading income because the partnership has made a loss; any salaries paid to the partners would be appropriations of the profit or loss of the business and not employment income. The partners would pay no Class 2 or Class 4 national insurance contributions while the business was making losses.

(ii)   **Earlier relief for trading losses**

Tutorial note

Remember that losses made by a company can only be set against profits within the company, whereas losses made by a sole trader or partner may be set against the individual's other income too.

If the new business is operated as a company, its tax adjusted trading loss in the year ending 31 March 2015 would be as follows:

		£
Forecast loss		(44,000)
Purchase of equipment – capital		24,000
Capital allowances:		
Cost of equipment	24,000	
Less: AIA	(24,000)	(24,000)
		(44,000)
Cost of employing Cindy and Arthur:		
Salaries paid to Cindy and Arthur (£8,500 × 2)		(17,000)
Employer's national insurance ((£8,500 − £7,488) × 13·8% × 2)		(279)
Tax adjusted trading loss		(61,279)

The loss could not be offset in the current year as the company would have no other income or gains, and therefore, it would have to be carried forward for offset against future trading profits.

The profit for the year ending 31 March 2016, as reduced by the salaries payable to Cindy and Arthur, is expected to be less than the loss available for relief. Accordingly, the trading losses will not be fully relieved until the year ending 31 March 2017. This equates to 1 January 2018 from a cash flow point of view, i.e. the date on which the corporation tax liability for the year ending 31 March 2017 is payable.

It should also be recognised that the loss will never be relieved if the company ceases to trade before it has made sufficient taxable profits.

If the new business is operated as a partnership, any salaries paid to the partners would not be deductible for the purposes of computing trading profit and would not be subject to Class 1 national insurance contributions.

Accordingly, the tax adjusted trading loss in the year ending 31 March 2015 would be £44,000 (as shown above)

Arthur and Cindy would share the loss equally and could each choose how to relieve their share in order to obtain relief as early as possible at the highest rate of tax.

The loss could be offset against total income:

–   of 2014/15, the year of the loss; or

–   of 2013/14, the previous year; or

–   of 2011/12 the year three years prior to the year of the loss.

Following the gift of the shares from Cindy, Arthur will be a higher rate taxpayer in 2014/15 but not in the earlier years. Accordingly, he would choose to offset the loss in 2014/15 to obtain the highest rate of relief.

Cindy is a higher rate taxpayer in all three years and is therefore indifferent in terms of the rate of relief. However, she would claim to relieve the loss in the earliest possible year, 2011/12 for cash flow purposes, to obtain a repayment of tax and repayment supplement.

Tutorial note

Remember that the requirement says you should assume that the FA2012 rates and allowances apply throughout.

(c) **Reduction of income tax liability by investing in unquoted shares**

Tutor's top tips

Read the information in the question carefully – Arthur and Cindy want to invest in unquoted shares, but they are concerned about risk, so VCT is more suitable than EIS or SEIS.

The possible forms of investment

Income tax relief is available for investments in venture capital trusts (VCTs), enterprise investment scheme (EIS) shares and also seed enterprise investment scheme (SEIS) shares.

For both VCTs and EIS shares, a tax credit of 30% of the amount invested is available. For investment in SEIS shares, a tax credit of 50% is available. However, the SEIS scheme is to promote investment in smaller start up companies and is therefore much more risky.

A VCT is a quoted company that invests in shares in a number of unquoted trading companies. EIS and SEIS shares are shares in qualifying unquoted trading companies.

Recommendation

The most suitable investment for Arthur and Cindy is a VCT for the following reasons.

– An investment in a VCT is likely to be less risky than investing directly in EIS/SEIS companies as the risk will be spread over a greater number of companies.

– Dividends from a VCT are not taxable whereas dividends on EIS/SEIS shares are taxed in the normal way.

Tutorial note

Tax relief for investing in a VCT is capped at a maximum amount of £200,000, but for EIS/SEIS the maximum investment is £1,000,000/£100,000 respectively.

However, as Arthur and Cindy are only considering an investment of £50,000, this is not an issue.

(d)   **Gift of £130,000 cash to Cindy**

Income tax implications

The pre-owned asset anti-avoidance legislation applies in this case as Elsa has gifted an asset (cash) which is used by her daughter to acquire another asset (land) which Elsa will occupy.

As a result, Elsa must pay income tax on the benefit she receives which is determined in a similar way to benefits under employment income rules.

Elsa must pay income tax on the annual rental value of the property which is basically the market rent that she might expect to pay for such a property.

In 2013/14 Elsa must pay income tax of £2,400 (£6,000 × 40%) and for each tax year that she uses the house rent-free.

This anti-avoidance legislation can be avoided if Elsa pays the daughter full market rent while occupying the property.

Inheritance tax implications

For IHT purposes the gift of cash to Cindy is a PET, which means no IHT is payable at the time of the gift but may become chargeable to IHT if Elsa dies within 7 years.

It is possible for Elsa to elect to disapply the annual income tax charge and have the property treated as subject to a reservation instead. It would then become part of Elsa's estate on death for IHT purposes.

Tutorial note

The idea of the pre-owned asset legislation is to prevent people from trying to artificially bypass the normal gift with reservation rules.

If Elsa had given Cindy the family home and carried on living there, this would be a gift with reservation. Instead, Elsa is selling the house and giving the cash, which is then used to buy her another house – effectively the same thing!

Tutor's top tips

Even if you did not know the pre-owned asset rules, you could still get a mark for discussing the IHT treatment of a PET.

(e)   **Responsibilities under self assessment**

Tutor's top tips

Probably the easiest section of the whole question provided you have learnt the rules. The number of marks available should be a guide as to the amount the examiner expects you to write.

The self assessment return for 2012/13 must be completed and submitted by 31 January 2014 in electronic format (or by 31 October 2013 in paper format).

There is an initial £100 penalty and if the return is not submitted by 30 April 2014 (i.e. more than three months late) a daily penalty of £10 per day can be imposed.

Submission after 31 July 2014 (i.e. more than six months late) may lead to a penalty of 5% of the tax due, subject to a minimum of £300.

Failure to pay any IT, Class 2 and 4 NIC by the due date of 31 January 2014 may lead to interest charges and penalties.

Interest charges will be due on any final payment for 2012/13 due on 31 January 2014 and on the late paid first payment on account for 2013/14, also due on that date. Any outstanding tax for 2012/13, still unpaid within one month of 31 January 2014 will be subject to a 5% penalty.

28   CORAL (ADAPTED)

Key answer tips

In part (a) there are some easy marks for calculating pension contributions but the tricky thing is to make sure you answer the question and calculate the after tax cost to both Coral and Reef Ltd.

As mentioned below, the advent of FA2008 made (b) much more difficult than when first set. You should first explain Coral's tax status in terms of her residence, ordinary residence and domicile. Your answer needs to be specific to Coral and not just general points that could apply to many people.

(a)   **Minimising the total after tax cost of the pension contributions**

Reef Ltd makes the pension contributions

The pension contributions will not give rise to any national insurance implications and are an exempt benefit for the purposes of income tax.

	£
Contributions made by Reef Ltd	15,000
Reduction in corporation tax liability (£15,000 × 25%)	(3,750)
Total after tax cost	11,250

Coral and Reef Ltd make the pension contributions between them

The maximum gross tax allowable pension contributions that can be made by Coral are equal to her relevant UK earnings of £11,400 (£950 × 12). The dividend income and any rental income from the overseas property are not relevant earnings.

Coral will make the contributions net of 20% income tax. Accordingly, her contributions will be £9,120 (£11,400 × 80%) and she will require a dividend from Reef Ltd of this amount. HMRC will contribute £2,280 (£9,120 × 20/80) such that the gross contributions will be £11,400.

The dividend will not be allowable for the purposes of corporation tax.

The dividend will not give rise to an income tax liability as Coral's basic rate band will be extended by the gross amount of pension contributions made (£11,400) which is more than the taxable dividend income received of £10,133 (£9,120 × 100/90). Coral is not currently a higher rate tax payer as shown in the working below. Accordingly, the dividend income will be taxed at 10% with a 10% tax credit.

	£
Contributions made by Coral	9,120
Contributions made by Reef Ltd (£15,000 − £11,400)	3,600
Reduction in corporation tax liability (£3,600 × 25%)	(900)
	———
Total after tax cost	11,820
	———

The calculations indicate that Reef Ltd should make all of the pension contributions as this results in the lower tax cost.

Working: 2013/14 income

	£
Director's fees	11,400
Dividends (£13,500 × 2) × 100/90	30,000
	———
Total income	41,400
Personal allowance	(8,105)
	———
Taxable income	33,295
	———

As Coral's taxable income is less than £34,370, she is a basic rate taxpayer.

Tutorial note

Rental income in respect of furnished holiday accommodation is relevant earnings but such furnished holiday accommodation must be situated in the UK or EEA.

(b) **UK tax on the rental income**

Coral is UK resident in 2013/14 because she is present in the UK for more than 182 days. She will have been treated as UK resident since 2004 when she moved here.

Coral is ordinarily resident in the UK in 2013/14 as she is habitually resident in the UK, has lived here since 2004 and does not intend to leave the UK until 2018.

Coral has therefore been resident for more than 7 out of the previous 9 tax years before 2013/14.

Coral will have acquired a domicile of origin in Kalania from her father. She has not acquired a domicile of choice in the UK as she has not severed her ties with Kalania and does not intend to make her permanent home in the UK. Therefore, she is not UK domiciled for tax purposes.

Accordingly, Coral will be taxed on her rental income from the house in Kalania as follows:

2013/14

If the unremitted overseas rental income ≤ £2,000 in a tax year the implications are:

– taxed in the UK on the remittance basis

– personal allowances are available in full

This is likely to be the case in 2013/14 as the maximum rental income earned will be £1,650 (£550 x 3 months)

Any rental income remitted to the UK will fall into the basic rate band and will be subject to income tax at 20% on the gross amount (before deduction of Kalanian tax). Unilateral double tax relief will be available in respect of the 8% tax suffered in Kalania such that the effective rate of tax suffered by Coral in the UK on the grossed up amount of income remitted will be 12%.

In order to minimise the total income tax suffered on the rental income Coral should ensure that it is not remitted (i.e. brought into or used in the UK). It will therefore not be subject to income tax in the UK.

Coral should retain evidence, for example bank statements, to show that the rental income has not been removed from Kalania. Coral can use the money whilst she is on holiday in Kalania with no UK tax implications.

Tutorial note

Note that if Coral does spend her unremitted income whilst abroad on items which she later takes to the UK, the importation of these items back into the UK may be treated as a remittance. However, there are exemptions such as personal items and items costing less than £1,000.

Subsequent years

The treatment outlined above may not apply in subsequent years however as the income earned will exceed £2,000, therefore the amount of unremitted income is important.

If the unremitted overseas rental income is > £2,000 in a tax year Coral has a choice of treatment, the arising or remittance basis

Arising basis

– Arising basis is mandatory unless an election is made

– Coral will be taxed in the UK on the rental income on an arising basis

- Potential taxable income is therefore £5,500 (i.e. £550 × 10 months)

- Personal allowances are available in full

- Double tax relief will be available as above.

Election for remittance basis

- Coral can choose to be assessed on a remittance basis and therefore only pay tax when cash is brought into the UK

- She is unlikely to do so however as she would lose the availability of her personal allowances, which are greater than the amount of rental income

- In addition to any tax levied on amounts actually remitted into the UK, she will be subject to an annual £30,000 tax charge payable for every year she wishes the remittance basis to apply. The charge will increase to £50,000 once she is resident for 12 out of the previous 14 tax years.

Tutorial note

This question was set prior to recent changes in the taxation of non domiciled individuals. As a result of those changes the question has been made more difficult.

Examiner's Comments

Part (a) required candidates to determine whether pension contributions should be made by the employee or by the employer and the employee together 'with the objective of minimising the total after tax cost'. This requirement was trickier than it appeared and could not be easily satisfied by simply preparing a series of corporation tax and income tax calculations. Instead, it was necessary to focus on the tax savings resulting from the pension contributions.

Many candidates demonstrated poor knowledge of the tax treatment of pension contributions and consequently did not score well. Others took the opportunity to explain the tax aspects of pension contributions in a general manner rather than attempting to satisfy the particular requirements of the question.

Part (b) concerned the resident, ordinarily resident and domicile status of the taxpayer and the taxation of overseas income. This was answered fairly well by many candidates.

Candidates should note the following points in connection with part (b).

1   The following explanation is not incorrect but is not as clear as it could be.

'The overseas income is taxable on the remittance basis because Coral (the individual in the question) is resident, ordinarily resident but not domiciled in the UK.'

It is better to explain the situation in the following manner.

'The overseas income is taxable because Coral is UK resident. However, it will be taxed on the remittance basis because she is not domiciled in the UK and her unremitted income and gains are no more than £2,000.'

2   The rules concerning deemed domicile relate to inheritance tax and not to income tax. They were referred to by many candidates but were not relevant to this question.

		ACCA marking scheme	
			Marks
(a)		Reef Ltd makes the pension contributions	
		Amount of contributions to be made to achieve objective	1.0
		Corporation tax saving	1.0
		No national insurance or income tax implications	1.0
		Coral and Reef Ltd make the pension contributions between them	
		Coral's contributions	
		Maximum tax allowable amount equals relevant earnings	0.5
		Salary but not dividends or rental income	1.0
		Amount of dividend required from Reef Ltd	1.5
		Corporation tax implications of dividend	0.5
		Income tax implications of dividend	1.5
		Contributions from HMRC	0.5
		Reef Ltd's contributions	
		Amount	0.5
		Corporation tax saving	0.5
	Conclusion		1.0
			————
			10.5
		Maximum	10.0
			————
(b)		UK resident with reason	1.0
		Taxed on overseas income	0.5
		Ordinarily resident with reason	1.0
		Domiciled in Kalania because of domicile of origin	1.0
		Domicile of choice with reason	1.0
		2013/14	
		Rental income taxed on the remittance basis	1.0
		Basic rate band	0.5
		Double tax relief	1.0
		Do not remit income to the UK	1.0
		No income tax	0.5
		Evidence	0.5
		Subsequent years	
		Importance of unremitted income figure	1.0
		Arising basis	1.0
		Personal allowance available	0.5
		Election for remittance basis	1.0
		Loss of personal allowance	0.5
		Annual £30,000 charge	1.0
		Charge increases to £50,000 in future	0.5
			————
			14.5
		Maximum	10.0
			————
	Total		20
			————

29 NUCLEUS RESOURCES (ADAPTED) *Walk in the footsteps of a top tutor*

 Online question assistance

Key answer tips

This question is really two unconnected questions.

The first part is all about a sole trader expanding her business, either by taking on some employees or paying a company to do some work for her. You need to work out which option will leave her financially better off.

The second part covers mainly IHT and CGT. There are a couple of issues here: you need to think about the impact of domicile on IHT, and the tax implications of a lifetime transfer into a trust. In addition, there is a small section on ethical issues.

The highlighted words in the written sections are key phrases that markers are looking for.

Tutor's top tips

Read the memorandum in the question carefully. The examiner gives you some helpful tips on how to approach this part of the question.

You need to check whether Maria is already an additional rate taxpayer, to avoid the need to prepare full income tax computations.

You also need to think about VAT as this is a partially exempt business. The examiner indicates that the recoverability of input VAT is bound to be affected.

If the amount of VAT recoverable changes as a result of the expansion, this will affect the amount of after tax income for Maria.

Remember also that you are considering the options from Maria's point of view, so you do not need to consider the tax position of the employees or company doing the work for Maria, just the extra income after tax generated for Maria herself.

Make sure that you show your workings clearly, so that if you do make some mistakes you can still gain marks for consistency.

Notes for meeting with Maria Copenhagen

(a) **After tax income generated by the expansion of Nucleus Resources**

Maria is an additional rate taxpayer, as the current net income from the business and IIP trust of £168,000 (£40,000 + £90,000 − £37,000 − £35,000 + £110,000) exceeds £150,000. Maria's personal allowance would already be reduced to £Nil as her net income exceeds £116,210.

Accordingly, the profit generated by the expansion will be subject to tax at a total of 52% (income tax at 50% and Class 4 national insurance at 2%).

Tutorial note

In the real exam answer the examiner worked out the net after tax income at £168,000 (i.e. ignoring the VAT impact). However, the net after tax income before considering the options is in fact £162,894 (£168,000 less irrecoverable VAT £5,106 (W1)). Either way, with £168,000 or £162,894, the purpose of this first paragraph is just to establish that she is an additional rate taxpayer and therefore the impact of each option can be calculated at the marginal rates.

Employ additional employees :

	£
Additional turnover	190,000
Existing irrecoverable VAT will be recoverable (W1, W2)	5,106
	195,106
Salaries (£55,000 + £40,000)	95,000
Class 1 NIC ((£95,000 − (£7,488 × 2)) × 13.8%)	11,043
Cost in respect of car (W4)	2,443
Additional overheads	20,000
	128,486
Net additional income (£195,106 − £128,486)	66,620
Additional income after tax (£66,620 × 48% (see Tutorial note))	31,978

Tutorial note

If the total tax rate at the margin is 52%, the after tax income generated by the expansion will be 48% (100% − 52%).

Use Quantum Ltd :

	£
Additional turnover	190,000
Additional irrecoverable VAT (£9,912 (W3) − £5,106 (W1))	4,806
Quantum Ltd annual fee	140,000
	144,806
Net additional income (£190,000 − £144,806)	45,194
Additional income after tax (£45,194 × 48%)	£21,693

Tutor's top tips

Don't worry if you didn't get this completely right. If you have calculated after tax income correctly based on your figures, you will still score marks here. There were some very easy marks for just putting in the extra income and expenses.

Workings

(W1) Existing business – Irrecoverable VAT due to partial exemption

	%
Partial exemption percentage (£40,000/£130,000) (Note)	31

	£
Total input tax (£37,000 × 20%)	7,400
Attributable to taxable supplies (£7,400 × 31%)	(2,294)
Attributable to exempt supplies	5,106

De minimis tests:

(1)   Total monthly input tax is £617 (£7,400 ÷ 12) on average, which is less than £625. However, as the value of exempt supplies is more than 50% of the total supplies, test 1 is not satisfied.

(2)   Total input tax less input tax directly attributable to taxable supplies is £7,400 (£7,400 – £Nil), which gives a monthly average of £617, as above, but again the value of exempt supplies is more than 50% of the total supplies, so test 2 is not satisfied.

(3)   Monthly input tax relating to exempt supplies is £425 (£5,106 ÷ 12) on average, which is less than £625. However, as the input VAT relating to exempt supplies is more than 50% of the total input VAT, test 3 is not satisfied either.

Therefore the VAT attributable to exempt supplies cannot be recovered.

Tutorial note

Remember that when a business makes a mixture of both taxable and exempt supplies, input VAT can usually only be reclaimed on purchases attributable to taxable supplies.

Any mixed input VAT needs to be apportioned using the formula:

Taxable supplies/total supplies = % recoverable.

This % is always rounded up to the next whole %

However, if the input VAT relating to exempt supplies is very small (i.e. below the de minimis limits), then the whole amount can be reclaimed.

(W2) **Expanded business with employees – Irrecoverable VAT due to partial exemption**

	%
Partial exemption percentage	
((£40,000 + £190,000)/(£130,000 + £190,000))	72

	£
Total input tax ((£37,000 + £20,000) × 20%)	11,400
Attributable to taxable supplies (£11,400 × 72%)	(8,208)
Attributable to exempt supplies	3,192

This is below the annual de minimis limit of £7,500 (£625 × 12) and is less than half of the total input tax. Accordingly, all of the input tax can be recovered.

Tutorial note

As this de minimis test is satisfied, there is no need to consider the two further tests.

Therefore, as a result of expanding the business and taking on employees, £5,106 (W1) of irrecoverable VAT becomes recoverable.

Tutorial note

The approach in this answer is that used by the examiner in his model answer and was therefore the way in which he expected you to deal with the situation, given his hint that the recoverability of input VAT is 'bound to be affected'.

However, you may have assumed that the examiner's comment in Note 4 that 'the expenditure cannot be attributed to particular supplies' only related to the existing business and that all of the input VAT on the additional overheads of £20,000 is fully recoverable as they directly relate to a wholly taxable supply (i.e. the new project).

If so, this is a very valid assumption. If you stated this assumption and prepared you answer on this basis, you should still have gained full marks.

(W3) **Expanded business using Quantum Ltd – Irrecoverable VAT due to partial exemption**

	%
Partial exemption percentage (W2)	72

	£
Total input tax ((£37,000 + £140,000) × 20%)	35,400
Attributable to taxable supplies (£35,400 × 72%)	(25,488)
Attributable to exempt supplies	9,912

De minimis tests:

(1)   Total monthly input tax is £2,950 (£35,400 ÷ 12) on average. As this exceeds £625, test 1 is not satisfied.

(2)   Total input tax less input tax directly attributable to taxable supplies is £35,400 (£35,400 – £Nil), which gives a monthly average of £2,950, as above. As this exceeds £625 test 2 is not satisfied.

(3)   Monthly input tax relating to exempt supplies is £826 (£9,912 ÷ 12) on average. As this exceeds £625, test 3 is not satisfied either.

Therefore the VAT attributable to exempt supplies cannot be recovered.

Tutorial note

As in (W2), you may have assumed that the examiner's comment in Note 4 that 'the expenditure cannot be attributed to particular supplies' only related to the existing business and that all of the input VAT on the annual charge of £140,000 is fully recoverable as it directly relates to a wholly taxable supply (i.e. the new project).

If so, this is a very valid assumption. The examiner has said that if you stated this assumption and prepared you answer on this basis, you should still have gained full marks.

(W4) **Cost in respect of car**

	£
Annual cost ((£12,800 – £2,000) ÷ 5) (Note)	2,160
Class 1A NIC (£2,048 (W5) × 13.8%)	283
	2,443

Tutorial note

*The examiner specifically tells you to spread the effect of the capital allowances evenly. All you need to remember is that the **total** capital allowances available will be equal to the net cost of the car to the business (i.e. the proceeds less the original cost). This effect will actually be spread over a longer period than 5 years, as the car will be added to the general pool and no balancing allowance will be given on disposal, and instead WDAs will continue to be claimed on a reducing balance basis. However you have been told in the question to spread the allowances over the period of ownership of the car.*

Don't forget that as an employer, Maria will have to pay Class 1A NICs as she will be providing a benefit to an employee.

(W5) **Car benefit**

CO_2 emissions 129 g/km, available all tax year

	%
Basic petrol percentage	11
Plus (125 – 100) x 1/5	5
Appropriate percentage	16

Car benefit (£12,800 x 16%)	£2,048

(b) (i) **Inheritance tax on the quoted shares**

Tutor's top tips

Make sure that you answer the specific question here. In the first part, the examiner asks you for the 'issues to be considered' in order to determine whether the gift will be subject to UK IHT.

What he is really asking you to consider is two things:

'is Neil's uncle UK domiciled', and

'are the shares UK or overseas assets'?

Consideration of the availability of double taxation relief is then required.

*There are six marks available, so try to make sure that you have at least six separately identifiable points in your answer, and show that you have **applied** your knowledge by using facts provided in the information in the question.*

The inheritance tax position depends on the domicile of the uncle and the location of the quoted shares.

- If the uncle was domiciled in the UK when he made the gift in October 2011, the value of the shares at the time of the gift will be subject to inheritance tax.

- If the uncle was domiciled in Heisenbergia, the gift will only be subject to UK inheritance tax if the shares are UK assets.

Uncle's domicile

- If the uncle was not UK domiciled in 1992 it seems very unlikely from what we know that he would have acquired a UK domicile whilst living in Heisenbergia.

- If the uncle was UK domiciled at the time he left the UK in 1992, he will continue to be UK domiciled unless he acquired a domicile of choice in Heisenbergia.

- In order to have acquired a domicile of choice in Heisenbergia, the uncle would have had to have severed his ties with the UK and exhibited a clear intention of making Heisenbergia his permanent home.

Location of the quoted shares

- The shares are UK assets if the company is incorporated in the UK or the shares are registered in the UK.

Tutorial note

The location of the shares may also be affected by any double tax treaty between the UK and Heisenbergia.

Inheritance tax suffered in Heisenbergia

- Any UK inheritance tax due in respect of the gift can be reduced by double tax relief in respect of the inheritance tax charged in Heisenbergia.

(ii)   **Creation of the trust**

Tutor's top tips

The first part of the requirement simply asks for the 'tax implications' of transferring the shares to the trust. So, you need to consider all of the capital tax implications of the gift here: IHT, CGT and also stamp duty.

The second part requires an outline of the taxation of trust income received by a beneficiary.

Inheritance tax

- The lifetime transfer of shares to the trust would be a chargeable lifetime transfer.

- The value transferred would be reduced by the annual exemptions for the year of the gift and the previous year.

– As the company is quoted, business property relief (at 50%) will only be available in respect of the shares if Niels controls the company, which is unlikely to be the case.

– As Niels has not made any previous chargeable transfers, the transfer would be covered by his £325,000 nil rate band; there would be no inheritance tax due.

Capital gains tax

– The transfer of the shares to the trust represents a chargeable disposal at market value.

– Gifts holdover relief would be available (because the gift is immediately chargeable to inheritance tax) such that any gain arising could be deducted from the trustees' base cost of the shares rather than being charged.

Stamp duty

– There is no stamp duty on a gift.

Income tax

– Niels will be subject to income tax on any amounts received from the trust by his sons, subject to a *de minimis* limit of £100 per annum. This is because the boys are both minors and the trust was created with capital provided by their parent, Niels.

– A tax credit will be given in respect of the income tax paid by the trustees.

(iii) **Discussion of issues with Maria**

Tutor's top tips

The examiner always includes ethical issues in his exams, up to a maximum of 5 marks. These sections are usually very straightforward, as long as you have not run out of time!

– Maria and Niels are separate clients and must be treated as such from the point of view of confidentiality.

– We must not disclose information relating to Niels to anyone, including Maria, unless we have permission from Niels (or such disclosure as is required by law or professional duty). Accordingly, we should check to see if we have written permission from Niels to discuss his affairs with his wife.

– Unless we have permission from Niels, we should not discuss the situation relating to the proposed transfer of shares to the trust. This is because we cannot explain the situation to Maria without referring to Niels' tax position, i.e. the lack of previous chargeable transfers.

– Maria's question concerning inheritance tax on the gift from the uncle is different because it can be answered without making any reference to the tax affairs of Niels. It is, arguably, a general question on the workings of inheritance tax. There would be no breach of confidentiality if we discussed this matter with Maria.

– However, we know that it is not a general question and we should still consider the potential problems that could arise in discussing matters with Maria that relate to the personal affairs of Niels without first obtaining permission from Niels.

Examiner's comments

Part (a) required calculations of the annual additional after tax income generated by two alternative business expansion proposals. These calculations were made more complicated by the fact that the client's business was partially exempt for the purposes of VAT (value added tax).

This required an approach similar to that tested in question 2 of the Pilot paper but was only attempted by a minority of candidates. However, with the exception of the VAT aspects, the majority of candidates made a good attempt at this part of the question and produced clear, logical calculations which identified most of the relevant issues.

One surprising but common error was to treat the car benefit as a cost incurred by the business. In addition, a minority of candidates wasted time by providing lengthy explanations which were not asked for.

Part (b) tested three technical areas relating to the client. The general approach in this question was good, with well structured documents addressing the majority of the issues being prepared by many candidates.

Part (i) concerned the inheritance tax implications of a gift from an individual who may or may not have been domiciled in the UK. Somewhat surprisingly, many candidates struggled with this. The most common error was to focus on the domicile status of the recipient of the gift rather than the donor. There was also some discussion of the remittance basis which had no relevance here.

Stronger candidates began by stating the general rule as regards domicile and location of assets in relation to inheritance tax and then applied the rules to the specific facts in the question.

The majority of candidates made sensible comments about the availability of double tax relief.

Part (ii) concerned the transfer of shares to a trust. The inheritance tax aspects were handled well and the stronger candidates also addressed the capital gains tax and income tax aspects. As always, it was important to identify all of the issues first and then ensure that they were all addressed in the time available. Otherwise, the only issue covered was inheritance tax and too few marks were earned.

Part (iii) concerned the extent to which it is acceptable to discuss a client's affairs with that client's spouse. The majority of candidates were quite clear on the inappropriateness of such behaviour and scored well. However, a significant minority did not attempt this part demonstrating either a lack of time management or poor knowledge of this area of the syllabus.

ACCA marking scheme

			Marks
(a)		**VAT position**	
		Existing business	3.0
		Expand with employees	2.0
		Expand using Quantum Ltd	2.0
		Employ additional staff	
		Turnover	0.5
		Irrecoverable VAT	1.0
		Salaries and Class 1 NIC	1.5
		Car	
		Cost	1.0
		Class 1A NIC	1.5
		Additional overheads	0.5
		Income after tax	1.0
		Use Quantum Ltd	
		Turnover	0.5
		Irrecoverable VAT	1.0
		Annual fee	0.5
		Income after tax	0.5
			————
			16.5
		Maximum	14.0
			————
(b)	(i)	Relevance of domicile	1.0
		Relevance of location of shares	1.0
		Uncle's domicile in 1992	2.0
		Acquisition of domicile of choice in Heisenbergia	1.0
		Location of shares	1.0
		Double tax relief	1.0
			————
			7.0
		Maximum	6.0
			————
	(ii)	**Inheritance tax**	
		Chargeable lifetime transfer	1.0
		Annual exemptions	0.5
		Business property relief	0.5
		Covered by nil rate band	1.0
		Capital gains tax	
		Gain by reference to market value	1.0
		Gift relief available	1.0
		Income tax	
		Payable by Niels, with reasons	2.0
		Tax credit for tax paid by trustees	0.5
		Stamp duty	1.0
			————
			8.5
		Maximum	7.0
			————

			Marks
(b)	(iii)	Two separate clients	1.0
		Statement of general rule	1.0
		Transfer of shares to trust	1.5
		Inheritance tax on gift from uncle	2.0
			5.5
		Maximum	4.0
		Appropriate style and presentation	2.0
		Effectiveness of communication	1.0
		Logical structure	1.0
			4.0
	Total		35

30 BOSON (ADAPTED) *Walk in the footsteps of a top tutor*

Key answer tips

This question is mainly about overseas aspects of income tax and CGT. Overseas aspects of tax are tested regularly in P6, so you must make sure that you learn the rules. You cannot assume that they will always be tested in the optional section of the exam and can therefore be avoided!

The highlighted words in the written sections are key phrases that markers are looking for.

(a) Boson – Capital gains tax

Tutor's top tips

The danger here is that you simply write down the definitions of residency and ordinary residency, which will score very few marks.

You must apply your knowledge to the specific scenario and give advice per the detailed requirement.

Boson's capital gains tax position

Boson will have been non-resident and non-ordinarily resident whilst living in Higgsia as he has been abroad for more than three years (see Tutorial Note).

Accordingly, he will not be subject to capital gains tax on disposals made during that period unless he is classed as a temporary non-resident.

Boson will be treated as a temporary non-resident if he returns to the UK on or before 5 April 2014.

This is because:

- he was UK resident for four of the seven years prior to leaving the UK, and

- he will have been absent for less than five complete tax years.

As a temporary non-resident:

- Any capital gains made whilst overseas on assets owned at the time Boson left the UK will be subject to capital gains tax in the year of return (i.e. if he returns as planned on 20 January 2014 in 2013/14).

- Gains on assets purchased after he left the UK do not come within the temporary non-resident rules.

Boson will become UK resident and ordinarily resident from the date he returns to the UK as he is returning permanently. He will then be subject to capital gains tax on his worldwide assets.

Tax planning advice

Sale of the shares in Meson plc on 1 May 2009 and 1 November 2013

Boson owned the shares at the time he left the UK and has already made the disposals whilst abroad.

Accordingly, it would be advisable if Boson delayed his return to the UK until after 5 April 2014 in order to avoid the gains being charged to capital gains tax.

Tutorial note

As Boson returns to the UK within five years, he will be liable to CGT on the disposals of assets acquired before his departure, in the year he returns.

However, if he delayed his return until after five tax years (which in this case is only a matter of deferring his return for just over a couple of months), he would not be subject to CGT on any of his disposals whilst abroad.

Note that it is not enough to just stay out of the UK for 5 years.

*Boson must be absent for more than 5 complete **tax years** to avoid being caught by the temporary non residence rules.*

Sale of the house in Higgsia

Boson purchased the house after leaving the UK and is considering selling it in the future.

As he purchased it after leaving the UK, the disposal will not fall within the temporary non-resident rules. Therefore, the disposal will not be subject to capital gains tax if Boson sells the house in a tax year prior to his return.

However, if he sells the house after his return, he will be liable to CGT on the disposal.

So, again, it would be advisable if Boson deferred his return to the UK until after 5 April 2014 and sold the house prior to this date, in the tax year 2013/14.

(b)　(i)　**Rental income after deduction of all taxes**

	£
Rental income	11,000
Higgsian income tax suffered (£11,000 × 30%)	3,300

UK income tax:

£	
6,885 × 20% (W1)	1,377
4,115 × 40%	1,646
11,000	

	£	£
Income tax liability	3,023	
Less: Double tax relief (lower of UK and foreign tax)	(3,023)	
		Nil
Total tax on overseas rental income		3,300
Income after deduction of all taxes (£11,000 – £3,300)		7,700

Tutorial note

Watch out here. The rental income will have suffered £3,300 overseas tax at source. The question to ask yourself is whether or not any more UK tax is also due.

*The total tax suffered is the overseas tax, plus any **extra** tax due in the UK. As the UK tax is completely covered by DTR, it will not reduce Boson's net income.*

Working: Remainder of basic rate band

	£
Salary	35,590
Less: Personal allowance	(8,105)
Taxable income in the UK	27,485
Basic rate band	34,370
Remainder of basic rate band	6,885

(ii) **Dividend income after deduction of all taxes**

	£
Dividend income (£200,000 × 4.3%)	8,600
	———
Taxable dividend income (£8,600 × 100/90)	9,556
	———

UK income tax:

£	
6,885 × 10% (remaining BR band as before)	688
2,671 × 32.5%	868
———	
9,556	
———	

	———
Income tax liability	1,556
Less: Tax credit (£9,556 × 10%)	(956)
	———
Income tax payable	600
	———
Income after deduction of all taxes (£8,600 − £600)	8,000
	———

Tutorial note

Remember that UK dividends received are deemed to be net of 10% tax, so must be grossed up to calculate the tax, but the cash received will be the £8,600 cash dividend less the income tax payable.

Beware in your calculation of the income tax payable!

Because the dividend falls partly in the basic rate band and partly in the higher rate band, you cannot calculate the income tax payable on the dividends by applying the effective rate of 25% to the net dividend here.

(iii) **Maximum fall in rate of return on portfolio of quoted shares**

Tutor's top tips

This section of the question is somewhat unusual, and not something that has ever been tested before. The best advice is to have a go, but don't get bogged down – it's only worth 3 marks!

	£
Maximum fall in after tax income (£8,000 – £7,700)	300

	£
Maximum fall in dividend income (£300/0.75) (see Tutorial note)	400
Minimum dividend income (£8,600 – £400)	8,200

	%
Minimum rate of return (£8,200/£200,000)	4.1
Rate of return can fall by (4.3% – 4.1%)	0.2

Tutorial note

The effective rate of tax on dividend income that falls within the higher rate band is 25% ((32.5% – 10%) x 100/90). A reduction in net dividend income of £300 would all fall within the higher rate band

Examiner's comments

Part (a) required candidates to advise Boson on his liability to capital gains tax by reference to his residence and ordinary residence position. Candidates needed to be methodical here and begin by pointing out that someone who is neither resident nor ordinarily resident is not subject to capital gains tax on investments. It was then necessary to relate this rule to Boson and to consider the applicability of the temporary non-resident rules. It was important that candidates clearly addressed the specific assets in the question (the shares and the house) rather than making general comments that could apply to anyone.

This part of the question was done reasonably well despite being quite tricky. The majority of candidates were aware of the temporary non-resident rules and some good attempts were made to apply them. Two significant errors, which were relatively common, were to think that the relevant period for the temporary non-resident rules is five years as opposed to five tax years and to suggest that the remittance basis was also relevant to Boson.

Candidates sitting the exam in the future should read my article on the international aspects of personal taxation and ensure that they are confident of the detail of the rules and the situations in which the remittance basis applies.

Part (b) concerned the taxation of investment income and was in three parts.

The first part required a calculation of rental income in respect of a house situated overseas after deduction of all taxes. This was a straightforward calculation of income less income tax liability, incorporating double tax relief, and was done well. Candidates who identified the remainder of the basic rate band after taking account of the salary and the personal allowance were more likely to calculate the tax on the rental income (as opposed to the tax on all of the individual's income) and were thus in a better position to satisfy the requirement correctly.

Part (ii) required a calculation of dividend income after deduction of all taxes. Again, this was a straightforward task, but many candidates let themselves down by failing to address the basics of the UK tax system. In particular, the dividend was often not grossed up and the tax credit was often omitted. Many candidates seem to find it difficult to apply their basic knowledge when dealing with a single element of income as opposed to a full income tax computation. When reviewing the model answer you should note that those candidates who calculated the remainder of the basic rate tax band in part (i) were in a position to use that information to calculate the tax on the dividends in this part.

Part (iii) required candidates to use the 25% effective rate of tax on dividends (for a higher rate taxpayer) in order to calculate the amount by which the rate of return on a portfolio of shares could fall before the after tax income generated would cease to exceed the return from renting out the overseas house. This was a commercial, practical problem but was quite tricky and was not done well.

		ACCA marking scheme	
			Marks
(a)		Position whilst living in Higgsia	
		Not subject to UK capital gains tax with reason	2.0
		Circumstances giving rise to temporary non-resident status	2.0
		Implications of temporary non-resident status	2.0
		Position on returning to the UK	
		Subject to capital gains tax with reason	1.5
		Sales of shares	1.5
		Potential sale of house	2.0
			11.0
		Maximum	**10.0**
(b)	(i)	Higgsian income tax	0.5
		UK income tax	
		Remainder of basic rate band	
		Salary	0.5
		Personal allowance	0.5
		Excess over basic rate band	0.5
		Tax at appropriate rates	0.5
		Double tax relief	1.0
		Income after deduction of all taxes	0.5
			4.0
	(ii)	Taxable dividend income	1.0
		Tax at appropriate rates	1.0
		Tax credit	0.5
		Income after deduction of all taxes	0.5
			3.0
	(iii)	Maximum fall in dividend income	1.5
		Minimum rate of return required	1.0
		Maximum fall in rate of return	0.5
			3.0
Total			20

31 CHARLESTON DANCE (ADAPTED) *Walk in the footsteps of a top tutor*

Key answer tips

This is a lengthy question, and the key to scoring well on a question like this is sorting out the information and the requirements and then planning a well structured answer to deal with them. You are asked to write a letter; therefore it is important that you present your answer in this format.

Part (i) involves reviewing an inheritance tax calculation which is provided in the question. This is less time consuming than preparing a calculation from scratch, but is a different type of question to those you may have seen before. Different skills are required in reviewing the computation, as it is easy to miss errors that you may not have made if you had done the computation yourself. Be careful to review the calculation line by line.

Part (ii) is a simple written question on VCTs and pension contributions.

Part (iii) involves income tax planning, and comparing the tax consequences of holding an investment personally or through a company. This section also includes some ethics.

The highlighted words in the written sections are key phrases that markers are looking for.

Tutor's top tips

It can be useful to look at the email from the manager and the requirements at the end of the question before you look at the memorandum and the inheritance tax calculation. That way you know what you are being asked to do as you read the detailed information and you can pick out which information is relevant to which part of the question.

You should note that the requirement at the end of the question is not complete – more detail regarding what you need to do is given in the email.

Note also that there are four marks in this question for format and style. To get these marks, you need to set up your answer as a letter, make sure that you use headings, write in short sentences, and have a logical flow to your answer.

Letter

A & B Co
High Street
Birmingham

Mr C Dance
2 The Avenue
Birmingham

1 June 2013

Dear Charleston

Thank you for coming to see me last week. I set out below my findings following my review of the inheritance tax calculations prepared by Lindy, my comments on your plans and some further advice to help you reduce your tax liability.

(i)   Inheritance tax

In respect of the gift on 1 July 2006, the nil band available will not be reduced by the value of the gift on 1 November 2003 as the latter gift was a potentially exempt transfer that took place more than seven years prior to death.

Tutorial note

Potentially exempt transfers made more than 7 years before death never become chargeable, and are therefore ignored in all IHT calculations.

In respect of the death estate, the Balboan inheritance tax should be deducted from the UK inheritance tax due and not from the value of the investment properties.

I am pleased to tell you that the correction of these errors results in a reduction in the inheritance tax due of £111,520 as set out in the appendix to this letter.

(ii)   Investments and pensions

Tutor's top tips

It may not seem immediately obvious what is required here; however, the clues are dispersed within the question. The memo states that Charleston does not want to invest in EIS shares, therefore you should not spend any time considering these. The email mentions VCTs and it is the details in respect of these that are required.

You are asked to provide a summary of the tax reliefs available, therefore you should discuss all the tax implications from Charleston's perspective (IT and CGT).

Venture capital trusts

I appreciate that you do not wish to invest in enterprise investment scheme shares due to the level of risk involved. However, you may wish to consider investing in venture capital trusts (VCTs). VCTs are quoted investment companies, which hold investments in unquoted trading companies, thus spreading the risk over a portfolio of companies.

Your income tax liability would be reduced by 30% of the amount you invest in a VCT in any tax year up to a maximum of 30% of £200,000. This relief would be withdrawn if you were to sell the shares within five years.

There is no tax on the dividends received from a VCT and no taxable gains or allowable losses arise on the sale of VCT shares.

Pension contributions

Tutor's top tips

It is important to spot that Charleston and his wife currently have no relevant earnings for pension purposes.

Again, it is the manager's email that provides the clue as to what is required here. You should look at the email as a list of hints from the examiner!

He links the question of pension contributions to the possibility of purchasing rental properties. The memo also states that 'it may be possible to increase his tax allowable pension contributions depending on the property he buys'.

These are both pointing you in the direction of considering furnished holiday lettings, which generate relevant earnings for pension purposes.

Once you have spotted that this is the kind of investment they should consider, there are easy marks for listing the conditions to qualify as an FHL.

You and Betty can each make tax allowable pension contributions up to the higher of £3,600 and your relevant earnings. Relevant earnings consist of employment income, trading income and income from furnished holiday accommodation. Furnished holiday accommodation is property situated in the UK or EEA that satisfies the following conditions.

–   It is furnished and let on a commercial basis as holiday accommodation.

–   It is available for such lettings to members of the public for at least 210 days per year and is let for at least 105 days per year.

–   Long-term occupation of the property (continuous occupation by the same person for more than 31 days) is limited to no more than 155 days per tax year.

At present, neither you nor Betty is in receipt of any relevant earnings. However, if you were to purchase property in the UK, rather than in Balboa, and ensure that it satisfied the above conditions, you would be able to make additional tax allowable pension contributions.

The annual allowance is £50,000, meaning you and Betty could make contributions of £50,000 each. The tax saved would depend on your tax rate for the year.

Tutorial note

Where the annual allowance of £50,000 is not used the unused amount can be carried forward and added to the maximum amount in the next three years, as long as the pension scheme was in existence in the earlier years.

(iii) **Income tax planning**

Tutor's top tips

Your manager had stated in the email that holding the investments in a company would result in higher tax charges. You therefore already know what result you should get from your calculations. If you have calculated a different outcome, it is important not to waste too much time trying to get the correct result.

In order to simplify your calculations you need to identify the marginal rate of tax suffered by Charleston on his dividend and interest income. It is then not necessary to do full income tax computations. You could still score full marks if you did the calculations with full tax computations, but you would waste a considerable amount of time this way.

Transfer of assets to family members who have no income is basic tax planning, and it is important to be familiar with the benefits of this sort of tax avoidance.

You need to identify the correct tax treatment of overseas rental income, and as Charleston has been advised he doesn't need to disclose this income this leads into the classic question of tax avoidance vs. tax evasion.

Ownership of quoted shares and government stocks

You are a higher rate taxpayer due to the level of your rental income and bank interest.

If the quoted shares and government stocks are owned personally by you, your annual tax liability on the income received would be £19,292 as set out below. As your taxable income would be more than £116,210, your personal allowance would be fully withdrawn.

	£
Tax on dividend income (£21,000 × 25%)	5,250
Government stocks (£27,000 × 40%)	10,800
Extra tax due to loss of PA (£8,105 × 40%)	3,242
	———
Total tax suffered	19,292
	———

If the investments are transferred to a company, the company would pay corporation tax on the interest income (but not on the dividends) at the rate of 24% regardless of the level of its profits.

This is because it is a company controlled by you that does not carry on a trading activity.

A calculation of the annual total tax payable using this structure is set out below.

	Corporation tax computation £	Dividend payable to you £
Dividend income (exempt)	–	21,000
Government stocks	27,000	27,000
Taxable total profits	27,000	
Corporation tax at 24%	6,480	(6,480)
Profits paid as dividend		41,520
Income tax liability (£41,520 × 25%)		10,380
Extra tax due to loss of PA (£8,105 × 40%)		3,242
Total tax liability (£6,480 + £10,380 + £3,242)		20,102

It can be seen from the calculations above that it is more tax efficient for the investments to be owned by you personally.

Tutorial note

The effective rate of tax on dividend income that falls within the higher rate band is 25% ((32·5% – 10%)/0·9).

It is much quicker to do your calculations using this effective rate of tax than to do full calculations grossing up the income, then taxing it, before deducting the associated tax credit, and in this kind of comparative scenario it is acceptable to do it this way.

Transfer of assets to family members

You could reduce the tax due on your investments by making an absolute gift of some of them to Betty (or your children). Betty will pay no income tax on her first £8,105 of income and will pay tax at a maximum of 20% on the next £34,370 whereas you are paying income tax at up to 40%.

The same savings would be available if you were to transfer income generating assets to your adult children (on the assumption that they have no other income).

Tutorial note

Note that it states in the question that the children are both at university, therefore you can assume that they are both over 18 and any income from a parental disposition will be taxable on them directly.

However, if they were under 18 and unmarried, any income deriving from a source set up by the parents would be taxable on their parents unless it was less than £100 per year.

Tax avoidance schemes

Tax avoidance involves arranging one's affairs in such a way as to minimise one's tax liabilities and is perfectly legal. However, the promoter will provide details of the scheme to HM Revenue and Customs and may be issued with a reference number. You will need to include this reference number in your income tax return.

The rental income is taxable in the UK because you are a UK resident. Any tax suffered in Balboa can be deducted from the UK liability but this cannot lead to a repayment of the Balboan tax. Failure to disclose the rental income arising on the Balboan properties would amount to tax evasion, a criminal offence.

Tutorial note

The examiner always includes a requirement on ethical issues, up to a maximum of 5 marks.

These sections are usually very straightforward, as long as you have not run out of time!

The classic issue of tax avoidance vs. tax evasion is a very common question.

Please call me if you require any further explanations or advice.

Yours sincerely

Tax manager

APPENDIX:

Inheritance tax computation on death of father on 1 April 2013

Gifts of cash during father's lifetime

	£
1 July 2006 (£370,000 – £6,000 AEs)	364,000
Less: Nil band	(325,000)
Taxable amount	39,000
Inheritance tax at 40%	15,600
Tapered (£15,600 x 20%)	3,120
Death estate	
Per Lindy's calculation	3,484,000
Add: Balboan inheritance tax	160,000
Chargeable estate	3,644,000
Inheritance tax at 40%	1,457,600
Less: Relief for Balboan tax	
(less than UK tax at 40% on the Balboan properties)	(160,000)
	1,297,600
	£
Total inheritance tax due (£3,120 + £1,297,600)	1,300,720
Per Lindy's calculation	1,412,240
Reduction in inheritance tax due	111,520

Examiner's comments

This question required a letter covering a number of personal tax planning issues. Most candidates started off writing a letter but, by the end of their answers, a considerable number were addressing the client as 'he' rather than 'you' and failing to sign off. This is a test of candidates' professional skills and is an easy way for candidates to earn (or lose) marks.

Part (i) concerned inheritance tax and the identification of errors in a schedule prepared by a friend of the taxpayer. Many candidates did an excellent job of this and produced brief explanations and adjusted calculations although a minority failed to provide the necessary explanations. Weaker candidates wasted time describing the operation of inheritance tax in detail and reproducing all of the calculations. This was a time to read and think rather than write; eight relatively easy marks were available to those who stayed calm and applied their knowledge.

The question stated there were no errors in relation to the annual exemptions and the taper relief but many candidates insisted on checking these areas and some even found 'errors'. Candidates will benefit enormously from reading the question carefully and taking note of all advice given.

Part (ii) concerned investing in venture capital trusts (VCTs) and pension contributions. Candidates performed very well in connection with VCTs; the only weakness was an inability to resist summarising enterprise investment schemes at the same time.

Pension schemes were not handled as well as VCTs. This was perhaps because there was a need to address a specific area of pensions (maximum contributions for these particular taxpayers) as opposed to the rules in general. Many candidates described, unnecessarily, how tax relief is obtained for pension contributions.

Part (iii) concerned various aspects of income tax planning and was the most difficult part of the question. Candidates had to prepare calculations to show the effect on the total tax payable of transferring personal investments to a company. It was disappointing that only the best candidates recognised that the proposed company would be a close investment holding company and would therefore pay tax at 24%.

A large number of candidates made basic errors, for example, including dividend income in the corporation tax computation. Candidates also made life hard for themselves by calculating the tax on all of the income rather than on the income that related to the assets to be transferred. Candidates should pause before preparing calculations, consider any advice given in the question and the precise terms of the requirement and then think about the best way to solve the problem before putting pen to paper.

The income tax advantages of transferring assets to other family members and the issues relating to tax avoidance and tax evasion were handled well.

ACCA marking scheme		Marks
(i)	Identification of errors	
	Potentially exempt transfer	2.0
	Balboan inheritance tax	2.0
	Correction of errors	
	Potentially exempt transfer	2.0
	Balboan inheritance tax	2.0
	Effect on total inheritance tax due	1.0
		9.0
	Maximum	8.0
(ii)	Venture capital trusts	
	Suitability	2.0
	30% reduction in tax liability	1.0
	Maximum	0.5
	Withdrawal of relief	1.0
	Dividends received	0.5
	Gain or loss on sale	1.0
	Pension contributions	
	Maximum	1.0
	Relevant earnings	1.0
	Annual allowance	1.0
	Furnished holiday accommodation	
	Identification of possibility	1.0
	Conditions	3.0
		13.0
	Maximum	9.0

		Marks
(iii)	Ownership of investments	
	Investments owned personally	
	Higher rate taxpayer	1.5
	Calculations	1.0
	Investments owned via a new company	
	Explanations	2.0
	Calculations	2.0
	Conclusion	0.5
	Transfer of income generating assets to family members	
	Rationale	2.0
	Assumption re children	1.0
	Tax avoidance schemes	
	Legality	1.0
	Reporting	1.0
	Rental income from Balboan properties	
	Taxable with reason	1.5
	Double tax relief	1.5
	Reference to evasion	1.0
		———
		16.0
	Maximum	14.0
		———
	Appropriate style and presentation	1.0
	Effectiveness of communication, including correct use of appendix	2.0
	Logical structure	1.0
		———
		4.0
		———
Total		35
		———

32   GRIFTER (ADAPTED) *Walk in the footsteps of a top tutor*

Key answer tips

This is a huge question with an enormous amount of information to assimilate, so time pressure is likely to be a problem here.

It is really two completely separate questions, so you should allocate your time between them and keep a close eye on the clock.

Again, the detailed requirements are to be found in the email and letter provided, so you will need to read these to understand what the question is about.

From reading the requirements first, and then reading the question, it should be fairly clear that part (b) is a very straightforward briefing note on the remittance basis of taxation, which requires no application to the scenario. Easy if you have learnt the rules!

It may therefore be a good idea to start with this part of the question just in case you run out of time on part (a).

Part (a) requires a memorandum, so there will be marks for using the correct style. Note the examiner's instruction to 'keep any narrative to a minimum'. This means that you do not need to provide any explanations that the examiner does not specifically ask for, and can use short sentences. This will be vital in ensuring that you do not run out of time.

Part (a)(i) covers income tax on overseas income, IHT due on a PET which has become chargeable and ethics. This part of the question is fairly straightforward once you have identified the information that you need.

Part (a)(ii) requires some thought. Grifter plans to reduce his mortgage either by selling some cars, or by selling his existing house and buying a smaller one. There are a number of issues to consider here, including the badges of trade and principal private residence relief. It would be very easy to get bogged down with this part of the question, so try to keep moving all the time. If there is anything you are unsure of, have a guess and then move on.

The highlighted words in the written sections are key phrases that markers are looking for.

(a)   **Memorandum**

To	The files
From	Tax assistant
Date	7 December 2013
Subject	Grifter

(i)   **Property in Shadowsia**

Tutor's top tips

Read the question carefully – you are asked to calculate the TOTAL that Grifter owes to the tax authorities up to and including 2012/13, which is 5 years' worth of tax.

Don't forget to gross up the overseas income for the overseas tax deducted.

Make sure that you follow the examiner's instructions! He tells you to assume interest and penalties equal to 100% of the tax due, which simplifies the calculations greatly.

Income tax

The income tax due on the rental income is calculated below.

	£
Annual rent received (£484 × 12)	5,808
12% Shadowsian tax deducted (£5,808 × 12/88)	792
Taxable rental income per annum	6,600
Income tax at 40%	2,640
Relief for tax suffered in Shadowsia	
(clearly less than the UK tax on the income)	(792)
Tax due for one year	1,848
2008/09 to 2012/13 (£1,848 × 5 years)	9,240
Estimated interest and penalties (100% of tax liability)	9,240
Total amount due	18,480

Tutorial note

Where there is no double tax treaty, unilateral double tax relief can be claimed. This gives a tax credit for the lower of the UK tax or the overseas tax.

Inheritance tax on the PET

The death of Grifter's uncle within seven years of giving him the property in Shadowsia results in an inheritance tax liability as set out below.

Tutor's top tips

Read the question carefully before you calculate the IHT! You are told that there is no annual exemption or nil rate band available.

The question says to calculate the liability 'after any available reliefs', which is a clue that there must be some relief available!

The relief here is fall in value relief, but if you failed to spot this you would only lose one mark as long as you used the correct method in your calculations.

	£
Value of property (1 April 2008)	94,000
Less: Annual exemption	
(other gifts in February 2008 used annual exemptions)	Nil
Potentially exempt transfer (PET)	94,000
Less: Relief for fall in value (£94,000 – £48,000)	(46,000)
Revised value of PET	48,000
Less: NRB available	
(other gifts in February 2008 used nil rate band)	Nil
Taxable amount	48,000
Inheritance tax at 40%	19,200
Less: Taper relief (5–6 years)	
(£19,200 × 60%)	(11,520)
Inheritance tax payable	7,680

The tax refund

Tutor's top tips

The examiner has said that there will be up to 5 marks on ethical issues in every exam. These are often very easy marks, so make sure that you get them!

Grifter's tax affairs should be reviewed in order to determine whether there is any explanation for the refund.

If the tax refund has been made to him in error, he should repay it immediately. He may be committing a civil and/or a criminal offence if he fails to do so.

If Grifter does not return the refund, we would have to consider ceasing to act as his advisers.

In these circumstances we are required to notify the tax authorities that we no longer act for him, although we should not provide any reason for our action.

We should also consider the need to submit a money laundering report to the Serious Organised Crime Agency as the retention of the refund may amount to a crime.

(ii)   **Reduction in mortgage**

Tutor's top tips

This is the most time-consuming part of the question. There are two separate options to deal with here, so make sure that your answer is clearly labelled.

In each case, you need to work out the proceeds after tax, which is a very common P6 requirement. This really just requires you to do a cash flow computation, taking account of all cash in and cash out, remembering that tax is a cash outflow.

You also need to take into account the liabilities calculated in part (i).

Don't worry if you made a mistake in part (i), you will still be given credit for deducting your figures as long as the marker can see where they came from!

Sell the cars

	£
Sale proceeds (£84,000 + £127,000 + £68,000)	279,000
Less: Auctioneer's fees (£279,000 × 8%)	(22,320)
Net sales proceeds	256,680
Tax on profit on sale of cars (see note below)	Nil
Income tax due on rental income (as in (i) above)	(18,480)
Inheritance tax payable (as in (i) above)	(7,680)
Repayment of income tax refund	(14,600)
Amount available to reduce mortgage	215,920

The tax treatment of the proposed sale of the cars

Tutor's top tips

The examiner specifically asks for a 'detailed explanation' of the tax treatment of the sale of the cars. This is a clue that the sale may not be just a straightforward sale of assets! The examiner hoped that you would discuss the badges of trade here.

You must apply the badges to the scenario, not just list them.

Don't worry if you came to the conclusion that Grifter was trading. You could still get full marks for your calculations as long as they were consistent.

The tax implications of the proposed sale of the cars depend on whether Grifter is regarded as trading or not.

If he is regarded as trading, the profit on each of the cars would be subject to income tax.

If he is not regarded as trading, the profit on the sale of each car would be a capital profit. These capital profits would not be subject to tax because cars are exempt from capital gains tax.

It is my view that the profits from the sale of the cars would be treated as capital profits. This conclusion is based on reference to the 'badges of trade' which are used to determine whether or not a trade is being carried on.

The particular factors which have led me to this conclusion are:

- Cars are not a category of asset that is purchased solely with the intention of realising a profit. They can also be purchased to be used and enjoyed.

- The cars were purchased to be used (and have been so used) rather than to be resold at a profit.

- The proposed sale of the cars is not one of a series of disposals.

- The cars have been owned for considerable periods of time.

Sell the house

Tutor's top tips

There are easy marks here for picking out the cash flows from the question, and marks for consistency if you use the figures you calculated earlier in the question!

		£
Net proceeds from sale of house (£1,200,000 – £6,400)		1,193,600
Less: Capital gains tax payable (W1)		(79,449)
Other amounts payable as per (i)		
(£18,480 + £7,680 + £14,600)		(40,760)
Payment to reduce mortgage (see above)		(215,920)
Amount available to purchase house		857,471
Less: Professional fees in respect of purchase		(4,000)
		853,471
Less: Stamp duty land tax at 4% (£853,471 × 4/104)		(32,826)
Maximum capital cost of house		820,645

Tutorial note

Don't forget that stamp duty is payable at 4% on residential properties costing between £500,000 and £1,000,000. The cash available has to cover not only the professional fees in respect of the purchase, but also the cost of the new house PLUS the stamp duty. The stamp duty is therefore (4/104 × the total cash).

To prove that this works, if you multiply the capital cost of the house of £820,645 by 4% you will arrive at the correct stamp duty payable of £32,826.

Workings

(1) **Capital gains tax on the sale of the house**

	£
Proceeds	1,200,000
Less: Incidental costs of disposal	(6,400)
Net proceeds	1,193,600
Less: Cost	(500,000)
Gain before Principal Private Residence exemption	693,600
Less: Principal Private Residence exemption	
(78/132 × £693,600) (W2)	(409,855)
Chargeable gain = Taxable gain (Note)	283,745
Capital gains tax at 28%	79,449

Tutorial note

Note that the Chargeable gain = Taxable gain as the examiner has said to assume that the annual exempt amount is not available.

(2) **Principal Private Residence exemption**

	Exempt	Chargeable	Total
1.3.2003 to 31.8.2007 – Absent (Period of absence with no prior period of occupation)	–	54	54
1.9.2007 to 28.2.2014 – Period of occupation	78	–	78
	78	54	132

Tutorial note

The three years deemed occupation for 'any reason' is only available if the absence was both preceded and followed by actual occupation, so does not apply here.

None of the other periods of deemed occupation apply.

The last 36 months are already exempted with actual occupation.

(b) **Briefing note**

The remittance basis

Tutor's top tips

The examiner gives you three suggested headings here, so make sure that you use them!

Overseas aspects of tax are popular in the P6 exam, so you must learn the rules.

Who is entitled to be taxed on the remittance basis?

Individuals who are:

- not ordinarily resident; and/or
- non UK domiciled.

Is a claim required?

The remittance basis applies automatically to individuals with unremitted overseas income and gains of less than £2,000 in a tax year.

Other individuals are required to submit a claim for the remittance basis to apply in a tax year.

How does the remittance basis affect an individual's UK tax liability?

Tutor's top tips

Don't forget that the remittance basis affects capital gains tax as well as income tax.

Income tax

- UK resident individuals are normally taxed on the whole of their worldwide income.
- Under the remittance basis, such individuals will only be subject to tax on foreign income if it is remitted to the UK.
- Remitted income is taxed as non-savings income at 20%/40%/50%.

Capital gains tax

- Individuals who are resident or ordinarily resident in the UK are normally subject to capital gains tax on their worldwide assets.
- Under the remittance basis, individuals who are not domiciled in the UK will only be subject to tax in respect of gains on overseas assets if the gains are remitted to the UK.
- An individual who has claimed the remittance basis must make an election in order for capital losses in respect of overseas assets to be allowable. The election must be made in respect of the first year in which the remittance basis is claimed and applies to all future years.

Availability of allowances

An individual who claims the remittance basis will not be entitled to:

- the income tax personal allowance;
- the capital gains tax annual exempt amount.

Remittance basis charge

The remittance basis charge:

- must be paid by an individual who claims the remittance basis and;
- is an additional tax charge that is added to the individual's income tax liability and is paid under self-assessment
- the amount of the charge varies depending on how long the individual has been resident in the UK:

Additional charge:	UK resident for:
£30,000 p.a.	7 out of last 9 tax years
£50,000 p.a.	12 out of last 14 tax years

Examiner's comments

This was a substantial question representing 35 marks of the paper or 68 minutes. Candidates' performance in this question was good with some excellent answers being produced.

Part (a) required a memorandum concerning a number of personal tax issues relating to Grifter, a man who was considering two possible strategies to reduce his mortgage. The question included a letter from Grifter setting out various aspects of his financial position and the two options to be considered. There was also an email from the candidate's manager, which set out the steps to be carried out in order to evaluate the two options. It was very pleasing to note that the vast majority of candidates followed the instructions carefully such that many were able to score high marks for this part of the question.

The memorandum was in two parts. Part (i) required calculations of the income tax due in respect of undeclared income relating to an overseas investment property and calculations of the inheritance due in respect of the property following the death of the person who gave it to Grifter. It also required candidates to comment on the client's behaviour in relation to a tax refund that he had received.

This first part of the memorandum was done well by the majority of candidates with many scoring full marks in respect of the income tax and some scoring full marks for both the income tax and the inheritance tax. The most common error was the failure to gross up the income in respect of the tax suffered overseas. Most candidates identified the need for Grifter to determine whether or not the tax refund had been received in error and to refund it to the tax authorities if he was not entitled to it.

The second part of the memorandum concerned the two possible ways of reducing the mortgage; the sale by Grifter of either a number of motor cars or his house. The sale of the motor cars was not handled as well as expected due mainly to a lack of thought and self-belief. Whilst many candidates pointed out, correctly, that motor cars were exempt from capital gains tax, a large number then went on to calculate capital gains tax on the sale of Grifter's cars as if the rules somehow could not apply to this particular situation. There was also a failure by a significant minority of candidates to include the 'detailed explanation' of the tax treatment of the sale of the cars as requested by the manager, which required consideration of the badges of trade. This was not technically difficult and most candidates would probably have made a good job of it if they had taken sufficient care to identify the need to do so.

In questions of this type candidates need to start by identifying all of the tasks they have been asked to carry out by both the client and the manager. They should then ensure that all of these tasks are addressed in the time available. Sufficient time will be available provided candidates do not allow themselves to be sidetracked into discussing irrelevant issues.

The sale of the house was handled quite well by most candidates with the majority recognising the relief available because the property was Grifter's principal private residence. The only common mistake here was to allow three years of the period of absence as deemed residence. This was not available as the period of absence was not preceded by a period of actual occupation.

Despite many candidates scoring well on this question, I would make two general criticisms of their performance,

1. Many candidates could save themselves time by not providing explanations unless they are asked for. In his email the manager requested candidates to 'keep any narrative to a minimum unless I have specifically asked for it'. Unfortunately, this guidance was ignored by a large number of candidates who provided very time consuming step-by-step explanations of the calculations they were about to perform. A requirement to calculate means just that: calculate.

2. Candidates must recognise the commercial aspect of the tasks they are performing. In this question there was a need to think in terms of after tax proceeds, i.e. the cash proceeds less any tax liabilities as opposed to, in the case of Grifter's house, the taxable gain less the tax liability (which was a meaningless figure). A failure to do this led to some candidates reaching the conclusion that the Porsche should not be sold because 'it would result in a loss' whereas, of course, the Porsche should be sold because its sale would result in £62,560 (£68,000 x 92%) in the hands of Grifter.

Part (b) required a briefing note on the remittance basis. This is an area of the tax system that has recently been the subject of significant changes and candidates were clearly well prepared for it to be examined. Although there was often a lack of precision over the terminology used, candidates' knowledge of this complicated area was often very good with many scoring very high marks for this part of the question. Again, however, many candidates' exam technique let them down in that they were not satisfied in explaining the rules once but for some reason felt the need to repeat them, thus wasting time. In addition, many candidates wasted further time by explaining the meaning of residence, ordinary residence and domicile which was not required.

ACCA marking scheme				
				Marks
(a)	(i)	Amount payable in respect of rental income		
		Taxable rental income		1.5
		Tax, interest and penalties due		2.5
		Inheritance tax on property in Shadowsia		3.0
		Tax refund		5.0
				———
				12.0
			Maximum	9.0
				———
	(ii)	Sell the cars		
		Net sales proceeds		1.0
		Treatment of profit on sale of cars		
		Trading or capital		3.0
		Badges of trade		4.0
		Other adjustments		1.5
		Sell the house		
		Gain before principal private residence exemption		1.0
		Principal private residence exemption		2.0
		Capital gains tax		0.5
		Other adjustments		1.0
		Stamp duty land tax		2.0
				———
				16.0
			Maximum	13.0
				———

		Marks
	Appropriate style and presentation	1.0
	Effectiveness of communication	2.0
	Logical structure	1.0
		4.0
(b)	Who is entitled to be taxed on the remittance basis?	2.0
	Is it necessary to claim the remittance basis?	1.5
	How does claiming the remittance basis affect an individual's UK tax liability?	
	Income tax	3.0
	Capital gains tax	3.5
	Remittance basis charge	2.0
		12.0
	Maximum	9.0
Total		35

33 POBLANO (ADAPTED) *Walk in the footsteps of a top tutor*

Key answer tips

This is a lengthy question, and the biggest problem is sorting out the information and the requirements whilst also leaving enough time to answer the question. There are really four separate questions here, which could be attempted in any order, as there is no follow through of information.

Part (i) covers a comparison of net income for two different employment packages. This type of question is very popular at P6, and once you have seen one they are all very similar. The accommodation benefit is pure F6 knowledge, and illustrates how important it is to retain this knowledge. However, even without this you should still be able to score a good pass here.

Part (ii) deals with the rules for senior accounting officers, and there are easy marks here if you have learnt these rules.

Part (iii) covers the popular topic of inheritance tax, but in a rather unusual way. The '12 possible situations' may put you off attempting this section, but the examiner does provide guidance on how to approach it – so if you heed his words and do not panic you should be able to score some marks.

The final part of the question, part (iv), covers the income tax treatment of trusts. Trusts are generally not a popular area with students, although this section is actually very straightforward if you have learnt the rules.

The highlighted words in the written sections are key phrases that markers are looking for.

Tutor's top tips

Again, the requirements at the end of the question serve only to highlight the number of marks available for each section. The real requirements are mainly in the email from the manager and in the memorandum given at the start of the question.

Highlight the requirements as you come across them, and don't forget to keep looking back at them to make sure your answer is focused.

The first requirement asks for 'notes for a meeting', with the 'briefest possible notes' where the numbers are not self-explanatory. This means that you must keep narrative to a minimum and should write in very short sentences. Bullet points are ideal.

Meeting notes

Date   7 June 2013

Subject   Poblano

(i)   **Working in Manchester – Poblano's financial position**

Tutor's top tips

Poblano wants to know how much better or worse off he will be compared to his current position. This means that you need to think about the additional net cash (or deficit) after taking into account any tax charges and expenses.

The first paragraph of the question states that Poblano earns £60,000 per year, so it is clear that any extra taxable employment income will be subject to 40% income tax and 2% NIC.

Living in the company flat

The calculations set out below are based on the information currently available.

	£
Additional salary	15,000
Less: Income tax (£15,000 × 40%)	(6,000)
Class 1 primary NICs (£15,000 × 2%)	(300)
Petrol and depreciation (£1,400 + £1,500) (Note 1)	(2,900)
Additional salary after income tax, NICs and motoring expenses	5,800
Less: Income tax on benefit in respect of the use of the flat	
(£17,100 (W) × 40%)	(6,840)
Contribution towards the flat to be made by Poblano (£200 × 12)	(2,400)
Poblano would be worse off by	(3,440)
Additional salary required for Poblano not to be out of pocket	
(£3,440 ÷ 58%)	5,931

Tutor's top tips

Remember to state the additional salary needed, and remember that this will also be received net of 40% income tax and 2% NIC, so needs to be grossed up by 100/58 (or divided by 58%).

If Poblano's additional salary and benefits increased his adjusted net income to more than £100,000 he would start to lose his personal allowance but that is not the case here.

Not living in the company flat

		£
Additional salary after income tax, NICs and motoring expenses		5,800
Plus: Mileage allowance (9,200 × 50p)		4,600
Less: Income tax and NICs on mileage allowance		
(£4,600 × 42%) (Note 2)		(1,932)
Rent (£325 × 12) (Note 3)		(3,900)
Poblano would be better off by		4,568

Notes

1. The depreciation is not an immediate cost but will increase the funds needed by Poblano to purchase his next car.

    Poblano will not be able to claim a tax deduction for these costs as they relate to travelling to and from work and not to the performance of his duties.

2. The mileage allowance would be subject to tax and national insurance contributions as Poblano would be travelling to and from work and not in the performance of his duties.

    Manchester will not be a temporary workplace for Poblano because he expects to work there for more than two years.

Tutorial note

The mileage allowance is not exempt and the authorised mileage allowance of 45p per mile is irrelevant here, as the travel from home to work is private mileage, not a business trip.

If Poblano had been sent to Manchester for less than two years, then the travel would represent travel from home to a temporary workplace, and would qualify as a business trip.

In this case, only the excess allowance of 5p per mile (50p – 45p) would be taxable, rather than all of it.

3. Poblano's aunt will not be subject to income tax on the rent.

    This is because it will be in respect of a (presumably) furnished room in her house and the rent does not exceed £4,250 per year.

Tutor's top tips

The question specifically asks for an explanation of the tax treatment of the mileage allowance and the rent paid to Poblano's aunt, so make sure that you provide this.

Further information required

- The cost of the furniture provided in the flat – there will be an annual taxable benefit equal to 20% of the cost.

- Any running costs (utilities and maintenance etc) in respect of the flat borne by Capsicum Ltd – there will be a taxable benefit equal to the costs incurred.

- Any capital improvements made to the property before the start of the tax year for which the benefit is being calculated.

Working: Taxable benefit in respect of the use of the flat

	£
Annual value	8,500
Additional benefit (£350,000 – £75,000) × 4% (Note)	11,000
	19,500
Contribution to be made by Poblano (£200 × 12)	(2,400)
Accommodation benefit	17,100

Note: The cost of £350,000 will be increased by any capital improvements made to the property before the start of the tax year for which the benefit is being calculated.

Tutorial note

The current value of the property (when Poblano moves in) is not relevant in this case, as the property has been owned by the employer for less than six years.

(ii) **Responsibilities of a senior accounting officer**

The rules require the senior accounting officer of a qualifying company or group of companies to:

- Ensure that a company's accounting systems are adequate for the purposes of calculating the company's tax liabilities.
- Certify to HM Revenue and Customs that such accounting systems exist for each financial year.
- Notify HM Revenue and Customs of any inadequacies in the accounting systems.

The rules apply to a company, or a group of companies, with turnover of more than £200 million and/or a balance sheet total of more than £2 billion.

Penalties apply for non-compliance with the rules.

The senior accounting officer of Capsicum Ltd is the director or officer with overall responsibility for the company's financial accounting arrangements. This could be Poblano or another director within the group.

(iii) **Property in Chilaca**

Inheritance tax liabilities

Tutor's top tips

This section of the question may have appeared daunting, as there are 12 possible situations to deal with. However, there are actually very few calculations needed, as a number of the situations result in the same amount of tax.

The examiner does hint at this in the question, and often does give advice concerning the approach he wants you to take with parts of his questions.

Make sure that you follow his advice!

Key answer tips

Watch out for the following:

–   There is no annual exemption, as Paprikash already makes gifts each year that use this.

–   There is no lifetime tax, as a gift to an individual is a PET. The issue therefore revolves around charges arising as a result of death.

–   In all cases, the nil band will be reduced by the gift in 2012, as this is less than seven years before the date of the gift/death.

–   Death tax on a lifetime gift is usually based on the value of the gift at the date of gift, not at the date of death (*unless* the property falls in value), so any increases in value since the date of the gift are irrelevant for calculating death tax on a lifetime gift.

–   Taper relief will be available for lifetime gifts, but only if the donor survives for at least three years.

Lifetime on 1 August 2013 – PET

Assumed Value at death (Note 1)	Death on 31 December 2015: IHT arising: (Note 2)		Death on 31 December 2017: IHT arising (Note 3)	
£		£		£
450,000	(£450,000 – £35,000) × 40% =	166,000	(£166,000 × 60%) =	99,600
600,000	(£600,000 – £35,000) × 40% =	226,000	(£226,000 × 60%) =	135,600
900,000	(£600,000 – £35,000) × 40% =	226,000	(£226,000 × 60%) =	135,600

Gift via will on 31 December 2015 or 31 December 2017 (Note 4)

Assumed Value at death (Note 1)	Death on 31 December 2015 or 2017: IHT arising: (Note 2)	
£		£
450,000	(£450,000 – £35,000) × 40% =	166,000
600,000	(£600,000 – £35,000) × 40% =	226,000
900,000	(£900,000 – £35,000) × 40% =	346,000

Notes

1. When made the gift will be a potentially exempt transfer, thus, if the value of the property at the time of death is less than it was at the time of the gift, the inheritance tax payable will reflect the fall in value.

  If the value at the time of death is higher than at the time of the gift, the 'frozen' value at the time of the gift is charged to tax at the death rates.

2. The nil band remaining following the gift into trust on 1 June 2012 will be:

  (£325,000 – £290,000 CLT in June 2012) = £35,000.

Tutorial note

The value of the CLT on 1 June 2012 is £290,000 as:

- *the gift is a gift of a minority shareholding in quoted shares, which does not qualify for Business Property Relief (BPR), and*

- *the annual exemptions have already been utilised.*

3. 31 December 2017 would be between four and five years after the gift such that 40% taper relief would be available. Accordingly, the liability will be 60% of the liability calculated in respect of death occurring on 31 December 2015.

4. The date of death will not affect the amount of inheritance tax due.

Tutorial note

Note 4 is true, but only because it is assumed in the answer that the nil rate band does not change in the future.

In practice, the nil rate band can change in each tax year and therefore the amount of tax payable will normally be affected by the date of death.

Inheritance tax liabilities – conclusions

If the property is gifted on 1 August 2013, the inheritance tax due on death will never be more than the amount due if the property is transferred via Paprikash's will, even if the value of the property falls prior to the date of death.

Making a lifetime gift would turn out to be particularly beneficial if:

- The value of the property increases, as the tax would be based on the value as at 1 August 2013 rather than the value at the time of death.

- Paprikash survives the gift by more than three years such that taper relief would be available.

Tutor's top tips

Even if your calculations are not correct, you will still be able to score marks for drawing sensible conclusions.

Other issues

Tutor's top tips

The examiner asks for any 'other issues' that should be drawn to Poblano's attention. The most obvious issue is the continuing use of the property by Paprikash, which is mentioned a couple of times in the question.

There is also the issue of capital gains tax potentially arising on lifetime gifts.

Gift with reservation

Once the property has been given to Poblano, the occasional use of it by Paprikash may result in the gift being treated as a gift with reservation.

In these circumstances, the gift would be ignored for inheritance tax purposes and the property would then be included in Paprikash's death estate at its value at the time of death.

In order to ensure that the gift is effective for inheritance tax purposes Paprikash should have only minimal use of the property unless he pays Poblano a market rent.

Tutorial note

There is HMRC guidance that suggests that visits of up to two weeks a year without the son, and up to a month with the son, would be acceptable as 'minimal' use for these purposes. Knowledge of this guidance is not expected in the exam, but is of interest!

If the father pays a full commercial rent for the use of the property gifted, the gift with reservation rules will not apply.

Capital gains tax

Lifetime gift

If Paprikash is resident or ordinarily resident in the UK in the year in which he gives the property to Poblano, it will be necessary to calculate a capital gain on the gift of the property.

The gain would be the market value of the property less its cost. The gain, less any available annual exempt amount, would be taxed at 18% or 28% depending on Paprikash's taxable income.

Tutorial note

If Paprikash is not resident or ordinarily resident in the UK in the year in which he gives the property to Poblano, the gain will be exempt from capital gains tax (subject to the temporary residence overseas rule).

Gift on death in the will

There would be no capital gains tax if the property were given to Poblano on death, via Paprikash's will.

(iv) **Tax treatment of trust income received by Poblano's daughter**

Tutor's top tips

*Be careful that you don't waste time here. The examiner only wants you to talk about the tax treatment of the **income** received from the trust by Poblano's daughter.*

There are six marks available, so your answer needs to reflect this. Note that the examiner does not tell you what type of trust it is, so you need to discuss the different types of trust and the tax treatment of income received from each.

The question clearly states that the income is dividend income, so don't bother discussing any other types of income.

The trust will be either an interest in possession trust or a discretionary trust:

- It will be an interest in possession trust if Piri has an absolute right to the income generated by the trust assets.

- It will be a discretionary trust if the trustees have the right to accumulate the income and pay it to Piri when they choose.

It is understood that the only income received by the trustees of the trust is dividend income.

Interest in possession trust

- The income to which Piri is entitled must be grossed up at 100/90.

- Where the income falls into Piri's basic rate band (after calculating the tax on her salary) it will be taxed at 10%.

- The balance of the income will be taxed at 32·5%.

- There will be a 10% tax credit.

Discretionary trust

- The income received must be grossed up at 100/50.

- Where the income falls into Piri's basic rate band it will be taxed at 20%.
- The balance of the income will be taxed at 40%.
- There will be a 50% tax credit.

Examiner's comments

This was a substantial question in four parts. Although some of the question parts could be seen as easier or harder than others, all of the parts had some easily accessible marks and candidates benefited from attempting all parts rather than only attempting those that appeared to be straightforward.

Part (i) concerned the implications of a change to an employee's location of work. On the whole this part of the question was done reasonably well. However, in order to score a high mark for this part it was necessary to focus on the client's financial position and calculate how much better or worse off he was going to be as a result of the change. This required candidates to think in terms of income and costs (with tax as a cost) and to recognise that costs that are not tax deductible are still costs and are therefore still relevant. This aspect of the question was not handled particularly well.

The calculation of the benefit in respect of the flat provided by the company was done well. However, the majority of candidates failed to recognise that the mileage allowance related to travel to and from work and was therefore taxable in full.

It was pleasing to note that fewer candidates than in the past provided lengthy explanations of what they were going to do before getting on and doing it. However, the question asked for an explanation of the tax treatment of two particular points; the receipt of the mileage allowance and the receipt of the rent. Many candidates failed to provide these explanations. As noted above, in respect of question 1, candidates must identify and carry out all of the tasks in the question in order to maximise their marks.

Part (ii) concerned the rules introduced in the Finance Act 2009 in relation to senior accounting officers. These rules were a significant development in the personal responsibility of individuals for the behaviour of their employing companies and were covered in great detail in the financial press at the time. However, the majority of candidates were not aware of them and, consequently, found it difficult to score well on this part of the question.

Part (iii) of the question concerned inheritance tax and the advantages of lifetime giving. At first sight it was a daunting question requiring the consideration of three possible property values, two dates of death and a lifetime gift or gift via will; a total of 12 possible situations. However, there was guidance from the 'manager' as to where to start together with the reassurance that 'you should find that the calculations do not take too long'.

It was very pleasing to find that the majority of candidates had no problem with this part of the question and that their knowledge of the basic mechanics of inheritance tax was sound. Candidates benefited from thinking rather than writing such that they were then able to realise that, for example, with a lifetime gift, the only difference between the two possible dates of death was the availability of taper relief. The best answers were admirably short and to the point.

The one area where candidates could have done better was in identifying the possible gift with reservation. The failure by many candidates to do this indicates, yet again, that some candidates do not take enough care in identifying all that has been asked of them.

The final part of the question concerned the tax treatment of income received from a trust. This was a test of knowledge, as opposed to application of knowledge, and candidates should have scored well.

However, the marks for this part were not as high as expected because candidates were not sufficiently careful in their approach. As always, the advice here is to stop and think. The question made it clear that the nature of the trust was not known and therefore candidates were expected to consider the income tax position of receipts from both an interest in possession trust and a discretionary trust. There was also the need to be specific and precise, as regards grossing up fractions and tax rates, rather than superficial and general in order to maximise the marks obtained.

		ACCA marking scheme	
			Marks
(i)		Salary less tax, national insurance contributions and motoring expenses	2.0
		Living in the company flat	
		Tax on the benefit	2.0
		Contribution	0·5
		Additional salary required	1.0
		Further information required	2.0
		Staying with aunt in Manchester	
		Calculations	1·5
		Mileage allowance	1·5
		Rent paid to aunt	1·5
			———
			12.0
		Maximum	10.0
			———
(ii)		Senior accounting officer	3·5
			———
			3.5
		Maximum	3.0
			———
(iii)		Inheritance tax liabilities	
		Nil band	1.0
		Lifetime gift	
		Value at time of gift and tax rate	1.0
		Fall in value post gift	1.0
		Taper relief	1.0
		Gift via will	1·5
		Full set of outcomes	0·5
		Conclusions (1 mark each, maximum 2 marks)	2.0
		Explanatory notes (½ mark each)	2.0
		Gift with reservation	2·5
		Capital gains tax	1·5
			———
			14.0
		Maximum	12.0
			———
(iv)		Nature of the trust	2.0
		Tax treatment – 2 × 2 marks	4.0
			———
			6.0
			———
		Appropriate style and presentation	2.0
		Effectiveness of communication	2.0
			———
			4.0
			———
	Total		35
			———

34   SUSHI (ADAPTED) *Walk in the footsteps of a top tutor*

Key answer tips

This question is in two separate parts.

Part (i) deals with inheritance tax, in particular the impact of domicile on an individual's inheritance tax liability. Domicile has been a very popular area in recent exams, so you must learn the rules in detail.

Part (ii) covers the remittance basis. This is another popular area in the exam. The rules are complex, and again must be learnt.

The highlighted words in the written sections are key phrases that markers are looking for.

Tutor's top tips

As with question 1 in this exam, the requirement at the end of the question just tells you how many marks are available for each section. The detailed requirements are all within the email from the manager.

You may find it useful to number these requirements so that you can tick them off as you attempt them.

Think about how you will structure your answer before you start; address only the questions set and do not deviate, otherwise you are likely to run out of time!

(i)   **UK inheritance tax and the statue**

On the death of Sushi's mother

Sushi's mother was not UK domiciled, and would therefore only be subject to UK inheritance tax on UK assets.

As Sushi's mother had no UK assets, there will be no UK inheritance tax due on her death.

Tutorial note

*It is the domicile of the **donor** that is important in determining whether or not inheritance tax is due on overseas assets, not the domicile of the recipient.*

On Sushi's death

Tutor's top tips

Sushi has both UK and overseas assets, both of which should be considered.

You do not know whether or not Sushi has acquired UK domicile, and you do not know when she will die, so you need to discuss all possibilities.

*Make sure that you **apply** the domicile rules to Sushi and give clear advice.*

UK assets

Sushi's UK assets will be subject to UK inheritance tax, regardless of her domicile status.

Overseas assets

However, her overseas assets will only be subject to tax if she is UK domiciled or deemed to be UK domiciled.

Domicile

A person's domicile is the country in which they have their permanent home.

At birth, a person's domicile of origin is inherited from their father. Sushi would therefore have inherited the domicile of Zakuskia.

Even though she has been living in the UK for a number of years, she will remain domiciled in Zakuskia unless she acquiresa domicile of choice in the UK.

To do this, she must acquire a permanent home in the UK and sever all ties with Zakuskia.

However, even if Sushi has not chosen to be UK domiciled, she will be deemed to be domiciled in the UK, for inheritance purposes only, once she has been resident in the UK for 17 out of the last 20 tax years (ending with the tax year in which any assets are transferred).

As Sushi has been resident in the UK since May 1999, she will be deemed domiciled in the UK from 2015/16 onwards.

This means that from 2015/16 onwards, both her UK assets and her overseas assets will be subject to UK inheritance tax.

Should Sushi die before 2015/16, her overseas assets will only be subject to UK inheritance tax if she has acquired a domicile of choice in the UK.

Land and buildings in Zakuskia

Tutor's top tips

*You are asked to explain **how** the inheritance will be calculated, should the overseas land and buildings be taxable in the UK.*

Think about the steps you would take if you were preparing an inheritance tax computation, and try to put these into words.

Valuation

The land and buildings will be valued at the date of Sushi's death. This value will be converted to sterling using the exchange rate on that day that gives the lowest sterling figure.

Any additional administration expenses incurred in Zakuskia will be deducted, subject to a maximum of 5% of the property value.

Calculation of inheritance tax

The nil rate band will be deducted from Sushi's death estate, including the land and buildings, and the excess will be subject to tax at 40%.

Double tax relief will be available for the lower of the overseas tax suffered, or the UK tax on the land and buildings.

The UK tax on the land and buildings will be calculated at the average estate rate.

Gift of the statue

Tutor's top tips

Read the instructions carefully!

*You are not asked to describe potentially exempt transfers in detail, just to state **why** this transfer will be a PET, and how this treatment could be avoided.*

Potentially exempt transfer

As the transfer of the statue is a lifetime gift of a UK asset from one individual to another, it will be a potentially exempt transfer.

How to avoid this treatment

Sushi can only avoid this treatment if she is not UK domiciled (i.e. she has not acquired a domicile of choice in the UK), and if the statue is an overseas asset.

As long as the statue is transferred to Sushi's son whilst it is in Zakuskia, it will not be subject to UK inheritance tax.

Tutorial note

It may also be possible to avoid UK inheritance tax by varying Sushi's mother's will, within 2 years of her death, so that the statue was left directly to Sushi's son, although the will would be subject to Zakuskian law.

The examiner has stated that you would have been given credit if you had discussed this as a possibility.

(ii)   **The Zakuskian income**

Tutor's top tips

Again, there are specific instructions to follow here, and you must try to address all of them.

Remittance basis

Under the remittance basis, overseas income is only taxed in the UK when it is remitted, or brought in, to the UK.

The remittance basis is only available to individuals who are not UK domiciled and/or not ordinarily resident in the UK. Accordingly, it will only be available to Sushi if she has not chosen to acquire UK domicile.

Meaning of remittance

The most obvious example of a remittance is when income is brought directly into the UK.

However, the definition of remittance also includes:

*   Using overseas income to settle debts in the UK

*   Using overseas income to purchase goods and services which are subsequently bought into the UK with the exception of:
    –   Personal items (e.g. clothes, shoes, jewellery)
    –   Items brought to the UK for repair
    –   Items costing no more than £1,000
    There are also exceptions for amounts remitted to the UK to:
    –   Acquire shares in or make a loan to an unquoted trading company or member of a trading group
    –   Pay the remittance basis charge

Tutor's top tips

You would not have to list all the above examples of a remittance and the exceptions to gain full marks in the exam.

Increase in UK tax liability due to Zakuskian income

Tutor's top tips

You only need to calculate the increase in Sushi's UK tax liability, not her total tax liability. This can be achieved very quickly by working in the margin.

The question states that Sushi is an additional rate taxpayer, so any additional UK tax will be levied at the rate of 50%.

Make sure that you add brief footnotes to your calculations as these are specifically requested, and therefore will score marks.

Remittance basis not available

	£
Gross Zakuskian income	200,000
UK income tax (50% × £200,000)	100,000
Less: Double tax relief for Zakuskian tax (lower than UK tax)	
(£200,000 × 10%)	(20,000)
Additional UK tax payable	80,000

Remittance basis available and claimed (Note 1)

	£
Gross Zakuskian income remitted	100,000
UK income tax (50% × £100,000)	50,000
Less: Double tax relief for Zakuskian tax (lower than UK tax)	
(£100,000 × 10%)	(10,000)
	40,000
Plus: Remittance basis charge (Note 2)	50,000
Plus: Loss of capital gains tax annual exempt amount (Note 3)	
(£10,600 × 28%)	2,968
Additional UK tax payable	92,968

Notes

1. As Sushi's unremitted overseas income is more than £2,000, the remittance basis is not automatically available. She will have to elect to use it.

2. The remittance basis charge is due because Sushi is claiming the remittance basis, and she has been resident in the UK for 12 of the previous 14 tax years.

3. If Sushi claims the remittance basis, she will lose her entitlement to the capital gains tax annual exempt amount.

   She also loses her entitlement to the income tax personal allowance, but this will already have been reduced to £Nil due to the level of Sushi's income, and therefore has no effect on the additional tax payable as a result of making a remittance basis claim.

Tutorial note

The fact that Sushi is an additional rate taxpayer tells you that she must have taxable income of more than £150,000.

Once an individual's net income exceeds £116,210, the personal allowance is fully withdrawn.

Conclusion

If Sushi remits £100,000 to the UK, it would not be beneficial for her to claim the remittance basis, if it is available.

Her UK income tax liability will increase by £92,968 if the remittance basis is claimed, but by £80,000 if it is not.

Tutor's top tips

Make sure that you clearly show your conclusion, if required.

Even if your answer is wrong, you will still be given credit if your conclusion is consistent with your analysis.

Examiner's comments

Part (i) concerned inheritance tax and, in particular, the relevance of domicile to an individual's tax position. The level of knowledge here was good with some very strong, thorough answers. However, many candidates who scored well for this part of the question often did so in an inefficient manner which may have left them short of time for the remainder of the exam. As always, there was a need to pause; this time in order to determine the best way to say what needed to be said. Weaker candidates simply kept writing, often repeating themselves, until they finally got to where they wanted to be. Stronger candidates wrote short, precise phrases which earned all of the marks despite using very few words. Candidates should practise explaining areas of taxation making sure that their explanations are concise and clear.

There was a need to address the position of both the mother and the daughter but many candidates simply addressed 'inheritance tax' rather than the situation of the individuals. Candidates will be more successful in the exam if they think in terms of providing advice to individuals and companies rather than addressing technical issues as this will help them to stick to the point and to satisfy the questions' requirements.

A substantial minority of candidates produced muddled explanations confusing the importance of domicile with residence and ordinary residence. This confusion was also evident in answers to part (ii). The three factors of residence, ordinary residence and domicile all have various implications depending on the taxes concerned and candidates need to know where to start such that they can then avoid writing about all of the factors at once.

A somewhat surprising error made by a significant minority of candidates was to state that the inheritance tax position on the death of Sushi's mother depended on the domicile status of Sushi as opposed to that of her mother. It is, of course, the status of the person whose estate has fallen in value that is relevant.

A final thought on this part of the question is that many candidates wasted time calculating inheritance tax, despite not having sufficient information, whilst others provided a considerable amount of detail regarding the taxation implications of making a potentially exempt transfer, despite being specifically told not to in the question.

Part (ii) concerned overseas income and the remittance basis. The performance of candidates for this part was mixed. To begin with there was much confusion regarding the conditions that must be satisfied in order for the remittance basis to be available with candidates mixing up domicile, residence and ordinary residence with the seven out of nine years/12 out of 14 years rule (and the 17 out of 20 years rule in respect of inheritance tax deemed domicile).

The application of the £2,000 rule was also misunderstood by many. There is no doubt that there is plenty to be confused about in this area but that is why candidates need to learn it rather than acquire a hopeful understanding of it.

Candidates were asked to explain the meaning of 'remittance' and the 'remittance basis'. Most candidates attempted to do this, which was very encouraging, but few had much knowledge beyond the absolute basics. Similarly, most candidates were aware of the remittance basis charge but a significant number were confused as to the situation in which the charge would be levied.

On the plus side, the vast majority of candidates provided a conclusion (as requested) and many produced neat and reasonably accurate calculations.

ACCA marking scheme		
		Marks
(i)	Assets subject to inheritance tax	1.5
	Mother's death	1.0
	Sushi's death	
	UK assets	0.5
	Foreign assets	0.5
	Domicile of origin	1.0
	Domicile of choice	1.0
	Deemed domicile	2.5
	UK IHT on land and buildings in Zakuskia	
	Valuation	1.5
	UK IHT and double tax relief	2.0
	The statue	2.5
		———
		14.0
	Maximum	12.0
		———
(ii)	Meaning and availability of remittance basis	1.5
	Meaning of remittance	3.0
	Calculations	
	Remittance basis not available	2.0
	Remittance basis available	
	Remittance basis charge	1.0
	Loss of annual exempt amount	1.0
	Loss of personal allowance has no effect	1.0
	Tax on remitted income	1.0
	Explanatory notes (1 mark per sensible point) – maximum	3.0
	Conclusion	1.0
		———
		14.5
	Maximum	13.0
		———
	Total	25
		———

PERSONAL FINANCE, BUSINESS FINANCE AND INVESTMENTS

35   JOHN AND MAUREEN ROBINSON (ADAPTED) *Walk in the footsteps of a top tutor*

Key answer tips

This question is based around a "real life" situation, where income and gains of a husband have been included, incorrectly, on his wife's tax return. It is a good example of a question which covers fairly basic F6 knowledge, but tested in a more advanced way.

The most daunting thing about the requirement is the lack of breakdown – part (a) is worth a massive 24 marks, so you will need to think carefully about how to structure your answer.

There is also a written section on VAT, which should be reasonably straightforward - as long as you don't get too bogged down in the numbers in part (a) to have time to attempt it. Once again, the advice would be to do this part first.

The highlighted words in the written sections are key phrases that markers are looking for

Tutor's top tips

There are several different ways that you could approach part (a). The most time-consuming would be to prepare income tax computations for John and Maureen both with and without the investment income, for each of the two tax years, and compare the tax payable. Whilst this would be awarded the same marks as the examiner's answer, it would require 8 income tax computations, and would not represent efficient use of your time!

The examiner does give some guidance as to how to approach the question, and the key to arriving at the answer quickly was to work out what rate of tax would apply to the investment income by considering which tax band it would fall into.

However you decide to approach the question, it is very important that your answer is clearly labelled so that the marker can follow your calculations. You will only be penalised once for any mistake you make, and will score follow-through marks if you answer the rest of the question correctly based on your numbers – as long as the marker can see what you have done.

(a) **John and Maureen Robinson – Additional tax payable**

Additional income tax payable – 2010/11

	£	£
2,550 × 20% (property income (W1))		510
669 × 20% (interest income (W1))		134
3,219 (remainder of basic rate band (W2))		
2,361 × 40% (interest income (£3,030 – £669))		944
9,840 × 32·5% (dividend income (W1))		3,198
15,420		
Additional income tax liability		4,786
Less: Tax credits		
On dividends (£9,840 × 10%)		(984)
On interest (£3,030 × 20%)		(606)
		3,196
Tax paid by Maureen (W4)		(510)
Additional income tax payable		2,686

Tutorial note

All of the income declared by John (W2) is classified as 'other income' and therefore the additional income that should have been included (W1) will be taxed in the following order:

1. Property income

2. Interest income (including the children's income)

3. Dividend income

Additional capital gains tax payable – 2010/11

	£
Chargeable gain	13,470
Less: Annual exempt amount	(10,600)
Taxable gain	2,870

The gain is taxable at 28% if it is taxed on John, as he is a higher rate taxpayer, rather than at 18% if it is taxed on Maureen.

Therefore there is additional CGT payable of £287 (£2,870 x (28% – 18%)).

Tutorial note

The gift of property to Maureen would not be effective for capital gains tax purposes due to the prior agreement whereby Maureen gave the sale proceeds to John.

Entrepreneurs' relief is not available as the asset is not a qualifying business asset disposal.

Additional income tax payable – 2011/12

	£	£
789 × 20% (interest income in remaining basic rate band (W2))		158
2,431 × 40% (rest of interest income (W1))		972
144 × 40% (interest income – Penny (W1))		58
10,120 × 32.5% (dividend income (W1))		3,289
13,484		
Additional income tax liability		4,477
Less: Tax credits		
On dividends (£10,120 × 10%)		(1,012)
On interest (£3,220 × 20%)		(644)
		2,821
Less: Tax paid by Maureen (W5)		(561)
Additional income tax payable		2,260
Total additional tax payable (£2,686 + £287 + £2,260)		5,233

Workings

(W1) John – Additional taxable income

	2010/11 £	2011/12 £
Arising on inherited assets:		
Property income	2,550	–
Interest income (£2,424/£2,576 × 100/80)	3,030	3,220
Dividend income (£8,856/£9,108 × 100/90)	9,840	10,120
Children's bank accounts:		
Will – below *de minimis* limit of £100	–	–
Penny	–	144
	15,420	13,484

Tutorial note

Income from a parental disposition of over £100 per annum is taxed on the parent instead of on the child, if the child is under 18 and unmarried.

(W2) **John – Remainder of basic rate band**

	2010/11 £	2011/12 £
Salary	32,040	31,362
Car benefit (W3)		
(£17,400 × 24% × 8/12)	2,784	
(£17,400 × 24%)		4,176
Fuel benefit (W3)		
(£20,200 × 24% × 8/12)	3,232	
(£20,200 × 24%)		4,848
Trust income (£600/£650 × 100/50)	1,200	1,300
Declared total income	39,256	41,686
Less: Personal allowance	(8,105)	(8,105)
Declared taxable income	31,151	33,581
Basic rate band	34,370	34,370
Remainder of basic rate band	3,219	789

(W3) **Car and fuel benefit – appropriate percentage**

CO_2 emissions = 166 g/km

Available for 8 months in 2010/11, all year in 2011/12

	%
Petrol	11
Plus (165 − 100) × $^1/_5$	13
Appropriate percentage	24

(W4) **Maureen – Tax paid on investment income 2010/11**

	£
Trading income (W6)	13,227
Property income (W1)	2,550
Interest income (W1)	3,030
Dividend income (W1)	9,840
Declared total income	28,647
Less: Personal allowance	(8,105)
Declared taxable income	20,542
Income tax on property income (£2,550 × 20%) (Note)	510

Note: All of the investment income fell into the basic rate band. The tax liability in respect of the interest and dividend income was covered by the related tax credits. Accordingly, in respect of the income arising on the inherited assets, only the property income gave rise to income tax payable.

(W5) **Maureen – Tax paid on investment income 2011/12**

	£
Trading income (W6)	31,630
Interest income (W1)	3,220
Dividend income (W1)	10,120
Declared total income	44,970
Less: Personal allowance	(8,105)
Declared taxable income	36,865
Tax on dividend income in higher rate band (Note)	
(£2,495 × 32·5%)	811
Less: Tax credit (£2,495 × 10%)	(250)
Tax paid on investment income	561

Note: The tax liability in respect of the investment income that fell into the basic rate band was covered by the related tax credits. Accordingly, income tax was payable in respect of the dividend income that fell into the higher rate band only (i.e. £2,495 (£36,865 – £34,370)).

(W6) **Maureen – Trading income**

		£
11 months ended 30 September 2011		29,100
Year ended 30 September 2012		30,360
2010/11 Actual basis of assessment		
(1 November 2010 to 5 April 2011)	(£29,100 x 5/11)	13,227
2011/12 First 12 months trading:		£
1 November 2010 to 31 October 2011		
(1 November 2010 to 30 September 2011)		29,100
(1 October 2011 to 31 October 2011)	(£30,360 x 1/12)	2,530
		31,630

(b)   **Advice on Maureen's VAT position**

Tutor's top tips

Part (b) required the answer to be presented as paragraphs suitable for incorporation into a letter to be sent to the client by your manager.

The answer should therefore be written as if writing to the client yourself and the appropriate style and language should be used.

When giving advice on an alternative strategy, don't just talk about all of the VAT schemes that you know - choose the one that will actually help Maureen.

Deregistration

In order to voluntarily deregister for VAT you must satisfy HMRC that the value of your taxable supplies in the next twelve months will not exceed £75,000. You will then be deregistered with effect from the date of your request or a later date as agreed with HMRC.

On deregistering you are regarded as making a supply of all inventory and equipment in respect of which input tax has been claimed. However, the VAT on this deemed supply need only be paid to HMRC if it exceeds £1,000.

Once you have deregistered, you must no longer charge VAT on your sales. You will also be unable to recover the input tax on the costs incurred by your business. Instead, the VAT you pay on your costs will be allowable when computing your taxable profits.

You should monitor your sales on a monthly basis in case you exceed the registration limit; if your sales in a twelve-month period exceed £77,000 you must notify HMRC within the 30 days following the end of the twelve-month period. You will be registered from the end of the month following the end of the twelve-month period.

Flat rate scheme

Rather than deregistering you may wish to consider operating the flat rate scheme. This would reduce the amount of administration as you would no longer need to record and claim input tax in respect of the costs incurred by your business.

Under the flat rate scheme you would continue to charge your customers VAT in the way that you do at the moment. You would then pay HMRC a fixed percentage of your VAT inclusive turnover each quarter rather than calculating output tax less input tax. This may be financially advantageous as compared with deregistering; I would be happy to prepare calculations for you if you wish.

Examiner's comments

Part (a) of this question required candidates to carry out a series of calculations to determine the income tax underpaid where the income of one spouse was incorrectly declared on the tax return of the other. This is an example of a question that tests fundamental tax knowledge (brought forward from Paper F6) in a Paper P6 context.

There was a large number of marks here for dealing with basic aspects of investment income, employment income and trading income and the calculation of income tax liabilities. Most of these matters were handled well by the majority of candidates although knowledge of the trading income opening years rules was noticeably weaker than that relating to other matters.

Further marks were then available for determining the additional tax due on the income declared in the incorrect tax return. This could be handled most efficiently by working at the margin; calculating the tax on the additional income only and comparing it with the tax already paid on that income. However, this approach was not taken by the majority of students who wasted time preparing full income tax computations both with and without the incorrectly declared income.

The need to compare the additional tax payable by the husband with that already paid by the wife was not identified by all candidates. This may have been partly due to the instructions in the body of the question not being repeated in the requirement. This matter was addressed during the marking process and the requirement has been altered in the exam paper on the ACCA website. (*The same amendment has been made to the requirement in this exam kit.*)

Part (b) required candidates to explain the implications of deregistration for the purposes of VAT and to identify an alternative strategy that would assist in reducing the administration of VAT. Although the rules regarding deregistration were known by many candidates, a considerable amount of time was wasted by some who went on to describe the advantages and disadvantages of being registered in detail. The identification of an alternative strategy was not done particularly well, with many candidates providing a comprehensive list of VAT schemes rather than identifying the flat rate scheme as the one which would genuinely help the client.

ACCA marking scheme		
		Marks
(a)	The additional income:	
	Interest – 0·5 for each year	1.0
	Dividends – 0·5 for each year	1.0
	Property income	0·5
	Children's interest – identification of issue	1.0
	De minimis	1.0
	John's income tax:	
	2010/11:	
	Car benefit	1.0
	Fuel benefit	0·5
	Trust income	1.0
	Personal allowance	0·5
	Remainder of basic rate band	0·5
	Additional tax liability	2.0
	Tax credits	1.0
	Comparison with the tax paid by Maureen	0·5
	2011/12:	
	Car	0·5
	Fuel benefit	0·5
	Trust income	0·5
	Personal allowance	0·5
	Remainder of basic rate band	0·5
	Additional tax liability	2.0
	Tax credits	1.0
	Comparison with the tax paid by Maureen	0·5
	Maureen's income tax:	
	Trading income:	
	2010/11 assessment	1.0
	2011/12 assessment	1·5
	Tax on investment income:	
	2010/11	2·5
	2011/12	2·5
	Additional capital gains tax due:	
	Annual exempt amount	0·5
	Additional tax	1·0
	Total additional tax due	0·5
		27.0
	Maximum	24.0
	Clarity of presentation and use of headings	2.0
	Logical structure	1.0
		3.0
(b)	Conditions for voluntary deregistration	1.0
	Effective date	0·5
	Deemed supply	1.0
	De minimis limit	1.0
	Stop charging VAT	0·5
	Cannot recover input tax	0·5
	Deductible for income tax	0·5
	Need to monitor turnover	1.0
	Suggestion of flat rate scheme	1.0
	Operation of the scheme	2.0
	Possible financial advantage	0·5
		9.5
	Maximum	7.0
	Effectiveness of communication	1.0
Total		35

36   ALICE AND ZARA (ADAPTED)

Key answer tips

Make sure you do not just give general points about each investment but tailor them to the individual requirements of Alice and Zara.

Income tax and CGT implications of proposed investments

Individual savings account (ISA)

Income tax and CGT

- Income and capital gains realised on investments held within an ISA are exempt from income tax and CGT.
- There is no minimum holding period so withdrawals can be made from an ISA at any time without affecting the tax relief.

Alice – Maximum investment and suitability

Alice can invest £11,280 in an ISA during 2012/13. Up to £5,640 can be invested in cash, and this includes those investments in National Savings products where the income is not exempt from tax.

The balance of the subscription limit of £5,640 (£11,280 – £5,640) can be invested into a stocks and shares ISA.

Qualifying low risk investments are

(1)   fixed interest preference shares and convertible preference shares,

(2)   gilts, fixed interest corporation bonds and convertible bonds with at least five years to run until maturity, and

(3)   investments in unit trusts, investment trusts and open-ended investment companies.

An ISA should result in capital growth, need not be high risk, and can be easily liquidated in ten years time. This type of investment therefore satisfies Alice's criteria.

Zara – Maximum investment and suitability

Zara can also invest £11,280 in a stocks and shares ISA during 2012/13. Ordinary shares will qualify provided they are listed on a stock exchange situated anywhere in the world.

An ISA can provide income (depending on the choice of investments), should be within the level of risk that Zara is prepared to accept, and can be easily liquidated in five years time. This type of investment therefore satisfies Zara's criteria.

Investment in pension schemes

Income tax and CGT

The maximum tax deductible pension contribution an individual can make is the higher of

(i)   £3,600, and

(ii)   100% of the individual's relevant earnings, chargeable to income tax in the year.

Where an individual contributes to more than one pension scheme, the annual limit applies to total contributions made by him into all schemes.

Provided the total contributions paid into a scheme by the individual member or any other party (e.g. employer, spouse) do not exceed the annual allowance, no further tax consequences apply in that year.

The basic annual allowance for 2012/13 is £50,000. However, where an individual has not contributed the maximum amount into their fund the unused amount can be carried forward and utilised in any of the following three years.

As Alice has been contributing 6% of her salary, and her employer 5% this gives annual contributions as follows:

2010/11   £45,000 x 11% £4,950   c/f unused relief £45,050 (£50,000 – £4,950)

2011/12   £52,000 x 11% £5,720   c/f unused relief £44,280 (£50,000 – £5,720)

For 2012/13 the annual allowance is therefore £139,330 (£50,000 + £45,050 + £44,280).

Tutorial note

Although total contributions <u>can</u> be £50,000 (or £139,330 in Alice's case), the maximum contribution that attracts tax relief is the higher of £3,600 and the individual's earnings for the year.

Assets within a registered pension fund can grow in value tax free (i.e. there is no income tax in respect of income earned from the assets and no capital gains tax in respect of any capital disposals made by the trustees of the fund).

Unless retiring through ill health, pensions will not normally be paid out until the individual is aged 55.

A tax free lump sum of up to 25% of the lower of the fund value and the lifetime allowance (£1,500,000 for 2012/13) can be drawn.

The remainder of the fund must be used to pay pension income which is taxable earned income in the hands of the recipient.

Alice – Maximum investment and suitability

Alice's maximum tax deductible contribution for 2012/13, based on her earnings, is £55,000. This is within the annual allowance of £139,330 (see above), so full tax relief will be available.

The contribution will reduce her income tax liability partly at 40% and partly at 20%. The tax relief is obtained via the PAYE system.

Alice has currently paid 6% into her scheme which is a contribution of £3,300.

She could therefore pay an additional voluntary contribution either into her employer's scheme, or pay into a separate free-standing scheme, an amount of £51,700 (£55,000 – £3,300).

The pension eventually received will be taxable as earned income.

Considering Alice's objectives, the pension contribution should result in capital growth, and should not be high risk.

Alice is 50 years old and she does not want to access the fund for at least ten years. Although the pension scheme cannot be liquidated in ten years time, she will be entitled to draw a 25% lump sum and pension.

Zara – Maximum investment and suitability

Zara's maximum tax deductible pension contribution for 2012/13 is £47,400.

The contribution will reduce Zara's 2012/13 income tax liability. Basic rate tax relief is given by deduction at source, therefore Zara will pay cash of £37,920 (80% × £47,400) to the pension fund. Higher rate relief is obtained by extending the basic rate band.

The pension eventually received will be taxable as earned income.

Considering Zara's objectives, a personal pension is within the level of risk that Zara is prepared to accept.

However, it will not provide income until she retires, and as she is currently aged 38 the capital lump sum will not be available in five years time.

Open-ended investment company (OEIC)

Income tax and CGT

Alice is to invest the balance of £12,020 (£75,000 – £11,280 – £51,700) in an OEIC.

This will not attract any tax relief, and dividends from the OEIC will be taxable, net of 10% tax. Disposals are also subject to CGT.

Alice – Maximum investment and suitability

There is no maximum investment.

An investment in an OEIC should result in capital growth, need not be high risk, and can easily be liquidated in ten years time.

Venture capital trust (VCT)

Income tax and CGT

Zara is to use the balance of £25,800 (£75,000 – £11,280 – £37,920) to subscribe for new ordinary shares in a VCT.

She will obtain income tax relief up to a maximum of £7,740 (£25,800 × 30%) for 2012/13 (the investment is below the annual limit of £200,000).

The shares must be held for five years or the tax relief will be withdrawn. Dividends received are exempt from income tax, and any disposal should be exempt from CGT.

Zara – Maximum investment and suitability

There is no maximum investment.

Although high risk, a VCT would appear to be within the level of risk that Zara is prepared to accept. However, the investment is unlikely to provide a high level of income, although a disposal in five years time will not result in a withdrawal of the tax relief.

37   ANDREW

Key answer tips

This question covers a number of investment issues.

You may not have been familiar with the accrued income scheme in part (a)(ii) but should have picked up the mark for stating that Government stock is exempt from capital gains tax.

Part (b)(i) requires a detailed discussion of the Enterprise Investment scheme. Structuring your answer under the three headings of Qualifying Individual, Eligible shares and Qualifying Company helps focus your answer. If you cannot remember all the details leave space and come back if you recall them later.

(a)   (i)   Assignment of residential property lease

	£
Proceeds (May 2013)	90,000
Less: Deemed cost (May 2001)	
(see Tutorial note)	
£50,000 × (91.981/98.902)	(46,501)
Chargeable gain	43,499

Tutorial note

Where a lease with less than 50 years to run is assigned, the deemed cost is calculated by applying the fraction X/Y to the original cost.

X and Y are the appropriate percentages from HMRC's lease table where:

X =   percentage for the years left at the date of assignment (35 years)

Y =   percentage for the years left at the date of acquisition by the seller (47 years)

(ii)   **Tax implications – disposal of Government stock**

Government stock is an exempt asset for the purposes of capital gains tax, however, as Andrew's holding has a nominal value in excess of £5,000, a charge to income tax will arise under the accrued income scheme.

This charge to income tax will arise in 2012/13, being the tax year in which the next interest payment following disposal falls due (20 April 2012) and it will relate to the income accrued for the period 21 October 2011 to 14 March 2012 of £279 (145/182 × £350).

As interest on Government Stock is paid gross (unless the holder applies to receive it net), the tax due of £112 (£279 × 40%) will be collected via the self-assessment system.

As Andrew is an employee, it is likely that he does not need to make payments on account, therefore the tax will be due on 31 January 2014.

However, as the interest was an ongoing source of income, if Andrew is required to pay half yearly payments on account, the tax will be included within his payments on account payable on 31 January and 31 July 2013.

Tutorial note

The exam instructions say that apportionments should be made to the nearest month unless told otherwise. The accrued income could have been calculated as £292 (5/6 × £350) with tax due at 40% of £117.

(b)   (i)   **Income tax and capital gains tax reliefs – Investment in Scalar Ltd**

Andrew may be able to take advantage of tax reliefs under the enterprise investment scheme (EIS) provided the necessary conditions are met. The conditions that have to be satisfied before full relief is available fall into three areas, and broadly require that a 'qualifying individual' subscribes for 'eligible shares' in a 'qualifying company'.

'Qualifying Individual'

To be a qualifying individual, Andrew must not be connected with the EIS company. This means that he should not be an employee (or, at the time the shares are issued, a director) or have an interest in (i.e. control) 30% or more of the capital of the company.

Andrew does not intend to become an employee (or director) of Scalar Limited, but he needs to exercise caution as to how many shares he subscribes for.

If only three investors subscribe for 100% of the shares, each will hold 33% of the share capital. This exceeds the 30% limit and will mean that EIS relief (other than deferral relief) will not be available.

Therefore, Andrew and the other two investors should ensure not only that the potential fourth investor is recruited, but that they subscribe for sufficient shares, such that none of them will hold 30% or more of the issued share capital, as only then will they all attain qualifying individual status.

'Eligible shares'

Qualifying shares need to be new ordinary shares which are subscribed for in cash and fully paid up at the time of issue.

On the basis of the information provided, the shares of Scalar Limited would qualify as eligible shares.

'Qualifying Company'

The company must be unquoted. It does not have to be resident in the UK, but must have a permanent establishment in the UK, and must be engaged in qualifying business activities.

While certain trading activities, such as dealing in shares or trading in land, are excluded, the manufacturing trade Scalar Limited proposes to carry on will qualify.

The company must have a maximum of 250 full-time employees.

It is necessary for the money raised to be used for the qualifying business activity within two years of the relevant date.

Andrew and the other investors will thus have to ensure that Scalar Limited has not raised more funds than it is able to employ in the business within the appropriate time periods.

There is also an annual maximum of £5 million which can be raised by the company under the EIS scheme.

Reliefs available:

Andrew can claim income tax relief at 30% income tax relief on the amount invested up to a maximum of £1,000,000 in any one tax year.

The relief is given in the form of a tax reducing allowance, which can reduce the investor's income tax liability to nil, but cannot be used to generate a tax refund.

All or part of the investment can be treated as having been made in the previous tax year provided the EIS investment limit for that year is not breached.

Any capital gains arising on the sale of EIS shares will be fully exempt from capital gains tax provided that income tax relief was given on the investment when made and has not been withdrawn.

If the EIS shares are disposed of at a loss, capital losses are still allowable, but reduced by the amount of any EIS relief attributable to the shares disposed of.

In addition, gains from the disposal of other assets can be deferred against the base cost of EIS shares acquired within one year before and three years after their disposal. Such gains will, thus, not normally become chargeable until the EIS shares themselves are disposed of.

Further, for deferral relief to be available, it is not necessary for the investment to qualify for EIS income tax relief (i.e. deferral is available even where the investor is not a qualifying individual).

Thus, Andrew could still defer the gain arising on the disposal of the residential property lease made in order to raise part of the funds for his EIS investment, even if no fourth investor were to be found and his shareholding were to exceed 30% of the issued share capital of Scalar Limited.

Withdrawal of relief:

Any EIS relief claimed by Andrew will be withdrawn (partially or fully) if, within three years of the relevant date:

(1)   he disposes of the shares;
(2)   he receives value from the company;
(3)   he ceases to be a qualifying individual; or
(4)   Scalar Limited ceases to be a qualifying company.

With regard to receiving value from the company, the definition excludes dividends which do not exceed a normal rate of return, but does include the repayment of any loans made to the company before the shares were issued, the provision of benefits and the purchase of assets from the company at an undervalue.

In this regard, Andrew and the other subscribers should ensure that the £50,000 they are to invest in Scalar Limited as loan capital is appropriately timed and structured relative to the issue of the EIS shares.

(ii) **Taxation implications of equity and loan finance**

A company needs to be aware of the following issues:

Equity

(1) Costs incurred in issuing share capital are not allowed as a trading deduction.

(2) Distributions to investors are not allowed as a trading deduction.

(3) The cost of making distributions to shareholders is disallowable.

Loan finance/debt

(1) The incidental costs of obtaining/raising loan finance are broadly deductible as a trading expense.

(2) Capital costs of raising loan finance (for example, loans issued at a discount) are not deductible for tax purposes.

(3) Interest incurred on a loan to finance a business is deductible from trading income.

Key answer tips

The question only asked for the tax consequences of equity and loan finance. Avoid wasting time by discussing other commercial aspects which are not required in this particular question.

(c) **Characteristics of pension schemes**

Defined benefit scheme

A defined benefit scheme is one in which the benefits to be received on retirement are determined by the terms of the scheme and the pension receivable is linked directly to the employee's earnings at retirement and their number of years' service.

As a consequence such schemes provide considerable certainty for the employee, but leave the employer with the financial risk if the combined contribution rate and/or the performance of the scheme's investments prove inadequate to fund the benefits promised.

Defined contribution scheme

A defined contribution scheme is one in which only the contributions to be made are determined by the terms of the scheme, so there is no guarantee as to the level of pension which will be payable at retirement, which is totally reliant on the adequacy of the contribution rate set and the performance of the scheme's investments.

As a consequence such schemes provide certainty for the employer in terms of the monetary commitment required, but transfer the financial risk to the employee, as the scheme may provide insufficient funds with which to purchase a reasonable level of pension relative to current earnings at the time of retirement.

38 SERGIO AND GERARD *Online question assistance*

Key answer tips

This is a tricky question on which to obtain high marks.

In part (a) you must be careful to distinguish figures which relate to the whole house and those which relate to the individual half shares.

In part (b) ensure you relate your points to Sergio's circumstances.

In part (c) you might find it difficult to see the advantages of delaying part of the pension payment. However you must pick up the easy marks for calculating the relief if the whole contribution were made in 2013/14.

(a) **Chargeable gains in respect of 'Hilltop'**

2011/12 – Receipt of insurance proceeds

	£
Insurance proceeds (£81,700 x 2)	163,400
Used for restoration (£55,500 x 2)	111,000
% insurance used to restore the asset (£111,000/£163,400)	68%

Tutorial note

Where an asset is damaged and insurance proceeds are received, a normal CGT part disposal arises.

If 95% or more of the insurance is used to restore the asset, the gain can be deferred until the later disposal of the asset if an election is made.

If less than 95% if the insurance is used to restore the asset, an election can be made to reduce the gain arising.

If the election is made, a part disposal arises but special rules apply; the calculation is carried out using values after the restoration of the asset.

The allowable cost = Cost x A/(A+B) where:

A = Insurance less restoration costs, and

B = Value of asset after restoration.

The question states that the necessary election has been made therefore the special part disposal rules are used to calculate the gain.

Chargeable gains arising in 2011/12:

	£
Insurance proceeds (£81,700 x 2)	163,400
Less: Used for restoration (£55,500 x 2)	(111,000)
	52,400
Less: Original cost	
(£124,000 x (£52,400/(£52,400 + £269,000)))	(20,217)
Restoration work	
(£111,000 x (£52,400/(£52,400 + £269,000)))	(18,097)
Chargeable gain	**14,086**

Sergio and Gerard will each have a capital gain of £7,043 (£14,086 x ½)
Base cost of asset:

	£
Original cost	124,000
Restoration work	111,000
Less: Used in part disposal (£20,217 + £18,097)	(38,314)
Restoration costs rolled over	(111,000)
Base cost of asset	**85,686**

2012/13 – Sale of Hilltop

	£
Sale proceeds	310,000
Less Base cost of asset	(85,686)
Chargeable gain	**224,314**

Sergio and Gerard will each have a chargeable gain of £112,157 (£224,314 × ½)

(b) **Sergio's investments**

Sergio aims to leave a substantial asset to his family on his death. Accordingly, in view of his age, he is right to be considering investing in an asset whose value is unlikely to fall suddenly, such as a domestic rental property.

However, it must be recognised that although the value of land and buildings can usually be relied on to increase over a long period of time, its value may fall over a shorter period.

The only investments that cannot fall in value are cash deposits, although they do, of course, fall in real terms due to the effects of inflation.

Sergio should consider whether or not he wishes to increase his annual income. The return on capital invested in a domestic rental property is likely to be uncertain due to the recent changes in the property market in the UK. Also, there are likely to be periods when the house is unoccupied during which no income will be generated.

Tutorial note

Depending on when you write your answer, UK house prices might be rising or falling. The important point is that they fluctuate in the short term.

If it is important to Sergio to generate additional income he should consider other low-risk investments with a more reliable and higher rate of return, for example, gilt edged stocks, unit trusts and cash deposits.

Sergio must also decide whether it is important to him to be able to access capital quickly, as it is usually not possible to realise the capital invested in land and buildings at short notice. If this is important, Sergio should consider holding some of his capital in cash deposits or other liquid investments (e.g. unit trusts).

Sergio could invest up to £11,280 each year in an individual savings account (ISA). A maximum of £5,640 can be held in a cash ISA with the balance invested in a stocks and shares ISA. The income and gains arising on the funds invested would be exempt from both income tax and capital gains tax. This would be a relatively low-risk investment and would also be accessible quickly if required.

(c) **Pension contributions**

Income tax relief in respect of proposed contributions

Gerard has pensionable income of £82,180 as set out below.

	£
Salary	70,500
Estimated bonus	4,500
Estimated benefits	7,180
Earned income	82,180

This amount exceeds the annual allowance of £50,000, and no relief is available on any additional contributions.

Gerard has no unused relief from earlier years as he only set-up his pension fund in August 2013.

This means the maximum contribution that Gerard should make is £50,000 (gross).

The contribution would be made net of 20% basic rate income tax providing Gerard with income tax relief of £10,000 (£50,000 x 20%).

Further tax relief will be available when Gerard's income tax liability for 2013/14 is computed as his basic rate band will be extended by the gross pension contributions of £50,000.

2013/14 – Taxable income

	£
Earned income (as above)	82,180
Bank interest (£648 x 100/80)	810
Dividends (£1,935 x 100/90)	2,150
Total income	85,140
Less: Personal allowance	(8,105)
Taxable income	77,035

Analysis of income

Dividends £2,150   Savings £810   Other income £74,075

2013/14 – Income tax liability (ignoring the pension contributions)

£	£
34,370 × 20% (other income)	6,874
39,705× 40% (other income)	15,882
74,075	
810 × 40% (savings)	324
2,150 × 32·5% (dividends)	699
77,035	
Income tax liability	23,779

2013/14 – Income tax liability (taking account of the pension contributions)

The extension of the basic rate band to £84,370 (£34,370 + £50,000) will mean that all of Gerard's income will fall within the basic rate band.

£	£
74,075× 20% (other income)	14,815
810 × 20% (savings)	162
2,150 × 10% (dividends)	215
77,035	
Income tax liability	15,192

The income tax relief in respect of the extension of the basic rate band is £8,587 (£23,779– £15,192). The total income tax relief is £18,587 (£10,000 + £8,587).

Advice on improving the position

If Gerard makes pension contributions of £50,000 in 2013/14, he will obtain relief at higher rates for only part of them, i.e. £42,665 (£77,035 – £34,370).

Accordingly, he should make pension contributions of £42,665 (gross) in 2013/14 and delay the balance of the contributions, i.e. £7,335 (£50,000 – £42,665), until 2014/15 so that he obtains higher rate tax relief in respect of all of the contributions.

In 2013/14 due to the extension of his basic rate band, all of Gerard's income will fall within the basic rate band. Accordingly, his income tax liability will be £15,192 as set out above.

In 2014/15, Gerard's basic rate band will be extended to £41,705 (£34,370 + £7,335). Accordingly, assuming the same income as for 2013/14, the tax payable will be:

	£	£
41,705 × 20% (other income)		8,341
32,370x 40% (other income)		12,948
74,075		
810 × 40% (savings income)		324
2,150 × 32·5% (dividends)		699
77,035		
Income tax liability		22,312

Gerard's total income tax relief consists of the basic rate relief together with the amounts saved in 2013/14 and 2014/15 in respect of the extension of the basic rate bands.

	£
Basic rate relief (as before)	10,000
Relief at higher rates:	
2013/14 (£23,779– £15,192)	8587
2014/15 (£23,779– £22,312)	1,467
	20,054
Less: Income tax relief (all contributions made in 2013/14)	(18,587)
Additional relief from delaying pension contributions	1,467

Gerard may consider making further contributions into his scheme in 2014/15 as the limit of £50,000 per annum would allow a further £42,665 (£50,000 − £7,335) to qualify for relief. However, this should again be restricted to achieve tax relief at the highest rate in his computation.

(d) **Implications for Gerard of the changes to Fizz plc's bonus scheme**

Value received

Under the existing scheme Gerard receives approximately £4,500 each year. This is subject to income tax at 40% and national insurance contributions at 2% such that Gerard receives £2,610 (£4,500 x 58%) after all taxes.

Under the proposed share incentive plan (SIP), Gerard expects to receive free shares worth £3,500 (£2,100 + £1,400). Provided the shares remain in the plan for at least five years there will be no income tax or national insurance contributions in respect of the value received. Gerard's base cost in the shares for the purposes of capital gains tax will be their value at the time they are withdrawn from the scheme.

In addition, the amount he spends on partnership shares will be allowable for both income tax and national insurance such that he will obtain shares with a value of £700 for a cost of only £406 (£700 x 58%).

Accordingly, Gerard will receive greater value under the SIP than he does under the existing bonus scheme. However, as noted below, he will not be able to sell the free or matching shares until they have been in the scheme for at least three years by which time they may have fallen in value.

Timing of receipt of benefit

Under the existing scheme Gerard receives a cash bonus each year.

The value of free and matching shares awarded under a SIP cannot be realised until the shares are withdrawn from the scheme and sold. This withdrawal cannot take place until at least three years after the shares are awarded to Gerard.

Accordingly, Gerard will not have access to the value of the bonuses he receives under the SIP until the scheme has been in operation for at least three years. In addition, if the shares are withdrawn within five years of being awarded, income tax and national insurance contributions will become payable on the lower of their value at the time of the award and their value at the time of withdrawal thus reducing the value of Gerard's bonus.

39 ADAM SNOOK (ADAPTED) *Walk in the footsteps of a top tutor*

Key answer tips

This question is all about an individual setting up in business as a sole trader, and covers virtually all the different taxes: capital gains tax, income tax, NICs, VAT and inheritance tax!

The first section requires you to calculate the external finance needed, which is a clever way of asking you to calculate the capital gains tax payable out of the proceeds from selling assets. You also need to recognise that, in order to find the appropriate rate of CGT, a computation of taxable income is required. There are some nice easy marks here.

There are also some straightforward NICs, and a simple explanation of inheritance tax on a PET.

The harder parts of this question are the section on VAT for land and buildings, the explanation of the income tax relief for the purchase and renovation of the theatre and the explanation of the effect of charitable bequests on IHT.

The highlighted words in the written sections are key phrases that markers are looking for.

Tutor's top tips

One of the hardest aspects of this question is that some of the information is scattered around, particularly the information about Adam's income. Once you have read the requirement and know which taxes you will be dealing with, run through the question and annotate it with 'IT', 'CGT' etc so that you know which bits of information are relevant for each part of your answer.

Make sure you cover all the points raised in the email – this is the real requirement! The requirements at the end of the question are a less detailed summary, and just set out how many marks are available.

The question specifically asks you to note any assumptions made, so make sure you do this as you go along as there will be marks for anything sensible.

MEMORANDUM

To	Tax manager
From	Tax assistant
Date	3 December 2013
Subject	Adam Snook

This memorandum considers the external finance required by Adam Snook (AS) to start his new business together with a number of related matters.

(a) (i) **External finance required**

Tutor's top tips

The examiner does remind you that you need to take into account capital gains tax – you will need to calculate this first. In addition, before you can calculate the CGT payable you need to calculate Adam's taxable income to see how much basic rate band remains.

Once you have calculated the CGT, whether it is right or wrong, you will be given credit here for netting the tax off the proceeds and comparing this to the total cost of the project.

	£	£
Total cost of project		310,000
Sale proceeds of shares/loan stock		
(£104,370 + £29,900)	134,270	
CGT on sale of shares/loan stock (W1)	(7,906)	
		(126,364)
External finance required		183,636

Assumptions:

AS has made no other disposals for the purposes of capital gains tax in 2013/14.

AS has no capital losses brought forward.

Tutor's top tips

The capital gains tax calculation is hard, as the shares and loan stock were acquired as a result of a takeover.

You need to break the computation down into three stages:

Step 1 Calculate the 'cost' (W4)

Step 2 Calculate the gains on disposal (W2/W3)

Step 3 Calculate the tax after deducting the annual exempt amount (W1/W5)

Remember that you don't need to get this completely right to pass and if your income tax computation is incorrect marks will be given here providing your answer is right using the income tax position you have calculated.

Workings: Capital gains tax

(W1) Capital gains tax on sale of shares/loan stock

		£
Gains realised (£36,114 (W2) + £8,616 (W3))		44,730
Less: Annual exempt amount		(10,600)
Taxable gains		34,130
Capital gains tax	£	
Gains in basic band (£34,370 – £17,865 (W5))	16,505 x 18%	2,971
Balance of gains (£34,130 – £16,505)	17,625 x 28%	4,935
	34,130	7,906

Tutor's top tips

You should have considered but dismissed the possibility of Entrepreneurs' relief being available on this disposal at this stage.

There is no Entrepreneurs' relief available as Snapper plc is not Adam's personal trading company. It is a public limited company and it is assumed that Adam has a less than 5% interest. In addition, Adam does not work for the company and has held the shares and loan stock for less than 12 months.

(W2) Gain on sale of shares

	£
Sale proceeds	104,370
Less Deemed cost (W4)	(68,256)
Capital gain	36,114

Tutorial note

There is no gain on the share for share exchange element at the time of the takeover.

> However, the original cost of the shares in Brill plc is allocated between the shares and the loan stock received in Snapper plc in proportion to their market values the day after the takeover (see W4).
>
> A gain arises on the subsequent disposal of the shares.

(W3) Gain crystallising on sale of loan stock

	£
Market value of loan stock on 1 November 2013	28,400
Less Deemed cost (W4)	(19,784)
Capital gain	8,616

Tutorial note

A capital gain is calculated when the shares in Brill plc are exchanged for the loan stock in Snapper plc. However, the gain is frozen and not charged until the loan stock is sold at a later date.

The increase in value of the loan stock from the time of the takeover to the disposal date does not give rise to a capital gain as the loan stock is a qualifying corporate bond and therefore an exempt asset for the purposes of capital gains tax.

(W4) Deemed cost of shares and loan stock

	Total consideration £	Allocation of cost £
Shares	97,980	
Deemed cost £88,040 x (£97,980/£126,380)		68,256
Loan stock	28,400	
Deemed cost £88,040 x (£28,400/£126,380)		19,784
	126,380	88,040

(W5) Remainder of basic rate band

Taxable income in 2013/14

Tutor's top tips

Make sure that you find all the different types of income from the information in the question, not just the salary and the car benefit. Watch the dates carefully!

		£
Salary:	full time (£25,200 × 9/12)	18,900
	part time (£1,050 × 3)	3,150
	Car benefit (W6)	2,720
Trading income – period ended 31 March 2014 (£400 × 3)		1,200
		25,970
Less: Personal allowance		(8,105)
Taxable income		17,865

Assumptions:

No tax adjustments are required to AS's net profit of £400 per month.

AS has no other sources of income.

Tutor's top tips

You may have assumed that Adam received some interest on the loan stock before the sale in November 2013 – this would have been a valid assumption, and earned marks accordingly.

(W6) **Car benefit**

CO_2 emissions 162 g/km, available for 9 months in 2013/14

	%
Diesel	14
Plus (160 – 100) × $^1/_5$	12
Appropriate percentage	26
Car benefit (£13,950 x 26% x 9/12)	£2,720

(ii) **Proposal to increase the after tax proceeds from the sale of the loan stock**

AS should delay the sale of the loan stock until after 5 April 2014. The gain made at the time of the takeover would then crystallise in 2014/15 and would be covered by the annual exempt amount for that year. The net proceeds would be increased by the capital gains tax saved of £2,412 (£8,616 × 28%).

Tutorial note

Delaying the sale is feasible as not all of the funding is required immediately. The theatre renovations (costing £45,000) will be carried out in April and May 2014.

Tutor's top tips

The other benefit of delaying the sale until after 5 April 2014 is that the CGT will not be payable until 31 January 2016. However, this question just asked for the increase in net proceeds.

More appropriate forms of external finance

A bank overdraft is not the most appropriate form of long term business finance. This is because the bank can demand repayment of the overdraft at any time and the rates of interest charged are fairly high.

AS should seek long term finance for his long term business needs, for example a bank loan secured on the theatre, and use a smaller bank overdraft to finance the working capital required on a day-to-day basis.

Tutor's top tips

Probably the easiest 2 marks in the whole question – you could probably just use your common sense!

(b) **Related matters**

   (i) **National insurance contributions in 2013/14**

Tutor's top tips

The NIC rates are provided in the tables. Don't forget to apply them to the question – Adam's trading profit will be below the thresholds

The profit for the period ending 31 March 2014 is expected to be £1,200 (£400 × 3).

No class 2 contributions will be due as the profit is less than the small earnings exception limit of £5,595.

No class 4 contributions will be due as the profit is less than the lower profits limit of £7,605.

Tutorial note

Adam will have paid Class 1 contributions in respect of his earnings from Rheims Ltd, thus preserving his entitlement to state benefits and pension, and therefore there is no disadvantage in claiming the small earnings exemption from Class 2 contributions.

(ii)   **Purchase and renovation of the theatre**

Tutor's top tips

Think carefully before answering this part of the question. It is all about capital versus revenue expenses. Remember that buildings do not qualify for capital allowances.

The theatre is a capital purchase that does not qualify for capital allowances as it is a building. Accordingly, the cost of purchasing the theatre will not give rise to a tax deduction for the purpose of computing AS's taxable trading income.

The tax treatment of the renovation costs may be summarised as follows:

- The costs will be disallowed if the renovations are necessary before the theatre can be used for business purposes. This is because they will be regarded as further capital costs of acquiring appropriate premises.

- Some of the costs may be allowable if the condition of the theatre is such that it can be used in its present state and the renovations are more in the nature of cosmetic improvements.

Tutorial note

Capital allowances will be available on any element of the purchase price which relates to fixtures and fittings or furniture, and on any renovations in relation to those items.

(iii)   **VAT position**

Tutor's top tips

Make sure you learn the VAT treatment of land and buildings, as this has been tested several times recently.

The grant of a right to occupy the theatre in exchange for rent is an exempt supply. Accordingly, as all of AS's activities will be regarded as one for VAT purposes, AS will become partially exempt once he begins to rent out the theatre.

AS will be able to recover the input tax that is directly attributable to his standard rated supplies (i.e. those in connection with the supply of children's parties). He will also be able to recover a proportion of the input tax on his overheads; the proportion being that of his total supplies that are standard rated.

The remainder of his input tax will only be recoverable if it is de-minimis. There are 3 different tests to determine if the blocked VAT is de minimis.

1   The total input tax is not more than £625 per month (on average) and the value of the exempt supplies is no more than 50% of the value of all its supplies

2   The total input tax less input tax directly attributable to taxable supplies is no more than £625 per month (on average) and the value of exempt supplies is no more than 50% of the value of all supplies.

3   The irrecoverable input tax is less than or equal to £625 per month on average, and is less than or equal to 50% of total input tax.

AS only needs to meet one test to be de minimis, and able to recover all the VAT on the inputs.

If AS were to opt to tax the theatre, the right to occupy the theatre in exchange for rent would then be a standard rated supply. AS could then recover all of his input tax, regardless of the amount attributable to the rent, but would have to charge VAT on the rent and on any future sale of the building.

The decision as to whether or not to opt to tax the theatre will depend on:

- the amount of input tax at stake; and
- whether or not those who rent the theatre are in a position to recover any VAT charged.

Tutorial note

Most supplies of land and buildings are exempt for VAT purposes. This means that input VAT on any related expenses is not recoverable. However, the trader has the 'option to tax', which can also be referred to as an option to 'waive the exemption'. If he opts to tax, he must add output VAT at 20% to ALL supplies of the building (rent and subsequent sale), but can then reclaim all input VAT. When deciding whether or not to opt to tax, it is important to consider who the supply is made to. If the tenant/purchaser is not VAT registered, the VAT will represent an extra cost to them.

(c)   **Inheritance tax payable by Adam**

Tutor's top tips

This section is fairly straightforward, but make sure you use the dates and figures from the question.

The gift by AS's aunt was a potentially exempt transfer. No tax will be due if she lives until 1 June 2020 (i.e. seven years after the date of the gift).

The maximum possible liability, on the assumption that there are no annual exemptions or nil band available, is £35,216 (£88,040 × 40%). This will only arise if AS's aunt dies before 1 June 2016.

The maximum liability will be reduced by taper relief of 20% for every full year after 31 May 2016 for which AS's aunt lives.

The liability will also be reduced if the chargeable transfers made by the aunt in the seven years prior to 1 June 2013 are less than £325,000 or if the annual exemption for 2012/13 and/or 2013/14 is/are available.

Effect of charitable bequests

Any gifts to charity comprised within AS's will are exempt legacies and will reduce the amount of the estate subject to inheritance at 40%.

However, if the value of the charitable gifts are at least 10% of the taxable death estate (after the nil rate band, but before the deduction of the exempt legacy) then inheritance tax on the death estate will be payable at 36% and not 40%.

Examiner's comments

This question principally concerned a number of issues relating to the establishment of an unincorporated business. It was pleasing that most candidates produced a memorandum as required and structured their answer in an appropriate manner.

In part (a) (i) candidates had to calculate the external finance required by the new business. This calculation had to be done in two stages.

First, it was necessary to calculate the capital gains arising on the sale of shares and loan stock acquired as a result of a paper for paper transaction. Whilst many candidates were aware that particular rules applied in this situation (and many described them, unnecessarily, in great detail) only a well prepared minority were able to calculate the gains correctly.

It was then necessary to use the information to determine the capital gains tax payable.

Part (a) (ii) required candidates to identify a strategy to increase the after tax proceeds from the sale of the loan stock and to suggest a form of external finance more appropriate than a bank overdraft. The first task was not done well as many candidates were of the opinion, incorrectly, that the sale of the loan stock would not give rise to a tax liability and therefore the position could not be improved. The second task was done well.

Part (b) required candidates to address various issues relating to the new business. This was not done particularly well. Candidates were happy to outline the national insurance position of unincorporated traders in general but, unfortunately, were less willing to apply their knowledge to the taxpayer's particular situation. The VAT implications of renting out the building were not well understood.

The final part of the question concerning the potential inheritance tax liability in respect of a lifetime gift was done well.

				Marks
ACCA marking scheme				
(a)	(i)	Total costs less after tax sale proceeds		1.0
		Calculation of gains:		
			On shares	1.0
			Crystallisation of gain on loan stock	2.0
			Annual exempt amount	0.5
			No Entrepreneurs' relief	0.5
		Remainder of basic rate band		
			Salary	1.5
			Car benefit	1.5
			Trading income	1.0
			Personal allowance	0.5
		Tax due		1.0
		Assumptions – 0.5 each – maximum 1.0		1.0
				11.5
			Maximum	10.0
	(ii)	Proposal to increase after tax sales proceeds:		
			Identification of strategy	1.0
			Tax saved	1.0
		More appropriate forms of finance:		
			Bank overdraft inappropriate with reason	1.0
			Longer term finance with reason	1.0
				4.0
			Maximum	3.0
(b)	(i)	National insurance contributions:		
			Class 2	1.0
			Class 4	1.0
	(ii)	Purchase and renovation of the theatre:		
			Purchase price	1.5
			Two possible treatments of renovations	2.0
	(iii)	VAT position:		
			Partial exemption with reason	1.5
			Recoverable input tax	1.5
			De minimis limits	1.0
			Effect of opting to tax	1.5
			Factors affecting decision – 1 each – maximum 2	2.0
				13.0
			Maximum	11.0
(c)		Gift is a PET, no tax if survives seven years		1.0
		Maximum possible liability		1.0
		Relevance of date of death/taper relief		1.5
		Annual exemption and nil rate band		1.0
		Charitable bequests exempt		1.0
		Possibility of 36% IHT rate		1.0
		Explanation of conditions		1.0
				7.5
			Maximum	7.0
		Appropriate style and presentation		2.0
		Effectiveness of communication		2.0
				4.0
Total				35

40   GAGARIN (ADAPTED)

Key answer tips

In part (a) it is very important to take note of the examiner's instructions. The question states that you can assume the company qualifies for EIS relief and you are not required to list any of the conditions. If you do then you will not earn any marks for them.

Part (b) requires knowledge of the capital goods scheme. Here the examiner asks for illustrative examples in your explanations. Even if you are not sure about the capital goods scheme, you should have picked up the marks for calculating the input tax recovery in the year of purchase

(a)   (i)   **The tax incentives immediately available**

Income tax

–   The investor's income tax liability for 2013/14 will be reduced by 30% of the amount subscribed for the shares.

–   The amount invested can be treated as if paid in 2012/13 rather than 2013/14. Relief can be claimed on a maximum of £1 million in any one tax year.

         This ability to carry back relief to the previous year is useful where the investor's income tax liability in 2013/14 is insufficient to absorb all of the relief available.

Tutorial note

There would be no change to the income tax liability of 2012/13 where an amount is treated as if paid in that year. This ensures that such a claim does not affect payments on account under the self assessment system. Instead, the tax refund due is calculated by reference to 2012/13 but is deducted from the next payment of tax due from the taxpayer or is repaid to the taxpayer.

Capital gains tax deferral

–   For every £1 invested in Vostok Ltd, an investor can defer £1 of capital gain and thus, potentially, 28 pence of capital gains tax.

–   The gain deferred can be in respect of the disposal of any asset.

–   The shares must be subscribed for within the four year period starting one year prior to the date on which the disposal giving rise to the gain took place.

(ii) **Answers to questions from potential investors**

Maximum investment

– For the relief to be available, a shareholder (together with spouse and children) cannot own more than 30% of the company.

– Accordingly, the maximum investment by a single subscriber will be £315,000 (15,000 (W) x £21).

Borrowing to finance the purchase

– There would normally be tax relief for the interest paid on a loan taken out to acquire shares in a close company such as Vostok Ltd. However, this relief is not available when the shares qualify for relief under the Enterprise Investment Scheme.

Implications of a subscriber selling the shares in Vostok Ltd

– The income tax relief will be withdrawn if the shares in Vostok Ltd are sold within three years of subscription.

– Any profit arising on the sale of the shares in Vostok Ltd on which income tax relief has been given will be exempt from capital gains tax provided the shares have been held for three years.

– Any capital loss arising on the sale of the shares will be allowable regardless of how long the shares have been held. However, the loss will be reduced by the amount of income tax relief obtained in respect of the investment.

– The loss may be used to reduce the investor's taxable income, and hence his income tax liability, for the tax year of loss and/or the preceding tax year.

– Any gain deferred at the time of subscription will become chargeable in the year in which the shares in Vostok Ltd are sold.

Working: Maximum investment

As 20,000 represents a 40% interest in the company, a 30% interest will be 15,000 shares (20,000 × 30/40).

Tutorial note

The theoretical maximum investment is £1 million but it would not be possible for an investor to make this amount of investment. See the examiner's comments in respect of this answer.

(b) **Recoverable input tax in respect of new premises**

Vostok Ltd will recover £54,720 (£456,000 × 1/6 (or 20/120) × 72%) in the year ending 31 March 2014.

The capital goods scheme will apply to the purchase of the building because it is to cost more than £250,000. Under the scheme, the total amount of input tax recovered reflects the use of the building over the period of ownership, up to a maximum of ten years, rather than merely the year of purchase.

Further input tax will be recovered in future years as the percentage of exempt supplies falls. If the percentage of exempt supplies were to rise, Vostok Ltd would have to repay input tax to HMRC.

The additional recoverable input tax will be computed by reference to the percentage of taxable supplies in each year including the year of sale.

For example, if the percentage of taxable supplies in a particular subsequent year were to be 80%, the additional recoverable input tax would be computed as follows.

£456,000 × 1/6 × 1/10 × (80% − 72%) = £608.

Further input tax will be recovered in the year of sale as if Vostok Ltd's supplies in the remaining years of the ten-year period are fully VATable.

For example, if the building is sold in year seven, the additional recoverable amount for the remaining three years will be calculated as follows.

£456,000 × 1/6 × 1/10 × (100% − 72%) × 3 = £6,384.

Tutorial note

If Vostok Ltd waives the VAT exemption in respect of the building (often referred to as 'opting to tax'), then when the building is sold, VAT must be charged and the previously partially exempt use of the building becomes fully taxable.

Examiner's comments

This question concerned a company that intended to raise finance under the Enterprise Investment Scheme to finance its expansion. The company intended to use a part of the funds raised to purchase new premises.

Part (a) of the question was in two parts. The first part required candidates to identify the tax incentives available to potential investors and the second part asked for the answers to questions that potential investors may raise.

In the first part, although most candidates had a good knowledge of the income tax deduction available to investors, many of them did not identify the possibility of investors deferring capital gains. A minority of candidates included information regarding the conditions that needed to be satisfied by the company despite a specific instruction in the question not to do so.

When it came to addressing the possible questions from investors, candidates did well on the implications of a future sale of the shares. However, when addressing the maximum investment by a potential shareholder, candidates resorted to making general comments in relation to the maximum investment of £1 million, when they should have applied the specific rules to the facts of the question. This would have led them to the need to restrict any investment to no more than 30% of the company, i.e. £315,000.

Although this part of the question was answered well, many candidates would have done better if they had written less and spent some time relating their knowledge to the particular situation in the question.

Part (b) concerned the recovery of VAT input tax in respect of a building acquired by a partially exempt company. It was not answered well with many candidates failing to identify the need to apply the capital goods scheme to the situation.

ACCA marking scheme				Marks
(a)	(i)	Income tax		
			Reduction in income tax	1.0
			Carry back	2.0
		Capital gains tax		
			Deferral	1.0
			Any asset	0·5
			Time period	1.0
				5·5
			Maximum	5.0
	(ii)	Maximum investment		1·5
		Borrowing to finance the purchase		1.0
		Sale of the shares		
			Importance of three-year period	1.0
			Withdrawal of income tax relief	1.0
			Treatment of gain arising	1.0
			Treatment of loss arising	
			Allowable	1.0
			Affect on loss of income tax relief	0·5
			Relief of loss against income	1.0
			Gain deferred at time of subscription	1.0
				9.0
(b)		Recoverable input tax in the year ending 31 March 2014		1.0
		Additional recoverable input tax		
			Capital goods scheme applies	1.0
			Explanatory rationale	1.0
			Input tax recoverable in future years	2.0
			Input tax recoverable following sale	2.0
				7.0
			Maximum	6.0
Total				20

TAXATION OF CORPORATE BUSINESSES

FAMILY COMPANY ISSUES

41 JAMES & MELVIN (ADAPTED)

Key answer tips

This question deals with the topics of close companies and purchase of own shares.

The technical details for part (a) are not too difficult, but since the requirement is a letter, you must be careful to explain them in a readable way. You should follow the question requirements to structure your answer with sections for each car, for the loan and for the effect on the company.

The purchase of own shares is trickier because you are not given the figure of shares to be sold back and must suggest a figure. You should calculate the minimum number to be sold back to achieve capital gains treatment.

Client address

Firm address

Date

Dear James and Melvin

Further to our recent meeting we are writing to set out the position regarding the queries raised.

Provision of Company Car to James

Special taxation rules apply when either a benefit (such as the provision of a company car) or a loan is made to a participator (i.e. a shareholder of a close company such as JM Limited).

As James is employed by JM Limited he will be assessed on the provision of the company car and fuel in 2012/13 under the 'normal assessable benefit' rules for employment income.

The following amounts will therefore form part of his assessable 2012/13 income.

	£
Company car benefit	3,600
Fuel benefit	3,636
	7,236

Appendix A sets out how these figures are derived.

As James is a higher rate taxpayer, his income tax liability will be increased by £2,894 (£7,236 × 40%). Tax on such benefits is usually collected by an adjustment to a taxpayer's PAYE code.

Provision of Company Car to Melvin

Melvin is not employed by JM Limited, nor is he a director of this company. He is, however, a participator in a close company and therefore the special close company provisions will apply.

In the case of benefits provided, the participator will be assessed on a deemed distribution (i.e. dividend) calculated in accordance with the normal benefit rules referred to above.

In 2012/13 Melvin will therefore be assessed on a gross distribution equal to the car benefit grossed up, calculated as follows:

£7,236 × 100/90 = £8,040

As Melvin is a higher rate taxpayer he will be assessed on this distribution via his 2012/13 self-assessment tax return at the special higher rate for dividends of 32.5%, giving a tax liability of £2,613 (£8,040 × 32.5%). A 10% tax credit will, however, attach to the gross dividend meaning that the net amount of additional tax payable amounts to £1,809 (£8,040 × 22.5%).

Settling of Melvin's personal bills

The settling by JM Limited of Melvin's personal bills is covered by the loans to participator rules. Under these rules the expression 'loan' is very widely defined and would include the company directly settling personal liabilities of a participator.

It is possible that HMRC will seek to assess Melvin on a benefit calculated under the beneficial loan rules. These rules usually apply where an employee is loaned money by their employer either without being charged any interest or being charged a below market value interest rate.

If HMRC were to seek an assessment in this manner the benefit would be calculated using the normal benefit rules and once again grossed up as a deemed distribution in a similar way to that described above. However, because Melvin is neither an employee nor a director of JM Limited and special close company rules specifically apply to such loans it is thought unlikely that a deemed distribution based on a beneficial loan benefit will arise.

It is considered more likely that Melvin will have no personal tax implications derived from this loan until the loan is written off. When this happens it will be treated as a gross distribution of £22,222 (£20,000 × 100/90) assessable in the tax year that the loan is written off. The distribution will carry a 10% tax credit as for other dividends.

As Melvin is a higher rate taxpayer this means that he will have to pay, via his self assessment tax return, an additional £5,000 (£22,222 × 22.5%).

Position for JM Limited

Provision of car to James

The cost of running the car provided to James is allowable for corporation tax purposes. In addition JM Limited will obtain capital allowances at 18% on the cost of the car, as its emissions level is between 111 and 160 g/km, to offset against its profits for the year ended 31 March 2013. The company will have to pay Class 1A National Insurance contributions of £999 (£7,236 × 13.8%) by 19 July 2013.

Tutorial note

As JM Limited is providing private fuel to James, there may be a VAT scale charge payable. This varies with the emission level of the car and is charged if the company reclaims all its input tax on petrol used for both private and business purposes.

Provision of car to Melvin

As Melvin is not an employee or director of JM Limited the company is unable to obtain any tax deductions (including capital allowances) for the car provided to him but no Class 1A NIC will arise on this car.

Settling Melvin's personal bills

JM Limited will be required to pay 25% of the net value of any loans made to participators which have not been repaid to the company or written off by the company's normal corporation tax due date.

This means that unless the loan is written off by 1 January 2014 an amount of £5,000 (£20,000 × 25%) will need to be paid to HMRC which will then only be refunded to the company when the loan is repaid by Melvin or he is formally released from having to repay it by the company (and then usually nine months after the end of the accounting period in which the loan is repaid or released).

As it is likely that the loan is going to be written off at some future point it is therefore recommended, to assist JM Limited's cash flow position, that the write-off occurs and is formally documented prior to 1 January 2014.

Direct Sale of Shares

If James sells his shares directly to Melvin this will result in a straightforward capital gain arising.

As James has owned at least 5% of the shares of JM Limited, and has been an employee, for at least 12 months, Entrepreneurs' relief will be available and the gain will be taxed at 10%. Capital gains tax will amount to between £3,930 and £16,405 (depending on the number of shares actually sold).

This will be payable either on 31 January 2014 if the sale occurs on 31 March 2013 or 31 January 2015 if the sale is deferred to 31 May 2013. From a cash flow perspective a deferral to the later date therefore appears preferable if possible. It may also be possible to sell some shares on 31 March 2013 and some on 31 May 2013 in order to utilise both annual exempt amounts.

Appendix B sets out the calculation of the capital gains tax liability.

If Melvin needs to borrow to raise the funds for the share purchase then the interest on such a loan will qualify for tax relief by deduction in arriving at his taxable income (as a relief) for the tax year in which the interest is paid.

Company Purchase of Own Shares

If the share sale proceeds via a company purchase of its own shares, assuming the conditions for a capital gains treatment are not satisfied (see below), the basic position is that this will be treated as an income distribution (i.e. dividend) in the hands of the recipient.

The distribution is calculated on the proceeds received for the shares less the amount originally subscribed for them. If James were to sell, for example, 100 shares he would therefore be deemed to receive net dividend income of £49,900 ((100 × £500) – £100) and would have an additional tax liability of £12,475 (£49,900 × 100/90 × 22.5%) collected through his self-assessment tax return.

If the following conditions are satisfied the share purchase by JM Limited will be subject to the capital gains tax rules rather than being treated as an income distribution.

- Company is an unquoted trading company

- Vendor is UK resident and ordinarily UK resident

- Shares have been owned for five years prior to the purchase date

- The purchase is for the benefit of the purchasing company's trade (which includes the position where an outside investor wishes to either partially or fully 'cash in' his investment)

- The transaction is not part of a scheme to avoid tax

- As a result of the purchase the vendor (and his associates):

    (i)   reduce their interest in the share capital to 75% or less of their percentage share immediately prior to the purchase (share reduction test); and

    (ii)   must not control more than 30% of the issued share capital (or voting rights) (connection test)

This is likely to be a more favourable tax treatment because capital gains tax is at a rate of only 10% due to the availability of Entrepreneurs' relief (less with the annual exempt amount), compared to 25% of the net dividend for the distribution route.

In this particular case the key conditions are the ownership period, the share reduction test and the connection test.

If James sells his shares on 31 March 2013 the five year test will not have been satisfied with the result that any sale will be subject to the income distribution rules outlined above. To access the CGT treatment it is therefore recommended, if possible, that the sale is deferred until 31 May 2013.

To satisfy the share reduction test at least 200 shares must be sold (see Appendix C).

To satisfy the connection test at least 286 shares will need to be sold giving a minimum capital gains tax charge of £13,211 (see Appendix C).

Conclusion

In conclusion, it would appear that if the purchase needs to proceed on 31 March 2013 (in which case a company purchase will be treated as an income distribution) a direct sale to Melvin would appear preferable, primarily because of the lower capital gains tax rate.

If the sale could be deferred to 31 May 2013, however, providing at least 286 shares are sold either a direct sale or company purchase of shares would be dealt with under the capital gains tax rules. In this case other deciding factors may therefore become important, for example the ability of Melvin to raise the funds for the share purchase personally.

We trust that the above is helpful but should you have any queries please do not hesitate to contact me.

Yours sincerely

A N Accountant

APPENDIX A: BENEFIT CALCULATIONS

Car Benefit Calculation

CO_2 emission level of car = 136 grams per kilometre

Base level CO2 emission for 2012/13 =100 grams per kilometre

Appropriate % = (135 – 100) $\times$ 1/5 + 11% = 18%

Benefit (£20,000 × 18%)   <u>£3,600</u>

Fuel Benefit Calculation

Benefit (£20,200 × 18%)   <u>£3,636</u>

APPENDIX B: CAPITAL GAINS TAX ARISING ON DIRECT SALE OF SHARES TO MELVIN

Sale of	*100 shares*	*350 shares*
Gains qualifying for Entrepreneurs' relief	£	£
Proceeds (@ £500 per share)	50,000	175,000
Less: Cost (May 2008)	(100)	(350)
Chargeable gain	49,900	174,650
Less: Annual exempt amount	(10,600)	(10,600)
Taxable gain	39,300	164,050
CGT at 10%	3,930	16,405

APPENDIX C: PURCHASE OF OWN SHARES

Share Reduction Test

Share % before disposal = 500/1,000	=	50%
Maximum % share permissible after buy back (50% × 75%)	=	37.5%

When shares are purchased back by the company they must be cancelled. Therefore James' holding and the total shareholding will be reduced.

$(500 - n/(1,000 - n)$	=	37.5% where n = number of shares purchased
500 – n	=	375 – 37.5n
500 – 375	=	62.5%n
125/62.5%	=	n
n	=	200 shares

Connection test

$(500 - n)/(1,000 - n)$	=	30% where n = number of shares purchased
500 – n	=	300 – 30%n
500 – 300	=	70%n
200/70%	=	n
n	=	286 shares

As a result to satisfy the requirements of CGT treatment at least 286 shares need to be sold.

Assuming 286 shares are sold the capital gains calculation will be as follows:

Gains qualifying for Entrepreneurs' relief	£
Proceeds (286 × £500)	143,000
Less: Cost (May 2008)	(286)
Chargeable gain	142,714
Less: Annual exempt amount	(10,600)
Taxable gain	132,114
CGT at 10%	13,211

Tutorial note

An alternative method of calculation of the minimum number to sell back is to say that if James' shareholding is to be 30% then Melvin's must be 70%. Since Melvin has 500 shares these must now represent 70% of the company's share capital and the total share capital must be 500 ×100/70 = 714. James shareholding is 30% which is 214 and since he started with 500 he must have sold back 286.

42 CHARLES AND JANE MIRO (ADAPTED)

Key answer tips

This question requires a good knowledge of the personal service company legislation (set out by HMRC in their press release IR 35). In part (a)(i) you are only required to give points in favour of Speak Write Ltd being treated as a personal service company and not to give any arguments against which would not earn any marks.

Make sure you pick up the easy marks for the administration points in part (b).

(a)   **Tax adviser**

1 Broad Street
Anytown

Mrs J Miro
Speak Write Ltd
1 The Avenue
Anytown

6 September 2013

Dear Jane

Personal Service Companies

I refer to our recent telephone conversation regarding the personal service companies (IR 35) legislation.

The legislation will apply if you would be regarded as an employee of the universities were you to contract with them directly, rather than via Speak Write Ltd. Accordingly, HM Revenue and Customs (HMRC) will consider the contracts between the universities and Speak Write Ltd and all of the factors surrounding the work carried out.

Based on the information you have supplied, HMRC could put forward the following points in support of an employer/employee relationship.

– In respect of all of the company's contracts the work must be done by you rather than by a substitute or assistant.

– In respect of the contract with Barnham University you use the university's office space and computer rather than those of Speak Write Ltd.

– In respect of some of the contracts the fee is by reference to the time taken to carry out the work and is not agreed in advance.

– The company obtains 70% of its gross income from one customer, Barnham University, and has only three other customers.

HMRC will consider each of the company's contracts separately when arguing whether the rules apply. However, in the computations in the appendix to this letter, I have assumed that the legislation applies to all of the company's income in 2013/14.

The consequence of the application of the IR 35 rules is that you would be treated as receiving additional salary from the company on the last day of the tax year of £44,736. The additional PAYE and Class 1 national insurance contributions on that deemed salary would be due on 19 April after the end of the tax year.

Please telephone me if you require any further information.

Yours sincerely

Tax consultant

APPENDIX – INCOME TAX AND NATIONAL INSURANCE DUE FOR 2013/14

		£
Gross fee income		110,000
Less: 5% × £110,000		(5,500)
Salary paid (£4,000 × 12)		(48,000)
Class 1 secondary national insurance contributions (£48,000 − 7,488) × 13·8%		(5,591)
		50,909
Deemed employment income payment (£50,909 ÷ $\frac{1}{1.138}$)		44,736
PAYE due at 40%		17,894

Employee's Class 1 national insurance contributions (£44,736 × 2%)

895
_____

Employer's Class 1 national insurance contributions (£44,736 × 13.8%)

6,174
_____

Tutorial note

A company deemed to be a personal service company must treat the income from relevant engagements as if it were salary paid to the employee. A deduction can be made for a flat 5% of the income to cover overheads. It does not matter if nothing has actually been spent on overheads. Deductions can also be made for pension contributions and any expenses borne by the company that would be allowable for an employee. Allowance must also be made for employer's NIC on the deemed salary payment. This is why the deemed employment income payment in the calculation above is 100/113.8 of the net fee income of £50,909

(b)   (i)   **Speak Write Ltd**

Corporation tax liability for the year ending 5 April 2014

	£
Estimated trading income	52,500
Deemed employment income payment	(44,736)
Employer's NIC on the deemed payment	(6,174)
	_____
Taxable total profits	1,590
	_____
Corporation tax liability at 20%	318
	_____

(ii)   **Administration of the company's tax affairs**

The corporation tax return must be submitted within 12 months of the end of the accounting period, i.e. by 5 April 2015.

Corporation tax is due nine months and one day after the end of the accounting period, i.e. by 6 January 2015.

HMRC have 12 months from the actual filing date to enquire into the corporation tax return. Once this deadline has passed the return can be regarded as agreed provided it includes all necessary information and there has been no loss of tax due to the company's fraud or negligence.

Jane should have notified HMRC by 5 July 2013 that Speak Write Ltd's first accounting period began on 6 April 2013. The penalty for failing to notify is a percentage of the revenue lost as a result of the inaccuracy and depends on the behaviour of the taxpayer as follows:

Taxpayer behaviour	Maximum penalty (% of revenue lost)
Genuine mistake	No penalty
Failure to take reasonable care	30%
Deliberate but no concealment	70%
Deliberate with concealment	100%

The penalties may be reduced depending on the type of penalty and whether the taxpayer makes an unprompted disclosure. If Jane makes an unprompted disclosure and the reason for the late notification was failure to take reasonable care, the penalty could be reduced to £Nil.

Tutorial note

There will be no penalty if there is no tax or NIC unpaid as a result of the failure to notify.

43 CARVER LTD

Key answer tips

This is a tricky question covering two areas; possible changes of activity for a company and the liquidation of the company either with or without a pre liquidation dividend.

In part (a) it is important to understand that the company will cease trading when it sells its assets, which will bring an accounting period to an end, and even though the examiner asks for the corporation tax liability for the year (in part (a)(iii)), this must be calculated in two parts. There is a clue in part (a)(i) with the reference to corporation tax return(s) implying there may be more than one. There are some easy marks to pick up for calculating the gain on the sale of the building and the balancing allowance on plant and machinery and you must make sure you get these even if you are not sure of all the technical points.

In part (b) the examiner is asking for discussion of four possible situations with two groups of taxpayers and two possible strategies. Child shareholders are unlikely to qualify for Entrepreneurs' relief, but will probably have no income and so would prefer a pre liquidation dividend. For adult shareholders the position is less clear-cut. Always try to identify the situations first, so that you can structure your discussion under those headings.

(a)　(i)　**Due date for submission of corporation tax return**

Carver Ltd intends to cease trading on 31 July 2013. This will bring to an end the accounting period that began on 1 January 2013. A new accounting period will commence on 1 August 2013 and end on the company's accounting reference date on 31 December 2013.

Carver Ltd is required to submit its corporation tax return by the later of:

– one year after the end of its accounting period; and

– one year after the end of the period of account in which the last day of the accounting period falls.

Accordingly, the company must submit its corporation tax returns for both accounting periods by 31 December 2014.

(ii) **Close investment holding company status**

Carver Ltd will not become a close investment-holding company if it purchases the office building as, although it will no longer be a trading company, it intends to rent out the building to a number of tenants none of whom is connected to the company.

Carver Ltd will become a close investment holding company if it purchases a portfolio of quoted shares as it will no longer be a trading company. As a result it will pay corporation tax at the main rate of 24% regardless of the level of its profits.

(iii) **Carver Ltd – Corporation tax liability for the year ending 31 December 2013**

Period from 1 January 2013 to 31 July 2013

	£
Trading profit	81,000
Profit on sale of goodwill	290,000
Less: Balancing allowance (£231,500 + £38,000 – £187,000)	(82,500)
Tax adjusted trading profit	288,500
Chargeable gain (W1)	190,552
Taxable total profits	479,052
Corporation tax liability	
£479,052× 24% (W2)	114,972
Marginal relief ((£875,000 – £479,052) × 1/100)	(3,959)
Corporation tax liability	111,013

Tutorial note

The profit on the sale of the goodwill falls within the regime governing intangible assets and is a trading profit.

The disposal of the machinery and equipment will not result in capital losses due to the availability of capital allowances.

Period from 1 August 2013 to 31 December 2013 – Purchase of building

	£
Accrued rental income for five months (£54,000/3 × 5)	90,000
Building maintenance	(7,500)
Property business income	82,500
Non-trading loan relationship deficit	(16,000)
Taxable total profits	66,500
Corporation tax liability	
£66,500 × 20% (W3)	13,300

Period from 1 August 2013 to 31 December 2013 – Purchase of share portfolio

	£
Indexed capital gains	10,000
Dividends (exempt)	–
Taxable total profits	10,000
Corporation tax liability	£
£10,000 × 24% (close investment-holding company)	2,400

Rollover relief

The business premises qualify for rollover relief because they are occupied and used for the purposes of the company's trade. However, neither of the proposed replacement assets qualifies for the relief. The new office building is to be held as an investment rather than being used for trading purposes and shares can never qualify for rollover relief.

Bank interest payable

The interest will be allowable on the accruals basis under the rules governing loan relationships. This is a non-trading loan relationship as the loan is to be taken out to finance the purchase of an investment as opposed to a trading asset. Accordingly, because Carver Ltd has no interest income, the interest payable amounts to a net deficit.

Carver Ltd can offset the deficit against

- its other income in the accounting period; or

- interest income in the previous 12 months; or

- future non-trading profits.

Carver Ltd did not have any interest income in the previous 12 months and therefore cannot carry back the deficit. The company will pay corporation tax at 20% in the accounting period ending 31 December 2013 and in future accounting periods, if it acquires the office building. Accordingly, it should offset the deficit in the current period, to obtain relief as early as possible

Tutorial note

The examiner asks for corporation tax liability assuming all beneficial elections are made. The only beneficial election possible is the use of the non-trading loan relationship deficit against current year profits.

(W1) **Chargeable gain on sale of premises**

	£
Disposal proceeds	2,165,000
Less: Cost	(1,708,000)
	457,000
Less: Indexation	
251.0 − 217.2/217.2 = 0.156 × £1,708,000	(266,448)
Chargeable gain	190,552

(W2) **Rate of corporation tax – Period from 1 January 2013 to 31 July 2013**

	£
Taxable total profits	479,052
Small profits rate lower limit (£300,000 × 7/12)	175,000
Small profits rate upper limit (£1,500,000 × 7/12)	875,000

Carver Ltd is a marginal rate company.

(W3) **Rate of corporation tax – Period from 1 August 2013 to 31 December 2013**

	£
Taxable total profits	66,500
Small profits rate lower limit (£300,000 × 5/12)	125,000

Carver Ltd is a small company.

(b) **Notes for meeting with directors of Carver Ltd**

(i) **Liquidation of Carver Ltd**

- The amount received from the liquidator represents a capital receipt.

- A capital gain must be computed by deducting the cost of the shares from the proceeds received.

- Cost of the shares:

  - Acquired as original subscriber: £1

  - Acquired by way of gift where gift relief was claimed: £1

  - Acquired by way of inheritance: Market value at date of inheritance (Probate value)

–	Acquired by way of gift where gift relief was not claimed:	Market value at date of gift

- If any of the shareholders own 5% or more and work for the company, they may qualify for Entrepreneurs' relief, provided they have held their shares for at least 12 months.

- The gains are reduced by the annual exempt amount of £10,600.

- If available, Entrepreneurs' relief would reduce the rate of tax on the gain to 10%.

- Any gains not qualifying for Entrepreneurs' relief will be taxed at 18% or 28%, depending on the income tax position of the taxpayer.

- Adults

  - The minimum gain will be £62,500 (500 × (£126 – £1))

- Children

  - The maximum gain will be £25,000 (200 × (£126 – £1)).

(ii) **Payment of a dividend followed by liquidation of Carver Ltd**

General rules re dividends

- Dividends received will be grossed up at 100/90 and taxed as the top slice of the individual's income.

- Tax rates:
  - Income falling into the lower or basic rate tax bands: 10%
  - Income falling into the higher rate band: 32.5%
  - Income falling into the additional rate band: 42.5%

- A 10% tax credit is available to reduce the tax liability. The tax credit cannot be refunded in cash.

- There is no income tax liability where the dividend income falls into the lower or basic rate tax bands.

Adults

- The rate of tax will depend on the individual's level of taxable income and the size of their shareholding but part at least is likely to fall within the higher rate band (500 × £125 × 100/90 = £69,444).

- The effective rate of tax on dividend income falling into the higher rate band is 25% of the amount received (36.1% for those paying at the additional rate)

Children

- Each child will receive maximum taxable dividend income of £27,778 (200 × £125 × 100/90).

- It is likely that the children will have little or no other income such that there will be no income tax to pay on the dividends received.

- The tax credit will not be repaid.

Liquidation of Carver Ltd

- The amount received from the liquidator represents a capital receipt.

- No gain will arise unless an individual acquired shares at a time when their market value was less than £1.

- Otherwise, a capital loss will arise being the excess of the individual's cost of the shares over the amount received.

- The loss will be offset against the individual's capital gains in the tax year 2013/14 or future gains.

44 BANDA ROSS (ADAPTED) *Walk in the footsteps of a top tutor*

Key answer tips

Parts (a) and (b) of this question are based on the scenario of an individual setting up a new business either as a sole trader or through a company, with the added twist that the company could be set up as a subsidiary of another company owned by the individual. There are lots of marks here for loss reliefs and calculation of the tax saved.

Part (c) is completely separate and much more straightforward, requiring discussion of a loan to a participator of a close company and the ethical issues related to the non-disclosure of this loan.

The highlighted words in the written sections are key phrases that markers are looking for.

Tutor's top tips

Parts (a) and (b) of this question are very tough, and it would be easy to get bogged down here and not have time to do part (c), which is actually very easy if you have learned the close company rules! There will be up to 5 marks on every exam for ethical issues, and these marks should always be easy to score.

The best approach would be to do part (c) first, and then move on to the opening sections.

The requirement specifically asks for 3 schedules, so make sure you label them as such. You can use the wording from the requirement as headings.

(a) **Banda Ross**

Tax adjusted profit/(loss) of the Aral business

Tutor's top tips

Don't forget to calculate the capital allowances for each accounting period on the equipment and the car, and note that the first accounting period is only 6 months long.

As there is no private use of any of the assets, the capital allowances and adjusted profits for the accounting periods will be exactly the same whether Banda sets up the business as a sole trader or a company.

	Period ending 30 June 2014	Year ending 30 June 2015	Year ending 30 June 2016
	£	£	£
Budgeted profit/(loss)	(25,000)	(13,000)	77,000
Pre trading expenditure (£6,000 × 1/2) (Note 1)	(3,000)		
Capital allowances:			
Equipment (Note 2)	(13,479)	(1,781)	(1,461)
Tax adjusted profit/(loss)	(41,479)	(14,781)	75,539

Notes

(1) Expenditure incurred in the seven years prior to the start of trading is treated as tax allowable as if incurred on the first day of trading if it would normally be allowable if incurred whilst trading. Entertaining expenditure however is not allowable whether incurred pre or post trading.

Tutor's top tips

The examiner informed us that candidates who stated as an assumption that the tax adjusted figure has already taken into account the pre-trading expenditure would be given appropriate credit.

(2)   **Capital allowances on equipment**

	£	General pool £	Allowances £
6 months ending 30 June 2014			
Additions: no AIA			
Car		9,875	
Additions qualifying for AIA:			
Cost in January 2014	13,500		
Less: AIA (see Tutorial note)	(12,500)		12,500
		1,000	
		10,875	
Less: WDA (£10,875 x 18% x 6/12)		(979)	979
TWDV c/f		9,896	
Total allowances			13,479

	General pool	Allowances
	£	£
Year ending 30 June 2015		
WDA (18%)	(1,781)	1,781
	8,115	
Year ending 30 June 2016		
WDA (18%)	(1,461)	1,461
TWDV c/f	6,654	

Tutorial note

1. Companies or businesses that are owned by the same person and are 'related' will only be entitled to one AIA which can be allocated between the businesses in whatever proportion the taxpayer chooses.

   'Related' means that the business or companies share premises and/or have similar activities.

2. It is assumed in this answer that of the £12,500, maximum AIA available (£25,000 x 6/12 as it is only a 6 month accounting period), Banda will choose to allocate £12,500 to the Aral business.

3. The car qualifies for a 18% WDA as it has CO_2 emissions of between 111 and 160 g/km.

(b) **Banda Ross**

Tax relief available in respect of the anticipated trading losses

Tutor's top tips

You need to think very carefully before attempting this section.

If Banda sets up the business as a sole trader, the losses must be matched to tax years before you start thinking about how to relieve them. As this is a new business, you will need to apply the opening year rules.

However, if the business is set up through a company, the loss reliefs will be for chargeable accounting periods, so no further adjustments will be needed.

It is vital that you clearly label your answer so that the marker can see which option you are dealing with.

(i)   **Business run as a sole trader**

The anticipated allowable losses for the business are set out below.

	Trading income £	Allowable Loss £
2013/14 (1 January 2014 to 5 April 2014)		
Allowable loss (– £41,479 loss × 3/6)	Nil	(20,740)
2014/15 (1 January to 31 December 2014)		
Allowable loss		
(– £41,479 loss + £20,740 used)		
+ (– £14,781 loss × 6/12)	Nil	(28,130)
2015/16 (Year ending 30 June 2015)		
Allowable loss		
(– £14,781 loss + (£14,781 × 6/12) used)	Nil	(7,390)

Tutorial note

Remember that when you apply the opening year rules to losses, there is no overlap! Losses can only be relieved once, and if they are matched with two tax years in the assessments, they must be removed from the later year.

Banda can offset the losses against her total income of:

• The year of loss and/or the previous year.

• The three years preceding the year of loss starting with the earliest year.

All of the losses can be used in this way and therefore the possibility of carrying the losses forward has not been considered.

Tutor's top tips

Don't just list all the loss reliefs you know for a sole trader, pick out the ones that are actually going to be useful.

Banda's income throughout the years in which the losses can be relieved (2010/11 to 2015/16) consists of her salary and dividends from Flores Ltd. In any year in which she claims loss relief, she will save the income tax on her employment income only. There will be no saving in respect of her dividend income because the 10% tax credit is not repayable.

The potential tax saving in a particular year is calculated below:

		£
Salary		13,140
Dividend income (£20,250 × 100/90)		22,500
Total income		35,640
Less Personal allowance		(8,105)
Taxable income (basic rate taxpayer)		27,535

Income tax on employment income of £5,035 (£13,140 − £8,105) at 20% is £1,007. This will have been collected under the PAYE system.

The tax refunded if a claim is made against total income is therefore £1,007.

Any loss relieved must be set off before the application of the personal allowance. Accordingly, in order to maximise the tax saved, Banda could claim to offset the losses of the first three tax years in each of three different tax years.

The total tax saved would be £3,021 (£1,007 × 3) as the losses would be set off against 'other non-savings income' in preference to dividend income.

Tutor's top tips

The examiner did not require any more detailed computation to prove that the tax saving would be £1,007 each year. He expected you to appreciate that dividend tax credits are non-repayable and therefore the tax saving would only be in respect of 'other non-savings income'.

To prove this is true, consider the carry back of the 2013/14 loss of £20,740 to the tax year 2010/11 as follows:

	Total £	Other £	Dividends £
Salary	13,140	13,140	
Dividends	22,500		22,500
Total income	35,640		
Less Losses	(20,740)	(13,140)	(7,600)
Net income	14,900	Nil	14,900
Less Personal allowance	(8,105)		(8,105)
Taxable income	6,795	Nil	6,795
Income tax liability (£6,795 x 10%)			680
Tax credits			
On dividends (£22,500 x 10%) (restricted)			(680)
PAYE			(1,007)
Income tax repayable			(1,007)

(ii)   **Business run as a company – Aral Ltd**

Tutor's top tips

There are two possibilities here: the company could either be owned by Banda directly, or could be set up as a 100% subsidiary of Flores Ltd.

The difference is that if it is owned directly by Banda, the losses will only be available for relief against Aral Ltd's profits, as an individual cannot link companies to form a 75% losses group.

However, if Aral Ltd is set up as a subsidiary of Flores Ltd, they would form a 75% group and the losses could be surrendered to Flores Ltd

The anticipated allowable losses for Aral Ltd are set out below.

	Trading income £	Allowable Loss £
6 months ending 30 June 2014	Nil	(41,479)
Year ending 30 June 2015	Nil	(14,781)

Aral Ltd owned by Banda

The losses would have to be carried forward and deducted from the trading profits of the year ending 30 June 2016. Aral Ltd cannot offset the loss in the current period or carry it back as it has no other income or gains.

Aral Ltd owned by Flores Ltd

The two companies will form a group relief group if Flores Ltd owns at least 75% of the ordinary share capital of Aral Ltd. The trading losses could be surrendered to Flores Ltd in the year ending 30 June 2014 and the year ending 30 June 2015. The total tax saved would be £11,252 ((£41,479 + £14,781) x 20%).

Tutor's top tips

Don't forget to include your recommendation. As always, marks will be given if this is consistent with your analysis, even if you have come to the wrong conclusion!

Recommended structure

The Aral business should be established in a company owned by Flores Ltd.

This will maximise the relief available in respect of the trading losses and enable relief to be obtained in the period in which the losses are incurred.

Tutorial note

The whole of the loss for the period ending 30 June 2014 can be surrendered to Flores Ltd as it is less than that company's profit for the corresponding period (i.e. £60,000 (£120,000 × 6/12)).

Tax will be saved at 20% as Flores Ltd's profits are below the lower limit. The limit for the year ending 30 June 2014 will be £150,000 (£300,000 ÷ 2) as there will be two associated companies.

(c) **Tax implications of there being a loan from Flores Ltd to Banda**

Tutor's top tips

You should have spotted that Flores is a close company, as it is wholly owned by Banda. (A close company is one that is controlled either by its directors, or up to 5 participators.)

Flores Ltd should have paid tax to HMRC equal to 25% of the loan (i.e. £5,250 (25% x £21,000)). The tax should have been paid on the company's normal due date for corporation tax in respect of the accounting period in which the loan was made (i.e. 1 April following the end of the accounting period).

The tax is due because Flores Ltd is a close company that has made a loan to a participator and that loan is not in the ordinary course of the company's business.

HMRC will repay the tax when the loan is either repaid or written off.

Flores Ltd should have included the loan on Banda's Form P11D in order to report it to HMRC.

Assuming that Banda is not paying interest on the loan, she should have paid income tax on an annual benefit equal to 4% of the amount of loan outstanding during each tax year. Accordingly, for each full year for which the loan was outstanding, Banda should have paid income tax of £168 (£21,000 × 4% × 20%).

Flores Ltd should have paid Class 1A NICs in respect of this benefit each year of £116 (£21,000 × 4% × 13.8%).

Interest and penalties may be charged in respect of the tax underpaid by both Flores Ltd and Banda and in respect of the incorrect returns made to HMRC.

Willingness to act for Banda

We would not wish to be associated with a client who has engaged in deliberate tax evasion as this poses a threat to the fundamental principles of integrity and professional behaviour. Accordingly, we should refuse to act for Banda unless she is willing to disclose the details regarding the loan to HMRC and pay the ensuing tax liabilities. Even if full disclosure is made, we should consider whether the loan was deliberately hidden from HMRC or Banda's previous tax adviser.

In addition, companies are prohibited from making loans to directors under the Companies Act. We should advise Banda to seek legal advice on her own position and that of Flores Ltd.

Examiner's comments

This question concerned a business venture where losses were anticipated. Candidates were asked to produce three distinct schedules, which should have had appropriate headings taken from the requirement; sadly, many failed to do so.

In part (a) candidates were required to calculate the tax adjusted trading profit/loss of the new business.

Part (b), representing almost half of the question, required candidates to determine the tax relief available in respect of the anticipated trading losses depending on the legal structure of the venture. This necessitated some clear thinking, ideally communicated to the examiner via the use of subheadings, such that a distinction was drawn between operating as an unincorporated trader and operating as a company. In many cases there was little evidence of such thinking taking place.

The majority of candidates either ignored the opening year rules for the unincorporated trader or failed to apply them to the situation. To be fair this was a relatively tricky situation due to the presence of the losses but it did seem as though many candidates had forgotten the basic rules governing the taxation of an unincorporated trader.

In order to calculate the potential tax relief it was necessary to determine the taxpayer's income tax liability for the years in which loss relief was available. Candidates had no problems calculating the income but were unsure how to proceed from there. In particular there was a lack of thought with many candidates performing calculations for all years rather than recognising that the income was the same in each year such that only one calculation was necessary.

Answers improved when considering the position of a company but there was a lack of precision when describing the loss reliefs available. There was also some confusion as to whether group relief would be available if the two companies were owned personally by the individual taxpayer (it wouldn't). Finally, there was a general unwillingness to satisfy the requirement and calculate the 'tax relief available'.

The final part of the question concerned a loan from a close company to a participator. Candidates did well in identifying the tax implications of the loan but many ignored the ethical considerations inherent within the question.

ACCA marking scheme		
		Marks
(a)	Three trading periods	0.5
	Capital allowances on equipment	3.0
	Pre-trading expenditure	1.5
		5.0
(b)	Business run as a sole trader:	
	Basis periods	1.5
	Losses	1.5
	Exclusion of overlap losses	1.0
	The reliefs available	2.5
	Total income	1.0
	Dividend credit not repayable	1.0
	Saving in any particular year	2.0
	Total potential tax saving	1.5
	Business run as a company:	
	Allowable losses	1.5
	Aral Ltd owned by Banda	1.5
	Aral Ltd owned by Flores Ltd:	
	Group relief	2.0
	Potential tax saving	1.5
	Recommendation	1.0
		19.5
	Maximum	18.0
(c)	Tax implications:	
	Tax payable to HMRC	1.0
	Due date	0.5
	Reasons for tax being due	1.5
	Repayment of tax by HMRC	1.0
	Report on Form P11D	1.0
	Income tax due	1.5
	Interest and penalties	1.0
	Class 1A NICs	1.0
	Willingness to act for Banda:	
	Threat to fundamental principles	1.0
	Require full disclosure	1.0
	Full disclosure may not be enough	0.5
	Legal issue	0.5
		11.5
	Maximum	8.0
	Appropriate style and presentation	2.0
	Effectiveness of communication	1.0
	Logical structure	1.0
		4.0
Total		35

45   SPICA (ADAPTED)

Key answer tips

This question is an exam favourite with the purchase of own shares comparing income and capital treatment. Since Spica has no other income, her personal allowance and basic rate band are available. This means you cannot use the shortcut method applicable to higher rate taxpayers of saying that tax on a dividend is 25% of the net dividend. With the capital route you must be careful not to use all the annual exempt amount as Spica has other gains. In (a)(ii) you must focus on points to be confirmed.

(i)   The most beneficial tax treatment of the payment received

The payment received by Spica will be treated as either an income distribution or as capital.

Income treatment

	£
Payment received (8,000 × £8)	64,000
Less: Original subscription price (8,000 × £1·25)	(10,000)
Distribution (Note 1)	54,000
Taxable dividend income (£54,000 × 100/90)	60,000
Less: Personal allowance	(8,105)
Taxable income	51,895

Income tax

	£	
34,370 × 10%		3,437
17,525 × 32·5%		5,696
51,895		
Income tax liability		9,133
Less: Income tax credit (£51,895 × 10%) (Note 2)		(5,190)
Income tax payable		3,943

Tutorial notes

(1)   Remember that to calculate the dividend income, you must deduct the original subscription price from the payment irrespective of who subscribed for the shares.

> (2) *The tax credit on the dividend is restricted to that on the dividend actually brought into the charge to tax. In this case, £8,105 of dividend income is covered by the personal allowance, therefore the tax credit is only available on £51,895, not £60,000. However, as this is a rather rare situation, you would still have gained full marks if you had shown the tax credit as £6,000 (£60,000 × 10%).*
>
> (3) *A capital loss of £21,600 [8,000 x (£3.95 – £1·25)] will also arise. Spica cannot claim to offset this capital loss against income as she did not subscribe for the shares. £2,300 of the loss will be offset against her gains in 2013/14 (wasting the annual exempt amount) and the remaining £19,300 will be carried forward.*

Capital treatment

Gain qualifying for Entrepreneurs' relief	£
Sales proceeds (8,000 × £8)	64,000
Less: Cost (8,000 × £3.95)	(31,600)
	32,400
Less: Remainder of the annual exempt amount (£10,600 – £2,300)	(8,300)
Taxable gain	24,100
Capital gains tax (£24,100 × 10%)	2,410

Tutorial note

Entrepreneurs' relief is available as the shares are shares in Spica's personal trading company. Spica has a holding of more than 5%, held for over a year, is an employee of the company and Acrux Ltd is a trading company.

The capital treatment gives rise to the lower tax liability.

(ii) **Ensuring capital treatment**

For the capital treatment to apply, a number of conditions need to be satisfied such that the following points need to be confirmed.

– Spica is UK resident and ordinarily resident despite living in both the UK and Solaris.

– The transaction is being carried out for the purpose of the company's trade and is not part of a scheme intended to avoid tax. This is likely to be the case as HMRC accept that a management disagreement over the running of the company has an adverse effect on the running of the business.

In addition, Spica must have owned the shares for at least five years so the transaction must not take place until 1 October 2013.

Key answer tips

The question asks for points that must be confirmed. Since Spica is selling back all her shares, the conditions for substantial reduction of her shareholding, and ceasing to be connected with the company, will automatically be met and will therefore not attract marks.

Examiner's comments

This question concerned a purchase by a company of its own shares.

The question was in two parts. The first part was a relatively straightforward test of the tax treatment of a purchase of own shares whilst the second part tested the conditions that needed to be satisfied for capital treatment to apply.

The first part was done well by the majority of candidates. The only common error was the general failure to recognise that, under the income distribution route, the distribution is the amount received less the amount *originally subscribed* for the shares (as opposed to the cost to the shareholder). A minority of candidates did not pick up easy marks by failing to include the personal allowance and/or the annual exemption or by using incorrect rates of tax.

Performance in the second part was not as good with many candidates simply listing all of the conditions they could think of as opposed to thinking and identifying the particular conditions that were relevant in these particular circumstances. This meant that time was wasted and that irrelevant conditions were provided at the expense of some that would have earned marks.

ACCA marking scheme			Marks
(i)	Income treatment		
	Calculation of distribution		1.0
	Gross up by 100/90		0·5
	Personal allowance		0·5
	Income tax liability		1.0
	Income tax credit		0·5
	Capital treatment		
	Capital gain		1.0
	Entrepreneurs' relief		1.5
	Annual exempt amount		1.0
	Capital gains tax liability		0.5
	Conclusion		0·5
			8.0
		Maximum	7.0
(ii)	Spica UK resident and ordinarily resident		1.0
	Benefit of company's trade		2.0
	Five year ownership period		1.0
			4.0
Total			11

46 JAMES (ADAPTED) *Walk in the footsteps of a top tutor*

Key answer tips

There are three main topic areas covered by this question: share incentive plans, redundancy payments, and the IR35 legislation.

When choosing which optional questions to attempt, you should always look at the number of marks available for each specific area of tax and gauge your knowledge to the level of detail you think the question requires.

In this question, 13 of the 20 marks available are for IR35. Therefore, if you have not studied IR35 in detail, you may find this question hard to pass!

The highlighted words in the written sections are key phrases that markers are looking for.

(a)   **Taxation of shares in Quark Ltd and redundancy payment**

   Shares in Quark Ltd

Tutor's top tips

Make sure you apply your knowledge to the specific scenario. James will have had some of the shares for more than three years, and some for less than three years, but will not have had any of the shares for more than five years.

There is, therefore, no need to consider or comment on the situation where the shares have been in the plan for five years or more as the first award was less than five years prior to the date on which they will be withdrawn.

No marks would have been given for such comments and time would have been wasted in doing so.

Withdrawal of shares

–   If the shares have been within the plan for less than three years, income tax and national insurance contributions will be charged on their market value at the time of withdrawal.

–   If the shares have been within the plan for more than three years, income tax and national insurance contributions will be charged on the lower of

   (i)   their value at the time they were awarded to James, and

   (ii)   their value at the time of withdrawal.

Sale of shares

–   The shares will have a base cost for the purposes of capital gains tax equal to their market value at the time of their withdrawal from the plan.

   Accordingly, no capital gain will have arisen on their immediate sale.

Redundancy payment

Any amount of statutory redundancy included within the payment is not subject to income tax or to national insurance contributions.

The first £30,000 of the balance of the payment, as reduced by any amount of tax-free statutory redundancy, will be exempt from income tax and national insurance contributions provided it relates solely to redundancy and is not simply a terminal bonus.

The remainder of the payment will be subject to income tax in full, but not to national insurance contributions.

The payment in lieu of notice will be subject to both income tax and national insurance contributions on the full amount, as it is the normal custom of Quark Ltd to make such payments.

(b) (i) **The effect on James's annual income, after deduction of all taxes, of working for Proton Ltd rather than Quark Ltd** .

Tutor's top tips

The examiner expected you to identify that James would be a higher rate taxpayer regardless of whether he was working for Quark Ltd or Proton Ltd.

Accordingly, he hoped that you would carry out your calculations of the effect on his income after deduction of all taxes 'at the margin'. A common theme in many of the examiner's recent questions.

The examiner also said that candidates who prepared full income tax computations were able to score full marks but may have spent more time on them than was necessary and possibly at the expense of time that should be spent on other questions.

	£
Reduction in salary (£70,000 – £48,000)	(22,000)
Reduction in income tax on salary (£22,000 × 40%)	8,800
Reduction in national insurance contributions (£22,000 × 2%)	440
Additional dividend	18,000
Tax on dividend (see Tutorial note)	–
Tax on deemed employment income (£18,373 (W) × 40%)	(7,349)
National insurance on deemed employment income (£18,373 × 2%)	(367)
Fall in James's annual income after all taxes	(2,476)

Tutorial note

A claim can be made by Proton Ltd for the dividend to be regarded as having been paid out of the deemed employment income and therefore not be subject to income tax in the hands of James.

Working: Deemed employment income

		£
Income of Proton Ltd in respect of relevant engagements		80,000
Less: 5% deduction		(4,000)
Reimbursed travel expenses		(1,500)
Salary paid to James		(48,000)
Employer's NIC ((£48,000 − £7,488) × 13.8%)		(5,591)
		—————
		20,909
Less: Employer's NIC on deemed employment income		
(£20,909 × 13.8/113.8)		(2,536)
		—————
Deemed employment income		18,373

Tutorial note

If you find it difficult to calculate the effect at the margin in this way, you could compare James' after tax income for each option as shown below.

Alternative approach:

	Working for Quark Ltd £	Working for Proton Ltd £
Income Tax		
Salary	70,000	48,000
Dividend	N/A	*Nil
Deemed salary (W)	Nil	18,373
	—————	—————
Total income	70,000	66,373
Less Personal allowance	(8,105)	(8,105)
	—————	—————
Taxable income	61,895	58,268
	—————	—————

* Dividend excluded as replaced by deemed salary.

			Working for Quark Ltd	Working for Proton Ltd
Income tax				
£	£			
34,370	34,370	x 20%	6,874	6,874
27,525	23,898	x 40%	11,010	9,559
―――	―――			
61,895	58,268			
―――	―――			
			―――	―――
Income tax liability			17,884	16,433
			―――	―――
National insurance				
(£42,475 – £7,605) x 12%			4,184	4,184
(£70,000 – £42,475) x 2%			551	
(£48,000 – £42,475) x 2%				111
£18,373 x 2%				367
			―――	―――
NIC liability			4,735	4,662
			―――	―――
			£	£
Net income (after all taxes)				
Salary			70,000	48,000
Dividend			Nil	18,000
Less: Income tax			(17,884)	(16,433)
Less: NIC			(4,735)	(4,662)
			―――	―――
Net income			47,381	44,905
			―――	―――
Difference: as above (£47,381– £44,905)			£2,476	
			―――	

Tutorial note:

Clearly this approach involves significantly more work for the same number of marks, although it does give the same answer!

(ii) **The effect on James's annual income, after deduction of all taxes, if the income of Proton Ltd were not regarded as being in respect of relevant engagements**

	£
Anticipated fall in annual income per part (b) (i)	(2,476)
Income tax and NIC on deemed employment income no longer payable (£7,349 + £367)	7,716
Income tax on dividends (£18,000 × 25%) (see Tutorial note)	(4,500)
Increase in James's annual income after all taxes	740

Tutorial note

The effective rate of tax on dividend income that falls within the higher rate band is 25% ((32.5% – 10%) x 100/90).

Tutorial note

It is quite acceptable to use the effective rate of tax on a net dividend in this kind of calculation, provided you make it clear where your figures are coming from. However, as above, if you find it difficult to calculate the effect at the margin in this way, you could calculate James' net income working for Proton Ltd and compare to his net income as an employee, as shown below.

Alternative approach:

Working for Quark Ltd

	£
Net income after all taxes (as above)	47,381

Working for Proton Ltd

	£
Income tax	
Salary	48,000
Dividend (£18,000 x 100/90)	20,000
Deemed salary (not applicable)	Nil
Total income	68,000
Less Personal allowance	(8,105)
Taxable income	59,895

Analysed as: Dividends £20,000, Other income (balance) £39,895

Income tax			£
£			
34,370	x 20%	*(Other income)*	6,874
5,525	x 40%	*(Other income)*	2,210
39,895			
20,000	x 32.5%	*(Dividend income)*	6,500
59,895			

Income tax liability	15,584
Less: Tax credit on dividends (£20,000 x 10%)	(2,000)
Income tax payable	13,584

National insurance	
(£42,475 – £7,605) x 12%	4,184
(£48,000 – £42,475) x 2%	111
Total national insurance	4,295

Net income after all taxes	
Salary	48,000
Dividend	18,000
	66,000
Less: Income tax	(13,584)
Less: NIC	(4,295)
Net income	48,121

Increase in net income (£48,121 – £47,381)	740

Tutorial note

Again, this gives the same answer but involves a great deal more work for the same number of marks.

(c)   **Specific contractual arrangements**

Tutor's top tips

The arguments to justify that the relationship between Proton Ltd and its customers do not count as 'relevant engagements' per IR35 are the same as the arguments that would be used to justify self employment as opposed to employment status. Therefore the usual factors that HMRC would look for need to be considered.

However, be careful!

'Having more than one customer' would not score marks here, as it is not something that could be built into a contract.   The requirement specifically asks for 'contractual arrangements' that would assist in the argument.

Any THREE of the following:

– Any necessary equipment or tools should be provided by Proton Ltd rather than its customers.

– The degree of the customers' control over when and how the work is carried out by James should be kept to a minimum.

– If James is unable to complete the work he would provide a mutually acceptable substitute.

– Proton Ltd should bear a degree of financial risk, e.g. by quoting fixed contract prices.

– Payments should be made under the contracts by reference to the work done rather than periods of time.

– Proton Ltd should be obliged to correct any unsatisfactory work at its own expense, and to insure against such matters.

– Payments should be made under the contracts in respect of the work carried out. The contracts should not include any provisions whereby payments will be made in respect of illness or holidays.

– Each contract should only come to an end when the work is completed or the contract has been breached in some way.

Tutorial note

The relationships between Proton Ltd and each of its customers will each have to be considered separately.

A contract may be regarded as a relevant engagement if it would have been an employer/employee relationship had it been between the customer and James.

Examiner's comments

This question concerned James who, on being made redundant by Quark Ltd, intended to form a new company, Proton Ltd, through which he would provide services to Quark Ltd and other companies. The question was in three parts.

Part (a) required candidates to identify the income tax, national insurance contribution and capital gains tax implications of the withdrawal and subsequent sale of shares obtained via a share incentive plan and the receipt of a redundancy payment and a payment in lieu of notice. On the whole, candidates had a better knowledge of redundancy payments than they did of share incentive plans. However, candidates with less than perfect knowledge were still able to do well provided they kept going and addressed every aspect of the question.

Weaker candidates wasted time by either writing too much or preparing unnecessary calculations of tax liabilities.

Part (b) required calculations of the effect on James' annual income, after deduction of all taxes, of working for Proton Ltd, a personal services company per the question, rather than Quark Ltd. The model answer shows how the difference between working for Proton Ltd as opposed to Quark Ltd can be calculated in one step but full marks were available to candidates who prepared separate calculations of the two situations and then found the difference between them. Those candidates who had memorised the proforma used to calculate the deemed employment payment from a personal services company were able to score well. Weaker candidates either did not know the proforma or failed to take sufficient time in order to understand the scenario and thus produced irrelevant corporation tax computations or incorrect income tax computations.

The final part of the question required three examples of contractual arrangements that would indicate that the relationships between Proton Ltd and its customers would not amount to an employer/employee relationship had they been between James and the customers. Candidates had a good knowledge of the features that distinguish an employer/employee relationship from other relationships where services are provided. However, many did not score as well as they could because they referred to the general situation, for example the bearing of financial risk, rather than specific contractual arrangements.

		ACCA marking scheme	
			Marks
(a)		Shares in Quark Ltd	
		Income tax where shares in plan for less than three years	1.0
		Income tax where shares in plan for three years or more	1.5
		Also subject to NIC	0.5
		Capital gains tax on sale	1.0
		Redundancy payment	
		Statutory redundancy	1.0
		£30,000 exemption	1.5
		Not subject to NIC	0.5
		Payment in lieu of notice	1.0
			———
			8.0
		Maximum	7.0
			———
(b)	(i)	Effect of fall in salary net of all taxes	2.5
		Dividend income	0.5
		No tax on dividend income	1.0
		Tax and NIC on deemed employment income	1.0
		Deemed employment income	
		Income	0.5
		5% deduction, travel expenses, salary (0·5 each)	1.5
		Employer's NIC on salary	1.0
		Employer's NIC on deemed payment	1.0
			———
			9.0
		Maximum	8.0
			———
	(ii)	Income tax and NIC no longer payable	1.0
		Income tax on dividends	1.0
			———
			2.0
			———
(c)		One mark for each contractual arrangement	3.0
			———
	Total		20

47 FEDORA AND SMOKE LTD (ADAPTED) *Walk in the footsteps of a top tutor*

Key answer tips

There are three separate parts to this question, all covering fairly mainstream areas.

Part (a) covers close company loans to participators.

Part (b) is a typical calculation of the net effect of employing someone. Marginal rates of tax can be used to save time here.

Part (c) requires calculation of a chargeable gain for a part disposal, with a detailed explanation of rollover relief.

The highlighted words in the written sections are key phrases that markers are looking for.

(a)   **Repayment of loan**

Tutor's top tips

Remember that a company controlled by five or fewer participators (shareholders) is a close company. There are special tax implications for loans to participators.

Even if you failed to spot that Smoke Ltd is a close company, you could still obtain the two and a half marks needed to pass this section by talking about the tax saved on the employment benefit for Fedora, and the Class 1A NIC saving for Smoke Ltd.

Smoke Ltd is a close company (as it is controlled by Fedora), that has made a loan to a participator (Fedora).

Accordingly, Smoke Ltd will have paid HM Revenue and Customs £4,600 (25% × £18,400) on 1 January 2009.

HM Revenue and Customs will repay the £4,600 to the company nine months after the end of the accounting period in which the loan is repaid.

The loan also gives rise to an annual employment income benefit for Fedora of £736 (£18,400 × 4 %). This benefit will no longer be charged to income tax once the loan is repaid, saving Fedora £294 (£736 x 40%) each year.

In addition, Smoke Ltd will no longer have to pay Class 1A national insurance contributions in respect of the loan benefit. This will save the company £81 (£736 × 13.8% × 80%).

Tutorial note

Class 1A NIC is tax deductible, so would have saved corporation tax at 20%.

If this NIC is no longer payable, the NIC saving is offset by the corporation tax saving lost, giving a net saving of 80% (100% − 20%).

(b)   **Annual net effect of Smoke Ltd employing Wanda**

Tutor's top tips

Label your answer clearly here: you need to consider the effect on
- *Fedora*
- *Wanda*
- *Smoke Ltd*

You are calculating the net effect on TAX LIABILITIES (not net income) – so think about how these are going to change.

Fedora is a higher rate taxpayer and is above the NIC upper limit, so a reduction in salary will save income tax at 40% and Class 1 NIC at 2%.

Wanda, however, still has part of her personal allowance available, so marginal rates cannot be used.

Smoke Ltd is a small company, so any corporation tax savings will be at 20%.

	Cost £	Saving £
Fedora		
Reduction in income tax liability (£20,000 × 40%)		8,000
Reduction in National insurance liability (£20,000 × 2%)		400
Wanda		
Increase in income tax liability (W1)	2,473	
National insurance liability ((£20,000 – £7,605) × 12%)	1,487	
Smoke Ltd		
Employer National insurance contributions		
Reduction in salary to Fedora (£20,000 × 13.8%)		2,760
Salary to Wanda ((£20,000 – £7,488) × 13.8%)	1,727	
Corporation tax effect (£1,727/£2,760 × 20%) (Note)	(345)	(552)
	5,342	10,608
Annual net saving (£10,608 – £5,342)		5,266

Tutorial note

Note that there is no 20% corporation tax saving in respect of paying the £20,000 to Wanda.

This is because previously this amount was paid to Fedora and so the total salary paid to Wanda and Fedora (£60,000 + £20,000) is the same as the total salary previously paid to Fedora (£80,000). As the total tax deductible amount in Smoke's corporation tax computation is the same, there is no saving.

The corporation tax saving is therefore only in respect of the increase and decrease in the Class 1 secondary NICs.

Tutor's top tips

Make sure that you highlight the total annual net effect. Even if you have made mistakes, you will still be given credit for consistency and for trying to answer the specific question asked!

Working: Wanda – Increase in income tax liability

	£
Employment income	20,000
Bank interest (Tutorial note)	470
Less: Personal allowance	(8,105)
Taxable income	12,365
Income tax (£12,365 × 20%)	2,473

Tutorial note

Before employment, this was Wanda's only source of income which was covered by her personal allowance and therefore she was a non-taxpayer.

As a non-taxpayer, Wanda will have been receiving the bank interest gross, therefore the £470 quoted in the question must be the gross amount.

(c)   **The sale of the land**

Taxable gain arising on the sale of the land

Tutor's top tips

This is a straightforward F6 level calculation of a chargeable gain on the part disposal of land, with rollover relief following partial reinvestment of the proceeds.

	£
Proceeds	22,000
Less: Cost (£174,000 × £22,000/(£22,000 + £491,000))	(7,462)
Indexation allowance	
((256.2 – 149.0)/149.0)) = 0.719 × £7,462	(5,365)
	9,173
Rollover relief:	
Proceeds not spent = £3,000 (£22,000 – £19,000)	
Relief available (£9,173 – £3,000)	(6,173)
Taxable gain = Chargeable gain (Note)	3,000

Tutorial note

Note that for a company the Taxable gain = Chargeable gain as there is no annual exempt amount available for companies.

The relief available

Tutor's top tips

Note the requirement here to explain 'in detail'. There are 8 marks available for part (c), so you will need to make your answer as full as possible.

The examiner also asks you to explain how the deferred part of the gain will be charged in the future – a clue that this is rollover relief for a depreciating asset, rather than a non-depreciating asset.

Rollover relief is available in respect of the gain because it has arisen on the disposal of a qualifying asset (land) that has been used for business purposes.

The gain can be rolled over if qualifying assets are purchased for use in the business in the four-year period commencing 1 February 2013.

Plant and machinery only qualifies for rollover relief if it is fixed rather than moveable.

On the assumption that the engineering machinery is fixed, and that Smoke Ltd will not purchase any other qualifying assets during the four-year period, the gain that will be charged will be equal to the amount of the proceeds from the sale of the land that has not been used to purchase qualifying assets, i.e. £3,000, with the balance of the gain of £6,173 (£9,173 – £3,000) being deferred.

Machinery has a statutory useful life of less than 50 years and is therefore a depreciating asset for the purposes of rollover relief (Tutorial note).

Accordingly, the deferred gain of £6,173 will become chargeable on the earliest of the following:

- the date on which the machinery is sold;

- the date on which the machinery is no longer used in the business; and

- ten years from the date on which the machinery is purchased, i.e. in March 2024.

Tutorial note

Technically, the definition of a depreciating asset is "a wasting asset or one which will become a wasting asset in the next ten years". A wasting asset has a life of 50 years.

Therefore, a depreciating asset is one which has a life of less than 60 years.

Machinery has a statutory life of less than 50 years so it is clearly a depreciating asset for rollover relief purposes.

Examiner's comments

This question concerned three possible ways by which an individual, Fedora, might improve his financial position. The question was in three parts.

Part (a) concerned the repayment of a loan by Fedora to his wholly-owned company, Smoke Ltd. Most candidates identified Smoke Ltd as a close company and went on to point out that the 25% charge paid when the loan was made would be refunded once the loan had been repaid. However, for many candidates that was the end of the story. Stronger candidates pointed out that there would no longer be an income tax liability for Fedora in respect of the employment benefit and the best candidates went on to point out that, consequently, there would no longer be a Class 1A liability for Smoke Ltd.

Identifying all of these points was not difficult; most of the candidates in the exam were fully aware of them. However, you will only pick up all of these points if you think about the issues before you start writing.

Part (b) required calculations of the tax implications of Smoke Ltd employing Fedora's wife. Although many candidates scored well here, a little bit of thought would have made things much easier. In particular, it was clear that Fedora was a higher rate tax payer and therefore, the tax saved if his salary was reduced by £20,000 would be £8,000 together with national insurance of £400 (at 2%). Many candidates prepared a page or more of calculations of the income tax and national insurance due on the both the old and the new salaries in order to arrive at the difference of £8,400. This represented a lack of thought and a waste of valuable time as the figure of £8,400 was only worth one mark.

The final part of the question required the calculation of the gain on a part disposal of land and a detailed explanation of the relief available. The calculation was done well. However, although the majority of candidates recognised that the relief available was rollover relief, the majority of explanations were not detailed and did not consider a sufficient number of the relevant rules. In particular, many candidates failed to identify that the engineering machinery would be a depreciating asset for the purposes of rollover relief. This may be explained in part by the fact that this was, for many candidates, their final question and time was running out.

	ACCA marking scheme		Marks
(a)	Close company loan to participator		1.0
	Payment made to HMRC will be repaid		1.5
	Annual benefit will cease		3.0
			————
			5.5
		Maximum	5.0
			————
(b)	Fedora		
	Income tax		0.5
	National insurance		0.5
	Wanda		
	Income tax		2.0
	National insurance		1.0
	Smoke Ltd		
	National insurance		1.5
	Corporation tax		1.0
	Annual net saving		0.5
			————
			7.0
		Maximum	7.0
			————
(c)	Calculation of gain before rollover relief		2.0
	Calculation of gain after rollover relief		1.0
	Land is a qualifying business asset		1.0
	Qualifying period		1.0
	Fixed plant and machinery is a qualifying asset		1.0
	Assumptions		1.0
	Plant and machinery is a depreciating asset		1.0
	Taxation of deferred gain		1.5
			————
			9.5
		Maximum	8.0
			————
Total			20

48 TRIFLES LTD, VICTORIA AND MELBA (ADAPTED) *Walk in the footsteps of a top tutor*

Key answer tips

This question covers two different areas: purchase of own shares by a company, and the tax implications of a close company. Whilst these areas tend not to appear in every exam, they are tested every few sittings.

Part (a) requires a discussion of the conditions for purchase of own shares, but focuses on just two conditions.

Part (b) requires the calculation of after tax proceeds for both the income and the capital treatment but for the purchase of Victoria's shares only. This section should provide some easy marks.

Part (c) is trickier. It appears to cover loans to participators due to the wording of the information in the question (i.e. 'loan of a motorcycle'), but actually covers the provision of benefits to participators (i.e. 'use of asset' benefit).

The highlighted words in the written sections are key phrases that markers are looking for.

(a)   **Purchase of own shares: Conditions for capital treatment**

Tutor's top tips

Read the requirement carefully. You are not required to consider all of the conditions for capital treatment, just the period of ownership and reduction in shareholding.

There will be no marks available for discussing any other conditions.

*To score marks here you must **apply** these conditions to Victoria and to Melba.*

Victoria

Ownership period

As Victoria inherited the shares from her husband, the required ownership period is reduced from five years to three years.

Victoria can include her husband's ownership as well as her own, giving a total ownership period from 1 February 2010 to 28 February 2014.

This is more than three years, therefore Victoria satisfies this condition.

Tutorial note

Even if you did not know that the ownership period was reduced to three years for inherited shares, you could still score some marks here for applying the condition to the facts.

Reduction in level of shareholding

Victoria sells all her shares, and therefore satisfies the two key conditions regarding share ownership:

*   she has had a 'substantial reduction' in her shareholding as she disposes of all of her shares, and

*   she has a lack of 'connection' to the company after the disposal as she no longer holds any shares in the company.

Melba

Ownership period

Melba has owned her shares since 1 February 2006. This is longer than the required five years, therefore Melba satisfies this condition.

Reduction in level of shareholding

Tutor's top tips

This is tricky! Remember that once shares are sold back to the company, they will be cancelled, so the total number of shares will be reduced.

*Victoria will sell her shares back to the company **before** Melba, so these shares will have already been cancelled.*

Before the buy back

Melba will have 1,700 shares from a total of 8,500 (10,000 – 1,500).

This represents a 20% share (1,700/8,500) in the company.

After the buy back

Melba will have 1,250 shares (1,700 – 450) from a total of 8,050 (8,500 – 450).

This represents a 15.5% share (1,250/8,050) in the company.

There are two tests that must be satisfied:

– 30% connection test:

Melba must own no more than 30% of the remaining shares after the repurchase.

This test is clearly satisfied.

– 75% test:

Melba's new percentage share in the company must be no more than 75% of her old share (i.e. no more than 15% (75% x 20%)).

15.5% is more than 15%, therefore this test is **not** satisfied.

Tutorial note

*The 75% (or 25% substantial reduction) test must be applied to the **percentage** shareholding, not the number of shares.*

If you got this wrong, or if you missed the fact that Victoria's shares had already been cancelled, you could still score follow-through marks here for applying the 30% and 75% tests and for coming to a conclusion.

(b)　**Victoria: after tax proceeds from purchase of shares**

Capital treatment

Gain qualifying for Entrepreneurs' relief (Note 1)

	£
Proceeds (1,500 × £30)	45,000
Less: Cost (probate value) (Note 2)	(16,000)
	29,000
Less: Capital loss brought forward	(4,300)
	24,700
Less: Annual exempt amount	(10,600)
Taxable gains	14,100
Capital gains tax (£14,100 × 10%)	1,410
After tax proceeds (£45,000 – £1,410)	43,490

Tutorial note

1.　*Victoria will have been a director of the company and held at least 5% of the shares for the 12 months prior to the disposal, and will therefore qualify for Entrepreneurs' relief.*

2.　*Where shares are inherited from a spouse, the deemed cost to the recipient for capital gains tax purposes is the probate value.*

　If the shares were transferred during lifetime, the transfer would be at no gain, no loss and the recipient would take over the original cost.

Income treatment

	£
Proceeds (1,500 × £30)	45,000
Less: Original subscription price (1,500 × £2)	(3,000)
Distribution (Note 1)	42,000
Income tax (£42,000 × 25%) (Note 2)	10,500
After tax proceeds (£45,000 – £10,500)	34,500

Tutorial note

1. *Remember that to calculate the deemed dividend income (i.e. distribution), you must deduct the original subscription price from the payment irrespective of who subscribed for the shares, and regardless of any price actually paid for the shares.*

2. *As Victoria is a higher rate taxpayer, the effective rate of tax suffered on the deemed dividend (i.e. distribution) is 25% (i.e. 100/90 × (32.5% – 10%)).*

    There would be no withdrawal of the personal allowance, as Victoria's total taxable income would be less than £100,000 (£50,000 + (£42,000 × 100/90) = £96,667).

3. *A capital loss of £13,000 (£3,000 – £16,000) will also arise. Victoria cannot claim to offset this capital loss against income as she did not subscribe for the shares. This loss therefore has no effect on the current period's after tax proceeds but may reduce tax on a future capital gain.*

(c)   **Tax implications of the loan of the motorcycle**

Tutor's top tips

The key to success here was to spot that Trifles Ltd is a close company.

Look out for this as many 'Ltd' companies are owned by only a few shareholders and are therefore close companies.

Remember that there are special rules governing the provision of loans and benefits to participators in a close company.

Trifles Ltd is controlled 5 or fewer shareholders (participators), and is therefore a close company.

Implications for Melba

The provision of the motorcycle to Melba will be treated as a distribution, as Melba will not be an employee of Trifles Ltd after the sale of her shares.

The value of the benefit, calculated using the income tax rules, will be treated as a net dividend:

	£
Use of asset (£9,000 × 20%) (Note 1)	1,800
Less: Contribution (£30 × 12)	(360)
	———
Distribution	1,440
	———
Income tax (£1,440 × 25%) (Note 2)	360
	———

Tutorial notes

1. The loan of the motorcycle will be treated as a 'use of asset' benefit each year Melba has the use of the motorcycle.

2. As Melba is a higher rate taxpayer, the effective rate of tax suffered on the deemed dividend (i.e. distribution) is 25% (i.e. 100/90 × (32.5% – 10%)).

    If Melba was still an employee, the motorcycle would be treated as a normal employment benefit, and would be taxed at 40% in the normal way.

Implications for Trifles Ltd

Tutor's top tips

You will be given marks here for consistency!

Remember that dividends are not allowable expenses for companies, so it follows that if the loan of the motorcycle is to be treated as a dividend, none of the associated expenses are deductible.

However, if you missed the fact that Trifles Ltd is a close company and that Melba will no longer be an employee, you may have treated the motorcycle as a normal employment benefit. In this case, you will be given marks here for saying that costs will be allowable and employer's Class 1A NIC will be due.

Trifles Ltd will not be able to claim capital allowances on the motorcycle, and there will be no allowable deduction for any running costs.

Examiner's comments

Part (a) required candidates to explain whether two of the conditions necessary to enable the amount received to be treated as capital were satisfied. Many candidates answered this part well but others, with similar knowledge levels, did not perform well because they failed to answer the question. Rather than addressing the two particular conditions set out in the question, this latter group attempted to address all of the conditions despite the majority of them being irrelevant.

Candidates had a good knowledge of the five-year rule and the 30% rule but were much less comfortable with the condition relating to the shareholder's interest in the company following the purchase. The rules require the shareholder's interest to be no more than 75% of the interest prior to the purchase – this is not the same as the shareholder selling 25% of his shares because the shares sold are cancelled thus reducing the number of issued shares.

Only a minority of candidates were aware that the ownership period of the husband could be added to that of the wife. Even fewer knew that the usual five-year ownership period is reduced to three where the shares are inherited.

Part (b) required calculations of the after tax proceeds depending on the tax treatment of the sum received. This part was answered well by the vast majority of candidates. The only point that many candidates missed was the availability of entrepreneurs' relief. It was particularly pleasing to see the majority of candidates correctly identify the after tax proceeds as the amount received less the tax liability (as opposed to the taxable amount less the tax liability).

The final part of the question was more difficult and, unsurprisingly, caused more problems. The question concerned the loan of a motorcycle to a shareholder in a close company who was not an employee. Candidates had no problem recognising that the company was a close company but many then decided that this was a loan to a participator as opposed to the loan of an asset.

Another relatively common error was to state, correctly, that the benefit would be treated as a distribution but to then give an incorrect tax rate of 40%. Candidates would benefit from slowing down and ensuring that they apply their basic tax knowledge correctly in the exam.

ACCA marking scheme			
			Marks
(a)	Victoria		
		Period of ownership	2.5
		Reduction in level of shareholding	0.5
	Melba		
		Period of ownership	1.0
		Reduction in level of shareholding	3.0
			7.0
(b)	Capital receipt		4.0
	Income receipt		3·0
			7.0
(c)	Close company		1.5
	Melba		
		Recognition of distribution	1.5
		Supporting calculations	2.0
	Trifles Ltd		1.0
			6.0
Total			20

49 ROBUSTO LTD (ADAPTED) *Walk in the footsteps of a top tutor*

Key answer tips

There are three areas covered by this question: VAT, employed vs. self-employed and personal service companies.

Part (a) requires consideration of the lowest cost option of obtaining market analysis. This requires an understanding of VAT for a partially exempt business, which is frequently tested in the exam, often as part of a Section A question.

Part (b) deals with employed vs. self-employed factors, but requires specific application to the scenario.

Part (c) covers the tax implications personal service companies. This section was tricky, and required a good understanding of the impact of the personal service company rules to score well.

The highlighted words in the written sections are key phrases that markers are looking for.

(a)   **Market analysis services**

        Lowest cost to Robusto Ltd

Tutor's top tips

Think carefully here – most of the marks are for the VAT implications.

Remember that VAT is a cost to the business if it cannot be reclaimed.

The question states that the irrecoverable VAT for the year will exceed the de minimis limits, which means that any VAT attributed to exempt supplies will represent an extra cost.

As Robusto Ltd is a partially exempt business, it will only be able to reclaim part of any VAT paid on the cost of the market analysis.

The percentage recoverable will based on taxable sales divided by total sales:

$$\frac{(£850,000 + £120,000)}{(£850,000 + £120,000 + £330,000)} = 75\% \text{ (rounded up to next whole \%)}$$

Therefore the irrecoverable VAT will be 25%.

This will increase the cost of the market analysis to Robusto Ltd.

Cognac Ltd

The cost of purchasing the services from Cognac Ltd is:

	£
Fixed fee (excluding VAT)	28,500
Add: Irrecoverable VAT (£28,500 × 20% × 25%)	1,425
Total cost	29,925

Fonseca Ltd

If the services were purchased from Fonseca Ltd, output VAT would be payable under the reverse charge procedure.

Again, only 75% of this VAT would be recoverable.

The cost of purchasing the services from Fonseca Ltd is:

	£
Fixed fee (excluding VAT)	29,000
Add: Irrecoverable VAT (£29,000 × 20% × 25%)	1,450
Total cost	30,450

Pisco

As Pisco is not VAT registered, there would be no VAT charged on the services.

The cost of purchasing the services from Pisco is:

	£
Fixed fee	29,500

Conclusion

The cheapest service provider is therefore Pisco.

However, it should be noted that if the fees increased Pisco's annual revenue above the VAT registration limit of £77,000, Pisco would have to register for VAT.

Tutorial note

Robusto Ltd would obtain a corporation tax saving for the cost incurred, but as this would be the case in each situation it would not affect the decision. There was not enough information provided in the question to actually calculate the saving.

Tutor's top tips

Make sure that you advise which service provider is cheapest. Even if your calculations are incorrect, you will still be given credit for a consistent conclusion.

Maximum salary

Tutor's top tips

*The calculations here are quite challenging. The **total** cost of taking on an employee must not be more than £29,500.*

*This total will be equal to the salary **plus employer's Class 1 NIC.** Employer's NICs are 13.8% but only on the excess over £7,488.*

Try not to get too bogged down in the computations – they are only worth 2.5 marks, and a reasonable attempt with a clearly identified salary should gain at least some marks.

The maximum salary (y) that would give a total cost (including employer's Class 1 NIC) of £29,500 is calculated as follows:

$$y + ((y - £7{,}488) \times 13.8\%) = £29{,}500$$
$$y + 0.138y - (£7{,}488 \times 13.8\%) = £29{,}500$$
$$1.138y - £1{,}033 = £29{,}500$$
$$1.138y = £29{,}500 + £1{,}033$$
$$1.138y = £30{,}533$$
$$y = £30{,}533/1.138$$
$$y = £26{,}830$$

The maximum salary is therefore £26,830.

(b) **Contractual arrangements that would indicate employer/employee relationship**

Tutor's top tips

*To score marks here you need to choose factors that could apply to **this** scenario, and only factors that could be embodied / written into a contract.*

You know from the information in the question that Pisco will be paid a fixed fee, so there is no point in discussing sick pay or holiday pay, for example.

- Tools and equipment to be provided by Robusto Ltd.
- Pisco must carry out the work himself, and cannot send a substitute.
- Robusto Ltd to control how and when the work is carried out by Pisco.
- Pisco does not have to correct unsatisfactory work in his own time, or at his own expense.
- Robusto Ltd can dismiss Pisco before the contract is completed.

Tutor's top tips

You only need to give four examples to score full marks here.

(c)   **Employer/employee relationship between Robusto Ltd and Offley/Pisco**

Tax implications for Robusto Ltd and Cognac Ltd

Tutor's top tips

Think carefully about the scenario here. Offley will be providing services to Robusto Ltd through Cognac Ltd.

If HMRC can argue that the relationship between Offley and Robusto Ltd is that of employer/employee, then Cognac Ltd will be treated as a personal service company and Offley will be taxed as if he is an employee.

Note that you are not required to prepare any calculations or to explain how the deemed salary would be calculated.

Robusto Ltd

The fee paid by Robusto Ltd will be a tax deductible expense.

Cognac Ltd

The fee received by Cognac Ltd will be taxable trading income.

Cognac Ltd will be subject to the personal service company rules.

The fee from Robusto Ltd will be treated as deemed salary payment from Cognac Ltd to Offley.

Offley will pay income tax and Class 1 NICs on this deemed salary.

Cognac Ltd will have to pay employer's Class 1 NIC on the deemed salary on 19 April following the end of the tax year..

The deemed salary and the employer's NIC will be tax deductible for Cognac Ltd.

Why Robusto Ltd may prefer Cognac Ltd

If Robusto Ltd pays Pisco and is deemed to be Pisco's employer, Robusto Ltd will be subject to employer's NIC on the fee paid.

However, if Robusto Ltd pays Cognac Ltd, then Cognac Ltd would suffer the employer's NIC as described above.

Robusto Ltd would therefore prefer to offer the contract to Cognac Ltd.

Examiner's comments

Part (a) required candidates to determine the cost of buying in services from three possible suppliers. Candidates were told that the purchasing company was partially exempt for the purposes of VAT and the vast majority realised that the key to the question was the impact of irrecoverable VAT on the cost.

There were minor errors in determining the percentage of input tax that could be recovered involving the need to include the zero rated supplies on the top and bottom of the fraction and also the requirement to round up the fraction to the nearest whole percentage; more care here could have earned some candidates an extra mark.

A more common error was a failure to realise that the purchasing company would need to account for output tax on the purchase of the services from overseas thus increasing the cost by the amount of irrecoverable VAT. Having said that, this was a tricky point and it was very pleasing that a large number of candidates identified this issue.

The calculation of the maximum salary that could be paid such that the total cost would be no more than the cheapest service provider was done well with the majority of candidates identifying the need to include employer's national insurance contributions in their calculations.

Part (b) required four examples of specific contractual arrangements that would indicate an employer/employee relationship. This was a simple test of knowledge and was done well by most candidates. Having said that, candidates were asked to give examples that related to the facts of this particular question as opposed to the first three that they thought of; the question made it clear that a fixed fee would be paid for the work so it was not appropriate to write about the payment of holiday pay or sick pay.

The final part of the question was more difficult. It required candidates to recognise that the personal service company rules would apply and to explain the implications for the various parties. Candidates' performance here was mixed. Many candidates identified that the issue related to personal service companies but got confused as to which of the companies would be regarded as making the deemed salary payment. Weaker candidates assumed that the question was still about VAT and repeated matters already covered in part (a).

	ACCA marking scheme		
			Marks
(a)	Partial exemption position		2.0
	Cognac Ltd		1.0
	Fonseca Inc		3.0
	Pisco		2.0
	Maximum salary		2.5
			10.5
		Maximum	10.0
(b)	One mark for each contractual arrangement		4.0
			4.0
		Maximum	4.0
(c)	Implications for Robusto Ltd and Cognac Ltd		
	Tax treatment of the fee		1.0
	Additional implications for Cognac Ltd		
	Personal service company rules apply		0.5
	Deemed salary payment		2.5
	Payment date for NIC		1.0
	Robusto Ltd's preference		
	Employer's Class 1 NIC		1.0
	Comparison with Cognac Ltd		1.0
			7.0
		Maximum	6.0
Total			20.0

GROUPS, CONSORTIA AND OVERSEAS COMPANY ASPECTS

50   JUGLANS LTD AND LARIX LTD (ADAPTED) 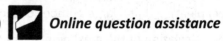 *Online question assistance*

> **Key answer tips**
>
> Part (a) is an interesting twist on the usual long period of account question. You must be very careful not to mix up the two situations given. If the company prepares accounts for a 3 month period, then a 12 month period, those form the basis of two separate accounting periods.
>
> With a 15 month set of accounts you must split it into two accounting periods covering the first 12 months and the following 3 months. Provided these rules are understood the actual computations are straightforward.
>
> In part (b) you should be able to pick up the easy marks for stating the reliefs available to groups.

(a)   **Most beneficial preparation of accounts**

Preparation of two sets of accounts

Under this option the two accounting reference dates will trigger the end of a chargeable accounting period for corporation tax purposes; one short accounting period to 31 March 2013 with the other of 12 months duration to 31 March 2014.

The corporation tax computations will therefore be as follows:

	CAP to 31/3/2013 £	CAP to 31/3/2014 £
Trading profits		
(3 × £25,000)	75,000	
(9 × £25,000 + 3 × £40,000)		345,000
Less: Capital allowances (W1)	(3,240)	(47,457)
Chargeable gain (Note)	92,000	Nil
	———	———
Taxable total profits	163,760	297,543
	———	———

Note:

The capital loss of CAP to 31/3/2014 cannot be set against the gain in CAP to 31/3/2013. The loss is carried forward and will be set against chargeable gains in the future.

	CAP to 31/3/2013 £	CAP to 31/3/2014 £
Corporation tax liability (W2)		
(£163,760 × 24%)	39,302	
(£297,543 × 24%)		71,410
Less: Marginal relief		
(£187,500 – £163,760) × $^1/_{100}$	(237)	
(£750,000 – £297,543) × $^1/_{100}$		(4,525)
Corporation tax liability	39,065	66,885
Total corporation tax liability	105,950	

Preparing one set of accounts for the fifteen month period to 31 March 2014

Under this option, as an accounting period cannot exceed 12 months in duration, the long period of account is divided into two accounting periods: the first to 31 December 2013, and the second to 31 March 2014.

Trading income before capital allowances is allocated on a time basis, with capital allowances and other items allocated by reference to the accounting period to which they relate.

The corporation tax computations will therefore be as follows:

CAP to:	31/12/2013 £	31/3/2014 £
Trading profit		
12/15 × (£300,000 + £120,000)	336,000	
3/15 × (£420,000)		84,000
Less: Capital allowances (W3)	(48,040)	(4,723)
Chargeable gain (£92,000 – £29,000) (Note)	63,000	–
Taxable total profits	350,960	79,277

Note: As both the chargeable gain and capital loss occur in the same CAP, the loss can be set against the gain.

Tutorial note

Strictly CAP to 31.12.13 is affected by FY2012 (3m) and FY2013 (9m) but the requirements stated that only FY 2012 rates were to be used throughout.

CAP to:	31/12/2013	31/3/2014
	£	£
Corporation tax liability (W4)		
(£350,960 × 24%)	84,230	
(£79,277 × 24%)		19,026
Less: Marginal relief		
(£750,000 − £350,960) × $^1/_{100}$	(3,990)	
(£187,500 − £79,277) × $^1/_{100}$		(1,082)
Corporation tax liability	80,240	17,944
Total corporation tax liability	98,184	

Conclusion

On the basis of the information provided it would appear preferable for Juglans Limited to opt for a single 15 month long period of account.

This will result in a corporation tax saving of £7,766 (£105,950 − £98,184).

Note that the saving is achieved mainly as a result of a timing difference from using up a capital loss of £29,000, and also due to the increase in capital allowances with a single 15 month period.

Workings

(W1) Capital allowances

	CAP to 31/3/2013			CAP to 31/3/2014	
	Pool	Allowance		Pool	Allowances
	£	£	£	£	£
TWDV b/f	72,000			68,760	
Additions			81,000		
AIA			(25,000)		25,000
				56,000	
	72,000			124,760	
WDA (18% × 3/12)	(3,240)	3,240			
WDA (18%)				(22,457)	22,457
Allowances claimed		3,240			47,457
TWDV c/f	68,760			102,303	

Tutorial note

It has been assumed that Juglans Limited and Larix Limited are not related businesses for capital allowance purposes. Since Bob owns all the share capital of both companies, they would be related if they shared premises or were engaged in similar activities. Related businesses only have one annual investment allowance which they can share between them as they see fit.

(W2) Small Profits Rate Limits

Juglans Limited and Larix Limited are associated companies as they are both under the control of Bob.

			£
CAP to 31/3/2013	Lower limit	(£300,000 × 3/12) ÷ 2	37,500
	Upper limit	(£1,500,000 × 3/12) ÷ 2	187,500
CAP to 31/3/2014	Lower limit	£300,000 ÷ 2	150,000
	Upper limit	£1,500,000 ÷ 2	750,000

(W3) Capital allowances

		CAP to 31/12/2014		CAP to 31/3/2014	
		Pool	Allowances	Pool	Allowances
	£	£	£	£	£
TWDV b/f		72,000		104,960	
Additions	81,000				
AIA	(25,000)		25,000		
	———	56,000			
		128,000			
WDA (18%)		(23,040)	23,040		
WDA (18% × 3/12)				(4,723)	4,723
Allowances claimed			48,040		4,723
TWDV c/f		104,960		100,237	

(W4) Small Profits Rate Limits

			£
CAP to 31/12/2013	Lower limit	300,000 ÷ 2	150,000
	Upper limit	1,500,000 ÷ 2	750,000
CAP to 31/3/2014	Lower limit	(300,000 × 3/12) ÷ 2	37,500
	Upper limit	(1,500,000 × 3/12) ÷ 2	187,500

(b)   (i)   **Reliefs available to groups**

It is possible for companies within a 75% group to transfer trading losses to other companies within the group. For these purposes two companies are within a 75% group if one company is a 75% subsidiary of the other *company* or both are 75% subsidiaries of a third *company*.

As Juglans Limited and Larix Limited are entirely owned by Bob (as individual) it will unfortunately not be possible to transfer the £45,000 trading loss from Larix Limited to Juglans Limited.

Companies which are in a capital gains group can elect to reallocate chargeable gains and losses to other group companies, to match gains and losses and obtain more immediate relief for capital losses than might otherwise have been the case.

Companies are within a capital gains group, however, as for the group relief, if one company is a 75% subsidiary of another *company* or both are 75% subsidiaries of a third *company*.

Again, as Juglans Limited and Larix Limited are entirely owned by Bob it will not therefore be possible to reallocate the capital loss of £30,000 made by Larix Limited to Juglans Limited (and thereby matching with the gain made by Juglans Limited in its accounting period ended 31 December 2013).

(ii)   **Group VAT registration**

Companies under common control may apply for group VAT registration. For these purposes control only needs to be via a 'person' which can include individuals as well as companies in traditional parent/subsidiary relationships.

As Bob controls both Juglans Limited and Larix Limited, therefore, it is possible for these two companies to be group VAT registered.

The effect of a group registration would be that the two companies are effectively treated as a single entity for VAT purposes. As Larix Limited predominantly makes exempt sales the group will therefore become partially exempt. The issue is, therefore, whether this will lead to an overall increase or reduction of input tax recovery under the partial exemption rules.

There are three de minimis tests which, if any are satisfied, mean that all VAT can be reclaimed:

(1)   Total input tax ≤ £625 per month on average, and
Value of exempt supplies ≤ 50% of value of total supplies

(2)   Total input tax less input tax directly attributable to taxable supplies ≤ £625 per month on average, and

Value of exempt supplies ≤ 50% of value of total supplies

(3)   Input tax relating to exempt supplies ≤ £625 per month on average, and
Input tax relating to exempt supplies ≤ 50% of total input VAT

Larix Limited clearly does not satisfy any of these tests, and therefore the input VAT attributable to exempt supplies cannot be reclaimed.

The current input tax recovery position is as follows:

	£
Juglans Limited (totally taxable supplies)	125,000
Larix Limited	
Relating to taxable supplies	12,000
Relating to unattributed supplies (£20,000 × 10%)	2,000
	139,000

With a group VAT registration the recovery of input tax will be as follows:

	£
Relating to taxable supplies (£123,000 + £12,000)	135,000
Relating to unattributed supplies (working)	10,560
	145,560

Conclusion

It would appear that, providing the information for the year ended 31 March 2014 is representative, a group VAT registration will result in an additional £6,560 (£145,560 – £139,000) of input tax recovery.

With this, together with possible administrative savings that may result, it would appear that a group VAT registration is worthwhile.

Working: Partial exemption recovery of unattributed VAT

	£
Taxable supplies	
– Juglans Ltd	1,100,000
– Larix Ltd (10% × £1,550,000)	155,000
	1,255,000
Exempt supplies	
– Larix Ltd (90% × £1,550,000)	1,395,000
Total supplies	2,650,000

Recoverable portion of unattributed VAT

$$\frac{1,255,000}{2,650,000} \times 100 = 47.358\%, \text{ rounded up to } 48\%$$

Recoverable unattributed VAT

$(20,000 + 2,000) \times 48\% = £10,560$

51 A, B, C AND D (ADAPTED)

Key answer tips

The first part of this question involves a group and consortium structure. Before starting to answer part (a) of this question it is important to understand the structure, the number of associated companies and which companies can surrender losses to which other companies.

There is an added complication to watch out for as the companies do not have the same year ends.

The report for part (b) is a straightforward explanation of the difference between selling shares in a company or selling the company's assets. Draw up an answer plan before you start to ensure you cover as many relevant points as possible.

(a)   **Corporation tax computations**

	A Ltd y/e 31.3.13 £	B Ltd y/e 31.12.12 £	D Ltd y/e 31.3.13 £
Trading profit	234,500	Nil	Nil
Property income (W2)	49,000	25,000	
Chargeable gain (W1)	Nil	30,000	20,000
	───────	───────	───────
	283,500	55,000	20,000
Loss relief		(53,500)	(20,000)
Consortium relief (W3)	(60,000)		
Group relief (W4)	(148,500)		
	───────	───────	───────
Taxable total profits	75,000	1,500	Nil
	───────	───────	───────
	£	£	£
Corporation tax @ 20% (W4)	15,000	300	Nil
Less: DTR (W5)	(7,350)	─────	─────
	───────		
Corporation tax payable	7,650		
	───────		

Beneficial reliefs

- Maximum consortium relief is taken by A Ltd from D Ltd of £60,000 (W3).

- Group loss relief is claimed by A Ltd from B Ltd of £148,500 (W4).

- B Ltd has a loss left after group relief of £53,500 which can be used by B Ltd in the current year against its property income of £25,000 and the balance of the gain (W1).

Tutorial note

Alternatively, the £53,500 loss remaining in B Ltd could be surrendered to A Ltd to set against its profits for the three months ended 31 March 2012. There is not enough information provided in the question to evaluate this course of action.

- D Ltd has a loss left after consortium relief of £60,000, of which £20,000 is used in the current year by D Ltd against its chargeable gain and the remainder is available to E Ltd, the other consortium member.

Workings

(W1) **Chargeable gain in A Ltd**

B Ltd has a capital loss brought forward of £20,000. This can be relieved against £20,000 of the gain realised by A Ltd if an election is made to reallocate that amount of the gain to B Ltd.

However, an election to transfer the whole gain is recommended as the balance of the gain not relieved by the remainder of B Ltd's loss will only be chargeable at 20% rather than 25% in A Ltd (before loss reliefs). (See W4 for explanation of group relief maximum to A Ltd.)

(W2) **Overseas property income**

	£	£
Rent received	41,650	
Withholding tax (£41,650 × 15/85)	7,350	7,350
Gross property income	49,000	
Overseas tax suffered		7,350

Tutorial note

The dividend received from C Inc is not taxable in the UK, therefore there is no double tax relief for the overseas tax suffered.

It is not included as franked investment income as C Inc is an associated company.

(W3) **Maximum consortium relief**

Lower of

(i) Available loss of D Ltd: (£120,000 – £20,000) × 60% = £60,000

(ii) Available taxable total profits of A Ltd: £283,500

Note that the amount of loss available for surrender up to A Ltd must be reduced by any possible claims against D Ltd's current period profits.

(W4) Maximum group relief

A Ltd and B Ltd have non–coterminous year ends, therefore the maximum group relief must be calculated for the corresponding accounting period of nine months (1 April 2012 to 31 December 2012).

Maximum group relief = lower of

(i)   Available loss of B Ltd: $(9/12 \times £202,000) = £151,500$

(ii)   Available taxable total profits of A Ltd: $(9/12 \times £283,500) = £212,625$

Note that unlike consortium relief, for group relief, the available loss that can be group relieved does not have to be reduced by any possible claims against B Ltd's total profits.

There are four associated companies (see Tutorial Note below), so the limits for corporation tax purposes are:

£1,500,000 ÷ 4 =   £375,000

£300,000 ÷ 4   =   £75,000

Before loss relief:

A Ltd is paying tax at 25%.

B Ltd is paying tax at an average rate of 20%. Although the year ended 31 December 2012 straddles the financial years 2011 and 2012, the small profits rate is 20% in both years.

D Ltd is also paying tax at 20%.

It is therefore advisable to allocate sufficient loss to A Ltd to reduce its taxable profits to £75,000 (the small profits rate limit), Thereafter, the remaining loss could be surrendered to A Ltd to save tax at 20%, or retained within B Ltd for the same effect.   IF the loss is retained in B Ltd, the group relief claimed = £223,500 − £75,000 = £148,500.

(W5) Double taxation relief

Lower of:

(1)	Overseas taxation (W2)	£7,350
(2)	UK taxation on overseas rent	
	£49,000 × 20% (rate after loss relief claims)	£9,800

Tutorial note

A Ltd, B Ltd, C Ltd and D Ltd are all associated companies (50% or more of shares owned).

A Ltd and B Ltd are in a group relief group (>75% of shares owned and resident in the UK).

A Ltd and E Ltd are eligible for consortium relief (together they own > 75% of D Ltd and neither company owns > 75%).

(b)   **Report to the managing director of A Ltd**

To: Managing Director of A Ltd
From: Tax advisors
Date: 1.5.13
Subject: The sales of B Ltd

(1)   **Sale of shares in B Ltd to a third party**

Corporation tax (CT)

(i)   *Chargeable gains implications*

A Ltd is disposing of its shares in B Ltd.

No gain arises on the disposal as the disposal is of a substantial shareholding. It is therefore exempt from CT under the substantial shareholding rules provided conditions are satisfied.

The company must have at least a 10% interest in the company and must have owned the shareholding throughout a 12 month period beginning not more than two years prior to the date of disposal.

The conditions appear to be satisfied and therefore the gain will be exempt.

(ii)   *Associated company*

B Ltd is an associated company. The limits for the purpose of calculating corporation tax are divided by the number of associated companies in a group.

If B Ltd is sold in December 2013 it will continue to be associated throughout the year to 31 March 2014 (the year of disposal) but not thereafter.

This means that for the A Ltd group the small company taxation limits will increase and will become £500,000 (£1,500,000 ÷ 3) and £100,000 (£300,000 ÷ 3) for the year to 31 March 2015 and thereafter.

Given current profit levels this may not affect the rate of tax each company pays.

(iii)   *Losses – group relief*

Only profits and losses that fall into the corresponding accounting period (period during which the group relationship exists) may be set off against each other.

Group relief is denied from the date that arrangements are made whereby a company might leave a group (this date may be earlier than the actual date of sale).

(iv)   *Losses – carry forward of trading losses by B Ltd*

Relief is denied when:

- there is both a change in ownership and a major change in the nature or conduct of the trade within a period of three years; or

- at any time after the scale of activities of the trade has become small or negligible, and before any considerable revival of the trade, there is a change in the ownership of the company.

Brought forward losses cannot be group relieved, but, as B Ltd has none this is not relevant.

(v) *Degrouping charge*

A degrouping charge will be assessed on A Ltd in the accounting period that B Ltd leaves the group, if B Ltd had acquired assets from other group members on a no gain/no loss basis within the six years preceding the company leaving the group.

The degrouping charge is added to the sales proceeds of the shares. If the disposal qualifies for the substantial shareholding exemption the degrouping charge will also therefore be exempt.

(vi) *Degrouping charge – intangibles*

There is also a degrouping charge where a company leaves a group having acquired an intangible fixed asset from another group company within the previous six years. This charge is taxed on B Ltd – the company leaving the group.

This degrouping gain may be reallocated to another A Ltd group company. A joint election must be made within two years of the end of the accounting period in which the company leaves the group.

Value added tax (VAT)

The sale of shares is exempt from VAT.

Stamp duty (SD)

Stamp duty at the rate of 0.5% will be charged on the consideration for the sale of the shares.

(2) **Selling the assets of B Ltd to a third party**

Corporation tax (CT)

(i) *Chargeable gains on disposal*

The individual chargeable assets disposed of may realise a chargeable gain or loss.

Rollover relief may be available if the proceeds of sale are reinvested by B Ltd, or by A Ltd, and if the sale and repurchase are of qualifying assets (such as land, fixed plant and machinery).

An election may be made (within two years of the end of accounting period of disposal) to treat any asset disposed of by B Ltd as being disposed of by A Ltd.

(ii) *Trading profits on disposal*

A trading profit or loss will arise on any inventory sold at more than cost. A trading profit will also arise on any goodwill which has been acquired or created since April 2002. (Goodwill acquired or created prior to this will result in a chargeable gain.)

(iii) *Associated company*

When the assets are sold, A Ltd retains its ownership of the shares in B Ltd. Therefore the number of associated companies remains unchanged.

However, if B Ltd becomes a dormant company, then it will cease to be an associated company, having the same effect as noted above concerning a sale of the shares.

(iv)   *Losses – group relief*

Group relief is available until the trade is sold. Thereafter, as the company is no longer trading, there will be no group relief claims allowed.

(v)   *Losses – carry forward of trading losses within B Ltd*

Trading losses are normally carried forward within B Ltd and can only be relieved against future profits of the same trade.

As the trade is sold, and therefore, does not continue, the benefit of any losses will be lost.

(vi)   *Capital allowances*

As the assets are sold, balancing adjustments will arise on the assets on which capital allowances are being claimed.

Value added tax (VAT)

The individual assets sold will be subject to output VAT, as sales by a VAT registered trader, unless the sale qualifies as a transfer of a business as a going concern.

If the conditions are satisfied so that the transfer is as a going concern, the sale will be outside the scope of VAT.

To be a transfer of a business as a going concern, the sale must be

- by a VAT registered trader to another VAT registered trader,
- of all or part of a business, which is capable of operating as a going concern.

Stamp duty and stamp duty land tax (SD/SDLT)

SD and SDLT can only be charged on the consideration for certain assets, primarily land and securities. Thus, if the assets of B Ltd include land, then SDLT will be charged on the value of the land at a rate ranging from 0% to 4% dependent on the value transferred.

52   GLOBAL PLC (ADAPTED)

Key answer tips

The structure of this question is straightforward with a series of numbered points that can be dealt with in turn.

It is important to read the whole question, as the last sentence tells you that Nouveau Inc is not a CFC, and therefore no discussion of the CFC rules is required.

Part (2) is a straightforward transfer pricing point.

In part (3) you are asked to deal with a foreign branch. Note that the overseas profits are taxed, unless an election to exempt those profits is made, in contrast with the foreign subsidiary in part (1) where Global is not taxed on profits remitted as dividends.

Part (4) is a well tested point about selling a company out of a gains group. There are two gains to consider – the disposal of the shares and a degrouping charge. The treatment of a de-grouping charge was changed by FA 2011.

The treatment of pre acquisition trade and capital losses is dealt with in part (5) and should be regarded as easy marks.

Part (b) simply requires a brief description of the corporation tax instalment system, specifically applied to Global plc's circumstances. Calculations are not required here.

(a) **Corporation tax implications of various transactions**

Rate of corporation tax

Global plc has significant profits such that it will pay corporation tax at the main rate.

The main rate of corporation tax for the year ended 30 September 2013 is 24%.

Shareholding in Nouveau Inc

The dividend received from Nouveau Inc. will be not be taxed.

There will be no double taxation relief available for the 5% withholding tax or for the underlying tax paid in Northia.

As Global plc owns 90% of Nouveau Inc, Nouveau Inc is an associated company and therefore the dividend received will not be treated as franked investment income.

Transfer pricing

Sales are going to be made to another group company, which is controlled by Global plc, at an undervalue. This will reduce UK trading profits and hence UK corporation tax. As Global plc is a large company, and the terms of the transaction would have been different if the companies were not connected then the transfer pricing rules apply and a true market price must be substituted for the transfer price.

The market price will be an 'arm's length' one that would be charged if the parties to the transaction were independent of each other. Under self assessment Global plc is required to make the adjustment in its tax return for the year to 30 September 2013.

An adjustment of £42,500 (£10,000 × £12.75 × 25/75) will be required, unless the discount is justified by different trading terms.

Tutorial note:

Under self-assessment the company has to decide if the transfer pricing rules apply with penalties if it transpires that they made the wrong decision. The company has to keep detailed evidence of the reasons for their decisions so that they can show they were not negligent even if with the benefit of hindsight, they got it wrong.

Branch in Eastina

The branch in Eastina is controlled from that country, and Global plc will therefore be assessed on the income as overseas trading profits. The branch profits would normally be subject to UK corporation tax in full regardless of the amount remitted to the UK.

However, an irrevocable election can be made to exempt the branch profits from UK corporation tax. The election applies to all branch profits, so careful consideration should be given before a decision is made.

The tax paid in Eastina of £70,000 (£175,000 at 40%) is more than the UK corporation tax on the overseas income of £42,000 (£175,000 at 24%), and so double taxation relief will be restricted to £42,000.

So, regardless of any election, there will be no additional UK tax to pay and tax at an effective rate of 40% will still be borne on the branch profits.

There seems little point, therefore, in making the election.

Sale of shareholding in Surplus Ltd

Degrouping charge

The factory was transferred from Global plc to Surplus Ltd, a 75% subsidiary, within six years of the date that Surplus Ltd is to leave the group.

The transfer would originally have been at no gain/no loss, but a chargeable gain, calculated as at the date of the intra-group transfer, of £300,320 (£630,000 – £260,000 – £69,680) will now be added by Global plc to the proceeds from the sale of shares in Surplus Ltd.

The issue is then whether the disposal will qualify for exemption as a substantial shareholding – see below.

Tutorial note

The degrouping charge arises because Surplus Ltd is to leave the gains group within 6 years of an earlier no gain no loss transfer from another gains group member. Note that if the sale of shares does not qualify for the substantial shareholding exemption, it is almost the sixth anniversary of the intra group transfer, so if the sale of Surplus Ltd took place after 20 June 2013 there would be no charge.

Disposal of shares

No gain will arise on the disposal of the shares due to the substantial shareholding exemption. As the degrouping charge is added to the sales proceeds it is included within this exemption.

Global plc and Surplus Ltd are trading companies, and Global plc has held at least 10% of the shares in Surplus Ltd for at least 12 months during the previous two years, so the gain on sale will be exempt.

Trading loss in Wanted Ltd

Wanted Ltd will be able to group relieve its trading loss to Global plc (and other 75% subsidiaries) once it has become a member of the Global plc group on 1 February 2013. It will be a member of the group for 8 months of the year ended 30 September 2013.

However, in the year ended 30 September 2013, the relief will be limited to the lower of Wanted Ltd's available loss of £160,000 (240,000 × 8/12) and 8/12 of the claimant company's taxable total profits (assuming they have coterminous accounting periods).

Capital loss in Wanted Ltd

The capital loss of £170,000 is a pre-entry loss.

The loss can be utilised by Wanted Ltd against its future gains on assets already owned when it joined the group, or assets acquired from a third party after it joined the group for use in Wanted Ltd's trade.

(b)   **Quarterly payments for corporation tax**

Global plc is a large company for the year ended 30 September 2013 as it will pay the main rate of corporation tax. Global plc will therefore have to pay its corporation tax liability by quarterly instalments.

However, an exception would apply if profits do not exceed £10 million (reduced according to the number of associated companies at the beginning of the accounting period), and Global plc was not a large company for the year ended 30 September 2012.

The four quarterly instalments for the year ended 30 September 2013 will be due on 14 April 2013, 14 July 2013, 14 October 2013 and 14 January 2014.

Instalments will be based on the expected corporation tax liability for the year ended 30 September 2013, and so Global plc will have to produce an accurate forecast of its corporation tax liability for the year.

Interest will be receivable/payable on any over/under payments of instalments. This interest is taxable/deductible in the corporation tax computation.

53   TAY LIMITED (ADAPTED)

Key answer tips

The first part of this question covers tax relief for an intangible asset. The availability of a 4% writing down allowance for purchased intangibles is important for companies, particularly when they buy goodwill which is usually not amortised through the accounts.

Part (a)(ii) to (iv) of this question deal with common corporation tax issues encountered when a company joins a group. You should always look out for the restrictions on the use of trading losses and capital losses that may apply in this situation.

Part (b) looks more complicated than it actually is. The examiner is asking you to compare the treatment of trading overseas through a subsidiary (share purchase) or a permanent establishment (asset purchase).

Notes for meeting

(a)   (i)   **Purchase of intellectual property**

Writing down allowances are available on intangible assets such as intellectual property. The allowance given is normally equivalent to the allowable depreciation charge to the accounts. However, in this case, Tay Ltd does not depreciate its intellectual property, so this basis is not available.

Nevertheless, Tay Ltd can elect to claim allowances at the rate of 4% on a straight line basis for tax purposes. The election is irrevocable and must be made within two years of the end of the accounting period in which the expenditure was incurred.

(ii) **Corporation tax payable – y/e 31 March 2013**

On the basis that the election in (i) is made, the trading profits for Tay Ltd will be as follows:

	£
Taxable trading profit before allowances	250,000
Less: Intellectual property amortisation (W1)	(10,000)
	240,000
Less: Group relief (W2)	(40,000)
Taxable total profits	200,000
Corporation tax at 24%	48,000
Less: Marginal relief	
(750,000 – 200,000) × 1/100	(5,500)
Corporation tax payable	42,500

Workings

(W1) WDA re intellectual property:

4% × £250,000

(W2) Losses of Trent Ltd prior to 1 September 2012 cannot be group relieved against the profits of Tay Ltd.

Group relief is available for the period 1 September 2012 to 31 December 2012, and is restricted to the lower of the following:

Profits of Tay Ltd	£80,000 (4/12 × 240,000)
Available losses of Trent Ltd	£40,000 (4/12 × (120,000))

i.e. £40,000

(iii) **Corporation tax implications of transferring work to Trent Ltd**

Trading losses may not be carried forward where, within a period of three years there is both a change in the ownership of a company and a major change in the nature or conduct of its trade.

The transfer of work from Tay Ltd to Trent Ltd could possibly constitute a major change in the nature or conduct of the latter's trade. As a consequence, any tax losses at the date of acquisition would be forfeited.

Assuming losses were incurred uniformly in 2012, the tax losses at the date of acquisition were £380,000 (£300,000 + 8/12 × £120,000)). This is worth £91,200 assuming a corporation tax rate of 24%.

Thus, Tay Ltd should not consider transferring any trade to Trent Ltd until after the third anniversary of the date of the change of ownership i.e. not before 1 September 2015. As the trades are similar, there should be little problem in transferring work from that date onwards.

Key answer tips

The email from the manager asks for suggestions on how the potential corporation tax implications can be minimised or eliminated. The answer suggests the usual remedy of waiting for 3 years before making any changes to Trent Ltd's trade.

If Trent Ltd and Tay Ltd carried out different trades the profits from the transferred contracts could not be relieved by the brought forward losses as they would not be from the same trade. However, as both companies manufacture engine components, hopefully this will not be the case here.

(iv) **Capital gains tax implications – sale of Trent Ltd's building**

Even though the factory was owned prior to the acquisition of Trent Ltd, as long as the capital loss is realised after 1 September 2012, when Trent Ltd joins the capital gains group, then it can be used against any gains arising from assets disposed of by Tay Ltd.

The calculation of the allowable loss is as follows:

	£
Proceeds	250,000
Less: cost	(400,000)
Allowable loss	(150,000)

This loss can be reallocated to Tay Ltd and will reduce the gain of £75,000 to £nil.

Tutorial note

The tax treatment of pre entry capital losses was changed in FA2011. Prior to this, where a pre entry asset was sold after the subsidiary joined the group, the pre entry proportion of the loss could not be set against group chargeable gains.

(b) **Corporation tax issues – acquiring shares or assets**

Memorandum to the management board of Tay Ltd.

To: Management Board
From: Tax advisers
Date: 3 May 2013
Subject: Proposed overseas investment in Tagus LDA

(1) **Acquisition of shares**

Status

The acquisition of shares in Tagus LDA will add another associated company to the group. This may have an adverse effect on the rates of corporation tax paid by the two existing group companies, particularly Tay Limited, as it will reduce the limits for deciding the relevant tax rate to be applied

Taxation of profits

Profits will be taxed in Portugal. If profits are remitted to the UK as dividends, they will not be taxed again in the UK, and there will be no double tax relief for the overseas tax suffered. They will not be treated as franked investment income ether, as Tagus LDA will be an associated company.

However, any other amounts paid to Tay Ltd, for example rent or interest, will be taxable in the UK, but will attract double tax relief.

Double tax relief will be available for any withholding tax deducted, not for the underlying tax on profits. Double tax relief is given as a tax credit at the lower rate of the UK tax and the foreign tax suffered.

Losses

As Tagus LDA is a non-UK resident company, losses arising in Tagus LDA cannot normally be group relieved against profits of the two UK companies. However as a non UK resident subsidiary in the European Economic Area, where trading losses cannot be utilised in any other way, they can be relieved to the UK group. This rule is not extended to UK trading losses which cannot be used against profits generated by Tagus LDA.

Gains

Tay Ltd will not be liable to UK corporation tax on any chargeable assets sold by Tagus LDA.

Tutorial note

Note that Tagus LDA is not a controlled foreign company as the tax rate in Portugal is not less than 75% of the UK rate payable by Tay Ltd. Even if the Portuguese tax rate were lower, Tagus LDA is a normal trading company and would be exempt.

(2) **Acquisition of assets**

Status

The business of Tagus will be treated as a branch of Tay Limited i.e. an extension of the UK company's activities. The number of associated companies will be unaffected.

Taxation of profits

Tay Limited will be treated as having a permanent establishment in Portugal. Profits attributable to the Tagus business will thus still be taxed in Portugal. In addition, the profits will be taxed in the UK as trading income, unless an election is made to exempt the branch profits. This election is irrevocable and will apply to all of Tay Limited's branches, so careful consideration should be given before this decision is made. Should the branch profits be taxable in the UK, double tax relief will be available for the tax already suffered in Portugal at the lower of the two rates.

Capital allowances will be available, should the election to exempt the branch profits not be made. As the assets in question will not previously have been subject to a claim for UK capital allowances, there will be no cost restriction and the consideration attributable to each asset will form the basis for the capital allowance claim.

Losses

The Tagus trade is part of Tay Limited's trade. Any losses incurred by the Portuguese trade will automatically be offset against the trading profits of the UK trade, and vice versa. However, if the election to exempt the branch profits is made, the losses will not be available for offset against trading profits of the UK trade.

Gains

Any disposals of chargeable assets by Tagus will be included in Tay Ltd's taxable total profits and liable to UK corporation tax, unless the branch exemption is made.

Key answer tips

It is important to make it clear in your answer which alternative (i.e. the purchase of shares or assets) you are addressing. Make good use of sub-headings to keep your answer focussed on the particular issues you are explaining.

(c)   **Consequences of submitting an incorrect VAT return**

Default surcharge

Although the VAT return was submitted on time (i.e. within one month of the end of the tax period), part of the quarterly VAT liability has not yet been paid. As a result this payment will be made late and a surcharge liability notice will be issued on the company.

The surcharge period will run from the date of the notice until the anniversary of the end of the period for which the VAT was paid late (i.e. until 31 March 2014).

During this period any further default will extend the surcharge period and any further late payments of VAT will attract a surcharge penalty of 2% on the first occasion, rising to 15% for successive late payments.

Standard penalty

As the return understates the VAT payable, a potential penalty arises. The penalty is determined in the same way as penalties on incorrect income tax and corporation tax returns i.e. according to:

– The amount of tax understated

– The reason for the understatement

– The extent of disclosure by the taxpayer

The level of the penalty is a percentage of the revenue lost as a result of the inaccuracy or under assessment and depends on the behaviour of the taxpayer as follows:

Taxpayer behaviour	Maximum penalty (% of revenue lost)
Genuine mistake	No penalty
Failure to take reasonable care	30%
Deliberate but no concealment	70%
Deliberate with concealment	100%

The penalties may be reduced depending on the type of penalty and whether the taxpayer makes an unprompted disclosure.

Assuming the error was not deliberate, the maximum penalty for Trent Limited would be 30% of the £55,000 VAT underpaid i.e. £16,500.

However, it would be advisable for Trent Limited to notify HMRC of the error immediately, in writing, as unprompted disclosure of 'failure to take reasonable care' could reduce the penalty to nil.

Default interest

Default interest is chargeable when an assessment to VAT arises for an amount that has been under declared in a previous period, whether as a result of voluntary disclosure or as identified by HMRC. Interest is charged on a daily basis from the date the under declaration should have been declared (i.e. 30 April 2013) to the date shown on the notice of assessment or notice of voluntary disclosure.

Given the size of the error the de minimis relief for voluntarily declared errors of less than £10,000 (or 1% of turnover, if greater, subject to a maximum of £50,000) is not applicable, the only way for Trent Limited to minimise the interest charge is by means of early disclosure and payment of the additional VAT due.

54   PALM PLC (ADAPTED)

Key answer tips

This is a question that needs a lot of reading to make sure you are clear on what is going on. Drawing diagrams of the group structure and timelines of events often helps in this process.

It is important for part (a) to note the relatively high mark allocation and to write enough detail to achieve the marks. Research and development relief is important for UK companies. Make sure you explain why the expenditure on Project Sabal will qualify. There is a tricky point regarding the degrouping charge in (a)(ii) but you should be able to pick up the marks for the treatment of the Date Inc dividends and the fact Nikau Ltd will suffer further tax on their share of the Date Inc profits.

Part (b) has a few marks for overseas VAT which should have been straightforward.

(a)   **Nikau Ltd and Palm plc**

Effect on corporation tax payable for the year ending 31 March 2014

(i)   **Project Sabal**

Research and development expenditure

The expenditure incurred in respect of research and development will give rise to an enhanced deduction for the purposes of computing the taxable trading profits of Nikau Ltd. The enhanced deduction is 130% of the qualifying expenditure as Nikau Ltd is a large enterprise for this purpose.

The expenditure will reduce the taxable total profits of Nikau Ltd by £91,000 (£70,000 × 1.30) and its corporation tax liability by £21,840 (£91,000 × 24%).

The budgeted expenditure will qualify for the enhanced deduction because it appears to satisfy the following conditions:

- It is likely to qualify as research and development expenditure within generally accepted accounting principles as it will result in new technical knowledge and a significant advance in technology for the industry.
- It relates to staff costs, consumable items or other qualifying expenditure as opposed to capital items.
- It will result in further trading activities for Nikau Ltd.

Use of brought forward trading losses

The development of products for the North American market and also for VAT-registered customers in the European Union (EU) is likely to represent a major change in the nature and conduct of the trade of Nikau Ltd. This is because the company is developing new products and intends to sell them in new markets. It is a major change as sales to North America and in the EU are expected to generate significant additional profits.

Because this change will occur within three years of the change in the ownership of Nikau Ltd on 1 November 2013, any trading losses arising prior to that date cannot be carried forward beyond that date.

Accordingly, the trading losses brought forward may only be offset against £156,917 ((£360,000 − £91,000) × 7/12) of the company's trading profits for the year. The remainder of the trading losses £38,783 (£195,700 − £156,917) will be lost resulting in lost tax relief of £9,308 (£38,783 × 24%).

Tutorial note

The profits for the year ending 31 March 2014 will be apportioned to the periods pre and post 1 November 2013 on either a time basis or some other basis that is just and reasonable.

However, it could be argued that the research and development costs of £91,000 do not arise until after the change in ownership, as Project Sabal does not commence until after the purchase of Nikau Ltd. Therefore profits of £210,000 (£360,000 × 7/12) would be treated as accruing before the change in ownership. This would enable full relief for the brought forward losses. This point would need to be clearly argued to receive full credit.

(ii)   **Date Inc**

Controlled foreign company

Date Inc is a controlled foreign company. The profits of such a company are attributed to its UK resident shareholders such that they are subject to UK corporation tax.

Nikau Ltd will therefore be subject to corporation tax on its share of the profits of Date Inc, i.e. £42,000 (£120,000 × 35%).   This will give a tax charge of £10,080 (£42,000 × 24%).

There will be double tax relief available for the 4% overseas withholding tax suffered on the dividend received, i.e. £1,592 (£38,200 × 4/96) leaving tax payable of £8,488 (£10,080 − £1,592).

Tutorial note

There are ways of avoiding attribution of the profits of the CFC: the motive test, taxable profits less than £50,000 or accounting profits less than £200,000, and exempt activities. However, the information clearly states that this is a CFC and that the chargeable profits arise from property investment activities, so there are no exemptions available here.

If Date Inc had not been a CFC, Nikau Ltd would include the dividend received, grossed up by 100/90, as franked investment income in its corporation tax computation. However, since the company is already paying tax at 24% due to being in such a large group this would have no further effect on their CT iiability.

(iii) **Sale of shares in Olive Ltd**

Degrouping charge

There will be a degrouping charge in the year ending 31 March 2014 in respect of the sale of the shares in Olive Ltd. This is because Olive Ltd has left the Palm Group within six years of the no gain, no loss transfer of the property from Spring Ltd whilst still owning the property.

The degrouping charge is calculated by treating the original no gain no loss transfer from Spring Ltd to Olive Ltd as a market value disposal. This will give rise to a gain, ignoring indexation allowance, of £520,000 (£900,000 − £380,000).

The gain is added to the sales proceeds of the Olive Ltd shares in order to calculate any gain arising in Palm plc on the disposal.

Disposal of shares in Olive Ltd

The disposal of the shares in Olive Ltd will not qualify for the Substantial Shareholding Exemption as Olive Ltd is not a trading company.

The gain will be calculated as follows:

	£
Proceeds of share disposal	1,400,000
Add: Degrouping charge	520,000
	1,920,000
Less: Cost (ignoring IA per question)	(338,000)
Gain	1,582,000

This gain will give rise to additional corporation tax of £379,680 (£1,582,000 × 24%).

Tutorial note

A property was transferred between two Palm plc group companies and then the company owning the property leaves the group within 6 years.

A degrouping charge therefore arises on 1 November 2013 when Palm plc sells the shares in Olive Ltd.

Following the changes in FA 2011 the degrouping charge is added to the proceeds of the sale of shares when calculating the gain on the disposal of those shares.

The substantial shareholding exemption does not apply to these shares as Olive Ltd is not a trading company.

(b)   **Recoverability of input tax**

Sales by Nikau Ltd of its existing products are subject to UK VAT at 20% because it is selling to domestic customers who will not be registered for VAT. Accordingly, at present, Nikau Ltd can recover all of its input tax.

Sales to customers in North America will be zero rated because the goods are being exported from the EU to a non-EU resident country. Sales to VAT-registered customers in the European Union will also be zero-rated.

Zero rated supplies are classified as taxable for the purposes of VAT and therefore Nikau Ltd will continue to be able to recover all of its input tax.

Tutorial note

Overseas VAT issues are important. You must remember that exports outside the EU and to VAT registered customers within the EU are zero rated, not exempt. Making zero rated supplies has no effect on input tax recovery.

Sales to non-VAT registered customers within the EU would be standard rated, and so would also have no effect on input tax recovery.

Examiner's comments

This question required candidates to identify various issues arising out of the acquisition of a subsidiary company. It was the least popular of the optional questions and was not done particularly well by those who attempted it.

Part (a) was in three parts. All parts required candidates to identify the implications of the proposed transactions and to apply their knowledge to the facts.

Part (i) concerned research and development and the use of brought forward losses. Whilst these issues were often successfully identified by candidates, the detail requested in the requirement was missing as was the effect of the issues on the amount of corporation tax payable. Some candidates thought, erroneously, that the restriction on the use of losses brought forward following the change in ownership and the major change in the nature of the trade related to group relief.

Parts (ii) and (iii) concerned the identification of a degrouping charge and the treatment of the profits of a controlled foreign company. Again, the issues were successfully identified by many candidates but there was a lack of precise knowledge of the rules and a tendency to describe the rules in general terms rather than to simply apply them to the facts.

Part (b) required candidates to understand the VAT implications of sales to domestic customers within and outside the European Union (standard rated and zero rated respectively). This was a straightforward test of important VAT rules but the majority of answers were poor and many confused the terms exempt and zero rated.

		ACCA marking scheme	
			Marks
(a)	(i)	Research and development	
		Enhanced tax deduction	0.5
		130% with reason	1.0
		Effect on tax liability	1.0
		Conditions 0.5 each – maximum 1.5	1.5
		Use of brought forward trading losses	
		Project Sabal will represent a major change in the nature and conduct of the trade with reasons	2.0
		Within three years of change of ownership	1.0
		Losses cannot be carried forward beyond date of change of ownership	1.0
		Tax effect of losses used/lost	2.0
			___
			10.0
			___
	(ii)	Controlled foreign company	
		Profits of CFC are attributed to UK resident shareholders	0.5
		Calculation of share of profits	0.5
		Corporation tax at 24% less double tax relief	1.5
			___
			2.5
		Maximum	2.0
			___
	(iii)	Sale of shares	
		Identification of degrouping charge	0.5
		Reason for charge and calculation	1.0
		No substantial shareholding exemption	0.5
		Gain on shares	1.5
			___
			3.5
		Maximum	3.0
			___
(b)		Current position	1.5
		Position in the future	3.5
			___
			5.0
			___
Total			20

55   SATURN LTD (ADAPTED) *Walk in the footsteps of a top tutor*

Key answer tips

This question is mainly about corporation tax groups, with some VAT and ethical issues thrown in at the end.

The groups section of the question really tests whether you know the definitions of associates, 75% groups and consortia. Without this knowledge, it would be hard to score well here.

There are some very easy marks available in part (b) for the issues to consider before accepting a new client.

The highlighted words in the written sections are key phrases that markers are looking for.

Tutor's top tips

Like many of these big scenario type questions, the second part is easier than the first, so you would be wise to start with this.

Before answering any groups question, it is always a good idea to draw a group structure diagram so that you can identify the relationships between the companies. It is also useful to annotate this diagram to show which companies have losses, which companies have joined or left during the year, which companies are overseas, and any other useful information you find whilst reading through the question. Don't spend too much time doing this though, as there probably won't be any marks available for the diagram itself!

MEMORANDUM

To	Tax manager
From	Tax assistant
Date	2 June 2013
Subject	Saturn Ltd group of companies

This memorandum considers a number of issues raised by Daniel Dare (DD), the managing director of Saturn Ltd.

(a)   (i)   **Dione Ltd – Value of tax loss**

Tutor's top tips

The requirement specifically asks you to include explanations, so make sure you explain the rationale behind your use of the losses as well as just preparing computations. By doing this, you should score some marks even if your solution is not the same as the examiner's.

Don't forget to give the dates for the loss relief claims where the question asks for them – these are very easy marks.

Remember also that the losses could be carried back in the loss-making company. The question tells you to assume the loss is not carried forward, but does not mention carrying back

- Any amount of the loss can be surrendered to the UK resident members of the 75% loss group (i.e. Saturn Ltd and Rhea Ltd). The loss cannot be surrendered to overseas subsidiaries (i.e. not to Titan Inc).

- The maximum tax saving will be obtained by offsetting the loss against profits between the limits for the small profits rate of corporation tax.

The limits are divided by four as there are four associated companies (Titan Inc is included as overseas companies are associated for the purposes of determining the rate of corporation tax). Accordingly, for the year ending 30 June 2013 the limits are £75,000 and £375,000.

– The maximum tax saving will be achieved by surrendering the loss to Saturn Ltd. The first £10,000 of loss will relieve profits at the main rate of tax and the balance of the loss will save tax at 25%. Surrendering the loss to Rhea Ltd would only save tax at 24%.

– The dividend received by Saturn Ltd does not affect its corporation tax liability. Dividends received are not subject to corporation tax and dividends received from a 51% subsidiary are not franked investment income.

– The corporation tax saved via the offset of the loss will be £46,650 ((£10,000 × 24%) + (£177,000 × 25%)).

– The claim must be submitted by 30 June 2015 (i.e. one year after the filing date of the corporation tax return).

Further information required:

– Income and gains of Dione Ltd for the year ended 30 June 2012

The loss could be carried back for offset against the total profits of Dione Ltd for the year ended 30 June 2012.

Whether or not this would be advantageous would depend on the company's total profits for that year. There would be a cash flow benefit of carrying back losses as tax already paid would be repaid

Tutorial note

Remember that overseas resident companies are counted as associates, but generally cannot transfer losses to/from UK companies as part of a 75% losses group. The only exception to this is where a loss-making subsidiary is resident in an EEA country and is unable to relieve its loss overseas, which clearly does not apply here.

*When claiming group relief for losses, the aim is always to save tax at the highest possible rate. Usually, this means targeting those companies whose profits already fall within the marginal band to save tax at the effective rate of 25%. The twist here was that both UK companies had profits above the upper corporation tax limit. In this case, you should surrender to the company with the lowest profit so that you can bring it down into the marginal band as quickly as possible and access the 25% saving. Doing this does not increase the amount of tax it will pay, as the **average** rate of tax will be between 20-24%.*

(ii) **Tethys Ltd – Use of trading loss**

Tutor's top tips

The requirement asks you to identify any further information that may be required. Look for clues in the question – it states that DD "cannot remember" who owns the balance of the share capital. This was really the key to scoring well in this section! A consortium is only formed where companies jointly own 75%.

– The two companies will not be in a group relief group as Saturn Ltd will not own 75% of Tethys Ltd.

– For a consortium to exist, 75% of the ordinary share capital of Tethys Ltd must be held by companies which each hold at least 5%. Accordingly, Tethys Ltd will be a consortium company if the balance of its share capital is owned by Clangers Ltd but not if it is owned by Edith Clanger.

– If Tethys Ltd qualifies as a consortium company: 65% of its trading losses in the period from 1 August 2013 to 31 December 2013 can be surrendered to Saturn Ltd, i.e. £21,667 (£80,000 × 5/12 × 65%).

– If Tethys Ltd does not qualify as a consortium company: none of its loss can be surrendered to Saturn Ltd.

– The acquisition of 65% of Tethys Ltd is a change in ownership of the company. If there is a major change in the nature or conduct of the trade of Tethys Ltd within three years of 1 August 2013, the loss arising prior to that date cannot be carried forward for relief in the future. Selling the factory and moving to rented premises should not constitute a major change in the conduct of the trade.

Further information required:

– Ownership of the balance of the share capital of Tethys Ltd.

(iii) **Tethys Ltd – Sale of the manufacturing premises**

Tutor's top tips

Make sure that you learn the VAT treatment of land and buildings, as this has been tested several times recently

Value added tax (VAT)

– The building is not a new building (i.e. it is more than three years old). Accordingly, the sale of the building is an exempt supply and VAT should not be charged unless Tethys Ltd has opted to tax the building in the past.

Taxable profits on sale

– The capital gain arising on the sale of the building will be £97,760 (W).

Rollover relief

- Tethys Ltd is not in a capital gains group with Saturn Ltd. Accordingly, rollover relief will only be available if Tethys Ltd, rather than any of the other Saturn Ltd group companies, acquires sufficient qualifying business assets.

- The amount of sales proceeds not spent in the qualifying period is chargeable, i.e. £40,000 (£240,000 – £200,000).

    The balance of the gain, £57,760 (£97,760 – £40,000), can be rolled over.

- Qualifying business assets include land and buildings and fixed plant and machinery. The assets must be brought into immediate use in the company's trade.

- The assets must be acquired in the four-year period beginning one year prior to the sale of the manufacturing premises.

Further information required:

- Whether or not Tethys Ltd has opted to tax the building in the past for the purposes of VAT.

- Whether the assets purchased to sustain a rollover claim are used in the trade or, for example in the case of building, might be rented out.

Tutorial note

*Remember that to form a 75% capital gains group, a company must have a direct share of 75% or more. For an **indirect** share, the percentage is reduced to 51%.*

Working: Chargeable gain on the sale of the building

	£
Sale proceeds	240,000
Less: Cost	(112,000)
Less: Indexation allowance (27% x 112,000)	(30,240)
Chargeable gain	97,760

(iv) **Stamp duty and stamp duty land tax**

- The purchase of Tethys Ltd will give rise to a liability to stamp duty of £1,175 (£235,000 × 0·5%).

    The stamp duty must be paid by Saturn Ltd within 30 days of the share transfer in order to avoid interest being charged.

- It is not an allowable expense for the purposes of corporation tax.

- If the group acquired land and buildings with the £200,000, stamp duty land tax would be payable at 1%

Tutor's top tips

Stamp duty land tax on the factory sold by Tethys Ltd is payable by the purchaser, not by the Saturn group.

(b)   **Before agreeing to become tax advisers to the Saturn Ltd group**

Tutor's top tips

There are 5 marks available for this section, so try to make sure that you have at least 5 separately identifiable points in your answer!

Information needed:

–   Proof of incorporation and primary business address and registered office.

–   The structure, directors and shareholders of the company.

–   The identities of those persons instructing the firm on behalf of the company and those persons that are authorised to do so.

Action to take:

–   Consider whether becoming tax advisers to the Saturn Ltd group would create any threats to compliance with the fundamental principles of professional ethics, for example integrity and professional competence.

Where such threats exist, we should not accept the appointment unless the threats can be reduced to an acceptable level via the implementation of safeguards.

–   Contact the existing tax adviser in order to ensure that there has been no action by the Saturn Ltd group that would, on ethical grounds, preclude us from accepting appointment.

Examiner's comments

This question was in two parts. In part (a) candidates had to write a memorandum, including explanations and calculations, consisting of four separate components. The general approach here was good, with well structured documents that addressed the majority of the issues being prepared by many candidates.

The first component concerned the tax efficient use of losses in a group situation. Whilst many candidates did this well, there were two particular areas where mistakes were common.

The first was the incorrect inclusion of Titan Inc, a non-UK resident company, in the group relief group. The second was the belief, held by a large number of candidates, that losses should not be surrendered to a company if to do so would make it subject to marginal relief.

Losses are used most tax effectively where they are offset against profits that fall between the limits. Accordingly, losses *should* be directed towards a company that is paying tax at the main rate if this will reduce its 'augmented profits' below the upper limit. Only a small minority of candidates identified the possibility of the losses being carried back for offset against the profits of the loss-making company in the previous 12 months.

The second component involved the acquisition of 65% of a loss-making company. The key here was to recognise that consortium relief would be available provided the remaining shares (or at least 10% of them) were held by a company. The possibility of consortium relief was identified by a significant number of candidates although many failed to recognise the importance of the identity of the other shareholder.

The third component required candidates to address the tax implications of the sale of a property. The capital gain and the possibility of rollover relief were handled well. The majority of candidates did not handle the VAT implications of the sale of the building well. Many of them missed the fact that the building was more than three years old or simply did not have sufficiently precise knowledge of the rules.

The final component of the memorandum concerned stamp duties and was handled well.

Part (b) concerned a firm's obligations in respect of money laundering and other matters when taking on a new client. This was done well by the majority of candidates.

				Marks
(a)	**(i)**	Identification of group members		1.0
		Identification of strategy		1.0
		Calculation of corporation tax rate limits		1.0
		Advice		1.0
		Relevance of dividend received by Saturn Ltd		1.0
		Tax saving		1.0
		Submission date for group relief claim		1.0
		Loss carry back		1·5
				8.5
			Maximum	8.0
	(ii)	Not in group relief group		1.0
		Recognition of condition for consortium to exist and information required		2.0
		Relief available if consortium exists		1·5
		Relief available if no consortium		1.0
		Possible restriction on ability to carry forward loss		2.0
				7.5
			Maximum	7.0
	(iii)	Value added tax/information required		4.5
		Capital gain		1.0
		Rollover relief:		
		Assets to be acquired by Tethys Ltd		1·5
		Amount of relief available		1.0
		Relevant assets		1.0
		Qualifying period		1.0
				10.0
			Maximum	9.0
	(iv)	Stamp duty		2.0
		Appropriate style and presentation		2.0
		Effectiveness of communication		2.0
				4.0
(b)		Information needed – 1 mark each		3.0
		Action to take		
		Threats and safeguards		2.0
		Contact existing tax adviser		1.0
				6.0
			Maximum	5.0
Total				**35**

56   PARTICLE LTD GROUP (ADAPTED) *Walk in the footsteps of a top tutor*

Key answer tips

This is a tough question on corporation tax for a group of companies. The largest single section covers a classic scenario encountered in practice; the sale of shares versus sale of assets. Not an easy topic and one you may find tricky if you have not seen it before.

There are, however, some easier marks in part (iii) of the question requiring detail about corporation tax payment dates.

The highlighted words in the written sections are key phrases that markers are looking for.

Tutor's top tips

Having read the whole question, you should have realised that the requirement at the end of the question does not give the complete detail of all that is required – more detail regarding what you need to do is given in the body of the question itself, mainly under the headings "Report" and "Advice required".

Before you start writing, you should spend time identifying the relationship between the parties involved, perhaps annotating the group diagram so that you know where assets have been transferred, which companies have losses, which are overseas and so on.

Note also that there are four marks in this question for format and style. To get these marks, you need to set up your answer as a report, make sure that you use headings, write in short sentences, and have a logical flow to your answer.

Report

To	The management of Particle Ltd
From	Tax advisers
Date	1 December 2013
Subject	Particle Ltd Group – Various group issues

(i)   Sale of Kaon Ltd

Tutor's top tips

The two alternatives for the sale of the business are very different.

> *Either Particle Ltd disposes of its shares in Kaon Ltd, so that the company Kaon Ltd leaves the group; or Kaon Ltd sells all of its individual assets but the company remains within the group as a dormant company.*
>
> *The split of marks in the requirement should give you a clue that there is much more to consider for the sale of individual assets than the sale of shares!*

Sale of share capital

A sale by Particle Ltd of the share capital of Kaon Ltd will not result in a tax liability due to the availability of the substantial shareholdings exemption.

This exemption is available because Particle Ltd is selling a trading company of which it has owned at least 10% for a year.

Accordingly, the after tax proceeds resulting from the sale will be £650,000.

Tutorial note

There will not be a degrouping charge arising in respect of Atom House, as Kaon Ltd is leaving the group more than six years after the no gain, no loss inter-group transfer.

Had there been a degrouping charge, this would be added to the proceeds from the sale of shares for Particle Ltd and would be exempt due to the availability of the substantial shareholdings exemption.

Sale of the trade and assets of the business

The sales proceeds of £770,000 will be reduced by the corporation tax payable on the sale as set out below.

Tutor's top tips

This is not a single disposal for tax purposes, so you need to consider each asset separately. Think about all the possible tax implications: capital gains for chargeable assets; capital allowances for plant and machinery; possibly VAT.

	Note	£
Chargeable gain on sale of Atom House (W1)	1	246,216
Balancing allowance (£65,000 – £46,000)	2	(19,000)
Profit on sale of goodwill	3	120,000
Additional taxable total profits		347,216
Corporation tax (£347,216 x 24%)	4	83,332

The after tax proceeds resulting from the sale will be £686,668 (£770,000 – £83,332).

Tutor's top tips

As always, as long as your after tax proceeds is consistent with your calculations, you will pick up the marks here.

This figure must then be reduced by £25,000 in respect of the payment of the company's net liabilities in order for it to be comparable with the net proceeds on the sale of shares.

Accordingly, the net after tax proceeds are £661,668 (£686,668 – £25,000).

Tutorial note

The approach in this answer is that used by the examiner in his model answer and was therefore the way in which he expected you to deal with the situation.

However, you may have spotted that the additional taxable profits arising on the sale of the business will cause the company to pay tax at the main rate. As a result, this will increase the corporation tax payable on its existing annual taxable profits by £1,200 (£30,000 x (24% - 20%)). This would further reduce the net after tax proceeds.

If you haved spotted this, the examiner will have been very impressed!

Notes

1. **Atom House**

    The purchase of Atom House from Baryon Ltd in March 2006 was a no gain, no loss transfer. Accordingly, Kaon Ltd's base cost for the building is its original cost to the group, as reduced by the claim for rollover relief, plus indexation allowance up to the date of transfer.

    The gain arising on the sale by Kaon Ltd can be reduced by the capital loss of £37,100 in Baryon Ltd, as the two companies are in a capital gains group. This will require a claim to be submitted to HM Revenue and Customs (HMRC) by 31 March 2016 (i.e. two years from the end of the accounting period).

    The claim will be to treat £37,100 of the capital gain as arising in Baryon Ltd in order to match the gain with the brought forward capital loss.

Tutorial note

A further corporation tax saving is available if sufficient of the gains realised by Kaon Ltd are treated as having been made by Baryon Ltd such that Kaon Ltd pays corporation tax at the small profits rate.

The examiner has stated that candidates were given credit for any sensible use of the capital loss of Baryon Ltd.

2. **Machinery and equipment**

   It has been assumed that no item of machinery or equipment will be sold for more than cost. The excess of the tax written down value over the sales proceeds will give rise to a tax allowable balancing adjustment.

3. **Goodwill**

   The profit on the sale of goodwill is taxed as a trading profit as the company began trading after 1 April 2002.

Tutorial note

If the company had started trading before 1 April 2002, then the sale of goodwill would give rise to a capital gain rather than a trading profit.

---

4. **Rate of corporation tax**

   In the year ended 31 March 2014 the limits used to determine the rate of corporation tax will be divided by six to reflect the number of associated companies in the group.

   Accordingly, Kaon Ltd will pay corporation tax at the main rate of 24% if its taxable profits exceed £250,000 (£1,500,000/6).

   The sale of the business will increase the taxable profits of the company such that they will exceed this limit.

VAT on the sale of the business

The sale of the business of Kaon Ltd will be outside the scope of VAT, such that no VAT should be charged, provided the following conditions are satisfied.

–   The business is transferred as a going concern.

–   The purchaser intends to use the assets to carry on the same kind of business as Kaon Ltd.

–   The purchaser is VAT registered or will become registrable as a result of the purchase.

As Kaon Ltd will cease making taxable supplies, the company will need to deregister for VAT and cannot remain in the VAT group.

Workings

(W1) Tax on gain on sale of Atom House

Tutor's top tips

Be very careful here!

> *Before you can work out Kaon Ltd's gain, you need to calculate the cost of Atom House. There has been a rollover relief claim, but only part of the original proceeds were reinvested, so only part of the gain on Bohr Square will have been rolled over.*

	£
Proceeds	604,000
Less: Deemed cost (W2)	(244,424)
Unindexed gain	359,576
Less: Indexation allowance (March 2006 to January 2014)	
(£244,424 × 0.312)	(76,260)
Chargeable gain	283,316
Less: Reallocated to Baryon Ltd to use capital loss	(37,100)
Net chargeable gain	246,216

(W2) Deemed cost of Atom House

	£
Original cost to Baryon Ltd	272,000
Less: Rollover relief (W3)	(51,600)
	220,400
Plus: Indexation allowance (July 2002 to March 2006)	
(£220,400 × 0·109)	24,024
Deemed cost	244,424

(W3) Rollover relief in respect of Atom House

	£
Gain on sale of Bohr Square	89,000
Less: Sales proceeds not reinvested in Atom House	
(£309,400 − £272,000)	(37,400)
Rollover relief claimed	51,600

Tutorial note

There is no degrouping charge if the assets are sold, as Kaon Ltd is still part of the original gains group.

Instead, Kaon Ltd will be taxed on the disposal as if they have always owned the asset.

Strictly, you should calculate two indexation allowances: one to the date of the intra-group transfer, then another from that date to the date of sale. However, if you simply indexed the base cost from July 2002 to January 2014 you would score most of the marks.

(ii)   **Muon Inc**

VAT

Tutor's top tips

You must learn the definitions of the different types of groups for corporation tax purposes and in particular, which types of group an overseas resident company can, and cannot, be a part of.

It will not be possible for Muon Inc to join the Particle Ltd group registration unless it has an established place of business in the UK.

This is not a problem, however, as there will be no VAT on the sales of components to Muon Inc; exports to countries outside the European Union (EU) are zero rated.

Tutor's top tips

Watch your terminology when you are writing about VAT. 'Zero rated' is very different from 'exempt'!

Interest on the loan from Particle Ltd

The profit or loss arising on transactions between Particle Ltd and Muon Inc must be determined as if the two companies are independent of each other because Particle Ltd controls Muon Inc.

This rule applies regardless of the size of Particle Ltd because Muon Inc is resident in a country that does not have a double tax treaty with the UK.

Accordingly, the taxable profit of Particle Ltd must be increased in order to reflect a market rate of interest on the loan.

(iii)   **Payment of corporation tax**

Tutor's top tips

The examiner did not specify which accounting periods he wanted you to discuss here, but the fact that there are eight marks available should make it obvious that you needed to consider all periods affected by the acquisitions, not just one year.

Year ended 31 March 2013

In the year ended 31 March 2013 there were three companies in the group. Accordingly, the limits would have been divided by three to determine the rate of corporation tax.

The taxable profit of each of the three companies was less than £500,000 (£1,500,000/3) such that no company will have to pay tax at the main rate.

Therefore, the tax is due on 1 January 2014, nine months and one day after the end of the accounting period.

Year ended 31 March 2014

In respect of the year ended 31 March 2014, some of the companies in the group will pay tax at the main rate, due to the additional associated companies and the consequent lowering of the limits.

However, this will not affect the date on which corporation tax is payable provided it is the first year in which it has occurred.

Corporation tax will therefore be payable on 1 January 2015.

Year ended 31 March 2015

In the year ended 31 March 2015 there will be five companies in the group.

Those companies with taxable profits in excess of £300,000 (£1,500,000/5) will have to pay their corporation tax liability in four equal instalments (if they paid tax at the main rate in the year ending 31 March 2014).

The instalments will be due on 14 October 2014, 14 January 2015, 14 April 2015 and 14 July 2015.

Quarterly payments

It should be noted that, under the instalment system, a company's tax liability has to be estimated because the first three payments are due during and shortly after the end of the accounting period.

Once the final liability is known, interest will be charged by HMRC on any amounts paid late and will be paid to the company on any amounts paid early or overpaid (albeit at a lower rate of interest).

Interest paid is allowable for tax purposes and interest received is taxable.

Group payment arrangement

In view of the difficulties involved in estimating the tax due, a system exists for groups of companies whereby a nominated company can pay instalments on behalf of the group and allocate them between the group members once the liabilities are known.

This enables underpayments and overpayments of tax that might have otherwise arisen in separate companies to be offset thus mitigating the effect of the differential between the interest charged and paid by HMRC.

The group for this purpose can include any of the companies in the Particle Ltd group required to pay tax in instalments.

Tutorial note

Under a group payment arrangement, it is only the instalments that can be paid as a group. Each company must still prepare a separate tax return to send to HMRC.

Examiner's comments

The majority of answers were well structured and logical such that many of the relevant issues were addressed.

Many candidates identified that the sale of the shares would be an exempt disposal due to the availability of the substantial shareholding exemption.

A number of aspects of the sale of the business was also handled well including the profit on the goodwill and the capital allowances.

The capital gain on the sale of the property was more difficult and was not dealt with particularly well. Candidates were inclined to charge the held over gain as a separate item rather than simply deducting it from the base cost of the building.

Credit was given for simply identifying the possibility of a degrouping charge with further credit for correct relevant statements. There was evidence of some confusion here with candidates referring to degrouping charges arising on a sale of assets whereas, of course, they can only arise on a sale of shares.

There was similar confusion concerning the VAT implications of the sale with a significant minority of candidates incorrectly describing a sale of shares as a transfer of a going concern.

The second part of the report concerned VAT and the interest being charged on a loan from the parent company to a subsidiary. Candidates needed to identify the issues, have precise knowledge of particular rules and to express that knowledge briefly as per the instructions in the tax manager's e-mail.

The majority of candidates identified the need to charge a market rate of interest under the transfer pricing rules.

However, the performance in respect of VAT was not as good. This was due in part to a lack of knowledge but also to candidates writing too much and not giving themselves time to think. Weaker candidates provided detailed, but irrelevant, explanations of the advantages and disadvantages of VAT groups. There was also a significant minority who thought, incorrectly, that exports outside the European Union are exempt as opposed to being zero rated.

The final part of the report required candidates to consider the dates on which corporation tax would be payable by the group companies. This was not a difficult requirement, as most candidates will have a good knowledge of the rules. However, many candidates failed to maximise their marks because they wrote about the general rules concerning payment dates and failed to take a logical approach that addressed the specifics of the companies in the question.

Candidates who thought about the circumstances surrounding the group identified the fact that the change in the number of associated companies would change the rate of tax paid by some of the companies and that this would, in turn, affect the date on which the corporation tax would be payable.

ACCA marking scheme

		Marks
(i)	**Sale of share capital:**	
	Availability of substantial shareholding exemption	1.0
	Reason for availability	1.0
	After tax proceeds	0.5
	Sale of business:	
	Atom House	
	Cost of Atom House	
	Use of original cost to Baryon Ltd	0.5
	Rollover relief	1.5
	IA to March 2006	1.0
	Gain on sale by Kaon Ltd	0.5
	Use of capital loss from Baryon Ltd	1.0
	Claim required	1.0
	Machinery and equipment	1.0
	Goodwill	1.0
	Rate of corporation tax	1.5
	Payment of net liabilities	1.0
	After tax proceeds	0.5
	Explanatory notes – 1 mark each – max 3 marks	3.0
	VAT	2.0
		────
		18.0
	Maximum	17.0
		────
(ii)	VAT group	1.0
	Zero rated	1.0
	Transfer pricing :	
	Identification of issue	1.0
	Why rules apply	2.0
	Effect	1.0
		────
		6.0
	Maximum	6.0
		────
(iii)	Year ended 31 March 2013	1.5
	Year ended 31 March 2014	1.5
	Year ended 31 March 2015	
	Reason for instalment basis	1.0
	Due dates	1.0
	Interest and need to estimate liabilities	1.5
	Group payment	
	Operation	1.0
	Why possibly beneficial	1.0
		────
		8.5
	Maximum	8.0
		────
	Appropriate style and presentation	1.0
	Effectiveness of communication	2.0
	Logical structure	1.0
		────
		4.0
		────
Total		35
		────

57   BAND PLC GROUP (ADAPTED) *Walk in the footsteps of a top tutor*

Key answer tips

This question is mainly about overseas aspects of corporation tax. Overseas aspects of tax are tested regularly in P6, so you must make sure that you learn the rules.

Although this topic commonly comes up in question 5, you cannot assume that it will always be tested in the optional section of the exam!

There were substantial changes to the taxation of overseas dividends in FA09 and this question has therefore been adapted from the question set in June 2009 to take account of these changes.

The highlighted words in the written sections are key phrases that markers are looking for.

(a)   (i)   Reliefs available

Tutor's top tips

Dealing with losses for companies is as important as dealing with losses for individuals.

It is important to be able to write about the possible uses of each type of loss, and not simply do the calculations.

Use of non-trading loan relationship deficits is less commonly tested, but as there are more options available for the use of this type of loss, it could come up in a planning scenario, and it is important that you are aware of the rules.

Trading loss

The trading loss brought forward must be offset against the next available profits of the same trade in Clarinet Ltd.

Tutorial note

Candidates were not expected to demonstrate an awareness of the possible restriction on the use of the loss due to the deemed change in ownership of Clarinet Ltd but credit was given to those who did.

Non-trading loan relationships deficit

The non-trading loan relationships deficit brought forward can be offset against the non-trading income and gains of Trumpet Ltd. The company can choose to offset some or none of the brought forward deficit in the year.

Tutorial note

Non-trading loan relationship deficits brought forward are unlike all other types of loss, in that they are NOT automatically offset against the first available profits.

It is an optional relief to utilise them, and therefore it may be beneficial to a company paying tax at a low rate in the current year, or with other reliefs available, to choose to carry the deficit forward.

(ii)   **Dividend payable by Trumpet Ltd to Band plc**

Tutor's top tips

This is a fairly complex calculation, and it is one which few students would be likely to get completely right. However, there are 9 marks available here, and many of these can be picked up if you take a systematic and logical approach.

It is best to start by drawing the group and noting on your diagram where there are anticipated dividend payments and tax liabilities. This is for your own understanding, and it is not necessary to include it in your answer.

You will need to work backwards in order to calculate the dividend payable by Trumpet Ltd, starting with calculations of the dividends received from the subsidiary companies. You then need to calculate Trumpet Ltd's own tax liability, taking into account DTR and relief for the non-trading loan relationship deficit.

Trumpet Ltd will pay a dividend equal to its taxable trading profit plus dividend and interest income, reduced by its corporation tax liability.

	£
Trading profit	40,000
Dividend received from Flugel Inc (W1)	134,320
Interest received from Flugel Inc (£180,000 × 80%)	144,000
Dividend received from Clarinet Ltd (W2)	89,000
Less: Corporation tax liability (W3)	(9,600)
	———
Dividend payable by Trumpet Ltd	397,720
	———

Workings

(W1) Dividend received from Flugel Inc

	£
Trading profit	182,500
Less: Corporation tax in Jazzerra (£182,500 x 20%)	(36,500)
	———
	146,000
Less: Withholding tax (£146,000 x 8%)	(11,680)
	———
	134,320
	———

Tutorial note

You do not need to consider double tax relief at this stage, because Flugel Inc is only paying tax in Jazzerra.

It is Trumpet Ltd which suffers the effective double tax charge on the interest received from Flugel Inc and therefore DTR is included in working 3.

(W2) Dividend received from Clarinet Ltd

	£	£
Taxable trading profit	107,000	107,000
Less: Trading loss brought forward	(32,000)	
Taxable total profits	75,000	
Corporation tax at 24%		(18,000)
		89,000

Tutorial note

Trading losses brought forward will affect the current year's tax liability, but not the dividend payable in the current year.

(W3) Trumpet Ltd – corporation tax liability

	£	£
Taxable trading profit		40,000
Interest income from Flugel Inc including withholding tax (£3,000,000 x 6%)	180,000	
Less: Non-trading loan relationships deficit brought forward (W4)	(30,000)	
		150,000
Taxable total profits		190,000
Corporation tax (£190,000 x 24%)		45,600
Double tax relief – lower of:		
UK tax on the foreign income (£150,000 x 24%)	36,000	
Foreign tax on the foreign income (£180,000 x 20%)	36,000	(36,000)
		9,600

Tutorial note

If you were able to correctly calculate the optimal use of the NTLR deficit brought forward in working 4, this part of the calculation is then fairly straightforward!

If instead you utilised the full deficit brought forward against the foreign interest income some of the foreign tax would not be relieved, but the end result will be the same (although there would be less NTLR deficit to carry forward) and you would only lose the 2 marks for working 4.

It is likely that your calculation would look something like this:

	£	£
Taxable trading profit		40,000
Interest income from Flugel Inc	180,000	
Less: Non-trading loan relationships deficit b/f	(174,000)	
	———	6,000
Taxable total profits		46,000
Corporation tax (£46,000 x 24%)		11,040
Double tax relief – lower of:		
UK tax on the foreign income (£6,000 x 24%)	1,440	(1,440)
Foreign tax on the foreign income (£180,000 x 20%)	36,000	
		9,600

Note: *Remember NTLR deficits can only be set against non-trading income and therefore there is no option to relieve the £40,000 of trading profits.*

(W4) **Use of non-trading loan relationships deficit against interest income from Flugel Inc**

Total foreign tax (£180,000 x 20%)   £36,000

Provided the UK corporation tax on the taxable foreign interest income equals £36,000, the whole of the foreign tax can be offset via double tax relief.

Accordingly, the taxable foreign interest income should be reduced to £150,000 (£36,000/24%).

This can be achieved via an offset of £30,000 (£180,000 – £150,000) of the non-trading loan relationships deficit brought forward.

Tutorial note

This is the most difficult part of the calculation.

You need to identify that not all of the non-trade loan relationship deficit needs to be utilised and that by claiming only part, the company will be able to get full relief for the foreign tax suffered.

In order to calculate the optimal claim you need to gross up the foreign tax suffered at the UK main rate (24%), to identify the taxable foreign income that will be required to get maximum DTR.

If you did not get this right, don't worry – you will not be alone and you only lost 2 marks!

(b)　**Overseas trading operation**

Tutor's top tips

This is a fairly standard exam topic – the choice of overseas expansion via a branch or a subsidiary company.

It is important to learn the main comparisons between these choices, but it is also very important to apply them to the circumstances in the question.

Here, the new operation is expected to be loss making in the first year, and it will be important to the group to be able to utilise those losses.

Overseas branch

A branch would be an extension of Band plc. Accordingly, provided the overseas operations do not amount to a separate trade carried on wholly overseas, the loss made in the first year of trading can be offset against Band plc's income and gains or surrendered to other group companies via group relief. This will save UK corporation tax at 24%.

An irrevocable election may be made to exempt the branch profits from UK corporation tax, but that would also mean that the loss in the first year of trading would not be available via group relief. In addition, the election would apply to all of Band plc's branches, so seems inadvisable at present.

Overseas subsidiary

A subsidiary company resident in Swingerra would be a separate legal entity and its losses would be subject to the tax regime of Swingerra.

The trading loss of the first year of trading will be carried forward and deducted from the company's future trading profits arising out of the same trade. This will save tax in Swingerra at 34%.

Advice

An extra 10% (34% – 24%) tax saving can be achieved by using a subsidiary in Swingerra rather than a branch. However, if the losses are carried forward, tax relief will not be available until the second year of trading. The management of Band plc will need to decide whether they wish to wait a year in order to achieve the extra tax saving.

Tutorial note

You may have suggested initially setting up a branch and later incorporating once the new operation is profit making.

Although this is often good tax planning advice, the point here was to compare how the loss made in the first year of trading overseas could be relieved, i.e.:

- *Immediately to save 24% (branch) assuming the election to exempt the branch profits were not made*
- *Delay until next year but save 34% (subsidiary).*

Examiner's comments

This question concerned a group of companies and the payment of dividends. It was in two parts.

The first part required an explanation of the use of brought forward losses and calculations of dividends payable to the holding company of the group.

The explanations were not done particularly well due to a lack of precise knowledge and a lack of care when reading the question. In particular, many candidates treated the brought forward losses as if they were current period losses and consequently wasted time providing comprehensive descriptions of the carry back of losses and group relief. There were only three marks for part (a)(i); three well-worded sentences would have been enough to earn full marks.

The calculations were relatively tricky and required a methodical approach in order to determine the post-tax profits of each company. Additional credit was given to candidates who calculated a dividend, thus demonstrating an intention to solve the problem, as opposed to those who simply prepared various corporation tax computations. The use of the brought forward non-trading loan relationship deficit made it particularly tricky to get the answer absolutely correct, but very respectable marks could be obtained without any reference to this point.

The second part concerned the use of a branch or subsidiary for a new overseas operation. Candidates knew quite a lot about this area of the syllabus but let themselves down by including all of their knowledge in their answers rather than applying it to the facts and answering the question set.

ACCA marking scheme			
			Marks
(a)	(i)	Offset of trading loss	1.0
		Offset of non-trading loan relationships deficit	2.0
			3.0
		Maximum	3.0
	(ii)	Dividend payable by trumpet Ltd	
		Trading income	0.5
		Dividend from Flugel Inc	1.5
		Dividend from Clarinet Inc	2.0
		Corporation tax liability of Trumpet Ltd	
		Trading income	0.5
		Gross interest income – Flugel Inc	1.0
		Use of non-trading loan relationship deficit against interest income	1.0
		Calculation of offset to preserve foreign tax credit	2.0
		Calculation of liability	1.5
			10.0
		Maximum	9.0
(b)		Use of branch and branch exemption	5.0
		Use of subsidiary	3.0
		Advice	2.0
			10.0
		Maximum	8.0
Total			20

58 AUTOMATIC LTD (ADAPTED) *Walk in the footsteps of a top tutor*

Key answer tips

This question is about the purchase of trade and assets by a company. The question is mainly written, with only 6 marks available for computational aspects. You are asked to write paragraphs for inclusion in a letter. So, make sure that your answer is well structured, written in appropriate professional language, and that the paragraphs are clearly labelled.

The key to scoring well in this question is to answer all the requirements. Most of the detailed requirements are to be found within the extracts from the emails provided, and not at the end of the question.

Look at the number of marks available for each section to get an idea of the number of points required. Generally, there is one mark per relevant point.

Part (i) requires discussion of the deal. The slight twist is that the company purchasing the trade and assets may either be:

- owned directly by Sirene, an individual who already owns an existing company, or

- set up as a subsidiary of Sirene's existing company.

You may find it useful to draw some diagrams here to help to visualise what each alternative structure will look like.

Part (ii) is a straightforward explanation of degrouping charges, although note that the tax treatment of degrouping charges changed in FA2011.

Part (iii) covers VAT on the transfer of the business.

Part (iv) is a basic corporation tax computation with rollover relief.

The highlighted words in the written sections are key phrases that markers are looking for.

Tutor's top tips

As you read through the information in the question, highlight any requirements and instructions that you find. They are somewhat scattered around in this question.

Keep looking back at these as you attempt each part of the question to ensure that you address all of them in your answer.

Paragraphs for inclusion in a letter to Sirene

(i)   **The Chase deal**

Tutor's top tips

There are really three different requirements to address here:

(i)   *Confirm whether or not Sirene owning Falcon Ltd personally will affect the rate of corporation tax paid by Automatic Ltd. This is really asking whether Falcon Ltd and Automatic Ltd will be associated companies under either structure.*

(ii)   *Confirm whether or not the purchase of the building will give rise to tax deductions from trading income.*

(iii)   *Discuss the tax advantages and disadvantages of Automatic Ltd owning Falcon Ltd. This is mainly just a straightforward discussion of corporation tax groups.*

Rate of corporation tax

Automatic Ltd and Falcon Ltd will be associated companies for the purposes of determining the rate of corporation tax payable regardless of whether Falcon Ltd is owned by you personally or by Automatic Ltd.

This is because, in both situations, you will have effective control of both companies.

Accordingly, the limits used to determine the rate of tax payable by Automatic Ltd (and Falcon Ltd) will be divided by two.

Tutorial note

Remember that although companies under the common control of an individual are deemed to be associated, they do not form a group relief group or a capital gains group for corporation tax purposes.

A group for corporation tax purposes cannot be formed unless there is corporate ownership at the top.

Automatic Ltd owning Falcon Ltd

From a corporation tax point of view it would be advantageous for Falcon Ltd to be owned by Automatic Ltd so that the two companies form a group.

This would enable the full gain made by Automatic Ltd on the sale of the storage building to be rolled over against the administrative head office purchased by Falcon Ltd from Chase Ltd as shown in the amended budgeted corporation tax computation below.

The rollover relief claim would reduce Falcon Ltd's base cost of the property purchased from Chase Ltd by the amount of the gain.

Tutor's top tips

There are some marks here for general discussion of groups, but to score full marks you must apply the rules to the specific scenario.

Wherever you see the sale of a building and the purchase of a building in the same question, think about whether rollover relief is possible!

Don't forget to reflect this in your corporation tax computation in part (iv).

There are further potential advantages to the two companies being in a group including:

- no gains or losses will arise on any future transfers of assets between the two companies;
- a capital loss made by one of the companies can be relieved against a chargeable gain made by the other; and
- if either of the companies were to make a trading loss in the future, the loss could be relieved against the taxable profits of the other group company.

There is a disadvantage in forming a group of companies in relation to capital allowances. The annual investment allowance will be split between the two companies if they are members of a group but would be available in full to each of them (unless they share premises or carry on similar activities) if you were to own them personally.

Cost of the head office

You are correct in thinking that there is no relief against trading profits for the cost of the administrative head office.

Tutorial note

The cost of the office is a capital cost and is therefore not tax allowable in the company's adjustment of profits computation.

In addition, it does not qualify for capital allowances. There is therefore no allowable deduction from trading income in respect of this cost.

(ii)   **Degrouping charges**

Tutor's top tips

This part of the question should be an absolute gift!

You just need to explain how a degrouping charge arises and how it is calculated and taxed.

The easiest way to explain how it is calculated is to write out a proforma calculation using 'X's instead of numbers.

Don't forget to apply your knowledge to the scenario though, and remember that Falcon Ltd is not buying the shares of Chase Ltd, but the trade and assets.

A degrouping charge can only arise on the sale of a company's shares. Accordingly, no such charge can arise in respect of the Chase deal.

I set out below the circumstances that will give rise to a degrouping charge on the sale of the shares of Target Ltd, a hypothetical company.

*   Target Ltd must be leaving its existing capital gains group.

*   An asset must have been transferred to Target Ltd at no gain, no loss from a company within its capital gains group.

*   The no gain, no loss transfer must have occurred within the six years prior to the purchase of Target Ltd.

*   Target Ltd must still own the asset at the time you acquire Target Ltd.

The degrouping charge would be calculated as follows:

		£
Market value of the asset at the time of the no gain, no loss transfer		X
Less:	Original cost to the group	(X)
	Indexation allowance from the date of the original purchase to the date of the no gain, no loss transfer	(X)
Degrouping charge in Target Ltd		XX

The charge is taxable in the accounting period in which Target Ltd is purchased, i.e. leaves the original group.

Where the degrouping charge arises on the disposal of shares in Target Ltd any gain is added to the sales proceeds of those shares. A degrouping loss would be added to the cost of the shares.

If the disposal qualified for exemption as a disposal of a substantial shareholding the degrouping charge would also be exempt.

Tutorial note

The recent changes to the tax treatment of a de-grouping charge mean this is a very important area for the exam.

It is important to understand that the de-grouping charge is now effectively added to any gain made on the disposal of the shares by the selling company. Providing the relevant conditions are met the substantial shareholding exemption will eliminate any tax charge.

(iii)   **VAT (Value added tax)**

Tutor's top tips

Think carefully before you answer this part of the question.

Although the examiner doesn't specifically mention it, you can assume that the trade and assets of Chase Ltd will be purchased as a going concern.

Most of the marks for this section are for discussing the VAT implications of a transfer of a going concern and the conditions that need to be satisfied.

VAT must be charged on the sale of a trade and assets unless it qualifies as a transfer of a going concern.

A transfer of a going concern is outside the scope of VAT such that no VAT should be charged.

For the sale of the trade and assets of Chase Ltd to be regarded as a transfer of a going concern the following conditions must be satisfied:

*   The trade and assets purchased from Chase Ltd must be a going concern.

*   Falcon Ltd must use the assets to carry on the same kind of business as that carried on by Chase Ltd.

*   Falcon Ltd must be VAT registered or be required to be VAT registered as a result of the purchase (based on the turnover of the purchased business in the previous 12 months).

*   There should be no significant break in trading before or after the purchase of the business.

Even if the transfer satisfies the above conditions, Chase Ltd is required to charge VAT on the administrative head office if it has opted to tax the building in the past or if the building is less than three years old at the date of sale.

The requirement to charge VAT in these circumstances is, however, removed if Falcon Ltd opts to tax the building at the time of purchase.

Tutor's top tips

Even if you missed the point about the transfer of a going concern, you would still score marks here for talking about the circumstances under which VAT should be charged on the sale of a building.

(iv) **Automatic Ltd**
Amended budgeted corporation tax computation – year ending 31 March 2014

Tutor's top tips

You are asked to amend the computation on the basis that Automatic Ltd owns Falcon Ltd and 'all beneficial claims are made'. This is a big clue that there must be a beneficial claim to make! Here, it is a group rollover claim.

The requirement specifically asks for brief explanations as well as an amended corporation tax computation, so make sure that you provide some.

	£
Original budgeted taxable total profits	280,000
Chargeable gain relieved by rollover relief	(34,000)
Amended budgeted taxable total profits (Note 1)	246,000
Corporation tax at 24% (W)	59,040
Less: Marginal relief	
1/100 × (£750,000 – £248,400 (W)) × £246,000/£248,400)	(4,968)
Corporation tax liability	54,072

Tutor's top tips

Even if you have the wrong figure for the revised taxable total profits, you can still score full marks for the calculation of tax as long as it is correct based on your figures.

You must make sure that your workings are clearly shown.

Explanatory notes to the amended computation

(1) *Dividends received*

It is correct to exclude the dividends received from Rye Ltd when calculating Automatic Ltd's taxable total profits.

However, as noted above, once Falcon Ltd has purchased the trade and assets of Chase Ltd, there will be two associated companies.

As a result of this, Automatic Ltd will be a marginal company and the dividends received from Rye Ltd will be relevant when calculating marginal relief.

(2) *Cost of investment in Rye Ltd*

The cost of investment in Rye Ltd does not qualify for any tax relief.

The percentage holding purchased will not qualify for the substantial shareholding exemption when sold, as a 10% stake is required.

Working: Rate of corporation tax

	£
Taxable total profits	246,000
Plus: Franked investment income (£2,160 × 100/90)	2,400
	———
Augmented profits	248,400
	———

The Augmented profits are between the limits of £150,000 (£300,000 x 1/2) and £750,000 (£1,500,000 x 1/2) such that the company is marginal.

Examiner's comments

This question required candidates to prepare paragraphs for inclusion in a letter to be written by a manager in connection with corporation tax and VAT. There were some very good answers to this question, particularly from those candidates who managed their time and addressed all aspects of all the parts of the question.

Part (i) concerned the acquisition of the trade and assets of a company, Chase Ltd. The client proposed to form a new company, Falcon Ltd, to acquire the trade and assets and to own the company personally so as 'not to affect the rate of corporation tax' paid by another company, Automatic Ltd, that she also owned. Candidates were required to respond to her proposals and to summarise the corporation tax advantages and disadvantages of Falcon Ltd being owned by Automatic Ltd rather than by the client.

Many candidates failed to recognise that this was a purchase of a trade as opposed to a purchase of shares. Because of the style of this particular question, this did not necessarily cost them too many marks but such an error could be more costly in a different style of question. Candidates are strongly advised to take sufficient time when starting a question to fully understand the facts of the situation in order to ensure that their response addresses appropriate issues.

The vast majority of candidates recognised that the question required them to consider the rules concerning associated companies and their effect on the rate of corporation tax payable. However, many of them did not have sufficient, precise knowledge of the rules in order to score well. Performance in relation to the advantages and disadvantages of forming a group was good.

Part (ii) required candidates to summarise the circumstances that can give rise to a degrouping charge and an explanation of how the charge is calculated and taxed. This was an opportunity for candidates to show off their knowledge without having to worry too much about applying it to particular circumstances.

Having said that, degrouping charges are not easy to explain and many candidates would have benefited from slowing down and thinking about what they were going to say before they started writing. Although most candidates had a reasonable understanding of degrouping charges, there was quite a bit of confusion as regards the purchase of shares versus the purchase of assets; only a small number of candidates were confident enough to state that a degrouping charge could not arise in the situation in the question as, because it was the purchase of a trade, no company was leaving a group.

In part (iii), candidates had to consider the VAT implications of the acquisition of the trade and assets. The majority of candidates missed the main point of this part of the question, which was that the transaction was likely to be a transfer of a going concern and therefore outside the scope of VAT. Many candidates compensated for this by setting out various aspects of the rules surrounding VAT including registration and the ability to recover input tax. Such candidates would have done better to stop writing and to think their way through their knowledge of VAT until they arrived at something which had particular relevance to the facts of the question, i.e. the transfer of a going concern.

Fortunately, the marks available for addressing the VAT treatment of the sale of the building were picked up by most candidates.

The final part of the question required an amended corporation tax computation based on the assumption that a group was formed. This was a relatively straightforward requirement and was performed well by the majority of candidates. Only a minority of candidates identified the possibility of group rollover relief.

ACCA marking scheme		Marks
(i)	Associated companies and the tax rate limits	2.0
	The advantages and disadvantages of forming a group	
	Rollover relief	2.0
	Other advantages and disadvantages (1 mark each)	3.0
	Tax relief in respect of the cost of the administrative head office	1.0
		8.0
	Maximum	8.0
(ii)	No degrouping charge on the Chase deal	1.0
	Circumstances giving rise to a degrouping charge	3.0
	Calculation of degrouping charge	1.0
	Explanation of how degrouping charge taxed	2.0
	Taxable period	0.5
		7.5
	Maximum	6.0
(iii)	Charge VAT unless transfer of a going concern	1.5
	Conditions (1 mark each, maximum 3 marks)	3.0
	Land and buildings	2.5
		7.0
	Maximum	6.0

		Marks
(iv)	Rollover relief	1.0
	Corporation tax liability	2.0
	Relief for investment in Rye Ltd	1.0
	Relevant explanations	2.5
		–––––
		5.5
	Maximum	5.0
		–––––
Total		25
		–––––

59 CACAO LTD GROUP (ADAPTED) *Walk in the footsteps of a top tutor*

Key answer tips

This question is really three independent short questions, which could be addressed in any order.

As is usual for Section A questions, the requirement at the end of the question really just tells you how many marks are available for each section. The real requirements can mainly be found in the emails in the question.

There are some easy marks available for basic corporation tax computations in part (i), and you should be able to score highly here.

Part (ii) requires detailed discussion of the CFC rules. If you have not revised these rules, you will find this part of the question difficult. There are also some marks here for discussing the treatment of interest under the loan relationship rules.

Part (iii) covers the capital goods scheme for VAT. As this is an area that the examiner has specifically mentioned as being important, you should make sure that you are able to explain how the scheme operates.

The highlighted words in the written sections are key phrases that markers are looking for.

Tutor's top tips

As you read through the information in the question, highlight any requirements and instructions that you find. Most of the requirements are in the email from the manager, but there are some additional requirements in Maya's email.

Keep looking back at these as you attempt each part of the question to ensure that you address all of them in your answer.

Make sure that you set out your answer as a memorandum, as there are marks available for this.

To   The files

From   Tax senior

Date   7 June 2013

Subject Cacao Ltd group of companies

(i)   **The corporation tax liability for the year ending 30 September 2014**

Tutor's top tips

There are two steps here:

*(i)   Calculate the total corporation tax liability for Ganache Ltd, Truffle Ltd and Fondant Ltd **without** the additional expenditure.*

(ii) Explain, with calculations, the effects of the additional expenditure on the tax liabilities. This means that you need to quantify any extra tax due or saved.

Note also the examiner's clue that you should 'take advantage of any opportunities available to reduce the total corporation tax liability'. This clearly means that there are some opportunities!

Based on the original budget

The corporation tax liabilities based on the original budget for the year ending 30 September 2014 are set out below.

These calculations do not reflect the projected scientific research costs or the capital expenditure.

	Ganache Ltd £	Truffle Ltd £	Fondant Ltd £
Taxable trading profit	45,000	168,000	55,000
Chargeable gain	–	42,000	–
Transfer of chargeable gain (Note 1)	14,000	(42,000)	28,000
Less: Capital loss brought forward			(23,000)
Taxable total profits	59,000	168,000	60,000
Corporation tax at 20%/24%/20% (Note 2)	11,800	40,320	12,000
Less: Marginal relief ((£300,000 – £168,000) × 1/100)		(1,320)	
Corporation tax liability	11,800	39,000	12,000

Subsidiaries' total corporation tax liability = (£11,800 + £39,000+ £12,000) = £62,800

Notes

1.   **Transfer of chargeable gain**

An election can be made to transfer £28,000 of Truffle Ltd's chargeable gain to Fondant Ltd in order to take advantage of that company's capital losses and its lower marginal rate of corporation tax.

The remainder of the gain can be transferred to Ganache Ltd in order to take advantage of that company's lower marginal rate of corporation tax.

Tutorial note

The aim here is to reduce the profits of the subsidiaries down to the small profits lower limit of £60,000 (see Note 2).

Transferring £27,000 of the gain to Fondant Ltd and the balance to Ganache Ltd would produce the same overall outcome. However, transferring more than £28,000 to Fondant Ltd or more than £15,000 to Ganache Ltd will put those companies into the marginal rate of tax and would not achieve the lowest possible total corporation tax liability.

However, even if you transferred all of the gain to Fondant Ltd, you would still score most of the marks available here for demonstrating your understanding of the possibility of transferring gains between group companies.

2.   **Rate of corporation tax**

There will be five associated companies in the group, including Praline Inc.

Accordingly the limits for the purposes of determining the rate of corporation tax payable are:

Lower limit: (£300,000 ÷ 5) = £60,000

Upper limit: (£1,500,000 ÷ 5) = £300,000.

Tutorial note

It may also be possible to reduce the taxable profits of one or more of the subsidiaries by surrendering the non-trading loan relationships deficit that will arise in Cacao Ltd.

However, there was no requirement to consider this issue in this part of the question.

Try to keep your answer simple and succinct and do not try to confuse your answer by interlinking ideas before you have stated the key obvious points on ideas in isolation.

Tutor's top tips

Don't worry if your taxable total profits were not correct.

You could still score full marks for the calculation of the corporation tax, and for stating the total liability based on your figures.

Research costs

The research costs will be tax deductible resulting in a corporation tax saving for Ganache Ltd of up to £2,200 (£11,000 × 20%).

A further tax deduction of 125% of the cost incurred will be available as staff costs are qualifying revenue expenses.

Accordingly, qualifying expenditure of £11,000 would give rise to an additional reduction in the company's tax liability of £2,750 (£11,000 × 125% × 20%).

Capital expenditure

The group is entitled to a 100% tax deduction for up to £25,000 of expenditure on manufacturing equipment. The balance will receive an 18% writing down allowance in the year ending 30 September 2014.

The £25,000 can be allocated between the companies in the group in the most tax efficient manner.

Truffle Ltd is expected to pay tax at a higher marginal rate than Ganache Ltd due to the level of its profits so its capital expenditure should be given priority for the 100% deduction before that of Ganache Ltd.

Therefore the 100% AIA should be given as follows:

	£
Truffle Ltd	16,000
Ganache Ltd	9,000
	25,000

The remaining £20,000 (£29,000 − £9,000) spent by Ganache Ltd will qualify for the 18% WDA.

Corporation tax liability – incorporating research costs and capital expenditure

	£	£
Total liability based on original budget		62,800
Tax relief for capital expenditure:		
Truffle Ltd		
AIA (£16,000 × 100% × 25%)		(4,000)
Ganache Ltd		
AIA (£9,000 × 100% × 20%)	1,800	
WDA (£20,000 × 18% × 20%)	720	
	———	(2,520)
Tax relief for research costs		
Deduction for expenditure (£11,000 × 20%)		(2,200)
Possible additional deduction (£11,000 × 125% × 20%)		(2,750)
		———
Revised total corporation tax liability		51,330
		———

Tutorial note

Truffle Ltd has profits between the upper and lower limits therefore any additional reduction in profits in the marginal band will result in a marginal rate of tax saving of 25%.

(ii) **Praline Inc**

Tutor's top tips

There are 13 marks available for this section, which indicates roughly how many points are required. Generally, there will be half to one mark available per relevant point.

Most of the marks here are for discussing CFCs. A good approach to such a question is to state the conditions and exceptions, then apply each one to the scenario. If you do not refer to the scenario, you are unlikely to pass.

Break your answer down into short paragraphs to make it easier to mark.

Make sure that you discuss the implications of Praline Inc. being a CFC and provide a summary of your findings, as requested. Remember also to discuss what would happen if Praline Inc. was not a CFC.

Consideration of whether or not Praline Inc is a controlled foreign company (CFC)

A company is a CFC if it satisfies all three of the following conditions.

- It is resident outside the UK.
- It is controlled by UK resident persons.
- Its tax payable is less than three quarters of the amount that would be payable if the company were resident in the UK.

Condition 1:

Although Praline Inc is incorporated in Noka it may not be resident there. For example, it will be resident in the UK if it is managed and controlled here.

Accordingly, we will need to consider where the main decisions are made in connection with the management of the company, the rules concerning residency in Noka and the terms of any double tax treaty between Noka and the UK in order to determine its residence status.

Condition 2:

The second condition will be satisfied as, following its purchase, Praline Inc will be controlled by Cacao Ltd, a UK resident person.

Condition 3:

The third condition is likely to be satisfied as the rate of corporation tax in Noka (12%) is considerably less than 75% of the rate that would be payable in the UK (20%).

However, it is not the tax rate that is relevant but rather the amount of tax payable.

Accordingly, it will be necessary to compare the tax payable in Noka (under Noka rules) with the amount that would be payable in the UK had the company been UK resident.

The implications of Praline Inc being a CFC

If Praline Inc is a controlled foreign company, Cacao Ltd must self assess UK corporation tax on Praline Inc's taxable income (calculated at the main rate under UK rules) unless Praline Inc can satisfy one of the following exceptions.

- Its taxable profits do not exceed £50,000 or its accounting profits do not exceed £200,000.

  Praline Inc currently satisfies these conditions but may not do so in the future.

- It is engaged in an exempt activity.

  This condition is not satisfied as Praline Inc's main activity, the receipt of royalty income, is not regarded as an exempt activity.

  However, there is an exemption for CFCs where their main business is the exploitation of intellectual property and where there is not a significant connection with the UK.

  Praline could be covered by this exemption, but only if an insubstantial proportion (less than 20%) of its gross income was obtained from UK resident persons.

- The main reason for the existence of Praline Inc was not to divert profits from the UK in order to reduce UK tax payable.

  It may be difficult to argue that this applies given Maya's intention to take advantage of the tax rate in Noka by transferring additional intellectual property to Praline Inc.

Conclusion

If Praline Inc is UK resident it will not be a CFC. However, Praline Inc would then be subject to UK corporation tax on its world-wide income such that the advantage of the low rate of tax in Noka would be lost.

If Praline Inc is not UK resident we will need to prepare the tax computations described above in order to determine whether or not it is a CFC.

If Praline Inc is a CFC, Cacao Ltd will pay corporation tax on its profits once they exceed £50,000 (or once its accounting profits exceed £200,000). A credit would be available to Cacao Ltd for the corporation tax suffered by Praline Inc in Noka.

Relief for interest on loan to acquire Praline Inc

Tutor's top tips

It would be easy to overlook this part of the question, as the requirement was in Maya's email, not the email from your manager. This reinforces the importance of highlighting all the requirements as you read through the question.

The loan is for the purpose of acquiring Praline Inc and not for the purposes of the trade of Cacao Ltd.

Accordingly, the interest on the loan, together with any fees incurred by Cacao Ltd in order to obtain the loan, represent non-trading debits under the loan relationship rules, which will be offset against any non-trading loan relationship credits of Cacao Ltd, for example, interest income.

There is likely to be a net debit, or deficit, as Cacao Ltd's taxable profits are very small. This deficit represents a form of loss that can be offset against the profits of Cacao Ltd or surrendered to Cacao Ltd's UK resident subsidiaries as group relief.

The subsidiary will deduct the amount surrendered from its taxable profits for the year in which the costs were incurred. The costs can be surrendered to the subsidiary with the highest marginal rate of tax in order to maximise the tax saved.

Tutorial note

Under the loan relationship rules, a loan to purchase an investment in a subsidiary is treated as a non trade loan.

(iii) **Fondant Ltd**

Tutor's top tips

There are two requirements to address here:

(i)   Outline the capital goods scheme and explain what would happen if Fondant Ltd purchased the building.

(ii)   Consider whether it would be advantageous to use last year's partial exemption percentage rather than the percentage for each quarter.

VAT on purchase of office premises

Purchasing the building would not solve the problem of irrecoverable VAT.

The landlord would be obliged to charge VAT on the purchase price because it is charging VAT on the rent.

Fondant Ltd would be able to recover a percentage of the VAT charged in the normal way by reference to its partial exemption percentage.

The capital goods scheme will apply because the cost of the building will be more than £250,000. Under the capital goods scheme, the total amount of input tax recovered reflects the use of the building over the period of ownership, up to a maximum of ten years, rather than merely the year of purchase.

In future years, as the percentage of exempt supplies increases, Fondant Ltd will have to repay HM Revenue and Customs some of the input tax recovered.

For example, if Fondant Ltd recovers 62% of the input tax in the year of purchase and the percentage of taxable supplies in a particular subsequent year were to be 52%, the input tax repayable to HM Revenue and Customs would be calculated as follows.

VAT charged × 1/10 × (62% – 52%)

Similarly, if the percentage of exempt supplies were to fall, Fondant Ltd would be able to recover additional input tax from HM Revenue and Customs.

Tutor's top tips

It is easier to explain the effect of the capital goods scheme using some figures, but you do not have to do this to score the marks.

Partial exemption percentage

If Fondant Ltd is preparing its VAT returns by reference to its supplies in each quarter it should consider using the percentage for the previous year instead.

This would simplify its administration and, whilst its percentage of exempt supplies is increasing, improve its cash flow position, as it would recover a greater percentage of VAT in each quarter.

There would be no change to the total VAT recovered as the annual adjustment would ensure that the amount of VAT recovered reflects the actual supplies made in the year.

Tax senior

Examiner's comments

This question concerned a number of issues relating to a group of companies. Candidates were required to prepare corporation tax computations and to provide detailed explanations of the rules regarding controlled foreign companies and the capital goods scheme.

Part (i) concerned the corporation tax liabilities of the three subsidiary companies and required knowledge of the rules in relation to research and development and the annual investment allowance.

The corporation tax computations were the straightforward marks in this part of the question and were prepared well. However, many candidates let themselves down by failing to satisfy the precise details of the requirement. The question asked for a calculation of the total of the liabilities of the three subsidiaries before taking account of the additional expenditure set out in the e-mail from the client, together with an explanation of the effects of that expenditure on the total of the liabilities. Unfortunately, many candidates simply calculated three corporation tax liabilities.

The manager's instructions required candidates to 'take advantage of any opportunities available to reduce the total corporation tax liability'. One of the companies, Truffle Ltd, had a chargeable gain. Candidates were expected to propose that some of that gain should be transferred to Fondant Ltd to take advantage of that company's capital loss. The remainder of the gain should also be transferred (to Ganache Ltd or Fondant Ltd) in order to take advantage of lower tax rates. Many candidates did not spot these opportunities and would perhaps have benefited from pausing for a moment in order to give themselves a chance to think about the situation presented to them.

Candidates demonstrated an excellent knowledge of the relief available in respect of expenditure on research and development and the rules concerning the annual investment allowance.

The second part of the question required a 'detailed analysis' of whether or not a proposed acquisition would be a controlled foreign company together with the implications of it being such a company. This was a chance for candidates to present detailed knowledge of this area in a structured manner and many answers were very good. Candidates who did not score well either did not know this area of the syllabus well enough or did not pick up on the instructions to provide a 'detailed analysis' such that their answers were too brief and superficial. Many candidates would have benefited from pausing and thinking before they started writing in order to ensure that they approached the question in a logical manner and thus identified more of the points that needed to be made.

Candidates need to ensure that they identify all of the elements of the requirements in each question. In part (ii) of this question the client questioned the tax treatment of the arrangement fees and interest relating to the loan taken out to purchase the overseas subsidiary. This was not a difficult point but it was not addressed by many candidates.

The final part of the question concerned a partially exempt company considering the purchase of a building and the workings of the capital goods scheme. This was reasonably straightforward and was done reasonably well. A small minority of candidates wasted time by providing detailed descriptions of partial exemption and other aspects of VAT and many candidates were confused about who was going to be charging VAT to whom. However, having said that, a good proportion of candidates understood the operation of the capital goods scheme and explained it well. Only a minority of candidates addressed the possible advantages of using the company's partial exemption percentage for the previous year.

		Marks
(i)	Reallocation of capital gain	2.0
	Use of capital loss brought forward	0.5
	Associated companies	1.0
	Corporation tax liabilities	2.0
	Research and development	
	Tax deduction for cost incurred	0.5
	Further deduction	2.0
	Capital allowances	
	Annual investment allowance and writing down allowance	1.0
	Allocation of annual investment allowance	1.5
	Tax savings	1.5
	Budgeted liability for the subsidiaries	1.0
		———
		13.0
	Maximum	12.0
		———
(ii)	Consideration of whether or not Praline Inc is a CFC	
	Definition of CFC	1·5
	Consideration of the rules	
	Resident	1.0
	Control	0·5
	Tax payable	1.0
	Implications of Praline Inc being a CFC	
	Apportionment of profits	1.0
	Unless exception applies	0·5
	Exceptions	
	Identification of exceptions	1·5
	Consideration of exceptions (1 mark each, maximum 2 marks)	2.0
	Conclusions	2.0
	Double tax relief	1.0
	Loan to acquire Praline Inc	
	Non-trading deficit	1.0
	Availability of group relief	1.0
	Maximisation of tax relief	0·5
		———
		14·5
	Maximum	13.0
		———
(iii)	Purchase of office premises	
	VAT charged and initial recovery	2.0
	Outline of capital goods scheme	3.0
	Partial exemption percentage	2.0
		———
		7.0
	Maximum	6.0
		———
	Appropriate style and presentation	2.0
	Effectiveness of communication	2.0
		———
	Maximum	4.0
		———
Total		35
		———

60   DAUBE GROUP (ADAPTED) *Walk in the footsteps of a top tutor*

Key answer tips

Part (a) is a typical corporation tax groups question covering: trading losses, capital gains aspects, VAT and stamp duty land tax.

The key to success is applying your knowledge to the scenario given and making sure that your answer only deals with the required issues; otherwise you are likely to run out of time.

You may not be familiar with the rules on pre-entry capital losses, as these have not been regularly tested in the past. However, there was a clue in the question.

Part (b) is a totally separate stand-alone section on the professional and ethical issues to consider before taking on a new client. Remember there will always be up to 5 marks in each exam on ethics.

There are easy marks available here, and it may therefore be a good idea to start with this part of the question just in case you run out of time on part (a).

The highlighted words in the written sections are key phrases that markers are looking for.

Tutor's top tips

As is usual for Section A questions, the requirement at the end of the question really just tells you how many marks are available for each section. The real requirements can all be found in the information provided in the question.

As you read through, highlight any requirements and instructions that you find. The requirements in this question are all in the email from the manager.

You may find it useful to number these requirements so that you can tick them off as you attempt them.

Make sure that you set out your answer to part (a) as a report, as there are marks available for this. You need to write in full sentences, but don't waste time preparing a lengthy introduction.

(a)   **Report**

To	Mr Daube
From	Tax advisers
Date	6 December 2013
Subject	Various corporate matters

(i)   **Sale of Shank Ltd**

Use of trading losses

Tutor's top tips

There are two different trading losses to consider here:

– *The loss brought forward from the year ended 31 March 2013*

– *The current year loss for the year ended 31 March 2014.*

You will need to deal with each of these separately in your answer, and clearly label them.

The examiner asks you to consider all possibilities, so make sure that you do that. However, you must ensure that you apply your knowledge to the scenario: there is no point in spending time discussing reliefs that are not actually possible.

Loss brought forward

The loss brought forward of £35,000 can only be set against future trading profits of the same trade within Shank Ltd.

However, there is a possible restriction on the use of this loss as Shank Ltd will change its owners when it is sold to Raymond Ltd on 1 February 2014.

If there is a major change in the nature or conduct of trade within three years of this change in ownership, the loss will not be allowed to be carried forward past 1 February 2014.

A major change would include a change in products or services offered, markets or customers.

As Mr Daube is of the opinion that the company will only become profitable if there are fundamental changes to its commercial operations, it seems likely that the restriction will apply.

Tutor's top tips

Look for clues in the question – you are specifically asked to consider any anti-avoidance legislation that may restrict the use of the losses. This is a big hint that there is some relevant anti-avoidance legislation here!

Make sure that you apply the rules to the scenario: there will be 'fundamental changes' to the company's commercial operations.

Tutorial note

A "change in ownership" occurs when more than 50% of the share capital in the company changes ownership. As Hock Ltd is disposing of all of the share capital in Shank Ltd, there clearly is a change in ownership.

However, for the restriction in use of losses to apply, there must be **both** a change in ownership and a major change in the nature and conduct of trade.

Current year loss

Tutor's top tips

Read the question carefully. The statement that Shank Ltd has surrendered the maximum possible losses to group companies applies to the losses in the past pre-31 March 2013, not the loss for the year ended 31 March 2014.

Therefore you need to include group relief as a key option available in your answer for the use of the loss in the year ended 31 March 2014.

The loss for the year ended 31 March 2014 cannot be set against current year profits or previous year profits of Shank Ltd, as there are none available. Shank Ltd has no other source of income.

All or part of this loss could be surrendered to other companies within Shank Ltd's 75% losses group. This group contains Hock Ltd, Shank Ltd, Rump Ltd and Brisket Ltd, but **not** Knuckle Ltd.

The loss available for surrender must be time apportioned, as Shank Ltd will only be part of the losses group for part of the year. For the purposes of group relief, Shank Ltd is deemed to leave the group once 'arrangements' for sale are in place. The contract for sale will represent such an 'arrangement', therefore Shank Ltd can only surrender losses up to 1 November 2013.

The maximum loss available for surrender to Hock Ltd and Rump Ltd is therefore £31,500 (7/12 × £54,000) from 1 April 2013 to 31 October 2013.

Brisket Ltd has only been part of the losses group since 1 May 2013, therefore the maximum loss available for surrender to Brisket Ltd is £27,000 (6/12 × £54,000), from 1 May 2013 to 31 October 2013.

The maximum loss that can be claimed by group companies will be limited to their taxable total profits for the corresponding period.

If group relieved, the losses should be allocated in such a way that saves the maximum corporation tax for the group as a whole.

Any remaining losses will be carried forward by Shank Ltd along with its £35,000 brought forward loss and the loss incurred between 1 November 2013 and 31 January 2014, as described above.

Tutor's top tips

This part of the question is all about explaining the reliefs available, not about giving advice on which relief might be best.

There is no information given about the profits of the other group companies for you to offer such advice.

Tutorial note

The requirement is to give advice to Mr Daube about the use of the trading loss within his group of companies, and so marks in the answer are going for advising on the loss incurred up to 31 January 2014 only, when Shank Ltd leaves the group.

There are therefore no marks for commenting on what can happen with the loss after Shank Ltd left Mr Daube's control.

However, were this a requirement, the loss for the year ended 31 March 2014 is actually divided into three parts:

- *1 April 2013 to 31 October 2013 (7 months loss = £31,500):*
  group relief possible within Hock Ltd group

- *1 November 2013 to 31 January 2014 (3 months loss = £13,500):*
  can only be used within Shank Ltd and as it has no other income, will be carried forward

- *1 February 2014 to 31 March 2014 (2 months loss = £9,000);*
  can be group relieved within the new group

Loss on sale of Shank Ltd

The sale of Shank Ltd will be covered by the substantial shareholding exemption, as Hock Ltd is disposing of shares and has held at least 10% of the shares in Shank Ltd for 12 months in the two years before the sale, and both companies are trading companies.

Accordingly, there will be no relief for the capital loss on the disposal of the shares.

Tutorial note

You are probably aware that gains on the sale of shares are covered by the substantial shareholding exemption. However, remember that the 'exemption' means that not only are there no chargeable gains, there are no allowable losses either!

Upper and lower limits for calculation of corporation tax

Tutor's top tips

Make sure that you read the verb in the question. You are asked to 'explain' the limits for **all** *of the companies. Just calculating the limits is not enough here.*

Also, remember that not all companies will necessarily have the same limits. Check the dates carefully to see which companies have joined or left during the year, as these may be associated with old or new groups too.

Companies are associated where one company controls another, or where companies are under common control of a 'person' (i.e. an individual or a company), for all or part of a chargeable accounting period.

As the Hock Ltd group companies and Knuckle Ltd are all under the control of Mr Daube, they are all associated for the year ended 31 March 2014.

Accordingly the limits for Hock Ltd, Rump Ltd and Knuckle Ltd for the purposes of determining the rate of corporation tax payable are:

Lower limit: (£300,000 ÷ 5) = £60,000

Upper limit: (£1,500,000 ÷ 5) = £300,000.

Shank Ltd will also be associated with its new owner, Raymond Ltd and may also be associated with other companies controlled by Raymond Ltd. Brisket Ltd will be associated with its previous owner and any other companies related to its previous owner. The limits for these companies will therefore be lower than those shown above.

The rate of corporation tax payable by each company will be found by comparing its augmented profits to these statutory limits.

Tutorial note

A company is associated if it has been a member of a group at any time in the chargeable accounting period. The upper and lower limits for Shank Ltd and Brisket Ltd will therefore be lower as they are associated with both their new and previous owners, and if applicable, other associated companies in those groups.

There is not enough information in the question, however, to specifically calculate the number of associated companies and therefore the upper and lower limits for these companies.

(ii) **Sales of buildings**

Gains/losses on sale

Gar building

The sale of the Gar building to Hock Ltd will be at no gain, no loss, as Shank Ltd and Hock Ltd are part of the same 75% capital gains group.

Tutor's top tips

There is no need to do a calculation here, it is enough to just state that the transfer will be at no gain, no loss.

There were no extra marks available for any calculations of the base cost of the deemed transfer.

Tutorial note

Although Shank Ltd is deemed to leave the 75% group losses group on 1 November 2013, it is still part of the 75% capital gains group until the sale is completed on 1 February 2014.

Had the base cost been requested, the transfer would have occurred at the base cost of £283,500 (£210,000 + IA (£210,000 x 0.350)). The estimated proceeds given in the question are irrelevant.

*There will be no degrouping charge in respect of the Gar building when Shank Ltd leaves the group. A degrouping charge only arises if the **recipient** company leaves the group less than 6 years after a no gain, no loss transfer, with the asset acquired.*

Cray building

	£
Proceeds	420,000
Less: Cost	(240,000)
	———
Unindexed gain	180,000
Less: Indexation allowance (£240,000 × 0.250)	(60,000)
	———
Chargeable gain	120,000

Monk building

	£
Proceeds	290,000
Less: Cost	(380,000)
	———
Capital loss	(90,000)

Indexation allowance is not available to increase the capital loss.

Sword building

Tutor's top tips

Be very careful here!

Before you can work out the gain on the Sword building, you need to calculate the allowable cost. There has been a rollover relief claim, but only part of the proceeds were reinvested, so only part of the gain on the Pilot building will have been rolled over.

	£
Proceeds	460,000
Less: Deemed cost (W1)	(210,000)
Unindexed gain	250,000
Less: Indexation allowance (£210,000 × 0.480)	(100,800)
Chargeable gain	149,200

Workings

(W1) Deemed cost of Sword building

	£
Original cost	255,000
Less: Rollover relief (W2)	(45,000)
Deemed cost	210,000

(W2) Rollover relief in respect of Sword building

	£
Gain on sale of the Pilot building	60,000
Less: Sale proceeds not reinvested in the Sword building (£270,000 – £255,000)	(15,000)
Rollover relief claimed	45,000

Tutorial note

The chargeable gains will arise in the company that made the disposal.

The chargeable gain arising in Knuckle Ltd's corporation tax computation cannot be moved to any other company.

However, the chargeable gain arising in Rump Ltd can be moved within the capital gains group to minimise the tax paid on gain.

Explaining this, however, is not mark earning as it is not specifically required in the question.

Use of capital losses

Tutor's top tips

Make sure that you provide the detailed explanations requested, and remember that capital losses are more restricted than trading losses.

The examiner is kind here, and tells you to watch out for the pre- loss on the Monk building. Even if you were unsure about the rules regarding pre-entry capital losses, you could still score some marks for a sensible attempt at describing its possible use.

Pre-entry loss

The Monk building was sold by Brisket Ltd before it joined the Hock Ltd group. Accordingly, the capital loss that arose before 1 May 2013 when Brisket Ltd joined the group is a restricted pre-entry loss.

It can only be set-off against gains on disposals made by Brisket Ltd on assets that it owned before it joined the group, or bought subsequently from unconnected persons for use in its own business.

Tutorial note

The question asks for the options available for the use of the loss only.

It does not ask for discussions re tax planning.

Therefore, no marks would be allocated to making such comments.

VAT on sale of buildings

Tutor's top tips

VAT on land and buildings and the option to tax are regularly tested in the exam. You must make sure that you learn the rules!

Inter-group transfer

Provided Hock Ltd and Shank Ltd are members of a VAT group, VAT should not be charged on the inter-group sale of the Gar building.

Other sales

VAT should only be charged on the sale of commercial buildings if:

– they are less than three years old; or

– the owner has opted to tax the building.

Stamp duty land tax

Tutor's top tips

The stamp duty rates and thresholds are given in the tax tables provided in the examination. To score marks here, you must make sure that you apply these rates to the buildings in the question.

Inter group transfer

There will be no stamp duty land tax payable on the transfer of the Gar building, as Shank Ltd and Hock Ltd are within the same 75% group.

Other sales

Stamp duty land tax will be payable at 3% on the sale price of other buildings, and will be payable by the purchaser.

Tutorial note

Even though Shank Ltd leaves the 75% group within three years of the transfer of the Gar building, there is still no stamp duty payable.

*Stamp duty is only payable where the **transferee** company leaves the group within three years.*

(iii) **Sales by Knuckle Ltd to overseas customers**

VAT implications

Tutor's top tips

Consideration of the VAT implications of imports and exports is another popular area in the exam.

Note that the examiner does not state whether the exports by Knuckle Ltd will be within the EU or outside the EU; so you must discuss both possibilities.

There are four marks available here, so you should try to make at least four separate points in your answer.

Sales outside the EU

Sales to customers outside the EU are zero rated.

Sales within the EU

Sales to VAT registered customers within the EU are also zero rated, provided the customer's VAT number is known.

Sales to customers who are not VAT registered will be standard rated.

If the level of sales to non-VAT registered customers in another EU country are above the relevant threshold limit in that country, Knuckle Ltd may have to register for VAT in that country.

The exports (whether zero rated or standard rated) will not affect Knuckle Ltd's ability to reclaim input VAT, as all sales will still be taxable sales.

Knuckle Ltd must retain evidence of the exports.

(b)   **Before agreeing to become tax advisers to Mr Daube and his companies**

Tutor's top tips

There are 5 marks available for this section, so try to make sure that you have at least 5 separately identifiable points available and address each of the requirements: information needed and actions to take!

Information needed:

–   Proof of identity for Mr Daube (e.g. passport), and proof of address (e.g. utility bill)

–   Proof of incorporation, primary business address and registered office for each company

–   The structure, directors and shareholders of the companies

–   The identities of those persons instructing the firm on behalf of the company and those persons that are authorised to do so.

Action to take:

Consider whether becoming tax advisers to Mr Daube and his companies would create any threats to compliance with the fundamental principles of professional ethics, for example integrity and professional competence.

Where such threats exist, we should not accept the appointment unless the threats can be reduced to an acceptable level via the implementation of safeguards.

Contact the existing tax adviser in order to ensure that there has been no action by Mr Daube or his companies that would, on ethical grounds, preclude us from accepting appointment.

Examiner's comments

Part (a) was in three parts and, on the whole, was done well by many candidates. The vast majority of candidates prepared their answer in the correct report format although a minority wasted time producing a long and unnecessary introduction.

Candidates' knowledge of the reliefs available in respect of trading losses was often very good but many let themselves down by addressing the issue in the abstract rather than in relation to the companies in the question.

This resulted in detailed explanations of reliefs that were simply not applicable (in particular the offset of losses against current and previous years' profits) such that candidates then had too little time to explain the relevant points properly.

As always, candidates benefited if they paused to allow themselves to identify the issues within the question.

There was to be a change of ownership of the loss making company and an apparent major change in the manner in which it would carry on its activities going forward. Accordingly, it is likely that it would be unable to carry forward its losses beyond the date of the change of ownership. There were also arrangements in force for the company to be sold such that it would leave the group relief group prior to the legal transfer of the shares.

Many candidates spotted both of these points but those that did not need to think about how they would do things differently such that they would spot them in the future. Finally, a surprising number of candidates thought, incorrectly, that Knuckle Ltd was a member of the group relief group.

The capital loss on the sale of the company was not available for offset due to the substantial shareholding exemption. Somewhat surprisingly, many candidates missed this and, of those that spotted the point, many thought that whilst a gain would not be subject to tax, a loss would still be allowable.

For the final element of this part of the question candidates were asked to explain the upper and lower limits of the companies. Many candidates simply stated the number of associates and the consequent limits; but that was not an explanation. What was needed were the reasons for the limits being what they were including references to the companies being controlled by the same person and the effect of companies joining and leaving the group. The limits were not the same for each of the companies. Candidates needed to consider each of the companies and apply their knowledge of the rules to that company's particular circumstances.

Part (ii) concerned the planned disposal of a number of buildings. The capital gains were reasonably straightforward with just an added complication of a gain rolled over into the cost of one of the buildings.

However, many candidates missed the fact that one of the buildings would be transferred at no gain, no loss as the vendor and the purchaser were in a capital gains group. Others made errors in connection with the indexation allowance (increasing a capital loss with indexation or applying the indexation factor to the unindexed gain rather than the cost) and the treatment of the held over gain. There was a sense here that some candidates had switched off in that some of the errors were very basic and were perhaps an indication of not paying sufficient attention as opposed to a lack of knowledge.

Candidates were told in the question that there was a pre-entry capital loss arising on the sale of one of the buildings. Only a small minority had a clear understanding of the manner in which the pre-entry loss could be used.

A minority of candidates wasted time on this part of the question explaining, often in some detail, how the gains and losses should be offset. This was not part of the requirements and there was insufficient information in the question to arrive at sensible conclusions. Candidates will always benefit from taking the time to read each requirement carefully and then taking care not to deviate from the tasks set.

The VAT and stamp duty land tax elements were handled well by many candidates. Those who did not do so well need to apply their knowledge to the facts as opposed to simply writing what they know. For example, the prices at which the buildings were to be sold meant that, where duty was payable, the rate would be 3%. Yet some candidates answered in the abstract and gave the various rates of duty for all possible prices that could be charged. Only a small number of candidates considered the possibility of there being a VAT group; slightly more identified that there would be no stamp duty land tax on the property transferred within the group.

Part (iii) concerned the VAT implications of selling goods overseas. There were many excellent answers to this part that, whilst being brief, often scored almost full marks. Weaker candidates either had not learned the rules or confused their terminology using the phrase 'no VAT will be charged' as opposed to 'zero- rated'; the two terms do not mean the same thing.

The majority of candidates scored well in part (b). Many took the sensible approach of starting the question with this part in order to ensure that they had sufficient time available to prepare an appropriate answer. A minority had not taken the time to learn this area of the syllabus with the result that they were unable to obtain some very straightforward marks.

ACCA marking scheme				
				Marks
(a)	(i)	Use of trading losses		
		Losses carried forward		3.5
		Current year loss		5.5
		Loss on sale of Shank Ltd		2.0
		Associates		3.5
				————
				14.5
			Maximum	12.0
				————
	(ii)	Gar building		2.0
		Cray building		1·0
		Sword building		2.5
		Monk building		
		Capital loss		1.0
		Use of pre-entry loss		2.0
		VAT		3.0
		Stamp duty land tax		2.0
				————
				13.5
			Maximum	10.0
				————
	(iii)	Customers situated outside the EU		1.0
		Customers situated within the EU		2.5
		Possibility of need to register in other countries		1.0
		Recoverability of input tax		1.0
				————
				5.5
			Maximum	4.0
				————
		Appropriate style and presentation		2.0
		Effectiveness of communication		2.0
				————
				4.0
				————
(b)		Information needed		3.0
		Action to take		3.0
				————
				6.0
			Maximum	5.0
				————
	Total			35
				————

Section 3

PILOT PAPER EXAM QUESTIONS

SECTION A – BOTH QUESTIONS ARE COMPULSORY AND MUST BE ATTEMPTED

1   Hutt plc has owned the whole of the ordinary share capital of Rainbow Ltd and Coronet Ltd since 2000. All three companies are resident in the UK. Their results for the year ended 31 March 2013 are as follows:

	Hutt plc £	Rainbow Ltd £	Coronet Ltd £
Taxable trading profit/(loss)	(105,000)	800,000	63,000
Capital gain	144,000	–	–
Rental income	65,000	–	–
UK bank interest receivable	2,000	57,000	18,000

Hutt plc's rental income of £65,000 per annum arises in respect of Hutt Tower, an office building acquired on 1 April 2012.

In the year ended 31 March 2012 Hutt plc had a trading profit of £735,000, UK bank interest receivable of £2,000 and a capital loss of £98,000, which was carried forward as at 31 March 2012.

Hutt plc and Coronet Ltd both carry on trades in the UK. Rainbow Ltd conducts both its manufacturing and trading activities wholly in the country of Prismovia. The system of corporation tax in Prismovia is mainly the same as that in the UK although the rate of corporation tax is 22%. There is no double taxation agreement between the UK and Prismovia.

Hutt plc has agreed that it will purchase the whole of the share capital of Lucia Ltd, a UK resident engineering component manufacturing company, on 1 July 2013 for £130,000.

Hutt plc will need to take out a loan to finance the purchase of Lucia Ltd. The company intends to borrow £190,000 from BHC Bank Ltd on 1 July 2013. BHC Bank Ltd will charge Hutt plc a £1,400 loan arrangement fee and interest at 7.25% per annum. Hutt plc only needs £130,000 of the loan to buy the share capital of Lucia Ltd and intends to use the balance of the loan as follows: £45,000 to carry out repairs to Hutt Tower; and the remainder to help fund the company's ongoing working capital requirements.

Lucia Ltd is a UK resident company. The scale of its activities in the last few years has been very small and it has made tax adjusted trading losses. As at 31 March 2013 Lucia Ltd has trading losses carried forward of £186,000. The company's activities from 1 April 2013 to 30 June 2013 are expected to be negligible and any profit or loss in that period can be ignored.

Because of the small scale of its activities Lucia Ltd has not been registered for value added tax (VAT) since March 2012. In arriving at the purchase price for the company, the owners of Lucia Ltd have valued the company's trading losses at £37,200 (£186,000 at 20%), as Lucia Ltd has always been a small company.

On the purchase of Lucia Ltd, Hutt plc has plans to return the company to profitability and the budgeted turnover of Lucia Ltd for the nine months ended 31 March 2014 is as set out below. All amounts relate to the sales of engineering components and are stated exclusive of VAT. It can be assumed that all categories of turnover will accrue evenly over the period.

		£
UK customers:	– VAT registered	85,000
	– non-VAT registered	25,000
European Union customers:	– VAT registered	342,000
	– non-VAT registered	70,000
Other non-UK customers		180,000
		702,000

Lucia Ltd will incur input VAT of £7,800 per month from 1 July 2013 in respect of purchases from UK businesses. It will also purchase raw materials from Dabet Gmbh for £17,000 in November 2013. Dabet Gmbh is resident and registered for VAT in Germany.

Lucia Ltd owns a number of properties but due to the reduced demand for its products has sold one property in Leeds in January 2013 realising a capital loss of £56,000. A second property in Manchester will be sold on 1 December 2013, and it is anticipated that a loss of £60,000 will arise on this disposal. It is proposed that an office building owned by Coronet Ltd be sold to Lucia Ltd in May 2014 at its market value. This building will then be sold on by Lucia Ltd, to Vac Ltd, an unconnected third party in June 2014, giving rise to a capital gain of £92,000. The intention is that this gain will be reduced by the capital losses arising on the sale of the properties.

Required:

(a) Describe and evaluate the options available in respect of the trading losses of Hutt plc for the year ended 31 March 2013.

Your answer should include a recommendation on the most tax efficient use of these losses, together with details of and time limits for any elections or claims that would need to be submitted, assuming that the losses are to be used as soon as possible and are not to be carried forward. **(13 marks)**

(b) Prepare a report for the management of Hutt plc concerning the acquisition of Lucia Ltd.

The report should be in three sections, addressing the three sets of issues set out below, and should, where appropriate, include supporting calculations.

(i) The purchase price

Comment on the valuation placed on Lucia Ltd's trading losses, by the owners of Lucia Ltd.

Provide an explanation of the tax treatment of the loan arrangement fee and the interest payable on the loan of £190,000, assuming that Hutt plc continues to have bank interest receivable, in the year ended 31 March 2014, of £2,000. **(9 marks)**

  (ii) **VAT issues**

Provide an explanation of the date by which Lucia Ltd will be required to register for VAT in the UK and any other relevant points in respect of registration.

Provide a calculation of the VAT payable by, or repayable to, Lucia Ltd in respect of the period from registration to 31 March 2014.

With reference only to the facts in the question, suggest ONE disadvantage of Lucia Ltd entering into a group VAT registration with Hutt plc.   **(6 marks)**

  (iii) **The office building**

Advise on the tax implications of the proposed sale of the office building by Coronet Ltd to Lucia Ltd in May 2014.

Your answer should consider all relevant taxes.

Evaluate the proposed strategy to reduce the capital gain arising on the sale of the office building by offsetting the capital losses on the sale of the properties in Leeds and Manchester, on the assumption that both Lucia Ltd and Coronet Ltd will pay corporation tax at the rate of 24%, for the year ended 31 March 2015.   **(9 marks)**

Appropriateness of the format and presentation of the report and the effectiveness with which its advice is communicated.   **(2 marks)**

You may assume that the tax rates and allowances for the Financial year to 31 March 2013 and for the tax year 2012/13 will continue to apply for the foreseeable future.

(Total: 39 marks)

2   Your manager has had a meeting with Pilar Mareno, a self-employed consultant, and has sent you a copy of the following memorandum.

To:	The files
From:	Tax manager
Date:	31 May 2013
Subject:	Pilar Mareno – Business expansion

Pilar Mareno (PM) has been offered a contract with DWM plc, initially for two years, which will result in fees of £80,000 plus VAT per annum.

In order to service this contract, PM would have to take on additional help in the form of either a part-time employee for two days a week, or the services of a self-employed contractor for 100 days per year. She would also have to acquire a van, which would be used wholly for business purposes. PM has decided that she will only enter into the contract if it generates at least an additional £15,000 per annum, on average, for the family after all costs and taxes.

PM's annual profitability and the profit generated by the contract (before taking into account the costs of the part-time employee/contractor and the van) are summarised below.

	Existing business	New contract
	£	£
Sales revenue	180,000	80,000
Less: Materials, wages and overheads	(120,000)	(33,000)
Profit per accounts and taxable profit	60,000	47,000

Supplies made under the contract will be 65% standard rated and 35% exempt for value added tax (VAT) purposes; this is the same as for PM's existing business. £31,500 of the costs incurred in relation to the contract will be subject to VAT at the standard rate. The equivalent figure for PM's existing business is £100,000.

PM has identified Max Wallen (MW) as a possible self-employed contractor. MW would charge £75 per day plus VAT for a contract of 100 days per year, with a rate of £25 per day plus VAT in respect of any days when he is ill (up to a maximum of 8 days per year). PM has a spare copy of the specialist software that MW would need but MW would use his own laptop computer.

Alternatively, PM could employ her husband, Alec (AM), paying him a gross annual salary of £8,600. AM would have to give up his current full time job, but would expect to do other part-time employed work earning a further £10,000 (gross) per annum.

PM estimates that a second hand van will cost £7,800 plus VAT or alternatively, a van could be leased for £300 plus VAT per month. We can assume that if the van is purchased, it will be sold at the end of the two year contract for £2,500 plus VAT.

Tax manager

An extract from an email from your manager is set out below.

Please prepare a memorandum for me, incorporating the following:

1   Calculations to demonstrate whether or not Pilar's desired annual after tax income from the new contract will be achievable depending on

    –   whether she leases or buys the van; and

    –   whether she employs Alec or uses Max Wallen.

    You may find it easier to:

    (i)   work out the after tax cost of buying or leasing the van. (When calculating the annual cost of the van, assume that the total cost can be averaged over the two years of the contract.)

    and then to consider:

    (ii)   the after tax income depending on whether Alec is employed or the self-employed contractor, Max, is used.

2   A rationale for the approach you have taken and a summary of your findings.

3   Any other issues we should be considering in respect of Pilar employing Alec, including any alternative to employment.

> 4   It seems to me that HM Revenue and Customs may be able to successfully contend that Max Wallen would be an employee, rather than a self-employed contractor.
>
> Prepare your figures on the basis that he is self-employed but include a list of factors in your memorandum, based on the information we have, that would indicate either employed or self-employed status.
>
> Take some time to think about your approach to this before you start. Also, as always when working on Pilar's affairs, watch out for the VAT as it can get quite tricky. I suspect the VAT will affect the costs incurred so you'll need to address VAT first. Pilar's estimate of the profit on the contract will have ignored these complications.
>
> Tax manager

You have extracted the following further information from Pilar Mareno's client file.

–   None of Pilar's VAT inputs is directly attributable to either standard rated or exempt supplies.

–   Alec has worked for a UK bank for many years and is currently paid an annual salary of £17,000.

–   The couple have no sources of income other than those set out above.

Required:

Prepare the memorandum requested by your manager.

Marks are available for the four components of the memorandum as follows:

1	**Relevant calculations.**	**(16 marks)**
2	**Rationale for the approach taken and summary of findings.**	**(2 marks)**
3	**Other issues in respect of Pilar employing Alec, together with any suggestions as to an alternative to employment.**	**(2 marks)**
4	**The employment status of Max Wallen.**	**(3 marks)**

Appropriateness of the format and presentation of the memorandum and the effectiveness with which the information is communicated. **(2 marks)**

You may assume that the rates and allowances for the tax year 2012/13 will continue to apply for the foreseeable future.

(Total: 25 marks)

SECTION B – TWO QUESTIONS ONLY TO BE ATTEMPTED

3 Stanley Beech, a self-employed landscape gardener, intends to transfer his business to Landscape Ltd, a company formed for this purpose.

The following information has been extracted from client files and from meetings with Stanley.

Stanley:

–   Acquired a storage building for £46,000 on 1 July 2003 and began trading.

–   Has no other sources of income.

–   Has capital losses brought forward from 2010/11 of £11,400.

The whole of the business is to be transferred to Landscape Ltd on 1 September 2013:

–   The market value of the assets to be transferred is £118,000.

–   The assets include the storage building and goodwill, valued at £87,000 and £24,000 respectively, and various small pieces of equipment and consumable stores.

–   Landscape Ltd will issue 5,000 £1 ordinary shares as consideration for the transfer.

Advice given to Stanley in respect of the sale of the business:

–   "No capital gains tax will arise on the transfer of your business to the company."

–   "You should take approximately 65% of the payment from Landscape Ltd in shares with the balance left on a loan account payable to you by the company, such that you can receive a cash payment in the future."

Advice given to Stanley in respect of his annual remuneration from Landscape Ltd:

–   "The payment of a dividend of £21,000 is more tax efficient than paying a salary bonus of £21,000 as you will pay income tax at only 25% on the dividend received, whereas you would pay income tax at 40% on a salary bonus. The dividend also avoids the need to pay national insurance contributions."

–   "There is no tax in respect of an interest free loan from an employer of less than £5,000."

–   "The provision of a company car is tax neutral as the cost of providing it is deductible in the corporation tax computation."

Stanley's proposed remuneration package from Landscape Ltd:

–   An annual salary of £50,000 and an annual dividend of approximately £21,000.

–   On 1 December 2013 an interest free loan of £3,600, which he intends to repay in two years time.

–   A company car with a cost when new of £11,400. The only costs incurred by the company in respect of this car will be lease rentals of £300 per month and business fuel of £100 per month.

–   The annual employment income benefit in respect of the car is to be taken as £3,420.

Landscape Ltd:

–   Will prepare accounts to 31 March each year.

–   Will pay corporation tax at the rate of 20%.

Required:

(a) (i)   Explain why there would be no capital gains tax liability on the transfer of Stanley's business to Landscape Ltd in exchange for shares.

Calculate the maximum loan account balance that Stanley could receive without giving rise to a capital gains tax liability and state the resulting capital gains tax base cost of the shares.   **(8 marks)**

(ii) Explain the benefit to Stanley of taking part of the payment for the sale of his business in the form of a loan account, which is to be paid out in cash at some time in the future.   **(1 mark)**

(b) Comment on the accuracy and completeness of the advice received by Stanley in respect of his remuneration package.

Supporting calculations are only required in respect of the company car.   **(9 marks)**

Ignore value added tax (VAT) in answering this question.

You may assume that the rates and allowances for the Financial year to 31 March 2013 and the tax year 2012/13 will continue to apply for the foreseeable future.

(Total: 18 marks)

4   Mahia Ltd is an unquoted, UK resident trading company formed in May 2005. One of its shareholders, Claus Rowen, intends to sell his shares back to Mahia Ltd on 31 July 2013. Another shareholder, Maude Brooke, intends to give some of her shares to her daughter, Tessa.

The following information has been extracted from client files and from meetings with the shareholders.

Mahia Ltd:

–   In May 2005 the company issued 40,000 shares at £3.40 per share as follows:

Claus Rowen	16,000
Charlotte Forde	12,000
Olaf Berne	12,000

–   Olaf sold his 12,000 shares to Maude Brooke on 1 October 2011 when they were worth £154,000.

Claus and Charlotte:

–   Have always lived in the UK.

–   Are higher rate taxpayers who use their capital gains tax annual exempt amount every year.

Maude:

–   Was born in the UK, but moved to Canada on 1 April 2009 with her daughter, Tessa.

–   Has not visited the UK since leaving for Canada, but will return to the UK permanently in December 2018.

–   Is employed in Canada with an annual salary equivalent to £70,000.

Sale of shares by Claus:

–   Charlotte and Maude want to expand the company's activities in the UK but Claus does not. The shareholders have been arguing over this matter for almost a year.

–   In order to enable the company to prosper, Claus has agreed to sell his shares to the company on 31 July 2013.

Gift of shares by Maude:

–   Maude will gift 4,000 shares in Mahia Ltd to her daughter, Tessa, on either 1 August 2013 or 1 June 2014.

–   She will delay the gift until 1 June 2014 (Tessa's wedding day) if this reduces the total tax due.

–   The tax due in Canada will be the same regardless of the date of the gift.

–   She has made no previous transfers of value for UK inheritance tax purposes.

–   For the purposes of this gift, you should assume that Maude will die on 31 December 2017.

Market values of shares in Mahia Ltd on all relevant dates are to be taken as:

Size of shareholding	Market value per share
%	£
< 25	10.20
25 – 35	14.40
> 35	38.60

Market values of the assets of Mahia Ltd on all relevant dates are to be taken as:

	£
Land and buildings used within the trade	1,400,000
Three machines of equal value used within the trade	15,000
Motor cars used by employees	45,000
Quoted shares	42,000
Inventory, trade receivables and cash	145,000

Required:

(a)   Advise Claus on the tax treatment of the proceeds he will receive in respect of the sale of his shares to Mahia Ltd.

Prepare a calculation of the net (after tax) proceeds from the sale based on your conclusions.   **(8 marks)**

(b)   Advise Maude on the UK tax consequences of gifting the shares to Tessa and prepare computations to determine on which of the two dates the gift should be made, if the total UK tax due on the gift is to be minimised.

Your answer should consider all relevant taxes.   **(10 marks)**

You may assume that the rates and allowances for the tax year 2012/13 will continue to apply for the foreseeable future.

(Total: 18 marks)

5 Vikram Bridge has been made redundant by Bart Industries Ltd, a company based in Birmingham. He intends to move to Scotland to start a new job with Dreamz Technology Ltd.

The following information has been extracted from client files and from meetings with Vikram.

Vikram Bridge:

− Is unmarried, but has been living with Alice Tate since 1999. The couple have four young children.

− Receives dividends of approximately £7,800 each year and makes annual capital gains of approximately £2,100 in respect of shares inherited from his mother.

− The couple have no sources of income other than Vikram's employment income and the £7,800 of dividends.

Made redundant by Bart Industries Ltd on 28 February 2013:

− Vikram's employment contract entitled him to two months' notice or two months salary in lieu of notice. On 28 February 2013 the company paid him his salary for the two-month period of £4,700, and asked him to leave immediately.

− On 30 April 2013 the company paid him a further £1,300 in respect of statutory redundancy, together with a non-contractual lump sum of £14,500, as a gesture of goodwill.

Job with Dreamz Technology Ltd:

− Starts on 1 October 2013 with an annual salary of £45,480.

− The company will contribute £9,400 in October 2013 towards Vikram's costs of moving to Scotland.

− In November 2014, the company will issue free shares to all of its employees. Vikram will be issued with 200 shares, expected to be worth approximately £2,750.

Moving house:

− Vikram's house in Birmingham is fairly small; he intends to buy a much larger one in Glasgow.

− The cost of moving to Glasgow, including the stamp duty land tax in respect of the purchase of his new house, will be approximately £12,500.

− To finance the purchase of the house in Glasgow Vikram will sell a house he owns in Wales, in August 2013.

House in Wales:

− Was given to Vikram by his mother on 1 September 2004, when it was worth £145,000.

− Vikram's mother continued to live in the house until her death on 1 May 2013, when she left the whole of her estate to Vikram.

− At the time of her death the house had severe structural problems and was valued at £140,000.

− Vikram has subsequently spent £18,000 improving the property and expects to be able to sell it for £195,000.

– Vikram is keen to reduce the tax payable on the sale of the house and is willing to transfer the house, or part of it, to Alice prior to the sale if that would help.

Required:

Prepare explanations, including supporting calculations where appropriate, of the following issues suitable for inclusion in a letter to Vikram.

(a) The taxable gain on the sale of the house in Wales in August 2013, together with the potential effect of transferring the house, or part of it, to Alice prior to the sale, and any other advice you consider helpful. **(3 marks)**

(b) The inheritance tax implications in respect of the house in Wales on the death of Vikram's mother. **(2 marks)**

(c) The income tax treatment of redundancy payments received from Bart Industries Ltd and Vikram's taxable income in 2013/14. **(4 marks)**

(d) The income tax treatment of the receipt by Vikram of the shares in Dreamz Technology Ltd. **(3 marks)**

(e) How Vikram's job with Dreamz Technology Ltd will affect the amount and date of payment of the income tax due on his dividend income for 2015/16 and future years.

(6 marks)

Ignore national insurance contributions in answering this question.

You may assume that the rates and allowances for the tax year 2012/13 will continue to apply for the foreseeable future. **(Total 18 marks)**

Section 4

ANSWERS TO PILOT PAPER EXAM QUESTIONS

SECTION A

1   HUTT PLC

Key answer tips

The first part of the question covers standard use of losses within a group to achieve the 'most tax efficient' result. However, you must be careful of the complication, which is that Rainbow has most of its profits taxed abroad, so any group relief claim must not prejudice the double tax relief available.

In the report section, the examiner has set out the structure and you need to stick with this. Use the headings given with sub headings for each separate issue.

In discussing Lucia's losses for (b)(i) the examiner has given you a clue to the fact that they will be disallowed by telling you that the company's activities immediately before the sale are negligible.

In discussing VAT registration in part (ii) it is always necessary to consider whether the future test may be applicable – students often miss this. VAT on exports is an important exam topic.

Finally in part (iii) note the instruction to consider all relevant taxes, which for a building transfer will always include stamp duty land tax and VAT.

(a)   **Options available in respect of the trading losses of Hutt plc of £105,000**

    (i)   **Within Hutt plc**

        The loss can be offset against the total profits of Hutt plc for the year ended 31 March 2013.

	£
Capital gain	144,000
Less: capital loss brought forward	(98,000)
	46,000
Rental income	65,000
Interest income	2,000
Taxable total profits	113,000

Hutt plc, Rainbow Ltd and Coronet Ltd are associated as Hutt plc controls the other two companies. As a result, the lower limit for the purposes of determining the rate of corporation tax is reduced from £300,000 to £100,000.

Accordingly, Hutt plc will pay corporation tax at 24% less marginal relief. This means that the first £100,000 of the company's profits will be taxed at 20% and the final £13,000 at the marginal rate of 25%.

A current period offset has to be made before losses can be carried back to the previous twelve months. The trading loss for the year ended 31 March 2013 is less than the taxable total profits and therefore a claim to carry back the losses cannot be made.

(ii) **Group relief**

Hutt plc, Rainbow Ltd and Coronet Ltd are in a group for group relief purposes as Hutt plc controls at least 75% of the other two companies. Any amount of the £105,000 loss can be surrendered to each of the two subsidiary companies in order to reduce their taxable total profits. However, the maximum surrender is restricted to the taxable total profits of the recipient company.

Coronet Ltd has taxable total profits of £81,000 (£63,000 + £18,000). As stated above, due to the number of associates, the lower limit is reduced to £100,000 (£300,000 × ⅓). Accordingly, Coronet Ltd will pay tax at 20%.

The taxable total profits of Rainbow Ltd exceed £500,000 (£1,500,000 × ⅓) and therefore, the company will pay UK corporation tax at the rate of 24%.

However, Rainbow Ltd has a permanent establishment in Prismovia as it manufactures and trades in that country. The profits arising in Prismovia will be taxed in that country at 22%. Double tax relief will be available in the UK in respect of the Prismovian tax suffered, up to a maximum of the UK tax on the Prismovian profits; any surrender to Rainbow Ltd must ensure that relief for the foreign tax suffered is not lost.

The maximum surrender that can be made to Rainbow Ltd whilst preserving relief for the foreign tax is calculated as follows.

	£
Trading profit ((£800,000 × 2%) / 24%)	66,667
Interest income	57,000
Maximum surrender	123,667

Tutorial note

The differential in tax rates in the UK and Prismovia is 2% (24% − 22%).

All of the interest income is taxable at 24% and and trading profits left to be charged to tax after loss relief will be taxable at an effective rate of 2%.

Therefore the trading profits that need to be included in taxable total profits to cover DTR will be 2/24ths of the trading profit for the year (see proof below).

(iii) **Recommendations**

In order to maximise the tax saved the losses should be offset against the profits taxed at 25% in Hutt plc and the profits taxed at 24% in Rainbow Ltd whilst preserving the relief for the foreign tax suffered.

Accordingly, £13,000 of the losses should be offset against the taxable total profits in Hutt plc with the balance of £92,000 (£105,000 – £13,000) surrendered to Rainbow Ltd. This is less than £123,667, and therefore, preserves relief for all of the foreign tax.

When making a claim to offset a company's trading loss against its total profits, it is not possible to specify the amount to be offset; all of the losses available will be offset subject to the level of taxable profits. Accordingly, in order to achieve the desired result, the two claims must be made in the following order.

1 An election to surrender losses of £92,000 to Rainbow Ltd. This must be made by 31 March 2015 (i.e. within one year of the filing date of the claimant company's tax return). Both Rainbow Ltd and Hutt plc must elect.

2 An election to offset the remaining losses (£13,000) against the total profits of Hutt plc should be submitted by the same date (i.e. within two years of the end of the period in which the loss was made).

Tutorial note

The tax computation of Rainbow Ltd for the year ended 31 March 2013 following the group relief claim is set out below. Group relief of £57,000 is offset against the interest income with the balance of £35,000 (£92,000 – £57,000) being offset against the trading profit in order to maximise the double tax relief

	£
Trading profit (£800,000 – £35,000)	*765,000*
Interest income (£57,000 – £57,000)	*–*
Taxable total profits	*765,000*
Corporation tax @ 24%	*183,600*
Less: Double tax relief (£800,000 × 22%)	*(176,000)*
Corporation tax payable	*7,600*

Tutorial note

Hutt plc has losses below the maximum surrender. However, if Hutt plc had trading losses in excess of £123,667, the maximum group relief claim that should be made to preserve DTR would be only £123,667 as shown below:

	£
Trading profit (£800,000 – £66,667)	*733,333*
Interest income (£57,000 – £57,000)	*–*
Taxable total profits	*733,333*
Corporation tax @ 24%	*176,000*
Less: Double tax relief (£800,000 × 22%)	*(176,000)*
Corporation tax payable	*Nil*

(b) **Report to the management of Hutt plc**

To: The management of Hutt plc

From: Tax advisers

Date: 1 June 2013

Subject: The acquisition of Lucia Ltd

(i)   **The purchase price**

Valuation of the trading losses in Lucia Ltd

Lucia Ltd has no profits in the year ended 31 March 2013 or the previous year against which to offset the losses.

The trading losses arose before Lucia Ltd joined the Hutt plc group, and therefore, they cannot be surrendered to any of the group members.

The losses cannot be carried forward as there will be a change of ownership of Lucia Ltd after its activities have become negligible. Losses arising prior to the change of ownership cannot be offset against profits arising once the trade has been revived.

The losses cannot be used, and therefore, they have no value to Hutt plc.

Loan from BHC Bank

Hutt plc is to enter into a loan relationship with BHC Bank. Any amounts charged to the company's profit and loss account in respect of the relationship are allowable deductions for tax purposes. Accordingly, a tax deduction is available for the interest and the loan arrangement fee on the accruals basis.

On the assumption that the loan arrangement fee is charged to the profit and loss account in full in the year ended 31 March 2014, the total amount charged in the accounts will be £11,731 (£1,400 + (£190,000 x 7.25% × 9/12)).

The income from which this amount can be deducted in the corporation tax computation depends on the use made of the finance obtained.

	Finance		Allowable cost
	£		£
For the purpose of investments:			
Acquisition of Lucia Ltd	130,000		
Repairs to Hutt Tower	45,000		
	175,000	175/190 × £11,731	10,805
For the purpose of the trade:			
Working capital requirements	15,000	15/190 × £11,731	926
Total finance obtained	190,000		11,731

Where the finance has been used for trading purposes, the cost of £926 is deductible in arriving at Hutt plc's taxable trading income.

Where the finance has been used for non-trading purposes, the cost of £10,805 is deductible from Hutt plc's interest income in respect of loan relationships. This results in a deficit, or loss, of £8,805 (£10,805 – £2,000) in the year ended 31 March 2014.

The deficit can be:

- Offset against other income and gains of Hutt plc of the same accounting period.
- Offset against the interest income of Hutt plc of the previous 12 months.
- Surrendered as group relief to companies within the group relief group.
- Carried forward and offset against future non-trading income and gains.

The most tax efficient use of the deficit will depend on the level of profits in Hutt plc and the other group companies in the year ended 31 March 2014.

(ii) **VAT issues**

Registration

All the supplies made by Lucia Ltd are taxable supplies for the purposes of VAT. The company must register for VAT:

- If its taxable supplies in the previous 12 months exceed £77,000; or
- If its taxable supplies in the next 30 days are expected to exceed £77,000.

It is anticipated that the company's supplies in the nine months ended 31 March 2014 will be £702,000 and that these supplies will accrue evenly over the period. This amounts to supplies of £78,000 per month. Accordingly, Lucia Ltd must register with effect from 1 July 2013 and must notify HMRC by 30 July 2013.

Lucia Ltd intends to make supplies to non-VAT registered customers in the European Union (EU). If Lucia Ltd is responsible for the delivery of the goods it should be aware that once its supplies in any one particular member state exceed that state's 'distance selling' threshold, it may be required to register for VAT in that state.

VAT in respect of the nine months ended 31 March 2014

	£
Output tax	
UK customers – VAT registered (£85,000 × 20%)	17,000
UK customers – non-VAT registered (£25,000 × 20%)	5,000
EU customers – VAT registered – zero-rated	–
EU customers – non-VAT registered (£70,000 × 20%)	14,000
Other non-UK customers – zero-rated	–
Acquisition from Dabet Gmbh (£17,000 × 20%)	3,400
	39,400
Input tax	
In respect of purchases from UK businesses (9 × £7,800)	70,200
Acquisition from Dabet Gmbh	3,400
	73,600
Repayment of VAT due (£73,600 – £39,400)	34,200

Tutorial note

VAT must be charged on supplies to all UK customers, whether or not they are registered for VAT.

Supplies to EU customers are zero-rated in the country of origin, unless the customer is not registered. In this case, VAT is charged at the point of origin at the appropriate rate. Therefore Lucia Ltd must charge 20% VAT in the normal way (i.e. the origin system).

All supplies to non-EU customers are zero-rated, regardless of whether or not the customer is registered.

An acquisition from a VAT registered EU supplier will be treated as zero-rated in the country of origin, however is chargeable at the appropriate rate in force in the country of destination. Therefore Lucia Ltd must account for output VAT at 20% on the purchase from Dabet Gmbh, but can reclaim the equivalent amount of input VAT in the same quarter (i.e. the destination system).

Disadvantage of entering into a group VAT registration

Lucia Ltd makes mainly zero-rated supplies and is in a VAT repayment position. It can improve its cash flow position by accounting for VAT monthly and receiving monthly repayments of VAT. It would not be in a position to do this if it were to register in a VAT group.

Under a group registration, the group's representative member will account for VAT payable to HMRC on behalf of all group companies. It may be some time before Lucia Ltd's accounting system is aligned with that of Hutt plc. The existence of two different systems may create administrative difficulties in preparing a group VAT return.

Note: Only one of the above disadvantages was required

(iii)   **The office building**

Tax implications of the sale of the office building from Coronet Ltd to Lucia Ltd

Corporation tax

At the time of the transfer, Coronet Ltd and Lucia Ltd will be in a capital gains group as they will both be 75% subsidiaries of Hutt plc. Therefore the transfer of the office building will be deemed to occur at no gain, no loss. Lucia Ltd will have a capital gains tax base cost in the building equal to the cost to Coronet Ltd plus indexation allowance up to the date of the transfer

Value added tax (VAT)

The transfer will be outside the scope of VAT if the two companies are in a VAT group.

If the two companies are registered separately, the treatment depends on whether the building is less than three years old or if Coronet Ltd has opted to tax the building. If so, then the transfer to Lucia Ltd will be standard rated and VAT must be charged. If not, the transfer will be an exempt supply.

Stamp duty land tax

There will be no stamp duty land tax on the transfer as both companies are 75% subsidiaries of Hutt plc.

Relief of the gain on the sale of the office building to Vac Ltd

Lucia Ltd has made two capital disposals at a loss.

The first property in Leeds was sold before Lucia Ltd became a member of the Hutt plc group. As a result, the capital loss can only be deducted from capital gains made by Lucia Ltd on assets it owned when it joined the group, or ones bought after from unconnected parties and used for the purposes of their own business.

The loss on the Manchester property will be realised after the company joined the group and can therefore be set-off against any gains made by Lucia Ltd or other group companies, including the gain on the sale of the office building to Vac Ltd.

It is not necessary to transfer the office building to Lucia Ltd before the sale as Lucia Ltd and Coronet Ltd can make a joint election to reallocate the gain to Lucia Ltd. The election must be submitted by 31 March 2017 (i.e. within two years of the end of the accounting period in which the disposal of the office building occurs).

Alternatively the loss on the Manchester property could be transferred to Coronet Ltd leaving the gain chargeable in their computation. The election to transfer the loss must be submitted by 31 March 2016, as the loss arises in the year ended 31 March 2014.

As both companies are paying tax at 24% either would produce the same tax cost for the group.

The tax saving would be £14,400 (£60,000 x 24%).

ACCA marking scheme		
		Marks
(a)	Hutt plc trading losses	
	Within Hutt plc	
	Current year offset	0.5
	Available profits	1.0
	Application of the corporation tax limits	1.0
	Effective rate of tax/relief	1.0
	No carry back opportunity	0.5
	Group Relief	
	Relevant companies	0.5
	Available relief	0.5
	Coronet Ltd:	
	Available profits	0.5
	Effective rate of tax	1.0
	Rainbow Ltd	
	Effective rate of UK tax	0.5
	Tax position in Prismovia	1.0
	Effect of DTR	2.0
	Recommendation	
	Identify correct objective	1.0
	Hutt plc – profits at 25%	0.5
	Rainbow Ltd – the balance	0.5
	Order of elections	1.0
	Group relief election – both companies/time limit	1.0
	Current year offset election/time limit	1.0
		15.0
	Maximum	13.0
(b) (i)	The purchase price	
	Trading losses:	
	No current relief in Lucia Ltd	0.5
	No group relief with reason	1.0
	No carry forward with reasons	1.5
	Conclusion	0.5
	Loan from BHC Bank	
	Tax deduction per accounts treatment	1.0
	Total amount allowable in the period	0.5
	Amount relating to trading purpose	1.0
	Amount relating to non-trading purpose	2.0
	Uses of deficit	2.0
	Recommendation	0.5
		10.5
	Maximum	9.0

				Marks
(b)	(ii)	VAT issues		
		Registration		
			Historic and future limits	1.0
			Registration and notification dates	1.0
			Distance selling thresholds	0.5
		Calculation		
			Output tax	2.5
			Input tax	1.0
		Disadvantage of group VAT registration		
			– either of Lucia Ltd in repayment position; or	
			administrative difficulties	1.0
				———
				7.0
			Maximum	6.0
				———
	(iii)	The office building		
		Sale from Coronet Ltd to Lucia Ltd		
			Capital gain	
			CGT group	0.5
			Consequences	1.0
			VAT	
			If group registration	0.5
			If no group registration	1.5
			Stamp duty land tax	1.0
		Sale of building to Vac Ltd		
			Pre-entry losses	
			Identify	0.5
			Consequences	1.0
			Loss on Manchester property	1.0
			Election re notional transfer – availability	1.0
			Impact of tax rates on transfer	0.5
		Both companies and time limit		1.0
				———
				9.5
			Maximum	9.0
				———
		Format and style		
		Appropriate style and presentation		1.0
		Effectiveness of communication		1.0
				———
				2.0
				———
Total				39
				———

2   PILAR MARENO

Key answer tips

This is a tricky question asking for a decision on whether a self employed consultant should take on a new contract and how the contract should be carried out.

The question requires quite careful calculations of the net of tax cost of each option and it is important to consider all relevant taxes – in this case NIC and VAT as well as income tax.

> Note also that the examiner gives marks for recognising the relevant issues as well as for calculations, so it is important to state relevant points even if you cannot see exactly how to calculate the tax implications.

To: The files

From: Tax assistant

Date: 1 June 2013

Subject: Pilar Mareno – Business expansion

This memorandum considers the implications of Pilar Mareno (PM) accepting the DWM plc contract.

Rationale and approach

PM has decided to accept the contract if it generates at least £15,000 per annum on average for the family after all costs and taxes.

PM will either employ her husband, Alec, or use the services of Max Wallen, and will either buy or lease a van. However, it can be seen from workings 3 and 4 that it is cheaper to buy rather than lease the van, and therefore, there are only two options to consider.

- Employ Alec and buy a van – Appendix 1
- Use Max Wallen and buy a van – Appendix 2.

Summary of findings

The contract generates sufficient after tax income whether PM buys a van and employs Alec or uses Max Wallen. However, the issues raised below in relation to PM employing Alec should be considered before a decision is made.

Issues in respect of Pilar employing Alec

1   Alec has worked for a UK bank for many years. It is risky to give up an apparently secure job in exchange for a two year contract requiring two days work a week and other, as yet unidentified, part-time work.

    Accordingly, Alec should obtain advice as regards his personal situation. If we are asked to provide this advice we must recognise that Pilar and Alec would be two separate clients. The work would have to be managed in such a way as to ensure that we do not allow the interests of Pilar to adversely affect those of Alec or vice versa.

2   PM and Alec should consider forming a partnership. This would reduce national insurance contributions as Alec would only pay 9% on his share of the profit plus Class 2 at £2.65 per week whereas the cost of employer and employee Class 1 contributions where Alec is an employee is 13.8% and 12% respectively.

    Alec's profit share could be more than £8,600. This would enable income currently taxed at 40% in PM's hands to be taxed at 20% in Alec's hands.

    However, this saving in income tax would be offset by increased national insurance costs as the national insurance on PM's marginal income is only 2% whereas Alec would pay 9%.

Employment status of Max Wallen

Max's employment status will be determined by reference to all of the facts surrounding his agreement with PM.

Factors indicating employee status

1   It appears that Max has to do the work himself and cannot use a substitute.

2   Max is to be paid by the day rather than by reference to the performance of particular tasks.

3   Max is to be paid for the days when he is sick.

4   Max is to be provided with the specialist software he needs to do the work.

Factors indicating self-employed status

1   Max provides his own laptop computer.

Tutorial note:

Remember that no one factor is conclusive. HMRC will look at all of the facts to decide Max's status.

There is insufficient information provided regarding other factors, such as the level of control over Max's work, to justify their inclusion within the terms of the brief provided.

Without further information a conclusion cannot be drawn.

APPENDIX 1 – EMPLOY ALEC AND BUY A VAN

	£
Profit on contract	47,000
Irrecoverable VAT due to partial exemption (W1)	(9,205)
Salary paid to Alec	(8,600)
Class 1 secondary NIC re Alec ((£8,600 – £7,488) × 13.8%)	(153)
	29,042
Income tax and Class 4 NIC due (£29,042 × (40% + 2%))	(12,198)
	16,844
Increase in Alec's income (W2)	1,088
Purchase of van (less than cost of leasing van) (W3 and W4)	(1,696)
Income of family after all taxes	16,236

Tutorial note:

Pilar requires additional income for the family of £15,000 before agreeing to enter into the contract. Consideration is therefore needed of the affect on both Pilar's and Alec's position.

The salary paid to Alec is a cost as far as Pilar is concerned and therefore tax allowable. The effect of the salary on Alec's income is calculated in (W2) below.

APPENDIX 2 – USE MAX WALLEN AND BUY A VAN

	£
Profit on contract	47,000
Irrecoverable VAT due to partial exemption (W1)	(9,205)
Fees paid to Max Wallen (100 × £75)	(7,500)
Irrecoverable VAT on fees (£7,500 × 20% × 35%)	(525)
	29,770
Income tax and Class 4 NIC due (£29,770 × (40% + 2%))	(12,503)
	17,267
Purchase of van (less than cost of leasing van) (W3 and W4)	(1,696)
	15,571
Income of family after all taxes	15,571

Tutorial note:

There are no NICs payable by Pilar on Max's fees if she uses Max on a self-employed contract basis.

Workings

(W1) Irrecoverable VAT due to partial exemption

Without the new contract:

	£
In respect of the existing business (£100,000 × 20% × 35%)	7,000

This is below the annual de minimis limit of £7,500 (£625 × 12) and is fully recoverable.

With the new contract:

	£
In respect of the existing business (as above)	7,000
In respect of the costs of the DWM contract (£31,500 × 20% × 35%)	2,205
	9,205

This exceeds the annual de minimis limit and is irrecoverable.

Tutorial note:

Pilar's taxable turnover is not affected by the sale of the van as it is a capital asset.

Neither of the other two de-minimis tests are relevant here as they require either the total input tax to be not more than £625 per month on average, or the difference between the total input tax and the input tax on directly attributable taxable supplies to be not more than £625 per month on average.

(W2) Increase in Alec's income

	£
Increase in gross salary ((£8,600 + £10,000) − £17,000)	1,600
Less: Income tax and NIC on additional salary (£1,600 × (20% + 12%))	(512)
Increase in after tax income	1,088

Tutorial note:

At the margin, Alec pays income tax at the basic rate of 20% and NIC at 12%.

Alec will also be better off because he now has two jobs, and Class 1 NIC is calculated independently for each employment (unless they are related). So in each job the first £7,605 of salary has no NIC and he would save £913 (£7,605 × 12%). This point has not been included in the calculation as the details of his other employment are not known.

(W3) Cost of purchasing van

	£
Net cost (£7,800 − £2,500) for two year period	5,300
Income tax and Class 4 NIC saved (£5,300 × (40% + 2%))	(2,226)
Irrecoverable VAT (£7,800 × 20% × 35%)	546
Income tax and Class 4 NIC saved (£546 × (40% + 2%))	(229)
	3,391
Average cost per year (£3,391 × ½)	1,696

Tutorial note:

The net cost of the van will be tax allowable through the capital allowances system and therefore Income tax and Class 4 NICs will be saved.

There will be irrecoverable VAT of 35% of the cost of the van as the business is partially exempt, but this will also be tax allowable and save both income tax and NICs.

(W4) Cost of leasing van (per year)

	£
Lease rentals (£300 × 12)	3,600
Income tax and Class 4 NIC saved (£3,600 × (40% + 2%))	(1,512)
Irrecoverable VAT (£3,600 × 20% × 35%)	252
Income tax and Class 4 NIC saved (£252 × (40% + 2%))	(106)
	2,234

As the annual cost of purchasing the van (W3) is less than the costs of leasing, all further calculations in the Appendices are based on the decision that Pilar will purchase the van.

ACCA marking scheme		
		Marks
(1)	Calculations	
	Employ Alec:	
	Net profit of contract	0.5
	Alec's salary and class 1 secondary NIC	1.5
	Irrecoverable VAT/purchase of van	0.5
	Tax and NIC saved	0.5
	Increase in Alec's income:	
	Identification of issue	1.0
	Calculation	1.5
	Use Max:	
	Fees paid	0.5
	Irrecoverable VAT on fees	0.5
	Tax and NIC saved	0.5
	Supporting calculations	
	Irrecoverable VAT:	
	Identification of issue	1.0
	Current partial exemption position	1.0
	Application of de minimis	1.0
	Irrecoverable amount with new contract	1.0
	Purchase of van:	
	Net cost	0.5
	Irrecoverable VAT	1.0
	Tax and NIC saved	1.0
	Cost per year	0.5
	Leasing van	
	Rentals	0.5
	Irrecoverable VAT	1.0
	Tax and NIC saved	1.0
		——
		16.5
	Maximum	16.0
		——
(2)	Rationale and summary	
	Reference to Pilar's income criterion	1.0
	Conclusion re van and implications	1.0
	Summary of findings	1.0
		——
		3.0
	Maximum	2.0
		——
(3)	Employment of Alec	
	Secure job, short-term contract	1.5
	Use of partnership	2.0
	Alec would be a separate client from Pilar	1.0
		——
		4.5
	Maximum	2.0
(4)	Employment status of Max	
	Depends on all of the facts	0.5
	Each valid factor – ½ mark (max 5 factors)	2.5
		——
		3.0
	Format and style	
	Appropriate style and presentation	1.0
	Effectiveness of communication	1.0
		——
	Maximum	2.0
		——
Total		25
		——

3 STANLEY BEECH

Key answer tips

The key to success in part (a) is understanding that Stanley can afford to have some chargeable gains after incorporation relief, because these can be covered by his capital losses and the annual exempt amount.

In part (b) it is important to answer the question set and not do unnecessary calculations. Also remember that an owner managed company like this will always be a close company and look out for any close company implications.

(a) **Transfer of the business to Landscape Ltd**

    (i) **Capital gains tax liability**

Where all of the assets of Stanley's business are transferred to Landscape Ltd as a going concern wholly in exchange for shares, any capital gains arising are relieved via incorporation relief such that no capital gains tax liability arises.

However, where part of the payment received from the company is in the form of a loan account, Stanley will have chargeable gains as set out below.

For Stanley to have no liability to capital gains tax in 2013/14, assuming he has no other capital gains in the year, his chargeable gains must be covered by his capital losses brought forward (£11,400) and the annual exempt amount of £10,600.

	£
Gain on building (£87,000 – £46,000)	41,000
Gain on goodwill	24,000
	─────
Total capital gains before reliefs	65,000
	─────

Incorporation relief should therefore be:	
(£65,000 – £11,400 – 10,600)	43,000

Therefore the MV of the shares to be accepted should be:

$$£43,000 = £65,000 \times \frac{\text{MV of shares}}{£118,000}$$

MV of shares = £78,062

Therefore the loan account to accept as part of the consideration can be up to the value of £39,938 (£118,000 − £78,062) and there will be no capital gains tax arising on the transfer.

The shares will have a capital gains tax base cost of £35,062 computed as:

	£
MV of shares (see above)	78,062
Less: Incorporation relief	(43,000)
Base cost of shares	35,062

Tutorial note:

Proof that incorporation relief of £43,000 will avoid a CGT liability is as follows:

	£
Total capital gains	*65,000*
Less: Incorporation relief	
$£65,000 \times \dfrac{£78,062}{£118,000}$	*(43,000)*
	22,000
Less: Capital losses	*(11,400)*
	10,600
Less: Annual exempt amount	*(10,600)*
Taxable gains	*Nil*

No Entrepreneurs' Relief is used as there is no chargeable gain. This should not be an issue providing Stanley retains the shares in the company for at least 12 months before he disposes of them.

(ii) **The benefit of using a loan account**

The loan account crystallises capital gains at the time of incorporation without giving rise to a tax liability due to the availability of capital losses, and the annual exempt amount.

This reduces the gains deferred against the base cost of the shares in Landscape Ltd from £65,000 to £43,000 such that any future gains on the disposal of the shares will be smaller.

Stanley can extract the loan account of £39,938 from Landscape Ltd in the future with no 'tax cost', by having the loan repaid.

Tutorial note:

The subsequent disposal of the shares will be eligible for Entrepreneurs' relief provided the conditions are satisfied, as none of Stanley's lifetime allowance of £10,000,000 has been utilised.

(b) **Advice on Stanley's remuneration package**

(i) **Dividend**

The advice in respect of the dividend is accurate but not complete as it ignores the cost to Landscape Ltd. Because Stanley owns Landscape Ltd, he must consider the effect on the company's position as well as his own.

Dividends are not tax deductible. The profits paid out as a dividend to Stanley will have been subject to corporation tax at 20%. On the other hand, Landscape Ltd will obtain a tax deduction at 20% for a salary bonus together with the related national insurance contributions.

There will be an overall tax saving from paying a dividend as opposed to a salary bonus. However the benefit will not be as great as suggested by the advice that Stanley has received due to the different treatment of the two payments in hands of the company.

(ii) **Interest free loan**

The advice in respect of the loan is again accurate but not complete. The loan will not give rise to an employment income benefit as it is for not more than £5,000, but the advice again ignores the position of the company.

As the company is controlled by Stanley, Landscape Ltd will be a close company. Accordingly, the loan to Stanley is a loan to a participator in a close company, and as Stanley owns more than 5% of the company's share capital there is no de minimis in this case.

Thus, Landscape Ltd must pay an amount equal to 25% of the loan (£900) to HMRC. The payment will be due on 1 January 2015 (i.e. nine months and one day after the end of the accounting period in which the loan is made).

When the loan is repaid by Stanley, Landscape Ltd may reclaim the £900. The repayment by HMRC will be made nine months and one day after the end of the accounting period in which the loan is repaid.

(iii) **Company car**

The advice in respect of the company car is not correct because of the difference in the tax rates applying to the company and to Stanley, and the liability to Class 1A national insurance contributions.

Tax cost of providing car:	£
Class 1A national insurance contributions (£3,420 × 13.8%)	472
Income tax on benefit (£3,420 × 40%)	1,368
	1,840

Tax saved:

Cost of providing car (£400 × 12)	4,800
Class 1A national insurance contributions	472
	5,272
Corporation tax @ 20%	1,054
Net tax cost (£1,840 – £1,054)	786

ACCA marking scheme			
			Marks
(a)	(i)	Split of consideration	
		Incorporation relief – 3 conditions	1.5
		Amount of future cash payment:	
		Rationale – gains to equal capital losses and annual exempt amount	1.5
		Gains on transfer of business	1.0
		Gains after incorporation relief:	
		Incorporation relief	1.0
		Calculation of gains after incorporation relief	0.5
		Solving to find value of the loan account	1.0
		Entrepreneurs' Relief	1.0
		CGT base cost of shares:	
		Value of assets transferred for shares	0.5
		Incorporation relief	1.0
	(ii)	Benefit of using a loan account	
		Capital gains	1.0
		Extract funds with no tax cost	0.5
			10.5
		Maximum	9.0
(b)		Advice on remuneration package	
		Dividend	
		Advice is correct but incomplete with reason	1.0
		CT position re dividend	0.5
		CT position re bonus	0.5
		Conclusion with reason	1.0
		Interest free loan	
		Advice is correct but incomplete with reason	1.0
		Close company	0.5
		Loan to a participator and reason	1.0
		Tax due /when	1.0
		Repayment position	0.5
		Company car	
		The advice is not correct with reason	1.0
		Calculation	
		Tax cost	1.0
		Tax saving	1.0
			10.0
		Maximum	9.0
Total			18

4   MAHIA LTD

Key answer tips

It is important when dealing with purchase of own shares to state all the factors that make a transaction either income or capital. Most of the marks for part (a) are available for this with only a few for the calculation of the after tax proceeds.

In part (b), even if you missed the tricky point that the percentage holdings of the remaining shareholders increase after the cancellation of Claus's shares, you could still pick up most of the marks for this section.

(a)   **Sale of shares in Mahia Ltd**

The proceeds received on a purchase by a company of its own shares are subject to either income tax or capital gains tax depending on the circumstances.

The normal assumption on a purchase of own shares by a company is that any payment you receive for the shares, over and above the amount originally subscribed for them, would be an income distribution, and treated in the same way as a payment of a dividend. The net amount received, less the amount originally subscribed, would be grossed up by 100/90 and included in your taxable income.

Alternatively, where the transaction satisfies the conditions set out below, the proceeds are treated as capital proceeds giving rise to a capital gain.

Your proposed sale of shares to Mahia Ltd satisfies these conditions and will therefore give rise to a capital gain.

- Mahia Ltd is an unquoted trading company.

- The purchase of shares is for the benefit of the company's trade as the disagreement between you and your sisters is having an adverse effect on the company's trade.

- You are resident and ordinarily resident in the UK.

- You have owned the shares for more than five years.

- You are selling all of your shares such that your holding is reduced by at least 25% and you will own less than 30% of Mahia Ltd following the sale.

- The purchase is not part of a scheme designed to avoid tax.

Advance clearance can be obtained from HM Revenue and Customs, to confirm that the capital treatment applies to a purchase of own shares.

The capital gains tax arising on the sale and the net cash proceeds after tax will be:

Number of shares sold (16,000 / 40,000)	40%

	£
Gain qualifying for Entrepreneurs' relief	
Proceeds (16,000 × £38.60)	617,600
Less: Cost (16,000 × £3.40)	(54,400)
Chargeable gain	563,200
Capital gains tax (£563,200 × 10%)	56,320
Proceeds after tax (£617,600 − £56,320)	561,280

Tutorial note:

Entrepreneurs' relief is available as Claus is disposing of shares in his personal trading company (i.e. he has more than a 5% holding) and he is an employee of the company.

Claus has already used his CGT annual exempt amount, therefore all of the remaining gain is taxed at 10%.

Following the purchase of its own shares from Claus, Mahia Ltd will cancel the shares. The company will therefore have 24,000 issued shares with effect from 1 August 2013.

(b) **Gift to Tessa**

Capital gains tax (CGT)

Maude lives in Canada and is non-UK resident and not-ordinarily resident. In addition, she is not a temporary non-resident for the purposes of capital gains tax as her stay in Canada will be for more than five tax years.

Accordingly, there will be no UK CGT on the gift of the shares to Tessa.

Even if Maude were a temporary non-resident, there would be no capital gains tax on the gift of the shares as she acquired them after she left the UK.

Inheritance tax (IHT)

As the shares are situated in the UK, UK IHT will be due on any transfers of value concerning them, regardless of the domicile of the transferor. Therefore, we do not need to consider Maude's domicile.

The gift by Maude to Tessa will be a potentially exempt transfer (PET) and no IHT will be payable. In addition, if Maude were to survive seven years from the date of the gift, there would be no IHT to pay on death.

However, the question asks us to assume that Maude will die on 31 December 2017. As this date is within seven years of the proposed dates of the gift, there would be a potential liability to IHT on death for each proposed date as follows:

Gift on 1 August 2013

	£
Value of shares before gift (12,000 × £38.60 (50% holding)) (Note 1)	463,200
Value of shares after gift (8,000 × £14.40 (33.3% holding))	(115,200)
Transfer of value	348,000
Less: BPR (Note 2)	(Nil)
Annual exemptions for 2013/14 and 2012/13	(6,000)
Taxable amount	342,000
IHT (40% × (£342,000 – £325,000 NRB available))	6,800
Less: Taper relief (4 to 5 years) (£6,800 × 40%)	(2,720)
Potential IHT payable (Note 3)	4,080

Tutorial note:

1. *On 1 August 2013 Mahia Ltd will have 24,000 issued shares as the shares sold by Claus to the company will have been cancelled, therefore Maude's holding before the gift will be a 50% holding.*

2. *BPR is not available as Maude acquired the shares on 1 October 2011 and therefore has not owned the shares for two years.*

3. *Double tax relief may be available to reduce this UK liability, in respect of any inheritance taxes payable in Canada.*

Gift on 1 June 2014

	£
Transfer of value (as above)	348,000
Less: BPR (W)	
$£348,000 \times \dfrac{£1,605,000}{£1,647,000}$	(339,126)
	8,874
Less: Marriage exemption	(5,000)
Annual exemptions for 2014/15 and 2013/14 (part only)	(3,874)
Taxable amount	Nil

Conclusion

Maude should therefore make the gift on 1 June 2014 as there would be no potential IHT liability due to the availability of BPR.

However, this presupposes that Tessa will continue to own the shares or replacement business property up to the date of Maude's death on 31 December 2017, and so preserve the entitlement to BPR.

If these conditions are not satisfied BPR is denied and a potential liability would arise. This would still be lower than potential liability if the gift were in August 2013, due to the availability of the marriage exemption.

Stamp duty

As the transfer of shares is made by way of gift (i.e. for no consideration), no stamp duty is payable.

Working: Restriction of BPR due to excepted assets in the company

	£
MV of assets	
(£1,400,000 + £15,000 + £45,000 + £145,000 + £42,000)	1,647,000
Less: MV of excepted assets (Quoted shares)	(42,000)
MV of assets excluding excepted assets	1,605,000

ACCA marking scheme		
		Marks
(a)	Sale of shares by Claus	
	Purchase of own shares	
	Identify and distinguish between the two possible treatments	1.0
	CGT treatment applies	1.0
	Reasons why:	
	Unquoted trading company	0.5
	Resident and ordinarily resident	0.5
	Owned for more than 5 years	0.5
	Not part of a scheme to avoid tax	0.5
	For benefit of company's trade with	1.0
	Reduction in holding criteria	1.0
	Availability of advance clearance	1.0
	Calculation	
	Gain	1.0
	Effect of Entrepreneurs' relief on tax charge	1.0
	Net of tax proceeds	0.5
		9.5
	Maximum	8.0

			Marks
(b)	**Gift to Tessa**		
	CGT		
		No CGT due	0.5
		Reasons why:	
		Not resident or ordinarily resident	0.5
		Asset acquired after becoming resident abroad	0.5
		Not temporarily non-resident	0.5
	IHT		
		IHT applies, shares are UK property	0.5
		Gift on 1 August 2013	
		Transfer of value	1.0
		No BPR with reason	1.0
		Chargeable transfer (2 x annual exemption)	0.5
		Taper relief available	0.5
		Calculation of tax due	0.5
		Reference to DTR	0.5
		Gift on 1 June 2014	
		Assumption re Tessa's continued ownership	1.0
		BPR	1.0
		Marriage and annual exemptions	1.0
	Advice		1.0
	Stamp duty		
		Not applicable, gift	0.5
			———
			11.0
		Maximum	10.0
			———
Total			18
			———

5 VIKRAM BRIDGE

Key answer tips

The question requires you to prepare explanations, with supporting calculations, suitable for inclusion in a letter to Vikram.

The answer should therefore adopt the appropriate language and style you would expect to use when writing to a client.

(a) **Taxable gain on the sale of the house in Wales**

Your taxable capital gain on the sale of the Welsh property will be computed as follows:

	£
Proceeds in August 2013	195,000
Less: Base cost (Note 1)	(145,000)
Enhancement expenditure	(18,000)
	———
Chargeable gain (Note 2)	32,000
Less: Annual exempt amount (£10,600 – £2,100)	(8,500)
	———
Taxable gain	23,500
	———

Tutorial note:

1. *The base cost is the market value as at 1 September 2004. The fact that his mother continued to live in it and it declined in value up to the date of her death is not relevant for capital gains tax.*

2. *Principal private residence relief is not available as Vikram never lived in the house, and Entrepreneurs' relief is not available as the house is not a qualifying business disposal. The gain would not, therefore, benefit from the 10% tax rate.*

Proposal to gift part of the house to Alice prior to disposal

Giving the house, or part of it, to Alice prior to the sale will not reduce the taxable gain. As you and Alice are not married, the inter spouse exemption is not available.

Therefore, if you make a gift to Alice, a capital gain will arise by reference to the market value of the property in exactly the same way as if you had sold the property to an unconnected third party.

The gain on such a gift cannot be deferred with a gift relief claim as the house is not a business asset for gift relief purposes.

(b) **Inheritance tax due in respect of the house in Wales**

Usually, where a gift is made to an individual more than seven years prior to the donor's death, as in the case of your mother's gift of the house to you, there are no inheritance tax (IHT) implications on the death of the donor.

However, because your mother continued to live in the house after she gave it to you, the gift will be taxed under the rules applying to 'gifts with reservation of benefit'.

In these circumstances, HM Revenue and Customs will ignore the original gift as, although the asset was gifted, your mother continued to use it as if it were her own. Therefore, the house will be included in your mother's death estate for IHT purposes at its market value at the date of her death (i.e. £140,000).

(c) **Income tax treatment of redundancy payments**

The payments you received on being made redundant from Bart Industries in 2013/14 are taxed as follows:

- The payment in lieu of notice of £4,700 is taxed in 2012/13, the year of receipt.
- Statutory redundancy pay is not taxable.
- A non-contractual lump sum up to a maximum of £30,000 is not subject to income tax.

The relocation costs paid by Dreamz Technology Ltd are exempt from income tax up to a maximum of £8,000.

Taxable income – 2013/14

	£
Employment income – Dreamz Technology Ltd	
Salary (£45,480 × 6/12)	22,740
Removal costs (£9,400 – £8,000)	1,400
Dividend income (£7,800 × 100/90)	8,667
Total income	32,807
Less: Personal allowance	(8,105)
Taxable income	24,702

(d) **Shares in Dreamz Technology Ltd**

The income tax treatment of the issue to you of shares in Dreamz Technology Ltd depends on whether or not the shares are issued via an approved share incentive plan.

Where there is no share incentive plan, the market value of the shares received (£2,750) will be taxable as employment income in 2014/15 (i.e. the year in which you receive them).

If there is a share incentive plan (SIP) approved by HM Revenue and Customs then an employer can give shares to its employees, up to a maximum value of £3,000 per employee per year, with no income tax consequences. However, the shares must be kept within the plan for a stipulated period and income tax will be charged if they are withdrawn within five years.

If you withdraw the shares from the plan within three years, income tax will be charged on their value at the time of withdrawal. If you withdraw them more than three years but within five years, income tax will be charged on the lower of their value when you acquired them and their value at the time of withdrawal.

(e) **Amount of income tax on dividend income**

When you worked for Bart Industries Ltd you were not a higher rate taxpayer as your taxable income was less than £34,370, as set out below. Accordingly, your dividend income was taxed at 10%, with a 10% tax credit such that there was no income tax payable.

	£
Employment income (£4,700 × ½ × 12)	28,200
Dividend income (£7,800 × 100/90)	8,667
Total income	36,867
Less: Personal allowance	(8,105)
Taxable income	28,672

In 2015/16 your annual salary from Dreamz Technology Ltd less the personal allowance is £37,375 (£45,480 – £8,105). As this exceeds £34,370, all of your dividend income will fall into the higher rate tax band such that it is taxed at 32½% less a 10% tax credit. This gives rise to income tax payable on the dividend income of £1,950 (£8,667 × 22½%).

Date of payment of income tax on dividend income

The tax due in respect of your dividend income must be paid on 31 January after the end of the tax year (i.e. on 31 January 2017 for 2015/16) under self-assessment.

You do not have to pay the tax earlier than this by instalments as the amount due is less than 20% of your total annual income tax liability as set out below.

The income tax on your employment income from Dreamz Technology Ltd will continue to be collected under the PAYE system.

	£
Taxable employment income (£45,480 – £8,105)	37,375
Income tax:	
£	
34,370 @ 20%	6,874
3,005 @ 40%	1,202
37,375	
Income tax liability on employment income	8,076
Income tax liability on dividend income (£8,667 × 32½%)	2,817
Total annual income tax liability	10,893
Less: PAYE (equal to liability on employment income)	(8,076)
Tax credit on dividend income (£8,667 × 10%)	(867)
Income tax payable via self-assessment	1,950
Threshold for payments by instalments (£10,893 × 20%)	2,179

Tutorial note

The important thing in this working is to determine the total income tax liability, and then assume that only the higher rate tax on the dividend will be payable by self assessment. It could have been set out as a standard income tax computation.

ACCA marking scheme		
		Marks
(a)	Taxable capital gain on the sale of the house	
	Computation of capital gain	
	Capital gain	0.5
	Annual exempt amount	0.5
	Effect of gift to Alice	1.0
	Style	1.0
		——
		3.0
		——
(b)	Inheritance tax due in respect of the house	
	Gift more than seven years prior to death	0.5
	Gift with reservation rules apply	0.5
	Consequences	1.0
		——
		2.0
(c)	Income tax	
	Treatment of redundancy payments	2.0
	Computation of taxable income	2.0
		——
		4.0
(d)	Shares in Dreamz Technology Ltd	
	Identify two possible treatments	0.5
	Treatment if no share incentive plan	1.0
	Exemption under share incentive plan	1.0
	Withdrawal from plan within five year	1.0
		——
		3.5
	Maximum	3.0
(e)	Amount of income tax on dividend income	
	Tax position whilst working for Bart Industries Ltd	
	No tax payable on dividends	1.0
	Computation	1.0
	Tax position whilst working for Dreamz Technology Ltd	1.5
	Date of payment of income tax on dividend income	
	Due date with reason	1.5
	Computation	2.5
		——
		7.5
	Maximum	6.0
		——
Total		18
		——